MW00785407

Siddhartha Rao

Sams **Teach Yourself**

C++

in **One Hour a Day**

Ninth Edition

SAMS

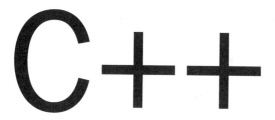

Sams Teach Yourself C++ in One Hour a Day, Ninth Edition

ISBN-13: 978-0-13-733468-1
ISBN-10: 0-13-733468-0

Library of Congress Control Number: 2021949810

1 2022

Trademarks

All terms mentioned in this book that are known to be trademarks or service marks have been appropriately capitalized. Sams Publishing cannot attest to the accuracy of this information. Use of a term in this book should not be regarded as affecting the validity of any trademark or service mark.

Warning and Disclaimer

Every effort has been made to make this book as complete and as accurate as possible, but no warranty or fitness is implied. The information provided is on an "as is" basis. The author and the publisher shall have neither liability nor responsibility to any person or entity with respect to any loss or damages arising from the information contained in this book.

Microsoft and/or its respective suppliers make no representations about the suitability of the information contained in the documents and related graphics published as part of the services for any purpose. All such documents and related graphics are provided "as is" without warranty of any kind. Microsoft and/ or its respective suppliers hereby disclaim all warranties and conditions with regard to this information, including all warranties and conditions of merchantability, whether express, implied or statutory, fitness for a particular purpose, title and non-infringement. In no event shall Microsoft and/or its respective suppliers be liable for any special, indirect or consequential damages or any damages whatsoever resulting from loss of use, data or profits, whether in an action of contract, negligence or other tortious action, arising out of or in connection with the use or performance of information available from the services.

The documents and related graphics contained herein could include technical inaccuracies or typographical errors. Changes are periodically added to the information herein. Microsoft and/ or its respective suppliers may make improvements and/or changes in the product(s) and/or the program(s) described herein at any time. Partial screenshots may be viewed in full within the software version specified.

Microsoft® and Windows® are registered trademarks of the Microsoft Corporation in the U.S.A. and other countries. Screenshots and icons reprinted with permission from the Microsoft Corporation. This book is not sponsored or endorsed by or affiliated with the Microsoft Corporation.

Special Sales

For information about buying this title in bulk quantities, or for special sales opportunities (which may include electronic versions; custom cover designs; and content particular to your business, training goals, marketing focus, or branding interests), please contact our corporate sales department at corpsales@pearsoned.com or (800) 382-3419.

For government sales inquiries, please contact governmentsales@pearsoned.com.

For questions about sales outside the U.S., please contact intlcs@pearson.com.

Editor-in-Chief
Mark Taub

Acquisitions Editor
Malobika Chakraborty

Development Editor
Chris Zahn

Managing Editor
Sandra Schroeder

Senior Project Editor
Tonya Simpson

Copy Editor
Kitty Wilson

Indexer
Tim Wright

Proofreader
Abby Manheim

Technical Editor
Adrian Ngo

Editorial Assistant
Cindy Teeters

Cover Designer
Chuti Prasertsith

Compositor
codeMantra

Dedication

In loving memory of my father.

Pearson's Commitment to Diversity, Equity, and Inclusion

Pearson is dedicated to creating bias-free content that reflects the diversity of all learners. We embrace the many dimensions of diversity, including but not limited to race, ethnicity, gender, socioeconomic status, ability, age, sexual orientation, and religious or political beliefs.

Education is a powerful force for equity and change in our world. It has the potential to deliver opportunities that improve lives and enable economic mobility. As we work with authors to create content for every product and service, we acknowledge our responsibility to demonstrate inclusivity and incorporate diverse scholarship so that everyone can achieve their potential through learning. As the world's leading learning company, we have a duty to help drive change and live up to our purpose to help more people create a better life for themselves and to create a better world.

Our ambition is to purposefully contribute to a world where

- Everyone has an equitable and lifelong opportunity to succeed through learning
- Our educational products and services are inclusive and represent the rich diversity of learners
- Our educational content accurately reflects the histories and experiences of the learners we serve
- Our educational content prompts deeper discussions with learners and motivates them to expand their own learning (and worldview)

While we work hard to present unbiased content, we want to hear from you about any concerns or needs with this Pearson product so that we can investigate and address them.

- Please contact us with concerns about any potential bias at https://www.pearson.com/report-bias.html.

Contents at a Glance

Table of Contents

PART III: Learning the Standard Template Library (STL)

PART IV: Lambda Expressions and STL Algorithms

Introduction

The rapid evolution of C++ has powered this age of machine learning and artificial intelligence. You can use C++20 to program simpler yet more powerful applications than ever before. This book, which analyzes nearly 300 compiling code examples in detail, introduces important C++20 language features and describes their inner workings.

In addition to explaining the basics of C++, this book teaches features of the language that are essential in professional C++ programming. You learn the fundamentals of object-oriented programming; essential Standard Template Library features and algorithms; and C++20 concepts, ranges, views, and adaptors, to mention a few. Whether you are a beginner or a professional programmer, you will find this book to be of immense value and support.

Who Should Read This Book?

To benefit from this book—which starts with the very basics of C++—you just need a desire to learn the C++ language and curiosity about how things works. An existing knowledge of C++ programming is not a prerequisite. You might also find this book helpful if you already know C++ and want to learn about the additions that have been made to the language in recent years. If you are a professional programmer, Part III, "Learning the Standard Template Library (STL)," Part IV, "Lambda Expressions and STL Algorithms," and Part V, "Advanced C++ Concepts," are bound to help you create better, more practical C++ applications.

NOTE

Visit the publisher's website and register this book at informit.com/register for convenient access to any updates, downloads, or errata that may be available for this book.

Organization of This Book

You can choose where to begin reading this book based on your current level of proficiency with C++. This book is organized into five parts:

- Part I, "The Basics," gets you started with writing simple C++ applications. In doing so, it introduces you to the keywords that you most frequently see in C++ code.

- Part II, "Fundamentals of Object-Oriented C++ Programming," teaches you object-oriented programming principles such as encapsulation, abstraction, inheritance, and polymorphism. Lesson 9, "Classes and Objects," also teaches you the importance of programming a copy constructor and using a move constructor to optimize performance. Lesson 12, "Operator Types and Operator Overloading," introduces you to the C++20 three-way comparison operator, which is referred to as the spaceship operator due to its shape (<=>). Lesson 14, "An Introduction to Macros and Templates," teaches you how to write powerful generic C++ code.
- Part III, "Learning the Standard Template Library (STL)," helps you write efficient and practical C++ code using STL classes and containers. For example, in this part, you will learn how `std::string` makes string concatenation operations safe and easy. Lessons 17, "STL Dynamic Array Classes," and 18, "STL `list` and `forward_list`," teach you how to use standardized dynamic arrays and linked lists so that you don't need to program your own. You will become familiar with using key/value pairs stored in associative containers such as `std::map` and `std::multimap` in Lesson 20, "STL map and multimap."
- Part IV, "Lambda Expressions and STL Algorithms," starts by explaining how to program function objects. Lesson 22, "Lambda Expressions," discusses the implementation of unnamed function objects. You'll learn to use various algorithms that help you perform operations on containers such as finding elements, removing elements, and sorting elements in Lesson 23, "STL Algorithms."
- Part V, "Advanced C++ Concepts," starts by explaining smart pointers and exception handling, which significantly contribute to application stability and quality. This part explains key features introduced in C++20. Lesson 29, "C++20 Concepts, Ranges, Views, and Adaptors" teaches you to validate template parameters by using concepts and construct views of elements in a range by using adaptors. Lesson 31, "C++20 Modules and C++23," teaches you about modules that will replace the traditional header files and ends with a note on language improvements expected to be released in the next version of the C++ standard, C++23.

Conventions Used in This Book

Within the lessons, you'll find the following elements that provide additional information:

NOTE

> These boxes provide additional information related to the surrounding material.

CAUTION

These boxes alert you to problems or side effects that can occur in special situations.

TIP

These boxes describe best practices in writing C++ programs.

DO	DON'T
DO use the "Do/Don't" boxes to find a quick summary of fundamental principles in a lesson.	**DON'T** overlook the useful information offered in these boxes.

This book uses different typefaces to differentiate between code and plain English. Throughout the lessons, code, commands, and programming-related terms appear in a computer `typeface`.

Sample Code for This Book

You can download code samples for free from https://github.com/learncppnow/9E.git

About the Author

Siddhartha Rao is the vice president in charge of product security at SAP SE, the world's most trustworthy supplier of enterprise software and cloud services. A software engineer at heart, Siddhartha is convinced that the rapid evolution of C++ has powered this age of machine learning and artificial intelligence. Features introduced by C++20 enable you to program simpler yet more powerful applications than ever before. In authoring this book, Siddhartha has taken care to ensure that this book's nearly 300 compiling code examples are accompanied by detailed analyses of how they work.

Siddhartha looks forward to your comments, reviews, and feedback!

Acknowledgments

I am thankful to my wife, Clara, and my family for their immense support, and to the editorial staff at Pearson for their spirited engagement in getting this book to you!

We Want to Hear from You!

As the reader of this book, *you* are our most important critic and commentator. We value your opinion and want to know what we're doing right, what we could do better, what areas you'd like to see us publish in, and any other words of wisdom you're willing to pass our way.

We welcome your comments. You can email or write to let us know what you did or didn't like about this book—as well as what we can do to make our books better.

Please note that we cannot help you with technical problems related to the topic of this book.

When you write, please be sure to include this book's title and author as well as your name and email address. We will carefully review your comments and share them with the author and editors who worked on the book.

Email: community@informit.com

Reader Services

Register your copy of *Sams Teach Yourself C++ in One Hour a Day* at informit.com for convenient access to downloads, updates, and corrections as they become available. To start the registration process, go to informit.com/register and log in or create an account.* Enter the product ISBN, 9780137334681, and click Submit. Once the process is complete, you will find any available bonus content under Registered Products.

*Be sure to check the box that you would like to hear from us in order to receive exclusive discounts on future editions of this product.

Figure Credits

Cover image rarrarorro/Shutterstock

Figure 8-2 © Microsoft 2021

Figure 9-2 © Microsoft 2021

Figure 1-1 © 2021 Apple Inc

Figure 1-2 © Microsoft 2021

LESSON 1

Getting Started

Welcome to *Sams Teach Yourself C++ in One Hour a Day*! You're ready to get started on becoming a proficient C++ programmer.

In this lesson, you find out

- Why C++ is a standard in software development
- How to enter, compile, and link your first working C++ program
- What's new in C++20

A Brief History of C++

The purpose of a programming language is to facilitate easy consumption of computational resources. C++ is not a new language but one that is popularly used and continuously evolving. As of this writing, the newest version of C++ is called C++20. It was ratified by the International Organization for Standardization (ISO) and published in December 2020. Previous amendments to the language were labeled C++17 (released in 2017), C++14 (released in 2014), and C++11 (released in 2011).

Connection to C

Initially developed by Bjarne Stroustrup at Bell Labs in 1979, C++ was designed to be a successor to C. In contrast to C, however, C++ was designed to be an object-oriented language that implements concepts such as inheritance, abstraction, polymorphism, and encapsulation. C++ features classes that are used to contain member data and member methods. These member methods are functions that can operate on member data. This organization helps a programmer model data along with the actions to perform on that data. Popular C++ compilers have continued to support C programming, too, offering seamless integration to both worlds, resulting in high backward compatibility.

NOTE

> Knowledge of C programming is not a prerequisite for learning C++. If your goal is to learn an object-oriented programming language like C++, then you can start directly with this book and don't need to learn a procedural language like C.

Advantages of C++

C++ is considered an intermediate-level programming language. It is versatile and can be used for high-level programming of applications that do not need to be aware of the specifics of the hardware they run on. C++ can also be used for low-level programming of libraries that work close to the hardware, such as device drivers. C++ therefore provides an optimal middle path that helps programmers develop complex applications that do not require any compromises in terms of performance or resource management.

Despite the existence of programming languages such as Java, C#, and others, C++ has not only remained relevant but has flourished and evolved. These other languages are *interpreted* by a runtime component that manages resources for the programmer. The runtime makes programming relatively easy, but it abstracts system resources to such an extent that the languages are unsuitable for many high-performance computing needs. Therefore, C++ remains the language of choice for situations that demand full control over memory consumption and performance. A tiered architecture where a web server programmed in C++ serves other components programmed in HTML, Java, JavaScript, or .NET is common. C++ is the language of choice for artificial intelligence and machine learning scenarios, device drivers, databases, operating systems, services, and even compilers and interpreters of other programming languages.

Evolution of the C++ Standard

Due to its popularity, years of evolution resulted in C++ being accepted and adopted on many different platforms (operating systems), most using their own C++ compilers. This evolution led to compiler-specific deviations and, therefore, interoperability problems and porting issues. Hence, there emerged a need to standardize the language and provide compiler manufacturers with a standard language specification to work with.

In 1998, the first standard version of C++ was ratified by the ISO Committee in ISO/IEC 14882:1998. Since then, the standard has undergone ambitious changes that have improved the usability of the language and extended the support of the standard library. As mentioned earlier, as of this writing, the current ratified version of the standard is ISO/IEC 14882:2020, popularly called C++20.

NOTE

> The current standard may not be completely supported by all popular compilers. Therefore, this book teaches the newest additions in C++20 and also explains well-supported language features that help you program good, functioning C++ applications.

Who Uses Programs Written in C++?

The list of applications, operating systems, interpreters, web services, databases, and enterprise software applications programmed in C++ is a long one. No matter who you are or how you consume computing resources, chances are that you use software programmed in C++. For example, the V8 JavaScript Engine by Google is programmed in C++. It is an integral part of popular browsers as well as server technologies such as Node.js.

C++ is a language of choice for research work by physicists, mathematicians, and data scientists. The rise of artificial intelligence using machine learning algorithms has been fueled by high-performance computing made possible by C++.

Programming a C++ Application

When you open your favorite browser or word processing application, you are instructing the processor to run an executable of that program. The executable is the finished product that should do what the programmer intended to achieve.

Steps in Building an Executable

Programming using C++ is the first step toward creating an executable that runs on your operating system. The basic steps in creating applications in C++ are the following:

1. Type C++ code using a text editor. This text editor is typically a code editor or an integrated development environment (IDE).
2. Compile code using a C++ *compiler* that creates a machine language version contained in "object files."
3. Link the object files by using a *linker* to get an executable (`.exe` in Windows, for example).

During the compilation step, code in C++, which is typically contained in text files with the extension `.cpp`, is converted into byte code that the processor can execute. The compiler converts one code file at a time, generating an object file with an `.o` or `.obj` extension and ignoring dependencies on code in another file.

> **TIP**
>
> Popular compilers include `g++` by the GNU Project, `clang++` by LLVM, and the Microsoft Visual C++ (MSVC) compiler. `g++` and `clang++` are frequently used in Linux and macOS environments, while MSVC is the compiler of choice for Windows.
>
> As of this writing, no compiler promises full C++20 support, but `g++` and MSVC are better than the rest.

A *linker* is a tool that resolves outstanding dependencies between `.obj` files. In the event of successful linkage, it creates an executable for the programmer to execute and distribute.

The process of successful compilation and linking is referred to as *building* an executable.

> **TIP**
>
> Using an online compiler accessible via your browser might be the fastest way to start editing, compiling, and executing simple C++ applications. Search for "online C++ compiler" and try out the options you find. With any compiler, pay attention to C++20 support when compiling new language features introduced in this book.

Analyzing Errors and Debugging

Applications rarely compile and execute as intended on the first run. A huge or complex application programmed in any language—C++ included—needs many runs as part of a testing effort to identify errors in code, called *bugs*. After the bugs are fixed, the executable is rebuilt, and the testing process continues. Thus, in addition to the three steps—programming, compiling, and linking—software development also involves a step called *debugging*, in which the programmer analyzes errors in code and fixes them. Good development environments supply tools and features that help with debugging.

Integrated Development Environments

Programmers often use an integrated development environment (IDE) that integrates programming, compiling, linking, and debugging in a unified user interface.

If you wish to program C++ using an IDE, you can install one of the many freely available C++ IDEs and compilers to get your learning started. Some popular IDEs are Eclipse and Code::Blocks for Linux, Xcode for macOS, and Microsoft Visual Studio for Windows.

DO	DON'T
DO save your C++ files with the `.cpp` extension.	**DON'T** use a `.c` extension for C++ files because some compilers compile such files as C rather than C++ programs.
DO use a simple text editor, a code editor, or an IDE to program code.	**DON'T** use word processors to write code because autocorrect and text formatting can cause compiler errors.

Programming Your First C++ Application

Now that you know the tools and the steps involved, it is time to program your first C++ application. You will follow tradition and have your first program display "Hello World!" on the screen.

If you are using Linux or macOS, you can use a text editor that you are familiar with (I used `gedit` on Ubuntu) to create a file with the contents shown Listing 1.1. Then save it with a name that ends with the extension `.cpp`, such as `Hello.cpp`.

If you are using macOS with Xcode, follow these steps to create a new C++ project:

1. Invoke the New Project Wizard via the menu option File, New, Project.
2. Select Command Line Tool and click Next.
3. Choose a product name, such as `Hello`. Select the language C++ and click Next.
4. Replace any automatically generated content in `main.cpp` with the code snippet shown in Listing 1.1.

If you are using Windows with Microsoft Visual Studio, follow these steps to create a new C++ project:

1. Invoke the New Project Wizard via the menu option File, New, Project.
2. Select C++, choose the type Console App, and click Next.
3. Give your project a name, such as `Hello`. Click Create.
4. Replace any automatically generated content in `Hello.cpp` with the code snippet shown in Listing 1.1.

LISTING 1.1 Hello.cpp, the Hello World Program

```
1: #include<iostream>
2:
3: int main()
4: {
5:     std::cout << "Hello World!" << std::endl;
6:     return 0;
7: }
```

This simple application does nothing more than display the customary "Hello World!" greeting on the screen using `std::cout`. `std::endl` instructs `cout` to end that line by inserting a line break, and the application exits by returning `0` to the operating system.

TIP

You might see variants of Line 5 in Listing 1.1 that appear as follows:

```
5:     std::cout << "Hello World!\n";
```

The output of the program would not change. `"Hello World!\n"` includes the line break in the form of `\n`, so it is not additionally inserted using a `cout::endl`.

Some code samples in this book use `'\n'` to help fit a line of code within a line on the printed page.

NOTE

To read a program to yourself, it might help if you know how to pronounce the special characters and keywords.

For instance, you can call `#include` "hash-include." You might also call it "sharp-include" or "pound-include," depending on where you come from.

Similarly, you can read `std::cout` as "standard-c-out." `endl` is "end-line."

CAUTION

The devil is in the details: You need to type your code in exactly the same way as shown in the listings. Compilers are strict, and if you mistakenly put a `:` at the end of a statement where a `;` is required, you can expect a compilation failure accompanied by an error report! For the same reason, you should not use word processing software to edit code.

TIP

Code editors like Visual Studio Code are available for Linux, macOS, and Windows for free. If you're not using an IDE, then Visual Studio Code might be the next best option for editing code.

Building and Executing Your First C++ Application

If you're using the `g++` compiler by GCC, you can open the terminal, navigate to the directory containing `hello.cpp`, and invoke the compiler and linker by using the command line:

```
g++ -o hello Hello.cpp -std=c++20
```

Alternatively, if you are using the `clang++` compiler on macOS, you can follow the steps mentioned above and execute the following command line:

```
clang++ -o hello Hello.cpp
```

These commands instruct `g++` and `clang++` to create an executable named `hello` by compiling your C++ file `Hello.cpp`.

Enable C++20 Features When Using g++ or clang++

To compile C++20–specific code using `g++` or `clang++`, append the parameter `-std=c++20` to the command line:

```
g++ -o hello Hello.cpp -std=c++20
```

or

```
clang++ -o hello Hello.cpp -std=c++20
```

You will need it when compiling code that uses C++20 features.

If you're using macOS with Xcode, then you can build and run your application by selecting Product, Run.

Your program composed in Xcode should look similar to the one illustrated in Figure 1.1.

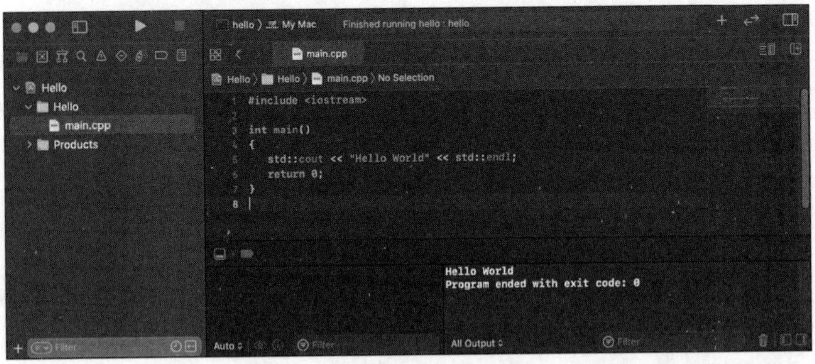

FIGURE 1.1
A simple "Hello World" C++ program edited in Xcode 12.5 on macOS.

TIP

> To compile C++20 code in Xcode, you need to explicitly enable it by setting C++ Language Dialect to c++20. You can find this option under Build Settings.

If you're using Microsoft Visual Studio on Windows, press Ctrl+F5 to run your program directly via the IDE. This compiles, links, and executes your application.

Your program composed in Microsoft Visual Studio should look similar to the one illustrated in Figure 1.2.

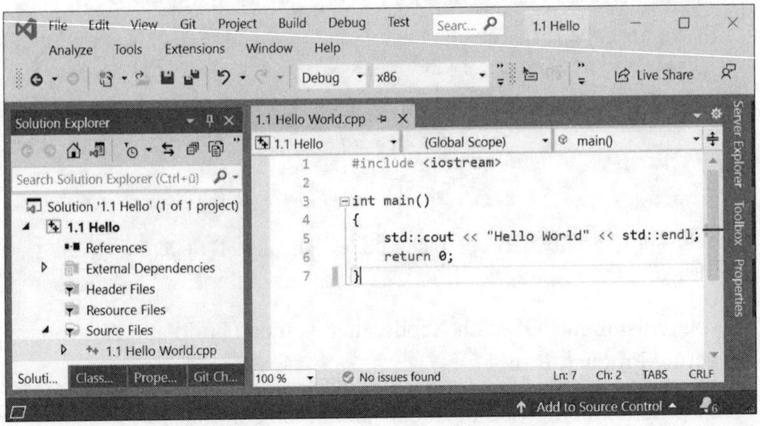

FIGURE 1.2
A simple "Hello World" C++ program edited in Microsoft Visual Studio 2019.

TIP

> To compile C++20 code in Microsoft Visual Studio, you need to explicitly enable it by setting the option C++ Language Standard to ISO C++20 Standard. You can find it under Project, Properties.

When you execute `./hello` or `Hello.exe`, you get the following output:

```
Hello World!
```

Congratulations! You have started on your way to learning one of the most popular and powerful programming languages of all time!

1

Significance of the C++ ISO Standard

Listing 1.1 demonstrates that adherence to the C++ ISO standard helps develop code that can be compiled for and executed on multiple operating systems.

The ISO standard for C++ enables consistent compiler support and cross-platform portability of code. Thus you as a developer can address a larger audience of users without needing to program specifically for every OS environment that they prefer.

Understanding Compiler Errors

Compilers are painfully exact in their requirements, but only the good ones make an effort to show you where the mistakes in code are. To see this in action, you can deliberately introduce an error in Listing 1.1 by deleting the semicolon (`;`) ending Line 5 before the `return` in Line 6. From a compiler's point of view, you have started a new statement in Line 6 without ending the previous one in Line 5—and this is against the rules. If you now try to compile the code, you get an error like this:

```
1.1 Hello World.cpp(6,2): error C2143: syntax error: missing ';' before 'return'
```

This error message from Visual C++ starts with the name of the file that contains the error, the line number where it encountered a new statement before closure of the previous one (6, in this case), and a description of the error and the error number (in this case, `C2143`). You can fix the problem by adding a semicolon at the beginning of the sixth line, and the program will compile just fine!

NOTE

Using a semicolon (`;`) is the valid way to terminate a statement in C++. Line breaks don't terminate statements in C++ as they do in languages such as VBScript.

C++ therefore allows you to have a statement spanning multiple lines. It is also possible to have multiple statements in a line, with each statement terminated by a semicolon.

What's New in C++20?

Revisions to the C++ standard have resulted in a language that is simpler to use for programming without compromising on the ability to write high-performance applications.

C++20, which was published by the ISO in December 2020, represents a quantum leap in the modernization of the language. It introduces the three-way comparison operator (also called the spaceship operator), validation of template parameters, a new ranges library that includes views and adapters that facilitate powerful operations on collections, further standardization of multithreading, synchronization support through coroutines, and improved lambda expressions. C++20 also introduces *modules*—a long-awaited feature that overcomes the drawbacks of including header (`.h`) files and greatly speeds up the compilation process in large projects. So drastic are the amendments in C++20 that no compiler promises complete C++20 standard support as of this writing, although the ones mentioned are making good progress to that end.

C++ is a language that's still evolving. Features that are expected in the next revision, which is expected to occur in 2023, are introduced at the end of the book, in Lesson 31, "C++20 Modules and C++23."

Summary

In this lesson, you learned how to program, compile, link, and execute your first C++ program. This lesson also gave you a brief overview on the evolution of C++ and demonstrated the effectiveness of the standard by showing that the same program can be compiled using different compilers on different operating systems.

Q&A

Q Can I ignore warning messages from my compiler?

A Compilers sometimes issue warning messages. Warnings are different from errors in that with a warning, the line in question is syntactically correct and compile-worthy. However, there may be a better way to write the line, and a good compiler will issue a warning with a recommendation for a fix.

You should heed these warnings and improve your programs accordingly. Don't ignore warning messages unless you are sure that they're false positives.

Q How does an interpreted language differ from a compiled language?

A Languages such as JavaScript, Ruby, and Python are interpreted languages. Such a language uses an interpreter that reads (interprets) code in a script file and performs the desired actions. Compiled languages like C++ use a build step to produce executables containing instructions that execute natively on the processor.

Q What are runtime errors, and how are they different from compile-time errors?

A Errors that happen when you execute an application are called *runtime errors*. You might have experienced the infamous "access violation" on Windows, which is a runtime error caused by a buggy executable. Compile-time errors break the build process. They indicate syntactical problems in code and need to be fixed by the programmer before compilation can proceed.

Q Why do I need to explicitly enable C++20 features when using g++, clang++, or MSVC? Why aren't they on by default?

A Amendments to C++ include new features and improvements to existing ones. Compilers need to ensure backward compatibility and execution stability of existing code. They do so by introducing new features (some still in experimental mode) that support the C++20 standard by using new command-line parameters so that existing build scripts are not jeopardized.

Workshop

The Workshop provides quiz questions to help you solidify your understanding of the material covered and exercises to provide you with experience in using what you've learned. Try to answer the quiz and exercise questions before checking the answers in Appendix E and be certain you understand the answers before continuing to the next lesson.

Quiz

1. Ignoring syntax, what is the difference between a compiled language like C++ and an interpreted language like JavaScript?
2. What does a linker do?
3. What are the steps in the normal program development cycle?

Exercises

1. Look at the following program and try to guess what it does without running it:

```
#include<iostream>
int main()
{
   int x = 8;
   int y = 6;
   std::cout << std::endl;
   std::cout << x - y << " " << x * y << " " << x + y;
   std::cout << std::endl;
   return 0;
}
```

2. Type in the program from Exercise 1 and then compile and link it. What does it do? Does it do what you guessed?

3. What do you think is the error in the following program?

```
include<iostream>
int main()
{
     std::cout << "Hello Buggy World " << std::endl;
     return 0;
}
```

4. Fix the error in the program in Exercise 3 and then compile, link, and run the program. What does it do?

LESSON 2

The Anatomy of a C++ Program

C++ programs are organized into classes comprising member functions and member variables. Most of this book is devoted to explaining these parts in depth, but to get a sense of how a program fits together, you must see a complete working program.

In this lesson, you learn

- The parts of a C++ program
- How the parts work together
- What a function is and what it does
- Basic input and output operations

Parts of the Hello World Program

Your first C++ program in Lesson 1, "Getting Started," did nothing more than display a simple "Hello World" statement on the screen. Yet this program contains some of the most important and basic building blocks of a C++ program. You use Listing 2.1 as a starting point to analyze components all C++ programs contain.

LISTING 2.1 `HelloWorldAnalysis.cpp`: Analyzing a Simple C++ Program

```
// Preprocessor directive that includes header iostream
#include<iostream>

// Start of your program: function block main()
int main()
{
   /* Write to the console output i.e. screen */
   std::cout << "Hello World" << std::endl;

   // Return a value to the OS
   return 0;
}
```

This C++ program can be broadly classified into two parts: the preprocessor directives that start with a # and the main body of the program, which starts with `int main()`.

> **NOTE**
>
> Lines 1, 4, 7, and 10, which start with a // or with a /*, are called *comments* and are ignored by the compiler. Comments are used to explain the code and are for humans to read.

Preprocessor Directive `#include`

As the name suggests, a *preprocessor* is a tool that runs before the actual compilation starts. Preprocessor directives are commands to the preprocessor and always start with a pound sign # (also called a hash symbol). In Line 2 of Listing 2.1, `#include<`*`filename`*`>` tells the preprocessor to take the contents of the file (`iostream`, in this case) and include them at the line where the directive is made. `iostream` is a standard header file that enables the usage of `std::cout` in Line 8 to display `"Hello World"` on the screen. In other words, the compiler was able to compile Line 8, which contains `std::cout`, because the preprocessor included the definition of `std::cout` in Line 2.

> **NOTE**
>
> Professionally programmed C++ applications include standard headers supplied by the development environment and those created by the programmer.
>
> Large applications are typically programmed in multiple files wherein some need to include others. So, if a variable or function declared in `FileA` needs to be used in `FileB`, you need to include the former in the latter. You would do that by inserting the following `include` statement in `FileB`:
>
> ```
> #include "...relative path to FileA\FileA"
> ```
>
> Use quotes (`""`) when including a self-programmed header file. Use angle brackets (`<>`) when including a standard header file—for example, `<iostream>`, `<string>`, and `<algorithm>`.

C++20 TIP

> The preprocessor directive `#include<file>` inserts the entire contents of the header *file* at the point in code where the inclusion is declared, even if no part of the file being included is relevant to the code being compiled. Large and complex C++ projects comprising many inclusions suffer long compilation times.
>
> C++20 has solved this problem by introducing *modules*. Modules help with efficient code reuse without compromising compilation times. As of this writing, modules are supported by some popular compilers in experimental mode. They are introduced in Lesson 31, "C++20 Modules and C++23."

2

The Body of Your Program: `main()`

Following the preprocessor directive(s) is the body of the program, characterized by the function `main()`. The execution of a C++ program always starts here. It is a standardized convention that function `main()` is declared with an `int` preceding it. `int` is the return value type of the function `main()` and stands for integer.

NOTE

> In many C++ applications, you find a variant of the `main()` function that looks like this:
>
> ```
> int main (int argc, char* argv[])
> ```
>
> This is also standard compliant and acceptable as `main()` returns `int`. The contents of the parenthesis are "arguments" supplied to the program. This variant allows the user to start the program with command-line arguments, such as
>
> ```
> program -DoSomethingSpecific
> ```
>
> `-DoSomethingSpecific` is the argument for that program passed by the operating system (OS) as a parameter to it, to be handled within `main (int argc, char* argv[])`.

Let's discuss Line 8, which fulfills the actual purpose of this program:

```
std::cout << "Hello World" << std::endl;
```

`cout` (which stands for "console-out" and is pronounced "see-out") is the statement that writes `"Hello World"` to the display console. `cout` is a *stream* defined in the standard `std` *namespace* (hence, `std::cout`), and what you are doing in this line is putting the text `"Hello World"` into this stream by using the insertion operator `<<`. `std::endl` is used to end a line, and inserting it into a stream is akin to inserting a carriage return. Note that the stream insertion operator `<<` is used every time a new entity needs to be inserted into the stream.

The good thing about streams in C++ is that different stream types support similar stream semantics to perform different operations with the same text. For example, insertion of the text `"Hello World"` into a file instead of a console would use the same insertion operator `<<` on an `std::fstream` instead of `std::cout`. Thus, working with streams becomes intuitive, and when you are familiar with one stream (such as `cout`, which writes text to the console), you will find it easy to work with others (such as `fstream`, which helps save files to the disk).

Streams are discussed in greater detail in Lesson 27, "Using Streams for Input and Output."

NOTE

> The actual text `"Hello World"`, including the quotes, is called a *string literal*.

Returning a Value

A function in C++ needs to return a value unless explicitly specified otherwise. `main()` is a function and always returns an integer. This integer value is returned to the OS and, depending on the nature of your application, can be very useful as most OSes provide for an ability to query on the return value of an application that has terminated naturally. In many cases, one application is launched by another, and the parent application (that launches) wants to know if the child application (that was launched) has completed its task successfully. A programmer can use the return value of `main()` to convey a success or error state to the parent application.

NOTE

> Programmers conventionally return `0` in the event of success or `-1` in the event of an error. However, the return value is an integer, and a programmer has the flexibility to convey many different states of success or failure by using the available range of integer return values.

CAUTION

> C++ is case-sensitive. So, expect compilation to fail if you write `Int` instead of `int` and `Std::Cout` instead of `std::cout`. This is why word processors aren't used to edit code!

The Concept of Namespaces

The reason you used `std::cout` in the program and not just `cout` is that the artifact (`cout`) that you want to invoke is in the standard (`std`) namespace.

So, what exactly are namespaces?

Assume that you didn't use the standard namespace qualifier `std` in invoking `cout` and assume that `cout` existed in two locations known to the compiler. Which one should the compiler invoke? This conflict will result in a compilation failure. Namespaces solve this problem by giving names to sections of code. In invoking `std::cout`, you are instructing the compiler to use the `cout` that is available in the `std` namespace.

NOTE

> You use the `std` (pronounced "standard") namespace to invoke functions, streams, and utilities that have been ratified by the ISO standards committee.

Many programmers find it tedious to repeatedly add the `std` namespace specifier to their code when using `cout` and other such features contained in the standard namespace. The `using namespace` declaration, as demonstrated in Listing 2.2, helps you avoid this repetition.

LISTING 2.2 The `using namespace` Declaration

```
// Preprocessor directive
#include<iostream>

// Start of your program
int main()
{
    // Tell the compiler what namespace to search in
    using namespace std;

    /* Write to the screen using std::cout */
```

```
11:     cout << "Hello World" << endl;
12:
13:     // Return a value to the OS
14:     return 0;
15: }
```

Analysis ▼

Note Line 8. By telling the compiler that you are using the namespace `std`, you don't need to explicitly mention the namespace on Line 11 when using `std::cout` or `std::endl`.

A more restrictive variant of Listing 2.2 is shown in Listing 2.3, where you do not include a namespace in its entirety. You explicitly include artifacts that you wish to use.

LISTING 2.3 Another Demonstration of the `using` Keyword

```
 1: // Preprocessor directive
 2: #include<iostream>
 3:
 4: // Start of your program
 5: int main()
 6: {
 7:     using std::cout;
 8:     using std::endl;
 9:
10:     /* Write to the screen using std::cout */
11:     cout << "Hello World" << endl;
12:
13:     // Return a value to the OS
14:     return 0;
15: }
```

Analysis ▼

Line 8 in Listing 2.2 has now been replaced by Lines 7 and 8 in Listing 2.3. The difference between `using namespace std` and `using std::cout` is that the former allows all artifacts in the `std` namespace (`cout`, `cin`, etc.) to be used without explicit inclusion of the namespace qualifier `std::`. With the latter, the convenience of not needing to disambiguate the namespace explicitly is restricted to only `std::cout`.

Comments in C++ Code

Lines 1, 4, 10, and 13 in Listing 2.3 contain text in a spoken language (English, in this case) yet do not interfere with the ability of the program to compile. They also do not alter the output of the program. Such lines are called *comments*. Comments are ignored by the compiler and are used by programmers to explain their code—hence, they are written in human-readable language.

C++ supports comments in two styles:

- // indicates the start of a comment, which is valid until the end of that line. For example:

```
// This is a comment and it ends at this line
```

- /* followed by */ indicates that the contained text is a comment, even if it spans multiple lines:

```
/* This is also a comment
and it spans two lines */
```

NOTE

> It might seem strange that a programmer needs to explain code, but the bigger a program gets or the larger the number of programmers working on a particular module gets, the more important it is to write code that can be easily understood. Comments help a programmer document what is being done and why it is being done in a particular manner.

DO	DON'T
DO add comments explaining the working of complicated algorithms and complex parts of your program. **DO** compose comments using language that other programmers can understand. **DO** review comments after updating code to ensure that they continue to be relevant.	**DON'T** use comments to explain or repeat the obvious. **DON'T** write obscure code and use comments to explain it because comments won't adequately compensate for poor coding practices.

Functions in C++

Functions help divide the content of an application into functional units that can be invoked in a sequence of your choosing. A function, when invoked, typically returns a value to the invoking/calling function. The most famous function is, of course, `int main()`. It is recognized by the compiler as the starting point of a C++ application and has to return an `int` (i.e., an integer).

As a programmer, you have the choice and usually the need to divide your code into logical units by composing functions. Listing 2.4 is a simple application that uses a function to display statements on the screen using `std::cout` with various parameters.

Input ▼

LISTING 2.4 Declaring, Defining, and Calling a Function That Demonstrates Capabilities of `std::cout`

```
#include<iostream>
using namespace std;

// Declare a function
int DemoConsoleOutput();

int main()
{
   // Call i.e. invoke the function
   DemoConsoleOutput();

   return 0;
}

// Define i.e. implement the previously declared function
int DemoConsoleOutput()
{
   cout << "This is a simple string literal" << endl;
   cout << "Writing number five: " << 5 << endl;
   cout << "Performing division 10 / 5 = " << 10 / 5 << endl;
   cout << "Pi is 22 / 7 = " << 22.0 / 7 << endl;

   return 0;
}
```

Output ▼

```
This is a simple string literal
Writing number five: 5
Performing division 10 / 5 = 2
Pi is 22 / 7 = 3.14286
```

Analysis ▼

Lines 5, 10, and 16 through 24 are the interesting lines in this listing. Line 5 is called a *function declaration*, and it basically tells the compiler that you want to create a function called `DemoConsoleOutput()` that returns an `int` (integer). This declaration enables the compiler to compile Line 10, where `DemoConsoleOutput()` is called inside `main()`. The compiler assumes that the *definition* (that is, the implementation of the function) is going to come up, which it does later, in Lines 16 through 24.

The function `DemoConsoleOutput()` demonstrates the capabilities of `cout`. Note that it prints not only text the same way as it displayed `"Hello World"` in previous examples, it also displays the results of simple arithmetic computations.

Function `DemoConsoleOutput()` is required to return an integer, as declared in Line 5, and therefore returns an integer value `0` in Line 12. Similarly, `main()` returns `0`, too. Given that `main()` has delegated all its activity to the function `DemoConsoleOutput()`, you can use the return value of the function also in returning from `main()`, as illustrated in Listing 2.5.

Input ▼

LISTING 2.5 Using the Return Value of a Function

```
#include<iostream>
using namespace std;

// Function declaration and definition
int DemoConsoleOutput()
{
    cout << "This is a simple string literal" << endl;
    cout << "Writing number five: " << 5 << endl;
    cout << "Performing division 10 / 5 = " << 10 / 5 << endl;
    cout << "Pi is 22 / 7 = " << 22.0 / 7 << endl;

    return 0;
}

int main()
{
    // Function call with return used to exit
    return DemoConsoleOutput();
}
```

Analysis ▼

The output of this application is the same as the output of the previous listing. However, there are slight differences in the way it is programmed. For example, because you have defined (that is, implemented) the function before `main()` in Lines 5–13, you don't need an extra declaration of it. The compiler accepts it as a function declaration and definition in one. `main()` is a bit shorter, too. Line 18 invokes the function `DemoConsoleOutput()` and also returns from `main()` using the return value of the function.

NOTE

In Listing 2.5, the function `DemoConsoleOutput()` is not required to make a decision. Therefore, you can declare the function to return type `void`:

```
void DemoConsoleOutput()
```

This variant cannot return a value.

Functions can take parameters, can be recursive, can contain multiple `return` statements, can be overloaded, can be expanded inline by the compiler, and more. These concepts are introduced in greater detail in Lesson 7, "Organizing Code with Functions."

Basic Input Using `std::cin` and Output Using `std::cout`

Your computer enables you to interact with applications running on it in various forms and allows those applications to interact with you in many forms, too. You interact with applications by using input devices. The keyboard and the mouse are popular examples. You can have information displayed on the screen as text, displayed in the form of graphics, printed on paper using a printer, or simply saved to the file system for later use. This section discusses the very simplest form of input and output in C++: using the console to write and read information.

You use `std::cout` (pronounced "standard see-out") to write simple text data to the console and use `std::cin` ("standard see-in") to read text and numbers (entered using the keyboard) from the console. In fact, in displaying `"Hello World"` on the screen, you have already encountered `cout`, as seen in Listing 2.1:

```
8:      std::cout << "Hello World" << std::endl;
```

This statement shows cout followed by the insertion operator << (which helps insert data into the output stream), followed by the string literal "Hello World" to be inserted, followed by a newline in the form std::endl (pronounced "standard end-line"). In addition to inserting a newline, std::endl also flushes the output buffer, making std::cout display all contents immediately.

The use of std::cin is simple, too. cin is used for input and is therefore accompanied by the variable you want to be storing the input data in:

```
std::cin >> variable;
```


Thus, cin is followed by the *extraction* operator >> (which extracts data from the input stream), which is followed by the variable where the data needs to be stored. If the user input needs to be stored in two variables, each containing data separated by a space, then you can store it by using one statement:

```
std::cin >> variable1 >> variable2;
```

Note that cin can be used for text as well as numeric inputs from the user, as shown in Listing 2.6.

Input ▼

LISTING 2.6 Using cin and cout to Display Number and Text Entered by a User

```
#include<iostream>
#include<string>
using namespace std;

int main()
{
    // Declare a variable to store an integer
    int inputNumber;

   cout << "Enter an integer: ";

   // store integer given user input
   cin >> inputNumber;

   // The same with text i.e. string data
   cout << "Enter your name: ";
   string inputName;
   cin >> inputName;

   cout << inputName << " entered " << inputNumber << endl;

   return 0;
}
```

Output ▼

```
Enter an integer: 42
Enter your name: Siddhartha
Siddhartha entered 42
```

Analysis ▼

Line 8 shows how a variable named `inputNumber` is declared to store data of type `int`. Line 10 uses `cout` to ask the user to enter a number. The entered number is then stored in the integer variable `inputNumber` using `cin` in Line 13. The same exercise is repeated to store the user's name in variable `inputName`, which of course is not an integer but a type called `string`, as seen in Lines 17 and 18. The reason you included header file `<string>` in Line 2 was to use type `std::string` later, inside `main()`. Finally, in Line 20, a `cout` statement is used to display the entered name with the number and intermediate text to produce the output `Siddhartha entered 42`.

This simple example demonstrates basic input and output in C++. Don't worry if the concept of variables is not clear to you yet, as it is explained in good detail in Lesson 3, "Using Variables, Declaring Constants."

NOTE

> If I had entered a couple of words as my name (for example, Siddhartha Rao) while executing Listing 2.6, `cin` would've still stored only the first word, `Siddhartha`, in the string. To be able to store entire lines, you use the function `getline()`, as demonstrated in Listing 4.7 in Lesson 4, "Managing Arrays and Strings."

Summary

This lesson introduced the basic parts of a simple C++ program. You learned what `main()` is, got an introduction to namespaces, and learned the basics of console input and output. You will be able to use a lot of these components in every program you write.

Q&A

Q What does `#include` do?

A This is a directive to the preprocessor that runs when you call your compiler. This specific directive causes the contents of the file named in `<...>` after `#include` to be inserted at that line as if it were typed at that location in your source code.

Q What is the problem with `#include`?

A Inclusion of many files results in slow compilation times, especially in large projects. This problem has been mitigated in C++20 by the introduction of modules.

Q What is the difference between `//` comments and `/*` comments?

A The double-slash comments (`//`) expire at the end of the line. Slash-star (`/*`) comments are in effect until a closing comment mark (`*/`) appears. The double-slash comments are also referred to as *single-line comments*, and the slash-star comments are often referred to as *multiline comments*. Remember, not even the end of the function terminates a slash-star comment. If you forget the closing comment mark (`*/`), you will have unintentionally commented away code that follows.

Q When do you need to program command-line arguments?

A You use command-line arguments to support options that may alter the execution of a program. For example, the command `format` in Windows helps format a drive, with a typical use being `format c:`. Here `c:` is the command-line argument sent to executable `format.exe`.

Workshop

The Workshop provides quiz questions to help you solidify your understanding of the material covered and exercises to provide you with experience in using what you've learned. Try to answer the quiz and exercise questions before checking the answers in Appendix E and be certain you understand the answers before continuing to the next lesson.

Quiz

1. What is the problem in declaring `Int main()`?
2. Can comments be longer than one line?

Exercises

1. **BUG BUSTERS:** Enter this program and compile it. Why does it fail? How can you fix it?

```
#include<iostream>
void main()
{
      std::Cout << Is there a bug here?";
}
```

2. Fix the bugs in Exercise 1 and recompile, link, and run it.
3. Modify Listing 2.4 to demonstrate subtraction (using -) and multiplication (using *).

LESSON 3
Using Variables, Declaring Constants

Variables help a programmer temporarily store data for a finite amount of time. *Constants* help a programmer define artifacts that are not allowed to change or make changes.

In this lesson, you find out

- How to declare and define variables and constants
- How to assign values to variables and manipulate those values
- How to write the value of a variable to the screen
- How to use the keywords `auto` and `constexpr`

What Is a Variable?

Before you actually explore the need for and use of variables in a programming language, take a step back and first think about what a computer contains and how it works.

Memory and Addressing in Brief

A computer, smart phone, or other programmable device contains a microprocessor and a certain amount of memory for temporary storage, called random access memory (RAM). In addition, many devices also allow for data to be persisted on a storage device such as a hard disk. The microprocessor executes instructions comprising your application. In doing so, it uses the RAM to fetch the application binary code to be executed, as well as the data associated with it.

The RAM itself can be visualized as a storage area akin to a row of lockers in a dorm, each locker having a number—that is, an address. To access a location in memory—such as location 578—the processor needs to be programmed using an instruction to fetch a value from the location or write a value to it.

Declaring Variables to Access and Use Memory

The following examples will help you understand what variables are. Assume you are writing a program to multiply two numbers supplied by the user. The user is asked to feed the multiplicand and the multiplier into your program, one after the other, and you need to store each of them so that you can use them later to multiply. Depending on what you want to be doing with the result of the multiplication, you might even want to store that result for later use in your program. Instead of painstakingly specifying memory addresses (such as 578) to store the numbers, you would use variables for the purpose. Defining a variable is simple and follows this pattern:

```
VariableType VariableName;
```

or

```
VariableType VariableName = InitialValue;
```

The `VariableType` attribute tells the compiler the nature of data the variable can store, and the compiler reserves the necessary space for it. The name chosen by the programmer is a friendly replacement for the address in memory where the variable's value is stored.

TIP

> Variable initialization is optional, but it's a good programming practice.

Listing 3.1 shows how variables are declared, initialized, and used in a program that multiplies two numbers supplied by the user.

Input ▼

LISTING 3.1 Using Variables to Store Numbers and the Result of Their Multiplication

```
#include<iostream>
using namespace std;

int main ()
{
    cout << "This program multiplies two numbers" << endl;

    cout << "Enter the first number: ";
    int firstNumber = 0;
    cin >> firstNumber;

    cout << "Enter the second number: ";
    int secondNumber = 0;
```

```
14:     cin >> secondNumber;
15:
16:     // Multiply two numbers, store result in a variable
17:     int multiplicationResult = firstNumber * secondNumber;
18:
19:     // Display result
20:     cout << firstNumber << " x " << secondNumber;
21:     cout << " = " << multiplicationResult << endl;
22:
23:     return 0;
24: }
```


Output ▼

```
This program multiplies two numbers
Enter the first number: 51
Enter the second number: 24
51 x 24 = 1224
```

Analysis ▼

This application asks the user to enter two numbers. The program multiplies these two numbers and displays the result. To use numbers entered by the user, it needs to store them in memory. Variables `firstNumber` and `secondNumber`, declared in Lines 9 and 13, do the job of temporarily storing integer values entered by the user. You use `std::cin` in Lines 10 and 14 to accept input from the user and to store them in the two integer variables. Line 17 performs the multiplication and stores result in variable `multiplicationResult`. The `cout` statement in Line 21 is used to display the result on the console.

Let's analyze a variable declaration further:

```
9: int firstNumber = 0;
```

This line declares a variable of type `int`, which indicates an integer, with the name `firstNumber`. Zero is assigned to the variable as an initial value.

The compiler does the job of mapping this variable `firstNumber` to a location in memory and takes care of the associated memory-address bookkeeping for you for all the variables that you declare. The programmer thus works with human-friendly names, while the compiler manages memory addressing and creates the instructions for the microprocessor to execute in working with the RAM.

TIP

> Naming variables appropriately is important for writing good, understandable, and maintainable code.
>
> Variable names in C++ can be alphanumeric, but they cannot start with a number. They cannot contain spaces and cannot contain arithmetic operators (such as `+`, `-`, and so on) within them. Variable names also cannot be reserved keywords. For example, a variable named `return` will cause compilation failure.
>
> Variable names may contain the underscore character (_), and it is popularly used in descriptive variable naming.

Declaring and Initializing Multiple Variables of a Type

In Listing 3.1, `firstNumber`, `secondNumber`, and `multiplicationResult` are all of the same type—integers—and are declared in three separate lines. If you wanted to, you could condense the declaration of these three variables to one line of code that looks like this:

```
int firstNumber = 0, secondNumber = 0, multiplicationResult = 0;
```

NOTE

> As you can see, C++ makes it possible to declare multiple variables of a type at once and to declare variables at the beginning of a function. However, declaring a variable when it is first needed is often better as it makes the code readable: People tend to notice the type of the variable when the declaration is close to its point of first use.

CAUTION

> Data stored in variables is data stored in RAM. This data is lost when the application terminates unless the programmer explicitly persists the data on a storage medium like a hard disk.
>
> Storing to a file on disk is discussed in Lesson 27, "Using Streams for Input and Output."

Understanding the Scope of a Variable

The *scope* of a variable is the region of code within which you can use that variable. An ordinary variable like the ones we have declared so far has a well-defined scope within which it's valid and can be used. When used outside its scope, a variable's name will not be recognized by the compiler, and your program won't compile. Beyond its scope, a variable is an unidentified entity that the compiler knows nothing of.

To better understand the scope of a variable, Listing 3.2 reorganizes the program in Listing 3.1 into a function `MultiplyNumbers()` that multiplies the two numbers and returns the result.

Input ▼

LISTING 3.2 Demonstrating the Scope of the Variables

```
#include<iostream>
using namespace std;

void MultiplyNumbers ()
{
    cout << "Enter the first number: ";
    int firstNumber = 0;
    cin >> firstNumber;

    cout << "Enter the second number: ";
    int secondNumber = 0;
    cin >> secondNumber;

    // Multiply two numbers, store result in a variable
    int multiplicationResult = firstNumber * secondNumber;

    // Display result
    cout << firstNumber << " x " << secondNumber;
    cout << " = " << multiplicationResult << endl;
}
int main ()
{
    cout << "This program multiplies two numbers" << endl;

    // Call the function that does all the work
    MultiplyNumbers();

    // cout << firstNumber << " x " << secondNumber;
    // cout << " = " << multiplicationResult << endl;

    return 0;
}
```

Output ▼

```
This program multiplies two numbers
Enter the first number: 51
Enter the second number: 24
51 x 24 = 1224
```

Analysis ▼

Listing 3.2 does exactly the same activity as Listing 3.1 and produces the same output. The only difference is that the bulk of the work is delegated to a function called `MultiplyNumbers()`, which is invoked by `main()`. Note that variables `firstNumber` and `secondNumber` cannot be used outside of `MultiplyNumbers()`. If you uncomment Lines 28 or 29 in `main()`, you experience compile failure of type `undeclared identifier`. This is because the scope of the variables such as `firstNumber` and `secondNumber` is limited to the function they're declared in—in this case `MultiplyNumbers()`. Such variables are therefore called *local* variables and can be used only within that function.

The curly brace (}) that indicates the end of a function also limits the scope of variables declared after the opening brace. When a function ends, all local variables are destroyed, and the memory they occupy is returned.

In Listing 3.2, therefore, variables declared within `MultiplyNumbers()` perish when the function ends. If they're used in `main()`, compilation fails as the variables have not been declared in there.

CAUTION

> If you declare another set of variables with the same name in `main()`, you can't expect them to carry a value that might have been assigned in `MultiplyNumbers()`.
>
> The compiler treats the variables in `main()` as independent entities even if they share their names with a variable declared in another function, as the two variables in question are limited by their scope.

Global Variables

If the variables used in function `MultiplyNumbers()` in Listing 3.2 were declared outside the scope of the function `MultiplyNumbers()` instead of within it, then they would be usable in both `main()` and `MultiplyNumbers()`. Listing 3.3 demonstrates global variables, which are the variables with the widest scope in a program.

Input ▼

LISTING 3.3 Using Global Variables

```
#include<iostream>
using namespace std;

// Declare three global integers
```

```
int firstNumber = 0;
int secondNumber = 0;
int multiplicationResult = 0;

void MultiplyNumbers ()
{
   cout << "Enter the first number: ";
   cin >> firstNumber;

   cout << "Enter the second number: ";
   cin >> secondNumber;

   // Multiply two numbers, store result in a variable
   multiplicationResult = firstNumber * secondNumber;

   // Display multiplicationResult
   cout << "Displaying from MultiplyNumbers(): ";
   cout << firstNumber << " x " << secondNumber;
   cout << " = " << multiplicationResult << endl;
}
int main ()
{
   cout << "This program multiplies two numbers" << endl;

   // Call the function that does all the work
   MultiplyNumbers();

   cout << "Displaying from main(): ";

   // This line will now compile and work!
   cout << firstNumber << " x " << secondNumber;
   cout << " = " << multiplicationResult << endl;

   return 0;
}
```


Output ▼

```
This program multiplies two numbers
Enter the first number: 65
Enter the second number: -3
Displaying from MultiplyNumbers(): 65 x -3 = -195
Displaying from main(): 65 x -3 = -195
```

Analysis ▼

Listing 3.3 displays the result of multiplication in two functions, neither of which has declared the variables `firstNumber`, `secondNumber`, and `multiplicationResult`. These variables are global because they have been declared in Lines 5–7, outside the scope of any function. Note Lines 22–23 and 35–36, which use these variables and display their values. Pay special attention to how `multiplicationResult` is first assigned in `MultiplyNumbers()` yet is effectively reused in `main()`.

CAUTION

> Indiscriminate use of global variables is considered poor programming practice. This is because global variables can be assigned values in any/every function and can contain an unpredictable state, especially when functions that modify them run in different threads or are programmed by different programmers in a team.
>
> An elegant version of Listing 3.3 would not use global variables but would instead have the function `MultiplyNumbers()` return the integer result of the multiplication to `main()`.

Naming Conventions

In case you haven't noticed, we named the function `MultiplyNumbers()` where every word in the function name starts with a capital letter (called *PascalCase*), while variables `firstNumber`, `secondNumber`, and `multiplicationResult` were given names where the first word starts with a lowercase letter (called *camelCase*). This book follows a convention where variable names follow camel casing, while other artifacts, such as function names, follow Pascal casing.

You may come across C++ code wherein a variable name is prefixed with characters that convey the type of the variable. This convention is called the *Hungarian notation*. So, `firstNumber` in Hungarian notation would be `iFirstNumber`, where the prefix `i` stands for integer. A global integer would be called `g_iFirstNumber`. Hungarian notation has lost popularity in recent years in part due to improvements in integrated development environments (IDEs) that display the type of a variable—on mouse hover, for instance.

Examples of commonly found bad variable names follow:

```
int i = 0;
bool b = false;
```

These variables are considered to be poorly named because their names do not convey their purpose. They would be better named as follows:

```
int totalCash = 0;
bool isLampOn = false;
```

CAUTION

Naming conventions are used to make code readable to programmers, not to compilers. Therefore, choose a convention and use it consistently.

When working as part of a team, it is a good idea to align on the convention to be used before starting a new project. When working on an existing project, adopt the established convention so that your new code remains readable to others.

Common Compiler-Supported C++ Variable Types

In most of the examples thus far, you have defined variables of type `int`—that is, integers. However, C++ programmers can choose from a variety of fundamental variable types supported directly by the compiler. Choosing the right variable type is important. An integer cannot be used to store values that contain decimals without loss of decimal data. If your program needs to store the value of pi, for instance, you can use the type `float` or `double`. Table 3.1 lists the various variable types and the data values they can contain.

TABLE 3.1 Variable Types

Type	Values
`bool`	`true` or `false`
`char`	256 character values
`unsigned short int`	0 to 65,535
`short int`	–32,768 to 32,767
`unsigned long int`	0 to 4,294,967,295
`long int`	–2,147,483,648 to 2,147,483,647
`unsigned long long`	0 to 18,446,744,073,709,551,615
`long long`	–9,223,372,036,854,775,808 to 9,223,372,036,854,775,807

Type	Values
`int` (16 bit)	–32,768 to 32,767
`int` (32 bit)	–2,147,483,648 to 2,147,483,647
`unsigned int` (16 bit)	0 to 65,535
`unsigned int` (32 bit)	0 to 4,294,967,295
`float`	1.2e–38 to 3.4e38
`double`	2.2e–308 to 1.8e308
`long double`	2.2e–308 to 1.8e308 (This is the same as a `double` variable type on Microsoft Visual C++ [MSVC] but is supported differently on other platforms.)

The following sections explain the important variable types in greater detail.

Using Type `bool` to Store Boolean Values

C++ provides a type `bool` that is specially created for containing Boolean values `true` or `false`, both of which are reserved words.

NOTE

Words such as `bool` are called *reserved* because you cannot use them in naming variables and functions.

Type `bool` is particularly useful for storing settings and flags that can be on or off, present or absent, available or unavailable, and the like.

A sample declaration of an initialized Boolean variable is

```
bool alwaysOn = true;
```

An expression that evaluates to a Boolean type is

```
bool deleteFile = (userSelection == "yes");
// evaluates to true if userSelection contains "yes", else to false
```

Conditional expressions are explained in Lesson 5, “Working with Expressions, Statements, and Operators.”

Using Type `char` to Store Character Values

You use type `char` to store a single character. A sample declaration is

```
char userInput = 'Y'; // initialized char to 'Y'
```

Memory is composed of bits and bytes. Bits evaluate to either state 0 or state 1. Bytes are the smallest unit of memory and comprise bits: 1 byte contains 8 bits. Thus bytes contain numeric data in binary format. When a program uses character data as shown in the example above, the compiler converts the character into a numeric representation that can be placed into memory. The numeric representation of Latin characters A–Z, a–z, numbers 0–9, some special keystrokes (for example, DEL), and special characters (such as backspace) has been standardized by the American Standard Code for Information Interchange, also called ASCII.

You can look up the table in Appendix D, "ASCII Codes," to see that the character Y assigned to variable `userInput` has the ASCII value `89` in decimal or `01011001` in binary. Thus, the compiler stores `01011001` in the memory space allocated for `userInput`.

3

TIP

> Visit Appendix A, "Working with Numbers: Binary and Hexadecimal," to learn about converting numbers between decimal and binary number systems.

The Concept of Signed and Unsigned Integers

Sign implies positive or negative. All numbers you work with using a computer are stored in memory in the form of bits and bytes. A memory location that is 1 byte in size contains 8 bits. Each bit can either be a 0 or 1 (that is, carry one of these two values, at best). Thus, a memory location that is 1 byte in size can contain a maximum of 2 to the power 8 values—that is, 256 unique values. Similarly, a memory location that is 16 bits in size can contain 2 to the power 16 values—that is, 65,536 unique values.

If these values were to be unsigned—that is, assumed to be only positive—then 1 byte could contain integer values ranging from 0 through 255, and 2 bytes could contain values ranging from 0 through 65,535. Referring to Table 3.1, you'll note that `unsigned short` is the type that supports this range and comprises 16 bits. Thus, it is quite easy to model positive values in bits and bytes (see Figure 3.1).

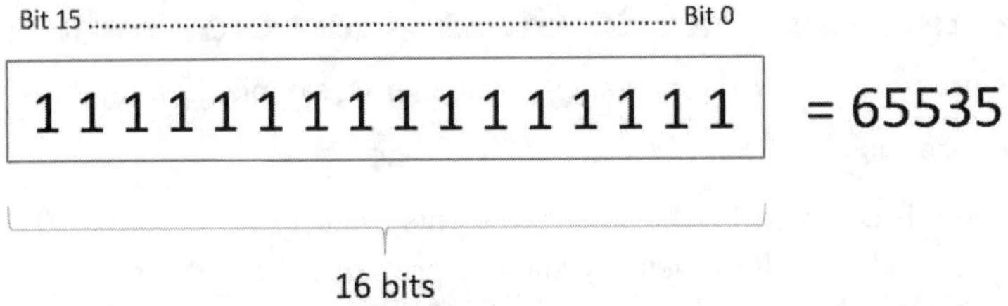

FIGURE 3.1 Organization of bits in a 16-bit unsigned short integer.

How do you model negative numbers in this space? One way is to "sacrifice" a bit as the sign bit that indicates whether the values contained in the other bits are positive or negative (see Figure 3.2). The sign bit needs to be the most-significant-bit (MSB) as the least-significant-bit is required for storing odd numbers. So, when the MSB contains sign information, it is assumed that 0 is positive and 1 means negative, and the other bytes contain the absolute value.

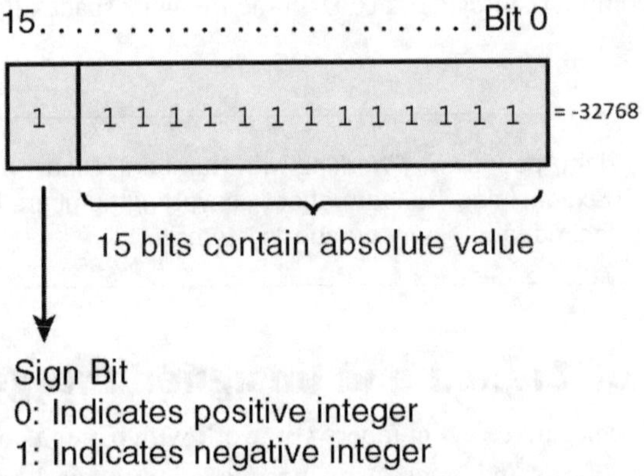

FIGURE 3.2 Organization of bits in a 16-bit signed short integer.

Thus, a signed number that stores 16 bits can contain values ranging from –32,768 through 32,767, and one that stores 8 bits can contain values ranging from –128 through 127. If you look at Table 3.1 again, note that (signed) `short` is the type that supports positive and negative integer values in a 16-bit space.

Signed Integer Types `short`, `int`, `long`, and `long long`

Integer types `short`, `int`, `long`, and `long long` differ in their sizes and the range of values they can contain. `int` is possibly the most used type and is 32 bits wide on most compilers. It is important to use the right type, based on your projection of the maximum value that a particular variable would be expected to hold.

Declaring a variable of a signed type is simple:

```
short int gradesInMath = -5; // not your best score
int moneyInBank = -70000; // overdraft
long populationChange = -85000; // reducing population
long long countryGDP_YoY = -70000000000; // GDP lower by 70 billion
```

Unsigned Integer Types `unsigned short`, `unsigned int`, `unsigned long`, and `unsigned long long`

Unlike their signed counterparts, unsigned integer variable types have not sacrificed a bit to store sign information, and therefore they support twice as many positive values.

Declaring a variable of an unsigned type is as simple as this:

```
unsigned short int numColorsInRainbow = 7;
unsigned int numEggsInBasket = 24; // will always be positive
unsigned long numCarsInNewYork = 700000;
unsigned long long countryMedicareExpense = 70000000000;
```


NOTE

> You use an unsigned variable type when you expect only positive values. So, if you're counting the number of apples harvested, don't use `int`; use `unsigned int`. The latter can hold twice as many values in the positive range as the former can.

CAUTION

> An unsigned type might not be suitable in every situation. For instance, a banking application is required to store negative account balance to support an overdraft facility. You wouldn't use an unsigned type in such a case.

Avoiding Overflow Errors by Selecting Correct Data Types

Data types such as `short`, `int`, `long`, `unsigned short`, `unsigned int`, `unsigned long`, and the like have a finite capacity for containing numbers. When you exceed the limit imposed by the type chosen in an arithmetic operation, you create an overflow.

Take `unsigned short` as an example. Data type `short` consumes 16 bits and can hence contain values from 0 through 65,535. When you add 1 to 65,535 in an `unsigned short`, the value overflows to 0. It's like the odometer of a car that suffers a mechanical overflow when it can support only five digits and the car has traveled 99,999 kilometers (or miles).

In this case, `unsigned short` was never the right type for such a counter. The programmer would have been better off using `unsigned int` to support numbers higher than 65,535.

In the case of a `signed short` integer, which has a range of –32,768 through 32,767, adding 1 to 32,767 may result in the `signed integer` taking the highest negative value. This behavior is compiler dependent.

Listing 3.4 demonstrates the overflow errors that you can inadvertently introduce via arithmetic operations.

Input ▼

LISTING 3.4 Examples of the Ill Effects of Signed and Unsigned Integer Overflow Errors

```
 1: #include<iostream>
 2: using namespace std;
 3:
 4: int main()
 5: {
 6:     unsigned short uShortValue = 65535;
 7:     cout << "unsigned short 65535 + 1 = ";
 8:     cout << ++uShortValue << endl;
 9:
10:     short signedShort = 32767;
11:     cout << "signed short 32767 + 1 = ";
12:     cout << ++signedShort << endl;
13:
14:     return 0;
15: }
```

Output ▼

```
unsigned short 65535 + 1 = 0
signed short 32767 + 1 = -32768
```

Analysis ▼

The output indicates that unintentional overflow situations result in unpredictable and unintuitive behavior for the application. Lines 8 and 12 increment an `unsigned short` and a `signed short` that have previously been initialized to their maximum supported values, –65,535 and 32,767, respectively. The output demonstrates the values the integers hold after the increment operation—namely an overflow of 65,535 to 0 in the `unsigned short` and an overflow of 32,767 to –32,768 in the `signed short`. You wouldn't expect the result of an increment operation to reduce the value in question, but that is exactly what happens when an integer type overflows. If you were using the values in question to allocate memory, then with the unsigned short, you could reach a point where you would request 0 bytes when your actual need is 65,536 bytes.

NOTE

> The increment operations `++uShortValue` and `++signedShort` seen in Listing 3.4 at lines 8 and 12 use the *prefix increment operator*. Operators are explained in detail in Lesson 5.

Floating-Point Types `float` and `double`

Floating-point types are used to store *real numbers*—that is, numbers that can be positive or negative and that can contain decimal values. So, if you want to store the value of pi (22 / 7, or 3.14) in a variable in C++, you use a floating-point type.

3

Declaring variables of these types follows exactly the same pattern as the `int` in Listing 3.1. So, a `float` that allows you to store decimal values would be declared as

```
float pi = 3.14;
```

And a double precision `float` (called simply a `double`) is defined as

```
double morePrecisePi = 22.0 / 7;
```

TIP

> You can use *chunking separators* in the form of a single quotation mark. This improves readability, as demonstrated in the following initializations:
>
> ```
> int moneyInBank = -70'000; // -70000
> long populationChange = -85'000; // -85000
> // -70 billion:
> long long countryGDPChange = -70'000'000'000;
> double pi = 3.141'592'653'59; // 3.14159265359
> ```

NOTE

> The data types mentioned thus far are often referred to as POD (plain old data).

Determining the Size of a Variable by Using `sizeof()`

Size is the amount of memory that the compiler reserves when a programmer declares a variable to hold the data assigned to it. The size of a variable depends on its type, and C++ has a very convenient operator called `sizeof()` that tells you the size, in bytes, of a variable or a type.

> **TIP**
>
> You will inevitably encounter `size_t`, which represents an unsigned integer. It is also the return type of `sizeof()` that gives you the size of the variable in bytes.

The use of `sizeof()` is simple. To determine the size of an integer, you invoke `sizeof()` with parameter `int` (the type), as shown here and further demonstrated in Listing 3.5:

```
cout << "Size of an int: " << sizeof (int);
```

Input ▼

LISTING 3.5 Finding the Sizes of Standard C++ Variable Types

```
#include<iostream>

int main()
{
   using namespace std;
   cout << "Computing the size of inbuilt variable types" << endl;

   cout << "sizeof bool: " << sizeof(bool) << endl;
   cout << "sizeof char: " << sizeof(char) << endl;
   cout << "sizeof unsigned short int: " << sizeof(unsigned short) << endl;
   cout << "sizeof short int: " << sizeof(short) << endl;
   cout << "sizeof unsigned long int: " << sizeof(unsigned long) << endl;
   cout << "sizeof long: " << sizeof(long) << endl;
   cout << "sizeof int: " << sizeof(int) << endl;
   cout << "sizeof uns. long long: "<< sizeof(unsigned long long)<< endl;
   cout << "sizeof long long: " << sizeof(long long) << endl;
   cout << "sizeof unsigned int: " << sizeof(unsigned int) << endl;
   cout << "sizeof float: " << sizeof(float) << endl;
   cout << "sizeof double: " << sizeof(double) << endl;

   cout << "The output changes with compiler, hardware and OS" << endl;

   return 0;
}
```

Output ▼

```
Computing the size of inbuilt variable types
sizeof bool: 1
sizeof char: 1
sizeof unsigned short int: 2
sizeof short int: 2
sizeof unsigned long int: 4
sizeof long: 4
sizeof int: 4
sizeof uns. long long: 8
sizeof long long: 8
sizeof unsigned int: 4
sizeof float: 4
sizeof double: 8
The output changes with compiler, hardware and OS
```


Analysis ▼

The output of Listing 3.5 reveals sizes of various types, in bytes, and is specific to my platform: compiler, OS, and hardware. This output in particular is a result of running the program in 32-bit mode (compiled by a 32-bit compiler) on a 64-bit operating system. Note that a 64-bit compiler probably creates different results, and the reason I chose a 32-bit compiler was to be able to run the application on 32-bit as well as 64-bit systems. The output indicates that the size of a variable doesn't change between unsigned and signed types; the only difference in the two is the MSB, which carries sign information in signed types.

TIP

> If you need to use fixed-width integer types, include header `<cstdint>`. It supplies types where the exact size is specified and assured. These are `int8_t` or `uint8_t` for 8-bit, `int16_t` and `uint16_t` for 16-bit, `int32_t` and `uint32_t` for 32-bit, and `int64_t` and `uint64_t` for 64-bit signed and unsigned integer types, respectively.

Avoid Narrowing Conversion Errors by Using List Initialization

When you initialize a variable of a smaller integer type (say, `short`) by using another variable of a larger type (say, an `int`), you are risking a narrowing conversion error because the compiler has to fit data stored in a type that can potentially hold much larger numbers into a type that doesn't have the same capacity (that is, it is narrower). Here's an example:

```
int largeNum = 5000000;
short smallNum = largeNum; // compiles OK, yet narrowing error
```

Narrowing isn't restricted to conversions between integer types only. You may face narrowing errors if you initialize a `float` using a `double`, a `float` (or `double`) using an `int`, or an `int` using a `float`. Some compilers may warn, but this warning will not cause an error that stops compilation. In such cases, you may be confronted by bugs that occur infrequently and at execution time.

To prevent errors due to narrowing, use *list initialization* techniques and insert initialization values/variables within braces {. . .}. List initialization works as follows:

```
int largeNum = 5000000;
short anotherNum{ largeNum }; // error! Amend types
int anotherNum{ largeNum }; // OK!
float someFloat{ largeNum }; // error! Type int being narrowed
float someFloat{ 5000000 }; // OK! 5000000 can be accommodated
```

It might not be immediately apparent, but this feature has the potential to prevent bugs that occur when data stored in a type undergoes a narrowing conversion at execution time. These bugs occur implicitly during an initialization and are tough to solve.

Automatic Type Inference Using `auto`

In some cases, the type of a variable is apparent, given the initialization value being assigned to it. For example, if a variable is being initialized with the value `true`, the type of the variable can be best estimated as `bool`. Compilers give you the option of not having to explicitly specify the variable type when using the keyword `auto`. In this example, we have left the task of defining an exact type for variable `coinFlippedHeads` to the compiler:

```
auto coinFlippedHeads = true;
```

The compiler checks the value the variable is being initialized to and then decides on the best possible type for this variable. In this particular case, it is clear that an initialization value of `true` best suits a variable that is of type `bool`. The compiler thus determines `bool` as the type that best suits variable `coinFlippedHeads` and internally treats `coinFlippedHeads` as a `bool`, as also demonstrated in Listing 3.6.

Input ▼

LISTING 3.6 Using the `auto` Keyword and Relying on the Compiler's Type-Inference Capabilities

```
 1: #include<iostream>
 2: using namespace std;
 3:
 4: int main()
 5: {
 6:     auto coinFlippedHeads = true;
 7:     auto largeNumber = 2500000000000;
 8:
 9:     cout << "coinFlippedHeads = " << coinFlippedHeads << ", ";
10:     cout << "sizeof(coinFlippedHeads) = " << sizeof(coinFlippedHeads);
11:     cout << endl << "largeNumber = " << largeNumber << ", ";
12:     cout << "sizeof(largeNumber) = " << sizeof(largeNumber) << endl;
13:
14:     return 0;
15: }
```

Output ▼

```
coinFlippedHeads = 1, sizeof(coinFlippedHeads) = 1
largeNumber = 2500000000000, sizeof(largeNumber) = 8
```

Analysis ▼

Note the use of the `auto` keyword in Lines 6 and 7, where the two variables have been declared. By using `auto`, you delegate the decision on the type of variable to the compiler, which uses the initialization value as a ballpark. `sizeof()` is used in Lines 10 and 12 to check whether the compiler created the types it was expected to, and the output confirms that it really did.

NOTE

> `auto` requires you to initialize the variable because the compiler uses this initial value in deciding what the type can be.
>
> When you don't initialize a variable of type `auto`, you get a compile error.

Even if `auto` seems to be a trivial feature at first sight, it makes programming a lot easier in cases where the variable is a complex type. The role of `auto` in writing simpler yet type-safe code is revisited in Lesson 15, "An Introduction to the Standard Template Library," and later chapters.

Using typedef to Substitute a Variable's Type

C++ enables you to substitute variable types with something that you might find convenient. You use the keyword typedef for that. Here is an example where a programmer wants to call an unsigned int a descriptive STRICTLY_POSITIVE_INTEGER:

```
typedef unsigned int STRICTLY_POSITIVE_INTEGER;
STRICTLY_POSITIVE_INTEGER numEggsInBasket = 45;
```

When this code is compiled, the first line tells the compiler that a STRICTLY_POSITIVE_INTEGER is nothing but an unsigned int. At later stages, when the compiler encounters the already defined type STRICTLY_POSITIVE_INTEGER, it substitutes it for unsigned int and continues compilation.

NOTE

> typedef or type substitution is particularly convenient when dealing with complex types that can have cumbersome syntax, such as types that use templates. Templates are discussed in Lesson 14, "An Introduction to Macros and Templates."

What Is a Constant?

Imagine that you are writing a program to calculate the area and the circumference of a circle. The formulas are

```
area = pi * radius * radius;
circumference = 2 * pi * radius
```

In these formulas, pi is a constant of value 22 / 7. You don't want the value of pi to change anywhere in your program. You also want to avoid any accidental assignments of possibly incorrect values to pi. C++ enables you to define pi as a constant that cannot be changed after declaration. In other words, after it's defined, the value of a constant cannot be altered. Assignments to a constant in C++ cause compilation errors.

Thus, constants are like variables in C++ except that they cannot be changed. Much like a variable, a constant also occupies space in memory and has a name to identify the address where the space is reserved. However, the content of this space cannot be overwritten. Constants in C++ can be

- Literal constants
- Declared constants using the const keyword

- Constant expressions using the `constexpr` keyword
- Enumerated constants using the `enum` keyword
- Defined constants (although they are not recommended and have been deprecated)

Literal Constants

Literal constants can be of many types: integer, string, and so on. In your first C++ program in Listing 1.1, you displayed "Hello World" using the following statement:

```
std::cout << "Hello World" << std::endl;
```

In this code, `"Hello World"` is a string literal constant. You literally have been using literal constants ever since then! When you declare an integer `someNumber`, like this:

```
int someNumber = 10;
```

the integer variable `someNumber` is assigned the initial value 10. Here decimal 10 is a part of the code, gets compiled into the application, is unchangeable, and is a literal constant, too. You can initialize the integer by using a literal in octal notation, like this:

```
int someNumber = 012 // octal 12 evaluates to decimal 10
```

You can also use binary literals, like this:

```
int someNumber = 0b1010; // binary 1010 evaluates to decimal 10
```

TIP

> C++ also allows you to define your own literals. For example, you can define temperature as `32.0_F` (Fahrenheit) or `0.0_C` (Celsius), distance as `16_m` (miles) or `10_km` (kilometers), and so on.
>
> The suffixes `_F`, `_C`, `_m`, and `_km` are called *user-defined literals* and are explained in Lesson 12, "Operator Types and Operator Overloading," after the prerequisite concepts are explained.

Declaring Variables as Constants Using `const`

The most important type of constants in C++ are declared by using the keyword `const` before the variable type. The syntax of a generic declaration looks like this:

```
const type-name constant-name = value;
```

Listing 3.7 shows a simple application that displays the value of a constant called `pi`.

Input ▼

LISTING 3.7 Declaring a Constant Called pi

```
 1: #include<iostream>
 2:
 3: int main()
 4: {
 5:    using namespace std;
 6:
 7:    const double pi = 22.0 / 7;
 8:    cout << "The value of constant pi is: " << pi << endl;
 9:
10:    // Uncomment next line to fail compilation
11:    // pi = 345; // error, assignment to a constant
12:
13:    return 0;
14: }
```

Output ▼

```
The value of constant pi is: 3.14286
```

Analysis ▼

Note the declaration of the constant `pi` in Line 7. You use the `const` keyword to tell the compiler that `pi` is a constant of type `double`. If you uncomment Line 11, which assigns a value to a constant, you get a compile failure that says something similar to, "You cannot assign to a variable that is `const`." Thus, using constants is a powerful way to ensure that certain data cannot be modified.

NOTE

> It is good programming practice to define variables that are not supposed to change their values as `const`. The usage of the `const` keyword indicates that the programmer has thought about ensuring the constant-ness of data where required and protects the application from inadvertent changes to this constant.
>
> This is particularly useful in a multi-programmer environment.

Constants are useful when declaring the length of a static array, which is fixed at compile time. Listing 4.2 in Lesson 4, "Managing Arrays and Strings," includes an example that demonstrates the use of a `const int` to define the length of an array.

Constant Expressions Using `constexpr`

The keyword `constexpr` instructs the compiler to compute the expression, if possible. For example, a simple function that divides two numbers may be declared as a `constexpr`:

```
constexpr double Div_Expr(double a, double b)
{
 return a / b;
}
```

The function can be used by a variable that is also declared as a `constexpr`:

```
constexpr double pi = Div_Expr(22, 7);
// Div_Expr() is executed by compiler, pi assigned at compile time
```

Thus, `constexpr` allows for optimization possibilities where some simple computation might be performed by the compiler. In the example above, `Div_Expr()` is invoked with arguments that are integral constants 22 and 7. Hence, the compiler is able to compute `pi`. If the arguments were not constants but plain integers, then you would still be able to use `Div_Expr()`, but the division would be performed at runtime, and you would not be able to assign it to a `constexpr`:

```
int a = 22, b = 7;
const double pi = Div_Expr(a, b);
// Div_Expr() executed at runtime because arguments are not constants
```

C++20 Immediate Functions Using `consteval`

In the previous section, you saw how `Div_Expr()` is treated by the compiler as a constant expression when invoked with constants, and you saw how the result of this constant expression is evaluated by the compiler. However, when `Div_Expr()` is invoked with plain integer variables, the compiler treats it as an ordinary function that is executed at runtime.

C++20 introduces *immediate functions* that are required to be executed by the compiler. You declare an immediate function by using keyword `consteval`:

```
consteval double Div_Eval(double a, double b)
{
   return a / b;
}
```

`Div_Eval()` can only be invoked with arguments that are constants themselves. The compiler performs the division and assigns the return value to the point in code where the function is called:

```
const double pi = Div_Eval(22, 7); // compiler assigns the value of pi
```

Unlike with `Div_Expr()`, if you were to invoke `DivEval()` using plain integers, the compilation would fail:

```
int a = 22, b = 7;
double pi = Div_Eval(a, b); // fail: non-const arguments to consteval fn.
```

Listing 3.8 demonstrates the use of `constexpr` and `consteval`.

Input ▼

LISTING 3.8 Using `consteval` and `constexpr` to Calculate Pi and Multiples of Pi

```
 0: #include<iostream>
 1: consteval double GetPi() { return 22.0 / 7; }
 2: constexpr double XPi(int x) { return x * GetPi(); }
 3:
 4: int main()
 5: {
 6:    using namespace std;
 7:    constexpr double pi = GetPi();
 8:
 9:    cout << "constexpr pi evaluated by compiler to " << pi << endl;
10:    cout << "constexpr XPi(2) evaluated by compiler to " << XPi(2) << endl;
11:
12:    int multiple = 5;
13:    cout << "(non-const) integer multiple = " << multiple << endl;
14:    cout << "constexpr is ignored when XPi(multiple) is invoked, ";
15:    cout << "returns " << XPi(multiple) << endl;
16:
17:    return 0;
18: }
```

Output ▼

```
constexpr pi evaluated by compiler to 3.14286
constexpr XPi(2) evaluated by compiler to 6.28571
(non-const) integer multiple = 5
constexpr is ignored when XPi(multiple) is invoked, returns 15.7143
```

Analysis ▼

In Lines 1 and 2, the program demonstrates the use of `consteval` and `constexpr`, respectively. `GetPi()` in Line 1 is an immediate function. When the compiler encounters `GetPi()` in Line 7, `consteval` instructs the compiler to compute the value of pi resulting from the division and initialize constant `pi` with this value, `3.14286`, in Line 7.

`GetPi()` never makes it to the compiled executable. Line 2 contains a `constexpr` in `XPi(int)`. Its usage in Line 10 results in the compiler substituting `XPi(2)` with `6.28571` because `XPi()` has been invoked with a constant, the integer value `2`. The same function `XPi()`, when invoked in Line 15 with the variable `multiple`, results in the compiler ignoring `constexpr` and integrating `XPi(multiple)` into the code as a regular function call.

If you were to change the declaration of `XPi()` in Line 2 from `constexpr` to `consteval`, you would require the compiler to necessarily compute its return value at every usage of `XPi()` in the code and replace it with the computed value. This would not be possible for the usage of `XPi` in Line 15 with a non-`const` integer, and the compilation would fail. This little example therefore also demonstrates the subtle differences between `consteval` and `constexpr`.

TIP

> The previous code samples define a constant `pi` to show the syntax involved in declaring constants and `constexpr`. However, most popular C++ compilers supply you with a reasonably precise value of `pi` in the constant `M_PI`. You can use this constant in your programs after including the header file `<cmath>`.

Enumerations

There are situations in which a particular variable should be allowed to accept only a certain set of values. For example, you might not want the colors of the rainbow to contain turquoise or the directions on a compass to contain left. In both these cases, you need a type of variable whose values are restricted to a certain set defined by you. *Enumerations*, which are characterized by the keyword `enum`, are exactly the tool you need in such situations. An enumeration comprises a set of constants called *enumerators*.

In the following example, the enumeration `RainbowColors` contains individual colors such as `Violet` as enumerators:

```
enum RainbowColors
{
   Violet = 0,
   Indigo,
   Blue,
   Green,
   Yellow,
   Orange,
   Red
};
```

Here's another enumeration for the cardinal directions:

```
enum CardinalDirections
{
   North,
   South,
   East,
   West
};
```

Enumerations are used as user-defined types. Variables of this type can be assigned a range of values restricted to the enumerators contained in the enumeration. So, if defining a variable that contains the colors of a rainbow, you declare the variable like this:

```
RainbowColors myFavoriteColor = Blue; // Initial value
```

In this line of code, you declare `myFavoriteColor` to be of type `RainbowColors`. This variable is restricted to store any of the specified VIBGYOR colors and no other values.

NOTE

> The compiler converts the enumerator such as `Violet` and so on into integers. Each enumerated value specified is one more than the previous value. You have the choice of specifying a starting value, and if this is not specified, the compiler evaluates it to `0`. So, `North` is evaluated as value `0`.
>
> If you want, you can also specify an explicit value against each of the enumerated constants by initializing them.

Listing 3.9 demonstrates how enumerated constants are used to hold the four cardinal directions, with an initializing value supplied to the first one.

Input ▼

LISTING 3.9 Using Enumerated Values to Indicate Cardinal Wind Directions

```
#include<iostream>
using namespace std;

enum CardinalDirections
{
   North = 25,
   South,
   East,
   West
};
```

```
11:
12: int main()
13: {
14:    cout << "Displaying directions and their symbolic values" << endl;
15:    cout << "North: " << North << endl;
16:    cout << "South: " << South << endl;
17:    cout << "East: " << East << endl;
18:    cout << "West: " << West << endl;
19:
20:    CardinalDirections windDirection = South;
21:    cout << "Variable windDirection = " << windDirection << endl;
22:
23:    return 0;
24: }
```

Output ▼

```
Displaying directions and their symbolic values
North: 25
South: 26
East: 27
West: 28
Variable windDirection = 26
```


Analysis ▼

Note that this listing enumerates the four cardinal directions but gives the first direction, `North`, an initial value of `25` (see Line 6). This automatically ensures that the following constants are assigned values `26`, `27`, and `28` by the compiler, as demonstrated in the output. In Line 20, you create a variable of type `CardinalDirections` that is assigned an initial value `South`. When displayed on the screen in Line 21, the compiler uses the integer value associated with `South`, which is `26`.

TIP

> You might want to take a look at Listings 6.4 and 6.5 in Lesson 6, "Controlling Program Flow." They use `enum` to enumerate the days of the week contained in the enumeration `DaysOfWeek`.

Scoped Enumerations

The enumerated type `CardinalDirections` is defined as an *unscoped* enumeration. The compiler lets you convert variables of this type into integers, and therefore the following statement would be valid:

```
int someNumber = South;
```

This flexibility, however, defeats the very purpose of using enumerations. You're therefore advised to use scoped enumerations instead. Introduced in 2011 as part of C++11, scoped enumerations are declared using the `class` or `struct` keyword following `enum`:

```
enum class CardinalDirections
{North, South, East, West};
```

When declaring a variable of type `CardinalDirections`, you then use the scope resolution operator `::` as follows:

```
CardinalDirections dir = CardinalDirections::South;
```

Scoped enumerations are safer because the compiler ensures strict type safety, which makes the following assignments invalid:

```
int someNumber = CardinalDirections::South; // error
int someNumber = dir; // error
```

As a scoped enumeration, `CardinalDirections` ensures that variables of its type can only be assigned directly to other variables of the same type:

```
CardinalDirections dir2 = dir; // OK
```

TIP

You might want to briefly visit Listing 9.16 in Lesson 9, "Classes and Objects." It uses the `enum class` construct in addition to concepts such as the `switch-case` construct, `struct` and `union`, that you will learn about later on.

Defining Constants by Using `#define`

First and foremost, don't use `#define` if you are writing a program from scratch. The only reason this book explains the definition of constants using `#define` is to help you understand legacy code that define constants using this format:

```
#define pi 3.14286
```

`#define` is a preprocessor macro. In the example above, it causes all following mentions of `pi` to be replaced by `3.14286` for the compiler to process. Note that this is a text replacement (read: non-intelligent replacement) done by the preprocessor. The compiler neither knows nor cares about the actual type of the constant in question.

CAUTION

> Defining constants using the preprocessor via `#define` is deprecated and should not be used.

Keywords You Cannot Use as Variable or Constant Names

Some words are reserved by C++, and you cannot use them as variable names. Keywords have special meaning to the C++ compiler. Keywords include `if`, `while`, `for`, and `main`. A list of keywords defined by C++ is presented in Table 3.2, as well as in Appendix B, "C++ Keywords." Your compiler might have additional reserved words, typically documented in its manuals.

TABLE 3.2 Major C++ Keywords and Reserved Words

Keywords			
asm	else	new	this
auto	enum	operator	throw
bool	explicit	private	true
break	export	protected	try
case	extern	public	typedef
catch	false	register	typeid
char	float	reinterpret_cast	typename
class	for	return	union
const	friend	short	unsigned
constexpr	goto	signed	using
continue	if	sizeof	virtual
default	inline	static	void
delete	int	static_cast	volatile
do	long	struct	wchar_t
double	mutable	switch	while
dynamic_cast	namespace	template	
Reserved Words			
and	bitor	not_eq	xor
and_eq	compl	or	xor_eq
bitand	not	or_eq	

DO	DON'T
DO give variables descriptive names, even if doing so makes them long.	**DON'T** give variables names that are too short or that contain just a character.
DO check whether your team is following certain naming conventions and follow them.	**DON'T** give variables names that use exotic acronyms known only to you.
DO initialize variables: Use list initialization to avoid narrowing conversion errors.	**DON'T** give variables names that are reserved C++ keywords as they won't compile.

Summary

In this lesson, you learned about using memory to store values temporarily in variables and constants. You learned that a variable has a size determined by its type and that the operator `sizeof()` can be used to determine the size of a variable. You got to know different types of variables, such as `bool`, `int`, and so on, and that they are to be used to contain different types of data. The right choice of a variable type is important in effective programming, and the choice of a variable that's too small for the purpose can result in a wrapping error or an overflow situation. You learned about the keyword `auto`, which you use to let the compiler decide the data type for you on the basis of the initialization value of the variable.

You also learned about the different types of constants and usage of the most important ones among them, using the keywords `const`, `constexpr`, and `enum`.

Q&A

Q Why define constants at all if you can use regular variables instead?

A Constants, especially those declared using the keyword `const`, give you a way of telling the compiler that the value of a particular variable should be fixed and should not be allowed to change. Consequently, the compiler always ensures that the constant variable is never assigned another value—not even if another programmer picks up your work and inadvertently tries to overwrite the value. So, declaring constants where you know the value of a variable should not change is a good programming practice and increases the quality of your application.

Q Why should I initialize the value of a variable?

A If you don't initialize, you don't know what the variable contains for a starting value. The starting value is just the contents of the location in the memory that are reserved for the variable. For example, initialization like this:

```
int myFavoriteNumber = 10;
```

writes the initial value of your choosing—in this case 10—to the memory location reserved for the variable `myFavoriteNumber` as soon as it is created.

Q Why does C++ give me the option of using `short int` and `int` and `long int`? Why not just always use the integer that can store the highest number?

A C++ is a programming language that is used to program for a variety of applications, many running on devices with little computing capacity or memory resources. A programmer can often save memory or speed or both by choosing the right kind of variable where high values are not needed. If you are programming on a regular desktop or a high-end smart phone, chances are that the performance gained or memory saved in choosing one integer type over another is going to be insignificant; in some cases there may be no difference.

Q Why should I avoid using global variables frequently? Isn't it true that they're usable throughout my application, and I can save some time otherwise lost to passing values around functions?

A Global variables can be read and assigned globally. The latter is the problem as they can be changed globally. Say that you are working on a project with a few other programmers in a team. You have declared your integers and other variables to be global. If any programmer on your team changes the value of your integer inadvertently in code—which even might be a different `.cpp` file than the one you are using—the reliability of your code is affected. Therefore, you are advised to use global variables as infrequently as possible.

Q I am using unsigned integers that are supposed to contain only positive integer values and zero. What happens if I decrement a zero value contained in an `unsigned int`?

A You see a wrapping effect. Decrementing an unsigned integer that contains 0 by 1 causes the variable to wrap to the highest value it can hold. Check Table 3.1, where you can see that an `unsigned short` can contain values from 0 to 65,535. When you declare an `unsigned short` instantiated to 0 and decrement it, expect it to contain 65,535!

```
unsigned short myShortInt = 0; // Initial Value
myShortInt = myShortInt - 1; // Decrement by 1
std::cout << myShortInt << std::endl; // Output: 65535!
```

Note that this is not a problem with `short`; it is only a problem with an `unsigned short`. An unsigned integral type is not to be used when negative values are within the specifications.

Workshop

The Workshop provides quiz questions to help you solidify your understanding of the material covered and exercises to provide you with experience in using what you've learned. Try to answer the quiz and exercise questions before checking the answers in Appendix E and be certain that you understand the answers before continuing to the next lesson.

Quiz

1. What is the difference between a signed integer and an unsigned integer?
2. Why should you not use `#define` to declare a constant?
3. Why would you initialize a variable?
4. Consider the `enum` below. What is the value of `Queen`?

   ```
   enum YourCards {Ace, Jack, Queen, King};
   ```

5. What is wrong with this variable name?

   ```
   int Integer = 0;
   ```

Exercises

1. Modify `enum YourCards` in Quiz Question 4 to demonstrate that the value of `Queen` can be `45`.
2. Write a program that demonstrates that the size of an unsigned integer and a normal integer are the same and that both are smaller in size than a long integer.
3. Write a program to calculate the area and circumference of a circle where the radius is supplied by the user.
4. In Exercise 3, if the area and circumference were to be stored in integers, how would the output be any different?
5. **BUG BUSTERS:** What is wrong in the following initialization?

   ```
   auto age;
   ```

LESSON 4

Managing Arrays and Strings

In previous lessons, you declared variables used to contain a single `int`, `char`, or `string`, to mention a few instances. However, you may want to declare a collection of objects, such as 20 `int`s or a string of characters to hold a name.

In this lesson, you learn

- What arrays are and how to declare and use them
- What strings are and how to use character arrays to make them
- A brief introduction to `std::string`

What Is an Array?

The dictionary definition of an *array* gets really close to what you need to understand in the context of C++. According to Merriam-Webster, an *array* is "a group of elements forming a complete unit, for example an array of solar panels."

The following are characteristics of an array:

- An array is a collection of elements.
- All elements contained in an array are of the same kind.
- This collection forms a complete set.

In C++, arrays enable you to store data elements of a type in memory, in a sequential and ordered fashion.

The Need for Arrays

Imagine that you are writing a program that asks the user to type in five integers and then displays those integers back to the user. One way to do this would be to have your program declare five distinct and unique integer variables and use them to store and display values. The declarations would look like this:

```
int firstNumber = 0;
int secondNumber = 0;
int thirdNumber = 0;
int fourthNumber = 0;
int fifthNumber = 0;
```

If a user needs this program to store and display 500 integers at a later stage, you need to declare 500 such integers using this system. This is doable, given generous amounts of patience and time. However, imagine that the user asks you to support 500,000 integers instead of 5. What would you do?

You would do it right and do it smart from the start by declaring an array of five integers, like this:

```
int myNumbers[5];
```

Then, if you were required to support 500,000 integers, the code for your array would scale up quite quickly, like this:

```
int manyNumbers[500'000];
```

An array of five characters would be defined as

```
char myCharacters[5];
```

Such an array is called a *static array* because the number of elements it contains and the memory the array consumes are fixed at the time of compilation.

Declaring and Initializing Static Arrays

In the preceding lines of code, you declared an array called `myNumbers` that contains five elements of type `int`—that is, integer. Array declaration in C++ follows this simple syntax:

```
ElementType arrayName[constant_number of elements] = {optional initial values};
```

You can even declare an array and initialize its contents on a per-element basis, as in this integer array, where each of the five integers is initialized to a different integer value:

```
int myNumbers[5] = {34, 56, -21, 5002, 365};
```

You can initialize all elements in an array of a numeric type to zero by using an empty initializer list { }, like this:

```
int myNumbers[5] = {}; // initializes all integers to 0
```

You can also partially initialize elements in an array, like this:

```
int myNumbers[5] = {34, 56};
// initialize first two elements to 34 and 56 and the rest to 0
```

You can define the length of an array (that is, the number of elements in an array) as a constant and use that constant in your array definition:

```
const int ARRAY_LENGTH = 5;
int myNumbers[ARRAY_LENGTH] = {34, 56, -21, 5002, 365};
```

This is particularly useful when you need to access and use the length of the array at multiple places in your code. Then, instead of having to correct the length at each of those places, you just change the initialization value at the `const int` declaration.

You can opt to leave out the number of elements in an array if you know the initial values of the elements in the array:

```
int myNumbers[] = {2016, 2052, -525}; // array of 3 elements
```

4

This code creates an array of three integers with the initial values `2016`, `2052`, and `-525`.

NOTE

The arrays declared so far in the lesson are called *static arrays* as the length of each array is a constant and fixed by the programmer at compile time. A static array cannot take more data than what the programmer has specified. It also does not consume any less memory if left half used or unused. Arrays where the length is decided at runtime are called *dynamic arrays*. Dynamic arrays are briefly introduced later in this lesson and are discussed in detail in Lesson 17, "STL Dynamic Array Classes."

How Data Is Stored in an Array

Think of books placed on a shelf, one next to the other. This is an example of a one-dimensional array, as it expands in only one dimension (that is, the number of books). Each book is an element in the array, and the shelf is akin to the memory that has been reserved to store this collection of books, as shown in Figure 4.1.

FIGURE 4.1
Books on a shelf: a one-dimensional array.

CAUTION

It is not an error that we started numbering the books with 0. As you'll later see, an index in C++ starts at 0 and not at 1.

Similar to the five books on a shelf, the array `myNumbers` containing five integers looks similar to Figure 4.2.

FIGURE 4.2
Organization of an array of five integers, *`myNumbers`*, in memory.

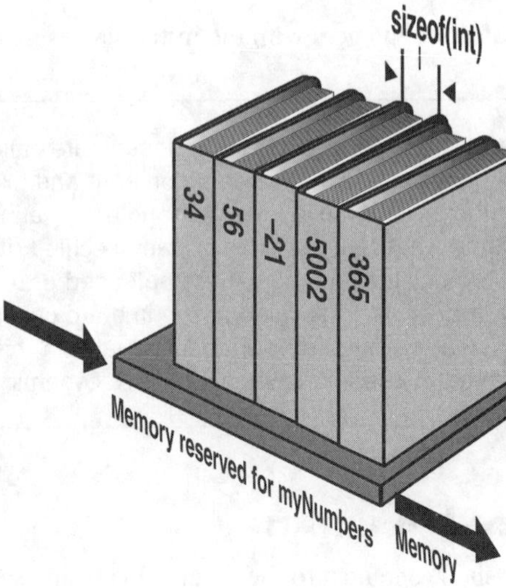

Note that the memory space occupied by the array is composed of five blocks, each of equal size, defined by the type of data to be held in the array—in this case, integer. Recall that you studied the size of an integer in Lesson 3, “Using Variables, Declaring Constants.” The amount of memory reserved by the compiler for the array `myNumbers` is hence `sizeof(int) * 5`. In general, the amount of memory reserved by the compiler for an array in bytes is

```
Bytes consumed by an array = sizeof(element-type) * Number of elements
```

Accessing Data Stored in an Array

Elements in an array can be accessed using their zero-based index. These indexes are called *zero-based* because the first element in an array is at index 0. So, the first integer value stored in the array `myNumbers` is `myNumbers[0]`, the second is `myNumbers[1]`, and so on. The fifth is `myNumbers[4]`. In other words, the index of the last element in an array is always (Length of array – 1).

When asked to access element at index `N`, the compiler uses the memory address of the first element (positioned at index 0) as the starting point and then skips *N* elements by adding the offset computed as `N*sizeof(element)` to reach the address containing the (N + 1)th element. The C++ compiler does not check if the index is within the defined bounds of the array. You can try fetching the element at index 1001 in an array of only 10 elements, but by doing so, you put the security and stability of your program at risk. The onus of ensuring that an array is not accessed beyond its bounds lies solely on the programmer.

CAUTION

Accessing an array beyond its bounds results in unpredictable behavior. In many cases, this causes the program to crash. Accessing arrays beyond their bounds should be avoided at all costs.

Listing 4.1 demonstrates how you declare an array of integers, initialize its elements to integer values, and access them to display them onscreen.

Input ▼

LISTING 4.1 Declaring an Array of Integers and Accessing Its Elements

```
#include<iostream>

using namespace std;

```

```
 4: int main ()
 5: {
 6:    int myNumbers[5] = {34, 56, -21, 5002, 365};
 7:
 8:    cout << "First element at index 0: " << myNumbers [0] << endl;
 9:    cout << "Second element at index 1: " << myNumbers [1] << endl;
10:    cout << "Third element at index 2: " << myNumbers [2] << endl;
11:    cout << "Fourth element at index 3: " << myNumbers [3] << endl;
12:    cout << "Fifth element at index 4: " << myNumbers [4] << endl;
13:
14:    return 0;
15: }
```

Output ▼

```
First element at index 0: 34
Second element at index 1: 56
Third element at index 2: -21
Fourth element at index 3: 5002
Fifth element at index 4: 365
```

Analysis ▼

Line 6 declares an array of five integers with initial values specified for each of them. The subsequent lines simply display the integers using `cout` and using the array variable `myNumbers` with an appropriate index.

NOTE

To familiarize you with the concept of zero-based indexes used to access elements in arrays, we started numbering lines of code in Listing 4.1 and beyond with the first line being numbered as Line 0.

Modifying Data Stored in an Array

In Listing 4.1, you did not enter user-defined data into the array. The syntax for assigning an integer to an element in that array is quite similar to the syntax for assigning an integer value to an integer variable.

For example, you assign the value `2016` to an integer like this:

```
int thisYear;
thisYear = 2016;
```

Assigning the value `2016` to the fourth element in an array looks like this:

```
myNumbers[3] = 2016; // Assign 2016 to the fourth element
```

Listing 4.2 demonstrates the use of constants in declaring the lengths of arrays and shows how individual array elements can be assigned values during the execution of the program.

Input ▼

LISTING 4.2 Assigning Values to Elements in an Array

```
#include<iostream>
using namespace std;
constexpr int Square(int number) { return number*number; }

int main()
{
   const int ARRAY_LENGTH = 5;

   // Array of 5 integers, initialized to 5 values
   int myNumbers[ARRAY_LENGTH] = {5, 10, 0, -101, 20};

   // Using a constexpr for array of 5*5=25 integers
   int moreNumbers[Square(ARRAY_LENGTH)];

   cout << "Enter index of the element to be changed: ";
   int elementIndex = 0;
   cin >> elementIndex;

   cout << "Enter new value: ";
   int newValue = 0;
   cin >> newValue;

   myNumbers[elementIndex] = newValue;
   moreNumbers[elementIndex] = newValue;

   cout << "Element " << elementIndex << " in array myNumbers is: ";
   cout << myNumbers[elementIndex] << endl;

   cout << "Element " << elementIndex << " in array moreNumbers is: ";
   cout << moreNumbers[elementIndex] << endl;

   return 0;
}
```


Output ▼

```
Enter index of the element to be changed: 3
Enter new value: 101
Element 3 in array myNumbers is: 101
Element 3 in array moreNumbers is: 101
```

Analysis ▼

The length of an array needs to be a constant integer. This can therefore also be specified in the constant `ARRAY_LENGTH`, used in Line 9, or the constant expression `Square()` used in Line 12. Thus, the array `myNumbers` is declared to be 5 elements in length, and the array `moreNumbers` is declared to be 25. Lines 14–20 ask the user to enter the index of the element in the array to be modified and the new value to be stored at that index. Lines 22 and 23 demonstrate how to modify a specific element in an array, given that index. Lines 26–29 demonstrate how to access elements in an array, given an index. Note that modifying the element at index 3 actually modifies the fourth element in the array, as indexes are zero-based entities. You have to get used to this.

NOTE

Many novice C++ programmers assign the fifth value at index 5 in an array of five integers. This exceeds the bound of the array as the compiled code tries accessing the sixth element in the array, which is beyond the defined bounds of the array.

This kind of error is called a fence-post error. This error is so named because the number of posts needed to build a fence is always one more than the number of sections in the fence.

CAUTION

Something fundamental is missing from Listing 4.2: It does not check whether the index entered by the user is within the bounds of the array. The program should actually verify whether `elementIndex` is within 0 and 4 for array `myNumbers` and within 0 and 24 for array `moreNumbers` and reject all other entries. This missing check allows the user to potentially assign and access a value beyond the bounds of the array. Such an entry could potentially cause the application—and the system, in a worst-case scenario—to crash.

Performing such checks is explained in Lesson 6, "Controlling Program Flow."

Using Loops to Access Array Elements

When working with arrays and their elements in serial order, you should access them (in other words, iterate) using loops. See Lesson 6, and Listing 6.10 in particular, to quickly learn how elements in an array can be efficiently inserted or accessed using a `for` loop.

DO	DON'T
DO remember that the first element in an array is accessed at index 0. **DO** always ensure that your arrays are used within their defined boundaries.	**DON'T** ever access the Nth element using index N in an array of N elements. Use index (N – 1).

Multidimensional Arrays

The arrays that we have seen thus far have been akin to books on a shelf. There can be more books on a longer shelf and fewer books on a shorter one. The length of the shelf is the only dimension defining the capacity of the shelf, and hence it is one-dimensional. Now, what if we were to use arrays to model an array of solar panels, as shown in Figure 4.3? Solar panels, unlike bookshelves, expand in two dimensions: in length and in breadth.

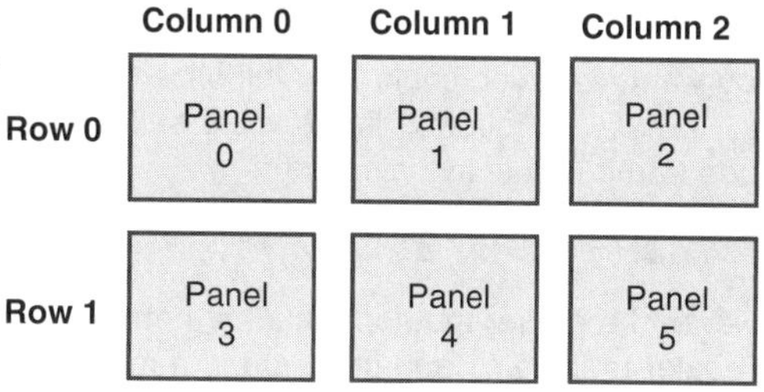

FIGURE 4.3
Array of solar panels on a roof.

As you see in Figure 4.3, six solar panels are placed in a two-dimensional arrangement composed of two rows and three columns. From one perspective, you can see this arrangement as an array of two elements, each element itself being an array of three panels—in other words, an array of arrays. You can use C++ to model two-dimensional arrays, but you are not restricted to just two dimensions. Depending on your need and the nature of the application, you can model multidimensional arrays in memory, too.

Declaring and Initializing Multidimensional Arrays

C++ enables you to declare multidimensional arrays by indicating the number of elements you want to reserve in each dimension. So, a two-dimensional array of integers representing the solar panels in Figure 4.3 is

```
int solarPanels[2][3];
```

Note that in Figure 4.3, each panel is assigned an ID ranging from 0 through 5 for the six panels in the solar array. If you were to initialize the integer array in the same order, it would look like the following:

```
int solarPanels[2][3] = {{0, 1, 2}, {3, 4, 5}};
```

As you see, the initialization syntax used is actually similar to one where we initialize two one-dimensional arrays. An array comprising three rows and three columns would look like this:

```
int threeRowsThreeColumns[3][3] = {{-501, 206, 2016}, {989, 101, 206}, {303,
456, 596}};
```

NOTE

Even though C++ enables you to model multidimensional arrays, the memory where the array is contained is one dimensional. So, the compiler maps the multidimensional array into the memory space, which expands only in one direction.

If you wanted to, you could also initialize the array called `solarPanels` as follows, and it would still contain the same values in the respective elements:

```
int solarPanels[2][3] = {0, 1, 2, 3, 4, 5};
```

However, the earlier method makes a better example because it's easier to imagine and understand a multidimensional array as an array of arrays.

Accessing Elements in a Multidimensional Array

Think of a multidimensional array as an array comprising elements that are arrays. So, when dealing with a two-dimensional array comprising three rows and three columns, each containing integers, visualize it as handling an array comprising three elements, where each element is an array comprising three integers.

When you need to access an element in this multidimensional array, you need to use a first subscript `[]` to address the array where the integer is and a second subscript `[]` to address that integer in this array. Consider this array:

```
int threeRowsThreeColumns[3][3] = {{-501, 205, 2016}, {989, 101, 206}, {303,
456, 596}};
```

This array has been initialized in such a way that you can visualize three arrays, each containing three integers. Here, the integer element with value `205` is at position `[0][1]`. The element with value `456` is at position `[2][1]`. Listing 4.3 illustrates how integer elements in this array can be accessed.

Input ▼

LISTING 4.3 Accessing Elements in a Multidimensional Array

```
 0: #include<iostream>
 1: using namespace std;
 2:
 3: int main()
 4: {
 5:    int threeRowsThreeColumns[3][3] = \
 6:    {{-501, 205, 2016}, {989, 101, 206}, {303, 456, 596}};
 7:
 8:    cout << "Row 0: " << threeRowsThreeColumns[0][0] << " "
 9:                      << threeRowsThreeColumns[0][1] << " "
10:                      << threeRowsThreeColumns[0][2] << endl;
11:
12:
13:    cout << "Row 1: " << threeRowsThreeColumns[1][0] << " "
14:                      << threeRowsThreeColumns[1][1] << " "
15:                      << threeRowsThreeColumns[1][2] << endl;
16:
17:    cout << "Row 2: " << threeRowsThreeColumns[2][0] << " "
18:                      << threeRowsThreeColumns[2][1] << " "
19:                      << threeRowsThreeColumns[2][2] << endl;
20:
21:    return 0;
22: }
```


Output ▼

```
Row 0: -501 205 2016
Row 1: 989 101 206
Row 2: 303 456 596
```

Analysis ▼

Note how you have accessed elements in the array row-wise, starting with the array that is Row 0 (the first row, with index 0) and ending with the array that is Row 2 (third row, with index 2). As each of the rows is an array, the code for addressing the third element in the first row (row index 0, element index 2) is in Line 10.

NOTE

In Listing 4.3, the length of the code increases dramatically with the increase in the number of elements in the array or dimensions thereof. This type of code is actually unsustainable in a professional development environment.

You can see a more efficient way to program accessing elements in a multidimensional array in Listing 6.14 in Lesson 6, in which you use a nested `for` loop to access all elements in such an array.

Dynamic Arrays

Consider an application that stores medical records for hospitals. There is no good way for the programmer to know the upper limits of the number of records the application might need to handle. She can make an assumption that is much higher than the reasonable limit for a small hospital to err on the safe side. In this case, the programmer would be reserving huge amounts of memory without reason and reducing the performance of the system.

The key is to not use static arrays like the ones we have seen thus far but, rather, to choose dynamic arrays that optimize memory consumption and scale up, depending on the demand for resources and memory at execution time. C++ provides you with convenient and easy-to-use dynamic arrays in the form `std::vector`, as shown in Listing 4.4.

Input ▼

LISTING 4.4 Creating a Dynamic Array of Integers and Inserting Values Dynamically

```
#include<iostream>
#include<vector>

using namespace std;

int main()
{
   vector<int> dynArray(3); // dynamic array of int

   dynArray[0] = 365;
   dynArray[1] = -421;
   dynArray[2] = 789;

   cout << "Number of integers in array: " << dynArray.size() << endl;

```

```
15:     cout << "Enter another element to insert" << endl;
16:     int newValue = 0;
17:     cin >> newValue;
18:     dynArray.push_back(newValue);
19:
20:     cout << "Number of integers in array: " << dynArray.size() << endl;
21:     cout << "Last element in array: ";
22:     cout << dynArray[dynArray.size() - 1] << endl;
23:     return 0;
24:
25: }
```

Output ▼

```
Number of integers in array: 3
Enter another element to insert
2017
Number of integers in array: 4
Last element in array: 2017
```

Analysis ▼

Don't worry about the syntax in Listing 4.4 as `vector` and templates have not been explained as yet. Just observe the output and try to correlate it to the code. The initial size of the array, according to the output, is 3, which is consistent with the declaration of the array (`std::vector`) in Line 7. Knowing this, you still ask the user to enter a fourth number in Line 15, and, interestingly, you are able to insert that number into the back of the array by using `push_back()` in Line 18. The `vector` dynamically resizes itself to accommodate more data. This can then be seen in the size of the array, which increases to 4. Note the usage of the familiar static array syntax to access data in the vector. Line 22 accesses the last element (wherever that might be, given a position calculated at runtime) by using the zero-based index, where the last element is at index `size() - 1`, where `size()` is the function that returns the total number of elements (integers) contained in the `vector`.

NOTE

To use the dynamic array class `std::vector`, you need to include the header `<vector>`, as in Line 1 of Listing 4.4.

Vectors are explained in greater detail in Lesson 17.

C-Style Character Strings

A C-style string is a special case of an array of characters. You have already seen some examples of C-style strings in the form of string literals that you have been writing in your code:

```
std::cout << "Hello World";
```

This is equivalent to using the array declaration

```
char sayHello[] = {'H','e','l','l','o',' ','W','o','r','l','d','\0'};
std::cout << sayHello << std::endl;
```

Note that the last character in the array is a null character `'\0'`. This is called the *string-terminating character* because it tells the compiler that the string has ended. Such C-style strings are a special case of character arrays in that the last character always precedes the null terminator `'\0'`. When you embed a string literal in your code, the compiler does the job of adding `'\0'` after it.

If you inserted `'\0'` anywhere in the middle of the array, it would not change the size of the array; it would only mean that string processing using the array as input would stop at that point. Listing 4.5 demonstrates this point.

NOTE

> `'\0'` might look like two characters contained within the single quotes, and it indeed is two characters typed using the keyboard. However, the backslash is a special escape code that the compiler understands, and `\0` means null—that is, it asks the compiler to insert a null or zero.
>
> You could not write `'0'` directly because that would be accepted as character zero, which has the nonzero ASCII code 48.
>
> Check the table in Appendix D, "ASCII Codes," to see this and other ASCII values.

Input ▼

LISTING 4.5 Analyzing the Null Terminator in a C-Style String

```
 0: #include<iostream>
 1: using namespace std;
 2:
 3: int main()
 4: {
 5:    char sayHello[] = {'H','e','l','l','o',' ','W','o','r','l','d','\0'};
 6:    cout << sayHello << endl;
 7:    cout << "Size of array: " << sizeof(sayHello) << endl;
 8:
 9:    cout << "Replacing space with null" << endl;
10:    sayHello[5] = '\0';
11:    cout << sayHello << endl;
12:    cout << "Size of array: " << sizeof(sayHello) << endl;
13:
14:    return 0;
15: }
```

Output ▼

```
Hello World
Size of array: 12
Replacing space with null
Hello
Size of array: 12
```


Analysis ▼

Line 10 is where you replace the space in `"Hello World"` with the null-terminating character. Note that the array now has two null terminators, but it's the first one that results in the display of the character array in Line 11 being truncated to just `"Hello"`. Operator `sizeof(...)` in Lines 7 and 12 indicates that the size of the array has not changed, even if the displayed data changed a lot.

CAUTION

> If you forget to add the `'\0'` when declaring and initializing the character array in Listing 4.5 at Line 5, then expect the output to contain garbled characters after printing `"Hello World"`. This occurs because `std::cout` does not stop with printing the array until it reaches a null character, even if it means exceeding the bounds of the array.
>
> This mistake can cause your program to crash and, in some cases, can compromise the stability of the system.

C-style strings are fraught with danger. Listing 4.6 demonstrates the risks involved in using such a string.

Input ▼

LISTING 4.6 A Risky Application Using C-Style Strings and User Input

```
 0: #include<iostream>
 1: #include<string.h>
 2: using namespace std;
 3: int main()
 4: {
 5:     cout << "Enter a word NOT longer than 20 characters:" << endl;
 6:
 7:     char userInput [21];
 8:     cin >> userInput;
 9:
10:     cout << "Length of your input was: " << strlen(userInput) << endl;
11:
12:     return 0;
13: }
```

Output

```
Enter a word NOT longer than 20 characters:
Don'tUseThisProgram
Length of your input was: 19
```

Analysis ▼

The danger is visible in the output. The program is begging the user to not enter data longer than 20 characters. The reason it does so is that the character buffer declared in Line 7 meant to store user input has a fixed—static—length of 21 characters. Because the last character in the string needs to be a null-terminator (`'\0'`), the maximum length of text stored by the buffer is 20 characters. However, `cin` will not verify the length of the character array `userInput` being used and will therefore exceed its bounds if the user enters a word that is 21 characters or longer.

TIP

> A bug wherein the bounds of an array are crossed is called a *buffer overflow*. In addition to compromising the stability of your application, a buffer overflow is considered a vulnerability that makes your C++ application insecure.

Note the use of `strlen()` in Line 10 to compute the length of the string. `strlen()` goes through the character array and counts the number of characters crossed until it reaches the null terminator that indicates the end of the string. This null terminator has been inserted by `cin` at the end of the user's input. This behavior of `strlen` makes it dangerous as it can easily walk past the bounds of the character array if the user has supplied text longer than the mentioned limit. One way to solve this problem would be to implement a check ensuring that the limits of the character buffer aren't crossed. Listing 6.2 in Lesson 6 implements one such check.

CAUTION

> Applications programmed in C (or in C++ by programmers who have a strong C background) often use string copy functions such as `strcpy()`, concatenation functions such as `strcat()`, and `strlen()` to determine the length of a string, in addition to other functions of this kind.
>
> These functions take C-style strings as input and are dangerous as they seek the null terminator and can exceed the boundaries of the character array they're using if the programmer has not ensured the presence of the terminating null.

The preferred way, however, is to avoid using character arrays for string operations. Use the C++ standard library class `std::string` instead.

C++ Strings: Using `std::string`

C++ standard strings are an efficient and safer way to deal with text input—and to perform string manipulations like concatenations. `std::string` is not static in size like a `char` array implementation of a C-style string is and can scale up when more data needs to be stored in it. Listing 4.7 shows the use of `std::string` to manipulate string data.

Input ▼

LISTING 4.7 Using `std::string` to Initialize, Store User Input, Copy, Concatenate, and Determine the Length of a String

```
#include<iostream>
#include<string>

using namespace std;

int main()
{
   string greetString ("Hello std::string!");
   cout << greetString << endl;

   cout << "Enter a line of text: " << endl;
   string firstLine;
   getline(cin, firstLine);

   cout << "Enter another: " << endl;
   string secondLine;
   getline(cin, secondLine);

   cout << "Result of concatenation: " << endl;
   string concatString = firstLine + " " + secondLine;
   cout << concatString << endl;

   cout << "Copy of concatenated string: " << endl;
   string aCopy;
   aCopy = concatString;
   cout << aCopy << endl;

   cout << "Length of concat string: " << concatString.length() << endl;

   return 0;
}
```

Output ▼

```
Hello std::string!
Enter a line of text:
I love
Enter another:
C++ strings
Result of concatenation:
I love C++ strings
Copy of concatenated string:
I love C++ strings
Length of concat string: 18
```

Analysis ▼

Try to understand the output and correlate it to the various elements in code. Don't let new syntax features bother you at this stage. The program starts by displaying a string that has been initialized in Line 7 to `"Hello std::string"`. It then asks the user to enter two lines of text, which are stored in variables `firstLine` and `secondLine` in Lines 12 and 16. The actual concatenation is simple and looks like an arithmetic addition in Line 19, where even a space has been added to the first line. The act of copying is a simple act of assigning in Line 24. Determining the length of the string is done by invoking `length()` on it in Line 27.

NOTE

> To use a C++ string, you need to include the header `string`:
>
> `#include<string>`
>
> This is also visible in Line 1 in Listing 4.7.

To learn the various functions of `std::string` in detail, take a quick look at Lesson 16, "The STL `string` Class." Because you have not learned about classes and templates yet, ignore sections that seem unfamiliar in that lesson and concentrate on understanding the gist of the samples.

Summary

This lesson taught you about the basics of arrays: what they are and where they can be used. You learned how to declare an array, initialize an array, access elements in an array, and write values to elements in an array. You learned how important it is to avoid exceeding the limits, also called *bounds*, of an array in order to avoid *buffer overflows*. You also learned the importance of ensuring that input is checked before using it to index elements to ensure that the limits of an array are not crossed.

Dynamic arrays are arrays in which the programmer doesn't need to worry about fixing the max length of an array at compile time. These arrays allow for better memory management if usage is less than the expected maximum.

You also learned that C-style strings are a special case of `char` arrays, where the end of the string is marked by the null-terminating character `'\0'`. More importantly, though, you learned that C++ offers a far better option in `std::string`, which provides convenient utility functions that enable you to determine the length, concatenate, and perform similar actions.

Q&A

Q Given a choice, would you use C-style strings that need a null terminator?

A Yes, but only if someone places a gun to your head. C++ `std::string` is a lot safer and supplies features that should make any good programmer stay away from using C-style strings.

Q Does the length of a string include the null terminator at the end of it?

A No, it doesn't. The length of the string `"Hello World"` is 11, including the space and excluding the (invisible) null character marking the end.

Q Well, I still want to use C-style strings in `char` arrays that I define. What should be the size of the array I am using?

A Here is one of the complications of using C-style strings. The size of the array should be one greater than the size of the largest string it will ever contain. This is essential so that it can accommodate the null character at the end of the largest string. If `"Hello World"` were the largest string your `char` array would ever hold, then the length of the array would need to be 11 + 1 = 12 characters. Clearly, this array would be less suited to containing user input because a user may easily exceed its bounds and cause a buffer overflow.

Workshop

The Workshop provides quiz questions to help you solidify your understanding of the material covered and exercises to provide you with experience in using what you've learned. Try to answer the quiz and exercise questions before checking the answers in Appendix E and be certain you understand the answers before continuing to the next lesson.

Quiz

1. Check the array `myNumbers` in Listing 4.1. What are the indexes of the first and last elements in that array?
2. If you needed to allow the user to input strings, would you use C-style strings?
3. How many characters does the compiler see in `'\0'`?
4. You forget to end your C-style string with a null terminator. What happens when you use it?
5. See the declaration of `vector` in Listing 4.4 and try composing a dynamic array that contains elements of the type `char`.

Exercises

1. Declare an array that represents the squares on the chessboard; the array should be an `enum` that defines the pieces that may possibly occupy the squares.

   Hint: The `enum` will contain enumerators (`Pawn`, `Rook`, `Bishop`, and so on), thereby limiting the range of possible values that the elements in the array can hold. Don't forget that a cell may also be empty!

2. **BUG BUSTERS:** What is wrong with this code fragment?

```
int myNumbers[5];
myNumbers[5] = 450; // Setting the 5th element to value 450
```

LESSON 5

Working with Expressions, Statements, and Operators

At its heart, a program is a set of commands executed in sequence. These commands are programmed into expressions and statements and use operators to perform specific calculations or actions.

In this lesson, you learn

- What statements are
- What blocks or compound statements are
- What operators are
- How to perform simple arithmetic and logical operations

Statements

Languages—spoken or programmed—are composed of statements that are executed one after another. Let's analyze the first important statement you learned:

```
cout << "Hello World" << endl;
```

A statement using `cout` displays text onscreen, via the console. Every statement in C++ ends with a semicolon (`;`), which defines the boundary of the statement. It is similar to the period (.) you add when ending a sentence in English. The next statement can start immediately after the semicolon. Therefore, this line comprises two statements in C++:

```
cout << "Hello World" << endl; cout << "Another hello" << endl;
```

However, for the sake of convenience and readability, programmers typically program statements one per line.

NOTE

> Whitespace—including spaces, tabs, line feeds, carriage returns, and so on—typically is not visible to the compiler. Whitespace within string literals, though, make a difference to the output.

The following would be invalid:

```
cout << "Hello
     World" << endl; // new line in string literal not allowed
```

Such code typically results in an error indicating that the compiler is missing a closing quote (`"`) and a statement-terminating semicolon (`;`) in the first line. If you need to spread a statement over two lines for some reason, you can do it by inserting a backslash (\) at the end of the first line:

```
cout << "Hello \
     World" << endl; // split to two lines is OK
```

Another way of writing the preceding statement in two lines is to write two string literals instead of just one:

```
cout << "Hello "
   "World" << endl; // two string literals is also OK
```

In the preceding example, the compiler notices two adjacent string literals and concatenates them for you.

NOTE

> Splitting a statement into many lines can be useful when you have long text elements or complex expressions composed of many variables that make a statement much longer than most displays allow.

Compound Statements, or Blocks

When you group statements together in braces {...}, you create a compound statement, or a block:

```
{
    int daysInYear = 365;
    cout << "Block contains an int and a cout statement" << endl;
}
```

A block typically groups many statements to indicate that they belong together. Blocks are particularly useful when programming conditional `if` statements or loops, which are explained in Lesson 6, "Controlling Program Flow."

Using Operators

Operators are tools that C++ provides to enable you to work with data, transform it, process it, and possibly make decisions on the basis of it.

The Assignment Operator (=)

The assignment operator is an operator that you have already been using intuitively in this book:

```
int daysInYear = 365;
```

This statement uses the assignment operator to initialize an integer to `365`. The assignment operator replaces the value contained by the operand to the left (unimaginatively called the *l-value*) with the one on the right (called the *r-value*).

Understanding l-Values and r-Values

An l-value typically refers to a location in memory. A variable such as `daysInYear` from the preceding example is actually a handle to a memory location and is an l-value. r-values, on the other hand, can be the very content of a memory location.

So, all l-values can be r-values, but not all r-values can be l-values. To understand it better, look at the following example, which doesn't make any sense and therefore won't compile:

```
365 = daysInYear;
```

Operators to Add (+), Subtract (-), Multiply (*), Divide (/), and Modulo Divide (%)

You can perform an arithmetic operation between two operands by using + for addition, - for subtraction, * for multiplication, / for division, and % for modulo operation:

```
int num1 = 22;
int num2 = 5;
int addNums = num1 + num2; // 27
int subtractNums = num1 - num2; // 17
int multiplyNums = num1 * num2; // 110
int divideNums = num1 / num2; // 4
int moduloNums = num1 % num2; // 2
```

Note that the division operator (/) returns the result of division between two operands. In the case of integers, however, the result contains no decimals as integers by definition cannot hold decimal data. The modulo operator (%) returns the remainder of a division operator, and it is applicable only on integer values. Listing 5.1 is a simple program that performs arithmetic functions on two numbers entered by the user.

Input ▼

LISTING 5.1 Demonstrating Arithmetic Operators on Integers Entered by the User

```
#include<iostream>
using namespace std;

int main()
{
    cout << "Enter two integers:" << endl;
    int num1 = 0, num2 = 0;
    cin >> num1;
    cin >> num2;

    cout << num1 << " + " << num2 << " = " << num1 + num2 << endl;
    cout << num1 << " - " << num2 << " = " << num1 - num2 << endl;
    cout << num1 << " * " << num2 << " = " << num1 * num2 << endl;
    cout << num1 << " / " << num2 << " = " << num1 / num2 << endl;
    cout << num1 << " % " << num2 << " = " << num1 % num2 << endl;

    return 0;
}
```

Output ▼

```
Enter two integers:
365
25
365 + 25 = 390
365 - 25 = 340
365 * 25 = 9125
365 / 25 = 14
365 % 25 = 15
```

Analysis ▼

Most of the program is self-explanatory. The line of most interest is possibly Line 14, which uses the `%` modulo operator. This returns the remainder that is the result of dividing `num1` (365) by `num2` (25).

Operators to Increment (++) and Decrement (--)

Sometimes you need to count in increments of one. This helps control loops where the value of a variable needs to be incremented or decremented every time a loop has been executed.

C++ includes the `++` (increment) and `--` (decrement) operators to help you with this task.

You use these operators as follows:

```
int num1 = 101;
int num2 = num1++; // Postfix increment operator
int num2 = ++num1; // Prefix increment operator
int num2 = num1--; // Postfix decrement operator
int num2 = --num1; // Prefix decrement operator
```

5

As this example indicates, there are two different ways to use the incrementing and decrementing operators: before and after the operand. Operators that are placed before the operand are called *prefix increment* or *prefix decrement* operators, and those that are placed after are called *postfix increment* or *postfix decrement* operators.

To Postfix or to Prefix?

It's important to understand the difference between prefix and postfix and use the one that works in a given situation. The result of execution of the postfix operators is that the r-value (the variable to the right) is first assigned to the l-value, and after that assignment, the r-value is incremented (or decremented). This means that in cases where a postfix operator has been used, the value of `num2` is the old value of `num1` (the value before the increment or decrement operation).

Prefix operators have exactly the opposite behavior. The r-value is first incremented and then assigned to the l-value. In cases where a prefix operator has been used, `num2` and `num1` carry the same value. Listing 5.2 demonstrates the effect of prefix and postfix increment and decrement operators on a sample integer.

Input ▼

LISTING 5.2 Demonstrating the Difference Between Postfix and Prefix Operators

```
#include<iostream>
using namespace std;

int main()
{
    int startValue = 101;
    cout << "Start value of integer being operated: " << startValue << endl;

    int postfixIncrement = startValue++;
    cout << "Result of Postfix Increment = " << postfixIncrement << endl;
    cout << "After Postfix Increment, startValue = " << startValue << endl;

    startValue = 101; // Reset
    int prefixIncrement = ++startValue;
    cout << "Result of Prefix Increment = " << prefixIncrement << endl;
    cout << "After Prefix Increment, startValue = " << startValue << endl;

    startValue = 101; // Reset
    int postfixDecrement = startValue--;
    cout << "Result of Postfix Decrement = " << postfixDecrement << endl;
    cout << "After Postfix Decrement, startValue = " << startValue << endl;

    startValue = 101; // Reset
    int prefixDecrement = --startValue;
    cout << "Result of Prefix Decrement = " << prefixDecrement << endl;
    cout << "After Prefix Decrement, startValue = " << startValue << endl;

    return 0;
}
```

Output ▼

```
Start value of integer being operated: 101
Result of Postfix Increment = 101
After Postfix Increment, startValue = 102
Result of Prefix Increment = 102
After Prefix Increment, startValue = 102
Result of Postfix Decrement = 101
After Postfix Decrement, startValue = 100
Result of Prefix Decrement = 100
After Prefix Decrement, startValue = 100
```

Analysis ▼

The results show that the postfix operators were different from the prefix ones in that the l-values being assigned in Lines 8 and 18 contain the original values of the integer before the increment or decrement operations. The prefix operations in Lines 13 and 23, on the other hand, result in the l-value being assigned the incremented or decremented value. This is the most important difference that needs to be kept in perspective when choosing the operator type.

Note that in the following statements, the prefix or postfix operators make no difference to the output of the program:

```
startValue++; // Is the same as…
++startValue;
```

This is because there is no assignment of an initial value, and the end result in both cases is just that the integer `startValue` is incremented.

> **NOTE**
>
> You often hear of cases where prefix increment or prefix decrement operators are preferred over their postfix variants on grounds of better performance. That is, `++startValue` is preferred over `startValue++`.
>
> This is true at least theoretically because with the postfix operators, the compiler needs to store the initial value temporarily in case it needs to be assigned. The effect on performance in these cases is negligible with respect to integers, but in the case of certain classes, this argument might have a point. Smart compilers may, however, optimize and reduce the differences in question.

5

Equality Operators (`==` and `!=`)

Often you need to check for a certain condition being fulfilled or not being fulfilled before you proceed to take action. The equality operators `==` (operands are equal) and `!=` (operands are unequal) help you with exactly that.

The result of an equality check is a `bool`—that is, `true` or `false`:

```
int personAge = 20;
bool checkEquality = (personAge == 20); // true
bool checkInequality = (personAge != 100); // true

bool checkEqualityAgain = (personAge == 200); // false
bool checkInequalityAgain = (personAge != 20); // false
```

Relational Operators

In addition to equality checks, you might want to check for inequality of a certain variable against a value. To assist you with that, C++ includes relational operators (see Table 5.1).

TABLE 5.1 Relational Operators

Operator Name	Description
Less than (<)	Evaluates to `true` if one operand is less than the other (`op1 < op2`); otherwise, evaluates to `false`
Greater than (>)	Evaluates to `true` if one operand is greater than the other (`op1 > op2`); otherwise, evaluates to `false`
Less than or equal to (<=)	Evaluates to `true` if one operand is less than or equal to another; otherwise, evaluates to `false`
Greater than or equal to (>=)	Evaluates to `true` if one operand is greater than or equal to another; otherwise, evaluates to `false`

As Table 5.1 indicates, the result of a comparison operation is always `true` or `false`—in other words, a `bool`. The following sample code indicates how the relational operators introduced in Table 5.1 can be put to use:

```
int personAge = 20;
bool checkLessThan = (personAge < 100);  // true
bool checkGreaterThan = (personAge > 100); // false
bool checkLessThanEqualTo = (personAge <= 20); // true
bool checkGreaterThanEqualTo = (personAge >= 20); // true
bool checkGreaterThanEqualToAgain = (personAge >= 100); // false
```

Listing 5.3 is a program that demonstrates the effect of using these operators by displaying the result onscreen.

Input ▼

LISTING 5.3 Demonstrating Equality and Relational Operators

```
#include<iostream>
using namespace std;

int main()
{
   cout << "Enter two integers:" << endl;
```

```
    int num1 = 0, num2 = 0;
    cin >> num1;
    cin >> num2;

    bool isEqual = (num1 == num2);
    cout << "equality test: " << isEqual << endl;

    bool isUnequal = (num1 != num2);
    cout << "inequality test: " << isUnequal << endl;

    bool isGT = (num1 > num2); // greater than
    cout << "" << num1 << " > " << num2 << " test: " << isGT << endl;

    bool isLT = (num1 < num2); // lesser than
    cout << "" << num1 << " < " << num2 << " test: " << isLT << endl;

    bool isGTE = (num1 >= num2); // greater than or equal to
    cout << "" << num1 << " >= " << num2 << " test: " << isGTE << endl;

    bool isLTE = (num1 <= num2); // lesser than or equal to
    cout << "" << num1 << " <= " << num2 << " test: " << isLTE << endl;

    return 0;
}
```

Output ▼

First run:

```
Enter two integers:
365
-24
equality test: 0
inequality test: 1
365 > -24 test: 1
365 < -24 test: 0
365 >= -24 test: 1
365 <= -24 test: 0
```

Next run:

```
Enter two integers:
101
101
equality test: 1
inequality test: 0
101 > 101 test: 0
101 < 101 test: 0
101 >= 101 test: 1
101 <= 101 test: 1
```

Analysis ▼

The program displays the binary results of the various operations, with the test result `0` indicating `false` and `1` indicating `true`. Note the output that occurs when the two supplied integers are identical: The operators `==`, `>=`, and `<=` produce identical results.

The fact that the output of equality and relational operators is binary makes these operators perfectly suited for use in statements that help in decision making and as loop condition expressions that ensure a loop executes only so long as the condition evaluates to `true`. You can learn more about conditional execution and loops in Lesson 6.

NOTE

The output of Listing 5.3 displays Boolean values containing `false` as `0`. Those containing `true` are displayed as `1`. From a compiler's point of view, an expression evaluates to `false` when it evaluates to `0`. A check against `false` is a check against zero. An expression that evaluates to a nonzero value is evaluated as `true`.

C++20 Three-Way Comparison Operator (<=>)

The three-way comparison operator is a modern addition to C++. Introduced formally in 2020, operator `<=>` compares two operands and reveals whether one is less than the other, whether one is greater than the other, or whether the two are equal to each other, as shown here:

```
Type var1 = value1, var2 = value2;
auto resultOfComparison = var1 <=> var2;
```

In this example,

- If `resultOfComparison` is less than zero, then `var1` is less than `var2`.
- If `resultOfComparison` is greater than zero, then `var1` is greater than `var2`.
- If `resultOfComparison` is zero, then `var1` is equal to `var2`.

Since this operator can be used to model both greater-than and less-than comparisons, it is considered to be rather fundamental and has been given higher precedence than various relational operators.

Listing 5.4 is a program that demonstrates the use of the three-way comparison operator.

Input ▼

LISTING 5.4 Demonstrating the Use of the Three-Way Comparison Operator (<=>) in Comparing Numbers

```
#include<iostream>
#include<compare>
using namespace std;

int main()
{
   int num1, num2;
   cout << "Enter two integers" << endl;
   cin >> num1;
   cin >> num2;

   auto resultofComparison = (num1 <=> num2); // introduced in C++20!

   if (resultofComparison < 0)
      cout << "num1 is less than num2" << endl;
   else if (resultofComparison > 0)
      cout << "num1 is greater than num2" << endl;
   else // comparison evaluates to zero
      cout << "They're equal" << endl;

   return 0;
}
```

Output ▼

First run:

```
Enter two integers
101
-5
num1 is greater than num2
```

Another run:

```
Enter two integers
-5
10
num1 is less than num2
```

Last run:

```
Enter two integers
2020
2020
They're equal
```

Analysis ▼

Focus on Line 11, which uses the three-way comparison operator <=>. The result of the comparison is assigned to the variable resultOfComparison. You use auto to let the compiler automatically deduce the type of the result from the nature of operands. For integer operands, as in this example, the result of the operation is stored by the compiler in a variable of type std::strong_ordering. The example demonstrates how one usage of the operator <=> produces results that otherwise needed three operations (<, >, and ==) in Listing 5.3.

NOTE

Some compilers (notably clang++ as of this writing) require you to include<compare> when using the three-way comparison operator <=>, as shown in Line 1 in Listing 5.4. This header defines the return types std::strong_ordering or std::partial_ordering.

TIP

The <=> operator is informally called the *spaceship operator* due to its appearance!

Logical Operations NOT, AND, OR, and XOR

Logical NOT operation is supported by the operator ! and works on a single operand. Table 5.2 is the truth table for a logical NOT operation, which, as expected, simply inverses the supplied Boolean flag.

TABLE 5.2 Truth Table of Logical NOT Operation

Operand	Result of NOT (Operand)
false	true
true	false

Other operators, such as AND, OR, and XOR, need two operands. Logical AND operation evaluates to `true` only when each operand evaluates to `true`. Table 5.3 demonstrates the functioning of a logical AND operation.

TABLE 5.3 Truth Table of Logical AND Operation

Operand 1	Operand 2	Result of Operand1 AND Operand2
`false`	`false`	`false`
`true`	`false`	`false`
`false`	`true`	`false`
`true`	`true`	`true`

Logical AND operation is supported by the operator `&&`.

Logical OR evaluates to `true` when at least one of the operands evaluates to `true`, as demonstrated in Table 5.4.

TABLE 5.4 Truth Table of Logical OR Operation

Operand 1	Operand 2	Result of Operand1 OR Operand2
`false`	`false`	`false`
`true`	`false`	`true`
`false`	`true`	`true`
`true`	`true`	`true`

Logical OR operation is supported by the operator `||`.

The exclusive OR (abbreviated XOR) operation is slightly different from logical OR as it evaluates to `true` when any one operand (but not both) is `true`, as demonstrated in Table 5.5.

TABLE 5.5 Truth Table of Logical XOR Operation

Operand 1	Operand 2	Result of Operand1 XOR Operand2
false	false	false
true	false	true
false	true	true
true	true	false

C++ provides a bitwise XOR in the form of the operator ^. This operator helps evaluate a result that is generated via an XOR operation on the operand's bits.

Using C++ Logical Operators NOT (!), AND (&&), and OR (||)

Consider these statements:

- "If it is raining AND if there are no buses, I cannot go to work."
- "If there is a deep discount OR if I am awarded a record bonus, I can buy that car."

You need such logical constructs in programming where the result of two operations is used in a logical context to decide the future flow of a program. C++ provides logical AND and OR operators that you can use in conditional statements to conditionally change the flow of the program.

Listing 5.5 demonstrates the workings of the logical AND and logical OR operators.

Input ▼

LISTING 5.5 Analyzing Logical AND (&&) and Logical OR (||)

```
#include<iostream>
using namespace std;

int main()
{
   cout << "Enter true(1) or false(0) for two operands:" << endl;
   bool op1 = false, op2 = false;
   cin >> op1;
   cin >> op2;

   cout << op1 << " AND " << op2 << " = " << (op1 && op2) << endl;
   cout << op1 << " OR " << op2 << " = " << (op1 || op2) << endl;

   return 0;
}
```

Output ▼

First run:

```
Enter true(1) or false(0) for two operands:
1
0
1 AND 0 = 0
1 OR 0 = 1
```

Next run:

```
Enter true(1) or false(0) for two operands:
1
1
1 AND 1 = 1
1 OR 1 = 1
```

Analysis ▼

The program demonstrates the use and function of the logical operators AND and OR in Lines 10 and 11. What the program doesn't show is how to use them in making decisions.

Listing 5.6 shows a program that executes different lines of code, depending on the values contained in variables. It uses conditional statement processing and logical operators to determine which statements to execute.

Input ▼

LISTING 5.6 Logical NOT (`!`) and Logical AND (`&&`) Operators in `if` Statements for Decision Making

```
#include<iostream>
using namespace std;

int main()
{
    cout << "Use boolean values(0 / 1) to answer" << endl;
    cout << "Is it raining? ";
    bool isRaining = false;
    cin >> isRaining;

    cout << "Do you have buses on the streets? ";
    bool busesPly = false;
```

```
    cin >> busesPly;

    // Conditional statement uses logical AND and NOT
    if (isRaining && !busesPly)
      cout << "You cannot go to work" << endl;
    else
      cout << "You can go to work" << endl;

    if (isRaining && busesPly)
      cout << "Take an umbrella" << endl;

    if ((!isRaining) && busesPly)
       cout << "Enjoy the sun and have a nice day" << endl;

    return 0;
}
```

Output ▼

First run:

```
Use boolean values(0 / 1) to answer
Is it raining? 1
Do you have buses on the streets? 1
You can go to work
Take an umbrella
```

Next run:

```
Use boolean values(0 / 1) to answer
Is it raining? 1
Do you have buses on the streets? 0
You cannot go to work
```

Last run:

```
Use boolean values(0 / 1) to answer
Is it raining? 0
Do you have buses on the streets? 1
You can go to work
Enjoy the sun and have a nice day
```

Analysis ▼

The program in Listing 5.6 shows conditional statements that use the `if` construct, which has not been introduced to you yet. For now, you can try to understand the behavior of this construct by correlating it against the output. Line 15 contains the logical expression `isRaining && !busesPly`, which can be read as "Raining AND NO buses." This uses the logical AND operator to connect the absence of buses (indicated by the logical NOT on presence of buses) to the presence of rain.

NOTE

> If you want to read a little about the `if` construct that helps in conditional execution, you can quickly visit Lesson 6.

Listing 5.7 uses logical NOT (`!`) and OR (`||`) operators to demonstrate conditional processing.

Input ▼

LISTING 5.7 Using Logical NOT and Logical OR Operators to Help Decide Whether You Can Buy That Dream Car

```
#include<iostream>
using namespace std;

int main()
{
    cout << "Answer questions with 0 or 1" << endl;
    cout << "Is there a discount on your favorite car? ";
    bool onDiscount = false;
    cin >> onDiscount;

    cout << "Did you get a fantastic bonus? ";
    bool fantasticBonus = false;
    cin >> fantasticBonus;

    if (onDiscount || fantasticBonus)
        cout << "Congratulations, you can buy that car!" << endl;
    else
        cout << "Sorry, waiting a while is a good idea" << endl;

    if (!onDiscount)
        cout << "Car not on discount" << endl;

    return 0;
}
```

Output ▼

First run:

```
Answer questions with 0 or 1
Is there a discount on your favorite car? 0
Did you get a fantastic bonus? 1
Congratulations, you can buy that car!
Car not on discount
```

Next run:

```
Answer questions with 0 or 1
Is there a discount on your favorite car? 0
Did you get a fantastic bonus? 0
Sorry, waiting a while is a good idea
Car not on discount
```

Last run:

```
Answer questions with 0 or 1
Is there a discount on your favorite car? 1
Did you get a fantastic bonus? 1
Congratulations, you can buy that car!
```

Analysis ▼

The program recommends buying a car if you get a discount or if you got a fantastic bonus (or both). Otherwise, it recommends waiting. Line 14 uses the `if` construct followed by an accompanying `else` in Line 16. The `if` construct executes the following statement in Line 15 when the condition `(onDiscount || fantasticBonus)` evaluates to `true`. This expression contains the logical OR operator and evaluates to `true` if there is a discount on your favorite car or if you have received a fantastic bonus. When the expression evaluates to `false`, the statement following `else` in Line 17 is executed. The listing uses the logical NOT operation in Line 19 to remind you that the car is not discounted.

Bitwise NOT (~), AND (&), OR (|), and XOR (^) Operators

The difference between the logical and bitwise operators is that bitwise operators don't return a Boolean result `true` or `false`, as logical operators do. Instead, they work at a bit level, returning a result wherein individual bits in the operand are modified. C++ allows you to perform operations such as NOT, OR, AND, and exclusive OR (that is, XOR) operations in a bitwise mode, where you can manipulate individual bits by negating them using `~`, ORing them using `|`, ANDing them using `&`, and XORing them using `^`. The latter three are performed against a number (typically a bit mask) of your choosing.

Listing 5.8 demonstrates the use of bitwise operators.

Input ▼

LISTING 5.8 Using Bitwise Operators to Perform NOT, AND, OR, and XOR on Individual Bits in an Integer

```
#include<iostream>
#include<bitset>
using namespace std;

int main()
{
    cout << "Enter a number (0 - 255): ";
    unsigned short inputNum = 0;
    cin >> inputNum;

    bitset<8> inputBits (inputNum);
    cout << inputNum << " in binary is " << inputBits << endl;

    bitset<8> bitwiseNOT = (~inputNum);
    cout << "Bitwise NOT ~" << endl;
    cout << "~" << inputBits  << " = " << bitwiseNOT << endl;

    cout << "Bitwise AND, & with 00001111" << endl;
    bitset<8> bitwiseAND = (0x0F & inputNum);// 0x0F is hex for 0001111
    cout << "0001111 & " << inputBits  << " = " << bitwiseAND << endl;

    cout << "Bitwise OR, | with 00001111" << endl;
    bitset<8> bitwiseOR = (0x0F | inputNum);
    cout << "00001111 | " << inputBits  << " = " << bitwiseOR << endl;

    cout << "Bitwise XOR, ^ with 00001111" << endl;
    bitset<8> bitwiseXOR = (0x0F ^ inputNum);
    cout << "00001111 ^ " << inputBits  << " = " << bitwiseXOR << endl;

    return 0;
}
```

Output ▼

```
Enter a number (0 - 255): 181
181 in binary is 10110101
Bitwise NOT ~
~10110101 = 01001010
Bitwise AND, & with 00001111
0001111 & 10110101 = 00000101
Bitwise OR, | with 00001111
00001111 | 10110101 = 10111111
Bitwise XOR, ^ with 00001111
00001111 ^ 10110101 = 10111010
```

Analysis ▼

This program uses `bitset`—a type you have not seen yet—to make displaying binary data easier. The role of `std::bitset` here is purely to help with displaying and nothing more. In Lines 10, 13, 18, and 22, you actually assign an integer to a `bitset` object, which is used to display that same integer data in binary mode. The operations are done on integers. For now, focus on the output, which shows the original integer 181 fed by the user in binary and then proceeds to demonstrate the effects of the bitwise operators `~`, `&`, `|`, and `^` on this integer. You see that the bitwise NOT used in Line 13 toggles the individual bits. The program also demonstrates how the operators `&`, `|`, and `^` work, performing the operations using each bit in the two operands to create the result. Correlate this result with the truth tables introduced earlier, and the workings should become clearer to you.

NOTE

> If you want to learn more about manipulating bit flags in C++, take a look at Lesson 25, "Working with Bit Flags Using STL." It introduces `std::bitset` in greater detail.

Bitwise Right Shift (>>) and Left Shift (<<) Operators

Shift operators move entire bit sequences to the right or to the left and thus can help with multiplication or division by multiples of two, in addition to having other uses in an application.

TIP

> Multiplication by two is achieved by shifting bits one position to the left. For example, `011` is binary for three. Shifting bits one position to the left gives you `110`, which is binary for six! Conversely, shifting bits one position to the right divides by two.

The following is an example of using a shift operator to multiply by two:

```
int doubledValue = num << 1; // shift bits one position left to double value
```

The following is an example of using a shift operator to divide by two:

```
int halvedValue = num >> 1; // shift bits one position right to halve value
```

Listing 5.9 demonstrates how you can use shift operators to effectively multiply and divide integer values.

Input ▼

LISTING 5.9 Using the Bitwise Right Shift Operator (>>) to Quarter and Half, and Left Shift (<<) to Double and Quadruple an Input Integer

```
#include<iostream>
using namespace std;

int main()
{
    cout << "Enter a number: ";
    int inputNum = 0;
    cin >> inputNum;

    int halfNum = inputNum >> 1;
    int quarterNum = inputNum >> 2;
    int doubleNum = inputNum << 1;
    int quadrupleNum = inputNum << 2;

    cout << "Quarter: " << quarterNum << endl;
    cout << "Half: " << halfNum << endl;
    cout << "Double: " << doubleNum << endl;
    cout << "Quadruple: " << quadrupleNum << endl;

    return 0;
}
```

Output ▼

```
Enter a number: 16
Quarter: 4
Half: 8
Double: 32
Quadruple: 64
```

Analysis ▼

The input number is 16, which in binary is `10000`. In Line 9, you move it 1 bit right to change it to `01000`, which is 8, effectively halving it. In Line 10, you move it 2 bits right, changing `10000` to `00100`, which is 4. The left shift operators in Lines 11 and 12 have exactly the opposite effect: You move the left shift operator 1 bit left to get `100000`, which is 32, and 2 bits left to get `1000000`, which is 64, effectively doubling and quadrupling the number!

> **NOTE** Bitwise shift operators don't rotate values. That is, the value contained in the most significant bit isn't rotated back to the least significant bit on a left shift or vice versa on a right shift.

Compound Assignment Operators

Compound assignment operators are assignment operators where the operand to the left is assigned the value resulting from the operation.

Consider the following code:

```
int num1 = 22;
int num2 = 5;
num1 += num2; // num1 contains 27 after the operation
```

This is similar to what's expressed in the following line of code:

```
num1 = (num1 + num2);
```

Thus, the effect of the += operator is that the sum of the two operands is calculated and then assigned to the operand on the left (which is `num1`). Table 5.6 provides a quick reference on the many compound assignment operators and explains their working.

TABLE 5.6 Compound Assignment Operators

Operator	Use	Equivalent
Addition assignment	`num1 += num2;`	`num1 = num1 + num2;`
Subtraction assignment	`num1 -= num2;`	`num1 = num1 - num2;`
Multiplication assignment	`num1 *= num2;`	`num1 = num1 * num2;`
Division assignment	`num1 /= num2;`	`num1 = num1 / num2;`
Modulo assignment	`num1 %= num2;`	`num1 = num1 % num2;`
Bitwise left-shift assignment	`num1 <<= num2;`	`num1 = num1 << num2;`
Bitwise right-shift assignment	`num1 >>= num2;`	`num1 = num1 >> num2;`
Bitwise AND assignment	`num1 &= num2;`	`num1 = num1 & num2;`
Bitwise OR assignment	`num1 |= num2;`	`num1 = num1 | num2;`
Bitwise XOR assignment	`num1 ^= num2;`	`num1 = num1 ^ num2;`

Listing 5.10 demonstrates the effects of using these operators.

Input ▼

LISTING 5.10 Using Compound Assignment Operators to Add, Subtract, Divide, Perform Modulus, Shift, Bitwise OR, Bitwise AND, and Bitwise XOR

```
#include<iostream>
using namespace std;

int main()
{
    cout << "Enter a number: ";
    int value = 0;
    cin >> value;

    value += 8;
    cout << "After += 8, value = " << value << endl;
    value -= 2;
    cout << "After -= 2, value = " << value << endl;
    value /= 4;
    cout << "After /= 4, value = " << value << endl;
    value *= 4;
    cout << "After *= 4, value = " << value << endl;
    value %= 1000;
    cout << "After %= 1000, value = " << value << endl;

    // Note: henceforth assignment happens within cout
    cout << "After <<= 1, value = " << (value <<= 1) << endl;
```

```
22:    cout << "After >>= 2, value = " << (value >>= 2) << endl;
23:
24:    cout << "After |= 0x55, value = " << (value |= 0x55) << endl;
25:    cout << "After ^= 0x55, value = " << (value ^= 0x55) << endl;
26:    cout << "After &= 0x0F, value = " << (value &= 0x0F) << endl;
27:
28:    return 0;
29: }
```

Output ▼

```
Enter a number: 440
After += 8, value = 448
After -= 2, value = 446
After /= 4, value = 111
After *= 4, value = 444
After %= 1000, value = 444
After <<= 1, value = 888
After >>= 2, value = 222
After |= 0x55, value = 223
After ^= 0x55, value = 138
After &= 0x0F, value = 10
```

Analysis ▼

Note that `value` is continually modified throughout the program via the various assignment operators. Each operation is performed using `value`, and the result of the operation is assigned back to it. Hence, at Line 9, the user input `440` is added to 8, which results in `448` and is assigned back to `value`. In the subsequent operation at Line 11, 2 is subtracted from 448, resulting in `446`, which is assigned back to `value`, and so on.

Using the `sizeof()` Operator to Determine the Memory Occupied by a Variable

The `sizeof()` operator determines the amount of memory, in bytes, consumed by a particular type or a variable. You use `sizeof()` as follows:

```
sizeof(variable);
```

or like this:

```
sizeof(type);
```

NOTE

> `sizeof(...)` might look like a function, but it is not a function. `sizeof()` is an operator. Interestingly, this operator cannot be defined by a programmer and hence cannot be overloaded.
>
> You'll learn more about defining your own operators in Lesson 12, "Operator Types and Operator Overloading."

Listing 5.11 demonstrates the use of `sizeof()` to determine memory space occupied by an array. In addition, you might want to revisit Listing 3.5 to analyze the use of `sizeof()` in determining memory consumed by the most familiar variable types.

Input ▼

LISTING 5.11 Using `sizeof()` to Determine the Number of Bytes Occupied by an Array of 100 Integers and by Each Element of the Array

```
#include<iostream>
using namespace std;

int main()
{
    cout << "Use sizeof to determine memory used by arrays" << endl;
    int myNumbers [100];

    cout << "Bytes used by an int: " << sizeof(int) << endl;
    cout << "Bytes used by myNumbers: " << sizeof(myNumbers) << endl;
    cout << "Bytes used by an element: " << sizeof(myNumbers[0]) << endl;

    return 0;
}
```


Output ▼

```
Use sizeof to determine memory used by arrays
Bytes used by an int: 4
Bytes used by myNumbers: 400
Bytes used by an element: 4
```

Analysis ▼

The program demonstrates how `sizeof()` is capable of returning the size of an array of 100 integers, in bytes, which is 400 bytes. The program also demonstrates that the size of each element is 4 bytes.

`sizeof()` can be useful when you need to dynamically allocate memory for *N* objects, especially of a type created by yourself. You would use the result of the `sizeof()` operation in determining the amount of memory occupied by each object and then dynamically allocate the memory by using the operator `new`.

Dynamic memory allocation is explained in detail in Lesson 8, "Pointers and References Explained."

Operator Precedence and Associativity

You possibly learned something in school about the order of arithmetic operations. You might have learned the acronym BODMAS, which stands for Brackets Orders Division Multiplication Addition Subtraction and indicates the order in which a complex arithmetical expression should be evaluated.

In C++, you use operators and expressions such as the following:

```
int myNumber = 10 * 30 + 20 - 5 * 5 << 2;
```

In what order is the expression to be evaluated? That is, which operations are to be resolved before the others? This order is not left to guesswork of any kind. The order in which the various operators are invoked is very strictly specified by the C++ standard. This order is referred to as operator *precedence*.

Another issue: Should operators of similar precedence be evaluated from right to left or from left to right? This order of evaluation is also defined in C++; it is called operator *associativity*. See Table 5.7.

TABLE 5.7 The Precedence of Operators

Rank	Name	Operator
1	Scope resolution (associativity: left to right)	`::`

2	Member selection, subscripting, increment, and decrement
	(associativity: left to right)
		`. ->`
		`()`
		`++ --`

3	`sizeof`, prefix increment and decrement, complement, and, not, unary minus and plus, address-of and dereference, `new`, `new[]`, `delete`, `delete[]`, casting
	(associativity: right to left)
		`++ --`
		`^ !`
		`- +`
		`& *`
		`()`

<table>
<tr><th>Rank</th><th>Name</th><th>Operator</th></tr>
<tr><td>4</td><td>Member selection for pointer
(associativity: left to right)</td><td>.* ->*</td></tr>
<tr><td>5</td><td>Multiply, divide, modulo
(associativity: left to right)</td><td>* / %</td></tr>
<tr><td>6</td><td>Add, subtract
(associativity: left to right)</td><td>+ -</td></tr>
<tr><td>7</td><td>Bitwise shift left, bitwise shift right
(associativity: left to right)</td><td><< >></td></tr>
<tr><td>8</td><td>C++20 three-way comparison</td><td><=></td></tr>
<tr><td>9</td><td>Inequality relational
(associativity: left to right)</td><td>< <= > >=</td></tr>
<tr><td>10</td><td>Equality
(associativity: left to right)</td><td>== !=</td></tr>
<tr><td>11</td><td>Bitwise AND
(associativity: left to right)</td><td>&</td></tr>
<tr><td>12</td><td>Bitwise exclusive OR
(associativity: left to right)</td><td>^</td></tr>
<tr><td>13</td><td>Bitwise OR
(associativity: left to right)</td><td>|</td></tr>
<tr><td>14</td><td>Logical AND
(associativity: left to right)</td><td>&&</td></tr>
<tr><td>15</td><td>Logical OR
(associativity: left to right)</td><td>||</td></tr>
<tr><td>16</td><td>Conditional
(associativity: right to left)</td><td>?:</td></tr>
<tr><td>17</td><td>Assignment
(associativity: right to left)</td><td>= *= /= %=
+= -=
>>=
&= |= ^=</td></tr>
<tr><td>18</td><td>Comma
(associativity: left to right)</td><td>,</td></tr>
</table>

Take another look at the complicated expression used as an example earlier:

```
int myNumber = 10 * 30 + 20 - 5 * 5 << 2;
```

In evaluating the result of this expression, you need to use the rules related to operator precedence, as shown in Table 5.7, to understand what value the compiler assigns. Because multiplication has priority over addition and subtraction, which in turn have priority over shift, you can simplify the preceding example to the following:

```
int myNumber = 300 + 20 - 25 << 2;
```

As addition and subtraction have priority over shift, you can further simplify to:

```
int myNumber = 295 << 2;
```

Finally, you perform the shift operation. Knowing that a shift 1 bit left doubles, and hence a shift 2 bits left quadruples, you can say that the expression evaluates to `295 * 4`, which is `1180`.

CAUTION

Use parentheses to make reading code easy.

The expression used earlier is deliberately composed poorly for the purpose of explaining operator precedence. It is easy for the compiler to understand, but you should write code that humans can understand, too.

The earlier expression is much better written this way:

```
int myNumber = ((10 * 30) - (5 * 5) + 20) << 2; // 1180
```

DO	DON'T
DO use parentheses to make your code and expressions readable. **DO** use the right variable types and ensure that your code will never reach overflow situations. **DO** understand that all l-values (for example, variables) can be r-values, but not all r-values (for example, `"Hello World"`) can be l-values.	**DON'T** program complicated expressions that rely on the operator precedence table; your code needs to be human readable, too. **DON'T** confuse `++variable` and `variable++` or think they're the same. They're different when used in assignments.

Summary

In this lesson, you learned what C++ statements, expressions, and operators are. You learned how to perform basic arithmetic operations such as addition, subtraction, multiplication, and division in C++. You also got an overview of logical operations such as NOT, AND, OR, and XOR. You learned about the C++ logical operators `!`, `&&`, and `||`, which help you in conditional statements, and the bitwise operators, such as `~`, `&`, `|`, and `^`, which help you manipulate data, 1 bit at a time.

You learned about operator precedence and how important it is to use parentheses to write code that can also be understood by humans. You took a look at integer overflow and why it must be avoided.

Q&A

Q Why do some programs use `unsigned int` if `unsigned short` takes less memory and compiles, too?

A `unsigned short` typically has a limit of 65,535, and if incremented, it overflows to 0. To avoid this behavior, well-programmed applications choose `unsigned int` when it is not certain that the value will stay well below this limit.

Q I need to calculate the double of a number after it's divided by three. Do you see any problem with using the following code to do this?

```
int result = Number / 3 << 1;
```

A Yes! Why didn't you simply use parentheses to make this line simpler for other programmers to read?

Q My application divides two integer values 5 and 2:

```
int num1 = 5, num2 = 2;
int result = num1 / num2;
```

On execution, the result contains the value 2. Isn't this wrong?

A Not at all. Integers are not meant to contain decimal data. The result of this operation is hence 2 and not 2.5. If 2.5 is the result you expect, change all data types to float or double, which are meant to handle floating-point (decimal) operations.

Workshop

The Workshop provides quiz questions to help you solidify your understanding of the material covered and exercises to provide you with experience in using what you've learned. Try to answer the quiz and exercise questions before checking the answers in Appendix E and be certain that you understand the answers before continuing to the next lesson.

Quiz

1. If you are writing an application to divide numbers, which data type would be best: int or float?
2. What is the value of 32 / 7?
3. What is the value of 32.0 / 7?
4. Is `sizeof(...)` a function?
5. You need to compute the double of a number, add 5 to it, and then double it again. Would the following line do this?

   ```
   int result = number << 1 + 5 << 1;
   ```
6. What is the result of an XOR operation where the XOR operands both evaluate to true?

Exercises

1. Improve on the code in Quiz Question 5, using parentheses to provide clarity.
2. What is the value of result stored by the following expression?

   ```
   int result = number << 1 + 5 << 1;
   ```
3. Write a program that asks the user to input two Boolean values and demonstrates the results of various bitwise operators on them.

LESSON 6

Controlling Program Flow

Most applications behave differently in different situations and with different user input. To program an application to respond differently, you need to code conditional statements that execute different code segments in different situations.

In this lesson, you find out

- How to make your program behave differently in certain conditions
- How to execute a section of code repeatedly in a loop
- How to better control the flow of execution in a loop

Conditional Execution Using `if...else`

Programs you have seen and composed thus far have a serial order of execution: from the top down. Every line has been executed, with no line ever ignored. However, serial execution of all lines of code in a top-down fashion rarely happens in applications.

Say that you want a program that multiplies two numbers if the user presses `m` or adds the numbers if the user presses anything else.

As you can see in Figure 6.1, not all code paths are executed in every run. If the user presses `m`, the code that multiplies the two numbers is executed. If the user enters anything other than `m`, the code that performs addition is executed. There is never a situation where both operations are executed.

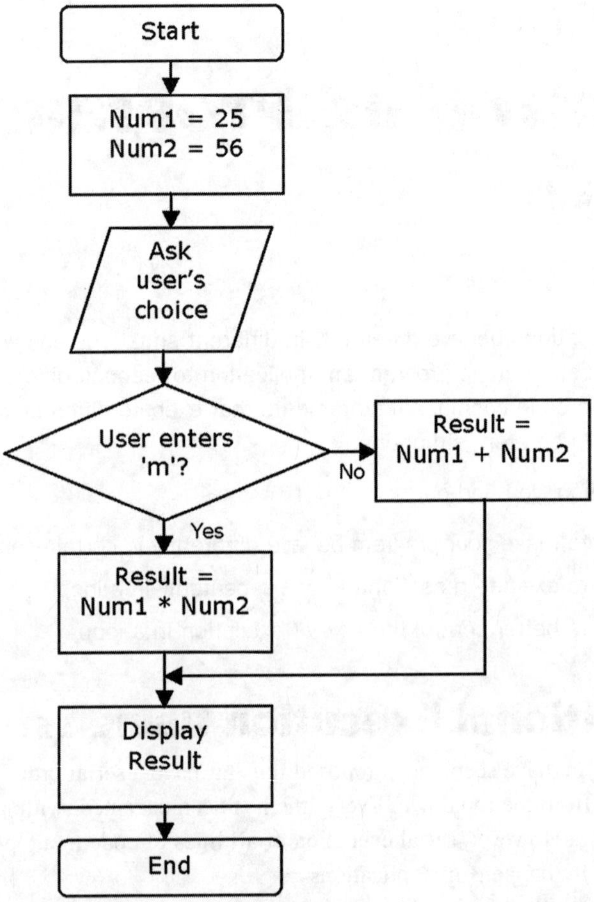

FIGURE 6.1
Example of conditional processing that occurs on the basis of user input.

Conditional Programming Using `if...else`

Conditional execution of code is implemented in C++ using the `if...else` construct, which looks like this:

```
if (conditional expression)
   Do something when expression evaluates true;
else     // optional
   Do something else when condition evaluates false;
```

So, an `if...else` construct that causes a program to multiply if the user enters *m* and adds otherwise looks like this:

```
if (userSelection == 'm')
```

```
   result = num1 * num2;  // multiply
else
   result = num1 + num2;  // add
```

NOTE

> Note that evaluation of an expression to `true` in C++ essentially means that the expression does not evaluate to `false` (where `false` is zero). So, an expression that evaluates to any nonzero number—negative or positive—is essentially considered to be evaluating to `true` when used in a conditional statement.

Let's analyze this construct in Listing 6.1, which enables the user to decide whether to either multiply or divide two numbers and uses conditional processing to generate the desired output.

Input ▼

LISTING 6.1 Multiplying or Adding Two Integers on the Basis of User Input

```
#include<iostream>
using namespace std;

int main()
{
   cout << "Enter two integers: " << endl;
   int num1 = 0, num2 = 0;
   cin >> num1;
   cin >> num2;

   cout << "Enter \'m\' to multiply, anything else to add: ";
   char userSelection = '\0';
   cin >> userSelection;

   int result = 0;
   if (userSelection == 'm')
      result = num1 * num2;
   else
      result = num1 + num2;

   cout << "result is: " << result << endl;

   return 0;
}
```

Output ▼

First run:

```
Enter two integers:
25
56
Enter 'm' to multiply, anything else to add: m
result is: 1400
```

Next run:

```
Enter two integers:
25
56
Enter 'm' to multiply, anything else to add: a
result is: 81
```

Analysis ▼

Note the use of `if` in Line 15 and `else` in Line 17. You are instructing the compiler to execute multiplication in Line 16 when the expression `(userSelection == 'm')` that follows `if` evaluates to `true` or to execute addition in Line 18 if the expression evaluates to `false`. `(userSelection == 'm')` is an expression that evaluates to `true` when the user has entered character *m* (case-sensitive); otherwise, it evaluates to `false`. Thus, this simple program models the flowchart in Figure 6.1 and demonstrates how an application can behave differently in different situations.

NOTE

The `else` part of the `if...else` construct is optional and doesn't need to be used in situations where there is nothing to be executed in the event of failure.

CAUTION

An inadvertent semicolon in Line 15:

```
15:     if (userSelection == 'm');
```

would make the `if` construct meaningless because it would be terminated by an empty statement (the semicolon). Be careful to avoid this situation, which essentially voids the attempt at conditional processing.

Some good compilers may warn you of an "empty control statement" in such a situation.

Conditional Execution of Statements Within a Block

If you want to execute multiple statements, based on a condition succeeding or failing, you need to enclose them within statement blocks. These are essentially braces {...} enclosing multiple statements to be executed as a block. For example:

```
if (condition)
{
   // condition success block
   Statement 1;
   Statement 2;
}
else
{
   // condition failure block
   Statement 3;
   Statement 4;
}
```

Such blocks are also called *compound statements.*

Listing 6.2 is a safer version of Listing 4.6 from Lesson 4, "Managing Arrays and Strings." It uses a compound statement that copies user input into a static character array if the length of user input is within the bounds of the array.

Input ▼

LISTING 6.2 Checking for Bounds Before Copying a String into a `char` Array in a Compound Statement

```
#include<iostream>
#include<string>
using namespace std;

int main()
{
   cout << "Enter a line of text: " << endl;
   string userInput;
   getline (cin, userInput);

   char copyInput[20] = {};
   if (userInput.length() < 20) // check bounds
   {
      cout << "Input within bounds, creating copy" << endl;
      userInput.copy (copyInput, userInput.length());
      cout << "copyInput contains: " << copyInput << endl;
   }
   else
      cout << "Bounds exceeded: cannot copy!" << endl;
```

```
19:
20:     return 0;
21: }
```

Output ▼

First run:

```
Enter a line of text:
Input within bounds
Input within bounds, creating copy
copyInput contains: Input within bounds
```

Next run:

```
Enter a line of text:
Input is too long for the buffer
Bounds exceeded: cannot copy!
```

Analysis ▼

Note how the length of the string is checked against the length of the buffer (`20`) in Line 11 before being copied into it. What is also special about this `if` check is the presence of a statement block (also called a compound statement) in Lines 12 through 16 that runs in the event of the check evaluating to `true`.

TIP

C++17 introduced the inclusion of initialization within the `if` statement. Applying it to lines 10 and 11 in Listing 6.2, you get

```
if (char copyInput[20] = {}; userInput.length() < 20)
{
    // statements
}
```

The scope of variable `copyInput` is now limited to the `if` statement where it is used. This feature is also supported by switch constructs that are introduced later in this lesson.

Nested `if` Statements

Often you have situations where you need to validate against a host of different conditions, many of which are dependent on the evaluation of a previous condition. C++ allows you to nest `if` statements to handle such requirements.

Nested `if` statements look like this:

```
if (expression1)
{
    DoSomething1;
    if(expression2)
        DoSomething2;
    else
        DoSomethingElse2;
}
else
     DoSomethingElse1;
```

Consider an application similar to Listing 6.1, in which the user can instruct the application to divide or multiply by pressing `d` or `m`. Now, division should be permitted only when the divisor is nonzero. So, in addition to checking the user input for the intended command, it is also important to check if the divisor is nonzero when the user instructs the program to divide. Listing 6.3 uses a nested `if` construct.

Input ▼

LISTING 6.3 Using Nested `if` Statements in Multiplying or Dividing a Number

```
#include<iostream>
using namespace std;

int main()
{
    cout << "Enter two numbers: " << endl;
    float num1 = 0, num2 = 0;
    cin >> num1;
    cin >> num2;

    cout << "Enter 'd' to divide, anything else to multiply: ";
    char userSelection = '\0';
    cin >> userSelection;

    if (userSelection == 'd')
    {
        cout << "You wish to divide!" << endl;
        if (num2 != 0)
            cout << num1 << " / " << num2 << " = " << num1 / num2 << endl;
        else
```

```
         cout << "Division by zero is not allowed" << endl;
   }
   else
   {
      cout << "You wish to multiply!" << endl;
      cout << num1 << " x " << num2 << " = " << num1 * num2 << endl;
   }

   return 0;
}
```

Output ▼

First run:

```
Enter two numbers:
45
9
Enter 'd' to divide, anything else to multiply: m
You wish to multiply!
45 x 9 = 405
```

Next run:

```
Enter two numbers:
22
7
Enter 'd' to divide, anything else to multiply: d
You wish to divide!
22 / 7 = 3.14286
```

Last run:

```
Enter two numbers:
365
0
Enter 'd' to divide, anything else to multiply: d
You wish to divide!
Division by zero is not allowed
```

Analysis ▼

The output is the result of running the program three times with three different sets of input, and as you can see, the program has executed different code paths for each of these three runs. This program has a few changes compared to Listing 6.1:

- The numbers are accepted as floating-point variables, to better handle decimals, which are important when dividing numbers.

- The `if` condition is different than in Listing 6.1. You no longer check whether the user has pressed `m`; rather, Line 14 contains an expression (`userSelection == 'd'`) that evaluates to `true` when the user presses `d`. If so, you proceed with division.
- Given that this program divides two numbers, and the divisor is entered by the user, it is important to check whether the divisor is nonzero. This is done using the nested `if` in Line 17.

Thus, this program demonstrates how nested `if` constructs can be very useful in performing different tasks, depending on the evaluation of multiple parameters.

TIP

> The nested tabs (whitespaces) in the code are optional, but they make a significant contribution to the readability of the nested `if` constructs. IDEs and code editors help indent code automatically.

Note that `if...else` constructs can also be grouped together. Listing 6.4 is a program that asks the user for the day of the week and then tells what that day is named after using grouped `if...else` constructs.

Input ▼

LISTING 6.4 Using a Grouped `if...else` Construct

```
 0: #include<iostream>
 1: using namespace std;
 2:
 3: int main()
 4: {
 5:    enum DaysOfWeek
 6:    {
 7:       Sunday = 0,
 8:       Monday,
 9:       Tuesday,
10:       Wednesday,
11:       Thursday,
12:       Friday,
13:       Saturday
14:    };
15:
16:    cout << "Find what days of the week are named after!" << endl;
17:    cout << "Enter a number for a day (Sunday = 0): ";
18:
19:    int dayInput = Sunday;   // Initialize to Sunday
```

```
20:     cin >> dayInput;
21:
22:     if (dayInput == Sunday)
23:        cout << "Sunday was named after the Sun" << endl;
24:     else if (dayInput == Monday)
25:        cout << "Monday was named after the Moon" << endl;
26:     else if (dayInput == Tuesday)
27:        cout << "Tuesday was named after Mars" << endl;
28:     else if (dayInput == Wednesday)
29:        cout << "Wednesday was named after Mercury" << endl;
30:     else if (dayInput == Thursday)
31:        cout << "Thursday was named after Jupiter" << endl;
32:     else if (dayInput == Friday)
33:        cout << "Friday was named after Venus" << endl;
34:     else if (dayInput == Saturday)
35:        cout << "Saturday was named after Saturn" << endl;
36:     else
37:        cout << "Wrong input, execute again" << endl;
38:
39:     return 0;
40: }
```

Output ▼

First run:

```
Find what days of the week are named after!
Enter a number for a day (Sunday = 0): 5
Friday was named after Venus
```

Next run:

```
Find what days of the week are named after!
Enter a number for a day (Sunday = 0): 9
Wrong input, execute again
```

Analysis ▼

Note the `if-else-if` construct used in Lines 22 through 37 to check user input and produce the corresponding output. The output in the second run indicates that the program is able to tell the user when she has entered a number that is outside the expected range 0–6 and hence does not correspond to any day of the week. The advantage of this construct is that it is perfectly suited to validating conditions that are mutually exclusive (for example, Monday can never be a Tuesday, and an invalid input cannot be any day of the week). Another interesting thing to note in this program is the use of the enumeration `DaysOfWeek` declared in Line 5 and used throughout the `if` statements. You could instead simply compare user input against integer values such as 0 for Sunday. However, the use of the enumerator Sunday makes the code more readable.

Conditional Processing Using switch-case

The switch-case construct enables you to check a particular expression against a host of possible constants and possibly perform a different action for each of those different values. The new C++ keywords you would find in such constructs are switch case, default, and break.

The following is the syntax of a switch-case construct:

```
switch(expression)
{
case LabelA:
    DoSomething;
    break;

case LabelB:
    DoSomethingElse;
    break;

// And so on...
default:
    DoStuffWhenExpressionIsNotHandledAbove;
    break;
}
```

The code evaluates the expression and checks against each of the case labels following it for equality. Each case label needs to be a constant. The program then executes the code following that label. When expression does not evaluate to LabelA, the program checks against LabelB. If that check evaluates to true, the program executes DoSomethingElse. This check continues until the program encounters a break. This is the first time we are using the keyword break. break causes execution to exit the code block. breaks are not compulsory; however, without a break, the execution simply continues checking against the next labels and so on, and you want to avoid that in this case. default is optional, too, and it is executed when the expression does not equate to any of the labels in the switch-case construct.

6

TIP

> switch-case constructs are well suited to being used with enumerators. The keyword enum was introduced in Lesson 3, "Using Variables, Declaring Constants."

Listing 6.5 is the `switch-case` equivalent of the program in Listing 6.4 that tells what the days of the week are named after and also uses enumerated constants.

Input ▼

LISTING 6.5 Telling What Days of the Week Are Named After Using `switch-case`, `break`, and `default`

```
#include<iostream>
using namespace std;

int main()
{
   enum DaysOfWeek
   {
      Sunday = 0,
      Monday,
      Tuesday,
      Wednesday,
      Thursday,
      Friday,
      Saturday
   };

   cout << "Find what days of the week are named after!" << endl;
   cout << "Enter a number for a day (Sunday = 0): ";

   int dayInput = Sunday;    // Initialize to Sunday
   cin >> dayInput;

   switch(dayInput)
   {
   case Sunday:
      cout << "Sunday was named after the Sun" << endl;
      break;

   case Monday:
      cout << "Monday was named after the Moon" << endl;
      break;

   case Tuesday:
      cout << "Tuesday was named after Mars" << endl;
      break;

   case Wednesday:
      cout << "Wednesday was named after Mercury" << endl;
      break;

   case Thursday:
      cout << "Thursday was named after Jupiter" << endl;
      break;
```

```
43:
44:     case Friday:
45:        cout << "Friday was named after Venus" << endl;
46:        break;
47:
48:     case Saturday:
49:        cout << "Saturday was named after Saturn" << endl;
50:        break;
51:
52:     default:
53:        cout << "Wrong input, execute again" << endl;
54:        break;
55:     }
56:
57:     return 0;
58: }
```

Output ▼

First run:

```
Find what days of the week are named after!
Enter a number for a day (Sunday = 0): 5
Friday was named after Venus
```

Next run:

```
Find what days of the week are named after!
Enter a number for a day (Sunday = 0): 9
Wrong input, execute again
```

Analysis ▼

Lines 22 through 55 contain the `switch-case` construct, which produces different output depending on the integer contained in `dayInput`, as entered by the user. When the user enters the number `5`, the application checks the `switch` expression `dayInput` that evaluates to `5` against the first four labels that are enumerators `Sunday` (value `0`) through `Thursday` (value `4`), skipping the code below each of them as none of them are equal to 5. It reaches the label `Friday`, where the expression evaluating to `5` equals the enumerated constant `Friday`. Thus, it executes the code under `Friday` until it reaches `break` in Line 46 and exits the `switch` construct. In the second run, when an invalid value is entered, the execution reaches `default` and runs the code under it, displaying the message asking the user to execute again.

This program, which uses `switch-case`, produces exactly the same output as Listing 6.4, which uses the `if-else-if` construct. However, the `switch-case` version looks a little more structured and is possibly well suited to situations where you want to be doing more than just writing a line to the screen.

TIP

> Use statement blocks using braces `{...}` to include multiple statements that need to be executed under a case.

Conditional Execution Using the `?:` Operator

C++ has an interesting and powerful operator called the *conditional operator*, which is similar to a compact `if-else` construct.

The conditional operator is also called a *ternary operator*, as it takes three operands:

```
(conditional expression evaluated to bool) ? expression1 if true : expression2
if false;
```

Such an operator can be used to compactly evaluate the greater of two given numbers, as seen here:

```
int max = (num1 > num2) ? num1 : num2; // max contains greater of num1 and num2
```

Listing 6.6 demonstrates conditional processing using the `?:` operator.

Input ▼

LISTING 6.6 Using the Conditional Operator (`?:`) to Find the Max of Two Numbers

```
#include<iostream>
using namespace std;

int main()
{
    cout << "Enter two numbers" << endl;
    int num1 = 0, num2 = 0;
    cin >> num1;
    cin >> num2;

    // using the ternary operator ?:
    int max = (num1 > num2)? num1 : num2;

    cout << "The greater of " << num1 << " and " \
         << num2 << " is: " << max << endl;

    return 0;
}
```

Output ▼

```
Enter two numbers
365
-1
The greater of 365 and -1 is: 365
```

Analysis ▼

Line 11 contains the statement of interest. It is a compact statement that makes a decision about which of the two numbers input is larger. This line can also be coded using `if-else`, as shown here:

```
int max;
if (num1 > num2)
   max = num1;
else
   max = num2;
```

You can see that using the conditional operators saves a few lines in this case. Saving lines of code, however, should not be a priority. Some programmers prefer conditional operators, and others don't. It is important to code conditional operators in a way that can be easily understood.

DO	DON'T
DO use enumerators in `switch` expressions to make code readable. **DO** remember to handle `default`, unless doing so is deemed totally unnecessary. **DO** check whether you inadvertently forgot to insert `break` in each `case` statement.	**DON'T** add two `cases` with the same label as it won't make sense and won't compile. **DON'T** complicate your `case` statements by including `cases` without `break` and relying on sequence. Doing so will break functionality in the future when you move the `case` statements without paying adequate attention to sequence. **DON'T** use complicated conditions or expressions when using conditional operators (`?:`).

TIP

C++17 introduced conditional compilation features using `if constexpr`. This is an advanced feature that gets the compiler to validate the conditional expression. The section of code within the conditional `if constexpr...else` statement that is not to be executed is then ignored by the compiler and doesn't make it to the executable. This optimization helps when using template classes. Templates are introduced in greater detail in Lesson 14, "An Introduction to Macros and Templates."

Getting Code to Execute in Loops

So far, you have seen how to make a program behave differently when certain variables contain different values; for example, in Listing 6.1 you multiplied when the user pressed `m`, and otherwise, you added. However, what if the user doesn't want the program to just end? What if a user wants to perform another add or multiply operation—or maybe five more? In such a case, you need to repeat the execution of existing code.

This is when you need to program a loop.

A Rudimentary Loop Using `goto`

As the name suggests, `goto` instructs execution to continue from a particular, labeled, point in code. You can use it to go backward and re-execute certain statements.

The syntax for the `goto` statement is

```
SomeFunction()
{
Start: // Called a label
   CodeThatRepeats;

   goto Start;
}
```

You declare a label called `Start` and use `goto` to repeat execution from this point on, as demonstrated in Listing 6.7. Unless you invoke `goto` given a condition that can evaluate to `false` under certain circumstances, or unless the code that repeats contains a `return` statement executed under certain conditions, the piece of code between the `goto` command and label will repeat endlessly and prevent the program from ending.

Input ▼

LISTING 6.7 Asking a User Whether to Repeat Calculations Using `goto`

```
#include<iostream>
using namespace std;

int main()
{
Start:
    int num1 = 0, num2 = 0;

    cout << "Enter two integers: " << endl;
    cin >> num1;
    cin >> num2;

    cout << num1 << " x " << num2 << " = " << num1 * num2 << endl;
    cout << num1 << " + " << num2 << " = " << num1 + num2 << endl;

    cout << "Do you wish to perform another operation (y/n)?" << endl;
    char repeat = 'y';
    cin >> repeat;

    if (repeat == 'y')
        goto Start;

    cout << "Goodbye!" << endl;

    return 0;
}
```

Output ▼

```
Enter two integers:
56
25
56 x 25 = 1400
56 + 25 = 81
Do you wish to perform another operation (y/n)?
y
Enter two integers:
95
-47
95 x -47 = -4465
95 + -47 = 48
Do you wish to perform another operation (y/n)?
n
Goodbye!
```

Analysis ▼

Note that the primary difference between Listing 6.7 and Listing 6.1 is that Listing 6.1 needs two runs (that is, two separate executions) to enable the user to enter a new set of numbers and see the result of the addition and multiplication. Listing 6.7 does that in one execution cycle by asking the user if she wishes to perform another operation. The code that actually enables this repetition is in Line 20, where `goto` is invoked if the user enters the character `y` for yes. Execution of `goto` in Line 20 results in the program jumping to the label `Start` declared in Line 5, which effectively reruns the program code.

CAUTION

> Using `goto` is not the recommended way to program loops because the prolific use of `goto` can result in unpredictable flow of code, where execution can jump from one line to another in no particular order or sequence—in some cases leaving variables in unpredictable states, too.
>
> A bad case of programming using `goto` results in what is called *spaghetti code*. You can avoid `goto` by using `while`, `do...while`, and `for` loops that are explained in the following pages.
>
> The only reason you were taught `goto` is so that you understand code that uses it.

The `while` Loop

The C++ keyword `while` can help you do what `goto` did in Listing 6.7 but in a refined manner. Its usage syntax is

```
while(condition)
{
   // Expression evaluates to true
   StatementBlock;
}
```

The statement block is executed repeatedly as long as the *`condition`* evaluates to `true`. It is hence important to code in such a way that there are situations where the expression would also evaluate to `false`; otherwise, the `while` loop would never end.

Listing 6.8 is equivalent to Listing 6.7 but uses `while` instead of `goto` in repeating a calculation cycle.

Input ▼

LISTING 6.8 Using a `while` Loop to Help the User Rerun Calculations

```
#include<iostream>
using namespace std;

int main()
{
   char userSelection = 'm';    // initial value

   while (userSelection != 'x')
   {
      cout << "Enter the two integers: " << endl;
      int num1 = 0, num2 = 0;
      cin >> num1;
      cin >> num2;

      cout << num1 << " x " << num2 << " = " << num1 * num2 << endl;
      cout << num1 << " + " << num2 << " = " << num1 + num2 << endl;

      cout << "Press x to exit(x) or any other key to recalculate" << endl;
      cin >> userSelection;
   }

   cout << "Goodbye!" << endl;

   return 0;
}
```

Output ▼

```
Enter the two integers:
56
25
56 x 25 = 1400
56 + 25 = 81
Press x to exit(x) or any other key to recalculate
r
Enter the two integers:
365
-5
365 x -5 = -1825
365 + -5 = 360
Press x to exit(x) or any other key to recalculate
x
Goodbye!
```

Analysis ▼

The `while` loop in Lines 7 through 19 contains most of the logic in this program. Note how the `while` checks the expression `(userSelection != 'x')` and proceeds only if this expression evaluates to `true`. To enable a first run, you initialized the `char` variable `userSelection` to `'m'` in Line 5. This needed to be any value that is not `'x'` (otherwise, the condition would fail at the very first loop, and the application would exit without letting the user do anything constructive). The first run is very simple, but the user is asked in Line 17 if he wishes to perform another set of calculations. Line 18 contains the user's input and is where you modify the expression that `while` evaluates, giving the program a chance to continue or to terminate. When the first loop is done, execution returns to evaluating the expression in the `while` statement at Line 7 and repeats if the user has not pressed `x`. When the user presses `x` at the end of a loop, the next evaluation of the expression, at Line 7, results in a `false`, and the execution exits the `while` loop, eventually ending the application after displaying a goodbye statement.

NOTE

A loop is also called an *iteration*. Statements involving `while`, `do...while`, and `for` are also called *iterative statements*.

The `do...while` Loop

There are cases (like the one in Listing 6.8) where you need to ensure that a certain segment of code repeats in a loop and that it executes at least once. This is where the `do...while` loop is useful.

The syntax of the `do...while` loop is

```
do
{
   StatementBlock; // executed at least once
} while(condition); // ends loop when condition evaluates to false
```

Note how the line containing `while(condition)` terminates with a semicolon. This is different from the previous `while` loop, in which a semicolon following `while` would've effectively terminated the loop in the very line, resulting in an empty statement.

Listing 6.9 demonstrates how `do...while` loops help in executing statements at least once.

Input ▼

LISTING 6.9 Using `do...while` to Repeat Execution of a Block of Code

```
#include<iostream>
using namespace std;

int main()
{
   char userSelection = 'x';    // initial value
   do
   {
      cout << "Enter the two integers: " << endl;
      int num1 = 0, num2 = 0;
      cin >> num1;
      cin >> num2;

      cout << num1 << " x " << num2 << " = " << num1 * num2 << endl;
      cout << num1 << " + " << num2 << " = " << num1 + num2 << endl;

      cout << "Press x to exit(x) or any other key to recalculate" << endl;
      cin >> userSelection;
   } while (userSelection != 'x');

   cout << "Goodbye!" << endl;

   return 0;
}
```

Output ▼

```
Enter the two integers:
654
-25
654 x -25 = -16350
654 + -25 = 629
Press x to exit(x) or any other key to recalculate
m
Enter the two integers:
909
101
909 x 101 = 91809
909 + 101 = 1010
Press x to exit(x) or any other key to recalculate
x
Goodbye!
```

Analysis ▼

This program is similar in behavior and output to Listing 6.8. Indeed, the only differences are the `do` keyword in Line 6 and the use of `while` in Line 18. The execution of code happens serially, one line after another, until the `while` is reached at Line 18. This is where `while` evaluates the expression `(userSelection != 'x')`. When the expression evaluates to `true` (that is, the user doesn't press character `x` to exit), execution of the loop repeats. When the expression evaluates to `false` (that is, the user presses `x`), execution quits the loop and continues with wishing goodbye and ending the application.

The `for` Loop

The `for` statement is a relatively sophisticated loop in that it allows for an initialization statement executed once (typically used to initialize a counter). It checks for an exit condition (typically using this counter) and performs an action at the end of every loop (typically incrementing or modifying this counter).

The syntax of the `for` loop is

```
for (initial expression executed only once;
     exit condition executed at the beginning of every loop;
     loop expression executed at the end of every loop)
{
    DoSomething;
}
```

The `for` loop is a feature that enables a programmer to define a counter variable with an initial value, check the value against an exit condition at the beginning of every loop, and change the value of the variable at the end of a loop.

Listing 6.10 demonstrates an effective way to access elements in an array by using a `for` loop.

Input ▼

LISTING 6.10 Using `for` Loops to Enter Elements in a Static Array and Display the Contents of the Array

```
#include<iostream>
using namespace std;

int main()
{
    const int ARRAY_LENGTH = 5;
    int myNums[ARRAY_LENGTH] = {0};

```

```
 8:     cout << "Populate array of " << ARRAY_LENGTH << " integers" << endl;
 9:
10:     for (int counter = 0; counter < ARRAY_LENGTH; ++counter)
11:     {
12:        cout << "Enter an integer for element " << counter << ": ";
13:        cin >> myNums[counter];
14:     }
15:
16:     cout << "Displaying contents of the array: " << endl;
17:
18:     for (int counter = 0; counter < ARRAY_LENGTH; ++counter)
19:        cout << "Element " << counter << " = " << myNums[counter] << endl;
20:
21:     return 0;
22: }
```

Output ▼

```
Populate array of 5 integers
Enter an integer for element 0: 365
Enter an integer for element 1: 31
Enter an integer for element 2: 24
Enter an integer for element 3: -59
Enter an integer for element 4: 65536
Displaying contents of the array:
Element 0 = 365
Element 1 = 31
Element 2 = 24
Element 3 = -59
Element 4 = 65536
```

Analysis ▼

There are two `for` loops in Listing 6.10—in Lines 10 and 18. The first helps enter elements into an array of integers, and the other handles the display. These two `for` loops are identical in syntax. Both declare an index variable `counter` to access elements in the array. This variable is incremented at the end of every loop; therefore, it helps access the next element in the next run of the loop. The middle expression in the `for` loop is the exit condition. It checks whether `counter`, which is incremented at the end of every loop, is still within the bounds of the array by comparing it against `ARRAY_LENGTH`. This way, it is also ensured that the `for` loop never exceeds the length of the array.

<table>
<tr><td>NOTE</td><td>A variable such as <code>counter</code> from Listing 6.10 that helps access elements in a collection such as an array is also called an iterator.

The scope of the iterator declared within the <code>for</code> construct is limited to the <code>for</code> loop. Thus, in the second <code>for</code> loop in Listing 6.10, this variable that has been re-declared is effectively a new variable from the compiler's point of view.</td></tr>
</table>

Using the initialization, conditional expression, and the expression to be evaluated at the end of every loop is optional. It is possible to have a `for` loop without some or any of these, as shown in Listing 6.11.

Input ▼

LISTING 6.11　Using a `for` Loop Without a Loop Expression to Repeat Calculations on User Request

```
 0: #include<iostream>
 1: using namespace std;
 2:
 3: int main()
 4: {
 5:     // without loop expression (third expression missing)
 6:     for(char userSelection = 'm'; (userSelection != 'x');)
 7:     {
 8:         cout << "Enter the two integers: " << endl;
 9:         int num1 = 0, num2 = 0;
10:         cin >> num1;
11:         cin >> num2;
12:
13:         cout << num1 << " x " << num2 << " = " << num1 * num2 << endl;
14:         cout << num1 << " + " << num2 << " = " << num1 + num2 << endl;
15:
16:         cout << "Press x to exit or any other key to recalculate" << endl;
17:         cin >> userSelection;
18:     }
19:
20:     cout << "Goodbye!" << endl;
21:
22:     return 0;
23: }
```

Output ▼

```
Enter the two integers:
56
```

```
25
56 x 25 = 1400
56 + 25 = 81
Press x to exit or any other key to recalculate
m
Enter the two integers:
789
-36
789 x -36 = -28404
789 + -36 = 753
Press x to exit or any other key to recalculate
x
Goodbye!
```

Analysis ▼

This program is identical to Listing 6.8, which uses the `while` loop, except that it uses the `for` construct in Line 6. The interesting thing about this `for` loop is that it contains only the initialization expression and the conditional expression; it ignores the option to change a variable at the end of each loop.

NOTE

You can initialize multiple variables in a `for` loop within the first initialization expression that is executed once. A `for` loop in Listing 6.11 with multiple initializations looks like this:

```
for (int counter1 = 0, counter2 = 5; // initialize
     counter1 < ARRAY_LENGTH;     // check
       ++counter1, --counter2)    // increment,
decrement
```

Note the new addition `counter2`, which is initialized to `5`. Interestingly, it is also possible to decrement it in the loop expression—once per loop.

6

The Range-Based `for` Loop

C++11 introduced a new variant of the `for` loop that makes operating over a range of values, such as those contained in an array, simpler to code and to read.

The syntax of the range-based `for` loop also uses the same keyword, `for`:

```
for (VarType varName : sequence)
{
   // Use varName that contains an element from sequence
}
```

For example, given an array of integers `someNums`, you would use a range-based `for` to read elements contained in the array like this:

```
int someNums[] = { 1, 101, -1, 40, 2040 };

for (int aNum : someNums) // range based for
   cout << "The array elements are " << aNum << endl;
```

TIP

> You can simplify this `for` statement further by using the automatic variable type deduction feature via the keyword `auto` to compose a generic `for` loop that will work for an array with elements of any type:
>
> ```
> for (auto anElement : elements) // range based for
>
>    cout << "Array elements are " << anElement << endl;
> ```

Listing 6.12 demonstrates the range-based `for` on ranges of different types.

Input ▼

LISTING 6.12 Using a Range-Based `for` Loop over Arrays and a `std::string`

```
#include<iostream>
#include<string>
using namespace std;

int main()
{
   int someNums[] = { 1, 101, -1, 40, 2040 };

   for (const int aNum : someNums)
      cout << aNum << ' ';
   cout << endl;

   for (auto anElement : { 5, 222, 110, -45, 2017 })
      cout << anElement << ' ';
   cout << endl;

   char charArray[] = { 'h', 'e', 'l', 'l', 'o' };
   for (auto aChar : charArray)
      cout << aChar << ' ';
   cout << endl;
```

```
20:
21:     double moreNums[] = { 3.14, -1.3, 22, 10101 };
22:     for (auto anElement : moreNums)
23:        cout << anElement << ' ';
24:     cout << endl;
25:
26:     string sayHello{ "Hello World!" };
27:     for (auto anElement : sayHello)
28:         cout << anElement << ' ';
29:     cout << endl;
30:
31:     return 0;
32: }
```

Output ▼

```
1 101 -1 40 2040
5 222 110 -45 2017
h e l l o
3.14 -1.3 22 10101
H e l l o   W o r l d !
```

Analysis ▼

This listing contains multiple implementations of the range-based `for` in Lines 8, 12, 17, 22, and 27. Each of these instances uses the loop to display the contents of a range on the screen, one element at a time. What's interesting is that, while the nature of the range changes from being an array of integers `someNums` in Line 8 to an unspecified range in Line 12 to an array of `char` (`charArray`) in Line 17, and even a `std::string` in Line 27, the syntax of the range-based `for` loop remains consistent.

This simplicity of implementation makes the range-based `for` one of the more popular features introduced by C++ in the past decade.

Modifying Loop Behavior Using `continue` and `break`

In a few cases—especially in complicated loops that handle many parameters with many conditions—you cannot program a loop condition efficiently and need to modify program behavior even within the loop. In such cases, `continue` and `break` can help you.

`continue` lets you resume execution from the top of the loop. The code following `continue` within the block is skipped. Thus, the effect of `continue` in a `while`, `do...while`, or `for` loop is that it results in the loop condition being reevaluated and the loop block being reentered if the condition evaluates to `true`.

NOTE

With a `continue` within a `for` loop, the loop expression (the third expression within the `for` statement typically used to increment the counter) is evaluated before the condition is reevaluated.

On the other hand, `break` exits the loop's block, thereby ending the loop when invoked.

CAUTION

Usually programmers expect all code in a loop to be executed when the loop conditions are satisfied. `continue` and `break` modify this behavior and can result in nonintuitive code.

Therefore, `continue` and `break` should be used sparingly.

Loops That Don't End: Infinite Loops

Remember that `while`, `do...while`, and `for` loops have a condition expression that results in a loop terminating when the condition evaluates to `false`. If you program a condition that always evaluates to `true`, the loop never ends.

An infinite `while` loop looks like this:

```
while(true)    // while expression fixed to true
{
   DoSomethingRepeatedly;
}
```

An infinite `do...while` loop would be

```
do
{
   DoSomethingRepeatedly;
} while(true);   // do...while expression never evaluates to false
```

An infinite `for` loop can be programmed the following way:

```
for (;;)    // no condition supplied = unending for
```

```
{
   DoSomethingRepeatedly;
}
```

Strange as it may seem, such loops do have a purpose. Imagine an operating system that needs to continually check whether you have connected a device such as a USB stick to the USB port. This is an activity that should not stop as long as the OS is running. Such cases warrant the use of loops that never end. Such loops are also called infinite loops as they execute forever, to eternity.

Controlling Infinite Loops

If you want to end an `infinite loop` (say the OS in the preceding example needs to shut down), you do so by inserting a `break` (typically used within an `if (condition)` block).

The following is an example of using `break` to exit an infinite `while`:

```
while(true)    // while condition fixed to true
{
   DoSomethingRepeatedly;
   if(condition)
      break;  // exit loop when expression evaluates to true
}
```

Using `break` inside an infinite `do...while`:

```
do
{
   DoSomethingRepeatedly;
   if(condition)
      break;  // exit loop when expression evaluates to true
} while(true);
```

Using `break` inside an infinite `for` loop:

```
for (;;)    // no condition supplied i.e. unending for loop
{
   DoSomethingRepeatedly;
   if(condition)
      break;  // exit loop when expression evaluates to true
}
```

Listing 6.13 shows how to program infinite loops using `continue` and `break` to control the exit criteria.

Input ▼

LISTING 6.13 Using `continue` to Restart and `break` to Exit an Infinite `for` Loop

```
#include<iostream>
using namespace std;

int main()
{
    for(;;)   // an infinite loop
    {
        cout << "Enter two integers: " << endl;
        int num1 = 0, num2 = 0;
        cin >> num1;
        cin >> num2;

        cout << "Do you wish to correct the numbers? (y/n): ";
        char changeNumbers = '\0';
        cin >> changeNumbers;

        if (changeNumbers == 'y')
           continue;  // restart the loop!

        cout << num1 << " x " << num2 << " = " << num1 * num2 << endl;
        cout << num1 << " + " << num2 << " = " << num1 + num2 << endl;

        cout << "Press x to exit or any other key to recalculate" << endl;
        char userSelection = '\0';
        cin >> userSelection;

        if (userSelection == 'x')
           break;   // exit the infinite loop
    }

    cout << "Goodbye!" << endl;

    return 0;
}
```

Output ▼

```
Enter two integers:
560
25
Do you wish to correct the numbers? (y/n): y
Enter two integers:
```

```
56
25
Do you wish to correct the numbers? (y/n): n
56 x 25 = 1400
56 + 25 = 81
Press x to exit or any other key to recalculate
r
Enter two integers:
95
-1
Do you wish to correct the numbers? (y/n): n
95 x -1 = -95
95 + -1 = 94
Press x to exit or any other key to recalculate
x
Goodbye!
```

Analysis ▼

The `for` loop in Line 5 is different from the one in Listing 6.11 in that this is an infinite `for` loop that contains no condition expression that is evaluated on every iteration of the loop. In other words, without the execution of a `break` statement, this loop (and hence this application) never exits. Note the output, which is different from the other output you have seen so far in that it allows the user to make a correction to the input before the program proceeds to calculate the sum and multiplication. This logic is implemented using a `continue`, given the evaluation of a certain condition in Lines 16 and 17. When the user presses character `y` when asked whether he wants to correct the numbers, the condition in Line 16 evaluates to `true`, hence executing the following `continue`. When `continue` is encountered, execution jumps to the top of the loop, and the program asks the user again whether he wants to enter two integers. Similarly, at the end of the loop, when the user is asked whether he wants to exit, his input is checked against `'x'` in Line 26, and if the user has pressed `x`, the following `break` is executed, ending the infinite loop.

NOTE

Listing 6.13 uses an empty `for(;;)` statement to create an infinite loop. You can replace that with `while(true)` or `do...while(true);` to generate the same output using a different loop type.

DO	DON'T
DO use `do...while` when the logic in the loop needs to be executed at least once.	**DON'T** use `goto`.
DO use `while`, `do...while`, or `for` loops with well-defined condition expressions.	**DON'T** use `continue` and `break` indiscriminately.
DO indent code in a statement block contained in a loop to improve readability.	**DON'T** program infinite loops terminated using `break` unless absolutely necessary.

Programming Nested Loops

Just as you saw nested `if` statements in the beginning of this lesson, often you need to nest one loop under another. Imagine two arrays of integers. If you want to find the multiple of each number in `array1` against each in `array2`, you use a nested loop to make programming it easy. The first loop iterates `array1`, and the second iterates `array2` under the first.

Listing 6.14 demonstrates the use of nested loops.

Input ▼

LISTING 6.14 Using Nested Loops to Multiply Each Element in an Array by Each Element in Another Array

```
#include<iostream>
using namespace std;

int main()
{
   const int ARRAY1_LEN = 3;
   const int ARRAY2_LEN = 2;

   int myNums1[ARRAY1_LEN] = {35, -3, 0};
   int myNums2[ARRAY2_LEN] = {20, -1};

   cout << "Multiplying each int in myNums1 by each in myNums2:" << endl;

   for(int index1 = 0; index1 < ARRAY1_LEN; ++index1)
      for(int index2 = 0; index2 < ARRAY2_LEN; ++index2)
         cout << myNums1[index1] << " x " << myNums2[index2] \
         << " = " << myNums1[index1] * myNums2[index2] << endl;

   return 0;
}
```

Output ▼

```
Multiplying each int in myNums1 by each in myNums2:
35 x 20 = 700
35 x -1 = -35
-3 x 20 = -60
-3 x -1 = 3
0 x 20 = 0
0 x -1 = 0
```

Analysis ▼

The nested `for` loops in question are in Lines 13 and 14. The first `for` loop iterates the array `myNums1`, whereas the second `for` loop iterates the other array, `myNums2`. The first `for` loop executes the second `for` loop within each iteration. The second `for` loop iterates over all elements in `myNums2` and, in each iteration, multiplies that element by the element indexed via `index1` from the first loop above it. So, for every element in `myNums1`, the second loop iterates over all elements in `myNums2`, resulting in the first element in `myNums1` at offset 0 being multiplied with all elements in `myNums2`. Then the second element in `myNums1` is multiplied by all elements in `myNums2`. Finally, the third element in `myNums1` is multiplied by all elements in `myNums2`.

Using Nested Loops to Walk a Multidimensional Array

In Lesson 4, you learned about multidimensional arrays. In Listing 4.3, you accessed elements in a two-dimensional array of three rows and three columns. What you did there was to individually access each element in the array, one element per line. There was no automation, and if you wanted to make the array larger, you would need to code a lot more—and also change the array's dimensions to access its elements. However, using loops can change all that, as demonstrated in Listing 6.15.

Input ▼

LISTING 6.15 Using Nested Loops to Iterate Elements in a Two-Dimensional Array of Integers

```
#include<iostream>
using namespace std;

int main()
{
   const int NUM_ROWS = 3;
   const int NUM_COLUMNS = 4;

```

```
 8:     // 2D array of integers
 9:     int MyInts[NUM_ROWS][NUM_COLUMNS] = { {34, -1, 879, 22},
10:                                           {24, 365, -101, -1},
11:                                           {-20, 40, 90, 97} };
12:
13:     // iterate rows, each array of int
14:     for (int row = 0; row < NUM_ROWS; ++row)
15:     {
16:        // iterate integers in each row (columns)
17:        for (int column = 0; column < NUM_COLUMNS; ++column)
18:        {
19:           cout << "Integer[" << row << "][" << column \
20:                << "] = " << MyInts[row][column] << endl;
21:        }
22:     }
23:
24:     return 0;
25: }
```

Output ▼

```
Integer[0][0] = 34
Integer[0][1] = -1
Integer[0][2] = 879
Integer[0][3] = 22
Integer[1][0] = 24
Integer[1][1] = 365
Integer[1][2] = -101
Integer[1][3] = -1
Integer[2][0] = -20
Integer[2][1] = 40
Integer[2][2] = 90
Integer[2][3] = 97
```

Analysis ▼

Lines 14 through 22 contain two `for` loops that you use to access and iterate through a two-dimensional array of integers. A two-dimensional array is, in effect, an array of an array of integers. Note how the first `for` loop accesses the rows (each of which is an array of integers), whereas the second accesses each element in this array—that is, accesses columns therein.

NOTE

> Listing 6.15 uses braces to enclose the nested `for` only to improve readability. This nested loop works just fine without the braces, too, as the loop statement is just a single statement to be executed (and not a compound statement that necessitates the use of enclosing braces).

Using Nested Loops to Calculate Fibonacci Numbers

The famed Fibonacci series is a set of numbers starting with 0 and 1, where every following number in the series is the sum of the previous two. So, a Fibonacci series starts with a sequence like this:

0, 1, 1, 2, 3, 5, 8,…and so on

Listing 6.16 demonstrates how to create a Fibonacci sequence comprising as many numbers as you want (but limited by the data-bearing capacity of the integer holding the final number).

Input ▼

LISTING 6.16 Using Nested Loops to Calculate a Fibonacci Sequence

```
#include<iostream>
using namespace std;

int main()
{
   const int numsToCalculate = 5;
   cout << "This program will calculate " << numsToCalculate \
        << " Fibonacci Numbers at a time" << endl;

   int num1 = 0, num2 = 1;
   char wantMore = '\0';
   cout << num1 << " " << num2 << " ";

   do
   {
      for (int counter = 0; counter < numsToCalculate; ++counter)
      {
         cout << num1 + num2 << " ";

         int num2Temp = num2;
         num2 = num1 + num2;
         num1 = num2Temp;
      }

```

```
24:         cout << endl << "Do you want more numbers (y/n)? ";
25:         cin >> wantMore;
26:     }while (wantMore == 'y');
27:
28:     cout << "Goodbye!" << endl;
29:
30:     return 0;
31: }
```

Output ▼

```
This program will calculate 5 Fibonacci Numbers at a time
0 1 1 2 3 5 8
Do you want more numbers (y/n)? y
13 21 34 55 89
Do you want more numbers (y/n)? y
144 233 377 610 987
Do you want more numbers (y/n)? y
1597 2584 4181 6765 10946
Do you want more numbers (y/n)? n
Goodbye!
```

Analysis ▼

The outer `do...while` in Line 13 is basically the query loop that repeats if the user wants to see more numbers. The inner `for` loop in Line 15 does the job of calculating the next Fibonacci number and displays five numbers at a time. In Line 19, you hold the value in `num2` in a temporary variable `num2Temp` so you can reuse it in Line 21. Note that if you didn't store this temporary value, you would be assigning the modified value in Line 20 directly to `num1`, which is not what you want. When the user presses `y` to get more numbers, the `do...while` loop executes once more, thereby executing the nested `for` loop that generates five more Fibonacci numbers.

Summary

This lesson taught you how to code conditional statements that create alternative execution paths and make code blocks repeat in a loop. You learned the `if...else` construct and how to use `switch-case` statements to handle different situations in the event that variables contain different values.

In learning about loops, you saw how to use `while`, `do...while`, and `for` constructs. You learned how to make the loops iterate endlessly to create infinite loops and to use `continue` and `break` to better control them. Last but not least, you learned about `goto`—but were warned against using it due to its ability to create code that cannot be understood.

Q&A

Q What happens if I omit a `break` in a `switch-case` statement?

A The `break` statement enables program execution to exit the `switch` construct. Without it, execution continues evaluating the following `case` statements.

Q How do I exit an infinite loop?

A Use `break` to exit a loop. Alternatively, use `return` to exit the function module.

Q My `while` loop looks like `while(Integer)`. Does the `while` loop execute when `Integer` evaluates to -1?

A Ideally, a `while` expression should evaluate to a Boolean value `true` or `false`. `false` is `0`. A condition that does not evaluate to `0` is considered to evaluate to `true`. Because `-1` is not `0`, the `while` condition evaluates to `true`, and the loop is executed. If you want the loop to be executed only for positive numbers, you can use the expression `while(Integer>0)`. This rule is true for all conditional statements and loops.

Q Is there an empty `while` loop equivalent to `for(;;)`?

A No. `while` always needs an accompanying conditional expression.

Q I changed a `do...while(exp);` to a `while(exp);` by copying and pasting. Should I anticipate any problems?

A Yes, big ones! `while(exp);` is already a valid yet empty `while` loop due to the null statement (the semicolon) following the `while`, even if it is followed by a statement block. The statement block in question is executed once—but outside of the loop. Exercise caution when copying and pasting code.

Workshop

The Workshop provides quiz questions to help you solidify your understanding of the material covered as well as exercises to provide you with experience using what you've learned. Try to answer the quiz and exercise questions before checking the answers in

Appendix E and be certain you understand the answers before continuing to the next lesson.

Quiz

1. Why should you bother to indent code within statement blocks, nested `if`s, and nested loops when it compiles even without indentation?
2. You can implement a quick fix using `goto`. Why would you want to avoid it?
3. Is it possible to write a `for` loop where the counter decrements? How would it look?
4. What is the problem with the following loop?

```
for (int counter=0; counter==10; ++counter)
    cout << counter << " ";
```

Exercises

1. Write a `for` loop to access elements in an array in reverse order.
2. Write a nested loop equivalent of Listing 6.14 that adds elements in two arrays but in reverse order.
3. Write a program similar to Listing 6.16 that displays Fibonacci numbers but that asks the user how many numbers she wants to compute.
4. Write a `switch-case` construct that tells whether a color is in the rainbow. Use enumerated constants.
5. **BUG BUSTERS:** What is wrong with this code?

```
for (int counter=0; counter=10; ++counter)
    cout << counter << " ";
```

6. **BUG BUSTERS:** What is wrong with this code?

```
int loopCounter = 0;
while(loopCounter <5);
{
    cout << loopCounter << " ";
    loopCounter++;
}
```

7. **BUG BUSTERS:** What is wrong with this code?

```
cout << "Enter a number between 0 and 4" << endl;
int input = 0;
cin >> input;
switch (input)
```

```
case 0:
case 1:
case 2:
case 3:
case 4:
cout << "Valid input" << endl;
default:
   cout << "Invalid input" << endl;
}
```

LESSON 7

Organizing Code with Functions

So far in this book, you have seen simple programs where all programming effort is contained in `main()`. This works well for really small programs and applications. The larger and more complex a program gets, the longer the contents of `main()` become—unless you choose to structure your program using functions.

Functions give you a way to compartmentalize and organize a program's execution logic. They enable you to split the contents of an application into logical blocks that are invoked sequentially.

A *function* is a subprogram that optionally takes parameters and returns a value, and it needs to be invoked to perform its task.

In this lesson you learn

- The need for programming functions
- Function prototypes and function definition
- Passing parameters to functions and returning values from them
- Overloading functions
- Recursive functions
- Lambda functions

The Need for Functions

Think of an application that asks the user to enter the radius of a circle and then computes the circumference and area of the circle. One way to do this is to have all the code inside `main()`. Another way is to break this application into logical blocks, as shown in Listing 7.1: one that computes area and one that computes circumference given radius.

Input ▼

LISTING 7.1 Two Functions That Compute the Area and Circumference of a Circle Given Radius

```
#include<iostream>
using namespace std;

const double Pi = 3.14159265;

// Function Declarations (Prototypes)
double Area(double radius);
double Circumference(double radius);

int main()
{
    cout << "Enter radius: ";
    double radius = 0;
    cin >> radius;

    // Call function "Area"
    cout << "Area is: " << Area(radius) << endl;

    // Call function "Circumference"
    cout << "Circumference is: " << Circumference(radius) << endl;

    return 0;
}

// Function definitions (implementations)
double Area(double radius)
{
    return Pi * radius * radius;
}

double Circumference(double radius)
{
    return 2 * Pi * radius;
}
```

Output ▼

```
Enter radius: 6.5
Area is: 132.732
Circumference is: 40.8407
```

Analysis ▼

`main()`, which is a function, is compact and delegates activity to functions such as `Area()` and `Circumference()` that are invoked in Lines 16 and 19, respectively.

The program demonstrates the following artifacts involved in programming using functions:

- Function prototypes are *declared* in Lines 6 and 7, so the compiler knows what the terms `Area` and `Circumference` mean when used in `main()`.
- Functions `Area()` and `Circumference()` are *invoked* in `main()` in Lines 16 and 19.
- Function `Area()` is *defined* in Lines 25 through 28, and `Circumference()` is defined in Lines 30 through 33.

Compartmentalizing the computation of area and circumference into different functions can potentially enable reuse as the functions can be invoked repeatedly, as and when required.

What Is a Function Prototype?

Let's take a look at Listing 7.1 again—Lines 6 and 7 in particular:

```
double Area(double radius);
double Circumference(double radius);
```

Figure 7.1 shows what a function prototype is composed of.

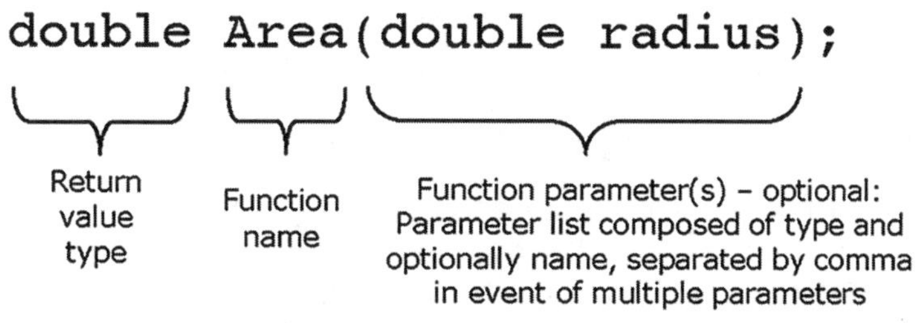

FIGURE 7.1 Parts of a function prototype.

The function prototype basically tells what a function is called (the name, `Area`), the list of parameters the function accepts (one parameter, a `double` called `radius`), and the return type of the function (a `double`). 7

Without the function prototype, on reaching Lines 16 and 19 in `main()`, the compiler wouldn't know what the terms `Area` and `Circumference` are. The function prototypes tell the compiler that `Area` and `Circumference` are functions; each of them takes one parameter of type `double` and returns a value of type `double`. The compiler then recognizes these statements as valid.

NOTE

A function can have multiple parameters separated by commas, but it can have only one return type.

When programming a function that does not need to return any value, specify the return type as `void`.

What Is a Function Definition?

The actual meat and potatoes of a function—the implementation of the function—is called the *definition*. Analyze the definition of the function `Area()`:

```
double Area(double radius)
{
   return Pi * radius * radius;
}
```

A function definition is always composed of a statement block. A return statement is necessary unless the function is declared with return type `void`. In this case, `Area()` needs to return a value because the function has been declared as one that returns a `double`. The statement block contains statements within open and closed braces ({ . . . }) that are executed when the function is called. `Area()` uses the input parameter `radius`, which contains the radius as an argument sent by the caller to compute the area of the circle.

What Is a Function Call, and What Are Arguments?

Calling a function is the same as invoking one. When a function declaration contains parameters, the function call needs to send *arguments*. Arguments are values the function requests within its parameter list. Let's analyze a call to `Area()` in Listing 7.1:

```
cout << "Area is: " << Area(radius) << endl;
```

Here, `Area(radius)` is the function call, and `radius` is the argument sent to the function `Area()`. When invoked, execution jumps to the function `Area()`, which uses the `radius` sent to compute the area of the circle.

Programming a Function with Multiple Parameters

Say that you are writing a program that computes the surface area of a cylinder, as shown in Figure 7.2.

FIGURE 7.2
A cylinder.

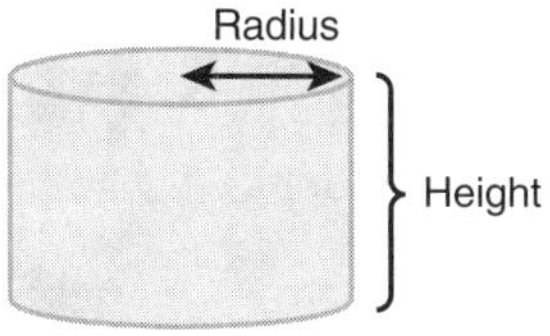

You need to use the following formula:

```
Area of Cylinder = Area of top circle + Area of bottom circle + Area of Side
             = Pi *  radius^2 + Pi * radius ^2 + 2 * Pi * radius * height
             = 2 * Pi * radius^2 + 2 * Pi * radius * height
```

Thus, you need to work with two variables—the radius and the height—to compute the area of the cylinder. When writing the function that computes the surface area of the cylinder, you specify at least two parameters in the parameter list within the function declaration. You do this by separating a pair of individual parameters with a comma, as shown in Listing 7.2.

Input ▼

LISTING 7.2 Function That Accepts Two Parameters to Compute the Surface Area of a Cylinder

```
#include<iostream>
using namespace std;

const double Pi = 3.14159265;

// Declaration contains two parameters
double SurfaceArea(double radius, double height);

int main()
{
    cout << "Enter the radius of the cylinder: ";
    double radius = 0;
    cin >> radius;
```

```
13:     cout << "Enter the height of the cylinder: ";
14:     double height = 0;
15:     cin >> height;
16:
17:     cout << "Surface area: " << SurfaceArea(radius, height) << endl;
18:
19:     return 0;
20: }
21:
22: double SurfaceArea(double radius, double height)
23: {
24:     double area = 2 * Pi * radius * radius + 2 * Pi * radius * height;
25:     return area;
26: }
```

Output ▼

```
Enter the radius of the cylinder: 3
Enter the height of the cylinder: 6.5
Surface Area: 179.071
```

Analysis ▼

Line 6 contains the declaration of the function `SurfaceArea()` with two parameters, `radius` and `height`, both of type `double`, separated by a comma. Lines 22 through 26 show the definition—that is, the implementation of `SurfaceArea()`. As you can see, the input parameters `radius` and `height` are used to compute the value stored in the local variable `area`, which is then returned to the caller.

NOTE

Function parameters are like local variables: They are valid within the scope of the function only. So in Listing 7.2, the parameters `radius` and `height` within the function `SurfaceArea()` are copies of variables with similar names within `main()`.

Programming Functions with No Parameters or No Return Values

If you delegate the task of saying “Hello World” to a function that does only that and nothing else, you can do it with a function that doesn’t need any parameters (as it doesn’t need to do anything apart from saying “Hello World”), and you may even be able to do it with one that doesn’t return any value (because you don’t expect anything from such a function that would be useful elsewhere). Listing 7.3 demonstrates one such function.

Input ▼

LISTING 7.3 A Function with No Parameters and No Return Values

```
 0: #include<iostream>
 1: using namespace std;
 2:
 3: void SayHello();
 4:
 5: int main()
 6: {
 7:    SayHello();
 8:    return 0;
 9: }
10:
11: void SayHello()
12: {
13:    cout << "Hello World" << endl;
14: }
```

Output ▼

```
Hello World
```

Analysis ▼

Note that the function prototype in Line 3 declares the function `SayHello()` as one with a return value of type `void`; that is, `SayHello()` doesn’t return a value. Consequently, in the function definition in Lines 11 through 14, there is no return statement. Some programmers prefer to insert a symbolic empty return statement at the end:

```
void SayHello()
{
   cout << "Hello World" << endl;
   return; // an empty return
}
```

Function Parameters with Default Values

In samples thus far, you have assumed the value of pi, fixed it as a constant, and never given the user an opportunity to change it. However, the user may be interested in a less or more accurate reading. How do you program a function that would use a default value of pi of your choosing unless another one is supplied?

One way of solving this problem is to supply an additional parameter in the function `Area()` for pi and supply a value that you choose as a default one. Such an adaptation of the function `Area()` from Listing 7.1 would look like the following:

```
double Area(double radius, double pi = 3.14);
```

Note that the second parameter, `pi`, is assigned the default value 3.14. This second parameter is therefore an optional parameter for the caller. The function `Area()` can be invoked as if the second parameter didn't exist:

```
Area(radius);
```

In this case, the second parameter defaults to the value 3.14. However, when required, the same function can be invoked using two arguments:

```
Area(radius, 3.14159); // more precise pi
```

Listing 7.4 demonstrates how you can program functions that contain default values for parameters that can be overridden with a user-supplied value, if available and desired.

Input ▼

LISTING 7.4 Function That Computes the Area of a Circle, Using Pi as a Second Parameter with Default Value 3.14

```
#include<iostream>
using namespace std;

// Function with default argument
```

```
double Area(double radius, double pi = 3.14);

int main()
{
   cout << "Enter radius: ";
   double radius = 0;
   cin >> radius;

   cout << "pi is 3.14, do you wish to change this (y / n)? ";
   char changePi = 'n';
   cin >> changePi;

   double circleArea = 0;
   if (changePi == 'y')
   {
      cout << "Enter new pi: ";
      double newPi = 3.14;
      cin >> newPi;
      circleArea = Area (radius, newPi);
   }
   else
      circleArea = Area(radius); // Ignore 2nd param, use default value

   // Call function "Area"
   cout << "Area is: " << circleArea << endl;

   return 0;
}

// Function definitions (implementations)
double Area(double radius, double pi)
{
   return pi * radius * radius;
}
```

Output ▼

First run:

```
Enter radius: 1
Pi is 3.14, do you wish to change this (y / n)? n
Area is: 3.14
```

Next run:

```
Enter radius: 1
Pi is 3.14, do you wish to change this (y / n)? y
Enter new Pi: 3.1416
Area is: 3.1416
```

Analysis ▼

In the two runs, the radius entered by the user is the same: 1. In the second run, however, the user opts to change the precision of pi, and hence the area computed is slightly different. Note that in both cases, as seen in Lines 22 and 25, you invoke the same function. Line 25 invokes `Area()` without the second parameter `pi`. In this case, the parameter `pi` in `Area()` contains the value 3.14, supplied as the default in the declaration in Line 4.

NOTE

> You can have multiple parameters with default values; however, they should all be at the tail end of the parameters list.

Recursion: Functions That Invoke Themselves

In certain cases, you can actually have a function call itself. Such a function is called a *recursive function*. Note that a recursive function should have a very clearly defined exit condition, where it returns without invoking itself again.

CAUTION

> In the absence of an exit condition or in the event of a bug in an exit condition, your program execution gets stuck at the recursive function that won't stop invoking itself. This eventually stops when the stack overflows, causing an application crash.

Recursive functions can be useful when determining a number in the Fibonacci sequence, as shown in Listing 7.5. This sequence starts with two numbers, 0 and 1:

```
F(0) = 0
F(1) = 1
```

The value of a subsequent number in the series is the sum of the previous two numbers. So, the nth value (for $n > 1$) is determined by the (recursive) formula:

```
Fibonacci(n) = Fibonacci(n - 1) + Fibonacci(n - 2)
```

As a result, the Fibonacci sequence expands to

```
F(2) = 1
F(3) = 2
F(4) = 3
F(5) = 5
F(6) = 8, and so on.
```

Input ▼

LISTING 7.5 Using Recursive Functions to Calculate a Number in the Fibonacci Sequence

```
 0: #include<iostream>
 1: using namespace std;
 2:
 3: int GetFibNumber(int fibIndex)
 4: {
 5:     if (fibIndex < 2)
 6:         return fibIndex;
 7:     else // recursion if fibIndex >= 2
 8:         return GetFibNumber(fibIndex - 1) + GetFibNumber(fibIndex - 2);
 9: }
10:
11: int main()
12: {
13:     cout << "Enter 0-based index of desired Fibonacci Number: ";
14:     int index = 0;
15:     cin >> index;
16:
17:     cout << "Fibonacci number is: " << GetFibNumber(index) << endl;
18:     return 0;
19: }
```

Output ▼

7

```
Enter 0-based index of desired Fibonacci Number: 6
Fibonacci number is: 8
```

Analysis ▼

The function `GetFibNumber()`, defined in Lines 3 through 9, is recursive as it invokes itself at Line 8. The exit condition programmed in Lines 5 and 6 ensures that the function will return without recursion if `fibIndex` is less than 2. Thus, `GetFibNumber()` invokes itself recursively with ever-reducing values of `fibIndex`. It ultimately reaches a state where the exit condition is satisfied, the recursion ends, and a Fibonacci value is determined and returned to `main()`.

Functions with Multiple Return Statements

You are not restricted to having only one `return` statement in a function definition. You can return from any point in the function—and multiple times if you want, as shown in Listing 7.6. Depending on the circumstances and the purpose of the function, this might or might not be poor programming practice.

Input ▼

LISTING 7.6 Using Multiple Return Statements in One Function

```
#include<iostream>
using namespace std;
const double Pi = 3.14159265;

void QueryAndCalculate()
{
   cout << "Enter radius: ";
   double radius = 0;
   cin >> radius;

   cout << "Area: " << Pi * radius * radius << endl;

   cout << "Do you wish to calculate circumference (y/n)? ";
   char calcCircum = 'n';
   cin >> calcCircum;

   if (calcCircum == 'n')
      return;

   cout << "Circumference: " << 2 * Pi * radius << endl;
   return;
}

```

```
23: int main()
24: {
25:     QueryAndCalculate ();
26:
27:     return 0;
28: }
```

Output ▼

First run:

```
Enter radius: 1
Area: 3.14159
Do you wish to calculate circumference (y/n)? y
Circumference: 6.28319
```

Next run:

```
Enter radius: 1
Area: 3.14159
Do you wish to calculate circumference (y/n)? n
```

Analysis ▼

The function `QueryAndCalculate()` contains multiple `return` statements: one at Line 17 and one at Line 20. If the user presses `n` for calculating circumference, the program quits by using the `return` statement. For all other values, it continues with calculating the circumference and then returning.

CAUTION

Use multiple returns in a function with caution. It is a lot easier to understand and follow a function that starts at the top and returns at the bottom than one that returns at multiple points in between. In Listing 7.6, use of multiple returns could be avoided simply by changing the `if` condition to testing for `'y'`, for yes:

```
if (calcCircum == 'y')
   cout << "Circumference: " << 2*Pi*radius <<
endl;
```

Using Functions to Work with Different Forms of Data

Functions don't restrict you to passing values one at a time; you can pass an array of values to a function. You can create two functions with the same name and return value but different parameters. You can program a function such that its parameters are not created and destroyed within the function call; instead, you use references that are valid even after the function has exited in order to manipulate more data or parameters in a function call. In this section, you'll learn about passing arrays to functions, function overloading, and passing arguments by reference to functions.

Overloading Functions

Functions with the same name and return type but with different parameters or sets of parameters are called *overloaded functions*. Overloaded functions can be quite useful in applications where a function with a particular name that produces a certain type of output might need to be invoked with different sets of parameters. Say you need to write an application that computes the area of a circle and the area of a cylinder. The function that computes the area of a circle needs a parameter: the radius. The other function that computes the area of the cylinder needs the height of the cylinder in addition to the radius of the cylinder. Both functions need to return data of the same type, containing the area. C++ enables you to define two overloaded functions, both called `Area`, both returning `double`, but one that takes only the radius as input and another that takes the height and the radius as input parameters. See Listing 7.7.

Input ▼

LISTING 7.7 Using an Overloaded Function to Calculate the Area of a Circle or a Cylinder

```
#include<iostream>
using namespace std;

const double Pi = 3.14159265;

double Area(double radius);    // for circle
double Area(double radius, double height); // for cylinder

int main()
{
    cout << "Enter z for Cylinder, c for Circle: ";
    char userSelection = 'z';
    cin >> userSelection;
```

```

    cout << "Enter radius: ";
    double radius = 0;
    cin >> radius;

    if (userSelection == 'z')
    {
        cout << "Enter height: ";
        double height = 0;
        cin >> height;

        // Invoke overloaded variant of Area for cylinder
        cout << "Area of cylinder is: " << Area (radius, height) << endl;
    }
    else
        cout << "Area of cylinder is: " << Area (radius) << endl;

    return 0;
}

// for circle
double Area(double radius)
{
    return Pi * radius * radius;
}

// overloaded for cylinder
double Area(double radius, double height)
{
    // reuse the area of circle
    return 2 * Area (radius) + 2 * Pi * radius * height;
}
```

Output ▼

First run:

```
Enter z for Cylinder, c for Circle: z
Enter radius: 2
Enter height: 5
Area of cylinder is: 87.9646
```

Next run:

```
Enter z for Cylinder, c for Circle: c
Enter radius: 1
Area of cylinder is: 3.14159
```

Analysis ▼

Lines 5 and 6 declare the prototype for the overloaded forms of `Area()`: The first overloaded variant accepts a single parameter: the radius of a circle. The next one accepts two parameters: the radius and height of a cylinder. The function is called *overloaded* because there are two prototypes with the same name, `Area()`; with the same return types, `double`; and different sets of parameters. The definitions of the overloaded functions are in Lines 34 through 44, where the two functions determine the area of a circle given the radius and the area of a cylinder given the radius and height, respectively. Interestingly, as the area of a cylinder is composed of the area of the two circles it contains (one on top and the other on the bottom) in addition to the area of the sides, the overloaded version for the cylinder is able to reuse `Area()` for the circle, as shown in Line 43.

Passing an Array of Values to a Function

A function that displays an integer can be represented like this:

```
void DisplayInteger(int Number);
```

A function that can display an array of integers uses a slightly different format:

```
void DisplayIntegers(int[] numbers, int Length);
```

The first parameter tells the function that the data being entered is an array, and the second parameter supplies the length of the array, such that you can use the array without crossing its boundaries. See Listing 7.8.

Input ▼

LISTING 7.8 Function That Takes an Array as a Parameter

```
#include<iostream>
using namespace std;

void DisplayArray(int numbers[], int length)
{
   for (int index = 0; index < length; ++index)
      cout << numbers[index] << " ";

   cout << endl;
}

void DisplayArray(char characters[], int length)
```

```
12: {
13:     for (int index = 0; index < length; ++index)
14:        cout << characters[index] << " ";
15:
16:     cout << endl;
17: }
18:
19: int main()
20: {
21:     int myNums[4] = {24, 58, -1, 245};
22:     DisplayArray(myNums, 4);
23:
24:     char myStatement[7] = {'H', 'e', 'l', 'l', 'o', '!', '\0'};
25:     DisplayArray(myStatement, 7);
26:
27:     return 0;
28: }
```

Output ▼

```
24 58 -1 245
H e l l o !
```

Analysis ▼

There are two overloaded functions called `DisplayArray()` here: one that displays the contents of elements in an array of integers and another that displays the contents of an array of characters. In Lines 22 and 25, the two functions are invoked using an array of integers and an array of characters, respectively, as input. Note that in declaring and initializing the array of characters in Line 24, you have intentionally included the null character—as a best practice and a good habit—even though the array is not used as a string in a `cout` statement or the like (`cout << characters;`) in this application.

Passing Arguments by Reference

Take another look at the function in Listing 7.1 that computes the area of a circle given the radius:

```
// Function definitions (implementations)
double Area(double radius)
{
   return Pi * radius * radius;
}
```

Here, the parameter `radius` contains a value that is copied into it when the function is invoked in `main()`:

```
// Call function "Area"
cout << "Area is: " << Area(radius) << endl;
```

This means that the variable `radius` in `main()` is unaffected by the function call, as `Area()` works on a copy of the value `radius` contains, held in `radius`. There are cases where you might need a function to work on a variable that modifies a value that is available outside the function, too, such as in the calling function. In such cases, you declare a parameter that takes an argument *by reference*. A form of the function `Area()` that computes and returns the area as a parameter by reference looks like this:

```
// output parameter 'result' by reference
void Area(double radius, double& result)
{
   result = Pi * radius * radius;
}
```

Note that `Area()` in this form takes two parameters. Don't miss the ampersand (`&`) next to the second parameter, `result`. This sign indicates to the compiler that the second argument should *not* be copied to the function; instead, it is a reference to the variable being passed. The return type has been changed to `void` as the function no longer supplies the area computed as a return value; rather, it supplies the area as an output parameter by reference. Returning values by references is demonstrated in Listing 7.9, which computes the area of a circle.

Input ▼

LISTING 7.9 Fetching the Area of a Circle as a Reference Parameter and Not as a Return Value

```
#include<iostream>
using namespace std;

const double Pi = 3.1416;

// output parameter result by reference
void Area(double radius, double& result)
{
   result = Pi * radius * radius;
}

int main()
```

```
12: {
13:     cout << "Enter radius: ";
14:     double radius = 0;
15:     cin >> radius;
16:
17:     double areaFetched = 0;
18:     Area(radius, areaFetched);
19:
20:     cout << "The area is: " << areaFetched << endl;
21:     return 0;
22: }
```

Output ▼

```
Enter radius: 2
The area is: 12.5664
```

Analysis ▼

Note Lines 17 and 18, where the function `Area()` is invoked with two parameters; the second is one that should contain the result. In Line 6, the function `Area()` takes the second parameter by reference. Therefore, the variable `result` used in Line 8 within `Area` points to the same memory location as `double areaFetched` declared in Line 17 within the caller `main()`. Thus, the result computed in the function `Area()` in Line 8 is available in `main()` and displayed on the screen in Line 20.

NOTE

> A function can return only one value by using the `return` statement. Passing arguments by reference is the best way to get a function to modify multiple values/variables that need to be available at the caller.

How Function Calls Are Handled by the Microprocessor

Although it is not extremely important to know exactly how a function call is implemented on a microprocessor level, you might find it interesting. Understanding this helps you understand why C++ gives you the option of programming inline functions, which are explained later in this section.

A function call essentially means that the microprocessor jumps to executing the next instruction belonging to the called function at a nonsequential memory location. After it is done executing the instructions in the function, it returns to where it left off. To implement this logic, the compiler converts your function call into a `CALL` instruction for the microprocessor. This instruction is accompanied by the address in memory that the next instruction needs to be taken from; this address belongs to your function routine. When the microprocessor encounters `CALL`, it saves the position of the instruction to be executed after the function call on the stack and jumps to the memory location contained in the `CALL` instruction.

Understanding the Stack

The stack is a last-in, first-out memory structure, quite like a stack of plates where you take the plate on top, which was the last one to be placed on the stack. Putting data onto the stack is called a *push* operation. Getting data out of the stack is called a *pop* operation. As the stack grows upward, the stack pointer always increments as it grows and points to the top of the stack. See Figure 7.3.

FIGURE 7.3
A visual representation of a stack containing three integers.

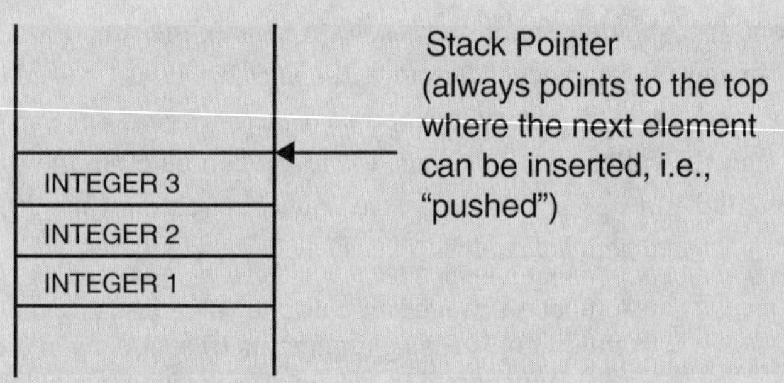

The nature of the stack makes it optimal for handling function calls. When a function is called, all local variables are instantiated on the stack—that is, pushed onto the stack. When the function ends, the variables are simply popped off it, and the stack pointer returns to where it originally was.

This memory location contains instructions belonging to the function. The microprocessor executes them until it reaches the `RET` statement (the microprocessor's code for `return` programmed by you). The `RET` statement results in the microprocessor popping that address from the stack stored during the `CALL` instruction. This address contains the location in the calling function from which the execution needs to continue. Thus, the microprocessor is back to the caller and continues where it left off.

Inline Functions

A regular function call is translated into a `CALL` instruction, which results in stack operations and microprocessor execution shift to the function and so on. This might sound like a lot of stuff happening under the hood, but it happens quite quickly—in most cases. However, what if a function is a very simple one, like the following?

```
double GetPi()
{
   return 3.14159;
}
```

The overhead involved in performing a function call in this case might be quite high for the amount of time spent actually executing `GetPi()`. This is why C++ compilers enable a programmer to declare such functions as inline. A programmer can use the keyword `inline` to request that these functions be expanded inline where called:

```
inline double GetPi()
{
   return 3.14159;
}
```

Functions that perform simple operations like doubling a number are good candidates for being inlined, too. Listing 7.10 demonstrates one such case.

Input ▼

LISTING 7.10 Using an Inline Function That Doubles an Integer

```
#include<iostream>
using namespace std;

// define an inline function that doubles
inline long DoubleNum (int inputNum)
{
   return inputNum * 2;
}

```

```
 9: int main()
10: {
11:     cout << "Enter an integer: ";
12:     int inputNum = 0;
13:     cin >> inputNum;
14:
15:     // Call inline function
16:     cout << "Double is: " << DoubleNum(inputNum) << endl;
17:
18:     return 0;
19: }
```

Output ▼

```
Enter an integer: 35
Double is: 70
```

Analysis ▼

The `inline` keyword is used in Line 4. Compilers typically see this keyword as a request to place the contents of the function `DoubleNum()` directly where the function has been invoked—in Line 16 in this case—which increases the execution speed of the code.

Classifying functions as inline can result in code bloat, especially if a function being inlined contains many instructions. The `inline` keyword should be used infrequently; it should be reserved for functions that have a simple task that needs to be executed quickly and with minimal overhead, as demonstrated earlier.

NOTE

> Most modern C++ compilers offer various performance optimization options. Some, such as the MSVC compiler, can optimize for size or speed. Optimizing for size may help in developing software for devices and peripherals where memory may be at a premium. When you optimize for size, the compiler might reject many inline requests, which might bloat code.
>
> When you optimize for speed, the compiler typically sees and takes opportunities to inline code where it would make sense to do so, and it does it for you—sometimes even in cases where you have not explicitly requested it.

Automatic Return Type Deduction

You learned about the keyword `auto` in Lesson 3, "Using Variables, Declaring Constants." This keyword, which was introduced in 2014, lets you leave variable type deduction to the compiler, and the compiler handles it on the basis of the initialization value assigned to the variable. The same principle applies to the use of `auto` in functions. Instead of specifying the return type, you can use `auto` and let the compiler deduce the return type for you on the basis of return values you program within the function body.

Listing 7.11 demonstrates the use of `auto` in a function that computes the area of a circle.

Input ▼

LISTING 7.11 Using `auto` as the Return Type of the Function `Area()`

```
#include<iostream>
using namespace std;

const double Pi = 3.14159265;

auto Area(double radius)
{
    return Pi * radius * radius;
}

int main()
{
    cout << "Enter radius: ";
    double radius = 0;
    cin >> radius;

    // Call function "Area"
    cout << "Area is: " << Area(radius) << endl;

    return 0;
}
```

Output ▼

```
Enter radius: 2
Area is: 12.5664
```

Analysis ▼

The line of interest is Line 5, which uses `auto` as the return type of the function `Area()`. The compiler deduces the return type on the basis of the return expression that uses `double`. Thus, despite using `auto`, `Area()` in Listing 7.11 compiles to the same code as `Area()` in Listing 7.1 with return type `double`.

NOTE

> Functions that rely on automatic return type deduction need to be defined (i.e., implemented) before they're invoked. This is because the compiler needs to know a function's return type at the point where it is used. If such a function has multiple return statements, they need to all deduce to the same type. Recursive calls need to follow at least one return statement.

Lambda Functions

Lambda functions are also called *lambda expressions*. This feature, which is a major upgrade since C++11, radically modernizes well-programmed C++ applications.

TIP

> This section provides an introduction to a concept that's not exactly easy for beginners. So, skim through it and try to learn the concept but don't be disappointed if you don't grasp it all. The topic is discussed in depth in Lesson 22, "Lambda Expressions."

Lambda functions, which were introduced in 2011, are frequently used in algorithms that are provided by the Standard Template Library (STL). For example, you might use a lambda function within a sort function that requires you to supply a binary predicate. The binary predicate is a function that compares two arguments and returns `true` if one is less than the other; otherwise, it returns `false`, thereby helping in deciding the order of elements in a sort operation. Lambda functions help in compact predicate definitions, as shown in Listing 7.12.

Input ▼

LISTING 7.12 Using Lambda Functions to Display Elements in an Array and to Sort Them

```
#include<iostream>
#include<algorithm>
#include<vector>
using namespace std;

void DisplayNums(vector<int>& dynArray)
{
   for_each (dynArray.begin(), dynArray.end(), \
            [](int Element) {cout << Element << " ";} );

   cout << endl;
}

int main()
{
   vector<int> myNums;
   myNums.push_back(501);
   myNums.push_back(-1);
   myNums.push_back(25);
   myNums.push_back(-35);

   DisplayNums(myNums);

   cout << "Sorting them in descending order" << endl;

   sort (myNums.begin(), myNums.end(),
         [](int Num1, int Num2) {return (Num2 < Num1); } );

   DisplayNums(myNums);

   return 0;
}
```

Output ▼

```
501 -1 25 -35
Sorting them in descending order
501 25 -1 -35
```

Analysis ▼

The program contains integers pushed into a dynamic array provided by the C++ Standard Library in the form of `std::vector` in Lines 15 through 19. The function `DisplayNums()` uses the STL algorithm `for_each` to iterate through the elements in the array and display the value of each one. In doing so, it uses a lambda function in Line 8. `std::sort` in Line 25 also uses a binary predicate (Line 26) in the form of a lambda function that returns `true` if the second number is smaller than the first, effectively sorting the collection in ascending order.

The syntax of a lambda function is the following:

```
[optional parameters](parameter list){ statements; }
```

NOTE

> Predicates and their use in algorithms such as `sort` are discussed at length in Lesson 23, "STL Algorithms." Listing 23.6 in particular is a code sample that uses a lambda function and a non-lambda variant in an algorithm, enabling you to compare the programming efficiency introduced by lambda functions.

Summary

In this lesson, you learned the basics of modular programming. You learned how functions can help you structure your code better and how they can help you reuse algorithms you write. You learned that functions can take parameters and return values, parameters can have default values that the caller can override, and parameters can contain arguments passed by reference. You learned how to pass arrays, and you also learned how to program overloaded functions that have the same name and return type but different parameter lists.

Last but not the least, you got a sneak preview into what lambda functions are. Lambda functions change how C++ applications are programmed, especially with STL.

Q&A

Q What happens if I program a recursive function that doesn't end?

A Program execution doesn't end. That might not be bad, per se, for there are `while(true)` and `for(;;)` loops that do the same thing; however, a recursive function call consumes more and more stack space, which is finite and runs out, eventually causing an application crash due to a stack overflow.

Q Why not inline every function? Doing so increases execution speed, right?

A The benefits of function inlining cannot be taken for granted. Inlining results in function code being inserted at the point where it's called, which causes code bloat.

Q Can I supply default parameter values to all parameters in a function?

A Yes, that is definitely possible and recommended when doing so makes sense.

Q I have two functions, both called `Area`. One takes a radius, and the other takes height. I want one to return `float` and the other to return `double`. Will this work?

A For function overloading to work, both functions with the same name must also have the same return type. In this case, your compiler will give you an error message as the name `Area` has been used twice in what it expects to be two functions with different names.

Workshop

The Workshop provides quiz questions to help you solidify your understanding of the material covered and exercises to provide you with experience in using what you've learned. Try to answer the quiz and exercise questions before checking the answers in Appendix E and be certain that you understand the answers before continuing to the next lesson.

Quiz

1. What is the scope of variables declared in a function's prototype?
2. What is the nature of the value passed to this function?
   ```
   int Func(int &someNumber);
   ```
3. You have a function that invokes itself. What is such a function called?
4. You have declared two functions, both with the same name and return type but different parameter lists. What are these called?
5. Does the stack pointer point to the top, middle, or bottom of the stack?

Exercises

1. Write overloaded functions that calculate the volume of a sphere and of a cylinder. The formulas are as follows:

```
Volume of sphere = (4 * Pi * radius * radius * radius) / 3
Volume of a cylinder = Pi * radius * radius * height
```

2. Write a function that accepts an array of `double` as input.
3. **BUG BUSTERS:** What is wrong with the following code?

```
#include<iostream>
using namespace std;
const double Pi = 3.1416;

void Area(double radius, double result)
{
   result = Pi * radius * radius;
}

int main()
{
   cout << "Enter radius: ";
   double radius = 0;
   cin >> radius;

   double areaFetched = 0;
   Area(radius, areaFetched);

   cout << "The area is: " << areaFetched << endl;
   return 0;
}
```

4. **BUG BUSTERS:** What is wrong with the following function declaration?

```
double Area(double Pi = 3.14, double radius);
```

5. Write a function with return type `void` that still helps the caller calculate the area and circumference of a circle when the radius is supplied.

LESSON 8

Pointers and References Explained

One of the biggest advantages of C++ is that it enables you to write high-level applications that are abstracted from the hardware as well as applications that work close to it. Indeed, C++ enables you to tweak the performance of an application on a bytes and bits level. Understanding how pointers and references work is one step toward being able to write programs that are effective in their consumption of system resources.

In this lesson, you find out

- What pointers are
- What the free store is
- How to use the operators `new` and `delete` to allocate and free memory
- How to write stable applications using pointers and dynamic allocation
- What references are
- Differences between pointers and references
- When to use pointers and when to use references

What Is a Pointer?

A *pointer* is a variable that stores an address in memory. Just as a variable of type `int` is used to contain an integer value, a pointer variable is used to contain a memory address, as illustrated in Figure 8.1.

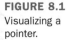

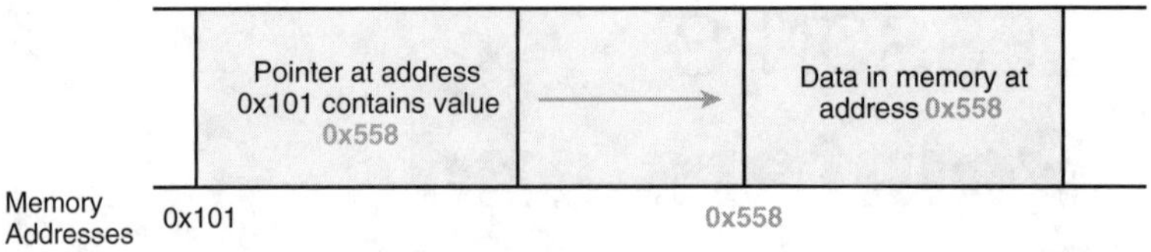

FIGURE 8.1
Visualizing a pointer.

Thus, a pointer is a variable, and like all other variables, a pointer occupies space in memory (in the case of Figure 8.1, at address 0x101). What's special about pointers is that the value contained in a pointer (in this case, 0x558) is interpreted as a memory address. So, a pointer is a special variable that *points to* a location in memory.

NOTE

Memory locations are typically addressed using *hexadecimal* notation. This is a number system with base 16—that is, a system featuring 16 distinct symbols from 0 to 9 followed by A through F. By convention, a hexadecimal number is prefixed with 0x. Thus, 0xA is hexadecimal for 10 in decimal, 0xF is hexadecimal for 15, and 0x10 is hexadecimal for 16. For more information, see Appendix A, "Working with Numbers: Binary and Hexadecimal."

Declaring a Pointer

As a variable, a pointer needs to be declared. You normally declare a pointer to point to a specific value type, such as `int`. This means that the address contained in the pointer points to a location in the memory that holds an integer. You can also declare a pointer to a block of memory of unspecified type (also called a `void` pointer).

Like every other variable, a pointer needs to be declared. A pointer declaration uses the following syntax:

```
PointedType* PointerVariableName;
```

As is the case with most other variables, unless you initialize a pointer, it will contain a random value. You don't want a random memory address to be accessed, so you initialize a pointer to `NULL`. `NULL` is a value that can be checked against and one that cannot be a memory address:

```
PointedType* PointerVariableName = NULL; // initializing value
```

Thus, you could declare a pointer to an integer like this:

```
int* pointsToInt = NULL;
```

CAUTION

> A pointer, like all other data types you have learned about, contains a junk value unless it has been initialized. This junk value is particularly dangerous in the case of a pointer because a pointer is expected to contain an address. Uninitialized pointers can result in a program accessing invalid memory locations, resulting in a crash.

Determining the Address of a Variable by Using the Reference Operator (`&`)

Variables are tools that C++ provides for you to work with data in memory. This concept is explained in detail in Lesson 3, "Using Variables, Declaring Constants."

If `varName` is a variable, `&varName` gives the address in memory where its value is placed.

So, if you have declared an integer, using the syntax that you're well acquainted with, such as

```
int age = 30;
```

`&age` would be the address in memory where the value (`30`) is placed. Listing 8.1 demonstrates the concept of the memory address of an integer variable that is used to hold the value it contains.

Input ▼

LISTING 8.1 Determining the Addresses of an `int` and a `double`

```
#include<iostream>
using namespace std;

int main()
{
    int age = 30;
    const double Pi = 3.1416;

    // Use & to find the address in memory
    cout << "Integer age is located at: 0x" << &age << endl;
    cout << "Double Pi is located at: 0x" << &Pi << endl;

    return 0;
}
```

Output ▼

```
Integer age is at: 0x0045FE00
Double Pi is located at: 0x0045FDF8
```

Analysis ▼

Note how the reference operator (`&`) is used in Lines 9 and 10 to reveal the addresses of the variable `age` and the constant `Pi`. The text `0x` has been appended as a convention that is used when displaying hexadecimal numbers.

NOTE

You know that the amount of memory consumed by a variable is dependent on its type. Listing 3.4 in Lesson 3 uses `sizeof()` to demonstrate that the size of an integer is 4 bytes (on my system, using my compiler). So, using the preceding output, which says that the integer `age` is located at address `0x0045FE00`, and using the knowledge that `sizeof(int)` is 4, you know that the 4 bytes located in the range `0x0045FE00` through `0x0045FE03` belong to the integer `age`.

NOTE

The reference operator (`&`) is also called the *address-of operator*.

Using Pointers to Store Addresses

You have learned how to declare pointers and how to determine the address of a variable. You also know that pointers are variables that are used to hold memory addresses. It's time to connect these dots and use pointers to store the addresses obtained using the reference operator (`&`).

Assume a variable declaration of the types you already know:

```
// Declaring a variable
Type Variable = InitialValue;
```

To store the address of this variable in a pointer, you would declare a pointer to the same `Type` and initialize the pointer to the variable's address by using the reference operator (`&`):

```
// Declaring a pointer to Type and initializing to address
Type* pointer = &Variable;
```

Thus, if you have declared an integer, using the syntax that you're well acquainted with, such as

```
int age = 30;
```

You would declare a pointer to the type `int` to hold the actual address where `age` is stored, like this:

```
int* pointsToInt = &age; // Pointer to integer age
```

In Listing 8.2 you see how a pointer can be used to store an address fetched using the reference operator (`&`).

Input ▼

LISTING 8.2 Demonstrating the Declaration and Initialization of a Pointer

```
#include<iostream>
using namespace std;

int main()
{
    int age = 30;
    int* pointsToInt = &age;   // pointer initialized to &age

    // Displaying the value of pointer
    cout << "Integer age is at: 0x" << hex << pointsToInt << endl;

    return 0;
}
```

Output ▼

```
Integer age is at: 0x0045FE00
```

Analysis ▼

Essentially, the output of this code snippet is the same as the output for the code in Listing 8.1 because both of these samples are displaying the same thing—the address in memory where the integer `age` is stored. The difference here is that the address is first assigned to a pointer in Line 6, and the value of the pointer (now the address) is displayed using `cout` in Line 9.

> **NOTE**
>
> Your output might differ in addresses from those you see in these examples. In fact, the address of a variable might change at every run of the application on the very same computer.

Now that you know how to store an address in a pointer variable, it is easy to imagine that the same pointer variable can be reassigned a different memory address and made to point to a different value, as shown in Listing 8.3.

Input ▼

LISTING 8.3 Pointer Reassignment to Another Variable

```
#include<iostream>
using namespace std;

int main()
{
   int age = 30;

   int* pointsToInt = &age;
   cout << "pointsToInt points to age now" << endl;

   // Displaying the value of pointer
   cout << "pointsToInt = 0x" << hex << pointsToInt << endl;

   int dogsAge = 9;
   pointsToInt = &dogsAge;
   cout << "pointsToInt points to dogsAge now" << endl;

   cout << "pointsToInt = 0x" << hex << pointsToInt << endl;

   return 0;
}
```

Output ▼

```
pointsToInt points to age now
pointsToInt = 0x002EFB34
pointsToInt points to dogsAge now
pointsToInt = 0x002EFB1C
```

Analysis ▼

This program demonstrates that one pointer to an integer, `pointsToInt`, can point to any integer. In Line 7, it has been initialized to `&age`, hence containing the address of the variable `age`. In Line 14 the same pointer is assigned `&dogsAge`, pointing to another location in memory that contains `dogsAge`. Correspondingly, the output indicates that the value of the pointer—that is, the address being pointed to—changes as the two integers `age` and `dogsAge` are, of course, stored in different locations in memory, `0x002EFB34` and `0x002EFB1C`, respectively.

Accessing Pointed Data Using the Dereference Operator (`*`)

If you have a pointer containing a valid address, how do you access that location—that is, get or set data at that location? The answer lies in using the dereference operator (`*`). Essentially, if you have a valid pointer `pData`, you use `*pData` to access the value stored at the address contained in the pointer. The use of the dereference operator (`*`) is demonstrated by Listing 8.4.

Input ▼

LISTING 8.4 Demonstrating the Use of the Dereference Operator (`*`) to Access Integer Values

```
#include<iostream>
using namespace std;

int main()
{
   int age = 30;
   int dogsAge = 9;

   cout << "Integer age = " << age << endl;
   cout << "Integer dogsAge = " << dogsAge << endl;
```

```
10:
11:     int* pointsToInt = &age;
12:     cout << "pointsToInt points to age" << endl;
13:
14:     // Displaying the value of pointer
15:     cout << "pointsToInt = 0x" << hex << pointsToInt << endl;
16:
17:     // Displaying the value at the pointed location
18:     cout << "*pointsToInt = " << dec << *pointsToInt << endl;
19:
20:     pointsToInt = &dogsAge;
21:     cout << "pointsToInt points to dogsAge now" << endl;
22:
23:     cout << "pointsToInt = 0x" << hex << pointsToInt << endl;
24:     cout << "*pointsToInt = " << dec << *pointsToInt << endl;
25:
26:     return 0;
27: }
```

Output ▼

```
Integer age = 30
Integer dogsAge = 9
pointsToInt points to age
pointsToInt = 0x0025F788
*pointsToInt = 30
pointsToInt points to dogsAge now
pointsToInt = 0x0025F77C
*pointsToInt = 9
```

Analysis ▼

In addition to changing the address stored within a pointer, as shown in Listing 8.3, the program in Listing 8.4 also uses the dereference operator (`*`) with the same pointer variable `pointsToInt` to display the different values at these two addresses. Note Lines 18 and 24. In both of these lines, the integer pointed to by `pointsToInt` is accessed using the dereference operator (`*`). As the address contained in `pointsToInt` is changed in Line 20, the same pointer after this assignment accesses the variable `dogsAge`, displaying `9`.

When the dereference operator (`*`) is used, the application essentially uses the address stored in the pointer as a starting point to fetch from memory 4 bytes that belong to an integer (as this is a pointer to integers, and `sizeof(int)` is 4). Thus, the validity of the address contained in the pointer is absolutely essential. By initializing the pointer to `&age` in Line 11, you have ensured that the pointer contains a valid address. When you don't initialize the pointer, it can contain any random value (that existed in the memory location where the pointer variable is located), and dereference of that pointer usually results in an access violation—which occurs when you use an application to access a memory location that the application was not authorized to access.

> **NOTE** The dereference operator (*) is also called the *indirection operator*.

You used the pointer in Listing 8.4 to read (get) values from the pointed memory location. Listing 8.5 shows what happens when `*pointsToInt` is used as an l-value—that is, when it is assigned to instead of just being accessed.

Input ▼

LISTING 8.5 Manipulating Data Using a Pointer and the Dereference Operator (*)

```
#include<iostream>
using namespace std;

int main()
{
    int dogsAge = 30;
    cout << "Initialized dogsAge = " << dogsAge << endl;

    int* pointsToAnAge = &dogsAge;
    cout << "pointsToAnAge points to dogsAge" << endl;

    cout << "Enter an age for your dog: ";

    // store input at the memory pointed to by pointsToAnAge
    cin >> *pointsToAnAge;

    // Displaying the address where age is stored
    cout << "Input stored at 0x" << hex << pointsToAnAge << endl;

    cout << "Integer dogsAge = " << dec << dogsAge << endl;

    return 0;
}
```

Output ▼

```
Initialized dogsAge = 30
pointsToAnAge points to dogsAge
Enter an age for your dog: 10
Input stored at 0x0025FA18
Integer dogsAge = 10
```

Analysis ▼

The key step here is in Line 14, where the age input by the user is saved at the location stored in the pointer `pointsToAnAge`. Line 19, which displays the variable `dogsAge`, shows the value you stored using the pointer. This is because `pointsToAnAge` points to `dogsAge`, as initialized in Line 8. Any change to that memory location where `dogsAge` is stored, and to which `pointsToAnAge` points, made using one is going to be reflected in the other.

What Is the Size of a Pointer?

You have learned that a pointer is basically a variable that contains a memory address. Hence, regardless of the type that is being pointed to, the content of a pointer is an address—that is, a number. The length of an address (that is, the number of bytes required to store it) is a constant for a given system. The size a pointer is hence dependent on the compiler and the operating system the program has been compiled for. This size can be computed using the operator `sizeof()`. The size of a pointer is *not* dependent on the nature of the data being pointed to, as Listing 8.6 demonstrates.

Input ▼

LISTING 8.6 Demonstrating That Pointers to Different Types Have the Same Sizes

```
#include<iostream>
using namespace std;

int main()
{
    cout << "sizeof fundamental types -" << endl;
    cout << "sizeof(char) = " << sizeof(char) << endl;
    cout << "sizeof(int) = " << sizeof(int) << endl;
    cout << "sizeof(double) = " << sizeof(double) << endl;

```

```
    cout << "sizeof pointers to fundamental types -" << endl;
    cout << "sizeof(char*) = " << sizeof(char*) << endl;
    cout << "sizeof(int*) = " << sizeof(int*) << endl;
    cout << "sizeof(double*) = " << sizeof(double*) << endl;

    return 0;
}
```

Output ▼

```
sizeof fundamental types -
sizeof(char) = 1
sizeof(int) = 4
sizeof(double) = 8
sizeof pointers to fundamental types -
sizeof(char*) = 4
sizeof(int*) = 4
sizeof(double*) = 4
```

Analysis ▼

The output clearly shows that even though `sizeof(char)` is 1 byte and `sizeof(double)` is 8 bytes, `sizeof(char*)` and `sizeof(double*)` are both 4 bytes. This is because the amount of memory consumed by a pointer that stores an address is the same, regardless of whether the memory at the address contains 1 byte or 8 bytes of data.

NOTE

> The output for Listing 8.6 that shows that the size of a pointer is 4 bytes might be different from what you see on your system. The output was generated when the code was compiled using a 32-bit compiler. If you use a 64-bit compiler and run the program on a 64-bit system, you might see that the size of your pointer variable is 64 bits—that is, 8 bytes.

Dynamic Memory Allocation

When you write a program that contains an array declaration such as

```
int myNums[100]; // a static array of 100 integers
```

your program has two problems:

- You are actually limiting the capacity of your program as it cannot store more than 100 numbers.
- You are reducing the performance of the system in cases where only 1 number needs to be stored but space has been reserved for 100.

These problems exist because the memory allocation in an array as declared earlier is static and fixed by the compiler.

To program an application that is able to optimally consume memory resources on the basis of the needs of the user, you need to use dynamic memory allocation. This enables you to allocate more memory when you need more and release memory that you have in excess. C++ supplies two operators, `new` and `delete`, to help you better manage the memory consumption of an application. Pointers, as variables that are used to contain memory addresses, play a critical role in efficient dynamic memory allocation.

Using the Operators `new` and `delete` to Allocate and Release Memory Dynamically

You use `new` to allocate new memory blocks. The most frequently used form of `new` returns a pointer to the requested memory if successful or else throws an exception. When using `new`, you need to specify the data type for which the memory is being allocated:

```
Type* pointer = new Type; // request memory for one element
```

You can also specify the number of elements you want to allocate that memory for (when you need to allocate memory for more than one element):

```
Type* pointer = new Type[numElements]; // request memory for numElements
```

Thus, if you need to allocate integers, you use the following code:

```
int* pointToAnInt = new int;  // get a pointer to an integer
int* pointToNums = new int[10];  // pointer to a block of 10 integers
```

NOTE

Note that `new` indicates a request for memory. There is no guarantee that a call for allocation always succeeds because it depends on the state of the system and the availability of memory resources.

Every allocation using `new` needs to eventually be released using an equal and opposite deallocation via `delete`:

```
Type* pointer = new Type; // allocate memory
delete pointer;  // release memory allocated above
```

This rule also applies when you request memory for multiple elements:

```
Type* pointer = new Type[numElements]; // allocate a block
delete[] pointer; // release block allocated above
```

NOTE

> Note the usage of `delete[]` when you allocate a block using `new[...]` and `delete` when you allocate just an element using `new`.

If you don't release allocated memory after you stop needing it, then that memory remains reserved and allocated for your application. This reduces the amount of system memory available for applications to consume and possibly even makes the execution of the application slower. This is called a *leak* and should be avoided at all costs.

Listing 8.7 demonstrates dynamic memory allocation and deallocation.

Input ▼

LISTING 8.7 Accessing Memory Allocated Using `new` via the `*` Operator and Releasing It Using `delete`

```
#include<iostream>
using namespace std;

int main()
{
   // Request for memory space for an int
   int* pointsToAnAge = new int;

   // Use the allocated memory to store a number
   cout << "Enter your dog's age: ";
   cin >> *pointsToAnAge;

   // use indirection operator* to access value
```

```
13:     cout << "Age " << *pointsToAnAge << " is stored at 0x"
14:          << hex << pointsToAnAge << endl;
15:
16:     delete pointsToAnAge; // release memory
17:
18:     return 0;
19: }
```

Output ▼

```
Enter your dog's age: 9
Age 9 is stored at 0x00338120
```

Analysis ▼

Line 6 demonstrates the use of the operator `new` to request space for an integer where you plan to store the dog's age, as entered by the user. Note that `new` returns a pointer, and that is the reason it is assigned to one. The age entered by the user is stored in this newly allocated memory using `cin` and the dereference operator (`*`) in Line 10. Line 13 displays this stored value using the dereference operator (`*`) again, and Line 14 displays the address in memory where the value is stored. Note that the address contained in `pointsToAnAge` in Line 14 is still what was returned by `new` in Line 6 and hasn't changed.

CAUTION

> The `delete` operator cannot be invoked on every address contained in a pointer. Rather, it can be invoked only on an address that has been returned by `new`.
>
> Thus, the pointers in Listing 8.5 contain valid addresses but should not be released using `delete` because the addresses were not returned by a call to `new`.

Note that when you allocate for a range of elements using `new[...]`, you deallocate by using `delete[]`, as demonstrated by Listing 8.8.

Input ▼

LISTING 8.8 Allocating Memory Using `new[...]` and Releasing It Using `delete[]`

```
 0: #include<iostream>
 1: #include<string>
 2: using namespace std;
 3:
 4: int main()
 5: {
 6:    cout << "How many integers shall I reserve memory for?" << endl;
 7:    int numEntries = 0;
 8:    cin >> numEntries;
 9:
10:    int* myNumbers = new int[numEntries];
11:
12:    cout << "Memory allocated at: 0x" << myNumbers << hex << endl;
13:
14:    // de-allocate before exiting
15:    delete[] myNumbers;
16:
17:    return 0;
18: }
```

Output ▼

```
How many integers shall I reserve memory for?
5001
Memory allocated at: 0x00C71578
```

Analysis ▼

The most important lines in this listing are Lines 10 and 15, which use the `new[]` and `delete[]` operators, respectively. What makes this sample different from Listing 8.7 is the dynamic allocation of a block of memory that can accommodate as many integers as the user requests. The output shows space requested for 5001 integers. In another run, it might be 20 or 55000. This program will allocate a different amount of memory required in every execution, depending on user input. Such allocations for an array of elements need to be matched by deallocation, with `delete[]` then used to free memory.

NOTE

> The operators `new` and `delete` allocate memory from the free store. The *free store* is a memory abstraction in the form of a pool of memory where an application can allocate (that is, reserve) memory from and deallocate (that is, release) memory to.

Effects of the Increment (++) and Decrement (--) Operators on Pointers

A pointer contains a memory address. For example, the pointer to an integer in Listing 8.3 contains `0x002EFB34`—the address where the integer is placed. The integer itself is 4 bytes long and hence occupies four places in memory, from `0x002EFB34` to `0x002EFB37`. Incrementing this pointer using the operator ++ would *not* result in the pointer pointing to `0x002EFB35` because pointing to the middle of an integer would be pointless.

An increment or decrement operation on a pointer is interpreted by the compiler as a need to point to the next value in the block of memory, assuming it to be of the same type, and *not* to the next byte (unless the value type is 1 byte large, like a `char`, for instance).

So, incrementing a pointer such as `pointsToInt` in Listing 8.3 results in its being incremented by 4 bytes, which is the size of an `int`. By using ++ on this pointer, you tell the compiler that you want it to point to the next consecutive integer. Hence, after incrementing, the pointer points to `0x002EFB38`. Similarly, adding 2 to this pointer result in its moving 2 integers ahead—that is, 8 bytes ahead. A correlation between this behavior displayed by pointers and indexes used in arrays is provided later in this chapter.

Decrementing pointers using the operator -- demonstrates the same effect: The address value contained in the pointer is reduced by the size of the data type it is being pointed to.

What Happens When You Increment or Decrement a Pointer?

When you increment or decrement a pointer, the address contained in the pointer is incremented or decremented by the sizeof() the type being pointed to (and not necessarily a byte). This way, the compiler ensures that the pointer never points to the middle or end of data placed in the memory; it only points to the beginning.

If a pointer has been declared as

```
Type* pType = Address;
```

`++pType` would mean that `pType` contains (and hence points to) `Address + sizeof(Type)`.

Listing 8.9 illustrates the effect of incrementing pointers or adding offsets to them.

Input ▼

LISTING 8.9 Using Offset Values and Operators to Increment and Decrement Pointers

```
#include<iostream>
using namespace std;

int main()
{
   cout << "How many integers you wish to enter? ";
   int numEntries = 0;
   cin >> numEntries;

   int* pointsToInts = new int[numEntries];

   cout << "Allocated for "" integers" << endl;
   for(int counter = 0; counter < numEntries; ++counter)
   {
      cout << "Enter number " << counter << ": ";
      cin >> *(pointsToInts + counter);
   }

   cout << "Displaying all numbers entered: " << endl;
   for(int counter = 0; counter < numEntries; ++counter)
      cout << *(pointsToInts++) << " ";

   cout << endl;

   // return pointer to initial position
   pointsToInts -= numEntries;

   // done with using memory? release
   delete[] pointsToInts;

   return 0;
}
```

Output ▼

First run:

```
How many integers you wish to enter? 2
Allocated for 2 integers
Enter number 0: 8774
```

```
Enter number 1: -5
Displaying all numbers entered:
8774 -5
```

Next run:

```
How many integers you wish to enter? 5
Allocated for 5 integers
Enter number 0: 543
Enter number 1: 756
Enter number 2: 2017
Enter number 3: -101
Enter number 4: 101010012
Displaying all numbers entered:
543 756 2017 -101 101010012
```

Analysis ▼

The program asks the user for the number of integers he wants to feed into the system before allocating memory for this in Line 9. This example demonstrates two methods of incrementing pointers. One uses an offset value, as shown in Line 15, where you store user input directly into the memory location, using the offset variable `counter`. The other uses the operator `++`, as in Line 20, to increment the address contained in the pointer variable to the next valid integer in the allocated memory. Operators are introduced in Lesson 5, "Working with Expressions, Statements, and Operators."

Lines 12 through 16 are a `for` loop where the user is asked to enter the numbers that are then stored in consecutive positions in the memory, using the expression in Line 15. It is here that the zero-based offset value (`counter`) is added to the pointer, causing the compiler to create instructions that insert the value fed by the user at the next appropriate location for an integer without overwriting the previous value. The `for` loop in Lines 19 and 20 is similarly used to display those values stored by the previous loop.

The original pointer address returned by `new` during allocation needs to be used in the call to `delete[]` during deallocation. As this value contained in `pointsToInts` has been modified by the operator `++` in Line 20, you bring the pointer back to the original position (address) by using the operator `-=` in Line 25 before invoking `delete[]` on that address in Line 28.

Using the `const` Keyword on Pointers

In Lesson 3, you learned that declaring a variable as `const` effectively ensures that the value of the variable is fixed as the initialization value for the life of the variable. The value of a `const` variable cannot be changed, and therefore it cannot be used as an l-value.

Pointers are variables, too, and hence the `const` keyword that is relevant to variables is relevant to pointers as well. However, a pointer is a special kind of variable as it contains a memory address and is used to modify memory at that address. Thus, when it comes to pointers and constants, you have the following combinations:

- The address contained in the pointer is constant and cannot be changed, but the data at that address can be changed:

```
int daysInMonth = 30;
int* const pDaysInMonth = &daysInMonth;
*pDaysInMonth = 31; // OK! Data pointed to can be changed
int daysInLunarMonth = 28;
pDaysInMonth = &daysInLunarMonth; // Not OK! Cannot change address!
```

- Data pointed to is constant and cannot be changed, but the address contained in the pointer can be changed (that is, the pointer can also point elsewhere):

```
int hoursInDay = 24;
const int* pointsToInt = &hoursInDay;
int monthsInYear = 12;
pointsToInt = &monthsInYear; // OK!
*pointsToInt = 13; // Not OK! Cannot change data being pointed to
int* newPointer = pointsToInt; //Error: const assigned to non-const
```

- Both the address contained in the pointer and the value being pointed to are constant and cannot be changed (most restrictive variant):

```
int hoursInDay = 24;
const int* const pHoursInDay = &hoursInDay;
*pHoursInDay = 25; // Not OK! Cannot change data being pointed to
int daysInMonth = 30;
pHoursInDay = &daysInMonth; // Not OK! Cannot change address
```

These different forms of `const` are particularly useful when passing pointers to functions. It is recommended that function parameters be declared to support the highest possible (restrictive) level of `const`-ness. This protects your application against unintended modifications using the function's arguments.

TIP

To easily identify the three `const` cases mentioned above, read them from right to left.

The first case is a constant pointer to an integer:

```
int* const pointerCannotChange = &value;
```

The second case is a pointer to a constant integer:

```
const int* pointedDataCannotChange = &value;
```

The third case is a constant pointer to a constant integer:

```
const int* const ptrAndDataCannotChange = &value;
```

Passing Pointers to Functions

Using pointers is an effective way to pass memory space that contains relevant data for functions to work on. The memory space shared can also return the result of an operation. When using a pointer with functions, it is important to ensure that the called function is only allowed to modify parameters that you want to let it modify—and not others. For example, a function that calculates the area of a circle given radius sent as a pointer should not be allowed to modify the radius. You can use the keyword `const` to control what a function is allowed to modify and what it isn't, as demonstrated in Listing 8.10.

Input ▼

LISTING 8.10 Using the `const` Keyword in Calculating the Area of a Circle

```
#include<iostream>
using namespace std;

void CalcArea(const double* const ptrPi, // const pointer to const data
              const double* const ptrRadius, // i.e. no changes allowed
              double* const ptrArea)  // can change data pointed to
{
   // check pointers for validity before using!
   if (ptrPi && ptrRadius && ptrArea)
      *ptrArea = (*ptrPi) * (*ptrRadius) * (*ptrRadius);
}

int main()
{
   const double Pi = 3.1416;

```

```
16:     cout << "Enter radius of circle: ";
17:     double radius = 0;
18:     cin >> radius;
19:
20:     double area = 0;
21:     CalcArea (&Pi, &radius, &area);
22:
23:     cout << "Area is = " << area << endl;
24:
25:     return 0;
26: }
```

Output ▼

```
Enter radius of circle: 10.5
Area is = 346.361
```

Analysis ▼

Lines 3 and 4 demonstrate the form of `const` where both `ptrRadius` and `ptrPi` are supplied as "const pointers to const data" so that neither the pointer address nor the data being pointed to can be modified. `ptrArea`, declared in Line 5, is evidently the parameter meant to store the output, for the value contained in the pointer (address) cannot be modified, but the data being pointed to can be. Line 8 shows how pointer parameters to a function are checked for validity before they are used. You don't want a function to calculate the area if the caller inadvertently sends a `NULL` pointer as any of the three parameters because that would risk an access violation followed by an application crash.

Similarities Between Arrays and Pointers

Don't you think that the code in Listing 8.9—where the pointer is incremented using a zero-based index to access the next integer in the memory—has too many similarities to the manner in which arrays are indexed? When you declare an array of integers like this:

```
int myNumbers[5];
```

you tell the compiler to allocate a fixed amount of memory to hold five integers and give you a pointer to the first element in that array that is identified by the name you assign to the array variable. In other words, `myNumbers` is a pointer to the first element, `myNumbers[0]`. Listing 8.11 highlights this correlation.

Input ▼

LISTING 8.11 Demonstrating That the Array Variable Is a Pointer to the First Element

```
 0: #include<iostream>
 1: using namespace std;
 2:
 3: int main()
 4: {
 5:    // Static array of 5 integers
 6:    int myNumbers[5];
 7:
 8:    // array assigned to pointer to int
 9:    int* pointToNums = myNumbers;
10:
11:    // Display address contained in pointer
12:    cout << "pointToNums = 0x" << hex << pointToNums << endl;
13:
14:    // Address of first element of array
15:    cout << "&myNumbers[0] = 0x" << hex << &myNumbers[0] << endl;
16:
17:    return 0;
18: }
```

Output ▼

```
pointToNums = 0x004BFE8C
&myNumbers[0] = 0x004BFE8C
```

Analysis ▼

This simple program demonstrates that an array variable can be assigned to a pointer of the same type, as shown in Line 9, essentially confirming that an array is akin to a pointer. Lines 12 and 15 demonstrate that the address stored in the pointer is the same as the address where the first element in the array (at index 0) is placed in memory. This program demonstrates that an array is a pointer to the first element in it.

If you need to access the second element via the expression `myNumbers[1]`, you can also access it by using the pointer `pointToNums` with the syntax `*(pointToNums + 1)`. The third element is accessed in the static array by using `myNumbers[2]`, and the third element is accessed in the dynamic array by using the syntax `*(pointToNums + 2)`.

Because array variables are essentially pointers, it should be possible to use the dereference operator (*) that you have used with pointers to work with arrays. Similarly, it should be possible to use the array operator ([]) to work with pointers, as demonstrated in Listing 8.12.

Input ▼

LISTING 8.12 Accessing Elements in an Array Using the Dereference Operator (*) and Using the Array Operator ([]) with a Pointer

```
#include<iostream>
using namespace std;

int main()
{
    const int ARRAY_LEN = 5;

    // Static array of 5 integers, initialized
    int myNumbers[ARRAY_LEN] = {24, -1, 365, -999, 2011};

    // Pointer initialized to first element in array
    int* pointToNums = myNumbers;

    cout << "Display array using pointer syntax, operator* \n";
    for (int index = 0; index < ARRAY_LEN; ++index)
       cout << "Element "<<index<< " = " << *(myNumbers + index) << endl;

    cout << "Display array using ptr with array syntax, operator[]\n";
    for (int index = 0; index < ARRAY_LEN; ++index)
       cout << "Element "" = " << index << " = " << pointToNums[index] << endl;

    return 0;
}
```

Output ▼

```
Display array using pointer syntax, operator*
Element 0 = 24
Element 1 = -1
Element 2 = 365
Element 3 = -999
Element 4 = 2011
Display array using ptr with array syntax, operator[]
Element 0 = 24
```

```
Element 1 = -1
Element 2 = 365
Element 3 = -999
Element 4 = 2011
```

Analysis ▼

The application contains a static array of five integers initialized to five initial values in Line 8. The application displays the contents of this array, using two alternative methods—one using the array variable `myNumbers` with the indirection operator (`*`) in Line 15 and the other using the pointer variable with the array operator (`[]`) in Line 19.

Thus, this program demonstrates that both the array `myNumbers` and the pointer `pointToNums` exhibit pointer behavior. In other words, an array declaration is similar to a pointer that is created to operate within a fixed range of memory. Note that you can assign an array to a pointer as in Line 11, but you cannot assign a pointer to an array. This is because, by its very nature, an array like `myNumbers` is static and cannot be used as an l-value; `myNumbers` cannot be modified.

CAUTION

It is important to remember that pointers that are allocated dynamically using the operator `new` still need to be released using the operator `delete`, even if you accessed data using syntax commonly used with static arrays.

If you forget this, your application leaks memory, and that's bad.

Common Programming Mistakes When Using Pointers

C++ lets you allocate memory dynamically so that you can optimize and control the memory consumption of an application. Unlike languages that use a runtime environment, such as C# and Java, C++ does not feature an automatic garbage collector that frees memory resources when they're no longer required. This incredible control over managing memory resources using pointers is accompanied by a host of opportunities to make mistakes.

Memory Leaks

This is probably one of the most common problems with poorly programmed C++ applications: The longer they run, the larger the amount of memory they consume and the slower the system gets. Memory leaks typically happen when the programmer did not ensure that the application releases memory allocated dynamically using `new` with a matching call to `delete` after the block of memory is no longer required.

It is up to you—the programmer—to ensure that all allocated memory is also released by an application. Something like this should never be allowed to happen:

```
int* pointToNums = new int[5]; // initial allocation
// use pointToNums
...
// forget to release using delete[] pointToNums;
...
// make another allocation and overwrite
pointToNums = new int[10]; // leaks the previously allocated memory
```

Pointers Pointing to Invalid Memory Locations

When you dereference a pointer using the operator `*` to access the pointed value, you need to be sure that the pointer contains a valid memory location, or else your program will either crash or misbehave. Logical as this may seem, invalid pointers are quite a common reason for application crashes. Pointers can be invalid for a range of reasons and are primarily due to poor programming and memory management. A typical case where a pointer might be invalid is shown in Listing 8.13.

Input ▼

LISTING 8.13 Poor Pointer Hygiene in a Program That Stores a Boolean Value Using Pointers

```
#include<iostream>
using namespace std;

int main()
{
   // uninitialized pointer (bad)
   bool* isSunny;

   cout << "Is it sunny (y/n)? ";
   char userInput = 'y';
   cin >> userInput;
```

```
11:
12:     if (userInput == 'y')
13:     {
14:        isSunny = new bool;
15:        *isSunny = true;
16:     }
17:
18:     // isSunny contains invalid value if user entered 'n'
19:     cout << "Boolean flag sunny says: " << *isSunny << endl;
20:
21:     // delete being invoked also when new wasn't
22:     delete isSunny;
23:
24:     return 0;
25: }
```

Output ▼

First run:

```
Is it sunny (y/n)? y
Boolean flag sunny says: 1
```

Second run:

```
Is it sunny (y/n)? n
<CRASH!>
```

Analysis ▼

This sample contains problems that have been intentionally programmed to explain poor pointer hygiene. Do not be surprised if your compiler complains. Note how memory is allocated and assigned to the pointer in Line 14, which is conditionally executed when the user presses `y` for yes. For all other inputs of the user, this `if` block is not executed, and the pointer `isSunny` remains invalid. Thus, when the user presses `n` in the second run, the application crashes because `isSunny` contains an invalid memory address, and dereferencing an invalid pointer in Line 19 causes problems.

Similarly, invoking `delete` on this pointer, as shown in Line 22, which has not been allocated for using `new`, is equally wrong. If you have a copy of a pointer, you need to be calling `delete` on only one of them; you also need to avoid having copies of a pointer floating around.

A better (that is, safer and more stable) version of this program would be one where pointers are initialized, used where their values are valid, and released only once and only when valid.

Dangling Pointers (Also Called Stray or Wild Pointers)

Note that any valid pointer is invalid after it has been released using `delete`. In other words, even the valid pointer `isSunny` in Listing 8.13 would be invalid after the call to `delete` in Line 22, and it should not be used after that point.

To avoid this problem, some programmers follow the convention of assigning `NULL` to a pointer when initializing it or after it has been deleted. They also always check a pointer for validity (by comparing against `NULL`) before dereferencing it using the operator `*`.

Having learned some typical problems that occur when using pointers, it's time to correct the faulty code in Listing 8.13. See Listing 8.14.

Input ▼

LISTING 8.14 Safer Pointer Programming: A Correction of Listing 8.13

```
#include<iostream>
using namespace std;

int main()
{
    cout << "Is it sunny (y/n)? ";
    char userInput = 'y';
    cin >> userInput;

    // declare pointer and initialize
    bool* const isSunny = new bool;
    *isSunny = true;

    if (userInput == 'n')
       *isSunny = false;

    cout << "Boolean flag sunny says: " << *isSunny << endl;

    // release valid memory
    delete isSunny;

    return 0;
}
```

Output ▼

First run:

```
Is it sunny (y/n)? y
Boolean flag sunny says: 1
```

Next run:

```
Is it sunny (y/n)? n
Boolean flag sunny says: 0
```

(Ends without crashing, regardless of user input.)

Analysis ▼

Minor restructuring has made the code safer for all combinations of user input. Note that the pointer is initialized to a valid memory address during declaration in Line 10. Here you use `const` to ensure that while the data being pointed to can be modified, the pointer value (that is, the address contained) remains fixed and unchangeable. You also initialize the Boolean value being pointed to, to `true` in Line 11. This data initialization adds not to the stability of the program but to the reliability of the output. These steps ensure that the pointer is valid for the rest of the program, and it is safely deleted in Line 19, for every combination of user input.

Checking Whether an Allocation Request Using `new` Succeeded

In the code to this point, we have assumed that `new` will return a valid pointer to a block of memory. Indeed, `new` usually succeeds unless the application asks for an unusually large amount of memory or the system is in such a critical state that it has no memory to spare. There are applications that need to make requests for large chunks of memory (for example, database applications). Therefore, C++ provides you with two possible methods to ensure that your pointer is valid before you use it. The default method—one that we have been using thus far—is to use *exceptions* wherein unsuccessful allocations result in an exception of the type `std::bad_alloc` to be *thrown*. An exception results in the execution of the application being disrupted, and unless you have programmed an *exception handler*, the application ends rather inelegantly with the error message "unhandled exception."

Exceptions are explained in detail in Lesson 28, "Exception Handling." Listing 8.15 gives you a sneak peek of how exception handling can be used to check for failed memory allocation requests. Don't be too worried if exception handling seems overwhelming at this stage: It's mentioned here only for the sake of completeness of the topic of memory allocation. You can revisit this sample after reading Lesson 28.

Input ▼

LISTING 8.15 Handling Exceptions and Exiting Gracefully When `new` Fails

```
 0: #include<iostream>
 1: using namespace std;
 2:
 3: // remove the try-catch block to see this application crash
 4: int main()
 5: {
 6:    try
 7:    {
 8:       // Request a LOT of memory!
 9:      int* pointsToManyNums = new int [0x1fffffff];
10:      // Use the allocated memory
11:
12:       delete[] pointsToManyNums;
13:    }
14:    catch (bad_alloc)
15:    {
16:       cout << "Memory allocation failed. Ending program" << endl;
17:    }
18:    return 0;
19: }
```

Output ▼

```
Memory allocation failed. Ending program
```

Analysis ▼

This program might execute differently on your computer. My environment could not successfully allocate the requested space for 536,870,911 integers! Without the exception handler (the `catch` block in Lines 14 through 17), the program would not end gracefully. You can experiment with the behavior of the program in the absence of the exception handler by commenting Lines 6 and 14. When using debug mode binaries built using Microsoft Visual Studio, program execution results in output like that shown in Figure 8.2.

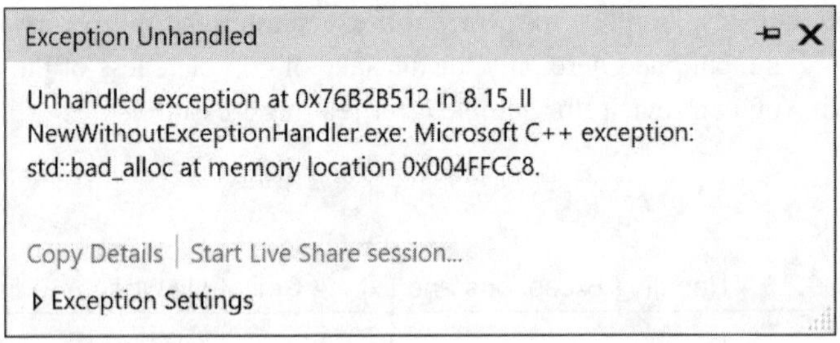

FIGURE 8.2
Program crash in the absence of exception handling in Listing 8.15 (with a debug build using the MSVC compiler).

The exception handling `try-catch` construct thus helps the application make a controlled exit after informing the user that a problem in memory allocation hampers normal execution.

For those who don't want to rely on exceptions, there is a variant of `new` called `new(nothrow)`. This variant does not throw an exception when allocation requests fail; rather, it results in the operator `new` returning `NULL`. The pointer being assigned, therefore, can be checked for validity against `NULL` before it is used. See Listing 8.16.

Input ▼

LISTING 8.16 Using `new(nothrow)`, Which Returns `NULL` When Allocation Fails

```
#include<iostream>
using namespace std;

int main()
{
   // Request LOTS of memory space, use nothrow
   int* pointsToManyNums = new(nothrow) int [0x1fffffff];

   if (pointsToManyNums) // check pointsToManyNums != NULL
   {
      // Use the allocated memory
      delete[] pointsToManyNums;
   }
   else
      cout << "Memory allocation failed. Ending program" << endl;

   return 0;
}
```

Output ▼

```
Memory allocation failed. Ending program
```

Analysis ▼

Listing 8.16 is the same function as Listing 8.15 except that it uses `new(nothrow)` in Line 6. As this variant of `new` returns `NULL` when memory allocation fails, you check the pointer before using it in Line 8. Both variants of `new` are good, and the choice is for you to make.

Pointer Programming Best Practices

There are some basic rules you need to keep in mind when it comes to using pointers in applications.

DO	DON'T
DO always initialize pointer variables, or else they will contain junk values. These junk values are interpreted as address locations that your applica tion is not authorized to access. If you cannot initialize a pointer to a valid address returned by `new` during variable declaration, initialize to `NULL`. **DO** ensure that your application is programmed in such a way that pointers are used when their validity is assured, or else your program might encounter a crash. **DO** remember to release memory allocated using `new` by using `delete`, or else your application will leak memory and reduce system performance.	**DON'T** access a block of memory or use a pointer after it has been released using `delete`. **DON'T** invoke `delete` on a memory address more than once. **DON'T** leak memory by forgetting to invoke `delete` when done using an allocated block of memory.

What Is a Reference?

A *reference* is an alias for a variable. When you declare a reference, you need to initialize it to a variable. Thus, using a reference variable is just a different way to access the data stored in the variable being referenced.

You declare a reference by using the reference operator (&), as shown in the following statement:

```
VarType original = Value;
VarType& referenceVariable = original;
```

To further understand how to declare references and use them, see Listing 8.17.

Input ▼

LISTING 8.17 Demonstrating That References Are Aliases for Assigned Values

```
#include<iostream>
using namespace std;

int main()
{
   int original = 30;
   cout << "original = " << original << endl;
   cout << "original is at address: " << hex << &original << endl;

   int& ref1 = original;
   cout << "ref1 is at address: " << hex << &ref1 << endl;

   int& ref2 = ref1;
   cout << "ref2 is at address: " << hex << &ref2 << endl;
   cout << "Therefore, ref2 = " << dec << ref2 << endl;

   return 0;
}
```

Output ▼

```
original = 30
original is at address: 0099F764
ref1 is at address: 0099F764
ref2 is at address: 0099F764
Therefore, ref2 = 30
```

Analysis ▼

The output demonstrates that references—regardless of whether they're initialized to the original variable as in Line 9 or to a reference as in Line 12—address the same location in memory where the original is contained. Thus, references are true aliases; that is, a reference is just another name for `original`. Displaying the value using `ref2` in Line 14 gets the same value as `original` in Line 6 because `ref2` aliases `original` and is contained in the same location in memory.

What Makes References Useful?

References enable you to work with the memory location they are initialized to. This makes references particularly useful when programming functions. As you learned in Lesson 7, "Organizing Code with Functions," a typical function is declared like this:

```
ReturnType DoSomething(Type parameter);
```

The function `DoSomething()` is invoked like this:

```
ReturnType result = DoSomething(argument); // function call
```

This code would result in the argument being copied into `parameter`, which is then used by the function `DoSomething()`. This copy step can result in overhead if the argument in question consumes a lot of memory. It would be ideal if you could avoid or eliminate the copy step and enable the function to work directly on the data in the caller's stack. References enable you to do just that.

A version of the function without the copy step looks like this:

```
ReturnType DoSomething(Type& parameter) // note the reference&
{
   // ...code
   return value;
}
```

This function would be invoked as follows:

```
ReturnType result = DoSomething(argument);
```

As the argument is being passed by reference, `parameter` is not a copy of `argument` but rather is an alias of it, much like `ref1` in Listing 8.17. In addition, a function that accepts a parameter as a reference can optionally return values using reference parameters.

NOTE

Copy elision has been guaranteed since C++17. To see what this means, let's review this code once again:

```
ReturnType result = DoSomething(argument);
```

Under normal circumstances, the return value of the function `DoSomething()` would be copied into `result`. This is an unnecessary step, and it can be quite an expensive step if `ReturnType` is a database table, for example. Since C++17, such unnecessary copy steps are elided (that is, eliminated) by default.

See Listing 8.18 to understand how functions can use references instead of return values.

Input ▼

LISTING 8.18 Function That Calculates Square Returned in a Parameter by Reference

```
#include<iostream>
using namespace std;

void Square(int& number)
{
   number *= number;
}

int main()
{
   cout << "Enter a number you wish to square: ";
   int number = 0;
   cin >> number;

   Square(number);
   cout << "Square is: " << number << endl;

   return 0;
}
```

Output ▼

```
Enter a number you wish to square: 5
Square is: 25
```

Analysis ▼

The function that performs the operation of squaring is in Lines 3 through 6. Note how it accepts the number to be squared as a parameter by reference and returns the result. If you forget to mark the parameter `number` as a reference (`&`), the result does not reach the calling function `main()` because `Square()` then performs its operations on a local copy of `number`, which is destroyed when the function exits. By using references, you ensure that `Square()` is operating in the same address space where `number` in `main()` is defined. Thus, the result of the operation is available in `main()` even after the function `Square()` has exited.

In this example, `Square()` modifies the number sent by the caller. If you need both values—the original and the square—you can have the function accept two parameters: one that contains the input and another that supplies the square.

Using the Keyword `const` on References

You might need to have references that are not allowed to change the value of the original variable being aliased. Using `const` when declaring such references is the way to achieve that:

```
int original = 30;
const int& constRef = original;
constRef = 40; // Not allowed: can't change value in original
int& ref2 = constRef; // Not allowed: ref2 is not const
const int& constRef2 = constRef; // OK, similar types
```

Passing Arguments by Reference to Functions

One of the major advantages of references is that they allow a called function to work on parameters that have not been copied from the calling function, resulting in significant performance improvements. However, as the called function works using parameters directly on the stack of the calling function, it is often important to ensure that the called function cannot change the value of the variable at the caller's end. References that are defined as `const` help you do just that, as demonstrated in Listing 8.19. A `const` reference parameter cannot be used as an l-value, so any attempt at assigning to it causes a compilation failure.

Input ▼

LISTING 8.19 Using a `const` Reference to Ensure That the Calling Function Cannot Modify a Value Sent by Reference

```
 0: #include<iostream>
 1: using namespace std;
 2:
 3: void Square(const int& number, int& result)
 4: {
 5:    result = number*number;
 6: }
 7:
 8: int main()
 9: {
10:    cout << "Enter a number you wish to square: ";
11:    int number = 0;
12:    cin >> number;
13:
14:    int square = 0;
15:    Square(number, square);
16:    cout << "Square of "" = " << number << " = " << square << endl;
17:
18:    return 0;
19: }
```

Output ▼

```
Enter a number you wish to square: 27
27^2 = 729
```

Analysis ▼

In contrast to the program in Listing 8.18, where the variable that sent the number to be squared also held the result, this one uses two variables: one to send the number to be squared and another to hold the result of the operation. To ensure that the number being sent cannot be modified, it has been marked as a `const` reference using the `const` keyword, as shown in Line 3. This automatically makes the parameter `number` an input parameter—one whose value cannot be modified.

As an experiment, you can modify Line 5 to return the square using the same logic shown in Listing 8.18:

```
number *= number;
```

You are now certain to face a compilation error that tells you that a `const` value cannot be modified. Thus, `const` references indicate that a parameter is an input parameter and ensure that its value cannot be modified. It might seem trivial at first, but in a multi-programmer environment where the person writing the first version might be different from the one enhancing it, using `const` references will add to the quality of the program.

Summary

In this lesson, you learned about pointers and references. You learned how pointers can be used to access and manipulate memory and how they assist in dynamic memory allocation. You learned about the operators `new` and `delete`, which can be used to allocate memory for an element. You learned that their variants `new...[]` and `delete[]` help you allocate memory for an array of data. You were introduced to traps in pointer programming and dynamic allocation and found out that releasing dynamically allocated memory is important to avoid leaks. References are aliases and are a powerful alternative to using pointers when passing arguments to functions in that references are guaranteed to be valid. You learned about "`const` correctness" when using pointers and references, and you will hopefully henceforth declare functions with the most restrictive level of `const`-ness in parameters as possible.

Q&A

Q Why dynamically allocate when you can make do with static arrays, where you don't need to worry about deallocation?

A Static arrays have a fixed size and will neither scale upward if your application needs more memory nor optimize if your application needs less. This is where dynamic memory allocation makes a difference.

Q I have two pointers:

```
int* pointToAnInt = new int;
int* pCopy = pointToAnInt;
```

Am I not better off calling `delete` using both to be sure that the memory used is released?

A Doing that would be wrong. You are allowed to invoke `delete` only once on the address returned by `new`. Also, you should ideally avoid having two pointers pointing to the same address because performing `delete` on any one would invalidate the other. Your program should also not be written in such a way that you have any uncertainty about the validity of pointers used.

Q When should I use `new(nothrow)`?

A If you don't want to handle the exception `std::bad_alloc`, you use the `nothrow` version of the operator `new`, which returns `NULL` when the requested allocation fails. If using the `nothrow` version, remember to check for pointer validity by checking against `NULL`.

Q I can call a function to calculate area using the following two methods:

```
void CalculateArea (const double* const ptrRadius, double* const
ptrArea);
void CalculateArea (const double& radius, double& area);
```

Which variant should I prefer?

A Use the latter one, which uses references, as references cannot be invalid, whereas pointers can be. In addition, it's simpler.

Q I have a pointer:

```
int number = 30;
const int* pointToAnInt = &number;
```

I understand that I cannot change the value of `number` using the pointer `pointToAnInt` due to the `const` declaration. Can I assign `pointToAnInt` to a non-`const` pointer and then use it to manipulate the value contained in the integer `number`?

A No, you cannot change the `const`-correctness of the pointer:

```
int* pAnother = pointToAnInt; // error
```

Q Why should I bother passing values to a function by reference?

A You don't need to so long as it doesn't affect your program performance much. However, if your function parameters accept objects that are quite heavy (that is, large in bytes), then passing by value would be quite an expensive operation. Your function call would be a lot more efficient in using references. Remember to use `const` generously, except where the function needs to store a result in a variable.

Q What is the difference between these two declarations?

```
int myNumbers[100];
int* myArrays[100];
```

A `myNumbers` is an array of integers—that is, `myNumbers` is a pointer to a memory location that holds 100 integers and points to the first one, at index 0. It is the static alternative to the following:

```
int* myNumbers = new int [100]; // dynamically allocated array
// use myNumbers
delete[] myNumbers;
```

`nmyArrays`, on the other hand, is an array of 100 pointers, where each pointer is capable of pointing to an integer or an array of integers.

Workshop

The Workshop provides quiz questions to help you solidify your understanding of the material covered and exercises to provide you with experience in using what you've learned. Try to answer the quiz and exercise questions before checking the answers in Appendix E and be certain you understand the answers before continuing to the next lesson.

Quiz

1. Why can't you assign a `const` reference to a non-`const` reference?
2. Are `new` and `delete` functions?
3. What is the nature of the value contained in a pointer variable?
4. What operator would you use to access the data pointed to by a pointer?

Exercises

1. What is displayed when these statements are executed:

```
int number = 3;
int* pNum1 = &number;
*pNum1 = 20;
int* pNum2 = pNum1;
number *= 2;
cout << *pNum2;
```

2. What are the similarities and differences between these three overloaded functions:

```
int DoSomething(int num1, int num2);
int DoSomething(int& num1, int& num2);
int DoSomething(int* pNum1, int* pNum2);
```

3. How would you change the declaration of `pNum1` in Exercise 1 at Line 1 to make the assignment at Line 3 invalid? (*Hint:* It has something to do with ensuring that `pNum1` cannot change the data pointed to.)

4. **BUG BUSTERS:** What is wrong with this code?

```
#include<iostream>
using namespace std;
int main()
{
   int* pointToAnInt = new int;
   pointToAnInt = 9;
   cout << "The value at pointToAnInt : " << *pointToAnInt;
   delete pointToAnInt;
   return 0;
}
```

5. **BUG BUSTERS:** What is wrong with this code?

```
#include<iostream>
using namespace std;
int main()
{
   int* pointToAnInt = new int;
   int* pNumberCopy = pointToAnInt;
   *pNumberCopy = 30;
   cout << *pointToAnInt;
   delete pNumberCopy;
   delete pointToAnInt;
   return 0;
}
```

6. What is the output of the program in Exercise 5 when that program is corrected?

LESSON 9
Classes and Objects

So far you have explored simple programs that start execution at `main()`, include local and global variables and constants, and feature execution logic organized into function modules that accept parameters and return values. The programming style thus far has been *procedural*, and you haven't seen an object-oriented approach yet. In this lesson, you will begin to learn the basics of object-oriented programming using C++.

In this lesson, you learn

- What classes and objects are
- How classes help you consolidate data with functions that work on them
- About constructors, copy constructors, and the destructor
- What move constructors are
- Object-oriented concepts of encapsulation and abstraction
- What the `this` pointer is about
- What a `struct` is and how it differs from a class

The Concept of Classes and Objects

Imagine that you are writing a program that models a human being, like yourself. This human being needs to have an identity, including a name, date of birth, place of birth, and gender—information that makes the person unique. In addition, the human should be able to perform certain functions, such as talk and introduce himself or herself, among others. Thus, a human being can be modeled as illustrated in Figure 9.1.

FIGURE 9.1
A broad representation of a human.

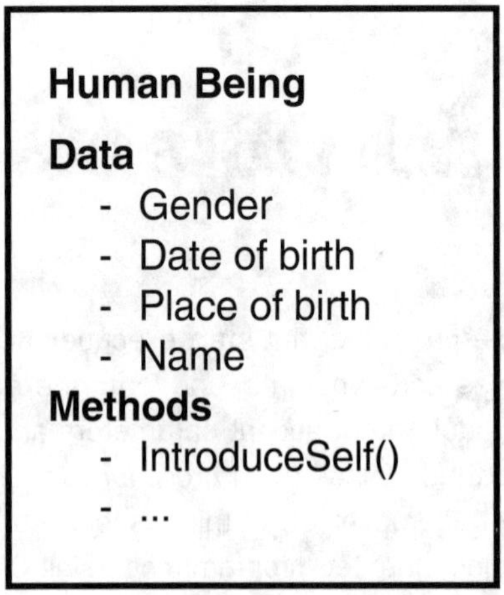

To model a human in a program, you need a construct that enables you to group within it the attributes that define a human (data) and the activities a human can perform (functions), using the available attributes. Such a construct is called a *class*.

Declaring a Class

You declare a class by using the keyword `class` followed by the name of the class and then a statement block {...} that encloses a set of member attributes and member functions within curly braces, terminated by a semicolon (`;`).

A declaration of a class tells the compiler about the class and its properties. Declaration of a class alone does not make a difference to the execution of a program, as the class needs to be used just the same way as a function would need to be invoked.

A class that models a human looks like this (though you should ignore the syntactic shortcomings for the moment):

```
class Human
{
    // Member attributes:
    string name;
    string dateOfBirth;
    string placeOfBirth;
    string gender;

    // Member functions:
    void Talk(string textToTalk);
```

```
    void IntroduceSelf();
    ...
};
```

Needless to say, IntroduceSelf() uses Talk() and some of the data attributes that are grouped within the class Human. Thus, in the keyword class, C++ provides a powerful way to create your own data type that enables you to *encapsulate* attributes and functions that work using those attributes. All attributes of a class—in this case name, dateOfBirth, placeOfBirth, and gender—and all functions declared within it—namely Talk() and IntroduceSelf()—are called members of the class Human.

Encapsulation, which is the ability to logically group data and functions that work using it, is an important property of object-oriented programming.

NOTE

You might often encounter the term *method*. A method is essentially a function that is member of a class.

An Object as an Instance of a Class

A class is like a blueprint, and declaring a class alone has no effect on the execution of a program. The real-world avatar of a class at program execution time is an *object*. To use the features of a class, you typically create an instance of that class, called an object. You use that object to access its member methods and attributes.

Creating an object of type class Human is similar to creating an instance of another type, say double:

```
double pi= 3.1415; // a variable of type double
Human firstMan;    // firstMan: an object of class Human
```

Alternatively, you can dynamically create an instance of the class Human by using new as you would for another type, say an int:

```
int* pointsToNum = new int;  // an integer allocated dynamically
delete pointsToNum;  // de-allocating memory when done using

Human* firstWoman = new Human(); // dynamically allocated Human
delete firstWoman;  // de-allocating memory
```

Accessing Members by Using the Dot Operator (.)

An example of a human would be Adam—a male, born in 1991 in California. You can create an instance called `firstMan` as seen below:

```
Human firstMan;   // an instance i.e. object of Human
```

Just like every instance of class `Human`, `firstMan` has attributes such as `dateOfBirth` that can be accessed using the dot operator (`.`):

```
firstMan.dateOfBirth = "1991";
```

This is because the attribute `dateOfBirth` belongs to the class `Human`; it is part of its blueprint, as shown in the class declaration. This attribute exists in reality—that is, at runtime—only when an object has been instantiated. The dot operator (`.`) helps you access attributes of an object. The same is true for methods such as `IntroduceSelf()`:

```
firstMan.IntroduceSelf();
```

If you have a pointer `firstWoman` to an instance of the class `Human`, you can either use the pointer operator (`->`) to access members, as explained in the next section, or use the indirection operator (`*`) to reference the object following the dot operator:

```
Human* firstWoman = new Human();
firstWoman->IntroduceSelf(); // same as (*firstWoman).IntroduceSelf();
```

NOTE

> Naming conventions continue to apply. A class name and member functions are declared in Pascal case (for example, `IntroduceSelf()`). Class member attributes are in camel case (for example, `dateOfBirth`).
>
> When you instantiate an object of a class, you declare a variable with the type of that class. You therefore use camel case, which you have been using for variable names thus far (for example, `firstMan`).

Accessing Members by Using the Pointer Operator (->)

If an object has been instantiated on the free store using `new` or if you have a pointer to an object, then you use the pointer operator (`->`) to access the member attributes and functions:

```
Human* firstWoman = new Human();
firstWoman->dateOfBirth = "1993";
firstWoman->IntroduceSelf();
delete firstWoman;
```

Listing 9.1 shows a compile-worthy form of the class `Human` featuring a new keyword, `public`.

Input ▼

LISTING 9.1 A Compile-Worthy Class `Human`


```
#include<iostream>
#include<string>
using namespace std;

class Human
{
public:
   string name;
   int age;

   void IntroduceSelf()
   {
      cout << "I am " + name << " and am ";
      cout << age << " years old" << endl;
   }
};

int main()
{
   // An object of class Human with attribute name as "Adam"
   Human firstMan;
   firstMan.name = "Adam";
   firstMan.age = 30;

   // An object of class Human with attribute name as "Eve"
   Human firstWoman;
   firstWoman.name = "Eve";
   firstWoman.age = 28;

   firstMan.IntroduceSelf();
   firstWoman.IntroduceSelf();
}
```

Output ▼

```
I am Adam and am 30 years old
I am Eve and am 28 years old
```

Analysis ▼

Lines 4 through 15 demonstrate the basic C++ class `Human`. Note the structure of the class `Human` and how this class has been used in `main()`.

This class contains two member variables: one of type `string` called `name` at Line 7 and another of type `int` called `age` at Line 8. It also contains the function (also called a method) `IntroduceSelf()` in Lines 10 through 14. Lines 20 and 25 in `main()` instantiate two objects of the class `Human`, named `firstMan` and `firstWoman`, respectively. The lines following this instantiation of objects set the member variables of the objects `firstMan` and `firstWoman` by using the dot operator. Note that Lines 29 and 30 invoke the same function `IntroduceSelf()` on the two objects to create two distinct lines in the output. In a way, this program demonstrates how the objects `firstMan` and `firstWoman` are unique and individually distinct real-world representatives of an abstract type defined by the class `Human`.

Did you notice the keyword `public` in Line 6? It's time you learned features that help you protect attributes your class should keep hidden from those using it.

The Keywords `public` and `private`

Information can be classified into at least two categories: data that you don't mind the *public* knowing and data that is *private*. Gender is an example of information that most people may not mind sharing. However, income may be a private matter.

C++ enables you to model class attributes and methods as public or private. Public class members can be used by anyone in possession of an object of the class. Private class members can be used only within the class (or its "friends"). The C++ keywords `public` and `private` help you as the designer of a class decide what parts of the class can be invoked from outside it—for instance, from `main()`—and which cannot.

What advantages does this ability to mark attributes or methods as `private` present you as the programmer? Consider the declaration of the class `Human` and the member attribute `age` in particular:

```
class Human
{
```

```
private:
   // Private member data:
   int age;
   string name;

public:
   int GetAge()
   {
      return age;
   }

   void SetAge(int humansAge)
   {
      age = humansAge;
   }

// ...Other members and declarations
};
```


Assume an instance of a `Human` called `eve`:

```
Human eve;
```

When the user of this instance tries to access member `age`:

```
cout << eve.age; // compile error
```

this user gets a compile error akin to "Error: `Human::age`—cannot access private member declared in class `Human`." The only permissible way to know the `age` would be to ask for it via the public method `GetAge()` supplied by the class `Human` and implemented in a way the programmer of the class thought was an appropriate way to share `age`:

```
cout << eve.GetAge(); // OK
```

`GetAge()` gives the programmer of the class `Human` the opportunity to know when `age` is being queried and share it in a way that suits. In other words, C++ allows the class to control what attributes it wants to expose and how it wants to expose them. If there were no `GetAge()` public member method implemented by the class `Human`, the class would effectively ensure that the user cannot query `age` at all. This feature can be useful in situations that are explained later in this lesson.

Note that `Human::age` cannot be assigned directly either:

```
eve.age = 22; // compile error
```

The only permissible way to set the age is via the method `SetAge()`:

```
eve.SetAge(22); // OK
```

This has many advantages. The current implementation of `SetAge()` does nothing but directly set the member variable `Human::age`. However, you can use `SetAge()` to verify that the `age` being set is nonzero and not negative and thus validate external input:

```
class Human
{
private:
   int age;

public:
   void SetAge(int humansAge)
   {
      if (humansAge > 0)
          age = humansAge;
   }
};
```

Thus, C++ enables the designer of the class to control how data attributes of the class are accessed and manipulated.

Abstraction of Data via the Keyword `private`

C++ empowers you to decide what information remains unreachable to the outside world (that is, unavailable outside the class) via the keyword `private`. At the same time, it enables you to control access to even information declared `private` via methods that you have declared as `public`. Your implementation of a class can therefore abstract member information that classes and functions outside this class don't need to have access to.

Going back to the example related to `Human::age` being a private member, you know that even in reality, many people don't like to reveal their true age. If the class `Human` were required to tell an age two years younger than the current age, it could do so easily via a public function `GetAge()` that uses the `Human::age` parameter, reduces it by two, and supplies the result, as demonstrated by Listing 9.2.

Input ▼

LISTING 9.2 A Model of the Class `Human` Where the True `age` Is Abstracted from the User, and a Younger `age` Is Reported

```
#include<iostream>
using namespace std;

class Human
{
private:
```

```
 6:     // Private member data:
 7:     int age;
 8:
 9: public:
10:     void SetAge(int inputAge)
11:     {
12:        age = inputAge;
13:     }
14:
15:     // Human lies about his / her age (if over 30)
16:     int GetAge()
17:     {
18:        if (age > 30)
19:           return (age - 2);
20:        else
21:           return age;
22:     }
23: };
24:
25: int main()
26: {
27:     Human firstMan;
28:     firstMan.SetAge(35);
29:
30:     Human firstWoman;
31:     firstWoman.SetAge(22);
32:
33:     cout << "Age of firstMan " << firstMan.GetAge() << endl;
34:     cout << "Age of firstWoman " << firstWoman.GetAge() << endl;
35:
36:     return 0;
37: }
```


Output ▼

```
Age of firstMan 33
Age of firstWoman 22
```

Analysis ▼

Note the public method `Human::GetAge()` in Line 16. As the actual age contained in the private integer `Human::age` is not directly accessible, the only resort external users of this class have in querying an object of the class `Human` for attribute `age` is via the method `GetAge()`. Thus, the actual age held in `Human::age` is abstracted from the outside world. Indeed, our Human lies about its age, and GetAge() returns a reduced value for all humans who are older than 30, as shown in Lines 18 through 21.

Abstraction is an important concept in object-oriented languages. It empowers programmers to decide what attributes of a class need to remain known only to the class and its members, with nobody outside it (with the exception of those declared as its "friends") having access to it.

Constructors

A *constructor* is a special function (or method) invoked during the instantiation of a class to construct an object. Just like functions, constructors can also be overloaded.

Declaring and Implementing a Constructor

A constructor is a special function that takes the name of a class and returns no value. So, the class Human would have a constructor that is declared like this:

```
class Human
{
public:
   Human(); // declaration of a constructor
};
```

This constructor can be implemented either inline within the class or externally outside the class declaration. An implementation (also called definition) inside the class looks like this:

```
class Human
{
public:
   Human()
   {
       // constructor code here
   }
};
```

A variant that enables you to define the constructor outside the class's declaration looks like this:

```
class Human
{
public:
   Human(); // constructor declaration
};
```

```
// constructor implementation (definition)
Human::Human()
{
   // constructor code here
}
```

NOTE

> `::` is called the *scope resolution operator*. For example, `Human::dateOfBirth` is referring to variable `dateOfBirth` declared within the scope of the class `Human`. Note that `::dateOfBirth` refers to another variable with the same name, `dateOfBirth`, in a global scope.

When and How to Use Constructors

A constructor is always invoked during object creation, when an instance of a class is constructed. This makes a constructor a perfect place to initialize class member variables such as integers, pointers, and so on to values you choose. Take another look at Listing 9.2. Note that if you forgot to use `SetAge()`, the integer variable `Human::age` might contain an unknown value as that variable would not have been initialized. (Try it by commenting out Lines 28 and 31.) Listing 9.3 uses constructors to implement a better version of the class `Human`, where the variable `age` has been initialized.

Input ▼

LISTING 9.3 Using Constructors to Initialize Class Member Variables

```
#include<iostream>
#include<string>
using namespace std;

class Human
{
private:
   string name;
   int age;

public:
   Human() // constructor
   {
      age = 1; // initialization
      cout << "Constructed an instance of class Human" << endl;
```

```
15:     }
16:
17:     void SetName (string humansName)
18:     {
19:        name = humansName;
20:     }
21:
22:     void SetAge(int humansAge)
23:     {
24:        age = humansAge;
25:     }
26:
27:     void IntroduceSelf()
28:     {
29:        cout << "I am " + name << " and am ";
30:        cout << age << " years old" << endl;
31:     }
32: };
33:
34: int main()
35: {
36:     Human firstWoman;
37:     firstWoman.SetName("Eve");
38:     firstWoman.SetAge (28);
39:
40:     firstWoman.IntroduceSelf();
41: }
```

Output ▼

```
Constructed an instance of class Human
I am Eve and am 28 years old
```

Analysis ▼

In the output, you see a line that indicates object construction. Now, take a look at `main()`, which is defined in Lines 34 through 41. You see that the first line in output results from the creation (construction) of the object `firstWoman` in Line 36. The constructor `Human::Human()` in Lines 11 through 15 contains the `cout` statement, which contributes to this output. Note that the constructor initializes the integer `age` to zero. If you forget to use `SetAge()` on a newly constructed object, you can rest assured that the constructor will ensure that the value contained in the variable `age` is not a random integer but a definitive `1`.

NOTE

> A constructor that is invoked without arguments is called the *default constructor*. Programming a default constructor is optional. If you don't program any constructor, as shown in Listing 9.1, the compiler creates one for you. (It constructs member attributes but does not initialize plain old data types such as `int` to any specific value.)

Overloading Constructors

Constructors can be overloaded just as functions can. You can therefore write a constructor that requires `Human` to be instantiated with a name as a parameter, for example:

```
class Human
{
public:
   Human()
   {
      // default constructor code here
   }

   Human(string humansName)
   {
      // overloaded constructor code here
   }
};
```

Listing 9.4 demonstrates the application of overloaded constructors in creating an object of the class `Human` with a name supplied at the time of construction.

Input ▼

LISTING 9.4 A `Human` Class with Multiple Constructors

```
#include<iostream>
#include<string>
using namespace std;

class Human
{
private:
   string name;
   int age;

public:
```

```
11:     Human() // default constructor
12:     {
13:        age = 0; // initialized to ensure no junk value
14:        cout << "Default constructor: name and age not set" << endl;
15:     }
16:
17:     Human(string humansName, int humansAge) // overloaded
18:     {
19:        name = humansName;
20:        age = humansAge;
21:        cout << "Overloaded constructor creates ";
22:        cout << name << " of " << age << " years" << endl;
23:     }
24: };
25:
26: int main()
27: {
28:     Human firstMan; // use default constructor
29:     Human firstWoman ("Eve", 20); // use overloaded constructor
30: }
```

Output ▼

```
Default constructor: name and age not set
Overloaded constructor creates Eve of 20 years
```

Analysis ▼

`main()` in Lines 26 through 30 is minimalistic and creates two instances of the class `Human`. `firstMan` uses the default constructor, and `firstWoman` uses the overloaded constructor, which supplies the name and age at instantiation. The output is the result of object construction only! You may appreciate that if the class `Human` had chosen not to support the default constructor, `main()` would've had no option but to construct every object of `Human` using the overloaded constructor, which takes `name` and `age` as a prerequisites—making it impossible to create a human without supplying a name or an age.

TIP

> You can choose not to implement the default constructor to enforce object instantiation with parameters that are required by the overloaded constructor, as explained in the next section.

A Class Without a Default Constructor

In Listing 9.5, see how the class `Human` without the default constructor enforces the availability of a name and age as a prerequisite to instantiating an object.

Input ▼

LISTING 9.5 A Class with Overloaded Constructors and No Default Constructor

```
#include<iostream>
#include<string>
using namespace std;

class Human
{
private:
   string name;
   int age;

public:
   Human(string humansName, int humansAge)
   {
      name = humansName;
      age = humansAge;
      cout << "Overloaded constructor creates " << name;
      cout << " of age " << age << endl;
   }

   void IntroduceSelf()
   {
      cout << "I am " << name << " and am ";
      cout << age << " years old" << endl;
   }
};

int main()
{
   Human firstMan("Adam", 25);
   Human firstWoman("Eve", 28);

   firstMan.IntroduceSelf();
   firstWoman.IntroduceSelf();
   return 0;
}
```

Output ▼

```
Overloaded constructor creates Adam of age 25
Overloaded constructor creates Eve of age 28
I am Adam and am 25 years old
I am Eve and am 28 years old
```

Analysis ▼

This version of the class `Human` has only one constructor that takes a `string` and an `int` as input parameters (see Line 11). There is no default constructor available, and given the presence of an overloaded constructor, the C++ compiler does not generate a default constructor for you. You therefore cannot create an object of the class `Human` like this:

```
Human firstMan; // error - no default constructor available
```

This example also demonstrates the ability to create an object of the class `Human` with `name` and `age` set at instantiation, and no possibility to change them later. This is because the `name` attribute of `Human` is stored as a `private` variable. `Human::name` cannot be accessed or modified by `main()` or by any entity that is not a member of the class `Human`. In other words, the user of the class `Human` is forced by the overloaded constructor to specify a name (and age) for every object she creates and is not allowed to change that name thereafter. This models a real-world scenario quite well, don't you think? You were named at birth; people are allowed to know your name, but nobody (except you) has the authority to change it.

Constructor Parameters with Default Values

Just as functions can have parameters with default values specified, so can constructors. What you see in the following code is a slightly modified version of the constructor from Listing 9.5 at Line 11, where the `age` parameter has a default value of `25`:

```
class Human
{
private:
   string name;
   int age;

public:
   // overloaded constructor (no default constructor)
   Human(string humansName, int humansAge = 25)
   {
      name = humansName;
      age = humansAge;
```

```
        cout << "Overloaded constructor creates " << name;
        cout << " of age " << age << endl;
    }

    // ... other members
};
```

Such a class can be instantiated as follows:

```
Human adam("Adam"); // adam.age is assigned a default value 25
Human eve("Eve", 18); // eve.age is assigned 18 as specified
```


NOTE

Note that a default constructor is a constructor that can be instantiated without arguments. A constructor with two parameters, both with default values as seen below, is hence a default constructor:

```
class Human
{
private:
    string name;
    int age;

public:
    // default values for both parameters
    Human(string humansName = "Adam", int humansAge = 25)
    {
        name = humansName;
        age = humansAge;
        cout << "Overloaded constructor creates ";
        cout << name << " of age " << age;
    }
};
```

The class `Human` can still be instantiated without arguments:

```
Human adam; // Human takes default name "Adam", age 25
```

Constructors with Initialization Lists

You have seen how useful constructors are in initializing member variables. Another way to initialize members is by using *initialization lists*. A variant of the constructor in Listing 9.5 using initialization lists would look like this:

```
class Human
{
private:
   string name;
   int age;

public:
   // two parameters to initialize members age and name
   Human(string humansName, int humansAge)
        :name(humansName), age(humansAge)
   {
      cout << "Constructed a human called " << name;
      cout << ", " << age << " years old" << endl;
   }
// ... other class members
};
```

Thus, the initialization list is characterized by a colon (`:`) following the parameter declaration contained in parentheses (`(...)`), followed by an individual member variable and the value it is initialized to. This initialization value can be a parameter such as `humansName` or can even be a fixed value. Initialization lists can also be useful in invoking base class constructors with specific arguments. These are discussed again in Lesson 10, "Implementing Inheritance."

You can see a version of the class `Human` that features a default constructor with parameters, default values, and an initialization list in Listing 9.6.

Input ▼

LISTING 9.6 A Default Constructor That Accepts Parameters with Default Values to Set Members Using Initialization Lists

```
#include<iostream>
#include<string>
using namespace std;

```

```
 4: class Human
 5: {
 6: private:
 7:    int age;
 8:    string name;
 9:
10: public:
11:    Human(string humansName = "Adam", int humansAge = 25)
12:          :name(humansName), age(humansAge)
13:    {
14:       cout << "Constructed a human called " << name;
15:       cout << ", " << age << " years old" << endl;
16:    }
17: };
18:
19: int main()
20: {
21:    Human adam;
22:    Human eve("Eve", 18);
23:
24:    return 0;
25: }
```


Output ▼

```
Constructed a human called Adam, 25 years old
Constructed a human called Eve, 18 years old
```

Analysis ▼

The constructor with initialization lists appears in Lines 11 through 16, where you can also see that the parameters have been given default values `Adam` for `name` and `25` for `age`. Hence, when an instance of the class `Human` called `adam` is created in Line 21, without arguments, its members are automatically assigned the default values. `eve` is supplied with arguments on Line 22; these arguments become values that are assigned to `Human::name` and `Human::age` during construction.

NOTE

It is possible to define a constructor as a constant expression, too, by using the keyword `constexpr`. In special cases where such a construct would be useful from a performance point of view, you could use it at the constructor declaration:

```
class Sample
{
const char* someString;
public:
    constexpr Sample(const char* input)
                    :someString(input)
    { // constructor code }
};
```

TIP

A constructor that contains parameters is also called a *converting constructor*. It implicitly converts the parameter list into the type being constructed. Before C++11, however, only constructors taking a single parameter were said to be converting. This changed with the support of initializer lists in C++11.

To avoid implicit conversions, you use the keyword `explicit` at the beginning of a constructor declaration.

Destructor

A destructor, like a constructor, is a special function. Whereas a constructor is invoked at object instantiation, a destructor is automatically invoked when an object is destroyed.

Declaring and Implementing a Destructor

A destructor looks like a function that takes the name of a class, and it has a tilde (~) preceding it. So, the class `Human` would have a destructor that is declared like this:

```
class Human
{
   ~Human(); // declaration of a destructor
};
```

This destructor can either be implemented inline in the class or externally, outside the class declaration. An implementation or definition inside the class looks like this:

```
class Human
{
public:
   ~Human()
   {
       // destructor code here
   }
};
```


A variant enabling you to define the destructor outside the class's declaration looks like this:

```
class Human
{
public:
   ~Human(); // destructor declaration
};
// destructor definition (implementation)
Human::~Human()
{
   // destructor code here
}
```

As you can see, the declaration of a destructor differs from the declaration of a constructor slightly in that it contains a tilde (~). The role of the destructor is, however, opposite that of the constructor.

When and How to Use a Destructor

A destructor is always invoked when an object of a class is destroyed when it goes out of scope or is deleted via `delete`. This property makes a destructor the ideal place to reset variables and release dynamically allocated memory and other resources. The constructors, the destructor, and well-programmed operators are widely used in the implementation of utility classes such as `std::string` (a smarter alternative to `char*`) and container classes such as `std::vector` provided by the Standard Template Library (STL).

NOTE

> Operators are explained in Lesson 12, "Operator Types and Operator Overloading."

Let us analyze the sample class `MyBuffer`, shown in Listing 9.7, which allocates memory for a dynamic array of integers using `new` in the constructor and releases it in the destructor.

Input ▼

LISTING 9.7 A Simple Class That Encapsulates a Pointer to Ensure Deallocation via the Destructor

```
#include<iostream>
using namespace std;

class MyBuffer
{
private:
    int* myNums;

public:
    MyBuffer(unsigned int length)
    {
       cout << "Constructor allocates " << length << " integers" << endl;
       myNums = new int[length]; // allocate memory
    }

    ~MyBuffer()
    {
       cout << "Destructor releasing allocated memory" << endl;
       delete[] myNums; // free allocated memory
    }

    // other set and get functions to work with myNums
};

int main()
{
    cout << "How many integers would you like to store?" << endl;
    unsigned int numsToStore = 0;
    cin >> numsToStore;

    MyBuffer buf(numsToStore);

    return 0;
}
```

Output ▼

First run:

```
How many integers would you like to store? 200
Constructor allocates 200 integers
Destructor releasing allocated memory
```

Another run:

```
How many integers would you like to store? 200000
Constructor allocates 200000 integers
Destructor releasing allocated memory
```

Analysis ▼

The class `MyBuffer` essentially encapsulates the pointer `MyBuffer::myNums` and relieves you of the task of allocating memory as well as deallocating it in good time. The lines of utmost interest in this case are the constructor `(..)` in Lines 9 through 13 and the destructor `~MyBuffer()` in Lines 15 through 19. The overloaded constructor enforces object creation with a compulsory input parameter `length` that contains the number of elements to be dynamically allocated. The destructor code does the job of ensuring that the memory allocated in the constructor is automatically returned to the system. It complements `new` in the constructor and performs `delete[]`. Note that nowhere in `main()` is there a `new` or a `delete`. In addition to abstracting the implementation of memory management from the user, the class `MyBuffer` also ensures technical correctness in releasing allocated memory. The destructor `~MyBuffer()` is automatically invoked when `main` ends, and this is demonstrated in the output that executes the `cout` statements in the destructor.

Lesson 26, "Understanding Smart Pointers," demonstrates the critical role the destructor plays in working with pointers in a smarter way.

NOTE

> A destructor cannot be overloaded. A class can have only one destructor. If you forget to implement a destructor, the compiler creates and invokes a dummy destructor—that is, an empty one (which does no cleanup of dynamically allocated memory).

The Copy Constructor

In Lesson 7, "Organizing Code with Functions," you learned that arguments passed to a function like `Area()` (shown in Listing 7.1) are copied:

```
double Area(double radius);
```

So, the argument sent as the parameter `radius` is copied when `Area()` is invoked. This rule applies to objects—that is, instances of classes—as well. However, *shallow copying* is a problem that needs to be addressed.

Shallow Copying and Associated Problems

Classes such as `MyBuffer`, shown in Listing 9.7, contain a pointer member `myNums`, which points to memory that is dynamically allocated in the constructor using `new` and deallocated in the destructor using `delete[]`. When an object of this class is copied, the pointer member is copied, but the pointed memory is not, resulting in two objects pointing to the same dynamically allocated buffer in memory. When an object is destroyed, `delete[]` deallocates the memory, thereby invalidating the pointer copy held by the other object. Such copies are *shallow* and are a threat to the stability of the program, as Listing 9.8 demonstrates.

Input ▼

LISTING 9.8 The Problem in Passing Objects of a Class Such as `MyBuffer` by Value

```
#include<iostream>
using namespace std;

class MyBuffer
{
private:
    int* myNums;

public:
    MyBuffer(unsigned int length)
    {
        cout << "Constructor allocates " << length << " integers" << endl;
        myNums = new int[length]; // allocate memory
    }

    ~MyBuffer()
    {
        cout << "Destructor releasing allocated memory" << endl;
        delete[] myNums; // free allocated memory
    }

    // other set and get functions to work with myNums
};

```

```
24: void UseMyBuf(MyBuffer copyBuf)
25: {
26:     cout << "Copy of buf will be destroyed when function ends" << endl;
27: }
28:
29: int main()
30: {
31:     cout << "How many integers would you like to store? ";
32:     unsigned int numsToStore = 0;
33:     cin >> numsToStore;
34:
35:     MyBuffer buf(numsToStore);
36:     UseMyBuf(buf); // send a copy
37:
38:     return 0; // crash, at destruction of buf
39: }
```


Output ▼

```
How many integers would you like to store? 25
Constructor allocates 25 integers
Copy of buf will be destroyed when function ends
Destructor releasing allocated memory
Destructor releasing allocated memory
```

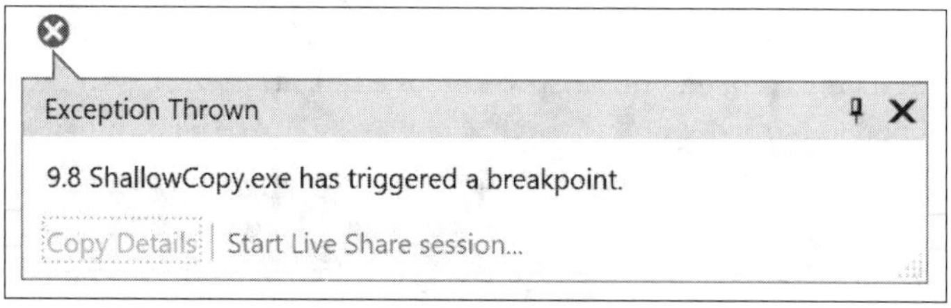

FIGURE 9.2 Screenshot of crash caused by executing Listing 9.8 (in Microsoft Visual Studio debug mode).

Analysis ▼

The error message when this code is compiled using g++ is a little more clear. It says:

```
free(): double free detected in tcache 2
Aborted (core dumped)
```

Apparently, it indicates that memory was freed twice. Why does the class `MyBuffer`, which worked just fine in Listing 9.7, crash in Listing 9.8? The only difference between Listing 9.7 and 9.8 is that a copy of `buf` was sent to `UseMyBuf()`, invoked in Line 36.

The compiler generates a copy because the function `UseMyBuf()` has been declared to take a parameter by value and not by reference. In copying `buf`, the compiler performs a binary copy of plain old data such as integers, characters, and pointers. So the pointer value contained in `buf.myNums` has simply been copied; that is, `copyBuf.myNums` within the function `UseMyBuf()` points to the same memory location as `buf.myNums`. This is illustrated in Figure 9.3.

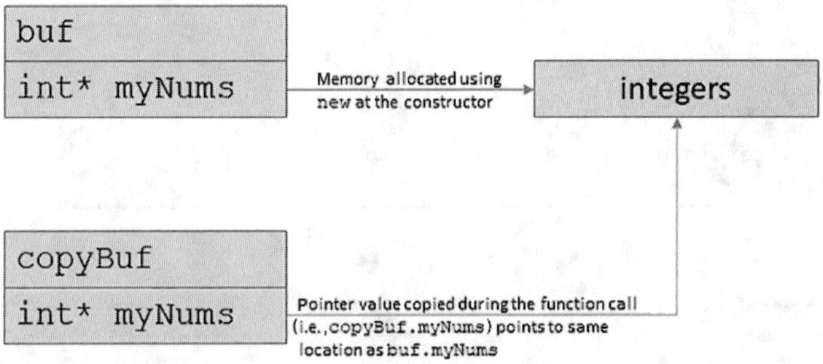

FIGURE 9.3
Shallow copy of `buf` into `copyBuf` when `UseMyBuf()` is invoked.

The binary copy does not perform a deep copy of data at the pointed memory location, and you now have two objects of the class `MyBuffer`, containing pointers to the same location in memory; that is, `buf.myNums` and `copyBuf.myNums` point to the same block of memory. Thus, when the function `UseMyBuf()` ends, `copyBuf`, which is local to the function, goes out of scope and is destroyed. In the process, the destructor of the class `MyBuffer` is invoked, and the destructor code in Line 19 in Listing 9.8 releases the memory pointed to by `copyBuf.myNums` by using `delete[]`. When `main()` ends, `buf` goes out of scope and is destroyed. This time, however, Line 19 repeats a call to `delete[]` on a memory address that is no longer valid (as it is released and invalidated via the previous destruction of `copyBuf`). This double `delete` results in a crash.

Ensuring a Deep Copy Using a Copy Constructor

The copy constructor is an overloaded constructor that you supply. It is invoked by the compiler every time an object of the class is copied. When correctly programmed, it solves the shallow copy problems demonstrated in Listing 9.8.

You declare a copy constructor for the class `MyBuffer` as follows:

```
class MyBuffer
{
   MyBuffer(const MyBuffer& copySource); // copy constructor
};
```

```
MyBuffer::MyBuffer(const MyBuffer& copySource)
{
   // Copy constructor implementation code
}
```

Thus, a copy constructor is characterized by a parameter that accepts an object of the same class type by *reference*. This parameter is an alias of the source object and is the handle you have in writing your custom copy code. You would use the copy constructor to ensure a deep copy of all buffers in the source, as Listing 9.9 demonstrates.

9

Input ▼
LISTING 9.9 Defining a Copy Constructor to Ensure a Deep Copy of Dynamically Allocated Buffers

```
 0: #include<iostream>
 1: #include<algorithm>
 2: using namespace std;
 3:
 4: class MyBuffer
 5: {
 6: private:
 7:     int* myNums;
 8:     unsigned int bufLength;
 9:
10: public:
11:     MyBuffer(unsigned int length)
12:     {
13:         bufLength = length;
14:         cout << "Constructor allocates " << length << " integers" << endl;
15:         myNums = new int[length]; // allocate memory
16:     }
17:
18:     MyBuffer(const MyBuffer& src) // copy constructor
19:     {
20:         cout << "Copy constructor creating deep copy" << endl;
21:         bufLength = src.bufLength;
22:         myNums = new int[bufLength];
23:         copy(src.myNums, src.myNums + bufLength, myNums); // deep copy
24:     }
25:
26:     ~MyBuffer()
27:     {
28:         cout << "Destructor releasing allocated memory" << endl;
29:         delete[] myNums; // free allocated memory
30:     }
```

```
   void SetValue(unsigned int index, int value)
   {
      if (index < bufLength) // check for bounds
         *(myNums + index) = value;
   }

   void DisplayBuf()
   {
      for (unsigned int counter = 0; counter < bufLength; ++counter)
         cout << *(myNums + counter) << " ";

      cout << endl;
   }
};

void UseMyBuf(MyBuffer copyBuf)
{
   cout << "Displaying copy of buf: " << endl;
   copyBuf.DisplayBuf();
}

int main()
{
   cout << "How many integers would you like to store? ";
   unsigned int numsToStore = 0;
   cin >> numsToStore;

   MyBuffer buf(numsToStore);
   for (unsigned int counter = 0; counter < numsToStore; ++counter)
   {
      cout << "Enter value: ";
      int valueEntered = 0;
      cin >> valueEntered;
      buf.SetValue(counter, valueEntered);
   }

   cout << "Numbers in the buffer buf: ";
   buf.DisplayBuf();
   UseMyBuf(buf); // function receives a deep copy of buf

   return 0; // no crash, at destruction of buf
}
```

Output ▼

```
How many integers would you like to store? 3
Constructor allocates 3 integers
Enter value: 2020
Enter value: -596
```

```
Enter value: 42
Numbers in the buffer buf: 2020 -596 42
Copy constructor creating deep copy
Displaying copy of buf: 2020 -596 42
Destructor releasing allocated memory
Destructor releasing allocated memory
```

Analysis ▼

9

Listing 9.9 contains a complete functional version of the class `MyBuffer`, including the `SetValue()` and `DisplayBuf()` functions. The most important part of it is the copy constructor in Lines 18 through 24. This copy constructor is implicitly invoked when line 70 is executed and a copy of `buf` is sent to the function `UseMyBuf()`. The copy constructor first allocates memory in the destination using `new` and then uses STL algorithm `std::copy` to perform a deep copy. This is illustrated in Figure 9.4.

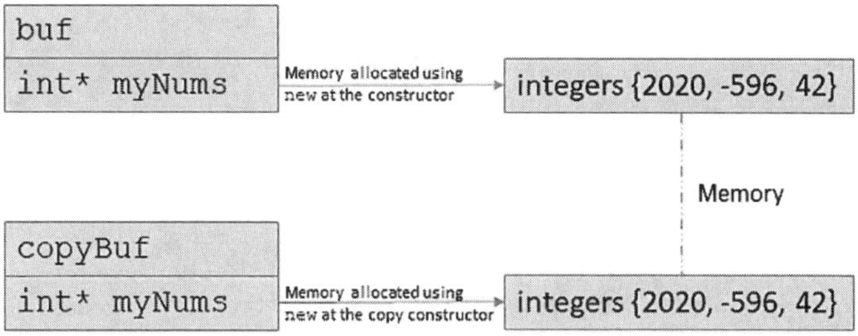

FIGURE 9.4
Illustration of a deep copy of the argument `buf` into `copyBuf` when the function `UseMyBuf()` is invoked.

The output of Listing 9.9 indicates that the memory address being pointed to by `buffer` is different in the copy; that is, two objects don't point to the same dynamically allocated memory address. As a result, when the function `UseMyBuf()` returns and the parameter `copyBuf` is destroyed, the destructor code does a `delete[]` on the memory address that was allocated in the copy constructor and that belongs to this object. In doing so, it does not touch memory that is being pointed to by the original `buf` in `main()`. So, both functions end, and their respective objects are destroyed successfully without the application crashing.

NOTE

The copy constructor ensures a deep copy in a case such as a function call:

```
UseMyBuf(buf);
```

However, what if you tried copying via assignment?

```
MyBuffer anotherCopy(numsToStore);
anotherCopy = buf; // assignment doesn't invoke
copy constructor
```

This would still result in a shallow copy because you haven't yet supplied a copy assignment `operator=`. In the absence of this operator, the compiler supplies a default operator that does a shallow copy.

The copy assignment operator is discussed in detail in Lesson 12. Listing 12.9 is an improved `MyBuffer` that implements the following:

```
MyBuffer::operator= (const MyBuffer& copySource)
{
   //... copy assignment operator code
}
```

CAUTION

Using `const` in the copy constructor declaration ensures that the copy constructor does not modify the source object being referred to.

In addition, the parameter in the copy constructor is passed by reference as a necessity. If this weren't a reference, the copy constructor would itself invoke a copy, thus invoking itself again and so on until the system ran out of memory.

DO	DON'T
DO always program a copy constructor and copy assignment operator when your class contains raw pointer members (`int*` and the like). **DO** always program the copy constructor with a `const` reference source parameter. **DO** use the keyword `explicit` while declaring constructors that should not permit implicit conversions.	**DON'T** use raw pointers as class members unless absolutely unavoidable.

NOTE

> The class `MyBuffer` with a raw pointer member, `int* myNums`, is used as an example to explain the need for copy constructors.
> If you were to program a class that needs to contain string data for storing names and so on, you could use `std::string` instead of `char*` and might not even need a copy constructor, given the absence of raw pointers. This is because the default copy constructor inserted by the compiler would ensure the invocation of all available copy constructors of member objects such as `std::string`.

Using Move Constructors to Improve Performance

In some cases, objects are subjected to copy steps automatically due to the nature and needs of the C++ language. Consider the following:

```
class MyBuffer
{
   // pick implementation from Listing 9.9
};
MyBuffer Copy(MyBuffer& source) // function
{
   MyBuffer copyForReturn(source. bufLength);  // create copy
   return copyForReturn;  // return by value invokes copy constructor
}
int main()
{
   MyBuffer buf1(5);
   MyBuffer buf2(Copy(buf1)); // invokes 2x copy constructor

   return 0;
}
```

As the comment indicates, in the instantiation of `buf2`, the copy constructor is invoked twice, and thus a deep copy is performed twice because of the call to the function `Copy(buf1)`, which returns `MyBuffer` by value. However, this value that is returned is very temporary and is not available outside this expression. So, the copy constructor that is invoked in good faith by the C++ compiler is a burden on performance. This impact becomes significant if the class contains objects of great size.

To avoid such a performance bottleneck, C++ introduced the *move constructor* in addition to the copy constructor in C++11. The syntax of a move constructor is

```
// move constructor
```

```
MyBuffer(MyBuffer&& moveSource)
{
   if(moveSource.myNums != NULL)
   {
      myNums = moveSource. myNums; // take ownership i.e. 'move'
      moveSource.myNums = NULL;    // set the move source to NULL
   }
}
```

When a move constructor is programmed, the compiler automatically opts to "move" the temporary resource and hence avoid a deep-copy step. With the move constructor implemented, the comment should be appropriately changed to the following:

```
MyBuffer buf2(Copy(buf1)); // invokes 1x copy, 1x move constructor
```

The move constructor is usually implemented with the move assignment operator, which is discussed in greater detail in Lesson 12. Listing 12.12 shows a better version of the class `MyBuffer` that implements the move constructor and the move assignment operator.

Different Uses of Constructors and the Destructor

You have learned a few important and basic concepts in this lesson, such as the concepts of constructors, destructor, and the abstraction of data and methods via keywords such as `public` and `private`. These concepts can be used to program classes that control how their instances can be constructed, copied, or destroyed, as well as how they expose data.

Let's look at a few interesting patterns that help you solve many important design problems.

A Class That Does Not Permit Copying

Say that you are asked to model the constitution of your country. Your constitution permits one president. Your class `President` risks the following:

```
President ourPresident;
DoSomething(ourPresident); // duplicate created in passing by value
President clone;
clone = ourPresident; // duplicate via assignment
```

Clearly, you need to avoid this situation. Beyond modeling a certain constitution, you might be programming an operating system and need to model one local area network, one processor, and so on. In such a situation, you need to ensure that certain resources cannot be copied or duplicated. If you don't declare a copy constructor, the C++ compiler inserts a default public copy constructor for you. This ruins your design and threatens your implementation. However, the C++ language gives you a solution to this design paradigm.

You can ensure that your class cannot be copied by declaring a `private` copy constructor. This ensures that the function call `DoSomething(ourPresident)` will cause a compile failure. To avoid assignment, you declare a `private` assignment operator.

Thus, the solution is as follows:

```
class President
{
private:
    President(const President&); // private copy constructor
    President& operator= (const President&); // private copy assignment operator

    // ... other attributes and methods
};
```

There is no need to implement the private copy constructor or assignment operator. Just declaring them as private is adequate and sufficient in fulfilling your goal of ensuring non-copyable objects of the class `President`.

A Singleton Class That Permits a Single Instance

The `President` class just discussed is good, but it cannot stop the creation of multiple presidents via instantiation of multiple objects:

```
President One, Two, Three;
```

Individually, these objects are non-copyable, thanks to the `private` copy constructors, but what you ideally need is a `President` class that has one, and only one, real-world manifestation; that is, you need to have only one object, and creation of additional ones needs to be prohibited. Welcome to the concept of a singleton class that uses private constructors, a private assignment operator, and a static instance member to create this (controversially) powerful pattern.

TIP

> When the keyword `static` is used on a class's data member, it ensures that the member is shared across all instances.
> When `static` is used on a method, the method is shared across all instances of the class.
>
> When `static` is used on a local variable declared within the scope of a function, it ensures that the variable retains its value between function calls.

The keyword `static` is an essential ingredient in creating a singleton class, as demonstrated in Listing 9.10.

Input ▼

LISTING 9.10 A Singleton Class `President` That Prohibits Copying, Assignment, and Multiple Instance Creation

```
#include<iostream>
#include<string>
using namespace std;

class President
{
private:
    President() {}; // private default constructor
    President(const President&); // private copy constructor
    const President& operator=(const President&); // assignment operator

    string name;

public:
    static President& GetInstance()
    {
        // static objects are constructed only once
        static President onlyInstance;
        return onlyInstance;
    }

    string GetName()
    { return name; }

    void SetName(string InputName)
    { name = InputName; }
};

```

```
28: int main()
29: {
30:     President& onlyPresident = President::GetInstance();
31:     onlyPresident.SetName("Abraham Lincoln");
32:
33:     // uncomment lines to see how compile failures prohibit duplicates
34:     // President second; // cannot access constructor
35:     // President* third= new President(); // cannot access constructor
36:     // President fourth = onlyPresident; // cannot access copy constructor
37:     // onlyPresident = President::GetInstance(); // cannot access operator=
38:
39:     cout << "The name of the President is: ";
40:     cout << President::GetInstance().GetName() << endl;
41:
42:     return 0;
43: }
```


Output ▼

```
The name of the President is: Abraham Lincoln
```

Analysis ▼

Take a quick look at `main()` in Lines 28 through 43. A host of commented lines show all the combinations possible in creating new instances or copies of a `President` class that won't compile. Let's analyze them one by one. Lines 34 and 35 try object creation on the stack and free store, respectively, using the `default` constructor, which is unavailable because it's `private`, as declared in Line 7:

```
34:     // President second; // cannot access constructor
35:     // President* third= new President(); // cannot access constructor
```

Line 36 is an attempt at creating a copy of an existing object via the copy constructor (as assignment at creation time invokes the copy constructor), which is unavailable in `main()` because it is declared `private` in Line 8:

```
36:     // President fourth = onlyPresident; // cannot access copy constructor
```

Line 37 makes an attempt at creating a copy via assignment, which does not work as the assignment operator is declared `private` in Line 9:

```
37:     // OnlyPresident = President::GetInstance(); // cannot access operator=
```

Therefore, `main()` can never create an instance of the class `President`, and the only option left is attempted in Line 30, which uses the static function `GetInstance()` to get an instance of the class `President`. Because `GetInstance()` is a static member, it is like a global function that can be invoked without having an object as a handle. `GetInstance()`, implemented in Lines 14 through 19, uses the static variable `onlyInstance` to ensure that there is one and only one instance of the class `President` created. To understand this better, imagine that Line 17 is executed only once (static initialization), and hence `GetInstance()` returns the only available instance of the class `President`, regardless of how often `President::GetInstance()` is invoked.

CAUTION

> Use the singleton pattern only where absolutely necessary, keeping future growth of the application and its features in perspective. Note that its very feature of restricting creation of multiple instances can become an architectural bottleneck when a use case comes up that requires multiple instances of the class. For example, if your project were to change from modeling a nation to modeling the United Nations, which currently includes 193 member nations, each with its own president, clearly you would have an architectural problem if you used the singleton class `President`, which permits the existence of only one instance.

A Class That Prohibits Instantiation on the Stack

As explained in Lesson 7, the stack is a last-in, first-out (LIFO) setup in memory that is used to house variables local to a function. Space on the stack is often limited. If you are writing a database that may contain terabytes of data in its internal structures, you might want to ensure that a client of this class cannot instantiate it on the stack; instead, you would want to force it to create instances only on the free store. The key to ensuring this is declaring the destructor `private`:

```
class MonsterDB
{
private:
   ~MonsterDB();   // private destructor

   //... members that consume a huge amount of data
};
```

Declaring a private destructor ensures that you are not allowed to create an instance like this:

```
int main()
{
   MonsterDB myDatabase; // compile error
   // ... more code
   return 0;
}
```

This instance, if successfully constructed, would be on the stack. All objects on the stack get popped when the stack is unwound, and therefore the compiler would need to compile and invoke the destructor `~MonsterDB()` at the end of `main()`. However, this destructor is private and therefore inaccessible, resulting in a compile failure.

A private destructor would not stop you from instantiating on the free store using `new` because such instances are not automatically destroyed:

```
int main()
{
   MonsterDB* myDatabase = new MonsterDB(); // no error
   // ... more code
   return 0;
}
```

Do you see the memory leak here? Because the destructor is not accessible from `main()`, you cannot do a `delete`, either. The class `MonsterDB` needs to support is a `public static` member function that destroys the instance. (A class member would have access to the private destructor.) See Listing 9.11.

Input ▼

LISTING 9.11 A Database Class `MonsterDB` That Allows Object Creation Only on the Free Store (Using `new`)

```
#include<iostream>
using namespace std;

class MonsterDB
{
private:
   ~MonsterDB() {}; // private destructor prevents instances on stack

public:
   static void DestroyInstance(MonsterDB* pInstance)
```

```
10:     {
11:        delete pInstance; // member can invoke private destructor
12:     }
13:
14:     void DoSomething() {} // sample empty member method
15: };
16:
17: int main()
18: {
19:     MonsterDB* myDB = new MonsterDB(); // on free store
20:     myDB->DoSomething();
21:
22:     // uncomment next line to see compile failure
23:     // delete myDB; // private destructor cannot be invoked
24:
25:     // use static member to release memory
26:     MonsterDB::DestroyInstance(myDB);
27:
28:     return 0;
29: }
```

Output ▼

The code snippet produces no output.

Analysis ▼

The purpose of the code is just to demonstrate the programming of a class that prohibits instance creation on the stack. A `private` destructor, as shown in Line 6, is key. The static function `DestroyInstance()` in Lines 9 through 12 is required for memory deallocation because `main()` cannot invoke `delete` on `myDB`. You can test this by uncommenting Line 23.

Using Constructors to Convert Types

Earlier in this lesson, you learned that constructors can be overloaded—that is, take one or more parameters. Overloading is often used to convert one type to another. Let's consider the class `Human`, which features an overloaded constructor that accepts an integer:

```
class Human
{
   int age;
public:
   Human(int humansAge): age(humansAge) {}
};
```

```
// Function that takes a Human as a parameter
void DoSomething(Human person)
{
   cout << "Human sent did something" << endl;
   return;
}
```

This constructor allows a conversion:

```
Human kid(10); // convert integer in to a Human
DoSomething(kid);
DoSomething(5); // implicitly convert integer to Human!
```


So, why does this line work? The compiler knows that the class `Human` supports a constructor that accepts an integer and performs an *implicit* conversion for you: It creates an object of type `Human` using the integer you supplied and sent it as an argument to the function.

To avoid implicit conversions, you use the keyword `explicit` when declaring the constructor:

```
class Human
{
   int age;
public:
   explicit Human(int humansAge): age(humansAge) {}
};
```

Using `explicit` is not required, but in many cases it is a good programming practice. Listing 9.12 demonstrates a version of the class `Human` that does not permit implicit conversions.

Input ▼

LISTING 9.12 Using the Keyword `explicit` to Block Unintentional Implicit Conversions

```
#include<iostream>
using namespace std;

class Human
{
   int age;
public:
```

```
 7:     // explicit constructor blocks implicit conversions
 8:     explicit Human(int humansAge) : age(humansAge) {}
 9: };
10:
11: void DoSomething(Human person)
12: {
13:     cout << "Human did something" << endl;
14:     return;
15: }
16:
17: int main()
18: {
19:     Human kid(10);     // explicit conversion is OK
20:     Human anotherKid = Human(11); // explicit, OK
21:     DoSomething(kid); // OK
22:
23:     // Human anotherKid2 = 11; // error: implicit conversion not OK
24:     // DoSomething(10); // implicit conversion, not OK
25:
26:     return 0;
27: }
```

Output ▼

```
Human did something
```

Analysis ▼

The lines of code that don't contribute to the output are as significant as those that do. `main()` in Lines 17 through 27 features variants of object instantiation of the class `Human` that is declared with an `explicit` constructor in Line 8. The lines that compile are attempts at explicit conversion, where an `int` has been used to instantiate a `Human`. Lines 23 and 24 are variants that involve implicit conversion. These lines, which are commented out, compile when you remove the keyword `explicit` in Line 8. Thus, this example demonstrates how the keyword `explicit` protects against implicit conversions.

TIP

> The problem of implicit conversions and avoiding them using the keyword `explicit` applies to operators, too. Remember to note the usage of `explicit` when you program conversion operators in Lesson 12.

The `this` Pointer

`this` is a reserved keyword that is applicable within the scope of a class and contains the address of the object. In other words, the value of `this` is `&object`. This is an important concept in C++. Within a class member method, when you invoke another member method, the compiler sends the `this` pointer as an implicit, invisible parameter in the function call:

```
class Human
{
private:
    void Talk (string statement)
   {
      cout << statement;
   }

public:
   void IntroduceSelf()
   {
      Talk("Bla bla"); // same as Talk(this, "Bla Bla")
   }
};
```

What you see here is the method `IntroduceSelf()` using the private member `Talk()` to print a statement on the screen. In reality, the compiler embeds the `this` pointer in calling `Talk`, which is invoked as `Talk(this, "Bla bla")`.

From a programming perspective, `this` does not have too many applications, except where it is usually optional. For instance, the code to access `age` within `SetAge()`, as shown in Listing 9.2, can have a variant:

```
void SetAge(int humansAge)
{
   this->age = humansAge;    // same as: age = humansAge
}
```

NOTE

> Note that the `this` pointer is not sent to class methods declared as `static` because static functions are not connected to instances of the class. Instead, they are shared by all instances.
>
> To use an instance variable in a static function, you explicitly declare a parameter and send the `this` pointer as an argument.

9

Using `sizeof()` with a Class

You have learned the fundamentals of defining your own type by using the keyword `class`, which enables you to encapsulate data attributes and methods that operate on that data. The operator `sizeof()`, covered in Lesson 3, “Using Variables, Declaring Constants,” is used to determine the memory requirement of a specific type, in bytes. This operator is valid for classes, too, and basically reports the sum of bytes consumed by each data attribute contained within the class declaration. Depending on the compiler you use, `sizeof()` might or might not include padding for certain attributes on word boundaries. Note that member functions and their local variables do not play a role in defining `sizeof()` for a class. See Listing 9.13.

Input ▼

LISTING 9.13 The Result of Using `sizeof()` on Classes and Their Instances

```
#include<iostream>
using namespace std;

class MyBuffer
{
private:
   int* myNums;

public:
   MyBuffer(unsigned int length)
   {
      myNums = new int[length]; // allocate memory
   }

   ~MyBuffer()
   {
      delete[] myNums; // free allocated memory
   }

   // other set and get functions to work with myNums
};

class Human
{
private:
   int age;
   string gender;
   string name;

public:
```

```
    Human(const string& inputName, int inputAge, string inputGender)
       : name(inputName), age (inputAge), gender(inputGender) {}

    int GetAge ()
    { return age; }
};

int main()
{
    MyBuffer buf1(5); // buffer initialized to 5 integers
    MyBuffer buf2(20);// buffer initialized to 20 integers

    cout << "sizeof(MyBuffer) = " << sizeof(MyBuffer) << endl;
    cout << "sizeof(buf1) = " << sizeof(buf1) << endl;
    cout << "sizeof(buf2) = " << sizeof(buf2) << endl;

    Human firstMan("Adam", 25, "man");
    Human firstWoman("Eve", 25, "woman");

    cout << "sizeof(Human) = " << sizeof(Human) << endl;
    cout << "sizeof(firstMan) = " << sizeof(firstMan) << endl;
    cout << "sizeof(firstWoman) = " << sizeof(firstWoman) << endl;

    return 0;
}
```


Output ▼

32-bit compiler output:

```
sizeof(MyBuffer) = 4
sizeof(buf1) = 4
sizeof(buf2) = 4
sizeof(Human) = 60
sizeof(firstMan) = 60
sizeof(firstWoman) = 60
```

64-bit compiler output:

```
sizeof(MyBuffer) = 8
sizeof(buf1) = 8
sizeof(buf2) = 8
sizeof(Human) = 88
sizeof(firstMan) = 88
sizeof(firstWoman) = 88
```

Analysis ▼

In this output, you can see that the result of using `sizeof()` on a class is the same as using an object of the class. Hence, `sizeof(MyBuffer)` is the same as `sizeof(buf1)` because the number of bytes consumed by a class is essentially fixed at compile time. Don't be surprised that `buf1` and `buf2` have the same size, in bytes, even though one contains 5 integers and the other 20; `MyBuffer::myNums` is an `int*`, a pointer whose size is fixed that is independent of the volume of data being pointed to. The output also demonstrates that a 64-bit compiler reserves more space in memory for the same type compared to a 32-bit compiler. This facilitates computations involving larger address and number ranges.

The Keyword `struct` and Its Differences from `class`

`struct` is a keyword from the days of C, and for all practical purposes, it is treated by a C++ compiler similarly to `class`. The exceptions are applicable to the access specifiers (`public` and `private`) when the programmer has not specified any. Unless specified, members in a `struct` are `public` by default (`private` for a class), and unless specified, a `struct` features `public` inheritance from a base `struct` (`private` for a class). Inheritance is discussed in detail in Lesson 10.

A `struct` form of the class `Human` from Listing 9.13 would be the following:

```
struct Human
{
private:
   int age;
   string gender;
   string name;

public:
   Human(const string& inputName, int inputAge, string inputGender)
      : name(inputName), age(inputAge), gender(inputGender) {}

   int GetAge()
   {
      return age;
   }
};
```

As you can see, `struct Human` is similar to `class Human`, and instantiation of an object of type `struct` would be similar to type `class` as well:

```
Human firstMan("Adam", 25, "man"); // an instance of struct Human
```

Declaring a `friend` of a `class`

A class does not permit external access to its data members and methods that are declared `private`. This rule is waived for classes and functions that are disclosed as friend classes or functions, using the keyword `friend`, as shown in Listing 9.14.

Input ▼

LISTING 9.14 Using the `friend` Keyword to Allow an External Function `DisplayAge()` Access to Private Data Members


```
#include<iostream>
#include<string>
using namespace std;

class Human
{
private:
    friend void DisplayAge(const Human& person);
    string name;
    int age;

public:
    Human(string humansName, int humansAge)
    {
       name = humansName;
       age = humansAge;
    }
};

void DisplayAge(const Human& person)
{
    cout << person.age << endl;
}

int main()
{
    Human firstMan("Adam", 25);
    cout << "Accessing private member age via friend function: ";
    DisplayAge(firstMan);

    return 0;
}
```

Output ▼

```
Accessing private member age via friend function: 25
```

Analysis ▼

Line 7 contains a declaration that indicates to the compiler that the function `DisplayAge()` in the global scope is a `friend` and therefore is permitted special access to the private members of the class `Human`. You can comment out Line 7 to see a compile failure at Line 21.

Like functions, external classes can also be designated as trusted friends, as Listing 9.15 demonstrates.

Input ▼

LISTING 9.15 Using the `friend` Keyword to Allow an External Class `Utility` Access to Private Data Members

```
#include<iostream>
#include<string>
using namespace std;

class Human
{
private:
    friend class Utility;
    string name;
    int age;

public:
    Human(string humansName, int humansAge)
    {
        name = humansName;
        age = humansAge;
    }
};

class Utility
{
public:
    static void DisplayAge(const Human& person)
    {
```

```
24:         cout << person.age << endl;
25:     }
26: };
27:
28: int main()
29: {
30:     Human firstMan("Adam", 25);
31:     cout << "Accessing private member age via friend class: ";
32:     Utility::DisplayAge(firstMan);
33:
34:     return 0;
35: }
```


Output ▼

```
Accessing private member age via friend class: 25
```

Analysis ▼

Line 7 indicates that the class `Utility` is a friend of the class `Human`. This `friend` declaration allows all methods in the class `Utility` access even to the private data members and methods in the class `Human`.

Union: A Special Data Storage Mechanism

A *union* is a special class type in which only one of the non-static data members is active at a time. Thus, a union can accommodate multiple data members, just like a class can, with the exception that only one of them can actually be used.

Declaring a Union

A union is declared using the keyword `union`, followed by the name of the union and its data members, within braces:

```
union UnionName
{
    Type1 member1;
    Type2 member2;
...
    TypeN memberN;
};
```

You could instantiate and use a union like this:

```
UnionName unionObject;
unionObject.member2 = value; // choose member2 as the active member
```

NOTE

> Similar to a `struct`, a union has members that are `public` by default. Unlike a `struct`, however, a union cannot be used in an inheritance hierarchy.
>
> In addition, the size of a union is always fixed at the size of the largest member contained in the union—even if that member is inactive in an instance of the union.

Where Would You Use a Union?

Often a union is used as a member of a `struct` to model a complex data type. In some implementations, the ability of a union to interpret the fixed memory space as another type is used for type conversions or memory reinterpretation—a practice that is controversial and not necessary, given alternatives.

Listing 9.16 demonstrates the declaration and use of unions.

Input ▼

LISTING 9.16 Declaration, Instantiation, and Size of Unions

```
#include<iostream>
using namespace std;

union SimpleUnion
{
   int num;
   char alphabet;
};

struct ComplexType
{
   enum class DataType
   {
      Int,
      Char
   } Type;
```

```

    union Value
    {
        int num;
        char alphabet;

        Value() {}
        ~Value() {}
    }value;
};

void DisplayComplexType(const ComplexType& obj)
{
    switch (obj.Type)
    {
    case ComplexType::DataType::Int:
        cout << "Union contains number: " << obj.value.num << endl;
        break;

    case ComplexType::DataType::Char:
        cout << "Union contains character: " << obj.value.alphabet << endl;
        break;
    }
}

int main()
{
    SimpleUnion u1, u2;
    u1.num = 2100;
    u2.alphabet = 'C';
    cout << "sizeof(u1) containing integer: " << sizeof(u1) << endl;
    cout << "sizeof(u2) containing character: " << sizeof(u2) << endl;

    ComplexType myData1, myData2;
    myData1.Type = ComplexType::DataType::Int;
    myData1.value.num = 2017;

    myData2.Type = ComplexType::DataType::Char;
    myData2.value.alphabet = 'X';

    DisplayComplexType(myData1);
    DisplayComplexType(myData2);

    return 0;
}
```

Output ▼

```
sizeof(u1) containing integer: 4
sizeof(u2) containing character: 4
Union contains number: 2017
Union contains character: X
```

Analysis ▼

The example demonstrates that `sizeof()` used with the union objects `u1` and `u2` returns the same amount of memory reserved for both objects, notwithstanding the fact that `u1` is used to hold an integer and `u2` a `char` (a `char` being smaller than an `int`). This is because the compiler reserves the amount of memory for a union that is consumed by the largest object it contains. `ComplexType`, defined in Lines 9 through 25, actually contains the enumeration `DataType` that is used to indicate the nature of the object stored in the union, in addition to the data member, which is a union called `Value`. This combination of a `struct` comprising an enumeration used to hold type information and a union used to hold value information is a popular application of the union. For example, the structure `VARIANT`, which is popularly used in Windows application programming, follows a similar approach. This combination is used by the function `DisplayComplexType()`, defined in Lines 27 through 39, which uses the enumeration in executing the right `case` in the supplied `switch-case` construct. For example, this union includes a constructor and a destructor; these are optional in Listing 9.16, given that the union contains plain old data types, but it may be required if a union is of another user-defined type, such as `class` or `struct`.

TIP

Unions give you the flexibility to store one among many permissible types. However, they do not stop you from accessing the contents of one type as another. That is, unions do not enforce type safety. C++17 introduced the ability to use a type-safe alternative to `union` called `std::variant`.

Using Aggregate Initialization on Classes and structs

The following initialization syntax is called an *aggregate initialization* syntax:

```
Type objectName = {argument1, ..., argumentN};
```

Alternatively, it can take this form:

```
Type objectName {argument1, ..., argumentN};
```


Aggregate initialization can be applied to an aggregate, and therefore it is important to understand what data types fall under this category.

You already saw examples of aggregate initialization in the initialization of arrays in Lesson 4, "Managing Arrays and Strings":

```
int myNums[] = { 9, 5, -1 }; // myNums is int[3]
char hello[6] = { 'h', 'e', 'l', 'l', 'o', ' \0' };
```

The term *aggregate*, however, is not limited to arrays of simple types like integers or characters but extends to classes (and therefore `structs` and unions), too. There are restrictions imposed by the standard on the specification of a `struct` or a `class` that can be called an aggregate. These restrictions can be nuanced, depending on the version of the C++ standard that you refer to. However, it can be safely said that `classes/structs` can be initialized as aggregates when they fulfill the following criteria: they do not contain a user-defined constructor; they comprise public and non-static data members; they do not contain private or protected data members; they do not contain virtual member functions; they do not use inheritance or only public inheritance (that is, no private, protected, or virtual inheritance).

TIP

> Inheritance is explained in detail in Lesson 10, "Implementing Inheritance," and Lesson 11, "Polymorphism."

Thus, the following `struct` fulfills the prerequisites of being an aggregate and, hence, can be initialized as one:

```
struct Aggregate1
{
   int num;
   double pi;
};
```

Initialization:

```
Aggregate1 a1{ 2017, 3.14 };
```

Another example:

```
struct Aggregate2
{
   int num;
   char hello[6];
   int impYears[5];
};
```

Initialization:

```
Aggregate2 a2 {42, {'h', 'e', 'l', 'l', 'o'}, {1998, 2003, 2011, 2014, 2017}};
```

Listing 9.17 demonstrates aggregate initialization applied to `classes` and `structs`.

Input ▼

LISTING 9.17 Aggregate Initialization on Class Type

```
#include<iostream>
#include<string>
using namespace std;

class Aggregate1
{
public:
    int num;
    double pi;
};

```

```
11: struct Aggregate2
12: {
13:     char hello[6];
14:     int impYears[3];
15:     string world;
16: };
17:
18: int main()
19: {
20:     int myNums[] = { 9, 5, -1 }; // myNums is int[3]
21:     Aggregate1 a1{ 2023, 3.14 };
22:     cout << "Pi is approximately: " << a1.pi << endl;
23:
24:     Aggregate2 a2{ {'h', 'e', 'l', 'l', 'o'}, {2017, 2020, 2023}, "world"};
25:
26:     // Alternatively
27:     Aggregate2 a2_2{'h', 'e', 'l', 'l', 'o', '\0', 2017, 2020, 2023, "world"};
28:
29:     cout << a2.hello << ' ' << a2.world << endl;
30:     cout << "C++ standard update scheduled in: " << a2.impYears[2] << endl;
31:
32:     return 0;
33: }
```


Output ▼

```
Pi is approximately: 3.14
hello world
C++ standard update scheduled in: 2023
```

Analysis ▼

The example demonstrates how you can use aggregate initialization in instantiating classes (or `structs`). `Aggregate1`, defined in Lines 4 through 9, is a class with public data members, and `Aggregate2`, defined in Lines 11 through 16, is a `struct`. Lines 21, 24, and 27 demonstrate aggregate initialization on the `class` and `struct`, respectively. Note how some members are an array and how a `std::string` member contained in `Aggregate2` has been initialized using this construct in Line 24.

CAUTION

> Aggregate initialization initializes only the first non-static member of a union. The aggregate initialization of the unions declared in Listing 9.16 would be
>
> ```
> 43:    SimpleUnion u1{ 2100 }, u2{ 'C' };
> // In u2, member num (type int) is initialized to 'C' (ASCII 67)
> // Although, you intended to initialize member alphabet (type char)
> ```
>
> Therefore, for the sake of clarity, it may be a good idea to avoid using aggregate initialization syntax on a union.

`constexpr` with Classes and Objects

You were introduced to `constexpr` in Lesson 3, where you learned that `constexpr` offers a powerful way to improve the performance of a C++ application. By marking functions that operate on constants or `const` expressions as `constexpr`, you instruct the compiler to evaluate those functions and insert their result instead of inserting instructions that compute the result when the application is executed. This keyword can also be used with classes and objects that evaluate as constants, as demonstrated in Listing 9.18. Note that the compiler ignores `constexpr` when a function or class is used with entities that are not constant.

Input ▼

LISTING 9.18 Using `constexpr` with the `Human` Class

```
#include<iostream>
using namespace std;

class Human
{
    int age;
public:
    constexpr Human(int humansAge):age(humansAge) {}
    constexpr int GetAge() const { return age; }
};

int main()
{
    constexpr Human somePerson(15);
```

```
14:     const int hisAge = somePerson.GetAge();
15:
16:     Human anotherPerson(45); // not constant expression
17:
18:     return 0;
19: }
```

Output ▼

The code snippet produces no output.

Analysis ▼

Note the slight modification in the class `Human` in Lines 3 through 9. It now uses `constexpr` in the declaration of its constructor and the member function `GetAge()`. This little addition tells the compiler to evaluate the creation and usage of instances of the class `Human` as a constant expression, where possible. `somePerson` in Line 13 is declared as a constant instance and used as one in Line 14. Therefore, this instance is likely to be evaluated by the compiler, and the code will be optimized for performance at execution. The instance `anotherPerson` in Line 16 is not declared to be a constant, and therefore its instantiation or usage may not be treated by the compiler as a constant expression.

Summary

This lesson taught you about one of the most fundamental concepts in C++: the class. You learned how a class encapsulates member data and member functions. You saw how access specifiers such as `public` and `private` help you abstract data and functionality that entities external to the class don't need to see. You learned the concept of copy constructors and the importance of using them to ensure a deep copy of dynamically allocated member data. You saw how move constructors help reduce unnecessary copy steps. You saw some special cases where all these elements come together to help you implement design patterns such as the singleton.

Q&A

Q What is the difference between an instance of a class and an object of that class?

A There is essentially no difference. When you instantiate a class, you get an instance that can also be called an object.

Q What is a better way to access members: using the dot operator (.) or using the pointer operator (->)?

A If you have a pointer to an object, the pointer operator is the best option. If you have instantiated an object as a local variable on the stack, the dot operator is the best option.

Q Should I always program a copy constructor?

A If your class's data members are well-programmed smart pointers, string classes, or STL containers such as `std::vector`, then the default copy constructor inserted by the compiler ensures that their respective copy constructors are invoked. However, if your class has raw pointer members (such as `int*` for a dynamic array instead of `std::vector<int>`), you need to supply a correctly programmed copy constructor that ensures a deep copy of an array during function calls where an object of the class is passed by value.

Q My class has only one constructor that has been defined with a parameter with a default value. Is this still a default constructor?

A Yes. If an instance of a class can be created without arguments, then the class is said to have a default constructor. A class can have only one default constructor.

Q Why do some code examples in this lesson use functions such as `SetAge()` to set the integer `Human::age`? Why not make `age` public and assign it as needed?

A From a technical viewpoint, making `Human::age` a `public` member would work as well. However, from a design point of view, keeping member data private is a good idea. Using accessor functions such as `GetAge()` and `SetAge()` is a refined and scalable way to access this private data, allowing you to perform error checks, for instance, before the value of `Human::age` is set or reset.

Q Why is the parameter of a copy constructor one that takes the copy source by reference?

A For one thing, the compiler expects the copy constructor to be that way. This is because a copy constructor would invoke itself if it accepted the copy source by value, which would result in an endless copy loop.

Q Are class and struct similar?

A In principle, yes, they are similar—with minor differences. When you don't specify the access qualifier (`private` or `public`) of a member, `class` assumes them to be `private` by default, whereas `struct` assumes them to be `public`. The same is true for `public` and `private` inheritances.

Workshop

The Workshop provides quiz questions to help you solidify your understanding of the material covered and exercises to provide you with experience in using what you've learned. Try to answer the quiz and exercise questions before checking the answers in Appendix E and be certain you understand the answers before continuing to the next lesson.

Quiz

1. When you create an instance of a class using `new`, where is the class created?
2. A class has a raw pointer `int*` that contains a dynamically allocated array of integers. Does `sizeof()` report different sizes, depending on the number of integers in the dynamic array?
3. All your class members are private, and your class does not contain any declared `friend` class or function. Who can access these members?
4. Can one class member method invoke another?
5. What is a constructor good for?
6. What is a destructor good for?

Exercises

1. **BUG BUSTERS:** What is wrong in the following class declaration?

```
Class Human
{
   int age;
   string name;

public:
   Human() {}
}
```

2. How would the user of the class in Exercise 1 access the member `Human::age`?
3. Write a better version of the class in Exercise 1 that initializes all parameters using an initialization list in the constructor.
4. Write a `Circle` class that computes the area and circumference, given a radius that is supplied to the class as a parameter at the time of instantiation. Pi should be contained in a constant private member that cannot be accessed from outside the circle.

LESSON 10
Implementing Inheritance

Object-oriented programming is based on four important concepts: encapsulation, abstraction, inheritance, and polymorphism. Inheritance is a powerful way to reuse attributes and is a stepping stone toward polymorphism.

In this lesson, you find out about

- Inheritance in the context of programming
- The C++ syntax of inheritance
- Public, private, and protected inheritance
- Multiple inheritance
- Problems caused by hiding base class methods and *slicing*

Basics of Inheritance

What Tom Smith inherits from his forefathers is first and foremost his family name that makes him a Smith. In addition, he inherits certain values that his parents have taught him and a skill at sculpting wood that has been the Smith family occupation for many generations. These attributes collectively identify Tom as a member of the Smith family tree.

In programming parlance, you are often faced with situations where components being managed have similar attributes, differing minutely in details or in behavior. One way to programmatically model this situation is by making every component a class, where each class implements all attributes and re-implements the common ones. Another solution is using inheritance to allow classes that are similar to derive from a base class that contains common attributes and implements common functionality. The derived classes overriding this base functionality implement behavior that makes each class unique; this is often the preferred way. Figure 10.1 illustrates inheritance in the world of object-oriented programming.

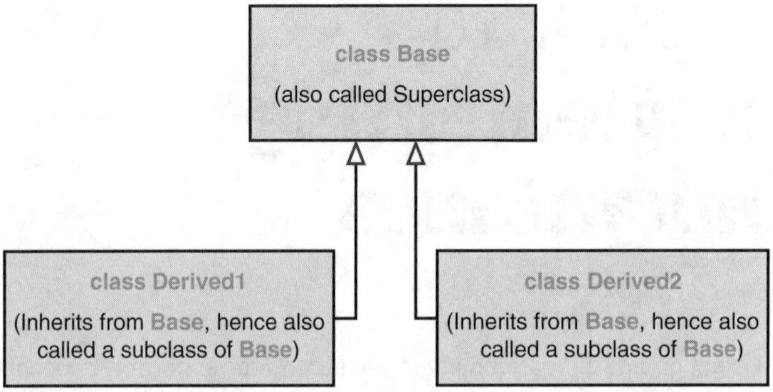

FIGURE 10.1
Inheritance between classes.

Inheritance and Derivation

Figure 10.1 shows a diagrammatic relationship between a base class and its derived classes. It might not be easy right now to visualize what a base class or a derived class could be. Try to understand that a derived class inherits from the base class and in that sense is a base class (just as Tom is a Smith).

> **NOTE** The "is-a" relationship between a derived class and its base class is applicable only to public inheritance. This lesson starts with public inheritance to help you understand the concept of inheritance using the most frequent form of inheritance before moving on to private or protected inheritance.

To make understanding this concept easy, think of a base class `Bird`. Classes derived from `Bird` include the classes `Crow`, `Parrot`, and `Kiwi`. A `Bird` class would define the most basic attributes of a bird, such as "is feathered," "has wings," "lays eggs," "can fly," and so on. Derived classes such as `Crow`, `Parrot`, and `Kiwi` inherit these attributes and customize them. (For example, a `Kiwi` class that represents a flightless bird would contain no implementation of `Fly()`.) Table 10.1 demonstrates a few more examples of inheritance.

TABLE 10.1 Examples of Public Inheritance Taken from Daily Life

Base Class	Examples of Derived Classes
`Fish`	`Goldfish`, `Carp`, `Tuna` (`Tuna` is a `Fish`)
`Mammal`	`Human`, `Elephant`, `Lion`, `Platypus` (`Platypus` is a `Mammal`)
`Bird`	`Crow`, `Parrot`, `Ostrich`, `Kiwi`, `Platypus` (`Platypus` is a `Bird`, too!)
`Shape`	`Circle`, `Polygon` (`Polygon` is a `Shape`)
`Polygon`	`Triangle`, `Octagon` (`Octagon` is a `Polygon`, which in turn is a `Shape`)

These examples show that when you put on your object-oriented programming glasses, you see examples of inheritance in many objects around you. `Fish` is a base class for a `Tuna` because a tuna, like a carp, is a fish. The `Fish` class presents all fish-like characteristics such as being cold-blooded. However, a tuna differs from carp in the way it looks and swims, as well as in the fact that it is a saltwater fish. Thus, `Tuna` and `Carp` inherit common characteristics from a common base class `Fish`, but they specialize the base class attributes to distinguish themselves from each other. This is illustrated in Figure 10.2.

FIGURE 10.2
Hierarchical relationship between `Tuna`, `Carp`, and `Fish`.

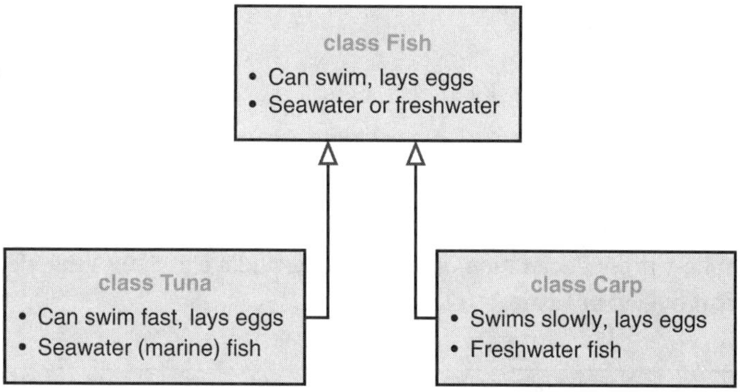

A platypus can swim, but it is a special animal with mammalian characteristics such as feeding its young with milk, avian (bird-like) characteristics such as laying eggs, and reptilian characteristics such as being venomous. Thus, you can imagine a class `Platypus` inheriting from two base classes, `Mammal` and `Bird`, to inherit mammalian and avian features. This form of inheritance is called *multiple inheritance*, and it is discussed later in this lesson.

C++ Syntax of Derivation

How would you inherit the class `Carp` from the class `Fish`, or, in general, a class `Derived` from a class `Base`? C++ syntax for doing this would be the following:

```
class Base
{
   // ... base class members
};

class Derived: access-specifier Base
{
   // ... derived class members
};
```

`access-specifier` can be `public` (most frequently used), where a "derived class is a base class" relationship; `private`; or `protected`, for a "derived class has a base class" relationship.

An inheritance hierarchical representation for a class `Carp` that derives from the class `Fish` would be

```
class Fish // base class
{
   // ... Fish's members
};

class Carp:public Fish // derived class
{
   // ... Carp's members
};
```

A compile-worthy declaration of a class `Carp` and a class `Tuna` that derive from the class `Fish` is provided in Listing 10.1.

A Note About Terminology

When reading about inheritance, you will come across terms such as *inherits from* and *derives from*, which essentially mean the same thing.

Similarly, the base class is also called the *superclass*. A class that derives from the base class, also known as a *derived class*, can be called a *subclass*.

Input ▼

LISTING 10.1 A Simple Inheritance Hierarchy Demonstrated Using the Piscean World

```
#include<iostream>
using namespace std;

class Fish
{
public:
   bool isFreshWaterFish;

   void Swim()
   {
      if (isFreshWaterFish)
         cout << "Swims in lake" << endl;
      else
         cout << "Swims in sea" << endl;
   }
};

class Tuna: public Fish
{
public:
   Tuna()
   {
      isFreshWaterFish = false;
   }
};

class Carp: public Fish
{
public:
   Carp()
   {
      isFreshWaterFish = true;
   }
};

int main()
{
   Carp myLunch;
   Tuna myDinner;

   cout << "About my food:" << endl;

   cout << "Lunch: ";
   myLunch.Swim();

```

```
45:     cout << "Dinner: ";
46:     myDinner.Swim();
47:
48:     return 0;
49: }
```

Output ▼

```
About my food:
Lunch: Swims in lake
Dinner: Swims in sea
```

Analysis ▼

Note Lines 37 and 38 in `main()`, which create instances of the classes `Carp` and `Tuna`, respectively, called `myLunch` and `myDinner`. Lines 43 and 46 are where you ask your lunch and dinner to swim by invoking the method `Swim()`. Now, look at the class definitions of `Tuna` in Lines 17 through 24 and `Carp` in Lines 26 through 33. As you can see, these classes are compact, with their constructors setting the Boolean flag in the base class `Fish::isFreshWaterFish` to the appropriate values. This flag is later used in the function `Fish::Swim()`. Neither of the two derived classes seems to define the method `Swim()` that you have managed to successfully invoke in `main()`. This is because `Swim()` is a public member of the base class `Fish` that the other classes inherit from, as defined in Lines 8 through 14. This public inheritance in Lines 17 and 26 automatically exposes the base class's public members, including the method `Swim()`, through instances of the derived classes `Carp` and `Tuna`, which you invoke in `main()`.

The Access Specifier Keyword `protected`

In Listing 10.1, the class `Fish` has a public attribute `isFreshWaterFish` that is set by the derived classes `Tuna` and `Carp` to customize (or *specialize*) the behavior of `Fish` and adapt it to saltwater and freshwater, respectively. However, Listing 10.1 exhibits a serious flaw: If you want, even `main()` could tamper with the Boolean flag `Fish::isFreshWaterFish`, which is public and hence open for manipulation from outside the class `Fish`:

```
myDinner.isFreshWaterFish = true; // but Tuna isn't a fresh water fish!
```

Apparently, you need a mechanism that allows derived class members to modify chosen attributes of the base class while denying access to these attributes for everyone else. This means that you want the Boolean flag `isFreshWaterFish` in the class `Fish` to be accessible to the classes `Tuna` and `Carp` but not accessible to `main()`, which instantiates the classes `Tuna` or `Carp`. This is where the keyword `protected` helps you.

NOTE

> `protected`, like `public` and `private`, is also an access specifier. When you declare a class attribute or function as `protected`, you are effectively making it accessible to classes that derive (and friends) from it and simultaneously making it inaccessible to everyone else outside the class, including `main()`.

`protected` is the access specifier you should use if you want a certain attribute in a base class to be accessible to classes that derive from this base class, as demonstrated in Listing 10.2.

Input ▼

LISTING 10.2 A Better `Fish` Class, Using the `protected` Keyword to Expose Its Member Attribute Only to the Derived Classes

```
#include<iostream>
using namespace std;

class Fish
{
protected:
   bool isFreshWaterFish; // accessible only to derived classes

public:
  void Swim()
   {
      if (isFreshWaterFish)
         cout << "Swims in lake" << endl;
      else
         cout << "Swims in sea" << endl;
   }
};

class Tuna: public Fish
{
public:
   Tuna()
   {
      isFreshWaterFish = false; // set protected member in base
   }
};

class Carp: public Fish
{
public:
   Carp()
```

```
31:     {
32:         isFreshWaterFish = true;
33:     }
34: };
35:
36: int main()
37: {
38:     Carp myLunch;
39:     Tuna myDinner;
40:
41:     cout << "About my food" << endl;
42:
43:     cout << "Lunch: ";
44:     myLunch.Swim();
45:
46:     cout << "Dinner: ";
47:     myDinner.Swim();
48:
49:     // uncomment line below to see that protected members
50:     // are not accessible from outside the class hierarchy
51:     // myLunch.isFreshWaterFish = false;
52:
53:     return 0;
54: }
```

Output ▼

```
About my food
Lunch: Swims in lake
Dinner: Swims in sea
```

Analysis ▼

Despite the fact that the output of Listing 10.2 is the same as the output of Listing 10.1, there are a good number of fundamental changes to the class `Fish`, as defined in Lines 3 through 16. The first and most important change is that the Boolean member `Fish::isFreshWaterFish` is now a `protected` attribute, and, hence, it is not accessible via `main()`, as shown in Line 51. (If you uncomment it, you get a compiler error.) All the same, this member of `Fish` with the access specifier `protected` is accessible from the derived classes `Tuna` and `Carp`, as shown in Lines 23 and 32, respectively. What this little program effectively demonstrates is the use of keyword `protected` in ensuring that base class attributes that need to be inherited are protected from being accessed outside the class hierarchy.

This is an important aspect of object-oriented programming. You can combine data abstraction and inheritance to ensure that derived classes can safely inherit base class attributes that cannot be tampered with by anyone outside the hierarchical system.

Base Class Initialization: Passing Parameters to the Base Class

What if a base class contains an overloaded constructor that requires arguments at the time of instantiation? How would such a base class be instantiated when the derived class is being constructed? The answer lies in using initialization lists and in invoking the appropriate base class constructor via the constructor of the derived class, as shown in the following code:

```
class Base
{
public:
   Base(int someNumber) // overloaded constructor
   {
      // Use someNumber
   }
};
Class Derived: public Base
{
public:
   Derived(): Base(25)  // instantiate Base with argument 25
   {
      // derived class constructor code
   }
};
```


This mechanism can be quite useful in the class `Fish`, where, by supplying a Boolean input parameter to the constructor of `Fish` that initializes `Fish::isFreshWaterFish`, this base class `Fish` can ensure that every derived class is forced to mention whether a fish is a freshwater one or a saltwater one, as shown in Listing 10.3.

Input ▼

LISTING 10.3 A Derived Class Constructor with Initialization Lists

```
#include<iostream>
using namespace std;

class Fish
{
protected:
   bool isFreshWaterFish; // accessible only to derived classes

```

```
public:
    // Fish constructor
    Fish(bool isFreshWater) : isFreshWaterFish(isFreshWater){}

    void Swim()
    {
        if (isFreshWaterFish)
            cout << "Swims in lake" << endl;
        else
            cout << "Swims in sea" << endl;
    }
};

class Tuna: public Fish
{
public:
    Tuna(): Fish(false) {} // constructor initializes base
};

class Carp: public Fish
{
public:
    Carp(): Fish(true) {}
};

int main()
{
    Carp myLunch;
    Tuna myDinner;

    cout << "About my food" << endl;

    cout << "Lunch: ";
    myLunch.Swim();

    cout << "Dinner: ";
    myDinner.Swim();

    return 0;
}
```

Output ▼

```
About my food
Lunch: Swims in lake
Dinner: Swims in sea
```

Analysis ▼

Fish now has a constructor that takes a default parameter that initializes Fish::isFreshWaterFish. Thus, the only way to create an object of Fish is by providing it a parameter that initializes the protected member. This way, the class Fish ensures that the protected member doesn't contain a random value, especially if a derived class forgets to set it. The derived classes Tuna and Carp are now forced to define a constructor that instantiates the base class instance of Fish with the right parameter (true or false, indicating freshwater or otherwise), as shown in Lines 24 and 30, respectively.

NOTE

> In Listing 10.3, you see that the Boolean member variable Fish::isFreshWaterFish was never accessed directly by a derived class, despite being a protected member, as this variable was set via the constructor of Fish.
>
> To ensure maximum security, if the derived classes don't need to access a base class attribute, remember to mark the attribute private. Therefore, a superior version of Listing 10.3 would feature Fish::isFreshWaterFish as private, for it is consumed only by the base class Fish. See Listing 10.4.

A Derived Class Overriding the Base Class's Methods

If the class Derived implements the same functions with the same return values and signatures as in the class Base from which it inherits, it effectively overrides that method in the class Base, as shown in the following code:

```
class Base
{
public:
   void DoSomething()
   {
      // implementation code... Does something
   }
};
class Derived:public Base
{
public:
   void DoSomething()
   {
      // implementation code... Does something else
   }
};
```

Thus, if the method `DoSomething()` were to be invoked using an instance of `Derived`, it would not invoke the functionality in the class `Base`.

If the classes `Tuna` and `Carp` were to implement their own `Swim()` method that also exists in the base class as `Fish::Swim()`, then a call to `Swim`, as shown in `main()` from the following excerpt from Listing 10.3 would result in the local implementation of `Tuna::Swim()` being invoked, which would essentially override the base class's `Fish::Swim()` method:

```
    Tuna myDinner;
// ...other lines
    myDinner.Swim();
```

This is demonstrated by Listing 10.4.

Input ▼

LISTING 10.4 The Derived Classes `Tuna` and `Carp` Overriding the Method `Swim()` in the Base Class `Fish`

```
#include<iostream>
using namespace std;

class Fish
{
private:
    bool isFreshWaterFish;

public:
    // Fish constructor
    Fish(bool isFreshWater) : isFreshWaterFish(isFreshWater){}

    void Swim()
    {
        if (isFreshWaterFish)
            cout << "Swims in lake" << endl;
        else
            cout << "Swims in sea" << endl;
    }
};

class Tuna: public Fish
{
public:
    Tuna(): Fish(false) {}

    void Swim()
    {
        cout << "Tuna swims real fast" << endl;
```

```
29:     }
30: };
31:
32: class Carp: public Fish
33: {
34: public:
35:     Carp(): Fish(true) {}
36:
37:     void Swim()
38:     {
39:         cout << "Carp swims real slow" << endl;
40:     }
41: };
42:
43: int main()
44: {
45:     Carp myLunch;
46:     Tuna myDinner;
47:
48:     cout << "About my food" << endl;
49:
50:     cout << "Lunch: ";
51:     myLunch.Swim();
52:
53:     cout << "Dinner: ";
54:     myDinner.Swim();
55:
56:     return 0;
57: }
```


Output ▼

```
About my food
Lunch: Carp swims real slow
Dinner: Tuna swims real fast
```

Analysis ▼

The output demonstrates that `myLunch.Swim()` in Line 51 invokes `Carp::Swim()`, defined in Lines 37 through 40. Similarly, `myDinner.Swim()` in Line 54 invokes `Tuna::Swim()`, defined in Lines 26 through 29. In other words, the implementation of `Fish::Swim()` in the base class `Fish`, as shown in Lines 12 through 18, is overridden by the identical function `Swim()`, which is defined by the classes `Tuna` and `Carp` that derive from `Fish`. The only way to invoke `Fish::Swim()` is by having `main()` use the *scope resolution operator* (`::`) in explicitly invoking `Fish::Swim()`, as shown later in this lesson.

Invoking Overridden Methods of a Base Class

In Listing 10.4, you saw an example of the derived class `Tuna` overriding the `Swim()` function in `Fish` by implementing its version of the function. Essentially:

```
Tuna myDinner;
myDinner.Swim(); // will invoke Tuna::Swim()
```

If you want to invoke `Fish::Swim()` in Listing 10.4 via `main()`, you need to use the scope resolution operator (::) in the following way:

```
myDinner.Fish::Swim(); // invokes Fish::Swim() using instance of Tuna
```

Listing 10.5 that follows shortly demonstrates the process of invoking a base class member using an instance of a derived class.

Invoking Methods of a Base Class in a Derived Class

Typically, `Fish::Swim()` would contain a generic implementation of swimming that is applicable to all fish—tuna and carp included. If your specialized implementations in `Tuna:Swim()` and `Carp::Swim()` need to reuse the base class's generic implementation of `Fish::Swim()`, you use the scope resolution operator (::), as shown in the following code:

```
class Carp: public Fish
{
public:
   Carp(): Fish(true) {}

   void Swim()
   {
      cout << "Carp swims real slow"
      Fish::Swim();  // invoke base class function using operator::
   }
};
```

This is demonstrated in Listing 10.5.

Input ▼

LISTING 10.5 Using the Scope Resolution Operator (`::`) to Invoke Base Class Functions from a Derived Class and `main()`

```
#include<iostream>
using namespace std;

class Fish
```

```
{
private:
   bool isFreshWaterFish;

public:
   // Fish constructor
   Fish(bool isFreshWater) : isFreshWaterFish(isFreshWater){}

   void Swim()
   {
      if (isFreshWaterFish)
         cout << "Swims in lake" << endl;
      else
         cout << "Swims in sea" << endl;
   }
};

class Tuna: public Fish
{
public:
   Tuna(): Fish(false) {}

   void Swim()
   {
      cout << "Tuna swims real fast" << endl;
   }
};

class Carp: public Fish
{
public:
   Carp(): Fish(true) {}

   void Swim()
   {
      cout << "Carp swims real slow" << endl;
      Fish::Swim();
   }
};

int main()
{
   Carp myLunch;
   Tuna myDinner;

   cout << "Getting my food to swim" << endl;

   cout << "Lunch: ";
   myLunch.Swim();

   cout << "Dinner: ";
```

```
55:     myDinner.Fish::Swim();
56:
57:     return 0;
58: }
```

Output ▼

```
Getting my food to swim
Lunch: Carp swims real slow
Swims in lake
Dinner: Swims in sea
```

Analysis ▼

`Carp::Swim()` in Lines 37 through 41 demonstrates calling the base class function `Fish::Swim()` using the scope resolution operator (`::`). Line 55, on the other hand, shows how you would use the scope resolution operator (`::`) to invoke the base class method `Fish::Swim()` from `main()`, given an instance of the derived class `Tuna`.

A Derived Class Hiding the Base Class's Methods

Overriding can take an extreme form where `Tuna::Swim()` can potentially hide all overloaded versions of `Fish::Swim()` that are available, even causing compilation failure when the overloaded versions are used; hence, this form is called *hidden*. See Listing 10.6.

Input ▼

LISTING 10.6 Using `Tuna::Swim()` to Hide the Overloaded Method `Fish::Swim(bool)`

```
0: #include<iostream>
1: using namespace std;
2:
3: class Fish
4: {
5: public:
6:     void Swim()
7:     {
8:         cout << "Fish swims... !" << endl;
9:     }
10:
11:     void Swim(bool isFreshWaterFish) // overloaded version
12:     {
13:         if (isFreshWaterFish)
14:             cout << "Swims in lake" << endl;
15:         else
16:             cout << "Swims in sea" << endl;
```

```
17:     }
18: };
19:
20: class Tuna: public Fish
21: {
22: public:
23:     void Swim()
24:     {
25:         cout << "Tuna swims real fast" << endl;
26:     }
27: };
28:
29: int main()
30: {
31:     Tuna myDinner;
32:
33:     cout << "About my food" << endl;
34:
35:     // myDinner.Swim(false);//failure: Tuna::Swim() hides Fish::Swim(bool)
36:     myDinner.Swim();
37:
38:     return 0;
39: }
```


Output ▼

```
About my food
Tuna swims real fast
```

Analysis ▼

This version of the class `Fish` is a bit different from the versions you have seen so far. Apart from being a minimal version to explain the problem at hand, this version of `Fish` contains two overloaded methods for `Swim()`: one that takes no parameters, shown in Lines 6 through 9, and another that takes a `bool` parameter, shown in Lines 11 through 17. As `Tuna` inherits `public` from `Fish`, as shown in Line 20, you would not be wrong to expect that both versions of the method `Fish::Swim()` would be available via an instance of the class `Tuna`. The fact is, however, that `Tuna` implementing its own `Tuna::Swim()`, as shown in Lines 23 through 26, results in the hiding of `Fish::Swim(bool)` from the compiler. If you uncomment Line 35, you get a compilation failure.

So, if you want to invoke the `Fish::Swim(bool)` function via an instance of `Tuna`, you can use any of the following solutions:

- Solution 1: Use the scope resolution operator in `main()`:
  `myDinner.Fish::Swim();`

- Solution 2: Use the keyword `using` in the class `Tuna` to unhide `Swim()` in the class `Fish`:

```
class Tuna: public Fish
{
public:
   using Fish::Swim;    // unhide all Swim() methods in class Fish

   void Swim()
   {
      cout << "Tuna swims real fast" << endl;
   }
};
```

- Solution 3: Override all overloaded variants of `Swim()` in the class `Tuna` (such as by invoking methods of `Fish::Swim(...)` via `Tuna::Fish(...)`):

```
class Tuna: public Fish
{
public:
   void Swim(bool isFreshWaterFish)
   {
      Fish::Swim(isFreshWaterFish);
   }

   void Swim()
   {
      cout << "Tuna swims real fast" << endl;
   }
};
```

Order of Construction

When you create an object of the class `Tuna` that derives from the class `Fish`, is the constructor of `Tuna` invoked before or after the constructor of the class `Fish`? In addition, during the instantiation of objects in the class hierarchy, what is the order of member attributes such as `Fish::isFreshWaterFish`? Thankfully, the instantiation sequence is standardized. Base class objects are instantiated before the derived class. So, the `Fish` part of `Tuna` is constructed first so that member attributes—especially the protected and public ones contained in the class `Fish`—are ready for consumption when the class `Tuna` is instantiated. Within the instantiation of the classes `Fish` and `Tuna`, the member attributes (such as `Fish::isFreshWaterFish`) are instantiated before the constructor `Fish::Fish()` is invoked, ensuring that member attributes are ready before the constructor works with them. The same applies to `Tuna::Tuna()`.

Order of Destruction

When an instance of `Tuna` goes out of scope, the sequence of destruction is the opposite of the sequence of construction. The destructor of the derived class `Tuna::~Tuna()` is invoked first, followed by the destructor of the base class `Fish::~Fish()`. Listing 10.7 is a simple example that demonstrates the order of construction and the order of destruction.

Input ▼

LISTING 10.7 The Order of Construction and the Order of Destruction of the Base Class and Derived Class and Their Members

```
#include<iostream>
using namespace std;

class FishDummyMember
{
public:
    FishDummyMember()
    {
        cout << "FishDummyMember constructor" << endl;
    }

    ~FishDummyMember()
    {
        cout << "FishDummyMember destructor" << endl;
    }
};

class Fish
{
protected:
    FishDummyMember dummy;

public:
    // Fish constructor
    Fish()
    {
        cout << "Fish constructor" << endl;
    }

    ~Fish()
    {
        cout << "Fish destructor" << endl;
    }
};

class TunaDummyMember
{
```

```
public:
    TunaDummyMember()
    {
        cout << "TunaDummyMember constructor" << endl;
    }

    ~TunaDummyMember()
    {
        cout << "TunaDummyMember destructor" << endl;
    }
};

class Tuna: public Fish
{
private:
    TunaDummyMember dummy;

public:
    Tuna()
    {
        cout << "Tuna constructor" << endl;
    }
    ~Tuna()
    {
        cout << "Tuna destructor" << endl;
    }

};

int main()
{
    Tuna myDinner;
}
```

Output ▼

```
FishDummyMember constructor
Fish constructor
TunaDummyMember constructor
Tuna constructor
Tuna destructor
TunaDummyMember destructor
Fish destructor
FishDummyMember destructor
```

Analysis ▼

main() in Lines 66 through 69 is pretty short given the volume of output it generates. Instantiation of the class Tuna is enough to generate these lines of output because of the cout statements inserted into the constructors and destructors of all the classes involved. For the sake of understanding how member variables are instantiated and destroyed, you defined two dummy classes, FishDummyMember and TunaDummyMember, with cout in their constructors and destructors. The classes Fish and Tuna each contain a member of each of these dummy classes, as shown in Lines 20 and 52. The output indicates that when an object of the class Tuna is instantiated, instantiation actually starts at the top of the hierarchy. So, the base class Fish part of the class Tuna is instantiated first, and in the process, the members of the class Fish—that is, Fish::dummy—are instantiated first. This is then followed by the constructor of the class Fish, which is rightfully executed after the member attributes such as dummy have been constructed. After the base class has been constructed, the instantiation of Tuna continues first with instantiation of the member Tuna::dummy, followed by the execution of the constructor code in Tuna::Tuna(). The output demonstrates that the sequence of destruction is exactly the reverse.

Private Inheritance

Private inheritance differs from public inheritance (which is what you have seen up until now) in that the keyword private is used in the line where the derived class declares its inheritance from a base class:

```
class Base
{
   // ... base class members and methods
};

class Derived: private Base     // private inheritance
{
   // ... derived class members and methods
};
```

Private inheritance of the base class means that all public members and attributes of the base class are private (that is, inaccessible) to anyone with an instance of the derived class. In other words, even public members and methods of the class Base can only be consumed by the class Derived but not by anyone else in possession of an instance of Derived.

This is in sharp contrast to the examples with Tuna and the base class Fish that you have been following since Listing 10.1. main() in Listing 10.1 could invoke the function

Fish::Swim() on an instance of Tuna because Fish::Swim() is a public method and because the class Tuna derives from the class Fish using public inheritance.

Thus, for the world outside the inheritance hierarchy, private inheritance essentially does not imply an is-a relationship. As private inheritance allows base class attributes and methods to be consumed only by the subclass that derives from the base class, this relationship is also called a "has-a" relationship. Table 10.2 lists a few examples of private inheritance in some things you see around you in daily life.

TABLE 10.2 Examples of Private Inheritance Taken from Daily Life

Base Class	Examples of Derived Classes
Motor	Car (Car has a Motor)
Heart	Mammal (Mammal has a Heart)
Bulb	Lamp (Lamp has a Bulb)

Listing 10.8 demonstrates private inheritance in a car's relationship to its motor.

Input ▼

LISTING 10.8 A Car Class Related to the Motor Class via Private Inheritance

```
#include<iostream>
using namespace std;

class Motor
{
public:
    void SwitchIgnition()
    {
        cout << "Ignition ON" << endl;
    }
    void PumpFuel()
    {
        cout << "Fuel in cylinders" << endl;
    }
    void FireCylinders()
    {
        cout << "Vroooom" << endl;
    }
};

```

```
20: class Car:private Motor // private inheritance
21: {
22: public:
23:     void Move()
24:     {
25:         SwitchIgnition();
26:         PumpFuel();
27:         FireCylinders();
28:     }
29: };
30:
31: int main()
32: {
33:     Car myDreamCar;
34:     myDreamCar.Move();
35:
36:     return 0;
37: }
```


Output ▼

```
Ignition ON
Fuel in cylinders
Vroooom
```

Analysis ▼

The class `Motor`, defined in Lines 3 through 18, is simple; it has three public member functions that switch ignition, pump fuel, and fire the cylinders. The class `Car`, as Line 20 demonstrates, inherits from `Motor`, using the keyword `private`. Thus, the public function `Car::Move()` invokes members from the base class `Motor`. If you try inserting the following in `main()`:

```
myDreamCar.PumpFuel(); // cannot access base's public member
```

it fails compilation with an error similar to error `C2247: Motor::PumpFuel not accessible because 'Car' uses 'private' to inherit from 'Motor'`.

NOTE

> If another class, RaceCar, had to inherit from Car, then regardless of the nature of inheritance between RaceCar and Car, RaceCar would not have access to any public member or function of the base class Motor. This is because the relationship between Car and Motor is one of private inheritance, meaning that all entities other than Car have private access (that is, no access) to public and protected members of Base when using an instance of Car.
>
> In other words, the most restrictive access specifier is dominant in the compiler's calculation of whether one class should have access to a base class's public or protected members.

Protected Inheritance

Protected inheritance differs from public inheritance in that the keyword `protected` is used in the line where the derived class declares its inheritance from a base class:

```
class Base
{
   // ... base class members and methods
};

class Derived: protected Base      // protected inheritance
{
   // ... derived class members and methods
};
```

Protected inheritance is similar to private inheritance in the following ways:

- It also signifies a has-a relationship.
- It also lets the derived class access all public and protected members of `Base`.
- Those outside the inheritance hierarchy with an instance of `Derived` cannot access public members of `Base`.

However, protected inheritance is a bit different when it comes to the derived class being inherited from:

```
class Derived2: protected Derived
{
   // can access public & protected members of Base
};
```

The protected inheritance hierarchy allows the subclass of the subclass (that is, `Derived2`) access to public and protected members of the `Base` class, as shown in

Listing 10.9. This would not be possible if the inheritance between `Derived` and `Base` were private.

Input ▼

LISTING 10.9 The `RaceCar` Class, Which Derives from the `Car` Class, Which Derives from the `Motor` Class, Using Protected Inheritance

```
#include<iostream>
using namespace std;

class Motor
{
public:
   void SwitchIgnition()
   {
      cout << "Ignition ON" << endl;
   }
   void PumpFuel()
   {
      cout << "Fuel in cylinders" << endl;
   }
   void FireCylinders()
   {
      cout << "Vroooom" << endl;
   }
};

class Car:protected Motor
{
public:
   void Move()
   {
      SwitchIgnition();
      PumpFuel();
      FireCylinders();
   }
};

class RaceCar:protected Car
{
public:
   void Move()
   {
      SwitchIgnition();  // RaceCar has access to members of
      PumpFuel();  // base Motor due to "protected" inheritance
      FireCylinders(); // between RaceCar & Car, Car & Motor
      FireCylinders();
      FireCylinders();
   }
};
```

```
43:
44: int main()
45: {
46:     RaceCar myDreamCar;
47:     myDreamCar.Move();
48:
49:     return 0;
50: }
```

Output ▼

```
Ignition ON
Fuel in cylinders
Vroooom
Vroooom
Vroooom
```

Analysis ▼

The class `Car` inherits using `protected` from `Motor`, as shown in Line 20. The class `RaceCar` inherits using `protected` from the class `Car` using `protected`, as shown in Line 31. As you can see, the implementation of `RaceCar::Move()` uses public methods defined in the base class `Motor`. This access to the ultimate base class `Motor` via intermediate base class `Car` is governed by the relationship between `Car` and `Motor`. If this were private instead of protected, `RaceCar` would have no access to the public members of `Motor` as the compiler would choose the most restrictive of the relevant access specifiers. Note that the nature of the relationship between the classes `Car` and `RaceCar` plays no role in access to the base class `Motor`, while the relationship between `Car` and `Motor` does. So, even if you change `protected` in Line 31 to `public` or to `private`, the fate of compilation of this program would remain unchanged.

CAUTION

Use private or protected inheritance only when you have to. In most cases where private inheritance is used, such as with `Car` and `Motor`, good alternatives exist. In this case, `Motor` could have been a member attribute of the class `Car` instead of being a superclass. By having it inherit from the class `Motor`, you have essentially restricted `Car` to having only one motor—for no significant gain over having an instance of the class `Motor` as a private member.

Cars have evolved, and a hybrid car, for instance, has an electric motor in addition to a conventional one. Our inheritance hierarchy for the class `Car` would be a bottleneck when used with such developments.

NOTE

Having an instance of `Motor` as a private member instead of inheriting from it is called *composition* or *aggregation*. The class `Car` might look like this:

```
class Car
{
private:
    Motor heartOfCar;  // private member

public:
    void Move()
    {
        heartOfCar.SwitchIgnition();
        heartOfCar.PumpFuel();
        heartOfCar.FireCylinders();
    }
};
```

This can be good design as it enables you to easily add more motors as member attributes to an existing `Car` class without changing its inheritance hierarchy or its design.

The Problem of Slicing

What happens when a programmer does the following?

```
Derived objDerived;
Base objectBase = objDerived;
```

Or, alternatively, what if a programmer does this?

```
void UseBase(Base input);
...
Derived objDerived;
UseBase(objDerived);  // copy of objDerived will be sliced and sent
```

In both cases, an object of type `Derived` is being copied into another object of type `Base`, either explicitly via assignment or by being passed as an argument. What happens in these cases is that the compiler copies only the `Base` part of `objDerived`—and not the complete object. The information contained by the data members belonging to `Derived` is lost in the process. This is not anticipated, and this unwanted reduction of that part of data that makes `Derived` a specialization of `Base` is called *slicing*.

CAUTION

> To avoid slicing problems, don't pass parameters by value. Pass them as pointers to the base class or as a reference (optionally using `const`) to the base class.

Multiple Inheritance

Earlier in this lesson, you learned that in certain cases, multiple inheritance might be relevant, such as with a platypus. A platypus is part mammal, part bird, and part reptile. For such cases, C++ allows a class to derive from two or more base classes:

```
class Derived: access-specifier Base1, access-specifier Base2
{
   // class members
};
```

The class diagram for the `Platypus` class, as illustrated by Figure 10.3, looks different from the diagram for `Tuna` and `Carp` (refer to Figure 10.2).

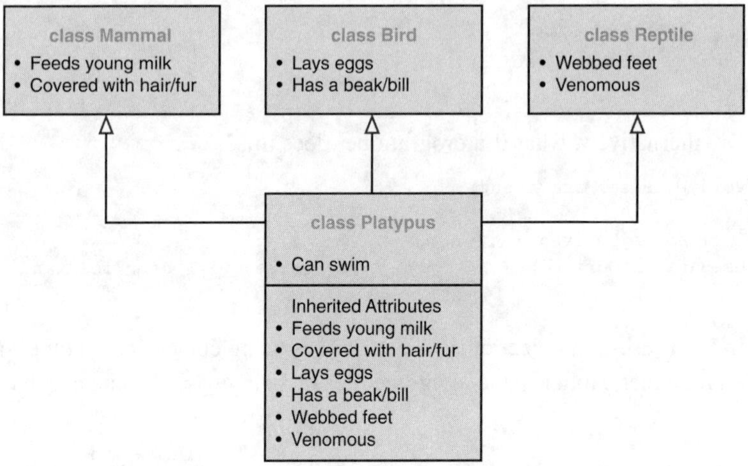

FIGURE 10.3
Relationship of the class `Platypus` to the classes `Mammal`, `Reptile`, and `Bird`.

Thus, the C++ representation of the class `Platypus` is as follows:

```
class Platypus: public Mammal, public Reptile, public Bird
{
   // ... platypus members
};
```

Listing 10.10 uses the `Platypus` class to demonstrate multiple inheritance.

Input ▼

LISTING 10.10 Using Multiple Inheritance to Model a Platypus That Is Part Mammal, Part Bird, and Part Reptile

```
#include<iostream>
using namespace std;

class Mammal
{
public:
    void FeedBabyMilk()
    {
        cout << "Mammal: Baby says glug!" << endl;
    }
};

class Reptile
{
public:
    void SpitVenom()
    {
        cout << "Reptile: Shoo enemy! Spits venom!" << endl;
    }
};

class Bird
{
public:
    void LayEggs()
    {
        cout << "Bird: Laid my eggs, am lighter now!" << endl;
    }
};

class Platypus: public Mammal, public Bird, public Reptile
{
public:
    void Swim()
```

```
34:     {
35:         cout << "Platypus: Voila, I can swim!" << endl;
36:     }
37: };
38:
39: int main()
40: {
41:     Platypus realFreak;
42:     realFreak.LayEggs();
43:     realFreak.FeedBabyMilk();
44:     realFreak.SpitVenom();
45:     realFreak.Swim();
46:
47:     return 0;
48: }
```

Output ▼

```
Bird: Laid my eggs, am lighter now!
Mammal: Baby says glug!
Reptile: Shoo enemy! Spits venom!
Platypus: Voila, I can swim!
```

Analysis ▼

Lines 30 through 37 provide a really compact definition of the class `Platypus`. This class essentially does nothing more than inherit from the three classes: `Mammal`, `Reptile`, and `Bird`. `main()` in Lines 41 through 44 is able to invoke these three characteristics of the individual base classes using an object of the derived class `Platypus` that is named `realFreak`. In addition to invoking the functions inherited from the classes `Mammal`, `Bird`, and `Reptile`, `main()` in Line 45 invokes `Platypus::Swim()`. This program demonstrates the syntax of multiple inheritance and also how a derived class exposes all the public attributes (in this case public member functions) of its many base classes.

Avoiding Inheritance Using `final`

There are instances when you need to ensure that absolutely no class can inherit from a class; that is, you want to be sure a particular class cannot be used as a base class. The specifier `final`, introduced with C++11, helps you do exactly this. A class declared as `final` cannot be used as a base class. In Listing 10.10, for instance, the class `Platypus` represents a well-evolved species. You may therefore want to ensure that this class is `final`, thereby blocking every possibility to inherit from it. A version of the class `Platypus` taken from Listing 10.10 and declared as `final` would look like this:

```
class Platypus final: public Mammal, public Bird, public Reptile
{
public:
   void Swim()
   {
      cout << "Platypus: Voila, I can swim!" << endl;
   }
};
```


In addition to being used with classes, `final` can also be used on member functions to control polymorphic behavior. This is discussed in Lesson 11, "Polymorphism."

NOTE

Although a platypus can swim, in Listing 10.10, you still did not inherit `Platypus` from `Fish`. This is because a platypus isn't a fish! That listing does not use inheritance for the convenience of reusing an existing `Fish::Swim()` function because that would be poor design. Public inheritance should signify an is-a relationship. It should not be used indiscriminately for the purpose of fulfilling goals related to code reuse. Those goals can still be achieved differently.

DO	DON'T
DO use a public inheritance hierarchy to establish an is-a relationship.	**DON'T** create an inheritance hierarchy just to reuse a trivial function.
DO use a private or protected inheritance hierarchy to establish a has-a relationship—but only after evaluating other design options.	**DON'T** use inheritance indiscriminately. Doing so can cause architectural bottlenecks that restrict the scalability of your application.
DO remember that private members in the base class cannot be accessed by any class deriving from it, notwithstanding the nature of the inheritance.	**DON'T** program derived class functions that hide those in the base class by having the same name but a different set of input parameters.
DO remember that public inheritance means that classes deriving from the derived class have access to the public and protected members of the base class. An object of the derived class can be used to access public members of the base class.	**DON'T** pass objects of a class as arguments to functions by value; instead, use references to avoid slicing errors.
DO remember that private inheritance means that even classes deriving from the derived class have no access to any member of the base class.	
DO remember that protected inheritance means that classes deriving from the derived class have access to the public and protected methods of the base class. However, an object of the derived class cannot be used to access public members of the base class.	

Summary

In this lesson, you learned the basics of inheritance in C++. You learned that public inheritance is an is-a relationship between the derived class and the base class, whereas private and protected inheritances create has-a relationships. You saw the application of the access specifier `protected` in exposing attributes of a base class only to the derived class but keeping them hidden from classes outside the inheritance hierarchy. You learned that protected inheritance differs from private in that the derived classes of the derived class can access public and protected members of the base class, which is not possible in private inheritance. You learned the basics of overriding methods and hiding them and how to avoid unwanted method hiding via the `using` keyword. Last but not the least, you became familiar with the specifier `final`, which ensures that a class cannot be derived from.

You are now ready to answer some questions and then continue to learning about the next major pillar of object-oriented programming: polymorphism.

Q&A

Q I have been asked to model the class `Mammal` along with classes for a few mammals, such as `Human`, `Lion`, and `Whale`. Should I use an inheritance hierarchy? If so, which one should I use?

A Because Human, Lion, and Whale are all mammals and essentially fulfill an is-a (mammal) relationship, you should use public inheritance where the class `Mammal` is the base class and classes such as `Human`, `Lion`, and `Whale` inherit from it.

Q What is the difference between the terms *derived class* and *subclass*?

A There is essentially no difference here. These terms are both used to refer to a class that derives from—that is, specializes—a base class.

Q A derived class uses public inheritance in relating to its base class. Can it access the base class's private members?

A No. Private member attributes and functions cannot be accessed outside the class—not even by a derived class. The compiler always ensures that the most restrictive of the applicable access specifiers is in force. An exception to this rule applies to classes and functions that have been declared as `friends`.

Workshop

The Workshop provides quiz questions to help you solidify your understanding of the material that was covered and exercises to provide you with experience in using what you've learned. Try to answer the quiz and exercise questions before checking the answers in Appendix E and be certain you understand the answers before continuing to the next lesson.

Quiz

1. You want some base class members to be accessible to the derived class but not outside the class hierarchy. What access specifier do you use?
2. If you pass an object of a derived class as an argument to a function that takes a parameter of the base class by value, what happens?
3. Which should you favor: private inheritance or composition?
4. How does the `using` keyword help you in an inheritance hierarchy?
5. The class `Derived` inherits `private` from the class `Base`. Another class, `SubDerived`, inherits `public` from the class `Derived`. Can `SubDerived` access public members of the class `Base`?

Exercises

1. In what order are the constructors invoked for the class `Platypus`, as shown in Listing 10.10?
2. Show how the classes `Polygon`, `Triangle`, and `Shape` are related to each other.
3. The class `D2` inherits from the class `D1`, which inherits from the class `Base`. To keep D2 from accessing the public members in Base, what access specifier would you use, and where would you use it?
4. What is the nature of inheritance with this code snippet? Would your answer be different if `Derived` were a `struct` instead?

```
class Derived: Base
{
    // ... Derived members
};
```

5. **BUG BUSTERS:** What is the problem in this code?

```
class Derived: public Base
{
    // ... Derived members
};
void SomeFunc (Base value)
{
    // ...
}
```

LESSON 11
Polymorphism

Having learned the basics of inheritance, creating an inheritance hierarchy, and understanding that public inheritance essentially models an is-a relationship, it's time to move on to consuming this knowledge in learning the holy grail of object-oriented programming: polymorphism.

In this lesson, you find out

- What polymorphism actually means
- What virtual functions do and how to use them
- What abstract base classes are and how to declare them
- What virtual inheritance means and where you need it

Basics of Polymorphism

"Poly" is Greek for *many*, and "morph" means *form*. Polymorphism is a feature of object-oriented languages that allows objects of different types to be treated similarly. This lesson focuses on polymorphic behavior that can be implemented in C++ via the inheritance hierarchy, also known as *subtype polymorphism*.

Need for Polymorphic Behavior

In Lesson 10, "Implementing Inheritance," you found out how `Tuna` and `Carp` inherit the public method `Swim()` from `Fish`, as shown in Listing 10.1. It is, however, possible that both `Tuna` and `Carp` provide their own `Tuna::Swim()` and `Carp::Swim()` methods to make `Tuna` and `Carp` different swimmers. However, as each of them is also a `Fish`, if a user with an instance of `Tuna` uses the base class type to invoke `Fish::Swim()`, he ends up executing only the generic part `Fish::Swim()` and not `Tuna::Swim()`, even though that base class instance `Fish` is a part of an instance of `Tuna`. This problem is demonstrated in Listing 11.1.

NOTE

All the code samples in this lesson have been stripped to the bare essentials required to explain the topic in question and to keep the number of lines of code to a minimum to improve readability.

When you are programming, you should program your classes correctly and create inheritance hierarchies that make sense, keeping the design and purpose of the application in perspective.

Input ▼

LISTING 11.1 Invoking Methods Using an Instance of the Base Class `Fish` That Belongs to `Tuna`

```
#include<iostream>
using namespace std;

class Fish
{
public:
    void Swim()
    {
        cout << "Fish swims! " << endl;
    }
};

class Tuna:public Fish
{
public:
    // override Fish::Swim
    void Swim()
    {
        cout << "Tuna swims!" << endl;
    }
};

void MakeFishSwim(Fish& inputFish)
{
    // calling Fish::Swim
    inputFish.Swim();
}

int main()
{
    Tuna myDinner;

    // calling Tuna::Swim
    myDinner.Swim();
```

```
34:
35:     // sending Tuna as Fish
36:     MakeFishSwim(myDinner);
37:
38:     return 0;
39: }
```

Output ▼

```
Tuna swims!
Fish swims!
```

Analysis ▼

The class `Tuna` specializes the class `Fish` via public inheritance, as shown in Line 12. It also overrides `Fish::Swim()`. `main()` makes a direct call to `Tuna::Swim()` in Line 33 and passes `myDinner` (of type `Tuna`) as a parameter to `MakeFishSwim()`, which interprets it as a reference `Fish&`, as shown in the declaration in Line 22. In other words, `MakeFishSwim(Fish&)` doesn't care if the object sent was a `Tuna`, handles it as a `Fish`, and invokes `Fish::Swim()`. So, the second line of output indicates that the same object `Tuna` produced the output of a `Fish`, not indicating any specialization thereof (and could as well be a `Carp`).

What the user would ideally expect is that an object of type `Tuna` behaves like a tuna even if the method invoked is `Fish::Swim()`. In other words, when `inputFish.Swim()` is invoked in Line 25, the user expects it to execute `Tuna::Swim()`. Such polymorphic behavior where an object of base class `Fish` can behave as its actual type; that is, derived class `Tuna` can be implemented by making `Fish::Swim()` a *virtual function.*

Polymorphic Behavior Implemented Using Virtual Functions

You have access to an object of type `Fish`, via pointer `Fish*` or reference `Fish&`. This object could have been instantiated solely as a `Fish`, or it could be part of a `Tuna` or `Carp` that inherits from `Fish`. You don't know (and don't care). You invoke the method `Swim()` using this pointer or reference, like this:

```
pFish->Swim();
myFish.Swim();
```

What you expect is that the object `Fish` swims as a `Tuna` if it is part of a `Tuna`, as a `Carp` if it is part of a `Carp`, or as an anonymous `Fish` if it wasn't instantiated as part of a specialized class such as `Tuna` or `Carp`. You can ensure this by declaring the function `Swim()` in the base class `Fish` as a virtual function:

```
class Base
{
   virtual ReturnType FunctionName (Parameter List);
};
class Derived: public Base
{
   ReturnType FunctionName (Parameter List);
};
```

Use of the keyword `virtual` means that the compiler ensures that any overriding variant of the requested base class method is invoked. Thus, if `Swim()` is declared `virtual`, invoking `myFish.Swim()` (`myFish` being of type `Fish&`) results in `Tuna::Swim()` being executed, as demonstrated in Listing 11.2.

Input ▼

LISTING 11.2 The Effect of Declaring `Fish::Swim()` as a `virtual` Method

```
#include<iostream>
using namespace std;

class Fish
{
public:
    virtual void Swim()
    {
        cout << "Fish swims!" << endl;
    }
};

class Tuna:public Fish
{
public:
    // override Fish::Swim
    void Swim()
    {
        cout << "Tuna swims!" << endl;
    }
};

class Carp:public Fish
{
public:
```

```
    // override Fish::Swim
    void Swim()
    {
        cout << "Carp swims!" << endl;
    }
};

void MakeFishSwim(Fish& inputFish)
{
    // calling virtual method Swim()
    inputFish.Swim();
}

int main()
{
    Tuna myDinner;
    Carp myLunch;

    // sending Tuna as Fish
    MakeFishSwim(myDinner);

    // sending Carp as Fish
    MakeFishSwim(myLunch);

    return 0;
}
```


Output ▼

```
Tuna swims!
Carp swims!
```

Analysis ▼

The implementation of the function `MakeFishSwim(Fish&)` has not changed one bit since Listing 11.1. However, the output it produces is dramatically different. For one thing, `Fish::Swim()` has not been invoked at all because of the presence of overriding variants `Tuna::Swim()` and `Carp::Swim()` that have taken priority over `Fish::Swim()` because the latter has been declared as a `virtual` function. This is a very important development. It implies that even without knowing the exact type of `Fish` being handled, the implementation `MakeFishSwim()` could result in different implementations of `Swim()` defined in different derived classes being invoked, given only a base class instance.

This is polymorphism: treating different fishes as a common type `Fish` but ensuring that the right implementation of `Swim()` supplied by the derived types is executed.

Need for Virtual Destructors

There is a more sinister side to the feature demonstrated by Listing 11.1: unintentionally invoking base class functionality of an instance of type derived, when a specialization is available. What happens when a function calls the operator `delete` using a pointer of type `Base*` that actually points to an instance of type `Derived`?

Which destructor would be invoked? See Listing 11.3.

Input ▼

LISTING 11.3 A Function That Invokes the Operator `delete` on `Base*`

```
#include<iostream>
using namespace std;

class Fish
{
public:
    Fish()
    {
        cout << "Constructed Fish" << endl;
    }
    ~Fish()
    {
        cout << "Destroyed Fish" << endl;
    }
};

class Tuna:public Fish
{
public:
    Tuna()
    {
        cout << "Constructed Tuna" << endl;
    }
    ~Tuna()
    {
        cout << "Destroyed Tuna" << endl;
    }
};

void DeleteFish(Fish* pFish)
{
    delete pFish;
}

```

```
34: int main()
35: {
36:     cout << "Allocating a Tuna on the free store:" << endl;
37:     Tuna* pTuna = new Tuna;
38:     cout << "Deleting the Tuna: " << endl;
39:     DeleteFish(pTuna);
40:
41:     cout << "Instantiating a Tuna on the stack:" << endl;
42:     Tuna myDinner;
43:     cout << "Automatic destruction as it goes out of scope: \n";
44:
45:     return 0;
46: }
```

Output ▼

```
Allocating a Tuna on the free store:
Constructed Fish
Constructed Tuna
Deleting the Tuna:
Destroyed Fish
Instantiating a Tuna on the stack:
Constructed Fish
Constructed Tuna
Automatic destruction as it goes out of scope:
Destroyed Tuna
Destroyed Fish
```


Analysis ▼

`main()` creates an instance of `Tuna` on the free store, using `new` at Line 37, and then releases the allocated memory by using the service function `DeleteFish()` in Line 39. For the sake of comparison, another instance of `Tuna` is created as a local variable `myDinner` on the stack in Line 42 and goes out of scope when `main()` ends. The output is created by the `cout` statements in the constructors and destructors of classes `Fish` and `Tuna`. Note that while `Tuna` and therefore `Fish` were both constructed on the free store because of the operator `new` in Line 37, the destruction of allocated memory by `DeleteFish()` in Line 39 was partial. Destructor of `Tuna` was not invoked during `delete`; rather, only the destruction of `Fish` was invoked. This is in stark contrast to the construction and destruction of local member `myDinner`, where all constructors and destructors are invoked. Lesson 10 demonstrated in Listing 10.7 the correct order of construction and destruction of classes in an inheritance hierarchy, showing that all destructors need to be invoked, including `~Tuna()`. Clearly, something is amiss.

This flaw means that the destructor of a deriving class that has been instantiated on the free store using `new` would not be invoked if `delete` is called using a pointer of type `Base*`. This can result in resources not being released, memory leaks, and so on and is a problem that is not to be taken lightly.

To avoid this problem, you use virtual destructors, as illustrated in Listing 11.4.

Input ▼

LISTING 11.4 Using Virtual Destructors to Ensure That Destructors in Derived Classes Are Invoked When Deleting a Pointer of Type `Base*`

```
#include<iostream>
using namespace std;

class Fish
{
public:
    Fish()
    {
        cout << "Constructed Fish" << endl;
    }
    virtual ~Fish()   // virtual destructor!
    {
        cout << "Destroyed Fish" << endl;
    }
};

class Tuna:public Fish
{
public:
    Tuna()
    {
        cout << "Constructed Tuna" << endl;
    }
    ~Tuna()
    {
        cout << "Destroyed Tuna" << endl;
    }
};

void DeleteFish(Fish* pFish)
{
    delete pFish;
}

```

```
34: int main()
35: {
36:     cout << "Allocating a Tuna on the free store:" << endl;
37:     Tuna* pTuna = new Tuna;
38:     cout << "Deleting the Tuna: " << endl;
39:     DeleteFish(pTuna);
40:
41:     cout << "Instantiating a Tuna on the stack:" << endl;
42:     Tuna myDinner;
43:     cout << "Automatic destruction as it goes out of scope: \n";
44:
45:     return 0;
46: }
```

Output ▼

```
Allocating a Tuna on the free store:
Constructed Fish
Constructed Tuna
Deleting the Tuna:
Destroyed Tuna
Destroyed Fish
Instantiating a Tuna on the stack:
Constructed Fish
Constructed Tuna
Automatic destruction as it goes out of scope:
Destroyed Tuna
Destroyed Fish
```


Analysis ▼

The key improvement in Listing 11.4 over Listing 11.3 is the addition of the keyword `virtual` in Line 10, where the destructor of base class `Fish` has been declared. Note that this small change resulted in the compiler essentially executing `Tuna::~Tuna()` in addition to `Fish::~Fish()` when the operator `delete` was invoked on `Fish*`, which actually points to a `Tuna`, as shown in Line 31. This output also demonstrates that the sequence and the invocation of constructors and destructors are the same, regardless of whether the object of type `Tuna` is instantiated on the free store using `new`, as shown in Line 37, or as a local variable on the stack, as shown in Line 42.

NOTE

Always declare the base class destructor as `virtual`:

```
class Base
{
public:
   virtual ~Base() {};   // virtual destructor
};
```

This ensures that a pointer `Base*` cannot be used to invoke `delete` in such a way that instances of the deriving classes are not correctly destroyed.

How Do Virtual Functions Work? Understanding the Virtual Function Table

NOTE

This section is not a prerequisite to using polymorphism. Feel free to skip it or read it to feed your curiosity.

The function `MakeFishSwim(Fish&)` in Listing 11.2 ends up invoking the `Carp::Swim()` or `Tuna::Swim()` methods even though the programmer calls `Fish::Swim()` within it. Clearly, all that the compiler knows is that the function `MakeFishSwim()` will be invoked with arguments of type `Fish&`, but the function ends up executing different `Swim()` methods belonging to different derived classes. The selection of the right `Swim()` method is evidently a decision made at runtime, using logic that implements polymorphism, which is supplied by the compiler at compile time.

Consider a class `Base` that declares *N* virtual functions:

```
class Base
{
public:
   virtual void Func1()
   {
      // Func1 implementation
   }
   virtual void Func2()
   {
      // Func2 implementation
   }
```

```
    // .. so on and so forth
    virtual void FuncN()
    {
        // FuncN implementation
    }
};
```

The class `Derived`, which inherits from `Base`, overrides `Base::Func2()`, exposing the other virtual functions directly from the class `Base`:

```
class Derived: public Base
{
public:
    virtual void Func1()
    {
        // Derived::Func1 overrides Base::Func1()
    }

    // no implementation for Func2()

    virtual void FuncN()
    {
        // FuncN implementation
    }
};
```


The compiler sees an inheritance hierarchy and understands that `Base` defines certain virtual functions that have been overridden in `Derived`. The compiler now creates a table called the virtual function table (VFT) for every class that implements a virtual function. Objects of classes `Base` and `Derived` get pointers to VFTs for `Base` and `Derived`. A VFT can be visualized as a static array containing function pointers, each pointing to the virtual function (or override) of interest, as illustrated in Figure 11.1.

Thus, each table is composed of function pointers, each pointing to the available implementation of a virtual function. In the case of the class `Derived`, all except one function pointer in its VFT point to local implementations of the virtual method in `Derived`. `Derived` has not overridden `Base::Func2()`, and hence that function pointer points to the implementation in the `Base` class.

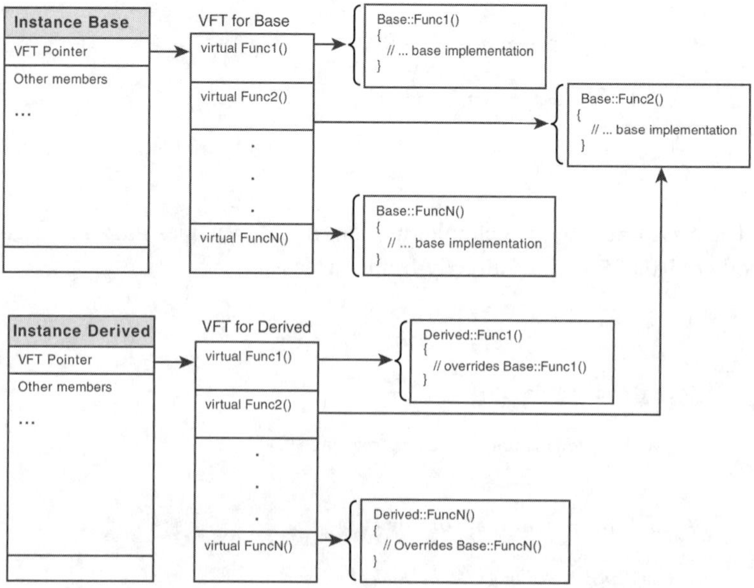

FIGURE 11.1 Visualization of a virtual function table for the classes `Derived` and `Base`.

This means that when a user of the class `Derived` calls

```
Derived objDerived;
objDerived.Func2();
```

the compiler ensures a lookup in the VFT of the class `Derived` and ensures that the implementation `Base::Func2()` is invoked. This also applies to calls that use methods that have been virtually overridden:

```
void DoSomething(Base& objBase)
{
   objBase.Func1();    // invoke Derived::Func1
}
int main()
{
   Derived objDerived;
   DoSomething(objDerived);
};
```

In this case, even though `objDerived` is being interpreted via `objBase` as an instance of the class `Base`, the VFT pointer in this instance is still pointing to the same table created for the class `Derived`. Thus, `Func1()`, which is executed via this VFT, is certainly `Derived::Func1()`.

You can see how VFTs help the implementation of (subtype) polymorphism in C++.

The proof of existence of a hidden VFT pointer is demonstrated in Listing 11.5, which compares the sizes of two identical classes—one that has virtual functions and another that doesn't.

Input ▼

LISTING 11.5 Demonstrating the Presence of a Hidden VFT Pointer in Comparing Two Classes Identical Except for a Function Declared Virtual

```
#include<iostream>
using namespace std;

class SimpleClass
{
   int a, b;

public:
   void DoSomething() {}
};

class Base
{
   int a, b;

public:
   virtual void DoSomething() {}
};

int main()
{
   cout << "sizeof(SimpleClass) = " << sizeof(SimpleClass) << endl;
   cout << "sizeof(Base) = " << sizeof(Base) << endl;

   return 0;
}
```


Output ▼

32-bit compiler output:

```
sizeof(SimpleClass) = 8
sizeof(Base) = 12
```

64-bit compiler output:

```
sizeof(SimpleClass) = 8
sizeof(Base) = 16
```

Analysis ▼

This example has been stripped to the bare minimum. You see two classes, `SimpleClass` and `Base`, that are identical in the types and number of members. However, `Base` has the function `DoSomething()` declared as virtual. The difference in adding this `virtual` keyword is that the compiler generates a virtual function table for the class `Base` and a reserved place for a pointer to the VFT in `Base` as a hidden member. This pointer consumes the 4 extra bytes in my 32-bit system. The output proves that the presence of a hidden pointer inserted by the compiler for a class has at least one virtual function.

> **NOTE**
>
> C++ also enables you to query a pointer `Base*` if it is of type `Derived*` by using the casting operator `dynamic_cast` and then performing conditional execution on the basis of the result of the query. This process, called runtime type identification (RTTI), should ideally be avoided even though it is supported by most C++ compilers. Needing to know the type of a derived class object behind a base class pointer is commonly considered poor programming practice.
>
> RTTI and `dynamic_cast` are discussed in Lesson 13, "Casting Operators."

Abstract Base Classes and Pure Virtual Functions

A base class that cannot be instantiated is called an *abstract base class*. Such a base class fulfills only one purpose: to be used in an inheritance hierarchy by a class that derives from it. C++ allows you to create an abstract base class using pure virtual functions.

A virtual method is said to be *pure virtual* when it has a declaration like this:

```
class AbstractBase
{
public:
   virtual void DoSomething() = 0;  // pure virtual method
};
```

This declaration essentially tells the compiler that `DoSomething()` needs to be implemented by the class that derives from `AbstractBase`:

```
class Derived: public AbstractBase
{
public:
   void DoSomething()    // pure virtual fn. must be implemented
   {
      cout << "Implemented virtual function" << endl;
   }
};
```

Thus, the `AbstractBase` class has ensured that the `Derived` class is required to supply an implementation for the virtual method `DoSomething()`. This functionality, where a base class can enforce support of methods with a specified name and signature in classes that derive from it, is that of an interface. Think of a `Fish` again. Imagine a `Tuna` that cannot swim fast because `Tuna` did not override `Fish::Swim()`. This would be a failed implementation and a flaw. Making the class `Fish` an abstract base class with `Swim` as a pure virtual function ensures that `Tuna`, which derives from `Fish`, implements `Tuna::Swim()` and swims like a `Tuna` and not like just any `Fish`. See Listing 11.6.

Input ▼

LISTING 11.6 The `Fish` Class as an Abstract Base Class for `Tuna` and `Carp`

```
#include<iostream>
using namespace std;

class Fish
{
public:
   // define a pure virtual function Swim
   virtual void Swim() = 0;
};

class Tuna:public Fish
{
public:
   void Swim()
   {
      cout << "Tuna swims fast in the sea! " << endl;
   }
};

class Carp:public Fish
{
   void Swim()
   {
```

```
23:         cout << "Carp swims slow in the lake!" << endl;
24:     }
25: };
26:
27: void MakeFishSwim(Fish& inputFish)
28: {
29:     inputFish.Swim();
30: }
31:
32: int main()
33: {
34:     // Fish myFish; // Fails, cannot instantiate an ABC
35:     Carp myLunch;
36:     Tuna myDinner;
37:
38:     MakeFishSwim(myLunch);
39:     MakeFishSwim(myDinner);
40:
41:     return 0;
42: }
```

Output ▼

```
Carp swims slow in the lake!
Tuna swims fast in the sea!
```

Analysis ▼

The first line in `main()`, Line 34 (which is commented out), is significant. It demonstrates that the compiler does not allow you to create an instance of an abstract base class `Fish`. It expects something concrete, such as a specialization of `Fish`—for example, `Tuna`—which makes sense even in the real-world arrangement of things. Thanks to the pure virtual function `Fish::Swim()` declared in Line 7, both `Tuna` and `Carp` are forced into implementing `Tuna::Swim()` and `Carp::Swim()`. Lines 27 through 30, which implement `MakeFishSwim(Fish&)`, demonstrate that even if an abstract base class cannot be instantiated, you can use it as a reference or a pointer. Abstract base classes are thus a very good mechanism for declaring functions that you expect derived classes to implement and fulfill. If a class `Trout` that derived from `Fish` forgets to implement `Trout::Swim()`, the compilation also fails.

NOTE

> Abstract base classes are often simply called *ABCs*. ABCs help enforce certain design constraints on a program.

Using Virtual Inheritance to Solve the Diamond Problem

In Lesson 10, you saw the curious case of a platypus that is part mammal, part bird, and part reptile. This is an example where a class, `Platypus`, needs to inherits from the classes `Mammal`, `Bird`, and `Reptile`. However, each of these in turn inherits from a more generic class, `Animal`, as illustrated in Figure 11.2.

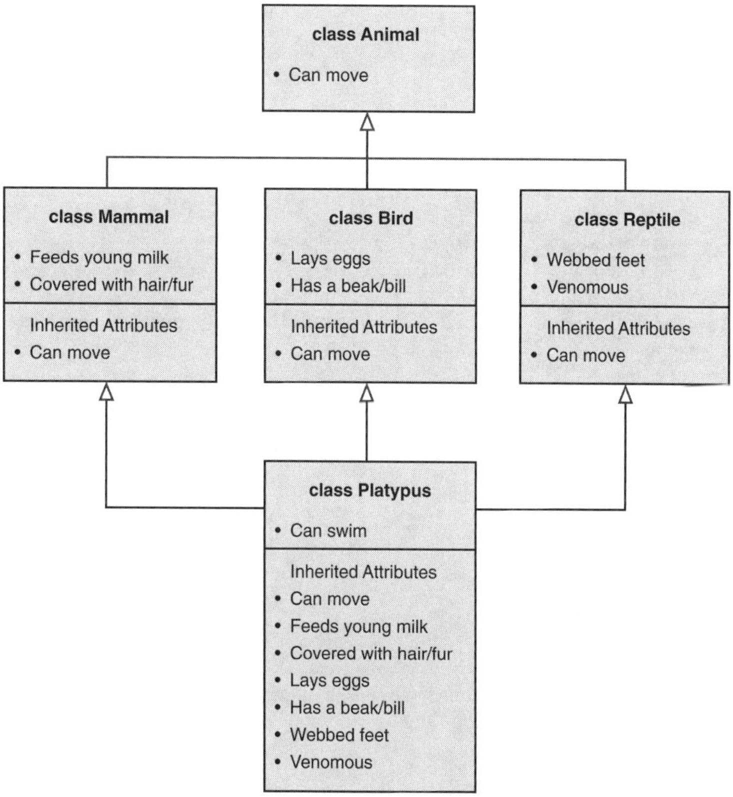

FIGURE 11.2
The class diagram of a platypus, demonstrating multiple inheritance.

So, what happens when you instantiate the `Platypus` class? How many instances of class `Animal` are instantiated for one instance of `Platypus`? Listing 11.7 helps answer this question.

Input ▼

LISTING 11.7 Checking for the Number of Base Class `Animal` Instances for One Instance of `Platypus`

```
#include<iostream>
using namespace std;

class Animal
{
public:
    Animal()
    {
        cout << "Animal constructor" << endl;
    }

    int age;
};

class Mammal:public Animal {};
class Bird:public Animal {};
class Reptile:public Animal {};

class Platypus :public Mammal, public Bird, public Reptile
{
public:
    Platypus()
    {
        cout << "Platypus constructor" << endl;
    }
};

int main()
{
    Platypus duckBilledP;

    // uncomment next line of code to see compile failure because
    // age is ambiguous: three instances of base Animal per Platypus
    // duckBilledP.age = 25;

    return 0;
}
```

Output ▼

```
Animal constructor
Animal constructor
Animal constructor
Platypus constructor
```

Analysis ▼

As the output demonstrates, due to multiple inheritance and all three base classes of `Platypus` inheriting in turn from the class `Animal`, you have three instances of `Animal` created automatically for every instance of `Platypus`, as demonstrated in Line 29. This is ridiculous because `Platypus` is still one animal that has inherited certain attributes from `Mammal`, `Bird`, and `Reptile`. The problem in the number of instances of base `Animal` is not limited to memory consumption alone. `Animal` has an integer member `Animal::age` (which has been kept public for explanation purposes). When you want to access `Animal::age` via an instance of `Platypus`, as shown in Line 33, you get a compilation error simply because the compiler doesn't know whether you want to set `Mammal::Animal::age` or `Bird::Animal::age` or `Reptile::Animal::age`. It can get even more ridiculous. If you so wanted, you could set all three:

```
duckBilledP.Mammal::Animal::age = 25;
duckBilledP.Bird::Animal::age = 2;
duckBilledP.Reptile::Animal::age = 5;
```

Clearly, one platypus should have only one `age`. However, you want class `Platypus` to also be `Mammal`, `Bird`, and `Reptile`. The solution is in virtual inheritance. If you expect a derived class to be used as a base class, it may be a good idea to define its relationship to the base class by using the keyword `virtual`:


```
class Derived1: public virtual Base
{
   // ... members and functions
};
class Derived2: public virtual Base
{
   // ... members and functions
};
```

Listing 11.8 shows a better class `Platypus` (actually, a better class `Mammal`, class `Bird`, and class `Reptile`).

Input ▼

LISTING 11.8 Demonstrating How the `virtual` Keyword in the Inheritance Hierarchy Helps Restrict the Number of Instances of the Base Class `Animal` to One

```
#include<iostream>
using namespace std;

class Animal
{
```

```
 5: public:
 6:     Animal()
 7:     {
 8:         cout << "Animal constructor" << endl;
 9:     }
10:
11:     int age;
12: };
13:
14: class Mammal:public virtual Animal {};
15: class Bird:public virtual Animal {};
16: class Reptile:public virtual Animal {};
17:
18: class Platypus final:public Mammal, public Bird, public Reptile
19: {
20: public:
21:     Platypus()
22:     {
23:         cout << "Platypus constructor" << endl;
24:     }
25: };
26:
27: int main()
28: {
29:     Platypus duckBilledP;
30:
31:     // no compile error as there is only one Animal::age
32:     duckBilledP.age = 25;
33:
34:     return 0;
35: }
```

Output ▼

```
Animal constructor
Platypus constructor
```

Analysis ▼

Do a quick comparison of this output against the output of Listing 11.7, and you see that the number of instances of the `Animal` class constructed has fallen to one, which is finally reflective of the fact that only one `Platypus` has been instantiated in Line 29. This is because of the keyword `virtual`, used in the relationship between classes `Mammal`, `Bird`, and `Reptile` in Lines 14 through 16. It ensures that when these classes are grouped together under `Platypus`, the common base `Animal` class exists only in a single instance. This solves a lot of problems; one of them is that Line 32 now compiles. Also note the use of keyword `final` in Line 18 to ensure that the class `Platypus` cannot be used as a base class.

NOTE

A problem caused in an inheritance hierarchy containing two or more base classes that inherit from a common base, which results in the need for ambiguity resolution in the absence of virtual inheritance, is called the *diamond problem*.

The name *diamond problem* was possibly inspired by the shape of the class diagram. (Refer to Figure 11.2, which has straight and slanted lines relating `Platypus` to `Animal` via `Mammal`, `Bird`, and `Reptile`. As you can see, this forms a diamond shape.)

NOTE

The `virtual` keyword in C++ is often used in different contexts for different purposes. (My best guess is that someone wanted to save time on inventing an apt keyword.) Here is a summary:

- A function declared as *virtual* means that an existing overriding function in a derived class is invoked.
- An inheritance relationship between the classes `Derived1` and `Derived2` that inherits using `virtual` from the class `Base` means that another class, `Derived3`, which inherits from `Derived1` and `Derived2`, still results in the creation of only one instance of `Base` during instantiation of type `Derived3`.

Thus, the same keyword `virtual` is used to implement two different concepts.

Using the Specifier `override` to Indicate the Intention to Override

Our versions of the base class `Fish` have featured a virtual function called `Swim()`, as shown in the following code:

```
class Fish
{
public:
   virtual void Swim()
   {
      cout << "Fish swims!" << endl;
   }
};
```

Assume that the derived class `Tuna` were to define a function `Swim()` but with a slightly different signature—one using `const` inserted unintentionally by a programmer who wants to override `Fish::Swim()`:

```
class Tuna:public Fish
{
public:
   void Swim() const
   {
      cout << "Tuna swims!" << endl;
   }
};
```

This function `Tuna::Swim()` actually does not override `Fish::Swim()`. The signatures are different due to the presence of `const` in `Tuna::Swim()`. Compilation succeeds, however, and the programmer may falsely believe that she has successfully overridden the function `Swim()` in the class `Tuna`. Starting in C++11, you can use the specifier `override` in the method declaration in the derived class, thereby explicitly stating your intention to override the method in the base class:

```
class Tuna:public Fish
{
public:
   void Swim() const override // Error: no virtual fn with this sig in Fish
   {
      cout << "Tuna swims!" << endl;
   }
};
```

Thus, `override` supplies a powerful way of expressing the explicit intention to override a base class virtual function, thereby getting the compiler to check whether

- The base class function is virtual.
- The signature of the base class virtual function exactly matches the signature of the derived class function declared to override.

Using `final` to Prevent Function Overriding

The specifier `final` was first presented to you in Lesson 10. A class declared as `final` cannot be used as a base class. Similarly, a virtual function declared as `final` cannot be overridden in a derived class.

Thus, a version of the class `Tuna` that doesn't allow any further specialization of the virtual function `Swim()` would look like this:

```
class Tuna:public Fish
{
public:
   // override Fish::Swim and make this final
   void Swim() override final
   {
      cout << "Tuna swims!" << endl;
   }
};
```

This version of `Tuna` can be inherited from, but `Swim()` cannot be overridden any further:

```
class BluefinTuna final:public Tuna
{
public:
   void Swim() // Error: Swim() was final in Tuna, cannot override
   {
   }
};
```


A demonstration of the specifiers `override` and `final` is available in Listing 11.9.

NOTE

We used `final` in the declaration of the class `BluefinTuna` as well. This ensures that the class `BluefinTuna` cannot be used as a base class. Therefore, the following would result in an error:

```
class FailedDerivation:public BluefinTuna {};
```

Virtual Copy Constructors?

Well, the question mark at the end of the section title is justified. It is technically impossible in C++ to have virtual copy constructors. However, such a feature would help you create a collection (for example, a static array) of type `Base*`, with each element being a specialization of that type:

```
// Tuna, Carp and Trout are classes that inherit public from base class Fish
Fish* pFishes[3];
Fishes[0] = new Tuna();
Fishes[1] = new Carp();
Fishes[2] = new Trout();
```

Then assigning it into another array of the same type, where the virtual copy constructor ensures a deep copy of the derived class objects as well, ensures that `Tuna`, `Carp`, and `Trout` are copied as `Tuna`, `Carp`, and `Trout` even though the copy constructor is operating on the type `Fish*`.

Well, that's a nice dream.

Virtual copy constructors are not possible because the `virtual` keyword in the context of base class methods being overridden by implementations available in the derived class are about polymorphic behavior generated at runtime. Constructors, however, are not polymorphic in nature as they can construct only a fixed type, and hence C++ does not allow use of the virtual copy constructors.

Having said that, there is a nice workaround in the form of defining your own clone function that allows you to do just that:

```
class Fish
{
public:
   virtual Fish* Clone() const = 0; // pure virtual function
};

class Tuna:public Fish
{
// ... other members
public:
   Fish* Clone() const  // virtual clone function
   {
      return new Tuna(*this);  // return new Tuna that is a copy of this
   }
};
```

Thus, the virtual function `Clone()` is a simulated virtual copy constructor that needs to be explicitly invoked, as shown in Listing 11.9.

Input ▼

LISTING 11.9 `Tuna` and `Carp` Classes, Which Support a `Clone()` Function as a Simulated Virtual Copy Constructor

```
#include<iostream>
using namespace std;

class Fish
{
public:
   virtual Fish* Clone() = 0;
   virtual void Swim() = 0;
```

```
   virtual ~Fish() {};
};

class Tuna: public Fish
{
public:
   Fish* Clone() override
   {
      return new Tuna (*this);
   }

   void Swim() override final
   {
      cout << "Tuna swims fast in the sea" << endl;
   }
};

class BluefinTuna final:public Tuna
{
public:
   Fish* Clone() override
   {
      return new BluefinTuna(*this);
   }

   // Cannot override Tuna::Swim as it is "final" in Tuna
};

class Carp final: public Fish
{
   Fish* Clone() override
   {
      return new Carp(*this);
   }
   void Swim() override final
   {
      cout << "Carp swims slow in the lake" << endl;
   }
};

int main()
{
   const int ARRAY_SIZE = 4;

   Fish* myFishes[ARRAY_SIZE];
   myFishes[0] = new Tuna();
   myFishes[1] = new Carp();
   myFishes[2] = new BluefinTuna();
   myFishes[3] = new Carp();

   Fish* myNewFishes[ARRAY_SIZE];
```

```
59:     for (int index = 0; index < ARRAY_SIZE; ++index)
60:        myNewFishes[index] = myFishes[index]->Clone();
61:
62:     // invoke a virtual method to check
63:     for (int index = 0; index < ARRAY_SIZE; ++index)
64:        myNewFishes[index]->Swim();
65:
66:     // memory cleanup
67:     for (int index = 0; index < ARRAY_SIZE; ++index)
68:     {
69:        delete myFishes[index];
70:        delete myNewFishes[index];
71:     }
72:
73:     return 0;
74: }
```

Output ▼

```
Tuna swims fast in the sea
Carp swims slow in the lake
Tuna swims fast in the sea
Carp swims slow in the lake
```

Analysis ▼

In addition to demonstrating virtual copy constructors via the virtual function `Fish::Clone()`, Listing 11.9 also demonstrates the use of the keywords `override` and `final`—the latter being applied to virtual functions and classes alike. It also features a virtual destructor for the class `Fish` in Line 8. Lines 52 through 56 in `main()` demonstrate how a static array of pointers to the base class `Fish*` has been declared and how individual elements have been assigned to newly created objects of type `Tuna`, `Carp`, `Tuna`, and `Carp`, respectively. Note how the array `myFishes` is able to collect seemingly different types that are all related by a common base type `Fish`. This is already cool, if you compare it against previous arrays in this book that have mostly been of a simple monotonous type `int`. If that isn't cool enough for you, keep in mind that you were able to copy into a new array of type `Fish*` called `myNewFishes` by using the virtual function `Fish::Clone()` within a loop, as shown in Line 60. Note that your array is quite small, at only four elements. It could've been a lot longer, but its size wouldn't make much difference to the copy logic, which would only need to adjust the loop-ending condition parameter. Line 64 invokes the virtual function `Fish::Swim()` on each stored element in the new array, and the output demonstrates that `Clone()` copied a `Tuna` as a `Tuna` and not just a `Fish()`. Also note that the output of `Swim()` used on an instance of

BluefinTuna was the same as that for a Tuna, because Tuna::Swim() was declared as final. Thus, BluefinTuna was not permitted to override Swim(), and the compiler executed Tuna::Swim() for it.

DO	DON'T
DO remember to mark base class functions that need to be overridden by the derived class as virtual.	**DON'T** forget to supply your base class with a virtual destructor.
DO remember that pure virtual functions make your class an abstract base class, and these functions must be implemented by a deriving class.	**DON'T** forget that the compiler does not allow you to create a standalone instance of an abstract base class.
DO mark functions in derived classes that are intended to override base functionality using the keyword override.	**DON'T** forget that virtual inheritance is about ensuring that the common base in a diamond hierarchy has only one instance.
DO use virtual inheritance to solve the diamond problem.	**DON'T** confuse the function of the keyword virtual when used in creating an inheritance hierarchy with the same keyword used in declaring base class functions.

Summary

In this lesson, you learned to tap the power of creating inheritance hierarchies in your C++ code by using polymorphism. You learned how to declare and program virtual functions—how they ensure that the derived class implementation overrides the implementation in the base class even if an instance of the base class is used to invoke the virtual method. You saw that pure virtual functions are a special type of virtual functions which ensure that the base class alone cannot be instantiated, making it a perfect place to define interfaces that derived classes must fulfill. Finally, you saw the diamond problem created by multiple inheritance and how virtual inheritance helps you solve it.

Q&A

Q Why use the virtual keyword with a base class function when code compiles without it?

A Without the virtual keyword, you are not able to ensure that someone calling objBase.Function() will be redirected to Derived::Function(). Besides, compilation of code is not the only measure of its quality.

Q Why does a compiler create a virtual function table?

A A compiler creates a VFT to store function pointers. Such a table ensures that the right virtual function supported in the hierarchy is invoked.

Q Should a base class always have a virtual destructor?

A Ideally, yes. Only then can you ensure that when someone does a

```
Base* pBase = new Derived();
delete pBase;
```

the `delete` on a pointer of type `Base*` results in the destructor `~Derived()` being invoked. This occurs when the destructor `~Base()` is declared `virtual`.

Q What is an abstract base class good for when I can't even instantiate it as a standalone class?

A An ABC is not meant to be instantiated as a standalone object; rather, it is always meant to be derived from. It contains pure virtual functions that define the minimal blueprint of functions that deriving classes need to implement, thus taking the role of an interface.

Q Given an inheritance hierarchy, do I need to use the keyword `virtual` on all declarations of a virtual function or just in the base class?

A It is enough to declare a function as `virtual` once, but that declaration has to be in the base class.

Q Can I define member functions and have member attributes in an ABC?

A Sure you can. Remember that you still cannot instantiate an ABC as it has at least one pure virtual function that needs to be implemented by a deriving class.

Workshop

The Workshop provides quiz questions to help you solidify your understanding of the material covered and exercises to provide you with experience in using what you've learned. Try to answer the quiz and exercise questions before checking the answers in Appendix E and be certain you understand the answers before continuing to the next lesson.

Quiz

1. You are modeling shapes—a circle and a triangle—and want every shape to compulsorily implement the functions `Area()` and `Print()`. How would you do it?
2. Does every class get its own virtual function table?
3. My class `Fish` has two public methods, one pure virtual function, and some member attributes. Is it still an abstract base class?

Exercises

1. Demonstrate an inheritance hierarchy that implements `Circle` and `Triangle` classes for Quiz Question 1.
2. **BUG BUSTERS:** What is the problem in the following code?

```
class Vehicle
{
public:
   Vehicle() {}
   ~Vehicle(){}
};
     class Car: public Vehicle
{
public:
   Car() {}
   ~Car() {}
};
```

3. In the (uncorrected) code in Exercise 2, what is the order of execution for constructors and destructors if an instance of `car` is created and destroyed like this:

```
Vehicle* myRacer = new Car;
delete myRacer;
```

LESSON 12
Operator Types and Operator Overloading

In addition to encapsulating data and methods, a class can also encapsulate *operators* that make it easy to operate on instances of the class. You can use these operators to perform operations such as assignment or addition on class objects similar to those on integers that you saw in Lesson 5, "Working with Expressions, Statements, and Operators." Just like functions, operators can also be overloaded.

In this lesson, you learn:

- The keyword `operator`
- Unary and binary operators
- Conversion operators
- The move assignment operator
- Operators that cannot be redefined

What Are Operators in C++?

On a syntactical level, there is very little that differentiates an operator from a function, save for the use of the keyword `operator`. An operator declaration looks quite like a function declaration:

```
return_type operator operator_symbol (...parameter list...);
```

operator _ symbol in this case could be any of the several operator types that a programmer can define: `+` (addition), `&&` (logical AND), and so on. The operands help the compiler distinguish one operator from another. So, why does C++ provide operators when functions are also supported?

Consider a utility class `Date` that encapsulates the day, month, and year:

```
Date holiday (12, 25, 2021);  // initialized to Dec 25, 2021
```

If you want to add a day and get the instance to contain the next day—December 26, 2021—which of these two options would be more intuitive?

- Option 1: Using the increment operator:
  ```
  ++ holiday;  // Dec 26, 2021
  ```
- Option 2: Using the member function `Increment()`:
  ```
  holiday.Increment();  // Dec 26, 2021
  ```

Clearly, Option 1 scores over method `Increment()`. The operator-based mechanism facilitates consumption by supplying ease of use and intuitiveness. Implementing the operator `<` in the class `Date` would help you compare two instances of the class `Date` like this:

```
if(date1 < date2)
{
   // Do something
}
else
{
   // Do something else
}
```

Operators can be used in more situations than just managing dates. They're essential to classes such as `std::string` that provide string concatenation features. Smart pointer classes leverage the operators `->` and `*` in helping a programmer with pointer and memory management.

NOTE

The effort involved in implementing relevant operators will be rewarded by the ease of consumption of a class.

On a broad level, operators in C++ can be classified into two types: unary operators and binary operators.

Unary Operators

As the name suggests, a *unary operator* is an operator that functions on a single operand. A unary operator that is implemented in the global namespace or as a static member function of a class uses the following structure:

```
return_type operator operator_type (parameter_type)
{
    // ... implementation
}
```

A unary operator that is a (non-static) member of a class has a similar structure but is lacking in parameters because the single parameter that it works on is the instance of the class itself (`*this`):

```
return_type operator operator_type()
{
    // ... implementation
}
```

The unary operators that can be overloaded (or redefined) are shown in Table 12.1.

TABLE 12.1 Overloadable Unary Operators

Operator Symbol	Name
++	Increment
--	Decrement
*	Pointer dereference
->	Member selection
!	Logical NOT
&	Address-of
~	One's complement
+	Unary plus
-	Unary negation
Conversion operators	Conversion into other types

TIP

`sizeof()` is a unary operator that cannot be overloaded!

Unary Increment (++) and Decrement (--) Operators

A unary prefix increment operator (++) can be programmed using the following syntax within the class declaration:

```
// Unary increment operator (prefix)
Date& operator ++ ()
```

```
{
    // operator implementation code
    return *this;
}
```

The postfix increment operator (++), on the other hand, has a different return type and an input parameter (which is not always used):

```
Date operator ++ (int)
{
   // Store a copy of the current state of the object, before incrementing day
   Date copy (*this);

   // increment code operating on 'this'

   // Return state before increment (because, postfix)
   return copy;
}
```

The prefix and postfix decrement operators have syntax similar to that of the increment operators; however, the declaration of a decrement operator contains a -- instead of a ++. Listing 12.1 shows a simple class `Date` that allows you to increment days by using the ++ operator.

Input ▼

LISTING 12.1 A Calendar Class That Handles Day, Month, and Year and Allows Incrementing and Decrementing of Days

```
#include<iostream>
using namespace std;

class Date
{
private:
    int day, month, year;

public:
    Date (int inMonth, int inDay, int inYear)
         : month (inMonth), day(inDay), year (inYear) {};

    Date& operator ++ () // prefix increment
    {
        ++day;
        return *this;
    }

    Date& operator -- () // prefix decrement
    {
        --day;
        return *this;
```

```
22:     }
23:
24:     void DisplayDate()
25:     {
26:        cout << month << " / " << day << " / " << year << endl;
27:     }
28: };
29:
30: int main ()
31: {
32:     Date holiday (12, 25, 2021); // Dec 25, 2021
33:
34:     cout << "The date object is initialized to: ";
35:     holiday.DisplayDate ();
36:
37:     ++holiday; // move date ahead by a day
38:     cout << "Date after prefix-increment is: ";
39:     holiday.DisplayDate ();
40:
41:     --holiday; // move date backwards by a day
42:     cout << "Date after a prefix-decrement is: ";
43:     holiday.DisplayDate ();
44:
45:     return 0;
46: }
```

Output ▼

```
The date object is initialized to: 12 / 25 / 2021
Date after prefix-increment is: 12 / 26 / 2021
Date after a prefix-decrement is: 12 / 25 / 2021
```


Analysis ▼

The operators of interest, which are defined in Lines 12 through 22, help in adding or subtracting a day at a time from instances of the class `Day`, as shown in Lines 37 and 41 in `main()`. Prefix increment operators, as demonstrated in this example, need to return a reference to the instance after the increment operation is complete.

NOTE

> This version of a date class has a bare minimum implementation to reduce the number of code lines and to explain how the prefix operators `++` and `--` are to be implemented. A professional version of this example would implement rollover functionalities for month and year and take into consideration leap years as well.

To support postfix increment or decrement, you simply add the following code to the Date class:

```
// postfix differs from prefix operator in return-type and parameters
Date operator ++ (int) // postfix increment
{
   Date copy(month, day, year);
   ++day;
   return copy; // copy of instance before increment returned
}

Date operator -- (int) // postfix decrement
{
   Date copy(month, day, year);
   --day;
   return copy; // copy of instance before decrement returned
}
```

When your version of the Date class supports both prefix and postfix increment and decrement operators, you can use objects of the Date class as follows:

```
Date holiday (12, 25, 2021);  // instantiate
++ holiday;  // using prefix increment operator++
holiday ++;  // using postfix increment operator++
-- holiday;  // using prefix decrement operator --
holiday --;  // using postfix decrement operator --
```

NOTE

> As the implementation of the postfix operators demonstrates, a copy containing the initial state of the object is created before the increment or decrement operation. This copy is returned to the caller.
>
> In other words, if you have a choice between using `++object;` and `object++;` to essentially only increment, you should choose the former to avoid creating a temporary copy that will not be used.

Conversion Operators

Say that you use Listing 12.1 and insert the following line in main():

```
cout << holiday;  // error in absence of conversion operator
```

The code would result in the following compile failure: `error: binary '<<' : no operator found which takes a right-hand operand of type 'Date' (or there is no acceptable conversion)`. This error essentially indicates that `cout` doesn't know how to interpret an instance of `Date` because the `Date` class does not support the operators that convert its contents into a type that `cout` would accept.

`cout` can work well with a `const char*`:

```
std::cout << "Hello world"; // const char* works!
```

So, getting `cout` to work with an instance of type `Date` might be as simple as adding an operator that returns a const `char*` version:

```
operator const char*()
{
   // operator implementation that returns a char*
}
```

Listing 12.2 shows a simple implementation of this conversion operator.

Input ▼

LISTING 12.2 Implementing the Conversion Operator `const char*` for the `Date` Class

```
#include<iostream>
#include<sstream> // new include for ostringstream
#include<string>
using namespace std;

class Date
{
private:
   int day, month, year;
   string dateInString;

public:
   Date(int inMonth, int inDay, int inYear)
      : month(inMonth), day(inDay), year(inYear) {};

   operator const char*()
   {
      ostringstream formattedDate; // assists string construction
      formattedDate << month << " / " << day << " / " << year;

      dateInString = formattedDate.str();
      return dateInString.c_str();
   }
};

int main ()
```

```
26: {
27:     Date holiday (12, 25, 2021);
28:
29:     cout << "Holiday is on: " << holiday << endl;
30:
31:     // string strHoliday (holiday); // OK!
32:     // strHoliday = Date(11, 11, 2021); // also OK!
33:
34:     return 0;
35: }
```

Output ▼

```
Holiday is on: 12 / 25 / 2021
```

Analysis ▼

The benefit of implementing the operator `const char*`, as shown in Lines 15 to 23, is visible in Line 29 in `main()`. Now, an instance of the `Date` class can be used directly in a `cout` statement because `cout` understands `const char*`. The compiler automatically uses the output of the appropriate (and, in this case, the only available) operator in feeding it to `cout`, which displays the date on the screen. In your implementation of the operator `const char*`, you use `std::ostringstream` to convert the member integers into a `std::string` object, as shown in Line 18. You could instead directly return `formattedDate.str()`, but you store a copy in the private member `Date::dateInString` in Line 20 because `formattedDate`, as a local variable, is destroyed when the operator returns. So, the pointer returned by `formattedDate.c_str()` would be invalidated on function return. `std::string::c_str()`, used in Line 21, returns the C-style `const char*` equivalent of the contents in the string object.

The `const char*` operator opens up new possibilities in terms of consuming the `Date` class. It allows you to even assign an instance of the `Date` class directly to a string:

```
string strHoliday (holiday);
strHoliday = Date(11, 11, 2021);
```

CAUTION

Note that such assignments cause implicit conversions. That is, the compiler uses the available conversion operator (in this case, `const char*`), thereby permitting unintended assignments that can be compiled without errors. To avoid implicit conversions, use the keyword `explicit` at the beginning of an operator declaration, as follows:

```
explicit operator const char*()
{
   // conversion code here
}
```

Using `explicit` would force a programmer to assert the intention to convert using a cast:

```
string strHoliday(static_cast<const char*>
(holiday));
strHoliday=static_cast<const char*>
(Date(11,11,2021));
```

Casting, including `static_cast`, is discussed in detail in Lesson 13, "Casting Operators."

NOTE

Program as many operators as you think your class would be used with. If an application needs an integer representation of a date, you could program it as follows:

```
explicit operator int()
{
   return day + month + year;
}
```

This would allow an instance of `Date` to be used or transacted as an integer:

```
FuncTakesInt(static_cast<int>(Date(12, 25, 2021)));
```

Listing 12.9, later in this lesson, also demonstrates conversion operators used with a string class.

The Dereference Operator (*) and Member Selection Operator (->)

The dereference operator (*) and member selection operator (->) are most frequently used in the programming of smart pointer classes. *Smart pointers* are utility classes that wrap regular pointers and simplify memory management by resolving ownership and copy issues using operators. In some cases, they can even help improve the performance of an application. Smart pointers are discussed in detail in Lesson 26, "Understanding Smart Pointers." This lesson takes a brief look at how overloading operators helps in making smart pointers work.

Analyze the use of `std::unique_ptr` in Listing 12.3 and observe how it uses the operators `*` and `->` to help you use the smart pointer class as you would any normal pointer.

Input ▼

LISTING 12.3 Using the Smart Pointer `unique_ptr` to Manage a Dynamically Allocated Instance of `Date` Class

```
#include<iostream>
#include<memory>  // new include to use unique_ptr
using namespace std;

class Date
{
private:
    int day, month, year;
    string dateInString;

public:
    Date(int inMonth, int inDay, int inYear)
        : month(inMonth), day(inDay), year(inYear) {};

    void DisplayDate()
    {
        cout << month << " / " << day << " / " << year << endl;
    }
};

int main()
{
    unique_ptr<int> smartIntPtr(new int);
    *smartIntPtr = 42;

    // Use smart pointer type like an int*
    cout << "Integer value is: " << *smartIntPtr << endl;

    unique_ptr<Date> smartHoliday (new Date(12, 25, 2021));
```

```
29:     cout << "The new instance of date contains: ";
30:
31:     // use smartHoliday just as you would a Date*
32:     smartHoliday->DisplayDate();
33:
34:     return 0; // smart pointers do the deallocation for you
35: }
```

Output ▼

```
Integer value is: 42
The new instance of date contains: 12 / 25 / 2021
```

Analysis ▼

Line 22 declares a smart pointer to type `int`. This line shows template initialization syntax for the smart pointer class `unique_ptr`. Similarly, Line 28 declares a smart pointer to an instance of the class `Date`. Focus on the pattern and ignore the details for the moment.

NOTE

> Don't worry if this template syntax looks awkward. Templates are introduced in Lesson 14, "An Introduction to Macros and Templates."

This example demonstrates how a smart pointer allows you to use normal pointer syntax, as shown in Lines 23 and 32. In Line 26, you display the value of the `int` using `*smartIntPtr`, and in Line 32, you use `smartHoliday->DisplayData()` as if these two variables were an `int*` and a `Date*`, respectively. The secret lies in the implementation of operators `*` and `->` in the pointer class `std::unique_ptr`, which makes the pointer smart.

NOTE

> Smart pointer classes can do a lot more than just behave as normal pointers or deallocate memory when they go out of scope. Find out more about this topic in Lesson 26.
>
> To see an implementation of a basic smart pointer class that has overloaded these operators, you may briefly visit Listing 26.1.

Binary Operators

An operator that functions on two operands is called a *binary operator*. You define a binary operator implemented as a global function or a static member function by using the following syntax:

```
return_type operator_type (parameter1, parameter2);
```

You define a binary operator implemented as a class member by using the following syntax:

```
return_type operator_type (parameter);
```

The reason the class member version of a binary operator accepts only one parameter is that the second parameter is usually derived from the attributes of the class itself.

Table 12.2 lists binary operators that can be overloaded or redefined in a C++ application.

TABLE 12.2 Overloadable Binary Operators

Operator Symbol	Name
,	Comma
!=	Inequality
%	Modulus
%=	Modulus/assignment
&	Bitwise AND
&&	Logical AND
&=	Bitwise AND/assignment
*	Multiplication
*=	Multiplication/assignment
+	Addition
+=	Addition/assignment
-	Subtraction
-=	Subtraction/assignment
->*	Pointer-to-member selection

Operator Symbol	Name
/	Division
/=	Division/assignment
<	Less than
<<	Left shift
<<=	Left shift/assignment
<=	Less than or equal to
=	Assignment, copy assignment, and move assignment
==	Equality
>	Greater than
>=	Greater than or equal to
>>	Right shift
>>=	Right shift/assignment
^	Exclusive OR
^=	Exclusive OR/assignment
|	Bitwise inclusive OR
|=	Bitwise inclusive OR/assignment
||	Logical OR
[]	Subscript operator

The Binary Addition (`a+b`) and Subtraction (`a-b`) Operators

Much like the increment/decrement operators, the binary plus and minus, when defined, enable you to add or subtract the value of a supported data type from an object of the class that implements these operators. Take a look at the calendar `Date` class again. Although you have already implemented the capability to increment `Date` so that it moves the calendar one day forward, you still do not support the capability to move it, say, five days ahead. To do this, you need to implement the binary operator (+), as the code in Listing 12.4 demonstrates.

Input ▼

LISTING 12.4 Calendar `Date` Class Featuring the Binary Addition Operator

```
#include<iostream>
using namespace std;

class Date
{
private:
   int day, month, year;
   string dateInString;

public:
   Date(int inMonth, int inDay, int inYear)
      : month(inMonth), day(inDay), year(inYear) {};

   Date operator + (int daysToAdd) // binary addition
   {
      Date newDate (month, day + daysToAdd, year);
      return newDate;
   }

   Date operator - (int daysToSub) // binary subtraction
   {
      return Date(month, day - daysToSub, year);
   }

   void DisplayDate()
   {
      cout << month << " / " << day << " / " << year << endl;
   }
};

int main()
{
   Date holiday (12, 25, 2021);
   cout << "Holiday on: ";
   holiday.DisplayDate ();

   Date previousHoliday (holiday - 19);
   cout << "Previous holiday on: ";
   previousHoliday.DisplayDate();

   Date nextHoliday(holiday + 6);
   cout << "Next holiday on: ";
   nextHoliday.DisplayDate ();

   return 0;
}
```

Output ▼

```
Holiday on: 12 / 25 / 2021
Previous holiday on: 12 / 6 / 2021
Next holiday on: 12 / 31 / 2021
```

Analysis ▼

Lines 13 through 22 contain the implementations of the binary operators + and - that permit the use of simple addition and subtraction syntax, as shown in `main()` in Lines 36 and 40, respectively.

The binary addition operator would also be useful in a class that manages dynamically allocated memory. In Lesson 9, "Classes and Objects," you analyzed a simple integer buffer class called `MyBuffer` that encapsulates memory management, copying, and the like, as shown in Listing 9.9. The `MyBuffer` class wouldn't support the concatenation of two buffers using a simple syntax as seen below:

```
MyBuffer buf1(3);  // space for 3 integers
MyBuffer buf2(2);  // 2 integers
MyBuffer bigBuf(buf1 + buf2);  // error: operator+ not defined
```

Defining the + operator in this case makes using `MyBuffer` extremely easy and is hence worth the effort:

```
MyBuffer operator + (const MyBuffer& bufToAppend)
{
   MyBuffer newBuf(this->bufLength + bufToAppend.bufLength);

   for (unsigned int counter = 0; counter < bufLength; ++counter)
      newBuf.SetValue(counter, *(myNums + counter));

   for (unsigned int counter = 0; counter < bufToAppend.bufLength; ++counter)
      newBuf.SetValue(counter + bufLength, *(bufToAppend.myNums + counter));

   return newBuf;
}
```

You can see a version of class `MyBuffer` with the + operator, among others, in Listing 12.12, later in this lesson.

The Addition Assignment (+=) and Subtraction Assignment (-=) Operators

The addition assignment operator allows syntax such as `a += b;`, which allows you to increment the value of an object `a` by an amount `b`. Then, the addition assignment operator can be overloaded to accept different types of parameter `b`. Listing 12.5 allows you to add an integer value to a `Date` object.

Input ▼

LISTING 12.5 Defining the Operators += and -= to Add or Subtract Days in the Calendar, Given an Integer Input

```
#include<iostream>
using namespace std;

class Date
{
private:
    int day, month, year;

public:
    Date(int inMonth, int inDay, int inYear)
        : month(inMonth), day(inDay), year(inYear) {}

   void operator+= (int daysToAdd) // addition assignment
   {
      day += daysToAdd;
   }

   void operator-= (int daysToSub) // subtraction assignment
   {
      day -= daysToSub;
   }

   void DisplayDate()
   {
       cout << month << " / " << day << " / " << year << endl;
   }
};

int main()
{
   Date holiday (12, 25, 2021);
   cout << "holiday is on: ";
   holiday.DisplayDate ();
```

```
33:
34:     cout << "holiday -= 19 gives: ";
35:     holiday -= 19;
36:     holiday.DisplayDate();
37:
38:     cout << "holiday += 25 gives: ";
39:     holiday += 25;
40:     holiday.DisplayDate ();
41:
42:     return 0;
43: }
```

Output ▼

```
holiday is on: 12 / 25 / 2021
holiday -= 19 gives: 12 / 6 / 2021
holiday += 25 gives: 12 / 31 / 2021
```

Analysis ▼

The addition and subtraction assignment operators of interest are in Lines 12 to 20. They allow you to add and subtract an integer value for days, as in `main()`, for instance:

```
35:     holiday -= 19;
39:     holiday += 25;
```

Your `Date` class now allows users to add or remove days from it as if they were dealing with integers by using addition or subtraction assignment operators that take an `int` as a parameter. You can even provide overloaded versions of the addition assignment operator (+=) that work with an instance of a fictitious class `Days`:

```
// operator that adds a Days to an existing Date
void operator += (const Days& daysToAdd)
{
    day += daysToAdd.GetDays();
}
```

NOTE

> The multiplication assignment `*=`, division assignment `/=`, modulus assignment `%=`, subtraction assignment `-=`, left-shift assignment `<<=`, right-shift assignment `>>=`, XOR assignment `^=`, bitwise inclusive OR assignment `|=`, and bitwise AND assignment `&=` operators have syntax similar to that of the addition assignment operator shown in Listing 12.5.
>
> Although the ultimate objective of overloading operators is making a class easy and intuitive to use, there are many situations where implementing an operator might not make sense. For example, the calendar class `Date` has absolutely no use for a bitwise AND assignment operator (`&=`). No user of this class should ever expect (or even think of) getting useful results from an operation such as `greatDay &= 20;`.

The Equality (==) and Inequality (!=) Operators

What would you expect when one instance of the class `Date` is compared to another?

```
if (date1 == date2)
{
    // Do something
}
else
{
    // Do something else
}
```

In the absence of an equality operator (==), the compiler simply performs a binary comparison of the two objects and returns `true` when they are exactly identical. This binary comparison will work for instances of classes containing simple data types (like the `Date` class as of now), but it will not work if the class in question has a non-static pointer member, such as the `int*` named `myNums` in class `MyBuffer` in Listing 9.9. When two instances of class `MyBuffer` are compared, a binary comparison of the member attributes would actually compare the member pointer values (`MyBuffer::myNums`). The two pointers being compared would never be equal. Comparisons involving two instances of `MyBuffer` would return `false` consistently because two members that are pointers are being compared, but not the content that they're pointing to. You solve this problem by defining comparison operators. A generic expression of the equality operator is as follows:

```
bool operator== (const ClassType& compareTo)
{
   // comparison code here, return true if equal else false
}
```

The inequality operator can reuse the equality operator:

```
bool operator!= (const ClassType& compareTo)
{
   // comparison code here, return true if inequal else false
}
```

The inequality operator can be the inverse (logical NOT) of the result of the equality operator. Listing 12.6 demonstrates comparison operators defined by the calendar class `Date`.

Input ▼

LISTING 12.6 Demonstrating the `==` and `!=` Operators

```
#include<iostream>
using namespace std;

class Date
{
private:
    int day, month, year;

public:
    Date(int inMonth, int inDay, int inYear)
        : month(inMonth), day(inDay), year(inYear) {}

   bool operator== (const Date& compareTo) const
   {
      return ((day == compareTo.day)
            && (month == compareTo.month)
            && (year == compareTo.year));
   }

   bool operator!= (const Date& compareTo) const
   {
      return !(this->operator==(compareTo));
   }

   void DisplayDate()
   {
```

```
26:      cout << month << " / " << day << " / " << year << endl;
27:    }
28: };
29:
30: int main()
31: {
32:    Date holiday1 (12, 25, 2021);
33:    Date holiday2 (12, 31, 2021);
34:
35:    cout << "holiday 1 is: ";
36:    holiday1.DisplayDate();
37:    cout << "holiday 2 is: ";
38:    holiday2.DisplayDate();
39:
40:    if (holiday1 == holiday2)
41:       cout << "Equality operator: The two are on the same day" << endl;
42:    else
43:       cout << "Equality operator: The two are on different days" << endl;
44:
45:    if (holiday1 != holiday2)
46:       cout << "Inequality operator: The two are on different days" << endl;
47:    else
48:       cout << "Inequality operator: The two are on the same day" << endl;
49:
50:    return 0;
51: }
```

Output ▼

```
holiday 1 is: 12 / 25 / 2021
holiday 2 is: 12 / 31 / 2021
Equality operator: The two are on different days
Inequality operator: The two are on different days
```

Analysis ▼

The equality operator (`==`) is a simple implementation that returns `true` if the day, month, and year are all equal, as shown in Lines 12 through 17. The inequality operator (`!=`) reuses the equality operator code, as shown in Line 21, and returns the opposite of it. The presence of these operators helps compare two `Date` objects, `holiday1` and `holiday2`, in `main()` in Lines 40 and 45.

The <, >, <=, and >= Operators

The code in Listing 12.6 made the `Date` class intelligent enough to be able to tell whether two `Date` objects are equal or unequal. You need to program the less-than (<), greater-than (>), less-than-or-equal-to (<=), and greater-than-or-equal-to (>=) operators to enable conditional checking akin to the following:

```
if (date1 < date2) {// do something}
```

or

```
if (date1 <= date2) {// do something}
```

or

```
if (date1 > date2) {// do something}
```

or

```
if (date1 >= date2) {// do something}
```

These operators are demonstrated in Listing 12.7.

Input ▼

LISTING 12.7 Demonstrates Implementing the <, <=, >, and >= Operators

```
#include<iostream>
using namespace std;

class Date
{
private:
   int day, month, year;

public:
   Date(int inMonth, int inDay, int inYear)
      : month(inMonth), day(inDay), year(inYear) {}

   bool operator< (const Date& compareTo)
   {
      if (year < compareTo.year)
         return true;
      else if ((year == compareTo.year) && (month < compareTo.month))
         return true;
      else if ((year == compareTo.year) && (month == compareTo.month)
               && (day < compareTo.day))
         return true;
      else
         return false;
   }

```

```
   bool operator<= (const Date& compareTo)
   {
      if (this->operator== (compareTo))
         return true;
      else
         return this->operator< (compareTo);
   }

   bool operator > (const Date& compareTo)
   {
      return !(this->operator<= (compareTo));
   }

   bool operator== (const Date& compareTo)
   {
      return ((day == compareTo.day)
         && (month == compareTo.month)
         && (year == compareTo.year));
   }

   bool operator>= (const Date& compareTo)
   {
      if(this->operator== (compareTo))
         return true;
      else
         return this->operator> (compareTo);
   }

   void DisplayDate()
   {
      cout << month << " / " << day << " / " << year << endl;
   }
};

int main()
{
   Date holiday1 (12, 25, 2016);
   Date holiday2 (12, 31, 2016);

   cout << "holiday 1 is: ";
   holiday1.DisplayDate();
   cout << "holiday 2 is: ";
   holiday2.DisplayDate();

   if (holiday1 < holiday2)
      cout << "operator<: holiday1 happens first" << endl;

   if (holiday2 > holiday1)
      cout << "operator>: holiday2 happens later" << endl;

   if (holiday1 <= holiday2)
```

```
76:         cout << "operator<=: holiday1 happens on or before holiday2" << endl;
77:
78:      if (holiday2 >= holiday1)
79:         cout << "operator>=: holiday2 happens on or after holiday1" << endl;
80:
81:      return 0;
82:  }
```

Output ▼

```
holiday 1 is: 12 / 25 / 2021
holiday 2 is: 12 / 31 / 2021
operator<: holiday1 happens first
operator>: holiday2 happens later
operator<=: holiday1 happens on or before holiday2
operator>=: holiday2 happens on or after holiday1
```

Analysis ▼

The operators of interest are implemented in Lines 12 through 51 and partially reuse the `==` operator that you saw in Listing 12.6.

The operators have been consumed inside `main()` between Lines 68 and 78, so you can see how easy it now is to compare two different dates.

The C++20 Three-Way Comparison Operator (<=>)

C++20 helps you write massively simplified comparison operations by using the three-way comparison operator (`<=>`) instead of using the `=`, `<`, `>`, `!=`, `<=`, and `>=` operators.

The syntax for defining this operator is as follows:

```
auto operator <=>(const Type& objToCompare)
{
   // comparison code, return type std::strong_ordering
}
```

This operator was first introduced in a simple example (refer to Listing 5.4 in Lesson 5). Listing 12.8 shows how to define a `<=>` operator—which is informally called a spaceship operator because of its shape—for the class `Date`.

Input ▼

LISTING 12.8 Programming a `<=>` Operator for the Class `Date` to Compare Two Dates

```
#include<iostream>
#include<compare>
using namespace std;

class Date
{
private:
   int day, month, year;

public:
   Date(int inMonth, int inDay, int inYear)
      : month(inMonth), day(inDay), year(inYear) {}

   auto operator <=>(const Date& rhs) const
   {
      if (year < rhs.year)
         return std::strong_ordering::less;
      else if (year > rhs.year)
         return std::strong_ordering::greater;
      else
      {
         // years are identical, compare months
         if (month < rhs.month)
            return std::strong_ordering::less;
         else if (month > rhs.month)
            return std::strong_ordering::greater;
         else
         {
            // months are identical, compare days
            if (day < rhs.day)
               return std::strong_ordering::less;
            else if (day > rhs.day)
               return std::strong_ordering::greater;
            else
               return std::strong_ordering::equal;
         }
      }
   }
};

int main()
{
   cout << "Enter a date: month, day & year" << endl;
   int month, day, year;
   cin >> month;
   cin >> day;
   cin >> year;
   Date date1(month, day, year);
```

```

    cout << "Enter another date: month, day & year" << endl;
    cin >> month;
    cin >> day;
    cin >> year;
    Date date2(month, day, year);

    auto result = date1 <=> date2;

    if (result < 0)
       cout << "Date 1 occurs before Date 2" << endl;
    else if (result > 0)
       cout << "Date 1 occurs after Date 2" << endl;
    else
       cout << "Dates are equal" << endl;

    return 0;
}
```

Output ▼

First run:

```
Enter a date: month, day & year
12
25
2021
Enter another date: month, day & year
1
1
2022
Date 1 occurs before Date 2
```

Next run:

```
Enter a date: month, day & year
6
2
2030
Enter another date: month, day & year
1
1
2001
Date 1 occurs after Date 2
```

Final run:

```
Enter a date: month, day & year
12
25
2021
Enter another date: month, day & year
12
25
2021
Dates are equal
```

Analysis ▼

For the sake of simplicity, the class doesn't validate the user input. Lines 13 through 37 define the spaceship operator for the `Date` class that is used within `main()` in Line 55. Note how the definition of class `Date` in Listing 12.8 is a good 20 lines shorter than the definition in Listing 12.7—without any loss of functionality! This is the power of the three-way comparison operator.

NOTE

> You may resort to using the compiler-defined three-way comparison operator by using the keyword `default` as follows:
>
> ```
> auto operator <=> (const T&) const = default;
> ```
>
> This might work for some trivial classes, but it won't work for our `Date` class because of the likelihood that the default comparison will not intelligently compare years, months, and days in that order before producing a result.

The Copy Assignment Operator (=)

There are times when you want to assign the contents of an instance of one class to another class, like this:

```
Date holiday(12, 25, 2021);
Date anotherHoliday(1, 1, 2022);
anotherHoliday = holiday; // uses copy assignment operator
```

This assignment invokes the default copy assignment operator that the compiler has built into a class when you have not supplied one. Depending on the nature of the class, the default copy assignment operator might be inadequate, especially if the class is managing a resource that will not be copied. This problem with the default copy assignment operator is similar to the problem with the default copy constructor discussed in Lesson 9. To ensure deep copies, as with the copy constructor, you need to specify an accompanying copy assignment operator:

```
ClassType& operator= (const ClassType& copySource)
{
   if(this != &copySource)  // protection against copy into self
   {
      // copy assignment operator implementation
   }
   return *this;
}
```

Deep copies are important if a class encapsulates a raw pointer, as does the `MyBuffer` class in Listing 9.9. To ensure deep copies during assignments, you define a copy assignment operator as shown in Listing 12.9.

Input ▼

LISTING 12.9 A Better `MyBuffer` Class from Listing 9.9 with a Copy Assignment Operator (=)

```
#include<iostream>
#include<algorithm>
using namespace std;
class MyBuffer
{
private:
   int* myNums;
   unsigned int bufLength;

public:
   MyBuffer(unsigned int length)
   {
      bufLength = length;
      myNums = new int[length]; // allocate memory
   }

   MyBuffer& operator= (const MyBuffer& src) // copy assignment
   {
      cout << "Copy Assignment creating deep copy" << endl;
      if (myNums != src.myNums) // avoid copy to self
      {
         if (myNums)
            delete myNums;

         bufLength = src.bufLength;
         myNums = new int[bufLength];
         copy(src.myNums, src.myNums + bufLength, myNums); // deep copy
```

```
      }

      return *this;
   }

   ~MyBuffer()
   {
      delete[] myNums; // free allocated memory
   }

   void SetValue(unsigned int index, int value)
   {
      if (index < bufLength) // check for bounds
         *(myNums + index) = value;
   }

   void DisplayBuf()
   {
      for (unsigned int counter = 0; counter < bufLength; ++counter)
         cout << *(myNums + counter) << " ";

      cout << endl;
   }
};

int main()
{
   cout << "How many integers would you like to store? ";
   unsigned int numsToStore = 0;
   cin >> numsToStore;

   MyBuffer buf(numsToStore);
   for (unsigned int counter = 0; counter < numsToStore; ++counter)
   {
      cout << "Enter value: ";
      int valueEntered = 0;
      cin >> valueEntered;
      buf.SetValue(counter, valueEntered);
   }

   MyBuffer anotherBuf(1); // initialize to contain just 1 int
   anotherBuf = buf;
   anotherBuf.DisplayBuf();

   return 0; // no crash, at destruction of buf
}
```

Output ▼

```
How many integers would you like to store? 3
Enter value: 101
Enter value: 202
Enter value: 303
Copy Assignment creating deep copy
101 202 303
```

Analysis ▼

I have purposely omitted the copy constructor in this example to reduce lines of code (but you should insert it when programming such a class; refer to Listing 9.9 as a guide). The copy assignment operator is implemented in Lines 16 through 27 and invoked by Line 68 in `main()`. It is similar in function to a copy constructor and performs a starting check to ensure that the same object is not both the copy source and destination. After the checks return `true`, the copy assignment operator for `MyBuffer` first deallocates its internal buffer `myNums` and then reallocates space for the text from the copy source and then uses `std::copy()` to copy, as shown in Line 26. The last line in the output contains the numbers entered by the user, generated using a copy of the initial object used to store them.

TIP

> `std::copy()` is one among many useful algorithms supplied by the Standard Template Library. You need to include the header `<algorithm>` to use it.
>
> These algorithms are discussed in detail in Lesson 23, "STL Algorithms."

CAUTION

> When implementing a class that manages a dynamically allocated resource such as an array allocated using `new`, always ensure that you have implemented (or evaluated the implementation of) the copy constructor and the copy assignment operator in addition to the constructor and the destructor.
>
> Unless you address the issue of resource ownership when an object of a class is copied, your class is incomplete and endangers the stability of the application when used.

TIP

> To create a class that cannot be copied, declare the copy constructor and copy assignment operator as private. Declaration as private without implementation is sufficient for the compiler to throw errors on all attempts at copying this class by passing to a function by value or assigning one instance into another.

The Subscript Operator (`[]`)

The operator that allows array-style (`[]`) access to a class is called a *subscript operator*. The typical syntax of a subscript operator is

```
return_type& operator [] (subscript_type& subscript);
```

So, when creating a class such as `MyBuffer` that encapsulates a dynamic array class of characters in a `char* buffer`, a subscript operator makes it really easy to randomly access individual characters in the buffer:

```
class MyBuffer
{
    // ... other class members
public:
    /*const*/ char& operator [] (int index) /*const*/
    {
        // return the char at position index in buffer
    }
};
```

Listing 12.10 demonstrates how the subscript operator (`[]`) helps a user iterate through the characters contained in an instance of `MyBuffer` using normal array semantics.

Input ▼

LISTING 12.10 Implementing a Subscript Operator (`[]`) in the `MyBuffer` Class to Allow Random Access to Characters Contained in `MyBuffer::myNums`

```
#include<iostream>
using namespace std;

class MyBuffer
{
private:
    int* myNums;
    unsigned int bufLength;

public:
    MyBuffer(unsigned int length)
```

```
    {
       bufLength = length;
       myNums = new int[length]; // allocate memory
    }

    int& operator[] (unsigned int index)
    {
       return myNums[index];
    }

    // Insert copy constructor & copy assignment operator
    // from previous listings here

    ~MyBuffer()
    {
       delete[] myNums; // free allocated memory
    }
};

int main()
{
    cout << "How many integers would you like to store? ";
    unsigned int numsToStore = 0;
    cin >> numsToStore;

    MyBuffer buf(numsToStore);
    for (unsigned int counter = 0; counter < numsToStore; ++counter)
    {
       cout << "Enter value: ";
       cin >> buf[counter];
    }

    for (unsigned int counter = 0; counter < numsToStore; ++counter)
       cout << "Value " << counter << " is " << buf[counter] << endl;

    return 0;
}
```


Output ▼

```
How many integers would you like to store? 3
Enter value: 101
Enter value: 202
Enter value: -101
Value 0 is 101
Value 1 is 202
Value 2 is -101
```

Analysis ▼

The program does the simple task of accepting numbers from the user, storing that information in the custom array `MyBuffer`, and then displaying the numbers from that array. The most important thing to note here is the introduction of the subscript operator (`[]`) in Lines 16 through 19, which helps with intuitive (that is, array-like) access, as shown in Lines 40 and 44 within `main()`.

CAUTION

Using the keyword `const` is important even when programming operators. To ensure that the subscript operator (`[]`) can be used only to read data and not to change data, you would do well to define the operator as

```
const int& operator[] (unsigned int index) const
{
     return myNums[index];
}
```

By using `const`, you protect the internal member `MyBuffer::myNums` against direct modification from the outside via `operator[]`. In addition to classifying the return value as `const`, you restrict the operator function type to `const` to ensure that it cannot modify the class's member attributes.

In general, use the maximum possible `const` restriction to avoid unintentional data modifications and increase protection of the class's member attributes.

You can improve on the version shown in Listing 12.10 by implementing a `const` version of the subscript operator :

```
const int& operator[] (unsigned int index) const
{
   return myNums[index];
}
```

This amendment is required to support `const` instances of the `MyBuffer` class, such as this:

```
const MyBuffer constBuf(20);
cout << constBuf[0];
```

There are other binary operators (refer to Table 12.2) that can be redefined or overloaded but that are not discussed further in this lesson. Their implementation, however, is similar to the implementations of those that have already been discussed.

Other operators, such as the logical operators and the bitwise operators, need to be programmed if the purpose of a class would be enhanced by having them. Clearly, a calendar class such as `Date` does not necessarily need to implement logical operators, whereas a class that performs numeric functions might need them.

Keep the objective of your class and its use in perspective when overloading operators or writing new ones.

The Function Operator (())

The operator `()`, which makes objects behave like functions, is called a *function operator*. Such operators are used in the Standard Template Library (STL), especially with STL algorithms. They can be used to make decisions; such function objects are typically called *unary* or *binary predicates*, depending on the number of operands they work on. Listing 12.11 shows a really simple function object to help you understand what gives these objects such an intriguing name.

Input ▼

LISTING 12.11 A Function Object Created Using the `()` Operator

```
#include<iostream>
#include<string>
using namespace std;

class Display
{
public:
   void operator() (string input) const
   {
      cout << input << endl;
   }
};

int main()
{
   Display displayFuncObj;

   // equivalent to displayFuncObj.operator () ("Display this string!");
   displayFuncObj("Display this string!");

   return 0;
}
```

Output ▼

```
Display this string!
```

Analysis ▼

Lines 7 through 10 implement `operator()`, which is then used inside the function `main()` in Line 18. Note that the compiler allows the use of the object `displayFuncObj` as a function in Line 18 by implicitly converting what looks like a function call to a call to `operator()`.

Hence, this operator is also called the function operator `()`, and the object of `Display` is also called a *function object*, or *functor*. This topic is discussed exhaustively in Lesson 21, "Understanding Function Objects."

The Move Constructor and Move Assignment Operator for High-Performance Programming

The move constructor and the move assignment operator are performance optimization features that became part of the standard in C++11. They ensure that temporary values (that is, *rvalues* that don't exist beyond the statement) are not wastefully copied. This is particularly useful when handling a class that manages a dynamically allocated resource, such as a dynamic array class or a string class.

The Problem of Unwanted Copy Steps

Take a look at the addition operator (+), as implemented in Listing 12.4. Notice that it actually creates a copy and returns it. If the `MyBuffer` class, as demonstrated in Listing 12.9, supported the addition operator, the following lines of code would be valid examples of easy concatenation:

```
MyBuffer buf1(5);
MyBuffer buf2(15);
MyBuffer buf3(buf1+buf2); // operator+, copy constructor
MyBuffer bufSum (1);
bufSum = buf1 + buf2 + buf3; // operator+, copy constructor, copy assignment
operator=
```

Thus, the useful operators that help with concatenation and assignment cause performance problems because multiple internal copy steps are required. The copy constructor, for instance, executes a deep copy to a temporary value that does not exist after the expression. This problem has been resolved through the introduction of move constructors and move assignment operators, which help avoid multiple internal resource copy/reassignment steps, thereby enhancing the performance of the copy or assignment steps.

Declaring a Move Constructor and Move Assignment Operator

You would program a move constructor as follows:

```
class Sample
{
private:
   Type* ptrResource;

public:
   Sample(Sample&& moveSource) // Move constructor, note &&
   {
      ptrResource = moveSource.ptrResource; // take ownership, start move
      moveSource.ptrResource = NULL;
   }

   Sample& operator= (Sample&& moveSource)//move assignment operator, note &&
   {
      if(this != &moveSource)
      {
         delete [] ptrResource;  // free own resource
         ptrResource = moveSource.ptrResource;  // take ownership, start move
         moveSource.ptrResource = NULL;  // free move source of ownership
      }
   }

   Sample(); // default constructor
   Sample(const Sample& copySource); // copy constructor
   Sample& operator= (const Sample& copySource); // copy assignment
};
```


Thus, the declaration of the move constructor and assignment operator are different from the declaration of the regular copy constructor and copy assignment operator in that the input parameter is of type `Sample&&`. In addition, as the input parameter is the move source, it cannot be a `const` parameter as it is modified. Return values remain the same; they are overloaded versions of the constructor and the assignment operator, respectively.

Standard-compliant compilers ensure that for rvalue temporaries, the move constructor is used instead of the copy constructor, and the move assignment operator is invoked instead of the copy assignment operator. In your implementation of these two, you ensure that instead of copying, you are simply moving the resource from the source to the destination. Listing 12.12 demonstrates the effectiveness of these two recent additions in optimizing the class `MyBuffer`.

Input ▼

LISTING 12.12 The `MyBuffer` Class with a Move Constructor and Move Assignment Operator in Addition to a Copy Constructor and Copy Assignment Operator

```
#include<iostream>
#include<algorithm>
using namespace std;
class MyBuffer
{
private:
    int* myNums;
    unsigned int bufLength;

public:
    MyBuffer(unsigned int length)
    {
        cout << "Constructing new instance with " \
              << length << " elements" << endl;
        bufLength = length;
        myNums = new int[length]; // allocate memory
    }

    MyBuffer(const MyBuffer& src) // copy constructor
    {
        cout << "Copy constructor creating deep copy" << endl;
        bufLength = src.bufLength;
        myNums = new int[bufLength];
        copy(src.myNums, src.myNums + bufLength, myNums); // deep copy
    }

    MyBuffer(MyBuffer&& src) // move constructor
    {
        cout << "Move constructor transferring ownership" << endl;

        if (src.myNums != NULL)
        {
            bufLength = src.bufLength;
            myNums = src.myNums; // take ownership

            src.myNums = NULL;
            src.bufLength = 0;
        }
    }

```

```
   MyBuffer& operator= (const MyBuffer& src) // copy assignment
   {
      cout << "Copy Assignment creating deep copy" << endl;
      if (myNums != src.myNums) // avoid copy to self
      {
         if (myNums)
            delete myNums;

         bufLength = src.bufLength;
         myNums = new int[bufLength];
         copy(src.myNums, src.myNums + bufLength, myNums); // deep copy
      }

      return *this;
   }

   MyBuffer& operator= (MyBuffer&& src) // move assignment
   {
      cout << "Move assignment transferring ownership" << endl;

      if ((src.myNums != NULL) && (myNums != src.myNums))
      {
         delete[] myNums;
         myNums = src.myNums; // take ownership
         bufLength = src.bufLength;

         src.bufLength = 0;
         src.myNums = NULL;
      }

      return *this;
   }

  MyBuffer operator + (const MyBuffer& bufToAppend)
   {
      cout << "Operator + concatenating" << endl;
      MyBuffer newBuf(this->bufLength + bufToAppend.bufLength);

      for (unsigned int counter = 0; counter < bufLength; ++counter)
         newBuf.SetValue(counter, *(myNums + counter));

      for (unsigned int counter = 0; counter < bufToAppend.bufLength;
      ++counter)
         newBuf.SetValue(counter + bufLength, *(bufToAppend.myNums +
         counter));

      return newBuf;
   }

   ~MyBuffer()
   {
```

```
      delete[] myNums; // free allocated memory
   }

   void SetValue(unsigned int index, int value)
   {
      if (index < bufLength) // check for bounds
         *(myNums + index) = value;
   }

   void DisplayBuf()
   {
      for (unsigned int counter = 0; counter < bufLength; ++counter)
         cout << *(myNums + counter) << " ";

      cout << endl;
   }
};

int main()
{
   MyBuffer buf1(5);
   MyBuffer buf2(15);

   cout << "Concatenation at object instantiation: " << endl;
   MyBuffer buf3(buf1 + buf2);
   MyBuffer bufSum(1);

   cout << "Concatenation at assignment: " << endl;
   bufSum = buf1 + buf2 + buf3;

   return 0;
}
```

Output ▼

Output without the move constructor and move assignment operator:

```
Constructing new instance with 5 elements
Constructing new instance with 15 elements
Concatenation at object instantiation:
Operator + concatenating
Constructing new instance with 20 elements
Copy constructor creating deep copy
Constructing new instance with 1 elements
Concatenation at assignment:
Operator + concatenating
Constructing new instance with 20 elements
Copy constructor creating deep copy
```

```
Operator + concatenating
Constructing new instance with 40 elements
Copy constructor creating deep copy
Copy Assignment creating deep copy
```

Output with the move constructor and move assignment operator enabled (MSVC):

```
Constructing new instance with 5 elements
Constructing new instance with 15 elements
Concatenation at object instantiation:
Operator + concatenating
Constructing new instance with 20 elements
Move constructor transferring ownership
Constructing new instance with 1 elements
Concatenation at assignment:
Operator + concatenating
Constructing new instance with 20 elements
Move constructor transferring ownership
Operator + concatenating
Constructing new instance with 40 elements
Move constructor transferring ownership
Move assignment transferring ownership
```

Output with the move constructor and move assignment operator enabled (g++):

```
Constructing new instance with 5 elements
Constructing new instance with 15 elements
Concatenation at object instantiation:
Operator + concatenating
Constructing new instance with 20 elements
Constructing new instance with 1 elements
Concatenation at assignment:
Operator + concatenating
Constructing new instance with 20 elements
Operator + concatenating
Constructing new instance with 40 elements
Move assignment transferring ownership
```


Analysis ▼

This is a long code sample, but most of it has already been demonstrated in previous examples and lessons. The most important part of this listing is in Lines 26 through 38, which implement the move constructor, and Lines 56 through 71, which contain the move assignment operator. Lines in the output that have been influenced by this addition have been marked in bold. Note that the output changes drastically when compared against the same class without these two entities: The unnecessary deep-copy steps have disappeared. If you look at the implementation of the move constructor and the move assignment operator again, you see that the move semantic is essentially implemented by taking ownership of the resources from the move source `src`, as shown in Line 33 for the move constructor and Line 63 for the move assignment operator. Then `NULL` is assigned to the move source pointer in Lines 35 and 67. This assignment to `NULL` ensures that the destructor of the instance that is the move source essentially does no memory deallocation via `delete` in Line 89 as the ownership has been moved to the destination object. Note that in the absence of the move constructor, the copy constructor is called, and it does a deep copy of the pointed string. Thus, the move constructor has saved a good amount of processing time in reducing unwanted memory allocations and copy steps.

Note that the move constructor and the move assignment operator are optional; they are not essential to the correct functioning of a program. However, they enable an immense improvement in performance and reduction in resource consumption. Unlike with the copy constructor and the copy assignment operator, the compiler does not add a default implementation of the move constructor or the move assignment operator for you.

TIP

Listing 12.12 also demonstrates that g++ (version 11.11) produces different output from MSVC (version 16.11). g++ elides some construction steps by default. You will get comparable output when you enable maximum optimization in Visual Studio.

User-Defined Literals

Literal constants were introduced in Lesson 3, "Using Variables, Declaring Constants." Here are some examples of literal constants:

```
int bankBalance = 10000;
long long companyNetWorth = 50'000'000'000; // 50 billion
double pi = 3.14;
char firstAlphabet = 'a';
const char* sayHello = "Hello!";
```

In this code, `10000`, `50'000'000'000`, `3.14`, `'a'`, and `"Hello!"` are all literal constants. Since C++11, the C standard has included features that enable you to define your own literals. For instance, if you are working on a scientific application that deals with thermodynamics, you might want all your temperatures to be stored using the Kelvin scale. You might then declare all your temperatures like this:

```
Temperature k1 = 32.15_F;
Temperature k2 = 0.0_C;
```

By using the literals `_F` and `_C`, which you have defined, you make your application a lot simpler to read and, therefore, maintain.

To define your own literal, you define `operator ""` like this:

```
ReturnType operator "" YourLiteral(ValueType value)
{
   // conversion code here
}
```

NOTE

> Depending on the nature of the user-defined literal, the `ValueType` parameter would be restricted to one of the following:
>
> - `unsigned long long int` for integral literal
> - `long double` for floating-point literal
> - `char`, `wchar_t`, `char16_t`, or `char32_t` for character literal
> - `const char*` for raw string literal
> - `const char*` together with `size_t` for string literal
> - `const wchar_t*` together with `size_t` for string literal
> - `const char16_t*` together with `size_t` for string literal
> - `const char32_t*` together with `size_t` for string literal

Listing 12.13 demonstrates a user-defined literal that converts temperatures to the Kelvin scale.

Input ▼

LISTING 12.13 Conversion from Fahrenheit and Centigrade to the Kelvin Scale

```
#include<iostream>
using namespace std;

struct Temperature
{
   double Kelvin;
   Temperature(long double kelvin) : Kelvin(kelvin) {}
};

Temperature operator"" _C(long double celsius)
{
   return Temperature(celsius + 273);
}

```

```
14: Temperature operator "" _F(long double fahrenheit)
15: {
16:     return Temperature((fahrenheit + 459.67) * 5 / 9);
17: }
18:
19: int main()
20: {
21:     Temperature k1 = 31.73_F;
22:     Temperature k2 = 0.0_C;
23:
24:     cout << "k1 is " << k1.Kelvin << " Kelvin" << endl;
25:     cout << "k2 is " << k2.Kelvin << " Kelvin" << endl;
26:
27:     return 0;
28: }
```

Output ▼

```
k1 is 273 Kelvin
k2 is 273 Kelvin
```

Analysis ▼

Lines 21 and 22 initialize two instances of `Temperature`: one using a user-defined literal `_F` to declare an initial value in Fahrenheit and the other using a user-defined literal to declare an initial value in Celsius (formerly called Centigrade). The two literals are defined in Lines 9 through 17 and do the work of converting the respective units into Kelvin and returning an instance of `Temperature`. Note that `k2` has intentionally been initialized to `0.0_C` and not to `0_C` because the literal `_C` has been defined (and is required) to take a `long double` as input value, and 0 would be interpreted as an integer.

Operators That Cannot Be Overloaded

C++ gives you a lot of flexibility in customizing the behavior of operators and making your classes easy to use. However, it does not allow you to change or alter the behavior of some operators that are expected to perform consistently. The operators that cannot be redefined are shown in Table 12.3.

TABLE 12.3 Operators That Cannot Be Overloaded or Redefined

Operator	Description
.	Member selection
.*	Pointer-to-member selection
::	Scope resolution
? :	Conditional ternary operator
sizeof	Gets the size of an object/class type

DO	DON'T
DO program as many operators as needed to make a class easy to consume—but not more.	**DON'T** rely on the default copy assignment operator and copy constructor supplied by the compiler as they perform deep copies of pointers that are members of the class.
DO mark conversion operators as `explicit` to avoid implicit conversions.	**DON'T** DON'T rely on the compiler to create a move assignment operator or move constructor. The compiler does not automatically create them for you but instead falls back on the regular copy assignment operator and copy constructor.
DO always program a copy assignment operator (with a copy constructor and destructor) in a class that contains pointer members.	
DO program a move assignment operator and move constructor for classes that manage dynamically allocated resources, such as an array of data.	

Summary

In this lesson, you learned how programming operators can make a significant difference in the ease with which your class can be consumed. When programming a class that manages a resource—for example, a dynamic array or a string—you need to supply at least a copy constructor and copy assignment operator, in addition to a destructor. A utility class that manages a dynamic array can do very well with a move constructor and a move assignment operator which ensures that the contained resource is not deep copied for temporary objects. Last but not least, you learned that operators such as `.`, `.*`, `::`, `?:`, and `sizeof` cannot be redefined.

Q&A

Q My class encapsulates a dynamic array of integers. What functions and operators should I implement at a minimum?

A When programming such a class, you need to clearly define the behavior in the scenario where an instance is being copied directly into another via assignment or copied indirectly by being passed to a function by value. You typically implement the copy constructor, copy assignment operator, and destructor. You also implement the move constructor and move assignment operator if you want to tweak the performance of this class in certain cases. To enable array-like access to elements stored inside an instance of the class, you need to overload the subscript operator (`[]`).

Q I have an instance object of a class. I want to support this syntax: `cout << object;`. What operator do I need to implement?

A You need to implement a conversion operator that allows your class to be interpreted as a type that `std::cout` can handle up front. One way is to define the operator `char*()`.

Q I want to create my own smart pointer class. What functions and operators do I need to implement at a minimum?

A A smart pointer needs to be able to be used as a normal pointer, as in `*pSmartPtr` or `pSmartPtr->Func()`. To enable this, you implement the operators `*` and `->`. In addition, to create a smart pointer, you need to take care of automatic resource release/returns by programming the destructor accordingly, and you need to clearly define how copy or assignment works by implementing the copy constructor and copy assignment operator. As an alternative, you could prohibit copying by declaring these as private.

Workshop

The Workshop contains quiz questions to help solidify your understanding of the material covered and exercises to provide you with experience in using what you've learned. Try to answer the quiz and exercise questions before checking the answers in Appendix E and be certain you understand the answers before going to the next lesson.

Quiz

1. In the following snippet, can the subscript operator (`[]`) return `const` and non-`const` variants of return types?

```
const Type& operator[](int index);
Type& operator[](int index); // is this OK?
```

2. Would you ever declare the copy constructor or copy assignment operator as private?
3. Would it make sense to define a move constructor and move assignment operator for the class `Date`?

Exercises

1. Program a conversion operator for the class `Date` that converts the date it holds into an integer.
2. Program a move constructor and move assignment operator for the class `DynamicFloats` that encapsulates a dynamically allocated array in the form of a private member `float*`.

LESSON 13
Casting Operators

Casting is a mechanism by which a programmer can temporarily or permanently change how the compiler interprets an object. (The programmer does not change the object itself but simply changes the *interpretation* of the object.) Operators that change the interpretation of objects are called *casting operators*.

In this lesson, you learn

- The need for casting operators
- Why C-style casts are not popular
- The four C++ casting operators
- The concepts of upcasting and downcasting
- Why C++ casting operators are not strongly recommended

The Need for Casting

A perfectly type-safe and type-strong world of well-written C++ applications has no need for casting or for casting operators. However, we live in a world where modules may be programmed by different people who used different environments. Newly programmed code is required to work with legacy code and libraries. To make this interoperability possible, compilers need to be instructed to interpret data in ways that make the application compile and function correctly. This interoperability is achieved using casting operators.

Let's take a real-world example. C++ compilers support `bool` as a native type, and they need to support linking to libraries that were programmed years ago in C. Such legacy code and libraries often used an integer type to hold Boolean data because type `bool` wasn't supported natively by the compiler back then. A Boolean type back in the day was something akin to

```
typedef unsigned short BOOL;
```

A function that returns Boolean data would be declared as

```
BOOL IsX ();
```

The programmer of a new C++ application consuming a legacy library needs to make the `bool` data type that is supported natively by his compiler function with the `BOOL` data type that is returned by the library. The way to make this interoperability work is by using casts:

```
bool Result = (bool)IsX(); // C-style cast interprets BOOL as bool
```

The evolution of C++ resulted in the emergence of C++ casting operators and continued support for the legacy C-style casting operator. You need to understand both casting styles because the world today uses both.

Why C-Style Casts Are Not Popular with Some C++ Programmers

Type safety is one of the attributes that adds quality to programming in C++. Most C++ compilers won't let you get away with this:

```
char* staticStr = "Hello World!";
int* intArray = staticStr;  // error: cannot convert char* to int*
```

—and rightfully so!

Having said that, compilers need to be backward compliant to support legacy code; therefore, they need to permit casting. In doing so, they permit code such as:

```
int* intArray = (int*)staticStr; // cast one problem away, create another
```

This C-style cast *forces* the compiler to interpret the destination as a type that the programmer wanted to assign to. The casting suppresses compile errors even though the types are totally incompatible. In this case, the programmer effectively muzzles the compiler and forces it to obey. In interpreting the `char*` as an `int*`, the compiler did not perform any conversion. In other words, in this example, a C-style cast compromised type safety and undermined the quality of the program.

The C++ Casting Operators

Despite the disadvantages of casting, the concept of casting cannot be discarded. In many situations, casts are legitimately required to solve important compatibility issues. In addition, C++ supplies a new casting operator specific to inheritance-based scenarios that did not exist with C programming.

The four C++ casting operators are

- static_cast
- dynamic_cast
- reinterpret_cast
- const_cast

The usage syntax of the casting operators is consistent:

```
destination_type result = cast_operator<destination_type> (object_to_cast);
```

Using `static_cast`

`static_cast` can be used to convert pointers between related types and perform explicit type conversions for standard data types that would otherwise happen automatically or implicitly. As far as pointers go, `static_cast` implements a basic compile-time check to ensure that a pointer is being cast to a related type. This is an improvement over a C-style cast, which allows a pointer to one object to be cast to an absolutely unrelated type without any complaint. With `static_cast`, a pointer can be upcasted to the base type or can be downcasted to the derived type, as the following code sample indicates:

```
Base* objBase = new Derived();
Derived* objDer = static_cast<Derived*>(objBase);  // ok!

// class Unrelated is not related to Base
Unrelated* notRelated = static_cast<Unrelated*>(objBase); // Error
// The cast is not permitted as types are unrelated
```

NOTE

Casting `Derived*` to `Base*` is called *upcasting* and can be done without any explicit casting operator:

```
Derived objDerived;
Base* objBase = &objDerived;  // ok!
```

Casting `Base*` to `Derived*` is called *downcasting* and cannot be done without the use of explicit casting operators:

```
Derived objDerived;
Base* objBase = &objDerived; // Upcast, ok!
Derived* objDer = objBase; // Error: Downcast, needs
explicit casting
```

However, note that `static_cast` verifies only that the pointer types are related. It does *not* perform any runtime checks. So, with `static_cast`, a programmer could still get away with this bug:

```
Base* objBase = new Base();
Derived* objDer = static_cast<Derived*>(objBase); // Still no errors!
```

Here, `objDer` points to a `Base` type but not to type `Derived`. `static_cast` performs a compile-time check by verifying that the types in question are related—which they are—and it therefore permits the casting. It does not perform a runtime check to ensure that the object being pointed to is of type `Derived`. Using this pointer `objDer` to call a method in the derived class `objDer->DerivedFunction()` would compile, but it would certainly result in unexpected behavior at execution.

In addition to helping in upcasting or downcasting, `static_cast` can, in many cases, help make implicit casts explicit and bring them to the attention of a programmer or reader:

```
double Pi = 3.14159265;
int num = static_cast<int>(Pi); // Making an otherwise implicit cast, explicit
```

In this code, `num = Pi` also works and would provide the same effect. However, using `static_cast` brings the nature of conversion to the attention of the reader and indicates (to someone who knows `static_cast`) that the compiler has performed the necessary adjustments based on the information available at compile time to perform the required type conversion. You also need to use `static_cast` when using conversion operators or constructors that have been declared using the keyword `explicit`. Avoiding implicit conversions via the keyword `explicit` is discussed in Lesson 9, "Classes and Objects," and Lesson 12, "Operator Types and Operator Overloading."

Using `dynamic_cast` and Runtime Type Identification

Dynamic casting, as the name suggests, is the opposite of static casting and actually executes the cast at runtime—that is, at application execution time. The result of a `dynamic_cast` operation can be checked to see whether the attempt at casting succeeded. The typical usage syntax of the `dynamic_cast` operator is

```
destination_type* Dest = dynamic_cast<class_type*>(Source);

if(Dest)     // Check for success of the casting operation
    Dest->CallFunc();
```

For example:

```
Base* objBase = new Derived();
```

```
// Perform a downcast
Derived* objDer = dynamic_cast<Derived*>(objBase);

if(objDer)    // Check for success of the cast
    objDer->CallDerivedMethod();
```

As shown in this short example, given a pointer to a base class object, the programmer can resort to using `dynamic_cast` to verify the type of the destination object being pointed to before proceeding to use the pointer as such. Note that in this code snippet, it is apparent that the destination object is a derived type. So, the sample is for demonstration only. However, this is not always the case—such as when a pointer of type `Derived*` is passed to a function that accepts type `Base*`. The function can use `dynamic_cast` given a base class pointer to detect the types and then perform operations specific to the types detected. Thus, `dynamic_cast` helps determine the type at runtime and makes it possible to use a casted pointer when it is safe to do so. See Listing 13.1, which uses the familiar hierarchy of classes `Tuna` and `Carp` related to the base class `Fish`, where the function `DetectFishType()` dynamically detects whether a `Fish*` is a `Tuna*` or a `Carp*`.

NOTE

> This mechanism of identifying the type of the object at runtime is called *runtime type identification* (*RTTI*).

Input ▼

LISTING 13.1 Using Dynamic Casting to Tell Whether a `Fish` Object Is a `Tuna` or a `Carp`

```
#include<iostream>
using namespace std;

class Fish
{
public:
   virtual void Swim()
   {
      cout << "Fish swims in water" << endl;
   }

   // base class should always have virtual destructor
   virtual ~Fish() {}
};

class Tuna: public Fish
{
public:
```

```
    void Swim()
    {
       cout << "Tuna swims real fast in the sea" << endl;
    }

    void BecomeDinner()
    {
       cout << "Tuna became dinner in Sushi" << endl;
    }
};

class Carp: public Fish
{
public:
    void Swim()
    {
       cout << "Carp swims real slow in the lake" << endl;
    }

    void Talk()
    {
       cout << "Carp talked Carp!" << endl;
    }
};

void DetectFishType(Fish* objFish)
{
    Tuna* objTuna = dynamic_cast <Tuna*>(objFish);
    if (objTuna) // check success of cast
    {
       cout << "Detected Tuna. Making Tuna dinner: " << endl;
       objTuna->BecomeDinner();
    }

    Carp* objCarp = dynamic_cast <Carp*>(objFish);
    if(objCarp)
    {
       cout << "Detected Carp. Making carp talk: " << endl;
       objCarp->Talk();
    }

    cout << "Verifying type using virtual Fish::Swim()" << endl;
    objFish->Swim(); // calling virtual function Swim
}

int main()
{
    Carp myLunch;
    Tuna myDinner;

    DetectFishType(&myDinner);
```

```
69:     cout << endl;
70:     DetectFishType(&myLunch);
71:
72:     return 0;
73: }
```

Output ▼

```
Detected Tuna. Making Tuna dinner:
Tuna became dinner in Sushi
Verifying type using virtual Fish::Swim()
Tuna swims real fast in the sea

Detected Carp. Making carp talk:
Carp talked Carp!
Verifying type using virtual Fish::Swim()
Carp swims real slow in the lake
```

Analysis ▼

This example uses a hierarchy in which the classes `Tuna` and `Carp` inherit from `Fish`. For the sake of explanation, not only do the two derived classes implement the virtual function `Swim()`, but each contains a function that is specific to its type (namely, `Tuna::BecomeDinner()` and `Carp::Talk()`). What is special in this example is that, given an instance of the base class `Fish*`, you are able to dynamically detect whether that pointer points to a `Tuna` or a `Carp`. This dynamic detection or runtime type identification happens in the function `DetectFishType()`, which is defined in Lines 43 through 61. In Line 45, `dynamic_cast` is used to test the nature of the input base class pointer of type `Fish*` for type `Tuna*`. If this `Fish*` points to a `Tuna`, the operator returns a valid address; otherwise, it returns `NULL`. Hence, the result of a `dynamic_cast` always needs to be checked for validity. After the check in Line 46 succeeds, you know that the pointer `objTuna` points to a valid `Tuna`, and you are able to call the function `Tuna::BecomeDinner()` using it, as shown in Line 49. With the `Carp`, you use the pointer to invoke the function `Carp::Talk()`, as shown in Line 56. Before returning, `DetectFishType()` does a verification of the type by invoking `Fish::Swim()`, which is virtual and redirects the call to the `Swim()` method implemented in `Tuna` or `Carp`, as applicable.

CAUTION

> The return value of a `dynamic_cast` operation should always be checked for validity. It is `NULL` when a cast fails.

Using `reinterpret_cast`

`reinterpret_cast` is the closest a C++ casting operator gets to a C-style cast. It really does allow a programmer to cast one object type to another, regardless of whether the types are related; that is, it forces a reinterpretation of type as shown in the following example:

```
Base* objBase = new Base();
Unrelated* notRelated = reinterpret_cast<Unrelated*>(objBase);
// The code above compiles, yet bad programming!
```

This cast actually forces the compiler to accept situations that `static_cast` would normally not permit. It finds usage in applications (such as device drivers, for example) where data needs to be converted to a simple type that an application programming interface (API) can accept. For example, some OS-level APIs require data to be sent as a byte array (that is, as an `unsigned char*`):

```
SomeClass* object = new SomeClass();
// Need to send the object as a byte-stream...
unsigned char* bytesFoAPI = reinterpret_cast<unsigned char*>(object);
```

The cast used in this code has not changed the binary representation of `object`. No other C++ casting operator would allow such a conversion that compromises type safety. `reinterpret_cast` is therefore the last resort when performing an otherwise unsafe conversion.

CAUTION

> Refrain from using `reinterpret_cast` in your applications because it suppresses type safety, allowing a type X to be interpreted as an unrelated type Y.

Using `const_cast`

`const_cast` enables you to turn off the `const` access modifier to an object. You are probably wondering why C++ needs this in the first place. In an ideal situation where programmers write their classes correctly, they remember to use the `const` keyword frequently and in the right places. The practical world is unfortunately way too different, and code like the following is prevalent:

```
class SomeClass
{
public:
    // ...
    void DisplayMembers(); //problem - display function isn't const
};
```

So, when you program a function such as

```
void DisplayAllData (const SomeClass& object)
{
    object.DisplayMembers ();  // Compile failure
    // reason: call to a non-const member using a const reference
}
```

You are correct in passing `object` as a `const` reference. After all, a display function should be read only and should not be allowed to call non-`const` member functions; that is, it should not be allowed to call a function that can change the state of the object. However, `SomeClass::DisplayMembers()` ought to be `const`, but unfortunately, it is not. Now, so long as `SomeClass` belongs to you and the source code is in your control, you can make corrective changes to `DisplayMembers()`. In many cases, however, it might belong to a third-party library, and you would not be able to make changes. In situations such as these, `const_cast` is your savior.

The code for invoking `DisplayMembers()` in such a scenario is

```
void DisplayAllData (const SomeClass& object)
{
    SomeClass& refData = const_cast<SomeClass&>(object);
    refData.DisplayMembers();    // Allowed!
}
```

CAUTION

> You should use `const_cast` to invoke non-`const` functions only as a last resort.

13

Note that `const_cast` can also be used with pointers:

```
void DisplayAllData (const SomeClass* data)
{
    // data->DisplayMembers(); Error: attempt to invoke a non-const function!
    SomeClass* pCastedData = const_cast<SomeClass*>(data);
    pCastedData->DisplayMembers();     // Allowed!
}
```

Problems with the C++ Casting Operators

Not everyone is happy with the C++ casting operators—not even those who swear by C++. Their reasons range from the syntax being cumbersome and nonintuitive to these operations being redundant. For instance:

```
double Pi = 3.14159265;

// C++ style cast: static_cast
int num = static_cast<int>(Pi);     // result: Num is 3

// C-style cast
int num2 = (int)Pi;                 // result: num2 is 3

// leave casting to the compiler
int num3 = Pi;                      // result: num3 is 3. No errors!
```

All three of these cases achieve the same result. The compiler is intelligent enough to convert such types correctly. This makes the cast syntax look redundant.

Similarly, every valid use of `static_cast` can be handled equally well by C-style casts:

```
// using static_cast
Derived* objDer = static_cast <Derived*>(objBase);

// But, this works just as well...
Derived* objDerSimple = (Derived*)objBase;
```

Thus, the advantage of using `static_cast` is often overshadowed by its cumbersome syntax.

Looking at other operators, `reinterpret_cast` is for forcing your way through when `static_cast` does not work. Ditto for `const_cast` with respect to modifying the `const` access modifiers. You can avoid `dynamic_cast` if your inheritance hierarchy is well designed and you invoke virtual functions using the base class instance. Thus, many experts hold the view that well-programmed, modern C++ applications can do without casting operators. These operators are necessary, however, when addressing interoperability issues with legacy code.

DO	DON'T
DO remember that casting a `Derived*` to a `Base*` is called upcasting and is inherently safe. **DO** remember that casting a `Base*` directly to a `Derived*` is called downcasting, and it can be unsafe unless you use `dynamic_cast` and check for success. **DO** remember that the objective of creating an inheritance hierarchy is typically to have virtual functions that, when invoked, use base class pointers to ensure that the available derived class versions are invoked.	**DON'T** forget to check a pointer for validity after using `dynamic_cast`. **DON'T** design an application around RTTI using `dynamic_cast`; use well-implemented virtual functions instead.

Summary

In this lesson, you learned the different C++ casting operators, as well as the arguments for and against using them. You also learned that, in general, you should avoid the use of casts.

Q&A

Q Is it okay to modify the contents of a `const` object by casting a pointer or reference to it using `const_cast`?

A Most definitely not. The result of such an operation is not defined and is certainly not desired.

Q I need a `Bird*` but have a `Dog*` at hand. The compiler does not allow me to use the pointer to the `Dog` object as a `Bird*`. However, when I use `reinterpret_cast` to cast the `Dog*` to `Bird*`, the compiler does not complain, and it seems that I can use this pointer to call `Bird`'s member function, `Fly()`. Is this okay?

A Again, definitely not. `reinterpret_cast` changes only the interpretation of the pointer; it does not change the object being pointed to (which is still a `Dog`). Calling a `Fly()` function on a `Dog` object will not give the results you are looking for, and it could possibly cause an application failure.

Q I have a `Derived` object being pointed to by an `objBase` that is a `Base*`. I am sure that `objBase` points to a `Derived` object, so do I really need to use `dynamic_cast`?

A Because you are sure that the object being pointed to is a `Derived` type, you can improve runtime performance by using `static_cast`.

Q C++ provides casting operators, but I am advised to avoid using them as much as possible. Why is that?

A Casting operators are useful when integrating legacy code, but you don't need them in well-programmed, modern C++ applications in most cases.

Workshop

The workshop contains quiz questions to help solidify your understanding of the material covered and exercises to provide you with experience in using what you've learned. Try to answer the quiz and exercise questions before checking the answers in Appendix E and be certain you understand the answers before going to the next lesson.

Quiz

1. You have a base class object pointer `objBase`. What cast would you use to determine whether it is a `Derived1` type or a `Derived2` type?
2. You have a `const` reference to an object and have tried calling a public member function that you wrote. The compiler does not allow this because the function in question is not a `const` member. Would you correct the function, or would you use `const_cast`?
3. True or false: `reinterpret_cast` should be used only when `static_cast` does not work and the cast is known to be required and safe.

4. True or false: Many instances of `static_cast`-based conversions, especially between simple data types, would be performed automatically by a good C++ compiler.

Exercises

1. **BUG BUSTERS:** What is the problem in the following code?

```
void DoSomething(Base* objBase)
{
   Derived* objDer = dynamic_cast <Derived*>(objBase);
   objDer->DerivedClassMethod();
}
```

2. You have a pointer `objFish*` that points to an object of class `Tuna`:

```
Fish* objFish = new Tuna;
Tuna* objTuna = <what cast?>objFish;
```

What cast would you use to get a pointer `Tuna*` to point to this object of type `Tuna`? Demonstrate using code.

LESSON 14

An Introduction to Macros and Templates

By now, you should have a solid understanding of basic C++ syntax. You are poised to learn language features that help you program C++ applications efficiently.

In this lesson, you learn

- An introduction to the preprocessor
- The `#define` keyword and macros
- An introduction to templates
- How to write template functions and classes
- The difference between macros and templates
- How to use `static_assert` to perform compile-time checks

The Preprocessor and the Compiler

Lesson 2, "The Anatomy of a C++ Program," introduced the preprocessor. The preprocessor, as the name indicates, runs before the compiler does. In other words, you use the preprocessor to influence what is compiled using preprocessor directives. These directives start with a # sign. For example:

```
// instruct preprocessor to insert contents of iostream here
#include<iostream>

// define a macro constant
#define ARRAY_LENGTH 25
int numbers[ARRAY_LENGTH]; // array of 25 integers

// define a macro function
#define SQUARE(x) ((x) * (x))
const int twentyFive = SQUARE(5);
```

This lesson focuses on two types of preprocessor directives shown in the code snippet above: one using `#define` to define a constant and another using `#define` to define a macro function. The directives instruct the preprocessor to replace every instance of the macro (`ARRAY_LENGTH` or `SQUARE`) with the value it defines.

NOTE

> Macros execute text substitution. The preprocessor does nothing intelligent. It simply replaces the identifier with other text—without validating the replacement.

Using the Macro `#define` to Define Constants

The syntax you use with `#define` to compose a constant is simple:

```
#define identifier replacement-text
```

For example, you define the constant `ARRAY_LENGTH` to be substituted with `25` as follows:

```
#define ARRAY_LENGTH 25
```

This identifier is now replaced by `25` wherever the preprocessor encounters the text `ARRAY_LENGTH`:

```
int numbers[ARRAY_LENGTH];
double radiuses[ARRAY_LENGTH];
std::string names[ARRAY_LENGTH];
```

After the preprocessor runs, the code above is visible to the compiler as follows:

```
int numbers[25];       // an array of 25 integers
double radiuses[25];  // an array of 25 doubles
std::string names[25];// an array of 25 std::strings
```

The replacement is applicable to every section of your code, including a `for loop` such as this one:

```
for(int index = 0; index < ARRAY_LENGTH; ++index)
    numbers[index] = index;
```

This `for` loop is visible to the compiler as

```
for(int index = 0; index < 25; ++index)
   numbers[index] = index;
```

To see exactly how such a macro works, review Listing 14.1.

Input ▼

LISTING 14.1 Declaring and Using Macros That Define Constants

```
 0: #include<iostream>
 1: #include<string>
 2: using namespace std;
 3:
 4: #define ARRAY_LENGTH 25
 5: #define PI 3.1416
 6: #define MY_DOUBLE double
 7: #define FAV_WHISKY "Jack Daniels"
 8:
 9: int main()
10: {
11:    int numbers [ARRAY_LENGTH] = {0};
12:    cout << "Array's length: " << sizeof(numbers) / sizeof(int) << endl;
13:
14:    cout << "Enter a radius: ";
15:    MY_DOUBLE radius = 0;
16:    cin >> radius;
17:    cout << "Area is: " << PI * radius * radius << endl;
18:
19:    string favoriteWhisky (FAV_WHISKY);
20:    cout << "My favorite drink is: " << FAV_WHISKY << endl;
21:
22:    return 0;
23: }
```

Output ▼

```
Array's length: 25
Enter a radius: 2.1569
Area is: 14.6154
My favorite drink is: Jack Daniels
```


Analysis ▼

`ARRAY_LENGTH`, `PI`, `MY_DOUBLE`, and `FAV_WHISKY` are the four macro constants defined in Lines 4 through 7, respectively. As you can see, `ARRAY_LENGTH` is used in defining the length of an array at Line 11, which has been confirmed indirectly by using the operator `sizeof()` in Line 12. `MY_DOUBLE` is used to declare the variable `radius` of type `double` in Line 15, and `PI` is used to calculate the area of the circle in Line 17. Finally, `FAV_WHISKY` is used to initialize a `std::string` object in Line 19 and is directly used in the `cout` statement in Line 20. All these instances show how the preprocessor simply makes a text replacement.

This simple text replacement by the preprocessor illustrated in Listing 14.1 has drawbacks.

TIP

In executing text substitutions, the preprocessor does not check for the correctness of the substitution (but the compiler always does). You could define `FAV_WHISKY` in Line 7 in Listing 14.1 like this:

```
#define FAV_WHISKY 42 // previously "Jack Daniels"
```

This would result in a compilation error in Line 19 for the `std::string` instantiation. However, in the absence of Line 19, the compiler would go ahead and print the following:

```
My favorite drink is: 42
```

This, of course, wouldn't make sense, and, most importantly, it would go through undetected. In addition, you wouldn't have much control over the macro-defined constant `PI`: Is it a `double` or a `float`? The answer is neither. To the preprocessor, `PI` is just a text substitution element 3.1416. It is not a defined data type.

Constants are best defined using the `const` keyword with data types instead. Here is a superior alternative:

```
const int ARRAY_LENGTH = 25;
const double PI = 3.1416;
const char* FAV_WHISKY = "Jack Daniels";
typedef double MY_DOUBLE;  // typedef aliases a type
```

Using Macros for Protection Against Multiple Inclusion

C++ programmers typically declare their classes and functions in *.H files*, also called *header files*. Functions are defined in .CPP files that include the header files using the

#include<*header*> preprocessor directive. If one header file—let's call it class1.h—declares a class that has another class declared in class2.h as a member, then class1.h needs to include class2.h. If the design were complicated, and the other class required the former as well, then class2.h would include class1.h, too!

For the preprocessor, however, two header files that include each other is a problem that is recursive in nature. To avoid this problem, you can use macros in conjunction with the preprocessor directives #ifndef and #endif.

header1.h, which includes <header2.h>, looks like the following:

```
#ifndef HEADER1_H _//multiple inclusion guard
#define HEADER1_H_ // preprocessor will read this and following lines once
#include<header2.h>

class Class1
{
   // class members
};
#endif  // end of header1.h
```

header2.h looks similar, but with a different macro definition, and it includes <header1.h>:

```
#ifndef HEADER2_H_//multiple inclusion guard
#define HEADER2_H_
#include<header1.h>

class Class2
{
   // class members
};
#endif // end of header2.h
```

NOTE

#ifndef can be read as "if-not-defined." It is a conditional processing command that instructs the preprocessor to continue only if the identifier has not been defined. This check ensures that the preprocessor works on the lines that follow only once.

#endif marks the end of this conditional processing instruction for the preprocessor.

Thus, when the preprocessor enters `header1.h` in the first run and encounters the `#ifndef` statement, it notices that the macro `HEADER1_H_` has not been defined and proceeds. The first line following `#ifndef` defines the macro `HEADER1_H_`, ensuring that a second preprocessor run of this file terminates at the first line containing `#ifndef`, as that condition now evaluates to `false`. The same is true for `header2.h`. This simple mechanism is arguably one of the most frequently used macro-based functionalities in the world of C++ programming.

TIP

> C++20 introduces *modules*. Modules provide a modern way of reusing code that was previously contained in header (`.H`) files. Modules don't need multiple inclusion guards and drastically reduce the time required for compilation of particularly large code bases. They are introduced in Lesson 31, "C++20 Modules and C++23."

Using `#define` to Write Macro Functions

A preprocessor can simply replace text elements identified by a macro, and so a preprocessor is often used to write simple functions, as in this example:

```
#define SQUARE(x) ((x) * (x))
```

This code determines the square of a number. Similarly, a macro that calculates the area of a circle looks like this:

```
#define PI 3.1416
#define AREA_CIRCLE(r) (PI*(r)*(r))
```

Macro functions are often used for very simple calculations such as these. They appear like regular function calls, but they are expanded inline before compilation. They can therefore help improve code performance in certain cases. Listing 14.2 demonstrates the use of these macro functions.

Input ▼

LISTING 14.2 Using Macro Functions That Calculate the Square of a Number, Area of a Circle, and Min and Max of Two Numbers

```
#include<iostream>
#include<string>
using namespace std;

```

```
 4: #define SQUARE(x) ((x) * (x))
 5: #define PI 3.1416
 6: #define AREA_CIRCLE(r) (PI*(r)*(r))
 7: #define MAX(a, b) (((a) > (b)) ? (a) : (b))
 8: #define MIN(a, b) (((a) < (b)) ? (a) : (b))
 9:
10: int main()
11: {
12:    cout << "Enter an integer: ";
13:    int num = 0;
14:    cin >> num;
15:
16:    cout << "SQUARE(" << num << ") = " << SQUARE(num) << endl;
17:    cout << "Area of a circle with radius " << num << " is: ";
18:    cout << AREA_CIRCLE(num) << endl;
19:
20:    cout << "Enter another integer: ";
21:    int num2 = 0;
22:    cin >> num2;
23:
24:    cout << "MIN(" << num << ", " << num2 << ") = ";
25:    cout << MIN (num, num2) << endl;
26:
27:    cout << "MAX(" << num << ", " << num2 << ") = ";
28:    cout << MAX (num, num2) << endl;
29:
30:    return 0;
31: }
```

Output ▼

```
Enter an integer: 36
SQUARE(36) = 1296
Area of a circle with radius 36 is: 4071.51
Enter another integer: -101
MIN(36, -101) = -101
MAX(36, -101) = 36
```

Analysis ▼

Lines 4 through 8 contain a few utility macro functions that return the square of a number, the area of a circle, and the min and max of two numbers. Note how `AREA_CIRCLE` in Line 6 evaluates the area using a macro constant `PI`, thus indicating that one macro can reuse another. After all, these are just plaintext replacement commands for the preprocessor. Let's analyze Line 25, which uses the macro `MIN`:

```
cout << MIN (num, num2) << endl;
```

This line is essentially fed to the compiler in the following format, where the macro is expanded in place:

```
cout << (((num) < (num2)) ? (num) : (num2)) << endl;
```

CAUTION

> Note that macros are not type sensitive, and macro functions can therefore cause problems. `AREA_CIRCLE`, for instance, should ideally be a function that returns `double` so that you are certain of the return value resolution of the area calculated.

Why All the Parentheses?

Take another look at the macro to calculate a circle's area:

```
#define AREA_CIRCLE(r) (PI*(r)*(r))
```

This calculation has curious syntax. Look at the number of parentheses used. Also, compare this syntax to the following syntax for the function `Area()` (which was originally presented in Listing 7.1 in Lesson 7, "Organizing Code with Functions"):

```
double Area(double radius)
{
   return Pi * radius * radius;  // look, no parentheses?
}
```

So, why do you use so many parentheses for the macro but not for the same formula in a function? The reason lies in the way the macro is evaluated: as a text substitution mechanism supported by the preprocessor.

Consider the macro without most of the brackets:

```
#define AREA_CIRCLE(r) (PI*r*r)
```

What happens when you invoke this macro using a statement like this:

```
cout << AREA_CIRCLE (4+6);
```

The compiler would expand it into

```
cout << (PI*4+6*4+6);  // not the same as PI*10*10
```

Thus, following the rules of operator precedence where multiplication happens before addition, the compiler actually evaluates the area like this:

```
cout << (PI*4+24+6);   // 42.5664 (which is incorrect)
```

In the absence of parentheses, plaintext conversion wreaks havoc on the programming logic! Parentheses help avoid this problem:

```
#define AREA_CIRCLE(r) (PI*(r)*(r))
cout << AREA_CIRCLE (4+6);
```

The compiler views the expression after substitution as follows:

```
cout << (PI*(4+6)*(4+6));  // PI*10*10, as expected
```

The parentheses automatically result in the calculation of an accurate area, making your macro code independent of operator precedence and its effects.

Using the `assert` Macro to Validate Expressions

Although it is good to test every path your code might execute and every potential data input, it might be unrealistic for programmers of large applications to be so meticulous. What is possible, though, is to check for valid expressions or variable values.

The `assert` macro enables you to do just that. You need to first include`<cassert>`, and then use `assert` as seen below:

```
assert(expression that evaluates to true or false);
```

A sample use of `assert()` that validates the contents of a pointer is

```
#include<cassert>
#include<cstddef>
#include<new>

int main()
{
   char* sayHello = new (std::nothrow) char[25];
   assert(sayHello != NULL); // throws a message if pointer is NULL

   // other code

   delete[] sayHello;
```

```
    return 0;
}
```

assert() ensures that you are notified if the pointer is invalid. For demonstration purposes, I initialized sayHello to NULL, and on execution in debug mode, the program produces the following output when compiled with g++:

```
int main(): Assertion 'sayHello != NULL' failed.
```

In certain configurations such as in Debug mode, Visual Studio might give you a visual alert.

Thus assert() is a handy debugging feature; for instance, you can validate input parameters of functions by using assert(). This is highly recommended and helps you improve the quality of your code over the long term.

Advantages and Disadvantages of Using Macro Functions

Macros enable you to reuse certain utility functions, regardless of the type of variables you are dealing with. Once again consider the following line from Listing 14.2:

```
#define MIN(a, b) (((a) < (b)) ? (a) : (b))
```

You can use this macro function MIN on integers:

```
cout << MIN(25, 101) << endl;
```

But you can reuse it on double, too:

```
cout << MIN(0.1, 0.2) << endl;
```

Note that if MIN() were a normal function, you would program two variants of it: MIN_INT(), which accepted int parameters and returned an int, and MIN_DOUBLE(), which does the same with type double instead. Defining MIN() as a macro reduces the number of lines of code and entices some programmers into using macros to define simple utility functions. These macro functions are expanded inline before compilation, and hence the performance of a simple macro is superior to that of an ordinary function call doing the same task. This is because the function call requires the creation of a call stack, passing arguments, and so on—administrative overload that often takes more CPU time than the calculation of MIN itself.

However, macros do not support any form of type safety, which compromises program quality and is a major disadvantage. In addition, debugging a complicated macro is not easy.

If you need the ability to program generic functions that are type independent yet type safe, you program a template function instead of a macro function. These functions are explained in the next section. If you need to boost performance, you call a function inline. (You have already been introduced to programming inline functions using the keyword `inline`. Refer to Listing 7.10 in Lesson 7.)

DO	DON'T
DO use macros as infrequently as possible. **DO** use `const` variables instead of macros where possible. **DO** remember that macros are not type safe, and the preprocessor performs no type checking.	**DON'T** forget to envelop variables in a macro function definition with parentheses `(...)`. **DON'T** forget to sprinkle your code with a generous number of `assert()` statements; they don't make it to the release version and are good at improving the quality of your code.

It's time to learn generic programming practices using templates!

An Introduction to Templates

Templates are arguably one of the most powerful features of C++.

A template in C++ enables you to define a behavior that you can apply to objects of varying types. This sounds ominously close to what macros let you do; think about the simple macro `MAX` that determined the greater of two numbers. However, macros are type unsafe, and templates are type safe.

Template Declaration Syntax

You begin the declaration of a template by using the `template` keyword followed by a type parameter list. The format of this declaration is

```
template <parameter list>
function or class declaration
```

The keyword `template` marks the start of a template declaration, and the template parameter list contains the keyword `typename`, which defines the template parameter objType, making it a placeholder for the type of the object that the template is being instantiated for:

```
template <typename T1, typename T2 = T1>
bool TemplateFunction(const T1& param1, const T2& param2);

// A template class
template <typename T1, typename T2 = T1>
class MyTemplate
{
private:
    T1 member1;
    T2 member2;

public:
    T1 GetMember1() {return member1; }
    // ... other methods
};
```

What you see here is a template function and a template class, each taking two template parameters, T1 and T2, where T2 has been given the default type T1.

The Different Types of Template Declarations

A template declaration can be

- A declaration or definition of a function
- A declaration or definition of a class
- A definition of a member function or a member class of a class template
- A definition of a static data member of a class template
- A definition of a static data member of a class nested within a class template
- A definition of a member template of a class or class template

Template Functions

Imagine a function that would adapt itself to suit parameters of different types, without requiring you to define an overloaded version for each type. Such a function is possible using template syntax! Let's analyze a sample template declaration that is the equivalent of the previously discussed macro MAX, which returns the greater of two supplied parameters:

```
template <typename objType>
const objType& GetMax(const objType& value1, const objType& value2)
{
    if (value1 > value2)
        return value1;
```

```
    else
        return value2;
}
```

Sample usage:

```
int num1 = 25;
int num2 = 40;
int maxVal = GetMax<int>(num1, num2);
double double1 = 1.1;
double double2 = 1.001;
double maxVal = GetMax<double>(double1, double2);
```

Note the detail `<int>` that is used in the call to `GetMax`. It effectively defines the template parameter `objType` as `int`. Based on the preceding code, the compiler generates two versions of the template function `GetMax`, which can be visualized as follows:

```
const int& GetMax(const int& value1, const int& value2)
{
    //...
}
const double& GetMax(const double& value1, const double& value2)
{
    // ...
}
```

In reality, however, template functions don't necessarily need an accompanying type specifier. So, the following function call works perfectly well:

```
int maxVal = GetMax(num1, num2);
```

Compilers are intelligent enough to understand that the template function is being invoked for the integer type. With template classes, however, you need to explicitly specify type, as shown in Listing 14.3.

Input ▼

LISTING 14.3 A Template Function `GetMax` That Helps Evaluate the Higher of Two Supplied Values

```
#include<iostream>
#include<string>
using namespace std;

template <typename Type>
const Type& GetMax(const Type& value1, const Type& value2)
{
    if (value1 > value2)
        return value1;
    else
```

```
10:         return value2;
11: }
12:
13: template <typename Type>
14: void DisplayComparison(const Type& value1, const Type& value2)
15: {
16:    cout << "GetMax(" << value1 << ", " << value2 << ") = ";
17:    cout << GetMax(value1, value2) << endl;
18: }
19:
20: int main()
21: {
22:    int num1 = -101, num2 = 2011;
23:    DisplayComparison(num1, num2);
24:
25:    double d1 = 3.14, d2 = 3.1416;
26:    DisplayComparison(d1, d2);
27:
28:    string name1("Jack"), name2("John");
29:    DisplayComparison(name1, name2);
30:
31:    return 0;
32: }
```

Output ▼

```
GetMax(-101, 2011) = 2011
GetMax(3.14, 3.1416) = 3.1416
GetMax(Jack, John) = John
```

Analysis ▼

This example features two template functions: `GetMax()` in Lines 4 through 11, which is used by `DisplayComparison()` in Lines 13 through 18. `main()` demonstrates in Lines 23, 26, and 29 how the same template function has been reused for very different data types: `integer`, `double`, and `std::string`. Not only are these template functions reusable (just like their macro counterparts), but they're easier to program and maintain and are type safe.

Note that you could also invoke `DisplayComparison` with the explicit type:

```
23:    DisplayComparison<int>(num1, num2);
```

However, this is unnecessary when calling template functions. You don't need to specify the template parameter type(s) because the compiler is able to infer it automatically. When using template classes, though, you do need to specify type.

Templates and Type Safety

The template functions `DisplayComparison()` and `GetMax()` in Listing 14.3 are type safe. This means that they would not allow a meaningless call like this one:

```
DisplayComparison(num1, name1);
```

Such a call would immediately result in a compile failure.

Template Classes

Lesson 9, "Classes and Objects," taught you that classes are programming units that encapsulate certain attributes and methods that operate on those attributes. Attributes typically are private members, such as `int age` in the class `Human`. Classes are design blueprints, and the real-world representation of a class is an object of the class. So, `Tom` can be thought of as an object of the class `Human` with the attribute `age` containing the value `15`, for example. It appears that in this case, age is provided in years. If you were required to store age as the number of seconds since birth for a certain reason unique to your application, then `int` might be insufficient. To be on the safe side, you might want to use a `long long` instead. This is where template classes could be handy. Template classes are templatized versions of C++ classes; they are blueprints of blueprints. When using a template class, you are given the option to specify the "type" you are specializing the class for. This enables you to create some humans with template parameter `Age` as a `long long`, some with `int`, and some with `Age` as an integer of type `short`.

A simple template class that uses a single template parameter `T` to hold a member variable of type `T` can be defined as follows:

```
template <typename T>
class HoldVarTypeT
{
private:
   T value;

public:
   void SetValue   (const T& newValue) { value = newValue; }
   T& GetValue() {return value;}
};
```

The type of the variable `value` is `T`, and `T` is resolved at the time the template is used—that is, when the template is *instantiated*. So, let's look at a sample usage of this template class:

```
HoldVarTypeT<int> holdInt;  // template instantiation for int
holdInt.SetValue(5);
cout << "The value stored is: " << holdInt.GetValue() << endl;
```

This example shows how to use this template class to hold and retrieve an object of type `int`; that is, the `Template` class is instantiated for a template parameter of type `int`. You can use the same class to deal with strings in a similar manner:

```
HoldVarTypeT<string> holdStr;
holdStr.SetValue("Sample string");
cout << "The value stored is: " << holdStr.GetValue() << endl;
```

Thus, the template class defines a pattern for classes and helps implement that pattern on different data types that the template may be instantiated with.

TIP

Template classes can be instantiated with types other than simple ones like `int` or classes supplied by the Standard Template Library. You can instantiate a template by using a class that you define. For example, when you add code that defines the template class `HoldVarTypeT` to Listing 9.1 in Lesson 9, you can instantiate the template for the class `Human` by appending the following code to `main()`:

```
HoldVarTypeT<Human> holdHuman;
holdHuman.SetValue(firstMan);
holdHuman.GetValue().IntroduceSelf();
```

Declaring Templates with Multiple Parameters

You can expand the template parameter list to declare multiple parameters, separated by commas. So, if you want to declare a generic class that holds a pair of objects that can be of different types, you can do so by using the construct shown in the following example (which displays a template class with two template parameters):

```
template <typename T1, typename T2>
class HoldsPair
{
private:
    T1 value1;
    T2 value2;
public:
```

```
    // Constructor that initializes member variables
    HoldsPair (const T1& val1, const T2& val2)
    {
        value1 = val1;
        value2 = val2;
    };
    // ... Other member functions
};
```

In this example, the class `HoldsPair` accepts two template parameters named `T1` and `T2`. You can use this class to hold two objects of the same type or of different types, as you can see here:

```
// A template instantiation that pairs an int with a double
HoldsPair<int, double> pairIntDouble(6, 1.99);

// A template instantiation that pairs an int with an int
HoldsPair<int, int> pairIntDouble(6, 500);
```

Declaring Templates with Default Parameters

You could modify the previous version of `HoldsPair <...>` to declare `int` as the default template parameter type:

```
template <typename T1=int, typename T2=int>
class HoldsPair
{
    // ... method declarations
};
```

This is similar in construction to functions that define default input parameter values except for the fact that, in this case, you define default *types*.

The use of `HoldsPair` can thus be compacted to

```
// Pair an int with an int (default type)
HoldsPair<> pairInts (6, 500);
```

Sample Template Class: `HoldsPair`

It's time to further develop the template version of `HoldsPair` that has been covered so far. Have a look at Listing 14.4.

Input ▼

LISTING 14.4 A Template Class with a Pair of Member Attributes

```
#include<iostream>
using namespace std;

// template with default params: int & double
```

```
template <typename T1=int, typename T2=double>
class HoldsPair
{
private:
   T1 value1;
   T2 value2;
public:
   HoldsPair(const T1& val1, const T2& val2) // constructor
      : value1(val1), value2(val2) {}

   // Accessor functions
   const T1& GetFirstValue() const
   {
      return value1;
   }

   const T2& GetSecondValue() const
   {
      return value2;
   }
};

int main ()
{
   HoldsPair<> pairIntDbl (300, 10.09);
   HoldsPair<short,const char*>pairShortStr(25,"Learn templates, love C++");

   cout << "The first object contains -" << endl;
   cout << "Value 1: " << pairIntDbl.GetFirstValue() <<  endl;
   cout << "Value 2: " << pairIntDbl.GetSecondValue() << endl;

   cout << "The second object contains -" << endl;
   cout << "Value 1: " << pairShortStr.GetFirstValue() <<  endl;
   cout << "Value 2: " << pairShortStr.GetSecondValue() << endl;

   return 0;
}
```

Output ▼

```
The first object contains -
Value 1: 300
Value 2: 10.09
The second object contains -
Value 1: 25
Value 2: Learn templates, love C++
```

Analysis ▼

This simple program illustrates how to declare the template class `HoldsPair` to hold a pair of values of types that are dependent on the template's parameter list. Line 4 contains a template parameter list that defines two template parameters `T1` and `T2`, with default types `int` and `double`, respectively. The accessor functions `GetFirstValue()` and `GetSecondValue()` can be used to query the values held by the object. Note how `GetFirstValue` and `GetSecondValue` get adapted on the basis of the template instantiation syntax to return the appropriate object types. You have managed to define a pattern in `HoldsPair` that you can reuse to deliver the same logic for different variable types. Thus, templates increase code reusability.

Template Instantiation and Specialization

A template class is a blueprint of a class, and it therefore doesn't truly exist for the compiler before it has been used in one form or another. That is, as far as the compiler is concerned, a template class you define but don't consume is code that is simply ignored. However, you *instantiate* a template class, like `HoldsPair`, by supplying template arguments like this:

```
HoldsPair<int, double> pairIntDbl;
```

Here you are instructing the compiler to create a class for you by using the template and to instantiate it for the types specified as template arguments (`int` and `double` in this case). Thus, in the case of templates, *instantiation* is the act or process of creating a specific type using one or more template arguments.

On the other hand, there may be situations that require you to explicitly define a (different) behavior of a template when instantiated with a specific type. In such cases, you specialize a template (or behavior thereof) for that type. A specialization of the template class `HoldsPair` when instantiated with template parameters of type `int` would look like this:

```
template<> class HoldsPair<int, int>
{
   // implementation code here
};
```

Needless to say, code that specializes a template must follow the template definition. Listing 14.5 is an example of a template specialization that demonstrates how different a specialized version can be from the template it specializes. 14

Input ▼

LISTING 14.5 Demonstrating Template Specialization

```
#include<iostream>
using namespace std;

template <typename T1 = int, typename T2 = double>
class HoldsPair
{
private:
    T1 value1;
    T2 value2;
public:
    HoldsPair(const T1& val1, const T2& val2) // constructor
        : value1(val1), value2(val2) {}

    // Accessor functions
    const T1& GetFirstValue() const;
    const T2& GetSecondValue() const;
};

// specialization of HoldsPair for types int & int here
template<> class HoldsPair<int, int>
{
private:
    int value1;
    int value2;
    string strFun;
public:
    HoldsPair(const int& val1, const int& val2) // constructor
        : value1(val1), value2(val2) {}

    const int & GetFirstValue() const
    {
        cout << "Returning integer " << value1 << endl;
        return value1;
    }
};

int main()
{
    HoldsPair<int, int> pairIntInt(222, 333);
    pairIntInt.GetFirstValue();

    return 0;
}
```

Output ▼

```
Returning integer 222
```

Analysis ▼

When you compare the behavior of the class `HoldsPair` in Listing 14.4 to the behavior of the class in this listing, you notice that the template is behaving remarkably differently. In fact, the function `GetFirstValue()` has been modified in the template instantiation for `HoldsPair<int, int>` to also display the value. A closer look at the specialization code in Lines 18 through 34 shows that this version also has a string member declared in Line 24—a member that is missing in the original template definition of `HoldsPair<>` in Lines 3 through 16. In fact, the original template definition doesn't even supply an implementation of the accessor functions `GetFirstValue()` and `GetSecondValue()`, and the program still compiles. This is because the compiler was only required to consider the template instantiation for `<int, int>`—for which you have supplied a specialized implementation that is complete enough. Thus, this sample not only demonstrates template specialization but also how template code is considered or even ignored by the compiler, depending on its use.

Template Classes and `static` Members

You learned that code in templates begins to exist for the compiler when used and not otherwise. So, how would `static` member attributes function within a template class? You learned in Lesson 9 that declaring a class member `static` results in the member being shared across all instances of a class. It's similar with a template class, too, save for the fact that a `static` member is shared across all objects of a template class with the same template instantiation. So a `static` member `X` within a template class is static within all instances of the class instantiated for `int`. Similarly, another instance of `X` is also static within all instances of the class specialized for `double`, independent of the other template instantiation for `int`. In other words, you can visualize it as the compiler creating two versions of the static member variable in a template class: `X_int` for template instantiation as `int` and `X_double` for template instantiation as `double`. Listing 14.6 demonstrates this.

Input ▼

LISTING 14.6 The Effect of Static Variables on Template Class and Instances Thereof

```
#include<iostream>
using namespace std;
```

```
 2:
 3: template <typename T>
 4: class TestStatic
 5: {
 6: public:
 7:     static T staticVal;
 8: };
 9:
10: // static member initialization
11: template<typename T> T TestStatic<T>::staticVal;
12:
13: int main()
14: {
15:     TestStatic<int> intInstance;
16:     cout << "Setting staticVal for intInstance to 2021" << endl;
17:     intInstance.staticVal = 2021;
18:
19:     TestStatic<double> dblnstance;
20:     cout << "Setting staticVal for dblnstance to 1011.022" << endl;
21:     dblnstance.staticVal = 1011.022;
22:
23:     cout << "intInstance.staticVal = " << intInstance.staticVal << endl;
24:     cout << "dblnstance.staticVal = " << dblnstance.staticVal << endl;
25:
26:     return 0;
27: }
```

Output ▼

```
Setting staticVal for intInstance to 2021
Setting staticVal for dblnstance to 1011.022
intInstance.staticVal = 2021
dblnstance.staticVal = 1011.02
```

Analysis ▼

In Lines 17 and 21, you set the member `staticVal` for an instantiation of the template for type `int` and type `double`, respectively. The output demonstrates that the compiler has stored two distinct values in two different static members, though both are called `staticVal`. Thus, the compiler ensures that the behavior of the static variable remains intact for the instantiation of the template class for a particular type.

NOTE

Note the static member instantiation syntax for a template class in Line 11 in Listing 14.6:

```
template<typename T> T TestStatic<T>::staticVal;
```

Variable Templates

Say that you want to write a generic function that adds two values. The template function `Sum()` achieves just that:

```
template <typename T1, typename T2, typename T3>
void Sum(T1& result, T2 num1, T3 num2)
{
   result = num1 + num2;
   return;
}
```

This function is simple. However, if you were required to write one single function that would be capable of adding any number of values, each passed as an argument, you would need to make use of *variable templates*, also called *variadic templates*, in defining such a function. C++ has supported variable templates since C++14. Listing 14.7 demonstrates the use of variable templates in defining such a function.

Input ▼

LISTING 14.7 Function Using Variadic Templates Demonstrating Variable Arguments

```
#include<iostream>
using namespace std;

template <typename Res, typename ValType>
void Sum(Res& result, ValType& val)
{
   result = result + val;
}

template <typename Res, typename First, typename... Rest>
void Sum(Res& result, First val1, Rest... valN)
{
   result = result + val1;
   return Sum(result, valN ...);
}

int main()
{
   double dResult = 0;
```

```
19:     Sum (dResult, 3.14, 4.56, 1.1111);
20:     cout << "dResult = " << dResult << endl;
21:
22:     string strResult;
23:     Sum (strResult, "Hello ", "World");
24:     cout << "strResult = " << strResult.c_str() << endl;
25:
26:     return 0;
27: }
```

Output ▼

```
dResult = 8.8111
strResult = Hello World
```

Analysis ▼

This example illustrates that the function `Sum()` that you defined using variable templates not only processed completely different argument types, as shown in Lines 19 and 23, but also processed a varying number of arguments. `Sum()` invoked by Line 19 uses four arguments, while that in Line 23 uses three arguments, of which one is `std::string` and the following two are `const char*`. During compilation, the compiler actually creates code for the right kind of `Sum()` to suit the call, and it does so recursively until all arguments have been processed.

> **NOTE**
>
> You might have noticed the use of the ellipsis (`...`) in Listing 14.7. An ellipsis used with a template tells the compiler that the template class or function may accept an arbitrary number of template arguments of any type.

Variable templates are a powerful addition to C++ that can be applied in mathematical processing as well as to accomplish certain simple tasks. Programmers using variable templates save themselves the repetitive effort of implementing functions in various overloaded versions; thus, they make it possible to create code that is shorter and simpler to maintain.

NOTE

> You can use the operator `sizeof...()` to determine the number of template arguments passed in a call to a variable template. In Listing 14.7, you could use this operator inside a function like `Sum()` as shown here:
>
> ```
> int arrNums[sizeof...(Rest)];
> // length of array evaluated using sizeof...() at
> compile time
> ```
>
> You must not confuse `sizeof...()` with `sizeof(Type)`. The latter returns the size of a type, while the former returns the number of template arguments sent to a variadic template.

The support of variable templates has also ushered in standard support for *tuples*. `std::tuple` is a class template that implements a tuple. It can be instantiated with a varying number of member elements and types. These may be individually accessed using the standard library function `std::get`. Listing 14.8 demonstrates the instantiation and use of a `std::tuple`.

Input ▼

LISTING 14.8 Instantiating and Using a `std::tuple`

```
#include<iostream>
#include<tuple>
#include<string>
using namespace std;

template <typename tupleType>
void DisplayTupleInfo(tupleType& tup)
{
   const int numMembers = tuple_size<tupleType>::value;
   cout << "Num elements in tuple: " << numMembers << endl;
   cout << "Last element value: " << get<numMembers - 1>(tup) << endl;
}

int main()
{
   tuple<int, char, string> tup1(make_tuple(101, 's', "Hello Tuple!"));
   DisplayTupleInfo(tup1);

   auto tup2(make_tuple(3.14, false));
   DisplayTupleInfo(tup2);

   auto concatTup(tuple_cat(tup2, tup1)); // contains tup2, tup1 members
   DisplayTupleInfo(concatTup);
```

```
23:
24:     double pi;
25:     string sentence;
26:     tie(pi, ignore, ignore, ignore, sentence) = concatTup;
27:     cout << "Unpacked! Pi: " << pi << " and \"" << sentence << "\"" << endl;
28:
29:     return 0;
30: }
```

Output ▼

```
Num elements in tuple: 3
Last element value: Hello Tuple!
Num elements in tuple: 2
Last element value: 0
Num elements in tuple: 5
Last element value: Hello Tuple!
Unpacked! Pi: 3.14 and "Hello Tuple!"
```

Analysis ▼

First and foremost, if the code in Listing 14.8 overwhelms you, do not worry! A tuple is used to hold a collection of elements of different types, where required. This example uses the `std::tuple` class to instantiate different tuples containing varying number and types of elements. Lines 15, 18, and 21 contain three different instantiations of a `std::tuple`. `tup1` contains three members: an `int`, a `char`, and a `std::string`. `tup2` contains a `double` and a `bool` and also uses the compiler's automatic type deduction feature via the keyword `auto`. `tup3` is actually a tuple with five members: `double`, `bool`, `int`, `char`, and `string`—a result of concatenation using the template function `std::tuple_cat`.

The template function `DisplayTupleInfo()` in Lines 5 through 11 demonstrates a use of `tuple_size` that resolves to the number of elements contained by that specific instantiation of `std::tuple` during compilation. `std::get` in Line 10 is the mechanism to access individual values stored in a tuple using their zero-based indexes. Finally, `std::tie` in Line 26 demonstrates how the contents of a tuple can be unpacked or copied into individual objects. You use `std::ignore` to instruct `tie` to ignore the tuple members that were not of any interest to the application.

Using `static_assert` to Perform Compile-Time Checks

`static_assert`, introduced in C++11, blocks compilation if a supplied condition is not fulfilled. `static_assert` is a compile-time assert that can display a custom message on your development environment (or console):

```
static_assert(expression being validated, "Error message when check fails");
```

This feature is quite useful with template classes. For example, you might want to ensure that your template class can only be instantiated for integer types. You would then use `static_assert()` as follows:

```
static_assert(std::is_integral<T>::value, "Only integers please!");
```

Introduced by C++11, `is_integral<>` defined in header `<type_traits>` checks whether the supplied template parameter is an integer type.

Listing 14.9 shows a template class that uses `static_assert` to allow compilation for integer types and block the rest.

Input ▼

LISTING 14.9 A Template Class That Protests Using `static_assert` When Instantiated for non-Integer Types

```
#include<type_traits>

template <typename T>
class OnlyInt
{
public:
   OnlyInt()
   {
      static_assert(std::is_integral<T>::value, "Only integers please!");
   }
};

int main()
{
   OnlyInt<int> test1; // OK!
   // OnlyInt<double> test2; // Error!

   return 0;
}
```

Output ▼

This code produces no output.

Analysis ▼

This example demonstrates how `static_assert` programmed in Line 8 ensures that the template class `OnlyInt<>` cannot be instantiated for a `double`, when you uncomment Line 15. The template instantiation shown in Line 15 is against the intended use of the class. Compilation hence fails, supplying reason:

```
Only integers please!
```

TIP

> C++20 introduced concepts, which you use to define rules that constrain the instantiation of your templates to certain allowed types. The compiler validates the fulfilment of these rules and delivers a simpler error message when the template uses parameter types that are not permitted.
>
> Concepts are explained in Lesson 29, "C++20 Concepts, Ranges, Views, and Adaptors."

Using Templates in Practical C++ Programming

An important and powerful application of templates is in the STL, which is a collection of template classes and functions containing generic utility classes and algorithms. These STL template classes enable you to implement dynamic arrays, lists, and key/value pair containers, whereas algorithms, such as `std::sort`, work on those containers and process the data they contain.

The knowledge of template syntax you gained earlier will greatly assist you in using STL containers and functions that are presented in greater detail in the following lessons of this book. A better understanding of STL containers and algorithms will, in turn, help you write efficient C++ applications that use the STL's tested and reliable implementation and help you avoid spending time on boilerplate details.

DO	DON'T
DO use templates for the implementation of generic concepts. **DO** choose templates over macros.	**DON'T** forget to use the principles of `const` correctness when programming template functions and classes. **DON'T** forget that a static member contained within a template class is static for every type specialization of the class.

Summary

In this lesson, you learned more details about working with the preprocessor. Each time you run the compiler, the preprocessor runs first and translates directives such as `#define`.

The preprocessor does text substitution, although with the use of macros, substitutions can be somewhat complex. Macro functions provide complex text substitution based on arguments passed at compile time to the macro. It is important to put parentheses around every argument in a macro to ensure that the correct substitution takes place.

Templates help you write reusable code that supplies a developer with a pattern that can be used for a variety of data types. They also make for a type-safe replacement of macros. With the knowledge of templates gained in this lesson, you are now poised to learn to use the STL.

Q&A

Q Why should I use inclusion guards in my header files?

A Inclusion guards using `#ifndef`, `#define`, and `#endif` protect a header from multiple or recursive inclusion errors, and in some cases they even speed up compilation.

Q When should I favor macro functions over templates if the functionality in question can be implemented in both?

A Ideally, you should always favor templates as they allow for generic implementation that is also type safe. Macros don't allow for type-safe implementations and are best avoided.

Q Do I need to specify template arguments when invoking a template function?

A Normally you do not because the compiler can infer this for you, given the arguments used in the function call.

Q How many instances of static variables exist for a given template class?

A This is entirely dependent on the number of types for which the template class has been instantiated. So, if your class has been instantiated for an `int`, a `string`, and a custom type `X`, you can expect three instances of your static variable to be available—one per template instantiation.

Workshop

The Workshop provides quiz questions to help you solidify your understanding of the material covered and exercises to provide you with experience in using what you've learned. Try to answer the quiz and exercise questions before checking the answers in Appendix E and be certain you understand the answers.

Quiz

1. What is an inclusion guard?
2. Consider the following macro:
   ```
   #define SPLIT(x) x / 5
   ```
   What is the result if this is called with `20`?
3. What is the result if the `SPLIT` macro in question 2 is called with `10+10`?
4. How would you modify the `SPLIT` macro in question 2 to avoid erroneous results?

Exercises

1. Write a macro that multiplies two numbers.
2. Write a template version of the macro in Quiz Question 2.
3. Implement a template function for `swap` that exchanges two variables.
4. **BUG BUSTERS:** How would you improve the following macro, which computes one-quarter of an input value?
   ```
   #define QUARTER(x) (x / 4)
   ```
5. Write a simple template class that holds two arrays of types that are defined via the class's template parameter list. The size of the array should be 10, and the template class should have accessor functions that allow for the manipulation of array elements.
6. Write a template function `Display()` that can be invoked with varying numbers and types of arguments and that displays each of them.

LESSON 15

An Introduction to the Standard Template Library

Put in simple terms, the Standard Template Library (STL) is a set of template classes and functions that supply a programmer with

- Containers for storing information
- Iterators for accessing the information stored
- Algorithms that comprise utility functions that work on containers using iterators

In this lesson, you get an overview of these three pillars of STL, which are explained in detail in forthcoming lessons.

STL Containers

Containers are STL classes that are used to store data. The STL supplies two types of container classes:

- Sequential containers
- Associative containers

In addition to these, the STL also provides classes called *container adapters* that are variants of containers with reduced functionality to support specific purposes.

Sequential Containers

As the name suggests, sequential containers are containers used to hold data in a sequential fashion; arrays and lists are examples of sequential containers. Sequential containers are characterized by fast insertion time, but they are relatively slow in `find` operations.

These are the STL sequential containers:

- **`std::vector`:** Operates like a dynamic array and grows at the end. Think of a vector as a shelf of books to which you can add or remove books on one end.
- **`std::deque`:** Similar to `std::vector` except that it allows for new elements to be inserted or removed at the beginning, too.
- **`std::list`:** Operates like a doubly linked list. Think of this like a chain, where an element is a link in the chain. You can add or remove links—that is, elements—at any position.
- **`std::forward_list`:** Similar to a `std::list` except that it is a singly linked list of elements that allows you to iterate in only one direction.

The STL `vector` class is akin to an array and allows for random access of an element; that is, you can directly access or manipulate an element in `vector`, given its position (index), by using the subscript operator (`[]`). In addition, `vector` is a dynamic array and can therefore resize itself to suit an application's runtime requirements. To keep the property of being able to randomly access an element in the array when given a position, most implementations of `vector` keep all elements in contiguous locations. Therefore, if `vector` needs to resize itself, it can often reduce the performance of the application, depending on the type of the object it contains. Lesson 4, "Managing Arrays and Strings," briefly introduced you to `vector` in Listing 4.4. This container is discussed extensively in Lesson 17, "STL Dynamic Array Classes."

You can think of the STL `list` as STL's implementation of a regular linked list. Although elements in `list` cannot be randomly accessed, as they can be in `vector`, `list` can organize elements in noncontiguous sections of memory. Therefore, `std::list` is not subject to the performance issues that are applicable to `vector` when `vector` needs to reallocate its internal array. The STL `list` class is discussed extensively in Lesson 18, "STL `list` and `forward_list`."

Associative Containers

Associative containers are containers that store elements in a sorted order—much like a dictionary. This results in slower insertion times but presents significant advantages when it comes to searching.

The associative containers supplied by STL are

- **`std::set`:** Stores unique values sorted on insertion in a container featuring logarithmic complexity.
- **`std::unordered_set`:** Stores unique values sorted on insertion in a container featuring near-constant-time complexity.

- **std::map:** Stores key/value pairs sorted by their unique keys in a container with logarithmic complexity.
- **std::unordered_map:** Stores key/value pairs sorted by their unique keys in a container with near-constant-time complexity.
- **std::multiset:** Akin to `set` and also supports the ability to store multiple items that have the same value; that is, the value doesn't need to be unique.
- **std::unordered_multiset:** Akin to `unordered_set` and also supports the ability to store multiple items that have the same value; that is, the value doesn't need to be unique. Features constant-time complexity.
- **std::multimap:** Akin to a `map` and also supports the ability to store key/value pairs where keys don't need to be unique.
- **std::unordered_multimap:** Akin to `unordered_map` and also supports the ability to store key/value pairs where keys don't need to be unique. Features constant-time complexity.

NOTE

Complexity in this case is an indication of the performance of the container in relation to the number of elements contained by it. Therefore, when we speak of *constant-time complexity*, as with `std::unordered_map`, we mean that the performance of the container is unrelated to the number of elements contained by it. Such a container would need as much time to perform on a thousand elements as it would on a million.

Logarithmic complexity, as with `std::map`, indicates that the performance is proportional to the logarithm of the number of elements contained in the container. Such a container would take twice as long to process a million elements as it would to process a thousand.

Linear complexity means that the performance is proportional to the number of elements. Such a container would be a thousand times slower to process a million elements as it would be to process a thousand.

For a given container, the complexities may be different for differing operations. For example, the element insertion complexity may be constant, while the search complexity is linear. Therefore, having an understanding of how a container may perform in addition to the functionality it will be used with is key to choosing the right container.

The sort criteria for STL containers can be customized by programming predicate functions.

> **TIP**
>
> Some implementations of STL also feature associative containers such as `hash_set`, `hash_multiset`, `hash_map`, and `hash_multimap`. These are similar to the `unordered_*` containers, which are supported by the C++ standard. In some scenarios, `hash_*` and the `unordered_*` variants can be better at searching as they offer constant time operations (independent of the number of elements in the container). Typically, these containers also supply public methods that are identical to those supplied by their standard counterparts and hence are as easy to use.
>
> Using the standard-compliant variants will result in code that is easier to port across platforms and compilers, and hence it should be preferred. It is also possible that the logarithmic reduction in performance of a standard-compliant container might not significantly affect an application.

Container Adapters

Container adapters are variants of sequential and associative containers that have limited functionality and are intended to fulfill particular purposes. The main adapter classes are

- **`std::stack:`** Stores elements in a LIFO (last-in, first-out) order, allowing elements to be inserted (pushed) and removed (popped) at the top.
- **`std::queue:`** Stores elements in FIFO (first-in, first-out) order, allowing elements to be removed in the order in which they were inserted.
- **`std::priority_queue:`** Stores elements in a sorted order, such that the one whose value is evaluated to be the highest is always first in the queue.

These containers are discussed in detail in Lesson 24, "Adaptive Containers: Stack and Queue."

STL Iterators

The simplest example of an iterator is a pointer. Given a pointer to the first element in an array, you can increment it and point to the next element or, in many cases, manipulate the element at that location.

Iterators are template classes, too. Think of them as a generalization of pointers. These template classes give a programmer a handle by which to work with elements in STL containers and perform operations on them. The STL supplies some operations called *algorithms* in the form of template functions. Iterators thus form the connecting bridge between algorithms and the containers they work on.

Iterators supplied by the STL can be broadly classified into the following categories:

- **Input iterator:** This is an iterator that can be dereferenced to reference an object. The object can be an element in a collection, for instance. Input iterators of the strictest types guarantee read-only access.
- **Output iterator:** This is an iterator that enables a programmer to change the content of a collection. Output iterators of the strictest types guarantee write-only access.

The basic iterator types mentioned above are further refined into the following categories:

- **Forward iterator:** This iterator is a refinement of the input and output iterators that allows both input and output. Forward iterators may be constant, allowing for read-only access to the object the iterator points to, and otherwise allow for both read and write operations, making them mutable. A forward iterator would typically be used in a singly linked list.
- **Bidirectional iterator:** This iterator is a refinement of the forward iterator in that it can be decremented to move backward as well. A bidirectional iterator would typically be used in a doubly linked list.
- **Random access iterators:** In general, this iterator is a refinement of a bidirectional iterator that allows addition and subtraction of offsets or allows one iterator to be subtracted from another to find the relative separation or distance between the two objects in a collection. A random iterator would typically be used in an array.

NOTE

At an implementation level, a *refinement* can be thought of as an *inheritance* or a *specialization*.

STL Algorithms

Finding, sorting, reversing, and the like are standard programming requirements that should not need to be programmed by every application. This is precisely why the STL supplies these functions in the form of STL algorithms that work well with containers using iterators to help a programmer with some of the most common requirements.

Some of the most used STL algorithms are

- **`std::find`:** Helps find a value in a collection.
- **`std::find_if`:** Helps find a value in a collection using a predicate supplied by the programmer.
- **`std::reverse`:** Reverses a collection.
- **`std::remove_if`:** Helps remove an item from a collection using a predicate supplied by the programmer.
- **`std::transform`:** Helps apply a transformation function supplied by the programmer to elements in a container.

These algorithms are template functions in the `std` namespace and require that the standard header `<algorithm>` be included.

Interaction Between Containers and Algorithms Using Iterators

Let's examine how iterators seamlessly connect containers and the STL algorithms by using an example. The program shown in Listing 15.1 uses the STL sequential container `std::vector`, which is akin to a dynamic array, to store some integers and then find one in the collection by using the algorithm `std::find`. Note that iterators form a bridge connecting a container to an algorithm. Don't worry about the complexity of the syntax or functionality. Containers such as `std::vector` and algorithms such as `std::find` are discussed in detail in Lesson 17, "STL Dynamic Array Classes," and Lesson 23, "STL Algorithms," respectively. If you find this part complicated, you can skip this section for the moment and come back to it after reading those lessons.

Input ▼

LISTING 15.1 Finding an Element and Its Position in a Vector

```
#include<iostream>
#include<vector>
#include<algorithm>
using namespace std;

int main ()
{
   // A dynamic array of integers
   vector<int> intArray;
```

```

    // Insert sample integers into the array
    intArray.push_back(50);
    intArray.push_back(2991);
    intArray.push_back(23);
    intArray.push_back(9999);

    cout < < "The contents of the vector are: " < < endl;

    // Walk the vector and read values using an iterator
    vector<int>::iterator arrIterator = intArray.begin();

    while (arrIterator != intArray.end())
    {
        // Write the value to the screen
        cout < < *arrIterator < < endl;

        // Increment the iterator to access the next element
        ++arrIterator;
    }

    // Find an element (say 2991) using the 'find' algorithm
    vector<int>::iterator elFound = find(intArray.begin(),
                                   intArray.end(), 2991);

    // Check if value was found
    if (elFound != intArray.end())
    {
        // Determine position of element using std::distance
        int elPos = distance(intArray.begin(), elFound);
        cout < < "Value "< < *elFound;
        cout < < " found in the vector at position: " < < elPos < < endl;
    }

    return 0;
}
```

Output ▼

```
The contents of the vector are:
50
2991
23
9999
Value 2991 found in the vector at position: 1
```

Analysis ▼

Listing 15.1 illustrates the use of iterators in walking through `vector` and as interfaces that help connect algorithms such as `find()` to containers like `vector` that contains the data on which the algorithm is meant to operate. The iterator object `arrIterator` is declared in Line 20 and is initialized to the beginning of the container—that is, the `vector` using the return value of the member function `begin()`. Lines 22 through 29 demonstrate how this iterator is used in a loop to locate and display the elements contained in `vector`, in a manner that is quite similar to how you can display the contents of a static array. The usage of the iterator is consistent across all STL containers. They all feature a function `begin()` that points to the first element, and a function `end()` that points to the end of the container after the last element. This also explains why the `while` loop in Line 22 stops at the element before `end()` and not at `end()`. Line 32 demonstrates how `find` is used to locate a value in `vector`. The result of the `find` operation is an iterator as well, and the success of the `find` is tested by comparing the iterator against the end of the container, as shown in Line 36. If an element is found, it can be displayed by dereferencing that iterator (much as a pointer would be dereferenced). The algorithm `distance` is applied to compute the offset position of the element found.

If you blindly replace all instances of `vector` with `deque` in Listing 15.1, your code will still compile and work perfectly. As you can see, iterators make it very easy to work with algorithms and containers.

Using the Keyword `auto` to Let a Compiler Define Type

Listing 15.1 shows a number of iterator declarations. They look similar to this:

```
20:    vector<int>::iterator arrIterator = intArray.begin();
```

This iterator type definition might look intimidating, but you can simplify this line to the following:

```
20:    auto arrIterator = intArray.begin(); // compiler detects type
```

Note that a variable defined as type `auto` needs to be initialized (so the compiler can detect type, depending on the type of the value the variable is being initialized to).

Choosing the Right Container

Clearly, an application might have requirements that can be implemented using many STL containers. There is a selection to be made, and that selection is important because a poor choice could result in performance issues and scalability bottlenecks. Therefore, it is important to evaluate the advantages and disadvantages of containers before selecting one. See Table 15.1 for more details.

TABLE 15.1 Properties of the STL's Container Classes

Container	Advantages	Disadvantages
Sequential Containers		
`std::vector`	Quick (constant time) insertion at the end. Array-like access.	Resizing can result in performance loss. Search time is proportional to the number of elements in the container. Insertion only at the end.
`std::deque`	All advantages of the `vector` and also offers constant-time insertion at the beginning of the container.	Disadvantages of `vector` with respect to performance and search are applicable to `deque`. Unlike `vector`, `deque` by specification does not need to feature the `reserve()` function, which allows a programmer to reserve memory space to be used—a feature that prevents frequent resizing to improve performance.
`std::list`	Constant time insertion at the front, middle, or end of the list. Removal of elements from a `list` is a constant-time activity, regardless of the position of the element. Insertion or removal of elements does not invalidate iterators that point to other elements in the `list`.	Elements cannot be accessed randomly given an index, as in an array. Accessing elements can be slower than with `vector` because elements are not stored in adjacent memory locations. Search time is proportional to the number of elements in the container.
`std::forward_list`	Singly linked list class that allows iteration only in one direction.	Allows insertion only at the front of the list via `push_front()`.

Container	Advantages	Disadvantages
Associative Containers		
`std::set`	Search is not directly proportional to the number of elements in the container; rather, it is proportional to the logarithm thereof and hence is often significantly faster than with sequential containers.	Insertion of elements is slower than in sequential counterparts, as elements are sorted at insertion.
`std::unordered set`	Search, insertion, and removal in this type of container are nearly independent of the number of elements in the container.	As elements are weakly ordered, you cannot rely on their relative positions within the container.
`std::multiset`	Should be used when a set needs to contain non-unique values, too.	Insertions may be slower than in a sequential container as elements (pairs) are sorted on insertion.
`std::unordered_multiset`	Should be preferred over `unordered_set` when you need to contain non-unique values, too. Performance is similar to `unordered_set`—that is, constant average time for search, insertion, and removal of elements, independent of size of container.	Elements are weakly ordered, so you cannot rely on their relative position within the container.
`std::map`	Key/value pairs container that offers search performance proportional to the logarithm of the number of elements in the container and hence often significantly faster than sequential containers.	Elements (pairs) are sorted on insertion, hence insertion will be slower than in a sequential container of pairs.
`std::unordered_map`	Offers the advantage of near constant time search, insertion, and removal of elements, independent of the size of the container.	Elements are weakly ordered and hence not suited to cases where order is important.
`std::multimap`	To be selected over `std::map` when requirements call for a key/value pairs container that holds elements with non-unique keys.	Insertion of elements will be slower than in a sequential equivalent as elements are sorted on insertion.

Container	Advantages	Disadvantages
`std::unordered_multimap`	To be selected over `multimap` when you need a key/value pairs container where keys can be non-unique. Allows constant average time insertion, search, and removal of elements, independent of the size of the container.	Is a weakly ordered container, so you cannot use it when you need to rely on the relative order of elements.

STL String Classes

STL supplies a template class that is especially designed for string operations. `std::basic_string<T>` is used popularly in its two template specializations:

- **`std::string`:** A `char`-based specialization of `std::basic_string` that is used for the manipulation of simple character strings.
- **`std::wstring`:** A `wchar_t`-based specialization of `std::basic_string` that is used for the manipulation of wide character strings and that is typically used to store Unicode characters that support symbols from different languages.

This utility class is extensively discussed in Lesson 16, "The STL String Class," where you will see how it makes working with and manipulating strings really simple.

Summary

In this lesson, you learned the concepts on which STL containers, iterators, and algorithms are based. You were introduced to `basic_string<T>`, which is discussed in detail in the upcoming lesson. Containers, iterators, and algorithms are some of the most important concepts in the STL, and having a thorough understanding of them will help you efficiently use STL in your applications. Lessons 17 through 25 explain the implementation of these concepts and their application in greater detail.

Q&A

Q I need to use an array. I don't know how many elements it needs to contain. What STL container should I use?

A `std::vector` or `std::deque` would be perfectly suited to this requirement. Both manage memory and can dynamically scale themselves to an application's increasing requirements.

Q My application has a requirement that involves frequent searches. What kind of container should I choose?

A An associative container like `std::map` or `std::set` or the unordered variants thereof are most suited to requirements that involve frequent searches.

Q I need to store key/value pairs for quick lookup. However, the use case may result in multiple keys that are not unique. What container should I choose?

A An associative container of type `std::multimap` is suited to this requirement. `multimap` can hold non-unique key/value pairs and can offer the quick lookup that is characteristic of associative containers.

Q An application needs to be ported across platforms and compilers. There is a requirement for a container that helps in a quick lookup based on a key. Should I use `std::map` or `std::hash_map`?

A Portability is an important constraint, and using standard-compliant containers is necessary. `hash_map` is not part of the C++ standard and therefore may not be supported across all platforms relevant to your application. Use `std::unordered_map` instead.

Workshop

The Workshop contains quiz questions to help solidify your understanding of the material covered. Try to answer the quiz questions before checking the answers in Appendix E and be certain you understand the answers before going to the next lesson.

Quiz

1. What would be your choice if you need a container that has to contain an array of objects with insertion possible at the top and at the bottom?
2. You need to store elements for quick lookup. What container would you choose?
3. You need to store elements in a `::set` but still also need to have the storage and lookup criteria altered, based on conditions that are not necessarily the value of the elements. Is this possible?
4. What feature in the STL is used to connect algorithms to containers?
5. Would you choose to use the container `hash_set` in an application that needs to be ported to different platforms and built using different C++ compilers?

LESSON 16
The STL `string` Class

The Standard Template Library (STL) supplies a container class that aids in string operations and manipulations. The `std::string` class not only dynamically resizes itself to cater to an application's requirement but also supplies useful functions (that is, methods that help manipulate a string and that work using it). Thus, it helps programmers make use of standard, portable, and tested functionality in applications and focus on developing features that are critical to their applications.

In this lesson, you learn

- Why string manipulation classes are necessary
- How to work with the STL `string` class
- How the STL helps you concatenate, append, find, and perform other string operations with ease
- How to use template-based implementation of the STL `string` class
- The `operator ""s`, which has been supported by the STL `string` class since C++14

The Need for String Manipulation Classes

In C++, a string is an array of characters. In Lesson 4, "Managing Arrays and Strings," a simple character array was defined as following:

```
char sayHello[] = {'H','e','l','l','o',' ','W','o','r','l','d','\0'};
```

`sayHello` is the declaration of a character array (also called a string) of a fixed (that is, static) length. As you see, this buffer can hold a string of limited length; it would soon be overrun if you tried to hold a greater number of characters in it. Resizing this statically allocated array is not possible. To overcome this constraint, C++ supplies dynamic allocation of data. Therefore, a more dynamic representation of a string array is

```
char* dynamicStr = new char[arrayLen];
```

`dynamicStr` is a dynamically allocated character array that can be instantiated to the length as stored in the value `arrayLen`, which can be determined at runtime, and hence it can be allocated to hold data of variable length. However, should you want to change the length of the array at runtime, you would first have to deallocate the allocated memory and then reallocate to hold the required data.

Things get complicated if these `char*` strings are used as member attributes of a class. Situations where an object of this class is assigned to another require the presence of a correctly programmed assignment operator and copy constructor. If these are not available, then two objects of the class might contain copies of a pointer, essentially pointing to the same `char` buffer in memory. The destruction of one object, releasing the buffer, can result in the invalidation of the pointer contained by the other object. This will cause an application malfunction.

String classes solve these problems for you. The STL string classes `std::string`, which models a character string, and `std::wstring`, which models a wide character string, help you in the following ways:

- Reduce the effort of string creation and manipulation
- Increase the stability of the application being programmed by internally managing memory allocation details
- Feature copy constructor and assignment operators that automatically ensure that member strings get correctly copied
- Supply useful utility functions that help in truncating, finding, and erasing
- Provide operators that help in comparisons
- Let you focus on your application's primary requirements rather than on string manipulation details

NOTE

Both `std::string` and `std::wstring` are actually template specializations of the same class—namely `std::basic_string<T>` for types `char` and `wchar_t`, respectively. When you have learned how to use one, you can use the same methods and operators on the other.

You will soon learn some useful helper functions that STL string classes supply, using `std::string` as an example.

Working with the STL string Class

The most commonly used string functions are

- Copying
- Concatenating
- Finding characters and substrings
- Truncating
- String reversal and case conversions, which are achieved using algorithms provided by the standard library

TIP

To use the class `std::string`, include the header:

```
#include<string>
```

Instantiating the STL string Class and Making Copies

The `string` class features many overloaded constructors and therefore can be instantiated and initialized in many different ways. For example, you can simply initialize or assign a constant character string literal to a regular STL `std::string` object:

```
const char* constCStyleString = "Hello String!";
std::string strFromConst(constCStyleString);
```

or

```
std::string strFromConst = constCStyleString;
```

The preceding is similar to

```
std::string str2("Hello String!");
```

As is apparent, instantiating a string object and initializing it to a value do not require supplying the length of the string or the memory allocation details; the constructor of the STL string class automatically provides this information.

Similarly, it is possible to use one `string` object to initialize another:

```
std::string str2Copy(str2);
```

You can also instruct the constructor of `string` to accept only the first *n* characters of the supplied input string:

```
// Initialize a string to the first 5 characters of another
std::string strPartialCopy(constCStyleString, 5);
```

You can also initialize a string to contain a specific number of instances of a particular character:

```
// Initialize a string object to contain 10 'a's
std::string strRepeatChars (10, 'a');
```

Listing 16.1 illustrates some popularly used `std::string` instantiation and string copy techniques.

Input ▼

LISTING 16.1 STL String Instantiation and Copy Techniques

```
#include<string>
#include<iostream>

int main ()
{
   using namespace std;
   const char* constCStyleString = "Hello String!";
   cout << "Constant string is: " << constCStyleString << endl;

   std::string strFromConst(constCStyleString);  // constructor
   cout << "strFromConst is: " << strFromConst << endl;

   std::string str2("Hello String!");
   std::string str2Copy(str2);
   cout << "str2Copy is: " << str2Copy << endl;

   // Initialize a string to the first 5 characters of another
   std::string strPartialCopy(constCStyleString, 5);
   cout << "strPartialCopy is: " << strPartialCopy << endl;

   // Initialize a string object to contain 10 'a's
   std::string strRepeatChars(10, 'a');
   cout << "strRepeatChars is: " << strRepeatChars << endl;

   return 0;
}
```

Output ▼

```
Constant string is: Hello String!
strFromConst is: Hello String!
str2Copy is: Hello String!
strPartialCopy is: Hello
strRepeatChars is: aaaaaaaaaa
```

Analysis ▼

This code example illustrates how you can instantiate an STL `string` object and initialize it to another string, creating a partial copy or initializing your STL `string` object to a set of recurring characters. `constCStyleString` is a C-style character string that contains a sample value, initialized in Line 6. Line 9 displays how easy `std::string` makes it to create a copy using the constructor. Line 12 copies another constant string into a `std::string` object `str2`, and Line 13 demonstrates how `std::string` has another overloaded constructor that allows you to copy a `std::string` object, to get `str2Copy`. Line 17 demonstrates how partial copies can be achieved, and Line 21 shows how `std::string` can be instantiated and initialized to contain repeating occurrences of the same character. This code example briefly demonstrates how `std::string` and its numerous copy constructors make it easy for a programmer to create strings, copy them, and display them.

NOTE

If you were to copy one C-style character strings into another, the equivalent of Line 9 in Listing 16.1 would be this:

```
const char* constCStyleString = "Hello World!";

// To create a copy, first allocate memory for one...
char* copy = new char[strlen(constCStyleString) + 1];
strcpy(copy, constCStyleString);  // The copy step

// deallocate memory after using copy
delete[] copy;
```

As you can see, the result is many more lines of code and a higher probability of introducing errors; in addition, you need to worry about memory management and deallocations. STL `string` does all this for you—and more! You don't need to use C-style strings at all.

Accessing Character Contents of `std::string`

The character contents of an STL `string` class can be accessed via iterators or via array-like syntax where the offset is supplied, using the subscript operator (`[]`). A C-style representation of `string` can be obtained via the member function `c_str()`. See Listing 16.2.

Input ▼

LISTING 16.2 Two Ways of Accessing Character Elements of an STL `string::operator[]` and Iterators

```
#include<string>
#include<iostream>

int main()
{
   using namespace std;

   string stlString("Hello String"); // sample

    // Access the contents of the string using array syntax
   cout << "Display elements in string using array-syntax: " << endl;
   for(size_t charCounter = 0;
       charCounter < stlString.length();
       ++charCounter)
    {
       cout << "Character[" << charCounter << "] is: ";
       cout << stlString[charCounter] << endl;
    }
   cout << endl;

    // Access the contents of a string using iterators
   cout << "Display elements in string using iterators: " << endl;
   int charOffset = 0;

   for(auto charLocator = stlString.cbegin();
       charLocator != stlString.cend();
       ++charLocator)
   {
      cout << "Character [" << charOffset ++ << "] is: ";
      cout << *charLocator << endl;
   }
   cout << endl;

   // Access contents as a const char*
   cout << "The char* representation of the string is: ";
   cout << stlString.c_str() << endl;

   return 0;
}
```

Output ▼

```
Display elements in string using array-syntax:
Character[0] is: H
Character[1] is: e
Character[2] is: l
Character[3] is: l
Character[4] is: o
Character[5] is:
Character[6] is: S
Character[7] is: t
Character[8] is: r
Character[9] is: i
Character[10] is: n
Character[11] is: g

Display elements in string using iterators:
Character[0] is: H
Character[1] is: e
Character[2] is: l
Character[3] is: l
Character[4] is: o
Character[5] is:
Character[6] is: S
Character[7] is: t
Character[8] is: r
Character[9] is: i
Character[10] is: n
Character[11] is: g

The char* representation of the string is: Hello String
```

Analysis ▼

This code displays multiple ways of accessing the contents of a string. Iterators are important in the sense that many of a string's member functions return their results in the form of iterators. Lines 11 through 17 display the characters in a string using array-like semantics via the subscript operator (`[]`), which is implemented by the `std::string` class. Note that with this operator, you need to supply the offset, as shown in Line 16. Therefore, it is important that you not cross the bounds of the `string`; that is, you do not read a character at an offset beyond the length of the string. Lines 24 through 30 also print the content of the string character by character—but using iterators.

Listing 16.2 smartly avoids the tedious iterator declaration in Line 24 by using the keyword auto, thereby telling the compiler to determine the type of iterator charLocator using the return value of std::string::cbegin(). If you were to explicitly program the type, the same line would appear as follows:

```
25: for(string::const_iterator charLocator = stlString.cbegin();
26:      charLocator != stlString.cend();
27:      ++charLocator)
28: {
29:    cout << "Character["<<charOffset++ <<"] is: ";
30:    cout << *charLocator << endl;
31: }
```

Concatenating One String to Another

String concatenation can be achieved by using either the += operator or the append() member function:

```
string sampleStr1("Hello");
string sampleStr2(" String! ");
sampleStr1 += sampleStr2;    // use std::string::operator+=
// alternatively use std::string::append()
sampleStr1.append(sampleStr2);   // (overloaded for char* too)
```

Listing 16.3 demonstrates the use of these two variants.

Input ▼

LISTING 16.3 Concatenating Strings Using the Addition Assignment Operator (+=) or append()

```
0: #include<string>
1: #include<iostream>
2:
3: int main()
4: {
5:    using namespace std;
6:
7:    string sampleStr1("Hello");
8:    string sampleStr2(" String!");
9:
10:    // Concatenate
11:    sampleStr1 += sampleStr2;
12:    cout << sampleStr1 << endl << endl;
```

```
13:
14:     string sampleStr3(" Fun is not needing to use pointers!");
15:     sampleStr1.append(sampleStr3);
16:     cout << sampleStr1 << endl << endl;
17:
18:     const char* constCStyleString = " You however still can!";
19:     sampleStr1.append(constCStyleString);
20:     cout << sampleStr1 << endl;
21:
22:     return 0;
23: }
```


Output ▼

```
Hello String!

Hello String! Fun is not needing to use pointers!

Hello String! Fun is not needing to use pointers! You however still can!
```

Analysis ▼

Lines 11, 15, and 19 show different methods of concatenating to an STL string. Note the use of the `+=` operator used in Line 11 to append from another `string` object. Lines 15 and 19 demonstrate overloaded variants of the `string::append()` function, with Line 19 concatenating a C-style character string.

Finding a Character or Substring in a String

The STL `string` class supplies a `find()` member function with a few overloaded versions that help find a character or a substring in a given `string` object:

```
// Find substring "day" in sampleStr, starting at position 0
size_t charPos = sampleStr.find("day", 0);

// Check if the substring was found, compare against string::npos
if(charPos != string::npos)
   cout << "First instance of \"day\" was found at position " << charPos;
else
   cout << "Substring not found." << endl;
```

Listing 16.4 demonstrates the use of `std::string::find()`.

Input ▼

LISTING 16.4 Using `string::find()` to Locate a Substring or `char`

```
#include<string>
#include<iostream>

int main()
{
   using namespace std;

   string sampleStr("Good day String! Today is beautiful!");
   cout << "Sample string is:" << endl << sampleStr << endl << endl;

   // Find substring "day" - find() returns position
   size_t charPos = sampleStr.find("day", 0);

   // Check if the substring was found...
   if(charPos != string::npos)
      cout << "First instance \"day\" at pos. " << charPos << endl;
   else
      cout << "Substring not found." << endl;

   cout << "Locating all instances of substring \"day\"" << endl;
   size_t subStrPos = sampleStr.find("day", 0);

   while(subStrPos != string::npos)
   {
      cout << "\"day\" found at position " << subStrPos << endl;

      // Make find() search forward from the next character onwards
      size_t searchOffset = subStrPos + 1;

      subStrPos = sampleStr.find("day", searchOffset);
   }

   return 0;
}
```

Output ▼

```
Sample string is:
Good day String! Today is beautiful!

First instance "day" at pos. 5
Locating all instances of substring "day"
"day" found at position 5
"day" found at position 19
```

Analysis ▼

Lines 11 through 17 display the simplest use of the `find()` function, where it ascertains whether a particular substring is found in a string. This is done by comparing the result of the `find()` operation against `std::string::npos` (which is actually `-1`) and indicates that the element searched for has not been found. When the `find()` function does not return `npos`, it returns the offset that indicates the position of the substring or character in the string. The code thereafter indicates how `find()` can be used in a `while` loop to locate all instances of a substring in an STL string. The overloaded version of the `find()` function used here accepts two parameters: the substring or character to search for and the search offset that indicates the point from which `find()` should search. You can manipulate the search by using this offset to get `find()` to search for the next occurrence of the substring, as shown in Line 29.

NOTE

> The STL string also features find functions such as `find_first_of()`, `find_first_not_of()`, `find_last_of()`, and `find_last_not_of()` that assist programmers in working with strings.

Truncating an STL String

The STL `string` class features a function called `erase()` that can erase

- A number of characters when given an offset position and count:

```
string sampleStr("Hello String! Wake up to a beautiful day!");
sampleStr.erase(13, 28);   // Hello String!
```

- A character when supplied with an iterator pointing to it:

```
sampleStr.erase(iCharS); // iterator points to a specific character
```

- A number of characters when given a range supplied by two iterators that bind the range:

```
sampleStr.erase(sampleStr.begin(), sampleStr.end()); // erase from begin
to end
```

Listing 16.5 demonstrates different applications of the overloaded versions of the `string::erase()` function.

Input ▼

LISTING 16.5 Using `string::erase()` to Truncate a String Starting at an Offset Position or Given an Iterator

```
#include<string>
#include<algorithm>
#include<iostream>

int main()
{
    using namespace std;

    string sampleStr("Hello String! Wake up to a beautiful day!");
    cout << "The original sample string is: " << endl;
    cout << sampleStr << endl << endl;

    // Delete characters given position and count
    cout << "Truncating the second sentence: " << endl;
    sampleStr.erase(13, 28);
    cout << sampleStr << endl << endl;

    // Find character 'S' using find() algorithm
    string::iterator iCharS = find(sampleStr.begin(),
                                   sampleStr.end(), 'S');

    // If character found, 'erase' to deletes a character
    cout << "Erasing character 'S' from the sample string:" << endl;
    if(iCharS != sampleStr.end())
        sampleStr.erase(iCharS);

    cout << sampleStr << endl << endl;

    // Erase a range of characters using an overloaded version of erase()
    cout << "Erasing a range between begin() and end(): " << endl;
    sampleStr.erase(sampleStr.begin(), sampleStr.end());

    // Verify the length after the erase() operation above
    if(sampleStr.length() == 0)
        cout << "The string is empty" << endl;

    return 0;
}
```

Output ▼

```
The original sample string is:
Hello String! Wake up to a beautiful day!

Truncating the second sentence:
Hello String!
```

```
Erasing character 'S' from the sample string:
Hello tring!

Erasing a range between begin() and end():
The string is empty
```

Analysis ▼

The listing indicates the three versions of the erase() function. One version erases a set of characters when supplied a starting offset and count, as shown in Line 14. Another version erases a specific character, given an iterator that points to it, as shown in Line 24. The final version erases a range of characters, given a couple of iterators that supply the bounds of the range, as shown in Line 30. As the bounds of the range are supplied by begin() and end() member functions of the string class that effectively include all the contents of the string, calling an erase() on this range clears the string object of its contents. Note that the string class also supplies a clear() function that effectively clears the internal buffer and resets the string object.

TIP

The iterator declarations in Listing 16.5 using auto are wordy:

```
string::iterator iCharS = find(sampleStr.begin(),
                               sampleStr.end(), 'S');
```

You can simplify them like this:

```
auto iCharS = find(sampleStr.begin(),
                   sampleStr.end(), 'S');
```

The compiler automatically deduces the type of the variable iCharS, given return value type information from std::find().

String Reversal

Sometimes it is important to reverse the contents of a string. Say you want to determine whether a string input by the user is a palindrome. One way to do it would be to reverse a copy of the string and then compare the two strings. You can easily reverse STL strings by using the generic algorithm std::reverse():

```
string sampleStr("Hello String! We will reverse you!");
reverse(sampleStr.begin(), sampleStr.end());
```

Listing 16.6 demonstrates the application of the `std::reverse()` algorithm to `std::string`.

Input ▼

LISTING 16.6 Reversing an STL String by Using `std::reverse`

```
 0: #include<string>
 1: #include<iostream>
 2: #include<algorithm>
 3:
 4: int main()
 5: {
 6:     using namespace std;
 7:
 8:     string sampleStr("Hello String! We will reverse you!");
 9:     cout << "The original sample string is: " << endl;
10:     cout << sampleStr << endl << endl;
11:
12:     reverse(sampleStr.begin(), sampleStr.end());
13:
14:     cout << "After applying the std::reverse algorithm: " << endl;
15:     cout << sampleStr << endl;
16:
17:     return 0;
18: }
```

Output ▼

```
The original sample string is:
Hello String! We will reverse you!

After applying the std::reverse algorithm:
!uoy esrever lliw eW !gnirtS olleH
```

Analysis ▼

The `std::reverse()` algorithm used in Line 12 works on the bounds of the container that are supplied to it using the two input parameters. In this case, these bounds are the starting and ending bounds of the `string` object, and the algorithm reverses the contents of the entire string. It would also be possible to reverse a string in parts by supplying the appropriate bounds as input. Note that the bounds should never exceed `end()`.

String Case Conversion

String case conversion can be effected by using the algorithm `std::transform()`, which applies a user-specified function to every element of a collection. In this case, the collection is the `string` object itself. Listing 16.7 shows how to switch the case of characters in a string.

Input ▼

LISTING 16.7 Converting an STL String to Uppercase by Using `std::transform()`


```
#include<string>
#include<iostream>
#include<algorithm>

int main()
{
    using namespace std;

    cout << "Please enter a string for case-conversion:" << endl;
    cout << "> ";

    string inStr;
    getline(cin, inStr);
    cout << endl;

    transform(inStr.begin(), inStr.end(), inStr.begin(), ::toupper);
    cout << "The string converted to upper case is: " << endl;
    cout << inStr << endl << endl;

    transform(inStr.begin(), inStr.end(), inStr.begin(), ::tolower);
    cout << "The string converted to lower case is: " << endl;
    cout << inStr << endl << endl;

    return 0;
}
```

Output ▼

```
Please enter a string for case-conversion:
> ConverT thIS StrINg!

The string converted to upper case is:
CONVERT THIS STRING!

The string converted to lower case is:
convert this string!
```

Analysis ▼

Lines 15 and 19 demonstrate how efficiently `std::transform()` can be used to change the case of the contents of an STL string.

Template-Based Implementation of an STL String

The `std::string` class, as you have learned, is actually a specialization of the STL template class `std::basic_string<T>`. The template declaration of the container class `basic_string` is as follows:

```
template<class _Elem,
    class _Traits,
    class _Ax>
    class basic_string
```

In this template definition, the parameter of utmost importance is the first one: `_Elem`. This is the type collected by the `basic_string` object. `std::string` is therefore the template specialization of `basic_string` for `_Elem=char`, whereas `wstring` is the template specialization of `basic_string` for `_Elem=wchar_t`.

In other words, the STL `string` class is defined as

```
typedef basic_string<char, char_traits<char>, allocator<char> >
    string;
```

and the STL `wstring` class is defined as

```
typedef basic_string<wchar_t, char_traits<wchar_t>, allocator<wchar_t> >
    string;
```

So, all string features and functions studied so far are actually those supplied by `basic_string`, and they are therefore also applicable to the STL `wstring` class.

TIP

> You would use `std::wstring` when programming an application that needs to better support non-Latin characters such as those in Japanese or Chinese.

operator ""s in std::string

Since C++14, the STL has supported `operator ""s`, which converts the string contained within the quotes, in its entirety, to `std::basic_string<t>`. This makes certain string operations intuitive and simple, as Listing 16.8 demonstrates.

Input ▼

LISTING 16.8 Using `operator ""s`

```
 0: #include<string>
 1: #include<iostream>
 2: using namespace std;
 3:
 4: int main()
 5: {
 6:    string str1("Conventional string \0 initialization");
 7:    cout << "Str1: " << str1 << " Length: " << str1.length() << endl;
 8:
 9:    string str2("Initialization \0 using literals"s);
10:    cout << "Str2: " << str2 << " Length: " << str2.length() << endl;
11:
12:    return 0;
13: }
```


Output ▼

```
Str1: Conventional string  Length: 20
Str2: Initialization  using literals Length: 31
```

Analysis ▼

Line 6 initializes an instance of `std::string` from a regular character string literal. Note the null character in the middle of the string, which results in the word `"initialization"` being completely missed by `str1`. Line 9 uses `operator ""s` to demonstrate how the instance `str2` can now be used to contain (and therefore also manipulate) character buffers containing null characters, too, for instance.

CAUTION

> Do not confuse the literal operator ""s working with std::string with that in std::chrono, as seen here:
>
> ```
> std::chrono::seconds timeInSec(100s); // 100 seconds
> std::string timeinText = "100"s; // string "100"
> ```
>
> The former indicates time in seconds and is an integer literal, while the latter gives a string.

Using std::string_view (Amended in C++20)

The std::string class can be used to create copies, like this:

```
string strOriginal("Hello string");
string strCopy(strOriginal);
string strCopy2(strCopy);
string strCopy3;
strCopy3 = strCopy2;
```

However, if you intend to use copies of strOriginal to just perform read operations, then the copy step in itself is an avoidably expensive operation. The string_view utility class allows you to view the original string without creating a copy of it:

```
string_strOriginal("Hello string view");
string_view strCopy(strOriginal);
string_view strCopy2(strCopy);
string_view strCopy3(strCopy2);
cout << strCopy3; // Hello string view
```

string_view provides a plethora of useful methods, as Listing 16.9 shows.

Input ▼

LISTING 16.9 Using str::string_view for Basic String Operations

```
#include<string_view>
#include<iostream>
using namespace std;

int main()
{
   string strOriginal("Use views instead of copies of strings");
```

```
 7:     string_view fullView(strOriginal); // a full view
 8:
 9:     cout << "The full view shows: " << fullView << endl;
10:
11:     cout << "The first instance of 'v' is at position: "
12:          << fullView.find_first_of('v') << endl;
13:
14:     cout << "Is view starting with \"Use\": " <<
15:        (fullView.starts_with("Use") ? "true" : "false") << endl; // C++20
16:
17:     cout << "Is view ending with \"strings\": " <<
18:        (fullView.ends_with("strings") ? "true" : "false") << endl; // C++20
19:
20:     string_view partialView(strOriginal.c_str(), 9); // partial view
21:     cout << "Partial view shows: " << partialView << endl;
22:
23:     return 0;
24: }
```


Output ▼

```
The full view shows: Use views instead of copies of strings
The first instance of 'v' is at position: 4
Is view starting with "Use": true
Is view ending with "strings": true
Partial view shows: Use views
```

Analysis ▼

Usage of the `string_view` class instead of `string` is optional, and you should do it only if you wish to optimize performance. Listing 16.9 shows how you can view the string data without actually needing to duplicate it. Lines 12 and 15 demonstrate the use of the methods `starts_with()` and `ends_with()`, respectively; these methods were added to `string_view` in C++20. Lines 20 and 21 demonstrate how a partial view of the original string may be constructed.

TIP

> Use the `string_view` class instead of a duplicate in `std::string` in any case where you need to be viewing (that is, reading) a string but do not need to be modifying it.

DO	DON'T
DO preferentially use `std::string` class where string operations are required.	**DON'T** use C-style character strings (`char*`) unless absolutely unavoidable.
DO use `std::string::length()` to compute the length of a string.	**DON'T** use insecure functions such as `strlen()` to compute the length of a string.
DO familiarize yourself with the different ways of copying and concatenating strings using methods and operators in the `std::string` class.	**DON'T** use insecure functions like `strcpy()` or `strcat()` to copy or concatenate strings respectively.

Summary

In this lesson, you learned that the STL `string` class is a container supplied by the Standard Template Library that helps with many string manipulation requirements. The advantage of using this class is apparent: This container class supplied by the STL framework implements memory management, string comparison, and string manipulation functions so programmers don't have to.

Q&A

Q Can I use a range-based `for` loop on a `std::string` object?

A Yes, you can use it to read one character after another, and it will make your code compact and readable! For example, in the code shown in Listing 16.2, a range version of the `for` loop in Lines 24 through 30 would be:

```
for(const auto& charLocator : stlString) // range-based for
{
   cout << "Character[" << charOffset ++ << "] is: ";
   cout << charLocator << endl;
}
```

Q I need to reverse a string by using `std::reverse()`. What header has to be included in order to be able to use this function?

A `<algorithm>` is the header that needs to be included for `std::reverse()` to be available.

Q What role does `std::transform()` play in converting a string to lowercase using the `tolower()` function?

A `std::transform()` invokes `tolower()` for the characters in the `string` object that are within the bounds supplied to the `transform` function.

Q Why do `std::string` and `std::wstring` feature exactly the same behavior and member functions?

A They do so because they are both template specializations of the template class `std::basic_string<T>`—for `T=char` and `T=wchar_t`, respectively.

Q Is the comparison operator < of the STL `string` class case-sensitive or is it not case-sensitive?

A The results of comparison using `string` class operator `<` are case-sensitive.

Workshop

The Workshop provides quiz questions to help you solidify your understanding of the material covered and exercises to provide you with experience using what you've learned. Try to answer the quiz and exercise questions before checking the answers in Appendix E and be certain you understand the answers before continuing to the next lesson.

Quiz

1. What STL template class does `std::string` specialize?
2. If you were to perform a case-insensitive comparison of two strings, how would you do it?

Exercises

1. Write a program to verify whether a word entered by a user is a palindrome. For example, ATOYOTA is a palindrome, as it reads the same backward and forward.
2. Write a program that tells the user the number of vowels in a sentence.
3. Write a program that converts every alternate character of a string into uppercase.
4. Write a program that has four string objects that are initialized to "I," "Love," "STL," and "String." Append them with a space in between and display the sentence.
5. Write a program that displays the position of every occurrence of the character `a` in the string `"Good day String! Today is beautiful!"`.

LESSON 17
STL Dynamic Array Classes

Unlike static arrays, dynamic arrays give a programmer flexibility in terms of storing data without needing to know the exact volume of the data when programming an application. Naturally, this is a frequently needed requirement, and the Standard Template Library (STL) supplies a ready-to-use solution in the form of the `std::vector` class.

In this lesson, you learn

- The characteristics of `std::vector`
- Typical `vector` operations
- The concepts of a vector's size and capacity
- The STL `deque` class

The Characteristics of `std::vector`

`vector` is a template class that supplies the generic functionality of a dynamic array and features the following characteristics:

- You can add elements to the end of the array in constant time; that is, the time needed to insert at the end is not dependent on the size of the array. The same goes for removal of an element at the end.
- The time required for the insertion or removal of elements in the middle of an array is directly proportional to the number of elements behind the element being removed.
- The number of elements held is dynamic, and the `vector` class manages the memory usage.

A *vector* is a dynamic array, as illustrated in Figure 17.1.

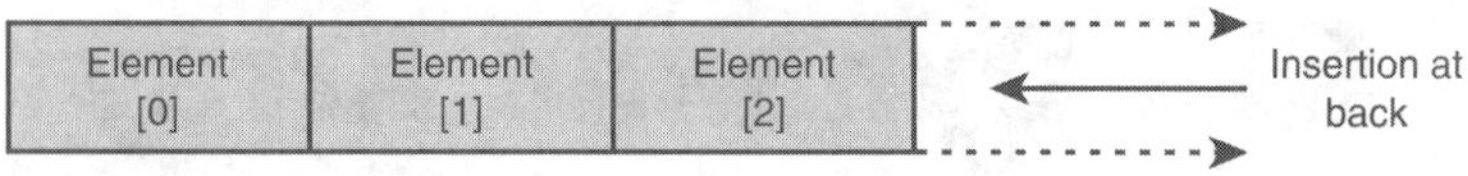

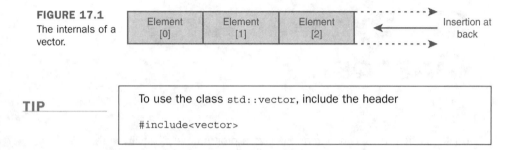

FIGURE 17.1
The internals of a vector.

TIP

To use the class `std::vector`, include the header

```
#include<vector>
```

Typical Vector Operations

The behavioral specifications and public members of the `std::vector` class are defined by the C++ standard. Consequently, operations on `vector` that you will learn in this lesson are supported by a variety of C++ programming platforms that are standard compliant.

Instantiating a Vector

`vector` is a template class that needs to be instantiated in accordance with template instantiation techniques that are covered in Lesson 14, "An Introduction to Macros and Templates." The template instantiation of `vector` needs to specify the type of the elements that you intend to collect in a dynamic array:

```
std::vector<int> dynIntArray;  // vector containing integers
std::vector<float> dynFloatArray;  // vector containing floats
std::vector<Tuna> dynTunaArray;  // vector containing Tunas
```

To declare an iterator that points to an element in the vector, you use

```
std::vector<int>::const_iterator elementInVec;
```

If you need an iterator that can be used to modify values or invoke non-`const` functions, you use `iterator` instead of `const_iterator`.

The overloaded constructors provided by `std::vector` let you specify the number of elements that the vector should be instantiated with and their initial values. You can even use part of a vector in instantiating another vector.

Listing 17.1 demonstrates a few vector instantiations.

Input ▼

LISTING 17.1 Different Ways of Instantiating `std::vector`: Specifying Size, Specifying the Initial Value, and Copying Values

```
 0: #include<vector>
 1:
 2: int main()
 3: {
 4:    // vector of integers
 5:    std::vector<int> integers;
 6:
 7:    // vector initialized using list initialization
 8:    std::vector<int> initVector{ 202, 2017, -1 };
 9:
10:    // Instantiate a vector with 10 elements (it can still grow)
11:    std::vector<int> tenElements(10);
12:
13:    // Instantiate a vector with 10 elements, each initialized to 90
14:    std::vector<int> tenElemInit(10, 90);
15:
16:    // Initialize vector to the contents of another
17:    std::vector<int> copyVector(tenElemInit);
18:
19:    // Vector initialized to 5 elements from another using iterators
20:    std::vector<int> partialCopy(tenElements.cbegin(),
21:                        tenElements.cbegin() + 5);
22:
23:    return 0;
24: }
```


Analysis ▼

This code features a template specialization of the `vector` class for type `int`; in other words, it instantiates a vector of integers. This vector, named `integers`, uses the default constructor in Line 5, which is useful when you do not know the minimal size requirements of the container—that is, when you do not know how many integers you want to hold in it. The second form of instantiation, which is shown in Line 8, uses the concept of list initialization introduced in C++11 to initialize `initVector` with three elements containing the values `202`, `2017`, and `-1`, respectively.

The vector instantiations in Lines 11 and 14 are ones where you know you need a vector that contains at least 10 elements. Note that these instantiations do not limit the size the container can grow to but just set the number of elements at initialization time.

Finally, Lines 17 and 20 demonstrate how a vector can be used to instantiate the contents of another vector—in other words, to create one `vector` object that is a copy of another vector or part of a vector. This is also a construct that works for all STL containers. The last form is the one that uses iterators. `partialCopy` contains the first five elements from `vecWithTenElements`.

NOTE

> The fourth construct can work only with objects of like types. So, you could instantiate `vecArrayCopy`—a vector of integer objects using another vector of integer objects. If one of them were to be a vector of, say, type `float`, the code would not compile.

Inserting Elements at the End of a Vector by Using `push_back()`

After you instantiate a vector of integers, the obvious next task is to insert elements (integers) into it. Insertion in a vector happens at the end of the array, and elements are "pushed" to the end of the array using the member function `push_back()`:

```
vector<int> integers;  // declare a vector of type int

// Insert sample integers into the vector:
integers.push_back(50);
integers.push_back(1);
```

Listing 17.2 demonstrates the use of `push_back()` to dynamically add elements to `std::vector`.

Input ▼

LISTING 17.2 Inserting Elements in a Vector by Using `push_back()`

```
#include<iostream>
#include<vector>
using namespace std;

int main()
{
    vector<int> integers;

    // Insert sample integers into the vector:
    integers.push_back(50);
    integers.push_back(1);
```

```
11:     integers.push_back(987);
12:     integers.push_back(1001);
13:
14:     cout << "The vector contains ";
15:     cout << integers.size() << " Elements" << endl;
16:
17:     return 0;
18: }
```

Output ▼

```
The vector contains 4 Elements
```

Analysis ▼

`push_back()`, as shown in Lines 9 through 12, is a `vector` class's public member function that inserts objects at the end of a dynamic array. Note the use of the function `size()`, which returns the number of elements held in the vector.

List Initialization

C++ features the class `std::initialize_list<>`, which, when supported, enables you to instantiate and initialize elements in a container as you would in a static array. `std::vector`, like most other containers, supports list initialization by allowing you to instantiate a vector with elements in one line (rather than many lines, as in Listing 17.2):

```
vector<int> integers = {50, 1, 987, 1001};
// alternatively:
vector<int> vecMoreIntegers {50, 1, 987, 1001};
```

Inserting Elements at a Given Position by Using `insert()`

You use `push_back()` to insert elements at the end of a vector. What if you need to insert elements in the middle of a vector? STL containers, including `std::vector`, feature an `insert()` function that has many overloads.

In one overload, you can specify the position at which an element can be inserted into the sequence:

```
// insert an element at the beginning
integers.insert(integers.begin(), 25);
```

In another overload, you can specify the position as well as the number of elements with a value that needs to be inserted:

```
// Insert 2 elements of value 45 at the end
integers.insert(integers.end(), 2, 45);
```

You can also insert the contents of one vector into another at a chosen position:

```
// Another vector containing 2 elements of value 30
vector<int> another(2, 30);

// Insert two elements from another container in position [1]
integers.insert(integers.begin() + 1,
                another.begin(), another.end());
```

You use an iterator, often returned by `begin()` or `end()`, to tell the `insert()` function the position where you want the new elements to be placed.

TIP

> Note that this iterator can also be the return value of an STL algorithm; for example, you can use the `std::find()` function to find an element and then insert another element at that position. Insertion will shift the element you found to the right. Algorithms such as `find()` are discussed in detail in Lesson 23, "STL Algorithms."

These forms of `vector::insert()` are demonstrated in Listing 17.3.

Input ▼

LISTING 17.3 Using the `vector::insert()` Function to Insert Elements at a Set Position

```
#include<vector>
#include<iostream>
using namespace std;

void DisplayVector(const vector<int>& inVec)
{
   for(auto element = inVec.cbegin();
         element != inVec.cend();
         ++ element)
       cout << *element << ' ';

   cout << endl;
}
```

```
13:
14: int main()
15: {
16:   // Instantiate a vector with 4 elements, each initialized to 90
17:     vector<int> integers(4, 90);
18:
19:     cout << "The initial contents of the vector: ";
20:     DisplayVector(integers);
21:
22:     // Insert 25 at the beginning
23:     integers.insert(integers.begin(), 25);
24:
25:     // Insert 2 numbers of value 45 at the end
26:     integers.insert(integers.end(), 2, 45);
27:
28:     cout << "Vector after inserting elements at beginning and end: ";
29:     DisplayVector(integers);
30:
31:     // Another vector containing 2 elements of value 30
32:     vector<int> another(2, 30);
33:
34:     // Insert two elements from another container in position [1]
35:     integers.insert(integers.begin() + 1,
36:        another.begin(), another.end());
37:
38:     cout << "Vector after inserting contents from another vector: ";
39:     cout << "in the middle:" << endl;
40:     DisplayVector(integers);
41:
42:     return 0;
43: }
```


Output ▼

```
The initial contents of the vector: 90 90 90 90
Vector after inserting elements at beginning and end: 25 90 90 90 90 45 45
Vector after inserting contents from another vector: in the middle:
25 30 30 90 90 90 90 45 45
```

Analysis ▼

This code demonstrates how the `insert()` function enables you to insert values in the middle of a container. The `vector` object in Line 17 is instantiated to contain four elements, all initialized to `90`. Taking this vector as a starting point, you use various overloaded forms of the `vector::insert()` member function. Line 23 shows how to add one element at the beginning. Line 26 shows how to add two elements of value `45` at the end. Line 35 demonstrates how elements can be inserted from one vector into the middle (in this example, the second position at offset 1) of another.

Although `vector::insert()` is a versatile function, using `push_back()` should be your preferred way of adding elements to a vector. This is because using `insert()` is an inefficient way to add elements to the `vector` (when adding in a position that is not the end of the sequence) because adding elements in the beginning or the middle makes the `vector` class shift all subsequent elements backward (after making space for the last ones at the end). Thus, depending on the type of the objects contained in the sequence, the cost of this shift operation can be significant in terms of the copy constructor or copy assignment operator invoked. The vector in Listing 17.3 is used to contain elements of type `int` that are relatively inexpensive to move around. This might not be the case with many other uses of the `vector` class, though.

TIP

> If a container needs to very frequently have insertions in the middle, you should ideally use `std::list`, explained in Lesson 18, "STL `list` and `forward_list`."

Accessing Elements in a Vector by Using Array Semantics

Elements in a vector can be accessed using the following methods: via array semantics using the subscript operator (`[]`), using the member function `at()`, or using iterators.

Listing 17.1 showed how an instance of `vector` can be created and initialized for 10 elements:

```
std::vector<int> tenElements(10);
```

You can access and set individual elements by using this array-like syntax:

```
tenElements[3] = 2011; // assign element at index 3 value 2011
```

Listing 17.4 demonstrates how elements in a vector can be accessed using the subscript operator (`[]`).

Input ▼

LISTING 17.4 Accessing Elements in a Vector by Using Array Semantics

```
 0: #include<iostream>
 1: #include<vector>
 2:
 3: int main()
 4: {
 5:    using namespace std;
 6:    vector<int> integers{ 50, 1, 987, 1001 };
 7:
 8:    for(size_t index = 0; index < integers.size(); ++index)
 9:    {
10:       cout << "Element[" << index << "] = " ;
11:       cout << integers[index] << endl;
12:    }
13:
14:    integers[2] = 2011; // change value of 3rd element
15:    cout << "After replacement: " << endl;
16:    cout << "Element[2] = " << integers[2] << endl;
17:
18:    return 0;
19: }
```


Output ▼

```
Element[0] = 50
Element[1] = 1
Element[2] = 987
Element[3] = 1001
After replacement:
Element[2] = 2011
```

Analysis ▼

In Lines 11, 14, and 16, `vector` is used to access and assign elements the same way you might use a static array using `vector`'s subscript operator (`[]`). The subscript operator accepts an element index that is zero-based, just as in a static array. Note how the `for` loop has been programmed in Line 8 to ensure that the index doesn't cross the bounds of the vector via comparison with `vector::size()`.

CAUTION

Accessing elements in a vector by using the subscript operator (`[]`) is fraught with the same dangers as accessing elements in an array; that is, you should not cross the bounds of the container. If you use `[]` to access elements in a vector at a position that is beyond the bounds of the vector, the result of the operation will be undefined (that is, anything could happen, possibly even an access violation).

A safer alternative is to use the `at()` member function:

```
// gets element at position 2

cout << integers.at(2);

// the vector::at() version of the code above in
// Listing   17.4, line 11:

cout << integers.at(index);
```

`at()` performs a runtime check against the size of the container and throws an exception if you cross the boundaries (which you shouldn't anyway).

It is safe to use the subscript operator (`[]`) when you can ensure bound integrity, as in the earlier example.

Accessing Elements in a Vector by Using Pointer Semantics

You can access elements in a vector by using pointer-like semantics via iterators, as shown in Listing 17.5.

Input ▼

LISTING 17.5 Accessing Elements in a Vector by Using Pointer Semantics (Iterators)

```
#include<iostream>
#include<vector>

int main()
{
   using namespace std;
   vector<int> integers{ 50, 1, 987, 1001 };

   vector<int>::const_iterator element = integers.cbegin();
   // auto element = integers.cbegin(); // auto type deduction

   while(element != integers.end())
```

```
12:     {
13:        size_t index = distance(integers.cbegin(), element);
14:
15:        cout << "Element at position ";
16:        cout << index << " is: " << *element << endl;
17:
18:        // move to the next element
19:        ++ element;
20:     }
21:
22:     return 0;
23: }
```

Output ▼

```
Element at position 0 is: 50
Element at position 1 is: 1
Element at position 2 is: 987
Element at position 3 is: 1001
```


Analysis ▼

The iterator in this example behaves like a pointer, as shown in Line 16, where the value stored in the vector is accessed using the dereference operator (*), and Line 19, where the iterator, when incremented using the operator ++, points to the next element. Notice how `std::distance()` is used in Line 13 to evaluate the zero-based offset position of the element in the vector (that is, position relative to the beginning), given `cbegin()` and the iterator pointing to the element. Line 9 presents a simpler alternative to the iterator declaration in Line 8, using the automatic type deduction capabilities of the compiler introduced in Lesson 3, "Using Variables, Declaring Constants."

Removing Elements from a Vector

Just the same way as a vector features insertion at the end via the `push_back()` function, it also features the removal of an element at the end via the `pop_back()` function. Removing an element from a vector by using `pop_back()` takes constant time; that is, the time required is independent of the number of elements stored in the vector. Listing 17.6 demonstrates the use of the function `pop_back()` to delete elements at the end of a vector.

Input ▼

LISTING 17.6 Using `pop_back()` to Delete the Last Element of a Vector

```
#include<iostream>
#include<vector>
using namespace std;

template <typename T>
void DisplayVector(const vector<T>& inVec)
{
   for(const auto& element : inVec)
      cout << element << ' ';

   cout << endl;
}

int main()
{
   vector<int> integers;

   // Insert sample integers into the vector:
   integers.push_back(50);
   integers.push_back(1);
   integers.push_back(987);
   integers.push_back(1001);

   cout << "Vector contains " << integers.size() << " elements: ";
   DisplayVector(integers);

   // Erase one element at the end
   integers.pop_back();

   cout << "After a call to pop_back()" << endl;
   cout << "Vector contains " << integers.size() << " elements: ";
   DisplayVector(integers);

   return 0;
}
```

Output ▼

```
Vector contains 4 elements: 50 1 987 1001
After a call to pop_back()
Vector contains 3 elements: 50 1 987
```

Analysis ▼

The output indicates that the `pop_back()` function used in Line 27 has reduced the elements in the vector by erasing the last element inserted into it. Line 30 calls `size()` again to demonstrate that the number of elements in the vector has been reduced by one, as indicated in the output.

NOTE

The function `DisplayVector()` in Lines 4 through 11 has taken a template form in Listing 17.6, whereas in Listing 17.3 it accepted only a vector for integers. The template form helps you reuse this function for a vector of any type, for example `float`:

```
vector <float> vecFloats;
```

```
DisplayVector(vecFloats);
```

This generic form of `DisplayVector()` would also support a vector of any class that features an operator that returns a value `cout` would understand. In addition, note how the range-based `for` loop in Line 7 simplifies the code.

Understanding the Concepts of Size and Capacity

The *size* of a vector is the number of elements stored in the vector. The *capacity* of a vector is the total number of elements that can potentially be stored in the vector before it reallocates memory to accommodate more elements. Therefore, a vector's size is less than or equal to its capacity.

You can query a vector for the number of elements by calling `size()`:

```
cout << "Size: " << integers.size();
```

You can query a vector for its capacity by calling `capacity()`:

```
cout << "Capacity: " <<  integers.capacity();
```

A vector that needs to frequently reallocate the memory of the internal dynamic array is likely to cause performance issues. This problem might be addressed by using the member function `reserve(number)`. What `reserve()` essentially does is increase the amount of memory allocated for the vector's internal array to accommodate the number of elements without needing to reallocate. Depending on the type of the objects stored in the vector, reducing the number of reallocations also reduces the number of times the objects are copied and improves performance. Listing 17.7 demonstrates the difference between `size()` and `capacity()`.

Input ▼

LISTING 17.7 Using `size()` and `capacity()`

```
#include<iostream>
#include<vector>

int main()
{
   using namespace std;

   // instantiate a vector object that holds 5 integers of default value
   vector<int> integers(5);

   cout << "Vector of integers was instantiated with " << endl;
   cout << "Size: " << integers.size();
   cout << ", Capacity: " << integers.capacity() << endl;

   // Inserting a 6th element in to the vector
   integers.push_back(666);

   cout << "After inserting an additional element... " << endl;
   cout << "Size: " << integers.size();
   cout << ", Capacity: " <<  integers.capacity() << endl;

   // Inserting another element
   integers.push_back(777);

   cout << "After inserting yet another element... " << endl;
   cout << "Size: " << integers.size();
   cout << ", Capacity: " <<  integers.capacity() << endl;

   return 0;
}
```

Output ▼

```
Vector of integers was instantiated with
Size: 5, Capacity: 5
After inserting an additional element...
Size: 6, Capacity: 7
After inserting yet another element...
Size: 7, Capacity: 7
```

Analysis ▼

Line 8 shows the instantiation of a vector of integers that contains five integers at the default value (0). Lines 11 and 12, which display the size and the capacity of the vector, respectively, show that the two are equal at instantiation time. Line 15 inserts a sixth element in the vector. Given that the capacity of the vector was 5 prior to the insertion, there isn't adequate memory in the internal buffer of the vector to support this new sixth element. In other words, for the `vector` class to scale itself and store six elements, it needs to reallocate the internal buffer. The implementation of the reallocation logic is smart: To avoid another reallocation on insertion of another element, it preemptively allocates a capacity greater than the requirements of the immediate scenario.

The output shows that when a sixth element is inserted in a vector that has capacity for five elements, the reallocation involved increases the capacity to seven elements. `size()` always reflects the number of elements in a vector, and it has a value of six at this stage in this example. The addition of a seventh element in Line 22 results in no increase in capacity; the existing allocated memory meets the demand sufficiently. The size and capacity values are equal at this stage, indicating that the vector is used to its full capacity, and insertion of the next element will cause the vector to reallocate its internal buffer, copying existing values before it inserts the new value.

NOTE

> The preemptive increase in the capacity of the vector when the internal buffer is reallocated is not regulated by any clause in the C++ standard. This level of performance optimization may vary depending on the provider of the STL in use, and therefore you may see different output when executing Listing 17.7.

The STL `deque` Class

`deque` (pronounced "deck") is an STL dynamic array class that is quite similar in properties to `vector` except that it allows for the insertion and removal of elements at the front and back of an array. You would instantiate a deque of integers like this:

```
// Define a deque of integers
std::deque<int> intDeque;
```

TIP

> To use `std::deque`, include the header `<deque>`:
>
> `#include<deque>`

A deque can be visualized as shown in Figure 17.2.

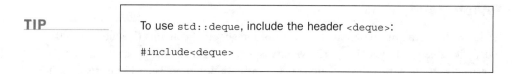

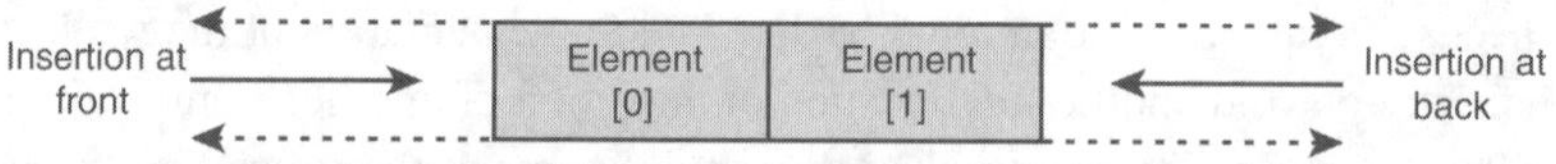

FIGURE 17.2 Internals of a deque.

A deque is similar to a vector in that it supports element insertions and deletions at the back via the `push_back()` and `pop_back()` functions. Just as with the `vector` class, you can access elements in the `deque` class by using array semantics via the subscript operator `[]`. `deque` is different from `vector`, however, in that it also permits insertion of elements at the front with `push_front()` and removal from the front with `pop_front()`, as demonstrated in Listing 17.8.

Input ▼

LISTING 17.8 Instantiating an STL `deque` Class and Using the `push_front()` and `pop_front()` Functions to Insert and Delete Elements at the Front

```
#include<deque>
#include<iostream>
#include<algorithm>

int main()
{
    using namespace std;

    // Define a deque of integers
    deque<int> intDeque;

    // Insert integers at the bottom of the array
    intDeque.push_back(3);
    intDeque.push_back(4);
    intDeque.push_back(5);

    // Insert integers at the top of the array
    intDeque.push_front(2);
    intDeque.push_front(1);
    intDeque.push_front(0);

    cout << "The contents of the deque after inserting elements ";
```

```
    cout << "at the top and bottom are:" << endl;

    // Display contents on the screen
    for(size_t count = 0;
        count < intDeque.size();
        ++ count)
    {
       cout << "Element [" << count << "] = ";
       cout << intDeque [count] << endl;
    }

    cout << endl;

    // Erase an element at the top
    intDeque.pop_front();

    // Erase an element at the bottom
    intDeque.pop_back();

    cout << "The contents of the deque after erasing an element ";
    cout << "from the top and bottom are:" << endl;

    // Display contents again: this time using iterators
    // if on older compilers, remove auto and uncomment next line
    // deque<int>::iterator element;
    for(auto element = intDeque.begin();
         element != intDeque.end();
         ++ element)
    {
       size_t Offset = distance(intDeque.begin(), element);
       cout << "Element [" << Offset << "] = " << *element << endl;
    }

    intDeque.clear();
    if(intDeque.empty())
       cout << "The container is now empty" << endl;

    return 0;
}
```


Output ▼

```
The contents of the deque after inserting elements at the top and bottom are:
Element [0] = 0
Element [1] = 1
Element [2] = 2
Element [3] = 3
Element [4] = 4
Element [5] = 5
```

```
The contents of the deque after erasing an element from the top and bottom are:
Element [0] = 1
Element [1] = 2
Element [2] = 3
Element [3] = 4
The container is now empty
```

Analysis ▼

Line 9 instantiates a deque of integers. Note how similar this syntax is to the instantiation of a vector of integers. Lines 12 through 14 display the use of the `deque` member function `push_back()` followed by `push_front()` in Lines 17 through 19. The latter distinguishes the `deque` from `vector`. As shown in Line 36, `pop_front()` deletes the first element in the deque. The mechanism that displays the contents of `deque` in Lines 25 through 31 uses array-like syntax to access elements using the operator `[]`, whereas Lines 47 through 53 demonstrate the use of iterators with the operator `*`. You can use a range-based `for` loop, as demonstrated in Listing 17.6, with `std::deque` as well. The algorithm `std::distance()` is used in Line 51 to evaluate the offset position of the element in the deque in the same manner that you have already seen work with a vector in Listing 17.5.

TIP

When you need to empty an STL container such as a vector or a deque—that is, delete all elements contained in it—you use the member function `clear()`.

The following code deletes all elements from the vector `integers` (refer to Listing 17.7):

```
integers.clear();
```

To delete all elements in the deque `intDeque`, you use the following (refer to Listing 17.8, Line 55):

```
intDeque.clear();
```

Note that both `vector` and `deque` also feature the member function `empty()`, which returns `true` when a container is empty. It doesn't actually delete existing elements the way `clear()` does.

DO	DON'T
DO use the dynamic arrays `vector` or `deque` when you don't know the number of elements you need to store. **DO** remember that a vector can grow only at one end via the function `push_back()`. **DO** remember that a deque can grow on both ends via the functions `push_back()` and `push_front()`.	**DON'T** access a dynamic array beyond its bounds. **DON'T** access a vector or a deque by using the subscript operator (`[]`) if you are not certain of being within bounds; use the member function `at()` instead.

Summary

In this lesson, you learned the basics of using the `vector` and `deque` classes for dynamic arrays. The concepts of size and capacity were explained, and you saw how the use of `vector` can be optimized to reduce the number of reallocations of a vector's internal buffer, which copies the objects contained and potentially reduces performance. `vector` is the simplest of the STL's containers, but it is frequently used and, arguably, among the most efficient container classes.

Q&A

Q Does the order of the elements stored in a vector change?

A A vector is a sequential container, which means elements are stored and accessed in it in the very order in which they were inserted.

Q What function is used to insert elements in a vector, and where is an element inserted?

A The member function `push_back()` inserts elements at the end of a vector.

Q What function gets the number of elements stored in a vector?

A The member function `size()` returns the number of elements stored in a vector. Incidentally, this is true for all STL containers.

Q Does the insertion or removal of elements at the end of a vector take more time if the vector contains more elements?

A No. Insertion and removal of elements at the end of a vector are constant-time activities.

Q What is the advantage of using the `reserve()` member function?

A `reserve()` allocates space in the internal buffer of a vector, and insertion of elements does not require the vector to reallocate the buffer and copy the existing contents. Depending on the nature of the objects stored in a vector, reserving space in a vector can result in performance improvements.

Q Are the properties of the `deque` class any different from those of the `vector` class when it comes to insertion of elements?

A No, the properties of the `deque` class are similar to those of the `vector` class when it comes to insertion, which is a constant-time activity for elements added at the end of a sequence and a linear-time activity for elements inserted in the middle. However, the `vector` class allows insertion only at the end, whereas `deque` allows insertion at the beginning and the end of the collection.

Workshop

The Workshop provides quiz questions to help you solidify your understanding of the material covered and exercises to provide you with experience using what you've learned. Try to answer the quiz and exercise questions before checking the answers in Appendix E and be certain you understand the answers before continuing to the next lesson.

Quiz

1. Can elements be inserted in the middle or at the beginning of a vector in constant time?
2. With a particular vector, `size()` returns `10`, and `capacity()` returns `20`. How many more elements can you insert in this vector without the `vector` class needing to trigger a buffer reallocation?
3. What does the `pop_back()` function do?
4. If `vector<int>` is a dynamic array of integers, `vector<Mammal>` is a dynamic array of what type?

5. Can elements in a vector be randomly accessed? If so, how?
6. What iterator type allows random access of elements in a vector?

Exercises

1. Write an interactive program that accepts integer input from the user and saves it in a vector. The user should be able to query a value stored in the vector at any time, given an index.
2. Extend the program from Exercise 1 so that it can tell a user whether a value she queries for already exists in the vector.
3. Jack sells jars on eBay. To help him with packaging and shipment, write a program in which he can enter the dimensions of each of these articles, store them in a vector, and have them printed on the screen.
4. Write an application that initializes a deque to the following three strings: `"Hello"`, `"Containers are cool!"`, and `"C++ is evolving!"`. You must display the strings by using a generic function that would work for a deque of any kind. Your application needs to demonstrate the use of list initialization introduced in C++11 and the operator "", which was introduced in C++14.

LESSON 18
STL `list` and `forward_list`

The Standard Template Library (STL) offers a doubly linked list: the template class `std::list`. The main advantages of a linked list are fast and constant time insertion and removal of elements. C++ also supports a singly linked list, the class `std::forward_list`, which can be traversed in only one direction.

In this lesson, you learn

- How to instantiate `list` and `forward_list`
- How to use the STL list classes, including for insertion and removal of elements
- How to reverse and sort elements

The Characteristics of `std::list`

A *linked list* is a collection of nodes in which each node, in addition to containing a value or an object of interest, also points to the next node; that is, each node links to the next one and the previous one, as shown in Figure 18.1.

The STL implementation of the `list` class allows for constant-time insertions at the beginning, end, or middle of a list.

FIGURE 18.1
Visual representation of a doubly linked list.

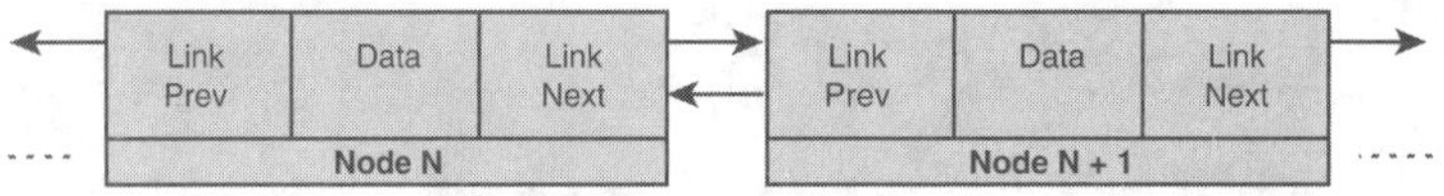

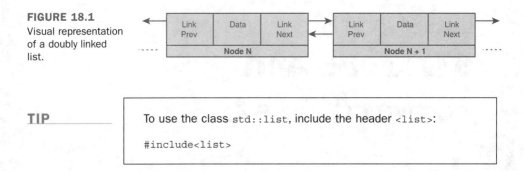

TIP

To use the class `std::list`, include the header `<list>`:

```
#include<list>
```

Basic `list` Operations

The template class `list` in the `std` namespace is a generic implementation that needs to be template instantiated before you can use any of its useful member functions.

Instantiating a `std::list` Object

The template instantiation of `list` needs to specify the type of object that you want to collect in the list. So, the initialization of a list would look like the following:

```
std::list<int> linkInts;  // list containing integers
std::list<float> listFloats;  // list containing floats
std::list<Tuna> listTunas;  // list containing objects of type Tuna
```

To declare an iterator that points to an element in the list, you would use

```
std::list<int>::const_iterator elementInList;
```

If you need an iterator that can be used to modify values or invoke non-`const` functions, you use `iterator` instead of `const_iterator`.

Given that an implementation of `std::list` provides a set of overloaded constructors, you can even create lists that are initialized to contain a number of elements of your choosing, each initialized to a value, as demonstrated in Listing 18.1.

Input ▼

LISTING 18.1 Different Forms of Instantiating `std::list`, Specifying Number of Elements and Initial Values

```
#include<list>
#include<vector>

int main()
```

```
 4: {
 5:     using namespace std;
 6:
 7:     // instantiate an empty list
 8:     list<int> linkInts;
 9:
10:     // instantiate a list with 10 integers
11:     list<int> listWith10Integers(10);
12:
13:     // instantiate a list with 4 integers, each value 99
14:     list<int> listWith4IntegerEach99(4, 99);
15:
16:     // create an exact copy of an existing list
17:     list<int> listCopyAnother(listWith4IntegerEach99);
18:
19:     // a vector with 10 integers, each 2017
20:     vector<int> vecIntegers(10, 2017);
21:
22:     // instantiate a list using values from another container
23:     list<int> listContainsCopyOfAnother(vecIntegers.cbegin(),
24:                                         vecIntegers.cend());
25:
26:     return 0;
27: }
```


Output ▼

The code snippet produces no output.

Analysis ▼

This program produces no output and demonstrates the application of the various overloaded constructors in creating a list of integers. Line 8 creates an empty list, whereas Line 11 creates a list that contains 10 integers. Line 14 shows a list, called `listWith4IntegersEach99`, that contains 4 integers that are each initialized to the value `99`. Line 17 creates a list that is an exact copy of the contents of another. Lines 20 through 24 are surprising and curious! They instantiate a vector that contains 10 integers, each containing the value `2017`, and then instantiate a list (in Line 23) that contains elements copied from the vector, using `const` iterators returned by `vector::cbegin()` and `vector::cend()`. Listing 18.1 also demonstrates how iterators help decouple the implementation of one container from another, enabling you to use their generic functionality to instantiate a list by using values taken from a vector, as shown in Lines 23 and 24.

NOTE

On comparing Listing 18.1 against Listing 17.1 from Lesson 17, "STL Dynamic Array Classes," you will note a remarkable similarity in the way containers of different types have been instantiated. The more you program using STL containers, the more reusable patterns you will see and the easier it will get.

Inserting Elements at the Front or Back of a List

As with a deque, with a list you insert elements at the front (or top, depending on your perspective) by using the member method `push_front()`. You insert elements at the end by using the member method `push_back()`. Each of these two methods takes one input parameter, which is the value to be inserted:

```
linkInts.push_back(-1);
linkInts.push_front(2001);
```

Listing 18.2 demonstrates the effect of using these two methods on a list of integers.

Input ▼

LISTING 18.2 Inserting Elements in a List by Using `push_front()` and `push_back()`

```
#include<list>
#include<iostream>
using namespace std;

template <typename T>
void DisplayContents(const T& container)
{
   for(auto element = container.cbegin();
        element != container.cend();
        ++ element )
      cout << *element << ' ';

   cout << endl;
}

int main()
{
   std::list<int> linkInts{ -101, 42 };

   linkInts.push_front(10);
   linkInts.push_front(2011);
   linkInts.push_back(-1);
   linkInts.push_back(9999);

   DisplayContents(linkInts);
```

```
25:
26:     return 0;
27: }
```

Output ▼

```
2011 10 -101 42 -1 9999
```

Analysis ▼

Line 17 features the template instantiation of a list for type `int` and uses list initialization syntax ({ . . . }) to ensure that `linkInts` is constructed with two integers (-101 and 42) linked within it. Lines 19 through 22 demonstrate the use of `push_front()` and `push_back()`. The value being supplied as an argument to `push_front()` takes the first position in the list, whereas that sent via `push_back()` takes the last position. The output displays the content of the list via the generic template function `DisplayContents()`, demonstrating the order of the inserted elements (and showing that they aren't stored in order of insertion).

NOTE

> `DisplayContents()` in Listing 18.2, Lines 4 through 13, is a more generic version of the method `DisplayVector()` in Listing 17.6 (note the changed parameter list). Whereas `DisplayVector()` works only for the `vector`, generalizing the type of elements stored in a vector, `DisplayContents()` is truly generic supporting multiple container types.
>
> You can invoke the version of `DisplayContents()` in Listing 18.2 by using a vector, a list, or a deque as an argument, and it will work just fine.

Inserting Elements in the Middle of a List

`std::list` can insert elements in the middle of the collection in constant time. This is done using the member function `insert()`.

The `list::insert()` member function is popularly used in the following three forms:

- Form 1:

  `iterator insert(const_iterator position, const T& value)`

  Here the insert function accepts the position of insertion as the first parameter and the value to insert as the second. This function returns an iterator pointing to the recently inserted element in the list.

- Form 2:

  ```
  void insert(const_iterator position, size_type n, const T& value)
  ```

  This function accepts the position of insertion as the first parameter, the value to insert as the last parameter, and the number of elements in variable `n`.

- Form 3:

  ```
  template <class InputIterator>
  void insert(const_iterator pos, InputIterator f, InputIterator l)
  ```

  This overloaded variant is a template function that accepts, in addition to the position, two input iterators that mark the bounds of the collection to insert into the list. Note that the input type `InputIterator` is a template-parameterized type and therefore can point to the bounds of any collection—be it an array, a vector, or another list.

Listing 18.3 demonstrates the use of these overloaded variants of the `list::insert()` function.

Input ▼

LISTING 18.3 Various Methods of Inserting Elements in a List

```
#include<list>
#include<iostream>
using namespace std;

template <typename T>
void DisplayContents(const T& container)
{
   for(auto element = container.cbegin();
        element != container.cend();
        ++ element )
      cout << *element << ' ';

   cout << endl;
}

int main()
{
   list<int> linkInts1;

   // Inserting elements at the beginning...
   linkInts1.insert(linkInts1.begin(), 2);
   linkInts1.insert(linkInts1.begin(), 1);

   // Inserting an element at the end...
   linkInts1.insert(linkInts1.end(), 3);

   cout << "The contents of list 1 after inserting elements:" << endl;
   DisplayContents(linkInts1);

```

```
    list<int> linkInts2;

    // Inserting 4 elements of the same value 0...
    linkInts2.insert(linkInts2.begin(), 4, 0);

    cout << "The contents of list 2 after inserting '";
    cout << linkInts2.size() << "' elements of a value:" << endl;
    DisplayContents(linkInts2);

    list<int> linkInts3;

    // Inserting elements from another list at the beginning...
    linkInts3.insert(linkInts3.begin(),
                     linkInts1.begin(), linkInts1.end());

    cout << "The contents of list 3 after inserting the contents of ";
    cout << "list 1 at the beginning:" << endl;
    DisplayContents(linkInts3);

    // Inserting elements from another list at the end...
    linkInts3.insert(linkInts3.end(),
                   linkInts2.begin(), linkInts2.end());

    cout << "The contents of list 3 after inserting ";
    cout << "the contents of list 2 at the end:" << endl;
    DisplayContents(linkInts3);

    return 0;
}
```


Output ▼

```
The contents of list 1 after inserting elements:
1 2 3
The contents of list 2 after inserting '4' elements of a value:
0 0 0 0
The contents of list 3 after inserting the contents of list 1 at the beginning:
1 2 3
The contents of list 3 after inserting the contents of list 2 at the end:
1 2 3 0 0 0 0
```

Analysis ▼

`begin()` and `end()` are member functions that return iterators pointing to the beginning and the end of the list, respectively. This is generally true for all STL containers, including `std::list`. The `list::insert()` function accepts an iterator that marks the position before which items are to be inserted. The iterator returned by the `end()` function, as used in Line 24, points to after the last element in the list. Therefore, Line 24 inserts integer value 3 before the end as the last value. Line 32 indicates the initialization of a list with four elements placed at the beginning—that is, at the front—each with the value 0. Lines 41 and 42 demonstrate the use of the `list::insert()` function to insert elements from one list at the end of another. Although this example inserts a list of integers into another list, the range inserted could as well have been within the limits of a vector, supplied by `begin()` and `end()`, as also shown in Listing 18.1, or a regular static array.

Erasing Elements from a List

The list member function `erase()` comes in two overloaded forms: one that erases one element given an iterator that points to it and another that accepts a range and therefore erases a range of elements from the list. You can see the `list::erase()` function in action in Listing 18.4, which demonstrates how you erase an element or a range of elements from a list.

Input ▼

LISTING 18.4 Erasing Elements from a List

```
#include<list>
#include<iostream>
using namespace std;

template <typename T>
void DisplayContents(const T& container)
{
   for(auto element = container.cbegin();
        element != container.cend();
       ++ element )
     cout << *element << ' ';

   cout << endl;
}

int main()
{
    std::list<int> linkInts{ 4, 3, 5, -1, 2017 };

   // Store an iterator obtained in using insert()
   auto val2 = linkInts.insert(linkInts.begin(), 2);

   cout << "Initial contents of the list:" << endl;
   DisplayContents(linkInts);

```

```
25:     cout << "After erasing element '"<< *val2 << "':" << endl;
26:     linkInts.erase(val2);
27:     DisplayContents(linkInts);
28:
29:     linkInts.erase(linkInts.begin(), linkInts.end());
30:     cout << "Number of elements after erasing range: ";
31:     cout << linkInts.size() << endl;
32:
33:     return 0;
34: }
```

Output ▼

```
Initial contents of the list:
2 4 3 5 -1 2017
After erasing element '2':
4 3 5 -1 2017
Number of elements after erasing range: 0
```

Analysis ▼

When `insert()` is used to insert a value, as shown in Line 20, it returns an iterator to the newly inserted element. This iterator pointing to an element with value `2` is stored in a variable `val2`, to be used later in a call to `erase()` in Line 26 to delete this very element from the list. Line 29 demonstrates the use of `erase()` to delete a range of elements. You clear a range from `begin()` to `end()`, effectively erasing the entire list.

TIP

> The quickest and simplest way to empty an STL container, such as `std::list`, is to call the member function `clear()`.
>
> A simpler Line 29 in Listing 18.4 would therefore be
>
> `linkInts.clear();`

NOTE

> Listing 18.4 demonstrates in Line 31 that the number of elements in `std::list` can be determined by using the list method `size()`, which is very similar to the same method for the `vector` class. `size()` is supported by all STL container classes.

Reversing and Sorting Elements in a List

`list` has a special property: Iterators that point to the elements in a list remain valid despite rearrangement of the elements or insertion of new elements and so on. To keep this important property intact, the `list` class features `sort()` and `reverse()` as member methods even though the STL supplies these as algorithms that will and do work on the `list` class. The member method versions of these algorithms ensure that iterators pointing to elements in a list are not invalidated when the relative position of an element is disturbed.

Reversing Elements by Using `list::reverse()`

The `list` class features the member function `reverse()`, which takes no parameters and reverses the order of the contents in a list for you:

```
linkInts.reverse();  // reverse order of elements
```

The use of `reverse()` is demonstrated in Listing 18.5.

Input ▼

LISTING 18.5 Reversing Elements in a List

```
#include<list>
#include<iostream>
using namespace std;

template <typename T>
void DisplayContents(const T& container)
{
     for(auto element = container.cbegin();
          element != container.cend();
          ++ element )
       cout << *element << ' ';

    cout << endl;
}

int main()
{
    std::list<int> linkInts{ 0, 1, 2, 3, 4, 5 };

    cout << "Initial contents of list:" << endl;
    DisplayContents(linkInts);

    linkInts.reverse();

    cout << "Contents of list after using reverse():" << endl;
```

```
25:     DisplayContents(linkInts);
26:
27:     return 0;
28: }
```

Output ▼

```
Initial contents of list:
0 1 2 3 4 5
Contents of list after using reverse():
5 4 3 2 1 0
```

Analysis ▼

As shown in Line 22, `reverse()` simply reverses the order of elements in the list. It is a simple call without parameters which ensures that iterators pointing to elements in the list, if you keep them, remain valid even after the reversal.

Sorting Elements

The `list` class member function `sort()` is available in a version that takes no parameters:

```
linkInts.sort();  // sort in ascending order
```

Another version allows you to define your own sort priorities via a binary predicate function as a parameter:

```
bool SortPredicate_Descending(const int& lhs, const int& rhs)
{
   // define criteria for list::sort: return true for desired order
   return(lhs > rhs);
}
// Use predicate to sort a list:
linkInts.sort(SortPredicate_Descending);
```

These two variants are demonstrated in Listing 18.6.

Input ▼

LISTING 18.6 Sorting a List of Integers in Ascending and Descending Order by Using `list::sort()`

```
#include<list>
#include<iostream>
```

```
using namespace std;

bool SortPredicate_Descending(const int& lhs, const int& rhs)
{
   // define criteria for list::sort: return true for desired order
   return(lhs > rhs);
}

template <typename T>
void DisplayContents(const T& container)
{
   for(auto element = container.cbegin();
        element != container.cend();
        ++ element )
      cout << *element << ' ';

   cout << endl;
}

int main()
{
   list<int> linkInts{ 0, -1, 2011, 444, -5 };

   cout << "Initial contents of the list are - " << endl;
   DisplayContents(linkInts);

   linkInts.sort();

   cout << "Order after sort():" << endl;
   DisplayContents(linkInts);

   linkInts.sort(SortPredicate_Descending);
   cout << "Order after sort() with a predicate:" << endl;
   DisplayContents(linkInts);

   return 0;
}
```

Output ▼

```
Initial contents of the list are -
0 -1 2011 444 -5
Order after sort():
-5 -1 0 444 2011
Order after sort() with a predicate:
2011 444 0 -1 -5
```

Analysis ▼

This example demonstrates the use of the `sort()` member function on a list of integers. Line 28 displays the use of a `sort()` function without parameters to sort elements in ascending order by default and compare integers by using the operator `<` (which, in the case of integers, is implemented by the compiler). However, if you want to override this default behavior, you must supply the `sort()` function with a binary predicate, as shown in Line 33. The function `SortPredicate_Descending()`, defined in Lines 4 through 8, is a binary predicate that helps the `list` class's `sort()` function decide whether one element is less than the other. Using this predicate you tell the list what's to be interpreted as less (which, in this case, is the first parameter being greater than the second), and the `list` class uses this decision to sort.

Sorting and Removing Elements from a List That Contains Instances of a Class

What if you have a list of a class type, and not a simple built-in type such as `int`? Say that you have a list of address book entries, where each entry is a class that contains name, address, and so on. How could you ensure that this list is sorted on name?

The answer is one of the following:

- Implement the operator < within the class type that the list contains.
- Supply a sort *binary predicate*—a function that takes two values as input and returns a Boolean value indicating whether the first value is smaller than the second.

Most practical applications involving STL containers rarely collect integers; instead, they collect user-defined types such as `class` or `struct`. Listing 18.7 demonstrates the use of a list where every element is a `class` type to create a contacts list. It seems rather long at first sight but is mostly simple code.

Input ▼

LISTING 18.7 A List of Class Objects: Creating a Contacts List

```
#include<list>
#include<string>
#include<iostream>
using namespace std;

template <typename T>
void displayAsContents(const T& container)
```

```
{
   for(auto element = container.cbegin();
         element != container.cend();
         ++ element )
     cout << *element << endl;

   cout << endl;
}

struct ContactItem
{
   string name;
   string phone;
   string displayAs;

   ContactItem(const string& conName, const string & conNum)
   {
      name = conName;
      phone = conNum;
      displayAs =(name + ": " + phone);
   }

   // used by list::remove() given contact list item
   bool operator ==(const ContactItem& itemToCompare) const
   {
      return(itemToCompare.name == this->name);
   }

   // used by list::sort() without parameters
   bool operator < (const ContactItem& itemToCompare) const
   {
      return(this->name < itemToCompare.name);
   }

   // Used by displayAsContents via cout
   operator const char*() const
   {
     return displayAs.c_str();
   }
};

bool SortOnphoneNumber(const ContactItem& item1,
                       const ContactItem& item2)
{
   return(item1.phone < item2.phone);
}

int main()
{
   list <ContactItem> contacts;
   contacts.push_back(ContactItem("Oprah Winfrey", "+1 7889 879 879"));
   contacts.push_back(ContactItem("Bill Gates", "+1 97 7897 8799 8"));
```

```
    contacts.push_back(ContactItem("Angi Merkel", "+49 23456 5466"));
    contacts.push_back(ContactItem("Vlad Putin", "+7 6645 4564 797"));
    contacts.push_back(ContactItem("John Travolta", "91 234 4564 789"));
    contacts.push_back(ContactItem("Angelina Jolie", "+1 745 641 314"));

    cout << "List in initial order: " << endl;
    displayAsContents(contacts);

    contacts.sort();
    cout << "Sorting in alphabetical order via operator<:" << endl;
    displayAsContents(contacts);

    contacts.sort(SortOnphoneNumber);
    cout << "Sorting in order of phone numbers via predicate:" << endl;
    displayAsContents(contacts);

    cout << "After erasing Putin from the list: " << endl;
    contacts.remove(ContactItem("Vlad Putin", ""));
    displayAsContents(contacts);

    return 0;
}
```

Output ▼


```
Sorting in alphabetical order via operator<:
Angelina Jolie: +1 745 641 314
Angi Merkel: +49 23456 5466
Bill Gates: +1 97 7897 8799 8
John Travolta: 91 234 4564 789
Oprah Winfrey: +1 7889 879 879
Vlad Putin: +7 6645 4564 797

Sorting in order of phone numbers via predicate:
Angelina Jolie: +1 745 641 314
Oprah Winfrey: +1 7889 879 879
Bill Gates: +1 97 7897 8799 8
Angi Merkel: +49 23456 5466
Vlad Putin: +7 6645 4564 797
John Travolta: 91 234 4564 789

After erasing Putin from the list:
Angelina Jolie: +1 745 641 314
Oprah Winfrey: +1 7889 879 879
Bill Gates: +1 97 7897 8799 8
Angi Merkel: +49 23456 5466
John Travolta: 91 234 4564 789
```

Analysis ▼

For a start, focus on main() in Lines 54 through 80. Line 56 instantiates a list of address book items of type ContactItem. Lines 57 through 62 populate this list with names and (fake) telephone numbers of celebrities; Line 56 displays this initial order. Line 67 uses list::sort() without a predicate function. In the absence of a predicate, this sort function seeks the presence of the operator < in ContactItem, which is defined in Lines 36 through 39. ContactItem::operator< helps list::sort() sort its elements in alphabetical order of the stored names (and not based on telephone numbers or using a random logic). To sort the same list based on the phone numbers, you use list::sort() and supply the binary predicate function SortOnPhoneNumber() as an argument in Line 71. This function, implemented in Lines 48 through 52, ensures that the input arguments of type ContactItem are compared to each other on the basis of the phone numbers and not the names. Thus, it helps list::sort() sort the list of celebrities on the basis of their phone numbers, as the output indicates. Finally, Line 76 uses list::remove() to remove a celebrity contact from the list. You supply an object with the celebrity's name as a parameter. list::remove() compares this object to other elements in the list, using ContactItem::operator==, which is implemented in Lines 30 through 33. This operator returns true if the names match, helping list::remove() decide what the criteria for a match should be.

This example demonstrates how STL's template version of a linked list can be used to create a list of any object type, and it also shows the importance of operators and predicates.

std::forward_list

Unlike the doubly linked std::list, std::forward_list is a singly linked list—that is, it allows iteration in only one direction, as shown in Figure 18.2.

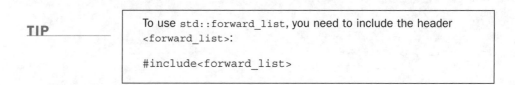

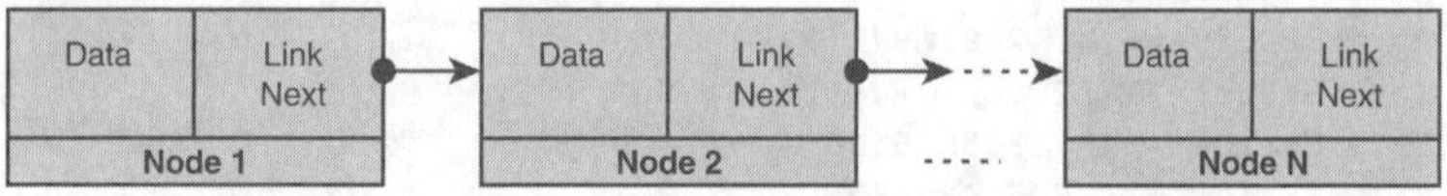

FIGURE 18.2 A visual representation of a singly linked list.

TIP

To use std::forward_list, you need to include the header <forward_list>:

```
#include<forward_list>
```

The usage of `forward_list` is similar to the usage of `list`, except for the fact that you can move iterators only in one direction, and you have a `push_front()` function to insert elements but no `push_back()` function. Of course, you can always use `insert()` and its overloaded functions to insert an element at a given position.

Listing 18.8 demonstrates some functions of the `forward_list` class.

Input ▼

LISTING 18.8 Basic Insertion and Removal Operations with `forward_list`

```
#include<forward_list>
#include<iostream>
using namespace std;

template <typename T>
void DisplayContents(const T& container)
{
    for(auto element = container.cbegin();
            element != container.cend();
            ++ element)
        cout << *element << ' ';

    cout << endl;
}

int main()
{
    forward_list<int> flistIntegers{ 3, 4, 2, 2, 0 };
    flistIntegers.push_front(1);

    cout << "Contents of forward_list: " << endl;
    DisplayContents(flistIntegers);

    flistIntegers.remove(2);
    flistIntegers.sort();
    cout << "Contents after removing 2 and sorting: " << endl;
    DisplayContents(flistIntegers);

    return 0;
}
```


Output ▼

```
Contents of forward_list:
1 3 4 2 2 0
Contents after removing 2 and sorting:
0 1 3 4
```

Analysis ▼

As the example shows, forward_list is similar in function to list. As forward_list doesn't support bidirectional iteration, you can use operator++, but not operator--, on an iterator. This example demonstrates the use of the function remove() in Line 23 to remove all elements with the value 2. Line 29 demonstrates sort() with the default sort predicate that uses std::less<T>.

The advantage of forward_list is that, because it is a singly linked list, its memory consumption is slightly lower than that of list (as an element needs to know only the next element but not the previous one).

DO	DON'T
DO choose std::list over std::vector if you need to frequently insert or delete elements, especially in the middle; whereas a vector needs to resize its internal buffer to allow array semantics and causes expensive copy operations, a list just links or unlinks elements. **DO** remember that you can insert in the beginning or end of a list by using the push_front() member method or the push_back() member method, respectively. **DO** remember to program the operators < and == in a class that will be collected in an STL container such as a list to supply the default sort or remove predicate. **DO** remember that you can always determine the number of elements in a list by using the list::size() method, as with any other STL container class. **DO** remember that you can empty a list by using the list::clear() method, as with any other STL container class.	**DON'T** use a list when you have infrequent insertions or deletions at the ends and no insertions or deletions in the middle; a vector or deque can be significantly faster in these cases. **DON'T** forget to supply a predicate function if you want to use sort() or remove() on the list with non-default criteria. **DON'T** confuse the method clear() with the method empty(); the latter is used to check if the container is empty (in which case it returns true) and makes no changes.

Summary

This lesson taught you the properties of the `list` and `forward_list` class functions and the different list operations. You now know some of the most useful list functions and can create a list of any object type.

Q&A

Q Why does the `list` class provide member functions such as `sort()` and `remove()`?

A The STL `list` class is required to ensure that iterators pointing to elements in the `list` should remain valid regardless of the position of the elements in the `list`. Although STL algorithms work on `list` too, `list's` member functions ensure that the aforementioned property of the list is assured.

Q I am using a list of type `CAnimal`, which is a class. What operators should `CAnimal` define for `list` member functions to be able to work on it accurately?

A You must provide the default comparison operator == and the default < operator to any class that can be used in STL containers.

Q How would I replace the keyword `auto` with an explicit type declaration in the following line:

```
list<int> linkInts(10);  // list of 10 integers
auto firstElement = linkInts.begin();
```

A You would replace `auto` with the following explicit type declaration:

```
list<int> linkInts(10);  // list of 10 integers
list<int>::iterator firstElement = linkInts.begin();
```

Workshop

The Workshop provides quiz questions to help you solidify your understanding of the material covered and exercises to provide you with experience using what you've learned. Try to answer the quiz and exercise questions before checking the answers in Appendix E and be certain you understand the answers before continuing to the next lesson.

Quiz

1. Is there any loss in performance when you insert items in the middle of an STL `list` object compared to at the beginning or the end?
2. Two iterators are pointing to two elements in an STL `list` object, and then an element is inserted between them. Are these iterators invalidated by the insert action?
3. How can the contents of `std::list` be cleared?
4. Is it possible to insert multiple elements in a list?

Exercises

1. Write a short program that accepts numbers from the user and inserts them at the top of a list.
2. Using a short program, demonstrate that an iterator pointing to an element in a `list` continues to remain valid even after another element has been inserted before it, thus changing the relative position of the former element.
3. Write a program that inserts the contents of a vector into an STL list by using the `list` class's `insert()` function.
4. Write a program that sorts and reverses a list of strings.

LESSON 19
STL set and multiset

The Standard Template Library (STL) offers container classes that help with frequent and quick searches. The classes `std::set` and `std::multiset` each contain a sorted set of elements with the ability to find elements given a logarithmic complexity. Their unordered counterparts offer constant-time insertion and search capabilities.

This lesson includes

- How STL `set` and `multiset`, `unordered_set`, and `unordered_multiset` containers can be of use to you
- Insertion, removal, and search of elements
- Advantages and disadvantages of using these containers

An Introduction to STL Set Classes

`set` and `multiset` are containers that facilitate quick lookups of keys in a container that stores them; that is, the keys are the values stored in a one-dimensional container. The difference between `set` and `multiset` is that the latter allows for duplicates, whereas the former can store only unique values.

Figure 19.1 is only demonstrative and indicates that `set` can be used to create a set of unique names, whereas `multiset` can be used to permit duplicates in a set.

To facilitate quick searching, STL implementations of `set` and `multiset` internally look like a binary tree. This means that elements inserted in a set or a multiset are sorted on insertion for quicker lookups. It also means that, unlike in a vector, where an element at a position can be replaced by another element, an element at a given position in a set cannot be replaced by a new element with a different value. This is because the set places the new element in a potentially different location, in accordance with its value relative to the elements in the internal tree.

FIGURE 19.1
Visual representation of using set and multiset for sets of names.

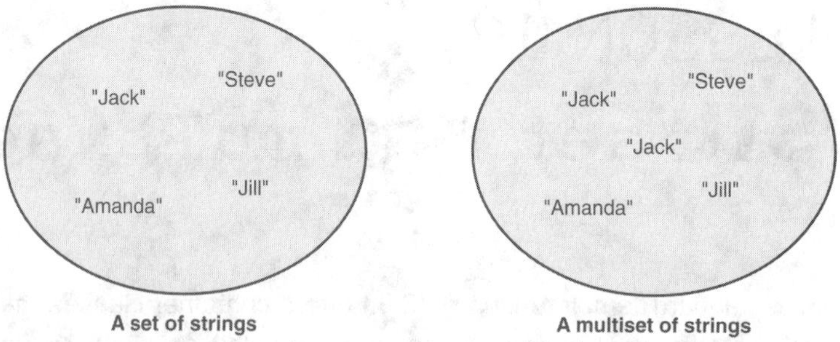

TIP

> To use the class `std::set` or the class `std::multiset`, include the header `<set>`:
>
> `#include<set>`

Basic STL set and multiset Operations

STL `set` and `multiset` are template classes that need to be instantiated before you can use any of their member functions.

Instantiating a std::set Object

Instantiating a set or a multiset of a type requires a specialization of the template class `std::set` or `std::multiset` for that type:

```
std::set<int>  setInts;
std::multiset<int> msetInts;
```

To define a set or multiset that contains objects of the class `Tuna`, you would program the following:

```
std::set<Tuna> tunaSet;
std::multiset<Tuna> tunaMSet;
```

You would declare an iterator that points to an element in a set or multiset like this:

```
std::set<int>::const_iterator element;
std::multiset<int>::const_iterator element;
```

If you need an iterator that can be used to modify values or invoke non-`const` functions, you use `iterator` instead of `const_iterator`.

Given that both `set` and `multiset` are containers that sort elements on insertion, they use the default predicate `std::less` when you don't supply sort criteria. This ensures that a set contains elements sorted in ascending order.

You create a binary sort predicate by using `operator()` to define a class that takes two values of the type contained in the set as input and returns `true`, depending on the criteria. One such sort predicate that sorts in descending order is the following:

```
// used as a template parameter in set / multiset instantiation
template <typename T>
struct SortDescending
{
   bool operator()(const T& lhs, const T& rhs) const
   {
      return (lhs > rhs);
   }
};
```

You then supply this predicate in the set or multiset instantiation as follows:

```
// a set and multiset of integers (using sort predicate)
set<int, SortDescending<int>> setInts;
multiset<int, SortDescending<int>> msetInts;
```

In addition to these variants, you can create a set or a multiset that copies from another set or multiset or that copies via a supplied range, as demonstrated in Listing 19.1.

Input ▼

LISTING 19.1 Different Instantiation Techniques with `set` and `multiset`

```
#include<set>

// used as a template parameter in set / multiset instantiation
template <typename T>
struct SortDescending
{
   bool operator()(const T& lhs, const T& rhs) const
   {
      return (lhs > rhs);
   }
};

int main()
{
```

```
14:     using namespace std;
15:
16:     // a simple set or multiset of integers (using default sort predicate)
17:     set<int> setInts1;
18:     multiset<int> msetInts1;
19:
20:     // set and multiset instantiated given a user-defined sort predicate
21:     set<int, SortDescending<int>> setInts2;
22:     multiset<int, SortDescending<int>> msetInts2;
23:
24:     // creating one set from another, or part of another container
25:     set<int> setInts3(setInts1);
26:     multiset<int> msetInts3(setInts1.cbegin(), setInts1.cend());
27:
28:     return 0;
29: }
```

Output ▼

This code snippet produces no output.

Analysis ▼

This program produces no output but demonstrates the various instantiation techniques for `set` and `multiset`, specialized to contain type `int`. In Lines 17 and 18, you see the simplest form, where the template parameters other than type have been ignored, resulting in the default sort predicate being taken, as implemented in `struct` (or `class`) `std::less<T>`. If you want to override the default sort, you need to specify a predicate like the ones defined in Lines 3 through 10 and used in `main()` in Lines 21 and 22. This predicate ensures that the sort is in descending order (as the default is ascending order). Finally, Lines 25 and 26 show instantiation techniques where one set is a copy of another, and a multiset instantiates from a range of values taken from a set (but could be a vector or a list or based on any STL container class that returns iterators that describe bounds via `cbegin()` and `cend()`).

Inserting Elements in a `Set` or `Multiset`

Most `set` and `multiset` functions work in a similar fashion. They accept similar parameters and return similar value types. For instance, you can insert elements in both kinds of containers by using the member function `insert()`, which accepts the value to be inserted or a range taken from another container, as shown here:

```
setInts.insert(-1);
msetInts.insert(setInts.begin(), setInts.end());
```

Listing 19.2 demonstrates the insertion of elements in these containers.

Input ▼

LISTING 19.2 Inserting Elements in STL set and multiset Containers

```
#include<set>
#include<iostream>
using namespace std;

template <typename T>
void DisplayContents(const T& container)
{
   for(auto element = container.cbegin();
         element != container.cend();
         ++element)
      cout << *element << ' ';

   cout << endl;
}

int main()
{
   set<int> setInts{ 202, 151, -999, -1 };
   setInts.insert(-1); // duplicate
   cout << "Contents of the set: " << endl;
   DisplayContents(setInts);

   multiset<int> msetInts;
   msetInts.insert(setInts.begin(), setInts.end());
   msetInts.insert(-1); // duplicate

   cout << "Contents of the multiset: " << endl;
   DisplayContents(msetInts);

   cout << "Number of instances of '-1' in the multiset are: '";
   cout << msetInts.count(-1) << "'" << endl;

   return 0;
}
```

Output ▼

```
Contents of the set:
-999 -1 151 202
Contents of the multiset:
-999 -1 -1 151 202
Number of instances of '-1' in the multiset are: '2'
```

Analysis ▼

Lines 4 through 13 contain the generic template function `DisplayContents()`, which you have also seen in Lesson 17, "STL Dynamic Array Classes," and Lesson 18, "STL `list` and `forward_list`." This function writes the contents of an STL container to the console or screen. Lines 17 and 22, as you already know, instantiate a `set` and a `multiset`, respectively, with the former using list initialization syntax. Lines 18 and 24 attempt to insert a duplicate value in the `set` and `multiset` containers. Line 23 demonstrates how `insert()` can be used to insert the contents of a set into a multiset, inserting in this case the contents of `setInts` into `msetInts`. The output demonstrates that the multiset is able to hold multiple values, while the set isn't. Line 30 demonstrates the `multiset::count()` member function, which returns the number of elements in the multiset that hold a particular value.

> **TIP**
>
> Use `multiset::count()` to find the number of elements in a multiset that have the same value as that supplied as an argument to this function.

Finding Elements in an STL `set` or `multiset` Container

Associative containers like `set` and `multiset` or `map` and `multimap` feature `find()`—a member function that enables you to find a value given a key:

```
auto elementFound = setInts.find(-1);

// Check if found...
if(elementFound != setInts.end())
   cout << "Element " << *elementFound << " found!" << endl;
else
   cout << "Element not found in set!" << endl;
```

The use of `find()` is demonstrated in Listing 19.3. With a multiset that allows multiple elements with the same value, this function finds the first value that matches the supplied key.

Input ▼

LISTING 19.3 Using the `find` Member Function

```
#include<set>
#include<iostream>
using namespace std;

```

```
 4: int main()
 5: {
 6:    set<int> setInts{ 43, 78, -1, 124 };
 7:
 8:    // Display contents of the set to the screen
 9:    for(auto element = setInts.cbegin();
10:         element != setInts.cend();
11:         ++ element)
12:       cout << *element << endl;
13:
14:    // Try finding an element
15:    auto elementFound = setInts.find(-1);
16:
17:    // Check if found...
18:    if(elementFound != setInts.end())
19:       cout << "Element " << *elementFound << " found!" << endl;
20:    else
21:       cout << "Element not found in set!" << endl;
22:
23:    // finding another
24:    auto anotherFind = setInts.find(12345);
25:
26:    // Check if found...
27:    if(anotherFind != setInts.end())
28:       cout << "Element " << *anotherFind << " found!" << endl;
29:    else
30:       cout << "Element 12345 not found in set!" << endl;
31:
32:    return 0;
33: }
```


Output ▼

```
-1
43
78
124
Element -1 found!
Element 12345 not found in set!
```

Analysis ▼

Lines 15 through 21 display the use of the `find()` member function. `find()` returns an iterator that needs to be compared against `end()`, as shown in Line 18, to verify whether an element was found. If the iterator is valid, you can access the value it points to by using `*elementFound`.

NOTE

> The example in Listing 19.3 works correctly for a multiset, too; that is, if Line 6 is a multiset instead of a set, it does not change the way the application works. A multiset may hold multiple elements of the same value at contiguous locations, and you can access them by using the iterator returned by `find()` and advancing it `count() - 1` times to access all elements with a particular value. The member method `count()` was demonstrated in Listing 19.2.

Erasing Elements in an STL `set` or `multiset` Container

Associative containers such as `set` and `multiset` or `map` and `multimap` containers feature `erase()`—a member method that allows you to delete a value given a key:

```
setObject.erase(key);
```

Another form of the `erase()` function allows the deletion of a particular element given an iterator that points to it:

```
setObject.erase(element);
```

You can erase a range of elements from a set or a multiset by using iterators that supply the bounds:

```
setObject.erase(iLowerBound, iUpperBound);
```

Listing 19.4 demonstrates the use of `erase()` in removing elements from a set or multiset.

Input ▼

LISTING 19.4 Using the `erase()` Member Function on a Multiset

```
#include<set>
#include<iostream>
using namespace std;

template <typename T>
void DisplayContents(const T& Input)
{
    for(auto element = Input.cbegin();
           element != Input.cend();
            ++ element)
```

```
10:         cout << *element << ' ';
11:
12:     cout << endl;
13: }
14:
15: typedef multiset<int> MSETINT;
16:
17: int main()
18: {
19:     MSETINT msetInts{ 43, 78, 78, -1, 124 };
20:
21:     cout << "multiset contains " << msetInts.size() << " elements: ";
22:     DisplayContents(msetInts);
23:
24:     cout << "Enter a number to erase from the set: ";
25:     int input = 0;
26:     cin >> input;
27:
28:     cout << "Erasing " << msetInts.count(input);
29:     cout << " instances of value " << input << endl;
30:
31:     msetInts.erase(input);
32:
33:     cout << "multiset now contains " << msetInts.size() << " elements: ";
34:     DisplayContents(msetInts);
35:
36:     return 0;
37: }
```


Output ▼

```
multiset contains 5 elements: -1 43 78 78 124
Enter a number to erase from the set: 78
Erasing 2 instances of value 78
multiset now contains 3 elements: -1 43 124
```

Analysis ▼

Note the use of `typedef` in Line 15. Line 28 demonstrates the use of `count()` to determine the number of elements with a specific value. The actual erase happens in Line 31, which deletes all elements that match the particular number input by the user.

TIP

The member function `erase()` is overloaded. When invoked with a value as shown in Listing 19.4, it deletes all elements that evaluate to it. When invoked using an iterator, such as one returned by a `find()` operation, it deletes that one element, as shown here:

```
MSETINT::iterator elementFound = msetInts.
find(numberToErase);
if(elementFound != msetInts.end())
   msetInts.erase(elementFound);
else
   cout << "Element not found!" << endl;
```

You can also use `erase()` to delete a range of values from a multiset:

```
MSETINT::iterator elementFound =
msetInts.find(valueToErase);

if(elementFound != msetInts.end())
   msetInts.erase(msetInts.begin(), elementFound);
```

This snippet removes all elements from the start to the element of value `valueToErase`, not including the latter. Both `set` and `multiset` can be emptied of their contents by using the member function `clear()`.

Now that you have had an overview of the basic `set` and `multiset` functions, it's time to review an example that features a practical application using this container class. Listing 19.5 shows the simplest implementation of a menu-based telephone directory that enables a user to insert names and telephone numbers, find them, erase them, and display them all.

Input ▼

LISTING 19.5 A Telephone Directory Featuring STL `set`, `find()`, and `erase()`

```
#include<set>
#include<iostream>
#include<string>
using namespace std;

template <typename T>
void DisplayContents(const T& container)
{
   for(auto iElement = container.cbegin();
```

```
         iElement != container.cend();
         ++ iElement)
      cout << *iElement << endl;

   cout << endl;
}

struct ContactItem
{
   string name;
   string phoneNum;
   string displayAs;

   ContactItem(const string& nameInit, const string & phone)
   {
      name = nameInit;
      phoneNum = phone;
      displayAs =(name + ": " + phoneNum);
   }

   // used by set::find() given contact list item
   bool operator ==(const ContactItem& itemToCompare) const
   {
      return(itemToCompare.name == this->name);
   }

   // used to sort
   bool operator <(const ContactItem& itemToCompare) const
   {
      return(this->name < itemToCompare.name);
   }

   // Used in DisplayContents via cout
   operator const char*() const
   {
      return displayAs.c_str();
   }
};

int main()
{
   set<ContactItem> setContacts;
   setContacts.insert(ContactItem("Oprah Winfrey", "+1 7889 879 879"));
   setContacts.insert(ContactItem("Bill Gates", "+1 97 7897 8799 8"));
   setContacts.insert(ContactItem("Angi Merkel", "+49 23456 5466"));
   setContacts.insert(ContactItem("Vlad Putin", "+7 6645 4564 797"));
   setContacts.insert(ContactItem("John Travolta", "91 234 4564 789"));
   setContacts.insert(ContactItem("Angelina Jolie", "+1 745 641 314"));
   DisplayContents(setContacts);

   cout << "Enter a name you wish to delete: ";
```

```
60:     string inputName;
61:     getline(cin, inputName);
62:
63:     auto contactFound = setContacts.find(ContactItem(inputName, ""));
64:     if(contactFound != setContacts.end())
65:     {
66:        setContacts.erase(contactFound);
67:        cout << "Displaying contents after erasing " << inputName << endl;
68:        DisplayContents(setContacts);
69:     }
70:     else
71:        cout << "Contact not found" << endl;
72:
73:    return 0;
74: }
```

Output ▼

```
Angelina Jolie: +1 745 641 314
Angi Merkel: +49 23456 5466
Bill Gates: +1 97 7897 8799 8
John Travolta: 91 234 4564 789
Oprah Winfrey: +1 7889 879 879
Vlad Putin: +7 6645 4564 797

Enter a name you wish to delete: John Travolta
Displaying contents after erasing John Travolta
Angelina Jolie: +1 745 641 314
Angi Merkel: +49 23456 5466
Bill Gates: +1 97 7897 8799 8
Oprah Winfrey: +1 7889 879 879
Vlad Putin: +7 6645 4564 797
```

Analysis ▼

This example is similar to Listing 18.7, which sorted a `std::list` in alphabetical order; however, in the case of `std::set`, the sort happens on insertion. As the output here indicates, you don't need to invoke any function to ensure that elements in the set are sorted because they're sorted on insertion, using the operator `<`, which is implemented in Lines 36 through 39. You give the user the choice to delete an entry, and Line 63 demonstrates the call to `find()` to locate that entry, which is deleted in Line 66 using `erase()`.

TIP

> This implementation of the telephone directory is based on the STL `set` class and therefore does not allow for multiple entries containing the same value. If you need your implementation of the directory to allow two people with the same name to be stored, you should instead use the STL `multiset` class. The code in Listing 19.5 would still work correctly if `setContacts` were a multiset. To make further use of the `multiset` class's capability to store multiple entries of the same value, you use the `count()` member function to determine the number of items that hold a particular value.

Pros and Cons of Using STL `set` and `multiset`

The STL `set` and `multiset` classes provide significant advantages in applications that need frequent lookups because their contents are sorted, and it's therefore quicker to locate items in them. However, to provide this advantage, a container needs to sort elements at insertion time. There is overhead in inserting elements because elements are sorted; this overhead might be a worthwhile compromise if you need to use features and functions such as `find()` often.

`find()` makes use of the internal binary tree structure. This sorted binary tree structure results in another implicit disadvantage over sequential containers such as a vector. In a vector, the element pointed to by an iterator (say, one returned by a `std::find()` operation) can be overwritten by a new value. In the case of a set, however, elements are sorted by the `set` class according to their respective values, and therefore overwriting an element using an iterator should never be done, even if doing so is programmatically possible.

STL Hash Set Implementation: `std::unordered_set` and `std::unordered_multiset`

STL `std::set` and `std::multiset` sort elements (which are simultaneously the keys) on the basis of `std::less<T>` or a supplied predicate. Searching in a sorted container is faster than searching in an unsorted container such as a vector, and `std::sort()` offers logarithmic complexity. This means that the time spent finding an element in a set is not directly proportional to the number of elements in the set; rather, it is proportional to the log of the number of elements. So, on average, it takes twice as long to search in a set of 10,000 elements as it would take in a set of 100 (as 100^2 = 10,000, or log(10000) = 2 × log(100)).

Yet, this dramatic improvement of performance over an unsorted container (where search time is directly proportional to the number of elements) is sometimes not enough. Programmers and mathematicians alike seek constant-time insertions and sort possibilities, and one of them uses a hash-based implementation, where a hash function is used to determine the sorting index. Elements inserted into a hash set are first evaluated by a hash function that generates a unique index, which is the index of the *bucket* they're placed in.

The hash set variant provided by STL is the container class `std::unordered_set`.

TIP

To use STL `std::unordered_set` or `std::unordered_multiset` containers, include
`#include<unordered_set>`

The use of this class doesn't change too much in comparison to the use of `std::set`:

```
// instantiation:
unordered_set<int> usetInt;

// insertion of an element
usetInt.insert(1000);

// find():
auto elementFound = usetInt.find(1000);

if(elementFound != usetInt.end())
   cout << *elementFound << endl;
```

However, one very important feature of `unordered_set` is the availability of a hash function that is responsible for deciding the sorting order:

```
unordered_set<int>::hasher HFn = usetInt.hash_function();
```

The decision to use `std::unordered_set` or a `std::set` is best made after the performance of the respective containers is measured in simulations involving operations and data volumes that closely resemble real-world usage. Listing 19.6 demonstrates the use of some of the common methods supplied by `std::unordered_set`.

Input ▼

LISTING 19.6 `std::unordered_set` and the Use of `insert()`, `find()`, `size()`, `max_bucket_count()`, `load_factor()`, and `max_load_factor()`

```
#include<unordered_set>
#include<iostream>
using namespace std;

template <typename T>
void DisplayContents(const T& cont)
{
   cout << "Unordered set contains: ";
   for(auto element = cont.cbegin();
        element != cont.cend();
        ++ element)
      cout<< *element << ' ';

   cout << endl;

   cout << "Number of elements, size() = " << cont.size() << endl;
   cout << "Bucket count = " << cont.bucket_count() << endl;
   cout << "Max load factor = " << cont.max_load_factor() << endl;
   cout << "Load factor: " << cont.load_factor() << endl << endl;
}

int main()
{
   unordered_set<int> usetInt{ 1, -3, 2017, 300, -1, 989, -300, 9 };
   DisplayContents(usetInt);
   usetInt.insert(999);
   DisplayContents(usetInt);

   cout << "Enter int you want to check for existence in set: ";
   int input = 0;
   cin >> input;
   auto elementFound = usetInt.find(input);

   if(elementFound != usetInt.end())
      cout << *elementFound << " found in set" << endl;
   else
      cout << input << " not available in set" << endl;

   return 0;
}
```

Output ▼

```
Unordered set contains: 9 1 -3 989 -1 2017 300 -300
Number of elements, size() = 8
Bucket count = 8
Max load factor = 1
Load factor: 1

Unordered set contains: 9 1 -3 989 -1 2017 300 -300 999
Number of elements, size() = 9
Bucket count = 64
Max load factor = 1
Load factor: 0.140625

Enter int you want to check for existence in set: -300
-300 found in set
```

Analysis ▼

Different compilers or different versions of the STL might produce slightly different output. The code in Listing 19.6 creates an unordered set of integers; inserts values into it using list initialization in Line 23; and then displays contents, including statistics supplied by the methods `max_bucket_count()`, `load_factor()`, and `max_load_factor()`, as shown in Lines 15 through 18. The output indicates that the bucket count is initially at eight, with eight elements in the container, resulting in a load factor of 1, which is the same as the maximum load factor. When a ninth element is inserted into the unordered set, the set reorganizes itself, creates 64 buckets, and re-creates the hash table; the load factor reduces. The rest of the code in `main()` demonstrates how the syntax for finding elements in an unordered set is similar to that in a set. `find()` returns an iterator that needs to be checked for the success of `find()`, as shown in Line 33, before it can be used.

NOTE

Hashes are typically used in a hash table to look up a value given a key. See the section on `std::unordered_map` in Lesson 20, "STL `map` and `multimap`," which demonstrates `std::unordered_map`—the STL implementation of a hash table.

DO

DO remember that STL set and multiset containers are optimized for situations that involve frequent searches.

DO remember that std::multiset allows multiple elements (keys) of the same value, whereas std::set permits only unique values.

DO use multiset::count(value) to find the number of elements of a particular value.

DO remember that set::size() or multiset::size() finds the number of elements in a container.

DON'T

DON'T forget to program the operators < and == for classes that can be collected in containers such as set or multiset. The former becomes the sort predicate, and the latter is used for functions such as set::find().

DON'T use std::set or std::multiset in scenarios with frequent insertions and infrequent searches. std::vector or std::list is usually better suited to such cases.

Summary

In this lesson, you learned about using the STL set and multiset classes, their significant member functions, and their characteristics. You also saw their application in the programming of a simple menu-based telephone directory that features search and erase functions.

Q&A

Q How would I declare a set of integers to be sorted and stored in order of descending magnitude?

A set<int> is a set of integers. It takes the default sort predicate std::less<T> to sort items in order of ascending magnitude and can also be expressed as set<int, less <int>>. To sort in order of descending magnitude, define the set as set <int, greater <int>>.

Q What would happen if, in a set of strings, I inserted the string "Jack" twice?

A A set is not meant to be used to contain non-unique values, and the set of strings would contain only one instance of "Jack".

Q In the preceding example, if I wanted to have two instances of "Jack", what would I need to change?

A By design, a set holds only unique values. You would need to change your selection of container to a multiset.

Q What `multiset` member function returns the count of items of a particular value in a container?

A `count(value)` is the function of interest.

Q I have found an element in a set by using the `find()` function and have an iterator pointing to it. Would I use this iterator to change the value being pointed to?

A Some STL implementations might allow the user to change the value of an element inside a set via an iterator returned by, for example, `find()`. However, this is not the correct thing to do. An iterator to an element in the set should be used as a `const` iterator—even when the STL implementation has not enforced it as such.

Workshop

The Workshop provides quiz questions to help you solidify your understanding of the material covered and exercises to provide you with experience using what you've learned. Try to answer the quiz and exercise questions before checking the answers in Appendix E and be certain you understand the answers before continuing to the next lesson.

Quiz

1. You declare a `set` of integers as `set<int>`. What function supplies the sort criteria?
2. Where would you find duplicate elements in a multiset?
3. What `set` or `multiset` function supplies the number of elements in a container?

Exercises

1. Extend the telephone directory example in this lesson to find a person's name, given a phone number. (*Hint:* Adjust the operators < and == and ensure that items are sorted and compared according to phone numbers.)
2. Define a multiset to store entered words and their meanings; that is, make a multiset work as a dictionary. (*Hint:* The multiset should be a structure that contains two strings: the word and its meaning.)
3. Demonstrate via a simple program that a set cannot accept duplicate entries, whereas a multiset can.

LESSON 20
STL `map` and `multimap`

The Standard Template Library (STL) supports container classes that help with applications that require frequent and quick searches.

This lesson covers

- How STL `map` and `multimap`, `unordered_map`, and `unordered_multimap` containers can be of use to you
- Inserting, removing, and searching for elements
- Supplying a custom sort predicate
- Basics of how hash tables work

An Introduction to STL Map Classes

`map` and `multimap` are key/value pair containers that allow for lookups on the basis of keys, as shown in Figure 20.1.

The difference between `map` and `multimap` is that the latter allows for duplicates, whereas the former can only store pairs with unique keys.

To facilitate quick searching, STL implementations of `map` and `multimap` internally look like binary trees. This means that elements inserted in a map or a multimap are sorted on insertion. It also means that, unlike in a vector, where an element at a position can be replaced by another, an element in a map at a given position cannot be replaced by a new element of a different value. This is because the map would ideally like to have it placed in a potentially different location, in accordance with its value relative to the elements in the internal tree.

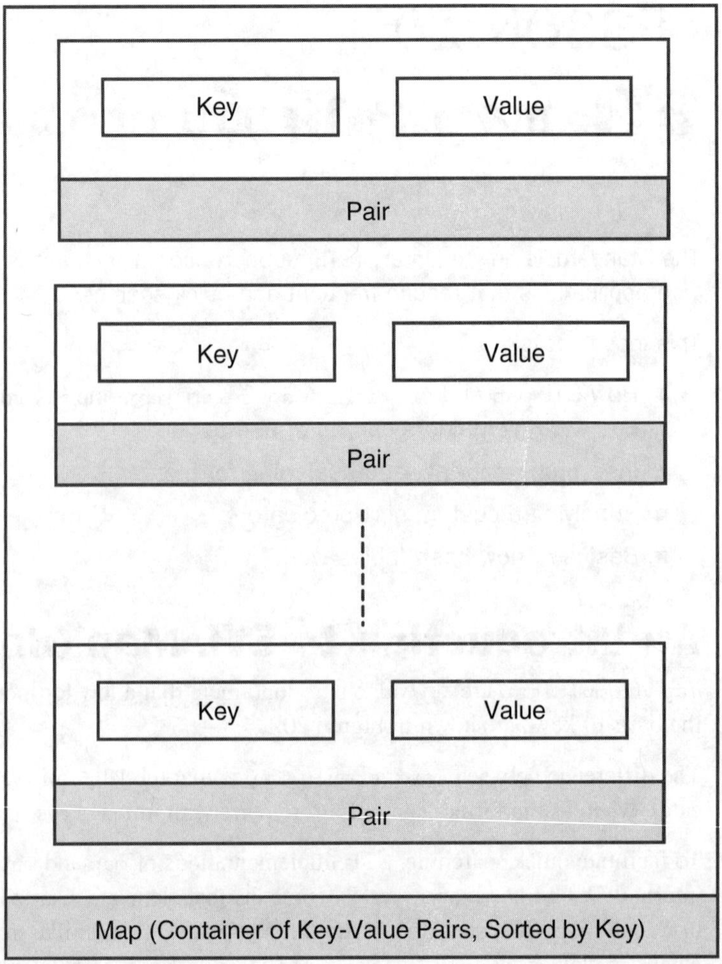

FIGURE 20.1
Visual illustration of a container for pairs, each holding a key and a value.

> **TIP**
>
> To use the class `std::map` or `std::multimap`, include the header:
> `#include<map>`

Basic `std::map` and `std::multimap` Operations

STL `map` and `multimap` are template classes that need to be instantiated before you can use any of their member functions.

Instantiating std::map or std::multimap

Instantiating a map or multimap for an integer as a key and a string as a value requires a specialization of the template class std::map or std::multimap. The template instantiation of the map class needs the programmer to specify the key type, the value type, and optionally a predicate that helps the map class to sort the elements on insertion. Therefore, typical map instantiation syntax looks like this:

```
#include<map>
using namespace std;
...
map <keyType, valueType, Predicate=std::less <keyType>> mapObj;
multimap <keyType, valueType, Predicate=std::less <keyType>> mmapObj;
```

Thus, the third template parameter is optional. When you supply only the key type and the value type and ignore the third template parameter, std::map and std::multimap default to class std::less<> to define the sort criteria. Thus, a map or multimap that maps an integer to a string looks like this:

```
std::map<int, string> mapIntToStr;
std::multimap<int, string> mmapIntToStr;
```

Listing 20.1 illustrates instantiation techniques in greater detail.

Input ▼

LISTING 20.1 Instantiating map and multimap Objects That Map an int Key to a string Value

```
#include<map>
#include<string>

template<typename keyType>
struct ReverseSort
{
   bool operator()(const keyType& key1, const keyType& key2) const
   {
      return(key1 > key2);
   }
};

int main()
{
   using namespace std;

   // map and multimap key of type int to value of type string
   map<int, string> mapIntToStr1;
```

```
18:     multimap<int, string> mmapIntToStr1;
19:
20:     // map and multimap constructed as a copy of another
21:     map<int, string> mapIntToStr2(mapIntToStr1);
22:     multimap<int, string> mmapIntToStr2(mmapIntToStr1);
23:
24:     // map and multimap constructed given a part of another map or multimap
25:     map<int, string> mapIntToStr3(mapIntToStr1.cbegin(),
26:                                   mapIntToStr1.cend());
27:
28:     multimap<int, string> mmapIntToStr3(mmapIntToStr1.cbegin(),
29:                                         mmapIntToStr1.cend());
30:
31:     // map and multimap with a predicate that inverses sort order
32:      map<int, string, ReverseSort<int> > mapIntToStr4
33:         (mapIntToStr1.cbegin(), mapIntToStr1.cend());
34:
35:     multimap<int, string, ReverseSort<int> > mmapIntToStr4
36:       (mapIntToStr1.cbegin(), mapIntToStr1.cend());
37:
38:     return 0;
39: }
```

Output ▼

This code snippet produces no output.

Analysis ▼

This example demonstrates instantiation and produces no output. Focus on `main()` in Lines 12 through 39. The simplest map and multimap of an integer key to a string value can be seen in Lines 17 and 18. Lines 25 through 28 demonstrate the creation of a map or a multimap initialized to a range of values from another as input. Lines 31 through 36 demonstrate how to instantiate a map or a multimap with your own custom sort criteria. Note that the default sort (in the previous instantiations) uses `std::less<T>`, which sorts elements in the increasing order. If you want to change this behavior, you supply a predicate that is a `class` or a `struct` that implements `operator()`. Such a predicate, `struct ReverseSort`, is in Lines 3 through 10 and has been used in the instantiation of a map in Line 32 and a multimap in Line 35.

Inserting Elements in an STL Map or Multimap

Most functions work in multimap much the same way they work in a map. They accept similar parameters and return similar value types. You can insert elements in both kinds of containers by using the `insert` member function:

```
std::map<int, std::string> mapIntToStr1;
// insert pair of key and value using make_pair function
mapIntToStr.insert(make_pair(-1, "Minus One"));
```

As these two containers maintain elements in key/value pairs, you can also directly supply a `std::pair` initialized to the key and value to be inserted:

```
mapIntToStr.insert(pair<int, string>(1000, "One Thousand"));
```

Alternatively, you can use array-like syntax to insert, which does appear quite user friendly and is supported via the subscript operator (`[]`):

```
mapIntToStr[1000000] = "One Million";
```

You can also instantiate a multimap as a copy of a map:

```
std::multimap<int, std::string> mmapIntToStr(mapIntToStr.cbegin(),
                                              mapIntToStr.cend());
```

Listing 20.2 demonstrates the various `map` and `multimap` instantiation methods.

Input ▼

LISTING 20.2 Inserting Elements in `map` and `multimap` Containers Using Overloads of `insert()` and Array Semantics via the `[]` Operator

```
#include<map>
#include<iostream>
#include<string>

using namespace std;

// Type-define the map and multimap definition for easy readability
typedef map <int, string> MAP_INT_STRING;
typedef multimap <int, string> MMAP_INT_STRING;

template <typename T>
void DisplayContents(const T& cont)
{
   for(auto element = cont.cbegin();
```

```
        element != cont.cend();
        ++element)
      cout << element->first << " -> " << element->second << endl;

   cout << endl;
}

int main()
{
   MAP_INT_STRING mapIntToStr;

   // Insert key-value pairs into the map using value_type
   mapIntToStr.insert(MAP_INT_STRING::value_type(3, "Three"));

   // Insert a pair using function make_pair
   mapIntToStr.insert(make_pair(-1, "Minus One"));

   // Insert a pair object directly
   mapIntToStr.insert(pair<int, string>(1000, "One Thousand"));

   // Use an array-like syntax for inserting key-value pairs
   mapIntToStr [1000000] = "One Million";

   cout << "The map contains " << mapIntToStr.size();
   cout << " key-value pairs. They are: " << endl;
   DisplayContents(mapIntToStr);

   // instantiate a multimap that is a copy of a map
   MMAP_INT_STRING mmapIntToStr(mapIntToStr.cbegin(),
                                mapIntToStr.cend());

   // The insert function works the same way for multimap too
   // A multimap can store duplicates - insert a duplicate
   mmapIntToStr.insert(make_pair(1000, "Thousand"));

   cout << endl << "The multimap contains " << mmapIntToStr.size();
   cout << " key-value pairs. They are: " << endl;
   DisplayContents(mmapIntToStr);

   // The multimap can return number of pairs with same key
   cout << "The number of pairs in the multimap with 1000 as their key: "
      << mmapIntToStr.count(1000) << endl;

   return 0;
}
```

Output ▼

```
The map contains 4 key-value pairs. They are:
-1 -> Minus One
3 -> Three
1000 -> One Thousand
1000000 -> One Million


The multimap contains 5 key-value pairs. They are:
-1 -> Minus One
3 -> Three
1000 -> One Thousand
1000 -> Thousand
1000000 -> One Million

The number of pairs in the multimap with 1000 as their key: 2
```

Analysis ▼

Note how `typedef` is used with the template instantiation of `map` and `multimap` in Lines 7 and 8. You can do this to make your code look a bit simpler (and reduce clutter caused by template syntax). Lines 10 through 19 are a form of `DisplayContents()` adapted for `map` and `multimap` in which the iterator is used to access `first`, which indicates the key, and `second`, which indicates the value. Lines 26 through 32 demonstrate the different ways of inserting a key/value pair into a `map` using overloaded variants of method `insert()`. Line 35 demonstrates how you can use array semantics via the operator `[]` to insert elements in a map. Note that these insert mechanisms work as well for a multimap, as demonstrated in Line 47, where you insert a duplicate into a multimap. Interestingly, the multimap is initialized as a copy of the map, as shown in Lines 42 and 43. The output demonstrates how the two containers have automatically sorted the input key/value pairs in ascending order of keys. The output also demonstrates that the multimap can store two pairs with the same key (in this case `1000`). Line 55 demonstrates the use of `multimap::count()` to determine the number of elements with a supplied key in the container.

Finding Elements in an STL `map` Container

Associative containers, such as `map` and `multimap`, feature the member function `find()`, which enables you to find a value given a key. The result of a `find()` operation is always an iterator:

```
multimap<int, string>::const_iterator pairFound = mapIntToStr.find(key);
```

You would first check this iterator for the success of `find()` and then use it to access the found value:

```
if(pairFound != mapIntToStr.end())
{
   cout << "Key " << pairFound->first << " points to Value: ";
   cout << pairFound->second << endl;
}
else
   cout << "Sorry, pair with key " << key << " not in map" << endl;
```

TIP

> The iterator declaration can be simplified using the keyword `auto`:
>
> `auto pairFound = mapIntToStr.find(key);`
>
> The compiler determines the type of the iterator automatically by inferring it from the declared return value of `map::find()`.

The example in Listing 20.3 demonstrates the use of `multimap::find()`.

Input ▼

LISTING 20.3 Using the `find()` Member Function to Locate a Key/Value Pair in a `map` Container

```
#include<map>
#include<iostream>
#include<string>
using namespace std;

template <typename T>
void DisplayContents(const T& cont)
{
    for(auto element = cont.cbegin();
         element != cont.cend();
         ++ element)
      cout << element->first << " -> " << element->second << endl;

   cout << endl;
}

int main()
{
    map<int, string> mapIntToStr;

```

```
       mapIntToStr.insert(make_pair(3, "Three"));
       mapIntToStr.insert(make_pair(45, "Forty Five"));
       mapIntToStr.insert(make_pair(-1, "Minus One"));
       mapIntToStr.insert(make_pair(1000, "Thousand"));

       cout << "The multimap contains " << mapIntToStr.size();
       cout << " key-value pairs. They are: " << endl;

       // Print the contents of the map to the screen
       DisplayContents(mapIntToStr);

      cout << "Enter the key you wish to find: ";
      int key = 0;
      cin >> key;

      auto pairFound = mapIntToStr.find(key);
      if(pairFound != mapIntToStr.end())
      {
         cout << "Key " << pairFound->first << " points to Value: ";
         cout << pairFound->second << endl;
      }
      else
         cout << "Sorry, pair with key " << key << " not in map\n";

       return 0;
 }
```

Output ▼

First run:

```
The multimap contains 4 key-value pairs. They are:
-1 -> Minus One
3 -> Three
45 -> Forty Five
1000 -> Thousand

Enter the key you wish to find: 45
Key 45 points to Value: Forty Five
```


Next run (where `find()` locates no matching key):

```
The multimap contains 4 key-value pairs. They are:
-1 -> Minus One
3 -> Three
45 -> Forty Five
1000 -> Thousand
```

```
Enter the key you wish to find: 2011
Sorry, pair with key 2011 not in map
```

Analysis ▼

Lines 20 through 23 in `main()` populate a map with sample pairs, each mapping an integer key to a string value. When the user supplies a key to be used in finding in the map, Line 35 uses the `find()` function to look up the supplied key in the map. `map::find()` always returns an iterator, and it is always wise to check for the success of the `find()` operation by comparing this iterator to `end()`, as shown in Line 36. If the iterator is indeed valid, you can use the member `second` to access the value, as shown in Line 39. In the second run, you input a key `2011` that is not represented in the map, and an error message is displayed to the user.

CAUTION

Never use the result of a `find()` operation without first checking the iterator returned for success.

Finding Elements in an STL `multimap` Container

If Listing 20.3 showed a `multimap` container, opening the possibility that the container contains multiple pairs with the same key, you would need to find the values that correspond to the repeating key. Hence, in the case of a multimap, you use `multimap::count()` to find the number of values corresponding to a key and increment the iterator to access those values:

```
auto pairFound = mmapIntToStr.find(key);

// Check if find() succeeded
if(pairFound != mmapIntToStr.end())
{
    // Find the number of pairs that have the same supplied key
    size_t numPairsInMap = mmapIntToStr.count(1000);

    for(size_t counter = 0;
        counter < numPairsInMap;  // stay within bounds
        ++ counter)
    {
        cout << "Key: " << pairFound->first;  // key
        cout << ", Value [" << counter << "] = ";
        cout << pairFound->second << endl;    // value
```

```
            ++ pairFound;
        }
    }
    else
        cout << "Element not found in the multimap";
```

Erasing Elements from an STL `map` or `multimap` Container

`map` and `multimap` feature a member function, `erase()`, which deletes an element from a container. The `erase()` is invoked with the key as the parameter to delete all pairs with a certain key:

```
mapObject.erase(key);
```

Another form of the `erase()` function allows the deletion of a particular element, given an iterator that points to it:

```
mapObject.erase(element);
```

You can erase a range of elements from a map or a multimap by using iterators that supply the bounds:

```
mapObject.erase(lowerBound, upperBound);
```

Listing 20.4 illustrates the use of the `erase()` function.

Input ▼

LISTING 20.4 Erasing Elements from a Multimap

```
#include<map>
#include<iostream>
#include<string>
using namespace std;

template<typename T>
void DisplayContents(const T& cont)
{
    for(auto element = cont.cbegin();
         element != cont.cend();
         ++ element)
      cout << element->first<< " -> " << element->second << endl;

   cout << endl;
```

```
}

int main()
{
   multimap<int, string> mmapIntToStr;

   // Insert key-value pairs into the multimap
   mmapIntToStr.insert(make_pair(3, "Three"));
   mmapIntToStr.insert(make_pair(45, "Forty Five"));
   mmapIntToStr.insert(make_pair(-1, "Minus One"));
   mmapIntToStr.insert(make_pair(1000, "Thousand"));

   // Insert duplicates into the multimap
   mmapIntToStr.insert(make_pair(-1, "Minus One"));
   mmapIntToStr.insert(make_pair(1000, "Thousand"));

   cout << "The multimap contains " << mmapIntToStr.size();
   cout << " key-value pairs. " << "They are: \n";
   DisplayContents(mmapIntToStr);

   // Erasing an element with key as -1 from the multimap
   auto numPairsErased = mmapIntToStr.erase(-1);
   cout << "Erased " << numPairsErased << " pairs with -1 as key.\n";

   // Erase an element given an iterator from the multimap
   auto pair = mmapIntToStr.find(45);
   if(pair != mmapIntToStr.end())
   {
      mmapIntToStr.erase(pair);
      cout << "Erased a pair with 45 as key using an iterator\n";
   }

   // Erase a range from the multimap...
   cout << "Erasing the range of pairs with 1000 as key." << endl;
   mmapIntToStr.erase(mmapIntToStr.lower_bound(1000),
                      mmapIntToStr.upper_bound(1000));

   cout << "The multimap now contains "<< mmapIntToStr.size();
   cout << " key-value pair(s)." << "They are: \n";
   DisplayContents(mmapIntToStr);

   return 0;
}
```

Output ▼

```
The multimap contains 6 key-value pairs. They are:
-1 -> Minus One
-1 -> Minus One
```

```
3 -> Three
45 -> Forty Five
1000 -> Thousand
1000 -> Thousand

Erased 2 pairs with -1 as key.
Erased a pair with 45 as key using an iterator
Erasing the range of pairs with 1000 as key.
The multimap now contains 1 key-value pair(s).They are:
3 -> Three
```

Analysis ▼

Lines 21 through 28 insert sample values into a multimap, some of them being duplicates (because a multimap, unlike a map, does support the insertion of pairs with duplicate keys). After pairs have been inserted into the multimap, the code erases items by using the version of the `erase()` function that accepts a key and erases all items with that key (`-1`), as shown in Line 35. The return value of `map::erase(key)` is the number of elements erased, which is displayed on the screen. In Line 39, the iterator returned by `find(45)` erases a pair from the map with key `45`. Lines 48 and 49 demonstrate how pairs with a key can be deleted, given a range specified by `lower_bound()` and `upper_bound()`.

Supplying a Custom Sort Predicate

The `map` and `multimap` template definition includes a third parameter that accepts the sort predicate for the map to function correctly. This third parameter, when not supplied (as in the preceding examples), is substituted with the default sort criterion provided by `std::less<>`, which essentially compares two objects by using the operator `<`.

To supply a different sort criterion than the key type supports, you typically program a binary predicate in the form of a class or a struct by using `operator()`:

20

```
template<typename keyType>
struct Predicate
{
   bool operator()(const keyType& key1, const keyType& key2) const
   {
      // your sort priority logic here
   }
};
```

A map that holds a `std::string` type as the key has a default sort criterion based on the operator `<` defined by the `std::string` class, triggered via the default sort predicate `std::less<T>`; it is therefore case-sensitive. For many applications, such as a telephone directory, it is important to feature an insertion and search operation that is not case sensitive. One way of solving this requirement is to supply the `map` with a sort predicate that returns either `true` or `false`, on the basis of a comparison that is not case-sensitive:

```
map <keyType, valueType, Predicate> mapObject;
```

Listing 20.5 illustrates this.

Input ▼

LISTING 20.5 Supplying a Custom Sort Predicate: A Telephone Directory

```
#include<map>
#include<algorithm>
#include<string>
#include<iostream>
using namespace std;

template <typename T>
void DisplayContents(const T& cont)
{
    for(auto element = cont.cbegin();
         element != cont.cend();
         ++ element)
      cout << element->first << " -> " << element->second << endl;

   cout << endl;
}

struct PredIgnoreCase
{
    bool operator()(const string& str1, const string& str2) const
    {
        string str1NoCase(str1), str2NoCase(str2);
         transform(str1.begin(), str1.end(), str1NoCase.begin(), ::tolower);
         transform(str2.begin(), str2.end(), str2NoCase.begin(), ::tolower);

        return(str1NoCase< str2NoCase);
    };
};

typedef map<string, string> DIR_WITH_CASE;
typedef map<string, string, PredIgnoreCase> DIR_NOCASE;

```

```
int main()
{
   // Case-sensitive directorycase of string-key plays no role
   DIR_WITH_CASE dirWithCase;

   dirWithCase.insert(make_pair("John", "2345764"));
   dirWithCase.insert(make_pair("JOHN", "2345764"));
   dirWithCase.insert(make_pair("Sara", "42367236"));
   dirWithCase.insert(make_pair("Jack", "32435348"));

   cout << "Displaying contents of the case-sensitive map:\n";
   DisplayContents(dirWithCase);

   // Case-insensitive mapcase of string-key affects insertion & search
   DIR_NOCASE dirNoCase(dirWithCase.begin(), dirWithCase.end());

   cout << "Displaying contents of the case-insensitive map:\n";
   DisplayContents(dirNoCase);

   // Search for a name in the two maps and display result
   cout << "Please enter a name to search\n> ";
   string name;
   cin >> name;

   auto pairWithCase = dirWithCase.find(name);
   if(pairWithCase != dirWithCase.end())
      cout << "Num in case-sens. dir: " << pairWithCase->second << endl;
   else
      cout << "Num not found in case-sensitive dir\n";

   auto pairNoCase = dirNoCase.find(name);
   if(pairNoCase != dirNoCase.end())
      cout << "Num found in CI dir: " << pairNoCase->second << endl;
   else
      cout << "Num not found in the case-insensitive directory\n";

   return 0;
}
```


Output ▼

```
Displaying contents of the case-sensitive map:
JOHN -> 2345764
Jack -> 32435348
John -> 2345764
Sara -> 42367236
```

```
Displaying contents of the case-insensitive map:
Jack -> 32435348
JOHN -> 2345764
Sara -> 42367236

Please enter a name to search
> jack
Num not found in case-sensitive dir
Num found in CI dir: 32435348
```

Analysis ▼

This code contains two directories with equal content: one that has been instantiated with the default sort predicate, using `std::less<T>` and the case-sensitive `std::string::operator<`, and another that has been instantiated with the predicate `struct PredIgnoreCase` defined in Lines 17 through 27. This predicate compares two strings after reducing them to lowercase, thereby ensuring a case-insensitive comparison that will evaluate `"John"` and `"JOHN"` as being equal. The output indicates that when you search the two maps for `"jack"` the map with the case-insensitive instantiation is able to locate `"Jack"` in its records, whereas the map with the default instantiation is unable to find this entry. Also note how the case-sensitive map has two entries for John, while the case-insensitive map identifies `"John"` and `"JOHN"` as duplicate elements and therefore stores only one.

NOTE

In Listing 20.5, `struct PredIgnoreCase` can also be a class if you add the keyword `public` for `operator()`. A struct is akin to a class with members that are public by default and inherit `public` by default.

This example demonstrates how you can use predicates to customize the behavior of a map. It also implies that the key could potentially be of any type and that the programmer can supply a predicate that defines the behavior of the map for that type. Note that the predicate is a struct that implements `operator()`. Such objects that double as functions are called *function objects* or *functors*. This topic is addressed in further detail in Lesson 21, "Understanding Function Objects."

NOTE

`std::map` is well suited for storing key/value pairs where you can look up a value given a key. A map does probably deliver better performance than an STL vector or list when it comes to searching. However, the performance slows down a bit when the number of elements increases. The operational performance of a map is said to be logarithmic in nature—that is, proportional to the log of the number of elements placed in the map.

In simple terms, logarithmic complexity means that a container such as `std::map` or `std::set` takes twice as long to find an element when it contains 10,000 elements as it takes to find an elements when it contains 100 elements (100^2 = 10,000).

An unsorted vector presents linear complexity when it comes to searching, which means it would be 100 times slower if it contained 10,000 elements instead of 100.

So, while logarithmic complexity already looks good, you should remember that insertions in a map (or multimap or set or multiset) get slower, too, as these containers sort on insertion. Thus, the search for faster containers continues, and mathematicians and programmers alike seek the holy grail of containers featuring constant-time insertions and searches. The hash table is one container that promises constant-time insertions and near-constant-time searches (in most cases), given a key, independent of the size of the container.

STL's Hash Table–Based Key/Value Container

The STL supports a hash map in the form of the class `std::unordered_map`. To use this template container class, include


```
#include<unordered_map>
```

`unordered_map` promises average constant-time insertion and the removal and lookup of arbitrary elements in a container.

How Hash Tables Work

Although it is not within the scope of this book to discuss hash tables in detail, this section describes the basics of what makes hash tables work.

A hash table can be viewed as a collection of key/value pairs, where given a key, the table can find a value. The difference between a hash table and a simple map is that a hash table stores key/value pairs in buckets, and each bucket has an index that defines its relative position in the table (akin to an array). This index is decided by a hash function that uses the key as input:

```
index = HashFunction(key, tableSize);
```

When performing a `find()` given a key, `HashFunction()` is used once again to determine the position of the element, and the table returns the value at the position, as an array would return an element stored within it. In cases where `HashFunction()` is not optimally programmed, more than one element would have the same index and land in the same bucket—which would, internally, be a list of elements. In such cases, called *collisions*, a search would be slower and not a constant time activity anymore.

Using `unordered_map` and `unordered_multimap`

The containers that implement hash tables, `std::unordered_map` and `std::unordered_multimap`, are not too different from `std::map` and `std::multimap`, respectively. Instantiation, insertion, and find follow similar patterns:

```
// instantiate unordered_map of int to string:
unordered_map<int, string> umapIntToStr;

// insert()
umapIntToStr.insert(make_pair(1000, "Thousand"));

// find():
auto pairFound = umapIntToStr.find(1000);
cout << pairFound->first << " - " << pairFound->second << endl;

// find value using array semantics:
cout << "umapIntToStr[1000] = " << umapIntToStr[1000] << endl;
```

However, one important feature of an unordered map is the availability of a hash function that is responsible for deciding the sorting order:

```
unordered_map<int, string>::hasher hFn =
        umapIntToStr.hash_function();
```

You can view the priority assigned to a key by invoking the hash function for a key:

```
size_t hashingVal = hFn(1000);
```

An unordered map stores key/value pairs in buckets. When the number of key/value pairs contained reaches or nearly reaches the total number of buckets available, it increases the number of buckets to automatically manage the load:

```
cout << "Load factor: " << umapIntToStr.load_factor() << endl;
cout << "Max load factor = " << umapIntToStr.max_load_factor() << endl;
cout << "Max bucket count = " << umapIntToStr.max_bucket_count() << endl;
```

`load_factor()` indicates the extent to which buckets in the unordered map have been filled. When `load_factor()` exceeds `max_load_factor()` due to an insertion, the map reorganizes itself to increase the number of available buckets and rebuilds the hash table, as demonstrated in Listing 20.6.

TIP

`std::unordered_multimap` is similar to `unordered_map` except that it supports multiple pairs with the same key.

Input ▼

LISTING 20.6 Instantiating the STL Hash Table Implementation `unordered_map`, Using `insert()`, `find()`, `size()`, `max_bucket_count()`, `load_factor()`, and `max_load_factor()`

```
#include<iostream>
#include<string>
#include<unordered_map>
using namespace std;

template <typename T1, typename T2>
void DisplayUnorderedMap(unordered_map<T1, T2>& cont)
{
   cout << "Unordered Map contains: " << endl;
   for(auto element = cont.cbegin();
        element != cont.cend();
        ++ element)
      cout << element->first << " -> " << element->second << endl;

   cout << "Number of pairs, size(): " << cont.size() << endl;
   cout << "Bucket count = " << cont.bucket_count() << endl;
   cout << "Current load factor: " << cont.load_factor() << endl;
   cout << "Max load factor = " << cont.max_load_factor() << endl;
}

int main()
{
   unordered_map<int, string> umapIntToStr;
   umapIntToStr.insert(make_pair(1, "One"));
```

```
   umapIntToStr.insert(make_pair(45, "Forty Five"));
   umapIntToStr.insert(make_pair(1001, "Thousand One"));
   umapIntToStr.insert(make_pair(-2, "Minus Two"));
   umapIntToStr.insert(make_pair(-1000, "Minus One Thousand"));
   umapIntToStr.insert(make_pair(100, "One Hundred"));
   umapIntToStr.insert(make_pair(12, "Twelve"));
   umapIntToStr.insert(make_pair(-100, "Minus One Hundred"));

   DisplayUnorderedMap<int, string>(umapIntToStr);

   cout << "Inserting one more element" << endl;
   umapIntToStr.insert(make_pair(300, "Three Hundred"));
   DisplayUnorderedMap<int, string>(umapIntToStr);

   cout << "Enter key to find for: ";
   int Key = 0;
   cin >> Key;

   auto element = umapIntToStr.find(Key);
   if(element != umapIntToStr.end())
      cout << "Found! Key pairs with value " << element->second << endl;
   else
      cout << "Key has no corresponding pair value!" << endl;

   return 0;
}
```

Output ▼

```
Unordered Map contains:
1 -> One
-2 -> Minus Two
45 -> Forty Five
1001 -> Thousand One
-1000 -> Minus One Thousand
12 -> Twelve
100 -> One Hundred
-100 -> Minus One Hundred
Number of pairs, size(): 8
Bucket count = 8
Current load factor: 1
Max load factor = 1
Inserting one more element
Unordered Map contains:
1 -> One
-2 -> Minus Two
45 -> Forty Five
1001 -> Thousand One
-1000 -> Minus One Thousand
12 -> Twelve
```

```
100 -> One Hundred
-100 -> Minus One Hundred
300 -> Three Hundred
Number of pairs, size(): 9
Bucket count = 64
Current load factor: 0.140625
Max load factor = 1
Enter key to find for: 300
Found! Key pairs with value Three Hundred
```

Analysis ▼

Different compilers or versions of the STL may produce slightly different output. Observe the output and note how `unordered_map`, which starts with an initial bucket count of eight, populated with eight pairs, resizes itself when a ninth pair is inserted. The bucket count is then increased to 64. Note the use of methods `bucket_count()`, `load_factor()`, and `max_load_factor()` in Lines 15 through 17. Apart from these, note that the rest of this code is similar to the code for `std::map`. One similarity is the use of `find()` in Line 42, which returns an iterator. This iterator needs to be checked against `end()` to confirm success of the operation.

CAUTION

> Don't rely on the order of elements in an unordered map (hence the name), regardless of the key. The order of an elements in a map depends on many factors, including the elements' keys, order of insertion, and number of buckets.
>
> `unordered_map` containers are optimized for search performance, and you should not rely on the order of elements when you iterate through them.

NOTE

> `std::unordered_map` supplies insertions and searches (in the event of no collisions) that are almost constant time, regardless of the number of elements contained. This, however, doesn't necessarily make `std::unordered_map` superior to `std::map`, which provides logarithmic complexity in all situations. The constant could be a lot longer, making an unordered map slow in cases where the number of elements contained is small.
>
> It is important to base your decision about the type of container to use on the outcomes of benchmark tests that simulate usage in a real scenario.

DO	DON'T
DO use `map` when you need a key/value pair where keys are unique. **DO** use `multimap` when you need a key/value pair where keys can repeat (for example, a telephone directory). **DO** remember that both `map` and `multimap`, like other STL containers, feature the member method `size()`, which finds the number of pairs a container contains. **DO** use `unordered_map` or `unordered_multimap` when constant-time insertions and searches are absolutely essential (typically when the number of elements is very high).	**DON'T** forget that `multimap::count(key)` can determine the number of pairs indexed using a key available in the container. **DON'T** forget to check the result of a `find()` operation by comparing it against the end of a container.

Summary

In this lesson, you learned about using the STL `map` and `multimap` containers, their significant member functions, and their characteristics. You also learned that these containers have logarithmic complexity and that STL supplies hash table containers in the form of `unordered_map` and `unordered_multimap`. The unordered variants of the containers feature `insert()` and `find()` operations that offer constant time performance independent of the number of elements contained within. You also learned the importance of being able to customize sort criteria using a predicate, as demonstrated in the directory application in Listing 20.5.

Q&A

Q How would I declare a map of integers to be sorted or stored in order of descending magnitude?

A `map<int>` defines a map of integers. It takes the default sort predicate `std::less <T>` to sort items in order of ascending magnitude and can also be expressed as `map <int, less <int>>`. To sort in order of descending magnitude, you define the map as `map <int, greater <int> >`.

Q What would happen if in a map of strings I inserted the string `"Jack"` twice?

A A map is not meant to be used to hold non-unique values. So, the map would still contain only one pair with a key called `"Jack"`.

Q In the preceding example, what would I change if I wanted to have two instances of `"Jack"`?

A By design, a map holds only unique values. You need to change your selection of container to a multimap.

Q What `multimap` member function returns the count of items of a particular value in the container?

A `count(value)` is the function that does this.

Q I have found an element in a map by using the `find()` function, and I have an iterator pointing to it. Would I use this iterator to change the value being pointed to?

A No. Some STL implementations might allow the user to change the value of an element inside a map via an iterator returned by `find()`. This, however, is not the correct thing to do. An iterator to an element in the map should be used as a `const` iterator—even when your implementation of STL has not enforced it as such.

Q I am using an older compiler that doesn't support the keyword `auto`. How should I declare a variable that holds the return value of `map::find()`?

A An iterator is always defined using this syntax:

```
container<Type>::iterator variableName;
```

So the iterator declaration for a map of integers would be the following:


```
std::map<int>::iterator pairFound = mapIntegers.find(1000);
if(pairFound != mapIntegers.end())
{ // Do Something }
```

Workshop

The Workshop provides quiz questions to help you solidify your understanding of the material covered and exercises to provide you with experience using what you've learned.

Try to answer the quiz and exercise questions before checking the answers in Appendix E and be certain you understand the answers before continuing to the next lesson.

Quiz

1. You declare a map of integers as `map<int>`. What function supplies the sort criteria?
2. Where would you find duplicate elements in a multimap?
3. What map or multimap function supplies the number of elements in the container?
4. Where would you find duplicate elements in a map?

Exercises

1. You need to write an application that works as a telephone directory where the names of the people need not be unique. What container would you choose? Write a definition of the container.
2. The following is a `map` template definition in your dictionary application:

   ```
   map<wordProperty, string, fPredicate> mapWordDefinition;
   ```

   where `WordProperty` is a structure:

   ```
   struct WordProperty
   {
       string word;
       bool isLatinBase;
   };
   ```

   Define the binary predicate `fPredicate`, which helps the map sort a key of type `WordProperty` according to the string attribute it contains.
3. Demonstrate via a simple program that a map cannot accept duplicate entries, whereas a multimap can.

LESSON 21
Understanding Function Objects

Function objects, or *functors*, might sound exotic or intimidating, but they are entities of C++ that you have probably seen, if not also used, without even realizing it.

In this lesson, you learn

- What function objects are
- How to use function objects as predicates
- How unary and binary predicates are implemented using function objects

Function Objects and Predicates

On a conceptual level, function objects are objects that work as functions. On an implementation level, however, function objects are objects of a class that implement `operator()`. Although functions and function pointers can also be classified as function objects, it is the capability of an object of a class that implements `operator()` to carry `state` (that is, values in member attributes of the class) that makes it useful with Standard Template Library (STL) algorithms.

Function objects can be classified into the following types:

- **Unary function:** A function called with one argument; for example, `f(x)`. When a unary function returns a `bool`, it is called a *predicate*.
- **Binary function:** A function called with two arguments; for example, `f(x, y)`. A binary function that returns a `bool` is called a *binary predicate*.

Function objects that return a Boolean type are naturally suited for use in algorithms that help in decision making. `find()` and `sort()` are two such algorithms that you learned about in previous lessons. A function object that combines two function objects is called an *adaptive function object.*

TIP

A function object is also called a *functor*.

Typical Applications of Function Objects

It is possible to explain function objects in pages and pages of theoretical explanations. It is also possible to understand how they look and work by examining tiny sample applications. Let's take the practical approach and dive straight into the world of C++ programming with function objects!

Unary Functions

A function that operates on a single parameter is a unary function. A unary function can do something very simple—for example, display an element on the screen. This can be programmed as follows:

```
// A unary function
template <typename elementType>
void FuncDisplayElement(const elementType& element)
{
    cout << element << ' ';
};
```

The function `FuncDisplayElement` accepts one parameter of templatized type `elementType`, which it displays using the console output statement `std::cout`. The following is another version, which contains the implementation of the function in `operator()` of a class or a struct:

```
// Struct that can behave as a unary function
template <typename elementType>
struct DisplayElement
{
    void operator()(const elementType& element) const
    {
        cout << element << ' ';
    }
};
```

TIP

> Note that `DisplayElement` is a struct. If it were a class, `operator()` would need to be given a `public` access modifier. A struct is akin to a class, and members are public by default.

Either of these implementations can be used with the STL algorithm `for_each()` to print the contents of a collection to the screen, an element at a time, as shown in Listing 21.1.

Input ▼

LISTING 21.1 Displaying the Contents of a Collection on the Screen by Using a Unary Function

```
#include<algorithm>
#include<iostream>
#include<vector>
#include<list>
using namespace std;

// struct that behaves as a unary function
template <typename elementType>
struct DisplayElement
{
    void operator()(const elementType& element) const
    {
        cout << element << ' ';
    }
};

int main()
{
   vector<int> numsInVec{ 0, 1, 2, 3, -1, -9, 0, -999 };
    cout << "Vector of integers contains: " << endl;

   for_each(numsInVec.begin(),    // Start of range
            numsInVec.end(),        // End of range
            DisplayElement<int>()); // Unary function object

    // Display the list of characters
   list <char> charsInList{ 'a', 'z', 'k', 'd' };
   cout << endl << "List of characters contains: " << endl;

   for_each(charsInList.begin(),
            charsInList.end(),
            DisplayElement<char>());

    return 0;
}
```

Output ▼

```
Vector of integers contains:
0 1 2 3 -1 -9 0 -999
List of characters contains:
a z k d
```

Analysis ▼

Lines 8 through 14 contain the function object `DisplayElement`, which implements `operator()`. The use of this function object is seen with the STL algorithm `std::for_each()` in Lines 21 through 23. `for_each()` accepts three parameters: The first is the starting point of the range, the second is the end of the range, and the third parameter is the function that is called for every element in the specified range. In other words, that code invokes `DisplayElement::operator()` for every element in the `vector` `numsInVec`. Lines 29 through 31 demonstrate the same functionality with a list of characters.

NOTE

In Listing 21.1, you could optionally use `FuncDisplayElement` instead of `struct DisplayElement` to the same effect:

```
for_each(charsInList.begin(),
         charsInList.end(),
         FuncDisplayElement<char>);
```

TIP

C++11 introduced *lambda expressions*, which are unnamed function objects.

A lambda expression version of `struct DisplayElement<T>` from Listing 21.1 compacts the entire code, including the definition of the struct and its usage, in three lines within `main()`, replacing Lines 21 through 23 with the following:

```
// Display elements using lambda expression
for_each(numsInVec.begin(), // Start of range
          numsInVec.end(),  // End of range
   [](int& Element) {cout << element << ' '; }); //
lambda
```

Thus, lambda expressions are a fantastic improvement to C++, and you should not miss learning about them in Lesson 22, "Lambda Expressions." Listing 22.1 demonstrates the use of lambda functions in a `for_each()` to display the contents of a container instead of the function object, as shown in Listing 21.1.

The real advantage of using a function object implemented in a struct becomes apparent when you are able to use the object of the struct to store information. This is something `FuncDisplayElement` cannot do the way a struct can because a struct can have member attributes in addition to `operator()`. A slightly modified version that makes use of member attributes is the following:

```
template <typename elementType>
struct DisplayElementKeepCount
{
    int count = 0;

    void operator()(const elementType& element)
    {
        ++ count;
        cout << element << ' ';
    }
};
```

In this snippet, `DisplayElementKeepCount` is a slight modification of the previous version. `operator()` is not a const member function anymore as it increments (hence, changes) the member `count` to keep a count of the number of times it was called to display data. This count is made available via the public member attribute `count`. The advantage of using such function objects that can also store state is illustrated in Listing 21.2.

Input ▼

LISTING 21.2 Using a Function Object That Holds State

```
#include<algorithm>
#include<iostream>
#include<vector>
using namespace std;

template<typename elementType>
struct DisplayElementKeepCount
{
    int count;

    DisplayElementKeepCount() : count(0) {} // constructor

    void operator()(const elementType& element)
    {
        ++ count;
        cout << element<< ' ';
    }
};

int main()
{
    vector<int> numsInVec{ 22, 2017, -1, 999, 43, 901 };
```

```
22:     cout << "Displaying the vector of integers: "<< endl;
23:
24:     DisplayElementKeepCount<int> result;
25:     result = for_each(numsInVec.begin(),
26:                       numsInVec.end(),
27:                       DisplayElementKeepCount<int>());
28:
29:     cout << endl << "Functor invoked " << result.count << " times";
30:
31:     return 0;
32: }
```

Output ▼

```
Displaying the vector of integers:
22 2017 -1 999 43 901
Functor invoked 6 times
```

Analysis ▼

The biggest difference between this example and Listing 21.1 is the use of `DisplayElementKeepCount()` as the return value of `for_each()`. `operator()`, implemented in `struct DisplayElementKeepCount`, is invoked by the algorithm `for_each()` for every element in the container. It displays the element and increments the internal counter stored in the member attribute `count`. After `for_each()` is done, you use the object in Line 29 to display the number of times elements were displayed. Note that a regular function used in this scenario instead of the function implemented in a struct would not be able to supply this feature in such a direct way.

Unary Predicates

A unary function that returns a `bool` is a predicate. Such functions help make decisions for STL algorithms. Listing 21.3 is a sample predicate that determines whether an input element is a multiple of an initial value.

Input ▼

LISTING 21.3 Using a Unary Predicate That Determines Whether a Number Is a Multiple of Another

```
// A struct as a unary predicate
template <typename numberType>
struct IsMultiple
{
    numberType Divisor;
```

```
 5:
 6:     IsMultiple(const numberType& divisor)
 7:     {
 8:        Divisor = divisor;
 9:     }
10:
11:     bool operator()(const numberType& element) const
12:     {
13:        // Check if the divisor is a multiple of the divisor
14:        return((element % Divisor) == 0);
15:     }
16: };
```

Output ▼

This code snippet produces no output

Analysis ▼

In this example, `operator()` returns `bool` and can work as a unary predicate. The structure has a constructor and is initialized with the divisor in Line 8. This value stored in the object is then used to determine whether the elements sent for comparison are divisible by it, as you can see in the implementation of `operator()`, using the math operation modulo (`%`), which returns the remainder of a division operation in Line 14. The predicate compares that remainder to zero to determine whether the number is a multiple.

Listing 21.4 makes use of the predicate from Listing 21.3 to determine whether numbers in a collection are multiples of a divisor input by the user.

Input ▼

LISTING 21.4 Using the Unary Predicate `IsMultiple` with `std::find_if()` to Find an Element in a Vector That Is a Multiple of a User-Supplied Divisor

```
#include<algorithm>
#include<vector>
#include<iostream>
using namespace std;
// insert code from Listing 21.3 here

int main()
{
   vector<int> numsInVec{ 25, 26, 27, 28, 29, 30, 31 };
   cout << "The vector contains: 25, 26, 27, 28, 29, 30, 31" << endl;

```

```
11:     cout << "Enter divisor (> 0): ";
12:     int divisor = 2;
13:     cin >> divisor;
14:
15:     // Find the first element that is a multiple of divisor
16:     auto element = find_if(numsInVec.begin(),
17:                            numsInVec.end(),
18:                            IsMultiple<int>(divisor));
19:
20:     if(element != numsInVec.end())
21:     {
22:        cout << "First element in vector divisible by " << divisor;
23:        cout << ": " << *element << endl;
24:     }
25:
26:     return 0;
27: }
```

Output ▼

```
The vector contains: 25, 26, 27, 28, 29, 30, 31
Enter divisor (> 0): 4
First element in vector divisible by 4: 28
```

Analysis ▼

This example starts with a sample container that is a vector of integers. The unary predicate is used in `find_if()`, as shown in Line 16. The function object `IsMultiple()` is initialized to a divisor value supplied by the user and stored in the variable `Divisor`. `find_if()` works by invoking the unary predicate `IsMultiple::operator()` for every element in the specified range. When `operator()` returns `true` for an element (which happens when that element is divided by 4 and does not produce a remainder), `find_if()` returns an iterator `element` to that element. The result of the `find_if()` operation is compared against the end of the container as returned by method `end()` to verify that an element was found, as shown in Line 20, and the iterator `element` is then used to display the value, as shown in Line 23.

TIP

> To see how using lambda expressions can compact the program shown in Listing 21.4, take a look at Listing 22.3 in Lesson 22.

Unary predicates find application in many STL algorithms, such as `std::partition()`, which can partition a range using the predicate, and `stable_partition()`, which does the same thing while keeping the relative order of the elements partitioned.

They're also used in find functions such as `std::find_if()` and functions that help erase elements, such as `std::remove_if()`, which erases elements in a range that satisfies the predicate.

Binary Functions

Functions of type `f(x, y)` are particularly useful when they return a value based on the input supplied. Such binary functions can be used for a host of arithmetic activity that involves two operands, such as addition, multiplication, subtraction, and other operations. A sample binary function that returns the multiple of input arguments can be written as follows:

```
template <typename elementType>
class Multiply
{
public:
    elementType operator()(const elementType& elem1,
                           const elementType& elem2)
    {
        return (elem1 * elem2);
    }
};
```

The implementation of interest is again `operator()`, which accepts two arguments, multiplies them, and returns the result. Such binary functions are used in algorithms such as `std::transform()`, where you can use `operator()` to multiply the contents of two containers. Listing 21.5 demonstrates the use of binary functions in `std::transform()`.

Input ▼

LISTING 21.5 Using a Binary Function to Multiply Two Ranges

```
#include<vector>
#include<iostream>
#include<algorithm>

template <typename elementType>
class Multiply
{
public:
    elementType operator()(const elementType& elem1,
                           const elementType& elem2)
    {
        return (elem1 * elem2);
    }
};

```

```
15: int main()
16: {
17:     using namespace std;
18:
19:    vector<int> multiplicands{ 0, 1, 2, 3, 4 };
20:    vector<int> multipliers{ 100, 101, 102, 103, 104 };
21:
22:     // A third container that holds the result of multiplication
23:     vector<int> vecResult;
24:
25:     // Make space for the result of the multiplication
26:     vecResult.resize(multipliers.size());
27:     transform(multiplicands.begin(), // range of multiplicands
28:               multiplicands.end(), // end of range
29:               multipliers.begin(),  // multiplier values
30:               vecResult.begin(), // holds result
31:               Multiply<int>());    // multiplies
32:
33:     cout << "The contents of the first vector are: " << endl;
34:     for(size_t index = 0; index < multiplicands.size(); ++ index)
35:         cout << multiplicands [index] << ' ';
36:     cout << endl;
37:
38:     cout << "The contents of the second vector are: " << endl;
39:     for(size_t index = 0; index < multipliers.size(); ++index)
40:         cout << multipliers [index] << ' ';
41:     cout << endl;
42:
43:     cout << "The result of the multiplication is: " << endl;
44:     for(size_t index = 0; index < vecResult.size(); ++ index)
45:         cout << vecResult [index] << ' ';
46:
47:     return 0;
48: }
```

Output ▼

```
The contents of the first vector are:
0 1 2 3 4
The contents of the second vector are:
100 101 102 103 104
The result of the multiplication is:
0 101 204 309 416
```

Analysis ▼

Lines 4 through 13 contain the class `Multiply`. This example uses the algorithm `std::transform()` to multiply the contents of two ranges and store the result in a third range. In this case, the ranges in question are held in `std::vector` as `multiplicands`, `multipliers`, and `vecResult`. You use `std::transform()` in Lines 27 through 31 to multiply every element in `multiplicands` by its corresponding element in `multipliers` and store the result of the multiplication in `vecResult`. The multiplication itself is done by the binary function `Multiply::operator()`, which is invoked for every element in the vectors that make the source and destination ranges. The return value of `operator()` is held in `vecResult`.

This example demonstrates the application of binary functions in performing arithmetic operations on elements in STL containers. The next example also uses `std::transform()`, but it uses this algorithm to convert a string to lowercase using the function `tolower()`.

Binary Predicates

A function that accepts two arguments and returns a `bool` is a binary predicate. Such functions find application in STL functions such as `std::sort()`. Listing 21.6 demonstrates the use of a binary predicate that compares two strings after reducing them both to lowercase. Such a predicate can be used in performing a case-insensitive sort on a vector containing elements of type `string`, for instance.

Input ▼

LISTING 21.6 Using a Binary Predicate for a Case-Insensitive String Sort

```
#include<algorithm>
#include<string>
using namespace std;

class CompareStringNoCase
{
public:
    bool operator()(const string& str1, const string& str2) const
    {
        string str1LowerCase;

        // Assign space
        str1LowerCase.resize(str1.size());

        // Convert every character to the lower case
        transform(str1.begin(), str1.end(), str1LowerCase.begin(),
                    ::tolower);

        string str2LowerCase;
        str2LowerCase.resize(str2.size());
        transform(str2.begin(), str2.end(), str2LowerCase.begin(),
                   ::tolower);

```

```
23:        return (str1LowerCase < str2LowerCase);
24:    }
25: };
```

Output ▼

This code snippet produces no output.

Analysis ▼

The binary predicate implemented in `operator()` first brings the input strings down to lowercase by using the algorithm `std::transform()`, as shown in Lines 15 and 20, before using the string's comparison operator, `<`, to return the result of the comparison.

You can use this binary predicate with the algorithm `std::sort()` to sort a dynamic array of strings contained in a vector, as demonstrated by Listing 21.7.

Input ▼

LISTING 21.7 Using the Function Object Class `CompareStringNoCase` to Perform a Case-Insensitive Sort on `vector<string>`

```
0: // Insert class CompareStringNoCase from Listing 21.6 here
1: #include<vector>
2: #include<iostream>
3:
4: template <typename T>
5: void DisplayContents(const T& container)
6: {
7:    for(auto element = container.cbegin();
8:        element != container.cend();
9:        ++ element)
10:        cout << *element << endl;
11: }
12:
13: int main()
14: {
15:    // Define a vector of string to hold names
16:    vector <string> names;
17:
18:    // Insert some sample names in to the vector
19:    names.push_back("jim");
20:    names.push_back("Jack");
21:    names.push_back("Sam");
22:    names.push_back("Anna");
23:
24:    cout << "The names in vector in order of insertion: " << endl;
```

```
25:     DisplayContents(names);
26:
27:     cout << "Names after sorting using default std::less<>: " << endl;
28:     sort(names.begin(), names.end());
29:     DisplayContents(names);
30:
31:     cout << "Sorting using predicate that ignores case:" << endl;
32:     sort(names.begin(), names.end(), CompareStringNoCase());
33:     DisplayContents(names);
34:
35:     return 0;
36: }
```

Output ▼

```
The names in vector in order of insertion:
jim
Jack
Sam
Anna
Names after sorting using default std::less<>:
Anna
Jack
Sam
jim
Sorting using predicate that ignores case:
Anna
Jack
jim
Sam
```

Analysis ▼

The output displays the contents of the vector in three stages. The first stage displays the contents of the vector in order of insertion. The second stage, after the use of `sort()` at Line 28, reorders by using the default sort predicate `less<T>`, and the output demonstrates that `jim` is not placed after `Jack` because this is a case-sensitive sort via `string::operator<`. The last stage uses the sort predicate class `CompareStringNoCase<>` in Line 32 (implemented in Listing 21.6), which ensures that `jim` comes after `Jack`, despite the difference in case.

Binary predicates are required in a variety of STL algorithms. For example, some of the STL algorithms that need a binary predicate are `std::unique()`, which erases duplicate neighboring elements; `std::sort()`, which sorts; `std::stable_sort()`, which sorts while maintaining relative order; and `std::transform()`, which can perform an operation on two ranges.

Summary

In this lesson, you got a look into the world of functors (or function objects). You learned that function objects are more useful when implemented in a structure or a class than are simple functions because functors can also be used to hold state-related information. You also learned about predicates, which are a special class of function objects, and saw some practical examples of their utility.

Q&A

Q A predicate is a special category of a function object. What makes it special?

A A predicate returns a `bool` and therefore suits algorithms that need decisions.

Q What kind of a function object should I use in a call to a function such as `remove_if()`?

A You should use a unary predicate that takes the value to be processed as the initial state via the constructor.

Q What kind of a function object should I use for a map?

A You should use a binary predicate that helps the map sort elements using a key.

Workshop

The Workshop provides quiz questions to help you solidify your understanding of the material covered and exercises to provide you with experience using what you've learned. Try to answer the quiz and exercise questions before checking the answers in Appendix E and be certain you understand the answers before continuing to the next lesson.

Quiz

1. What is the term used for a unary function that returns a `bool` result?
2. What would be the utility of a function object that neither modifies data nor returns `bool`? Explain by using an example.
3. Explain what *function objects* are.

Exercises

1. Write a unary function that can be used with `std::for_each()` to display the double of the input parameter.
2. Extend the predicate from Exercise 1 to indicate the number of times it was used.
3. Write a binary predicate that helps sort in ascending order.

LESSON 22

Lambda Expressions

Lambda expressions, which were introduced in C++11 and have been improved in more recent versions of C++, define function objects without requiring a class or a struct with a name. Recent amendments in C++20 add support for template arguments.

In this lesson, you find out

- How to program a lambda expression
- How to use lambda expressions as predicates
- What generic lambda expressions are
- How to program lambda expressions that can hold and manipulate state

What Is a Lambda Expression?

A lambda expression can be visualized as a compact version of an unnamed struct (or class) with a public `operator()` function. In that sense, a lambda expression is a function object. Before we get into programming lambda functions, let's revisit a function object from Listing 21.1 (from Lesson 21, "Understanding Function Objects") as an example:

```
// struct that behaves as a unary function
template <typename elementType>
struct DisplayElement
{
    void operator()(const elementType& element) const
    {
        cout << element << ' ';
    }
};
```

This function object displays the object `element` on the screen by using `cout`. It would be used in algorithms such as `std::for_each()`, as shown in this example:

```
// Display every integer contained in a vector
for_each(numsInVec.cbegin(),    // Start of range
```

```
         numsInVec.cend(),        // End of range
         DisplayElement<int>()); // Unary function object
```

A lambda equivalent of `struct DisplayElement` requires a single line of code:

```
auto lambda = [](const int& element) {cout << element << ' '; };
```

This is what it looks like when used with `for_each()`:

```
// Display elements in vector using a lambda expression
for_each(numsInVec.cbegin(),     // Start of range
         numsInVec.cend(),        // End of range
         lambda);  // display elements
```

TIP

Lambda expressions are also called *lambda functions*.

How to Define a Lambda Expression

A lambda expression always starts with square brackets (`[]`). C++20 introduced new capabilities such as support for template arguments to lambda expressions, making them more generic and, hence, more powerful.

Lambda expression syntax can be generalized to:

```
[optional captured variables]<optional template arguments> optional-lambda-
specifiers (arguments)
{ // lambda expression code; }
```

Capturing Variables

If you want to use variables that are declared outside the body of a lambda expression, you need to *capture* these variables. The capture list can include multiple variables separated by commas:

```
[var1, var2] <class Type> (Type& param) { // lambda code here; }
```

If you need to modify these variables within the lambda expression, you add the specifier `mutable`:

```
[var1, var2] <class Type> (Type& param) mutable
{ // lambda code here; }
```

CAUTION

A mutable lambda expression allows captured variables (`[...]`) to be modified within the lambda expression, but these changes are not reflected outside the expression.

If modifications to the captured variables within the lambda expression are required to be reflected outside it, too, then you use references:

```
[&var1, &var2] <class Type> (Type& param) { // lambda code here; }
```

TIP

> In addition to `mutable`, the other two specifiers that optionally enhance a lambda expression are `constexpr` and `consteval`. `constexpr` indicates the intention to have the lambda evaluated as a constant expression where possible, whereas `consteval` makes the lambda an *immediate function* to be evaluated by the compiler.

Parameters

C++20 allows lambda expressions to be extremely generic—akin to function objects programmed using template classes. You may optionally specify a template parameter list, as shown here:

```
[var1, var2] <typename Type1, typename Type2> (Type1 param1, Type2 param2)
{ // lambda code here; }
```

In addition, lambda expressions permit multiple input parameters, separated by commas:

```
[var1, var2] <class Type> (Type param1, Type param2)
{ // lambda code here; }
```

With automatic type deduction using the keyword `auto`, you can program a *generic lambda* expression that looks like this:

```
[var1, var2] (auto param1, auto param2)
{ // lambda code here; }
```

Return Types

A lambda expression that comprises a single `return` statement does not need to explicitly specify a return value type because the type is automatically deduced by the compiler. To explicitly declare a return type, you use `->` as follows:

```
[var1, var2] <class Type> (Type param1, Type param2) -> ReturnType
{ return (value or expression ); }
```

Finally, the compound statement `{}` can hold multiple statements, each separated by a `;`, as shown here:

```
[stateVar1, stateVar2](Type1 var1, Type2 var2) -> ReturnType
{
```

```
   Statement 1;
   Statement 2;
   return (value or expression);
}
```

A Lambda Expression for a Unary Function

A simple lambda version of the unary `operator(Type)` function that takes one parameter would be the following:

```
[](Type paramName) {  // lambda expression code;  }
```

Note that you can pass the parameter by reference if you so wish:

```
[](Type& paramName) {  // lambda expression code here;  }
```

Use Listing 22.1 to study the usage of a lambda function in displaying the contents of a Standard Template Library (STL) container using the algorithm `for_each()`.

Input ▼

LISTING 22.1 Displaying Elements in a Container via the Algorithm `for_each()` Invoked with a Lambda Expression Instead of a Function Object

```
#include<algorithm>
#include<iostream>
#include<vector>
#include<list>
using namespace std;

int main()
{
   vector<int> numsInVec{ 101, -4, 500, 21, 42, -1 };
   cout << "Display elements in a vector using a lambda: " << endl;

   // Display the array of integers
   for_each(numsInVec.cbegin(),     // Start of range
            numsInVec.cend(),        // End of range
            [](const int& element) {cout << element << ' '; }); // lambda

   cout << endl;

   list<char> charsInList{ 'a', 'h', 'z', 'k', 'l' };
   cout << "Display elements in a list using a lambda: " << endl;

   // Display the list of characters
   for_each(charsInList.cbegin(),     // Start of range
```

```
23:             charsInList.cend(),         // End of range
24:             [](auto& element) {cout << element << ' '; }); // lambda
25:
26:     return 0;
27: }
```


Output ▼

```
Display elements in a vector using a lambda:
101 -4 500 21 42 -1
Display elements in a list using a lambda:
a h z k l
```

Analysis ▼

There are two lambda expressions of interest, in Lines 14 and 24. They do similar tasks and are the same except for the type of the input parameter. They have been customized to the nature of the elements within the two containers. The first expression takes one parameter that is an `int`, as it is used to print one element at a time from a vector of integers; the second expression accepts a `char` (automatically deduced by the compiler) as it is used to display elements of type `char` stored in a `std::list`.

TIP

You might have noticed that the second lambda expression in Listing 22.1 is slightly different:

```
for_each(charsInList.cbegin(),     // Start of range
          charsInList.cend(),      // End of range
  [](auto& element) {cout << element << ' '; } );
// lambda
```

This lambda expression uses the compiler's automatic type deduction capabilities, which are invoked using the keyword `auto`. The compiler would interpret this lambda expression as

```
for_each(charsInList.cbegin(),     // Start of range
          charsInList.cend(),      // End of range
  [](const char& element) {cout << element << ' '; } );
```

NOTE

The code in Listing 22.1 is similar to that in Listing 21.1 except that the latter uses function objects. In fact, Listing 22.1 is a lambda version of the function object `DisplayElement<T>`.

If you compare the two listings, you can see that lambda functions make C++ code simple and compact.

A Lambda Expression for a Unary Predicate

A predicate helps make decisions. A unary predicate is a unary expression that returns a `bool`, conveying `true` or `false`. Lambda expressions can return values, too. For example, the following code is a lambda expression that returns `true` for numbers that are even:

```
[](int& num) {return ((num % 2) == 0); }
```

The nature of the return value in this case tells the compiler that the lambda expression returns a `bool`.

You can use a lambda expression that is a unary predicate in algorithms, such as `std::find_if()`, to find even numbers in a collection. See Listing 22.2 for an example.

Input ▼

LISTING 22.2 Finding an Even Number in a Collection Using a Lambda Expression for a Unary Predicate and the Algorithm `std::find_if()`

```
#include<algorithm>
#include<vector>
#include<iostream>
using namespace std;

int main()
{
   vector<int> numsInVec{ 25, 101, 2017, -50 };

   auto evenNum = find_if(numsInVec.cbegin(),
                          numsInVec.cend(),  // range to find in
                     [](const int& num){return ((num % 2) == 0); } );

   if (evenNum != numsInVec.cend())
      cout << "Even number in collection is: " << *evenNum << endl;

   return 0;
}
```

Output ▼

```
Even number in collection is: -50
```

Analysis ▼

The lambda function that works as a unary predicate is shown in Line 11. The algorithm `find_if()` invokes the unary predicate for every element in the range. When the predicate returns `true`, `find_if()` reports a find by returning an iterator `evenNum` to that element. The predicate in this case is the lambda expression that returns `true` when `find_if()` invokes it with an integer that is even; that is, the result of a modulo operation with 2 is zero.

TIP

> Listings 22.1 and 22.2 demonstrate not only a lambda expression as a unary predicate but also the use of `const` within a lambda expression.
>
> Remember to use `const` for input parameters, especially when they're references, to avoid unintentional changes to the value of elements in a container.

A Lambda Expression with State via Capture Lists ([...])

Listing 22.2 shows a unary predicate that returns `true` if an integer is divisible by 2—that is, if the integer is an even number. What if you need a more generic function that returns `true` when the number is divisible by a divisor of the user's choosing? You need to maintain that "state"—that is, the divisor—in the expression:

```
int divisor = 2; // initial value
...
auto element = find_if(begin of a range,
                       end of a range,
        [divisor](int dividend){return (dividend % divisor) == 0; } );
```

A list of arguments transferred as state variables (`[...]`) is also called the lambda's *capture list*.

NOTE

> The lambda expression shown above is a one-line equivalent of the 16 lines of code in Listing 21.3 that define the unary predicate `struct IsMultiple<>`.

Listing 22.3 demonstrates the application of a unary predicate, given a state variable, in finding a number in a collection that is a multiple of a divisor supplied by the user.

Input ▼

LISTING 22.3 Demonstrating the Use of Lambda Expressions That Hold State to Check Whether One Number Is Divisible by Another

```
#include<algorithm>
#include<vector>
#include<iostream>
using namespace std;

int main()
{
   vector<int> numsInVec{25, 26, 27, 28, 29, 30, 31};
   cout << "The vector contains: {25, 26, 27, 28, 29, 30, 31}";

   cout << endl << "Enter divisor (> 0): ";
   int divisor = 2;
   cin >> divisor;

   // Find the first element that is a multiple of divisor
   vector<int>::iterator element;
   element = find_if(numsInVec.begin(),
                          numsInVec.end(),
               [divisor](int dividend){return (dividend % divisor) == 0; } );

   if(element != numsInVec.end())
   {
      cout << "First element in vector divisible by " << divisor;
      cout << ": " << *element << endl;
   }

   return 0;
}
```

Output ▼

```
The vector contains: {25, 26, 27, 28, 29, 30, 31}
Enter divisor (> 0): 4
First element in vector divisible by 4: 28
```

Analysis ▼

The lambda expression that contains state and works as a predicate is shown in Line 18. `divisor` is the state variable, and it is comparable to `IsMultiple::Divisor` in Listing 21.3. Hence, state variables are akin to member attributes in a function object class. You are now able to pass states on to your lambda function and customize its usage on the basis of the state.

> **NOTE**
>
> Listing 22.3 features the lambda expression equivalent of Listing 21.4, without the function object class `IsMultiple`. This lambda expression eliminated 16 lines of code!

A Lambda Expression for a Binary Function

A binary function takes two parameters and optionally returns a value. A lambda expression equivalent of a binary function would be

```
[...](Type1& param1Name, Type2& param2Name)
{  // lambda code here;  }
```

Listing 22.4 shows a lambda expression that multiplies two equal-sized vectors element by element, using `std::transform()`, and stores the result in a third vector.

Input ▼

LISTING 22.4 Using a Lambda Expression as a Binary Function to Multiply Elements from Two Containers and Store the Result in a Third

```
#include<vector>
#include<iostream>
#include<algorithm>

int main()
{
   using namespace std;

   vector<int> vecMultiplicand{ 0, 1, 2, 3, 4 };
   vector<int> vecMultiplier{ 100, 101, 102, 103, 104 };

   // Holds the result of multiplication
   vector<int> vecResult;

   // Make space for the result of the multiplication
```

```
15:     vecResult.resize(vecMultiplier.size());
16:
17:     transform(vecMultiplicand.begin(), // range of multiplicands
18:               vecMultiplicand.end(), // end of range
19:               vecMultiplier.begin(),  // multiplier values
20:                vecResult.begin(), // range that holds result
21:                [](int a, int b) {return a * b; } );  // lambda
22:
23:     cout << "The contents of the first vector are: " << endl;
24:     for(size_t index = 0; index < vecMultiplicand.size(); ++index)
25:     cout << vecMultiplicand[index] << ' ';
26:     cout << endl;
27:
28:     cout << "The contents of the second vector are: " << endl;
29:     for(size_t index = 0; index < vecMultiplier.size(); ++index)
30:     cout << vecMultiplier[index] << ' ';
31:     cout << endl;
32:
33:     cout << "The result of the multiplication is: " << endl;
34:     for(size_t index = 0; index < vecResult.size(); ++index)
35:     cout << vecResult[index] << ' ';
36:
37:     return 0;
38: }
```

Output ▼

```
The contents of the first vector are:
0 1 2 3 4
The contents of the second vector are:
100 101 102 103 104
The result of the multiplication is:
0 101 204 309 416
```

Analysis ▼

The lambda expression in this example is shown in Line 21 as a parameter to `std::transform()`. This algorithm takes two ranges as input and applies a transformation algorithm that is contained in a binary function (the lambda expression of interest). The return value of the binary function is stored in a target container. The lambda expression accepts two integers as input and returns the result of the multiplication via the return value. This return value is stored by `std::transform()` in `vecResult`. The output demonstrates the contents of the two containers and the result of multiplying them element by element.

NOTE

Listing 22.4 demonstrates the lambda equivalent of the function object `class Multiply<>` from Listing 21.5.

A Lambda Expression for a Binary Predicate

A function that accepts two parameters and returns either `true` or `false` to help make a decision is called a *binary predicate*. Binary predicates find use in sort algorithms, such as `std::sort()`, that invoke the binary predicate for any two values in a container to determine which one should be placed after the other. The generic syntax of a binary predicate is

```
[...](Type1& param1Name, Type2& param2Name) {  // return bool expression; }
```

Listing 22.5 demonstrates a lambda expression being used with template parameters and another being used as a binary predicate with an explicit return type declaration.

Input ▼

LISTING 22.5 Using a Lambda Expression as a Binary Predicate in `std::sort()` to Enable Case-Insensitive Sorting

```
#include<algorithm>
#include<string>
#include<vector>
#include<iostream>
using namespace std;

int main()
{
   vector <string> namesInVe"{ ""im", "J"ck", ""am", "A"na" };

   // template lambda that displays object on screen
   auto displayElement = []<typename T>(const T& element)
                               { cout << element '<'' ';};

   cout << "The names in vector in order of insertion: " << endl;
   for_each(namesInVec.cbegin(), namesInVec.cend(), displayElement);

   cout "< "\nOrder after case sensitive sort:"\n";
   sort(namesInVec.begin(), namesInVec.end());
   for_each(namesInVec.cbegin(), namesInVec.cend(), displayElement);

```

```
21:     cout "< "\nOrder after sort ignoring case:"\n";
22:     sort(namesInVec.begin(), namesInVec.end(),
23:         [](const string& str1, const string& str2) -> bool  // lambda
24:         {
25:            string str1LC, str2LC; // LC = lowercase
26:            str1LC.resize(str1.size()); // create space to store result
27:            str2LC.resize(str2.size());
28:
29:            // Convert strings (each character) to the lower case
30:            transform(str1.begin(), str1.end(), str1LC.begin(),::tolower);
31:            transform(str2.begin(), str2.end(), str2LC.begin(), ::tolower);
32:
33:            return(str1LC < str2LC);
34:         } // end of lambda
35:       );  // end of sort
36:
37:     for_each(namesInVec.cbegin(), namesInVec.cend(), displayElement);
38:
39:     return 0;
40: }
```

Output ▼

```
The names in vector in order of insertion:
jim Jack Sam Anna
Order after case sensitive sort:
Anna Jack Sam jim
Order after sort ignoring case:
Anna Jack jim Sam
```

Analysis ▼

Listing 22.5 is quite novel in that it uses a template lambda expression `displayElement`, which is defined in Lines 11 and 12 and used by the algorithm `for_each()` in Lines 15, 19, and 37. `displayElement` is the lambda equivalent of `struct DisplayContents<>`, which you have used multiple times (for instance, in Listing 18.2 to display elements in `std::list` and in Listing 19.2 to display elements in `std::set`). This one-line lambda expression is generic and powerful.

A rather large lambda expression also spans Lines 23 through 34 as the third parameter of `std::sort()`! A lambda that spans multiple statements needs to explicitly declare the return value type (`bool`), as shown in Line 23. This lambda expression implements a binary predicate that assists with case-insensitive sorting by first converting the two strings to be compared to the same case (in this example, to lowercase, as shown in Lines 30 and 31) and then comparing the converted strings with each other. This case-insensitive sort helps place `"jim"` after `"Jack"`, as shown in the output.

NOTE

This extraordinarily large lambda expression in Listing 22.5 is a lambda version of class `CompareStringNoCase` from Listing 21.6, which is used in Listing 21.7.

DO	DON'T
DO remember that unless specified, state variables supplied within a capture list (`[]`) are not modifiable within the lambda expression unless you use the specifier `mutable`. **DO** use `const` generously when defining parameter types to ensure higher integrity.	**DON'T** forget that lambda expressions are unnamed representations of a class or a struct with `operator()`. **DON'T** forget to explicitly mention the return type when a lambda expression includes multiple statements within the statement block (`{}`).

Summary

In this lesson, you learned about an important feature that contributes to modern C++ programming: lambda expressions. You saw that lambda expressions are basically unnamed function objects that can take parameters, that have state, that return values, and that can be multiple lines. You learned how to use lambdas instead of function objects in STL algorithms, such as `find()`, `sort()`, or `transform()`. Lambda expressions make programming in C++ fast and efficient, and you should try to use them where applicable.

Q&A

Q How are the state parameters of a lambda expression transferred: by value or by reference?

A When a lambda expression is programmed with a capture list, like this:

```
[var1, var2, ... varN](Type& param1, ... ) { ...expression ;}
```

the state parameters `var1` and `var2` are copied (that is, not supplied as a reference). If you want to have them as reference parameters, you use this syntax:

```
[&Var1, &Var2, ... &varN](Type& param1, ... ) { ...expression ;}
```

In this case, you need to exercise caution as modifications to the state variables supplied within the capture list continue outside the lambda expression.

Q Can I use the local variables in a function in a lambda expression?

A You can pass the local variables in the capture list:

```
[var1, var2, ... varN](Type& param1, ... ) { ...expression ;}
```

If you need to capture all variables, you use this syntax:

```
[=](Type& Param1, ... ) { ...expression ;}
```

Workshop

The Workshop provides quiz questions to help you solidify your understanding of the material covered and exercises to provide you with experience using what you've learned. Try to answer the quiz and exercise questions before checking the answers in Appendix E and be certain you understand the answers before continuing to the next lesson.

Quiz

1. How does a compiler recognize the start of a lambda expression?
2. How do you pass state variables to a lambda function?
3. If you need to supply a return value in a lambda expression, how do you do it?

Exercises

1. Write a lambda binary predicate that helps sort elements in a container in descending order.
2. Write a lambda function that, when used in `for_each()`, adds a user-specified value in a container such as a vector.

LESSON 23
STL Algorithms

An important part of the Standard Template Library (STL) is a set of generic functions, supplied by the header `<algorithm>`, that help manipulate or work with the contents of a container.

In this lesson, you learn:

- Algorithms that help count, search, find, copy, and remove elements from a container
- How to set values in a range of elements to the return value of a generator function or a predefined constant
- How to sort or partition elements in a range
- How to insert elements at the correct position in a sorted range
- C++20 constrained algorithms

What Are STL Algorithms?

Finding, searching, removing, and counting are some generic algorithmic activities that find application in a broad range of programs. STL solves these and many other requirements with generic template functions that work on containers using iterators. To use STL algorithms, a programmer first has to include the header `<algorithm>`.

> **NOTE**
>
> Although most algorithms work via iterators on containers, not all algorithms necessarily work on containers, and hence not all algorithms need iterators. For example, `swap()` simply accepts a pair of values and swaps them. Similarly, `min()` and `max()` work directly on values, too.

Classification of STL Algorithms

STL algorithms can be broadly classified into two types: non-mutating and mutating algorithms.

Non-mutating Algorithms

Algorithms that change neither the order nor the contents of a container are called *non-mutating algorithms*. Some of the prominent non-mutating algorithms are shown in Table 23.1.

TABLE 23.1 Quick Reference of Non-mutating Algorithms

Algorithm	Description
Counting Algorithms	
`count()`	Finds all elements in a range whose values match a supplied value
`count_if()`	Finds all elements in a range whose values satisfy a supplied condition
Search Algorithms	
`search()`	Searches for the first occurrence of a given sequence within a target range, either on the basis of element equality (that is, with the operator `==`) or using a specified binary predicate
`search_n()`	Searches a specified target range for the first occurrence of `n` number of elements of a given value or those that satisfy a given predicate
`find()`	Searches for the first element in the range that matches the specified value
`find_if()`	Searches for the first element in a range that satisfies the specified condition
`find_end()`	Searches for the last occurrence of a particular subrange in a supplied range

Algorithm	Description
`find_first_of()`	Searches for the first occurrence of any element supplied in one range within a target range; or, in an overloaded version, searches for the first occurrence of an element that satisfies a supplied find criterion
`adjacent_find()`	Searches for two elements in a collection that are either equal or satisfy a supplied condition
Comparison Algorithms	
`equal()`	Compares two elements for equality or uses a specified binary predicate to determine equality
`mismatch()`	Locates the first difference position in two ranges of elements using a specified binary predicate
`lexicographical_compare()`	Compares the elements between two sequences to determine which is the lesser of the two

Mutating Algorithms

Mutating algorithms are algorithms that change the contents or the order of the sequence they are operating on. Some of the most useful mutating algorithms supplied by the STL are described in Table 23.2.

TABLE 23.2 A Quick Reference of Mutating Algorithms

Algorithm	Description
Initialization Algorithms	
`fill()`	Assigns the specified value to every element in the specified range.
`fill_n()`	Assigns the specified value to the first `n` elements in the specified range.
`generate()`	Assigns the return value of a specified function object to each element in the supplied range.
`generate_n()`	Assigns the value generated by a function to a specified count of values in a specified range.
Modifying Algorithms	
`for_each()`	Performs an operation on every element in a range. When the specified argument modifies the range, `for_each` becomes a mutating algorithm.
`transform()`	Applies a specified unary function on every element in the specified range.

Algorithm	Description
Copy Algorithms	
`copy()`	Copies one range into another.
`copy_backward()`	Copies one range into another, arranging elements in the destination range in the reverse order.
Removal Algorithms	
`remove()`	Removes an element of a specified value from a specified range.
`remove_if()`	Removes an element that satisfies a specified unary predicate from a specified range.
`remove_copy()`	Copies all elements from a source range to a destination range, except those of a specified value.
`remove_copy_if()`	Copies all elements from a source range to a destination range except those that satisfy a specified unary predicate.
`unique()`	Compares adjacent elements in a range and removes the following duplicates. An overloaded version works using a binary predicate.
`unique_copy()`	Copies all but adjacent duplicate elements from a specified source range to a specified destination range.
Replacement Algorithms	
`replace()`	Replaces every element in a specified range that matches a specified value with a replacement value.
`replace_if()`	Replaces every element in a specified range that matches a specified value, as determined by a predicate, with a replacement value.
Sort Algorithms	
`sort()`	Sorts elements in a range by using a specified sort criterion, which is a binary predicate that supplies a strict weak ordering. `sort` might change relative positions of equivalent elements.
`stable_sort()`	Works much like `sort` but preserves order, too.
`partial_sort()`	Sorts a specified number of elements in a range.
`partial_sort_copy()`	Copies elements from a specified source range to a destination range that holds them in a sort order.

Algorithm	Description
Partitioning Algorithms	
`partition()`	Given a specified range, splits elements into two sets within the range: Elements that satisfy a unary predicate come first and the rest after. Might not maintain the relative order of elements in a set.
`stable_partition()`	Partitions an input range into two sets—as `partition` does—but maintains relative ordering.
Algorithms That Work on Sorted Containers	
`binary_search()`	Determines whether an element exists in a sorted collection.
`lower_bound()`	Returns an iterator pointing to the first position where an element can potentially be inserted in a sorted collection based on its value or on a supplied binary predicate.
`upper_bound()`	Returns an iterator pointing to the last position where an element can potentially be inserted into a sorted collection based on its value or on a supplied binary predicate.

Usage of STL Algorithms

The usage of the STL algorithms mentioned in Tables 23.1 and 23.2 is best learned in a hands-on coding session. The code examples that follow give you a chance to practice with and start applying STL algorithms to your programs.

Finding Elements, Given a Value or a Condition

Given a container such as a `vector`, the STL algorithms `find()` and `find_if()` help you find an element that matches a value or fulfills a condition, respectively. The usage of `find()` follows this pattern:

```
auto element = find(numsInVec.cbegin(),    // Start of range
                    numsInVec.cend(),      // End of range
                    numToFind);            // Element to find

// Check if find() succeeded
if(element != numsInVec.cend())
    cout << "Result: Value found!" << endl;
```

`find_if()` is similar and requires you to supply a unary predicate (that is, a unary function that returns `true` or `false`) as the third parameter:

```
auto evenNum = find_if(numsInVec.cbegin(), // Start of range
                       numsInVec.cend(),     // End of range
                [](int element) { return (element % 2) == 0; } );
```

```
if(evenNum != numsInVec.cend())
   cout << "Result: Value found!" << endl;
```

Thus, both find functions return an iterator, which you need to compare by using `end()` or `cend()` in the container to verify the success of the find operation. If this check is successful, you can use the iterator further. Listing 23.1 demonstrates the use of `find()` to locate a value in a vector and `find_if()` to locate the first even value.

Input ▼

LISTING 23.1 Using `find()` to Locate an Integer Value in a Vector and `find_if()` to Locate the First Even Number Given a Unary Predicate in a Lambda Expression

```
#include<iostream>
#include<algorithm>
#include<vector>

int main()
{
   using namespace std;
   vector<int> numsInVec{ 2017, 0, -1, 42, 10101, 25 };

   cout << "Enter number to find in collection: ";
   int numToFind = 0;
   cin >> numToFind;

   auto element = find(numsInVec.cbegin(),  // Start of range
                       numsInVec.cend(),    // End of range
                       numToFind);          // Element to find

   // Check if find succeeded
   if(element != numsInVec.cend())
      cout << "Value " << *element << " found!" << endl;
   else
      cout << "No element contains value " << numToFind << endl;

   cout << "Finding the first even number using find_if: " << endl;

   auto evenNum = find_if(numsInVec.cbegin(), // Start range
                          numsInVec.cend(),   // End range
             [](int element) { return (element % 2) == 0; } );

   if(evenNum != numsInVec.cend())
   {
      cout << "Number '" << *evenNum << "' found at position [";
      cout << distance(numsInVec.cbegin(), evenNum) << "]" << endl;
   }

   return 0;
}
```

Output ▼

First run:

```
Enter number to find in collection: 42
Value 42 found!
Finding the first even number using find_if:
Number '0' found at position [1]
```

Next run:

```
Enter number to find in collection: 2016
No element contains value 2016
Finding the first even number using find_if:
Number '0' found at position [1]
```


Analysis ▼

`main()` starts by initializing a vector of integers to sample values in Line 7. `find()` in Lines 13 through 15 finds the integer entered by the user. The use of `find_if()` to locate the first even number in the range is shown in Lines 25 through 27. Line 27 is the unary predicate supplied to `find_if()` as a lambda expression. This lambda expression returns `true` when `element` is divisible by 2, thereby indicating to the algorithm that the element satisfies the criteria being checked for. Note the use of the algorithm `std::distance()` in Line 32 to find the relative position of an element found against the start of the container.

CAUTION

> Note how Listing 23.1 always checks the iterator returned by `find()` or `find_if()` for validity against `cend()`. This check should never be skipped, as it indicates the success of the `find()` operation, which should not be taken for granted.

Counting Elements Given a Value or a Condition

`std::count()` and `count_if()` are algorithms that help in counting elements in a range. `std::count()` helps you count the number of elements that match a value (tested via the equality operator, `==`):

```
size_t numZeroes = count(numsInVec.cbegin(), numsInVec.cend(), 0);
cout << "Number of instances of '0': " << numZeroes << endl;
```

`std::count_if()` helps you count the number of elements that fulfill a unary predicate supplied as a parameter (which can be a function object or a lambda expression):

```
// Unary predicate:
template <typename elementType>
bool IsEven(const elementType& number)
{
   return((number % 2) == 0); // true, if even
}
...
// Use the count_if algorithm with the unary predicate IsEven:
size_t numEvenNums = count_if(numsInVec.cbegin(),
                                        numsInVec.cend(), IsEven<int>);
cout << "Number of even elements: " << numEvenNums << endl;
```

The code in Listing 23.2 demonstrates the use of these functions.

Input ▼

LISTING 23.2 Using `std::count()` to Determine the Number of Elements with a Value and `count_if()` to Determine the Number of Elements That Fulfill a Condition

```
#include<algorithm>
#include<vector>
#include<iostream>

// unary predicate for *_if functions
auto IsEven = [](const auto& number) {return((number % 2) == 0); };

int main()
{
   using namespace std;
   vector<int> numsInVec{ 2017, 0, -1, 42, 10101, 25 };

   size_t numZeroes = count(numsInVec.cbegin(), numsInVec.cend(), 0);
   cout << "Number of instances of '0': " << numZeroes << endl;

   size_t numEvenNums = count_if(numsInVec.cbegin(),
                                 numsInVec.cend(), IsEven);

   cout << "Number of even elements: " << numEvenNums << endl;
   cout << "Number of odd elements: ";
   cout << numsInVec.size() - numEvenNums << endl;

   return 0;
}
```

Output ▼

```
Number of instances of '0': 1
Number of even elements: 2
Number of odd elements: 4
```

Analysis ▼

Line 12 uses `count()` to determine the number of instances of 0 in the `vector`. Similarly, Line 15 uses `count_if()` to determine the number of even elements in the vector. It uses the predicate `IsEven` that is implemented as a lambda expression in Line 5. Note the third parameter, which is a unary predicate `IsEven()`, defined in Lines 5 through 9. The number of elements in the vector that are odd is calculated by subtracting the return of `count_if()` from the total number of elements contained in the vector returned by `size()`.

Searching for an Element or a Range in a Collection

Listing 23.1 demonstrates how you can find an element in a container. Sometimes, you need to find a range of values or a pattern. In such situations, you should use `search()` or `search_n()`. `search()` can be used to check if one range is contained in another:

```
auto range = search(numsInVec.cbegin(), // Start range to search in
                    numsInVec.cend(),   // End range to search in
                    numsInList.cbegin(),// start range to search for
                    numsInList.cend()); // End range to search for
```

`search_n()` is used to find the first occurrence of `n` consecutive instances of a specified value in a range:

```
auto partialRange = search_n(numsInVec.cbegin(), // Start range
                             numsInVec.cend(),   // End range
                             3,  // num items to be searched for
                             9); // value to search for
```

Both functions return an iterator to the first instance of the pattern found, and this iterator needs to be checked against `end()` before it can be used. Listing 23.3 demonstrates the use of `search()` and `search_n()`.

Input ▼

LISTING 23.3 Finding a Range in a Collection by Using `search()` and `search_n()`

```
#include<algorithm>
#include<vector>
#include<list>
#include<iostream>
using namespace std;

template <typename T>
void DisplayContents(const T& container)
{
   for(auto element = container.cbegin();
       element != container.cend();
       ++ element)
     cout << *element << ' ';
```

```
    cout << endl;
}

int main()
{
    vector<int> numsInVec{ 2017, 0, -1, 42, 10101, 25, 9, 9, 9 };
    list<int> numsInList{ -1, 42, 10101 };

    cout << "The contents of the sample vector are:\n";
    DisplayContents(numsInVec);

    cout << "The contents of the sample list are:\n";
    DisplayContents(numsInList);

    cout << "search() for the contents of list in vector:\n";
    auto range = search(numsInVec.cbegin(), // Start range to search in
                        numsInVec.cend(), // End range to search in
                        numsInList.cbegin(), // Start range to search for
                        numsInList.cend()); // End range to search for

    // Check if search found a match
    if(range != numsInVec.end())
    {
       cout << "Sequence in list found in vector at position: ";
       cout << distance(numsInVec.cbegin(), range) << endl;
    }

    cout << "Searching {9, 9, 9} in vector using search_n():\n";
    auto partialRange = search_n(numsInVec.cbegin(), // Start range
                                 numsInVec.cend(),   // End range
                                 3,  // Count of item to be searched for
                                 9);   // Item to search for

    if(partialRange != numsInVec.end())
    {
       cout << "Sequence {9, 9, 9} found in vector at position: ";
       cout << distance(numsInVec.cbegin(), partialRange) << endl;
    }

    return 0;
}
```

Output ▼

```
The contents of the sample vector are:
2017 0 -1 42 10101 25 9 9 9
The contents of the sample list are:
-1 42 10101
```

```
search() for the contents of list in vector:
Sequence in list found in vector at position: 2
Searching {9, 9, 9} in vector using search_n():
Sequence {9, 9, 9} found in vector at position: 6
```

Analysis ▼

This example starts with two sample containers—a vector and a list—that are initially populated with sample integer values. `search()` is used to find the contents of the list in vector, as shown in Line 29. Because you want to search in the entire vector for the contents of the entire list, you supply a range, as returned by the iterators corresponding to the `cbegin()` and `cend()` member methods of the two container classes. This actually demonstrates how well iterators connect the algorithms to the containers. The physical characteristics of the containers that supply those iterators are of no significance to algorithms, which search the contents of a list in a vector seamlessly as they only work with iterators. `search_n()` is used in Line 42 to find the first occurrence of the series `{9, 9, 9}` in the vector.

Initializing Elements in a Container to a Specific Value

`fill()` and `fill_n()` are the STL algorithms that help set the contents of a given range to a specified value. `fill()` is used to overwrite the elements in a range, given the bounds of the range and the value to be inserted:

```
vector<int> numsInVec(3);

// fill all elements in the container with value 9
fill(numsInVec.begin(), numsInVec.end(), 9);
```

As the name suggests, `fill_n()` reassigns a specified `n` number of values. It needs a starting position, a count, and the value to fill:

```
fill_n(numsInVec.begin() + 3, /*count*/ 3, /*fill value*/ -9);
```

Listing 23.4 demonstrates how these algorithms make it easy to initialize elements in `vector<int>`.

Input ▼

LISTING 23.4 Using `fill()` and `fill_n()` to Set Initial Values in a Container

```
#include<algorithm>
#include<vector>
#include<iostream>

```

```
 4: int main()
 5: {
 6:     using namespace std;
 7:
 8:     // Initialize a sample vector with 3 elements
 9:     vector<int> numsInVec(3);
10:
11:     // fill all elements in the container with value 9
12:     fill(numsInVec.begin(), numsInVec.end(), 9);
13:
14:     // Increase the size of the vector to hold 6 elements
15:     numsInVec.resize(6);
16:
17:     // Fill the three elements starting at offset position 3 with value -9
18:     fill_n(numsInVec.begin() + 3, 3, -9);
19:
20:     cout << "Contents of the vector are: " << endl;
21:     for(size_t index = 0; index < numsInVec.size(); ++ index)
22:     {
23:         cout << "Element [" << index << "] = ";
24:         cout << numsInVec [index] << endl;
25:     }
26:
27:     return 0;
28: }
```

Output ▼

```
Contents of the vector are:
Element [0] = 9
Element [1] = 9
Element [2] = 9
Element [3] = -9
Element [4] = -9
Element [5] = -9
```

Analysis ▼

Listing 23.4 uses the `fill()` and `fill_n()` functions to initialize the contents of the container to two separate sets of values, as shown in Lines 12 and 18. Note the use of the `resize()` function in Line 15. You use it to create space for a total of six elements. The three new elements are later filled with the value `-9`, using `fill_n()` in Line 18. The `fill()` algorithm works on a complete range, whereas `fill_n()` can also work on a partial range.

TIP

> You might have noticed that code in Listings 23.1, 23.2, and 23.3 uses the constant versions of the iterators; that is, `cbegin()` and `cend()` are used in defining the bounds of elements accessed in a container. However, Listing 23.4 deviates by using `begin()` and `end()`. This is simply because the purpose of the algorithm `fill()` is to modify the elements in the container, and this cannot be achieved using constant iterators that don't allow changes to the element they point to.
>
> Using constant iterators is a good practice, but you can deviate from it when you need to modify the elements they point to.

Using `std::generate()` to Initialize Elements to a Value Generated at Runtime

Just as the `fill()` and `fill_n()` functions fill a collection with specific values, STL algorithms, such as `generate()` and `generate_n()`, are used to initialize collections using values returned by a unary function.

You can use `generate()` to fill a range using the return value of a generator function:

```
generate(numsInVec.begin(), numsInVec.end(),     // range
         rand);     // generator function, returns random values
```

`generate_n()` is similar to `generate()` except that you supply the number of elements to be assigned instead of the closing bound of a range:

```
generate_n(numsInList.begin(), 5, rand);
```

Thus, you can use these two algorithms to initialize the contents of a container to the contents of a file, for example, or to random values, as shown in Listing 23.5.

Input ▼

LISTING 23.5 Using `generate()` and `generate_n()` to Initialize Collections to Random Values

```
#include<algorithm>
#include<vector>
#include<list>
#include<iostream>
#include<ctime>

int main()
{
    using namespace std;
```

```
 9:     srand(static_cast<int>(time(NULL))); // seed random generator
10:
11:     vector<int> numsInVec(5);
12:     generate(numsInVec.begin(), numsInVec.end(),     // range
13:              rand);    // generator function
14:
15:     cout << "Elements in the vector are: ";
16:     for(size_t index = 0; index < numsInVec.size(); ++ index)
17:         cout << numsInVec [index] << " ";
18:     cout << endl;
19:
20:     list<int> numsInList(5);
21:     generate_n(numsInList.begin(), 3, rand);
22:
23:     cout << "Elements in the list are: ";
24:     for(auto element = numsInList.begin();
25:         element != numsInList.end();
26:         ++ element)
27:         cout << *element << ' ';
28:
29:     return 0;
30: }
```

Output ▼

```
Elements in the vector are: 41 18467 6334 26500 19169
Elements in the list are: 15724 11478 29358 0 0
```

Analysis ▼

The use of a random number generator seeded using the current time in Line 9 means that the output is likely to be different on every run of the application. Listing 23.5 uses `generate()` in Line 12 to populate all elements in the vector and uses `generate_n()` in Line 21 to populate the first three elements in the list with random values supplied by the generator function `rand()`. Note that the `generate()` function accepts a range as an input and then calls the specified function object `rand()` for every element in the range. `generate_n()`, in comparison, accepts only the starting position. It then invokes the specified function object `rand()`, the number of times specified by the `count` parameter to overwrite the contents of that many elements. The elements in the container that are beyond the specified offset are left untouched.

Processing Elements in a Range by Using `for_each()`

The `for_each()` algorithm applies a specified unary function object to every element in the supplied range. The usage of `for_each()` is

```
fnObjType retValue = for_each(start_of_range,
                              end_of_range,
                              unaryFunctionObject);
```

This unary function object can also be a lambda expression that accepts one parameter.

The return value indicates that `for_each()` returns the function object (or *functor*) used to process every element in the supplied range. The implication of this specification is that using a struct or a class as a function object can help in storing state information, which you can later query when `for_each()` is done. This is demonstrated in Listing 23.6, which uses the function object to display elements in a range and also uses it to count the number of elements displayed.

Input ▼

LISTING 23.6 Displaying the Contents of Sequences by Using `for_each()`

```
#include<algorithm>
#include<iostream>
#include<vector>
#include<string>
using namespace std;

template <typename elementType>
struct DisplayElementKeepcount
{
   int count;
   DisplayElementKeepcount(): count(0) {}

   void operator()(const elementType& element)
   {
      ++ count;
      cout << element << ' ';
   }
};

int main()
{
   vector<int> numsInVec{ 2017, 0, -1, 42, 10101, 25 };

   cout << "Elements in vector are: " << endl;
   DisplayElementKeepcount<int> functor =
      for_each(numsInVec.cbegin(),    // Start of range
               numsInVec.cend(),       // End of range
               DisplayElementKeepcount<int>());// functor
   cout << endl;

```

```
30:     // Use the state stored in the return value of for_each!
31:     cout << "'" << functor.count << "' elements displayed" << endl;
32:
33:     string str("for_each and strings!");
34:     cout << "Sample string: " << str << endl;
35:
36:     cout << "Characters displayed using lambda:" << endl;
37:     int numElements = 0;
38:     for_each(str.cbegin(),
39:              str.cend(),
40:             [&numElements](auto c) { cout << c << ' '; ++numElements; });
41:
42:     cout << endl;
43:     cout << "'" << numElements << "' characters displayed" << endl;
44:
45:     return 0;
46: }
```

Output ▼

```
Elements in vector are:
2017 0 -1 42 10101 25
'6' elements displayed
Sample string: for_each and strings!
Characters displayed using lambda:
f o r _ e a c h   a n d   s t r i n g s !
'21' characters displayed
```

Analysis ▼

This example demonstrates the utility of `for_each()` invoked in Lines 25 and 38, and the function object `functor` returned by `for_each()` that is programmed to hold the number of times it was invoked in the member `count`.

The code features two sample ranges: one contained in a vector of integers, `numsInVec`, and the other a `std::string` object `str`. The first call to `for_each()` uses `DisplayElementKeepCount` as the unary predicate, and the second uses a lambda expression. `for_each()` invokes `operator()` for every element in the supplied range, which in turn prints the element on the screen and increments an internal counter. The function object is returned when `for_each()` is done, and the member `count` determines the number of times the object was used. This facility of storing information (or state) in the object that is returned by the algorithm can be useful in practical programming situations. `for_each()` in Line 38 does exactly the same as its previous counterpart in Line 25 for `std::string`, using a lambda expression instead of a function object. Note that the lambda equivalent being used for type `char` in Line 38 is generic enough that you can use it in its current form in Line 25 for type `int`, too (with minor modifications to the code around).

Performing Transformations on a Range by Using `std::transform()`

`std::for_each()` and `std::transform()` are similar in that they both invoke a function object for every element in a source range. However, `std::transform()` has two versions. The first version accepts a unary function and is popularly used to convert a string to upper- or lowercase, using the functions `toupper()` or `tolower()`:

```
string str("THIS is a TEst string!");
transform(str.cbegin(), // start source range
          str.cend(), // end source range
          strLowerCaseCopy.begin(), // start destination range
          ::tolower); // unary function
```

The second version accepts a binary function that allows `transform()` to process a pair of elements taken from two different ranges:

```
// sum elements from two vectors and store result in a deque
transform(numsInVec1.cbegin(), // start of source range 1
          numsInVec1.cend(),   // end of source range 1
          numsInVec2.cbegin(), // start of source range 2
          sumInDeque.begin(),  // store result in a deque
           plus<int>());       // binary function plus
```

Both versions of `transform()` always assign the result of the specified transformation function to a supplied destination range, unlike `for_each()`, which works on only a single range. The use of `std::transform()` is demonstrated in Listing 23.7.

Input ▼

LISTING 23.7 Using `std::transform()` with Unary and Binary Functions

```
#include<algorithm>
#include<string>
#include<vector>
#include<deque>
#include<iostream>
#include<functional>

int main()
{
    using namespace std;

    string str("THIS is a TEst string!");
    cout << "The sample string is: " << str << endl;
```

```

    string strLowerCaseCopy;
    strLowerCaseCopy.resize(str.size());

    transform(str.cbegin(), // start source range
              str.cend(),   // end source range
              strLowerCaseCopy.begin(), // start destination range
              ::tolower);   // unary function

    cout << "Result of 'transform' on the string with 'tolower':\n";
    cout << "\"" << strLowerCaseCopy << "\"" << endl << endl;

    // Two sample vectors of integers...
   vector<int> numsInVec1{ 2017, 0, -1, 42, 10101, 25 };
   vector<int> numsInVec2(numsInVec1.size(), -1);

    // A destination range for holding the result of addition
    deque<int> sumInDeque(numsInVec1.size());

    transform(numsInVec1.cbegin(), // start of source range 1
              numsInVec1.cend(),   // end of source range 1
              numsInVec2.cbegin(), // start of source range 2
              sumInDeque.begin(),  // start of destination range
              plus<int>());        // binary function

    cout << "Result of 'transform' using binary function 'plus': \n";
    cout << "Index   Vector1 + Vector2 = Result(in Deque)\n";
    for(size_t index = 0; index < numsInVec1.size(); ++ index)
    {
        cout << index << "    \t " << numsInVec1 [index]   << "\t+   ";
        cout << numsInVec2 [index]  << " \t  =    ";
        cout << sumInDeque [index] << endl;
    }

    return 0;
}
```

Output ▼

```
The sample string is: THIS is a TEst string!
Result of 'transform' on the string with 'tolower':
"this is a test string!"

Result of 'transform' using binary function 'plus':
Index   Vector1 + Vector2 = Result (in Deque)
0        2017   +   -1    =    2016
1        0      +   -1    =    -1
2        -1     +   -1    =    -2
3        42     +   -1    =    41
```

```
4        10101   +   -1    =    10100
5        25      +   -1    =    24
```

Analysis ▼

This example demonstrates both versions of `std::transform()`: one that works on a single range using the unary function `tolower()`, shown in Line 20, and another that works on two ranges and uses the binary function `plus()`, shown in Line 36. The first changes the case of a string, character by character, to lowercase. If you use `toupper()` instead of `tolower()`, you effect a case conversion to uppercase. The other version of `std::transform()`, shown in Lines 32 through 36, acts on elements taken from two input ranges (two vectors in this case) and uses a binary predicate in the form of the STL function `plus()` (supplied by the header `<functional>`) to add them. `std::transform()` takes one pair at a time, supplies it to the binary function `plus`, and assigns the result to an element in the destination range—one that happens to belong to an `std::deque` container. Note that the change in container used to hold the result is purely for demonstration purposes, to show how well iterators can be used to abstract containers and their implementation from STL algorithms; `transform()`, which is an algorithm, deals with ranges and really does not need to know details about the containers that implement these ranges. So, the input ranges happened to be in `vector`, and the output ranges happened to be in `deque`, and it all works fine—as long as the bounds that define the range (supplied as input parameters to `transform`) are valid.

Copy and Remove Operations

STL supplies three prominent copy functions: `copy()`, `copy_if()`, and `copy_backward()`. `copy()` assigns the contents of a source range to a destination range in the forward direction:

```
auto lastElement = copy(numsInList.cbegin(),     // start source range
                        numsInList.cend(),       // end source range
                        numsInVec.begin());      // start dest range
```

`copy_if()` copies an element when a unary predicate supplied by you returns `true`:

```
// copy odd numbers from list into vector
copy_if(numsInList.cbegin(), numsInList.cend(),
        lastElement, // copy position in dest range
        [](int element){return((element % 2) == 1);});
```

`copy_backward()` assigns the contents to the destination range in the backward direction:

```
copy_backward(numsInList.cbegin(),
              numsInList.cend(),
              numsInVec.end());
```

`remove()`, on the other hand, deletes elements in a container that match a specified value:

```
// Remove all instances of '0', resize vector using erase()
auto newEnd = remove(numsInVec.begin(), numsInVec.end(), 0);
numsInVec.erase(newEnd, numsInVec.end());
```

`remove_if()` uses a unary predicate and removes from the container those elements for which the predicate evaluates to `true`:

```
// Remove all odd numbers from the vector using remove_if
newEnd = remove_if(numsInVec.begin(), numsInVec.end(),
           [](int num) {return ((num % 2) == 1);} ); //predicate

numsInVec.erase(newEnd, numsInVec.end());  // resizing
```

Listing 23.8 demonstrates the use of the copy and removal functions.

Input ▼

LISTING 23.8 Using `copy()`, `copy_if()`, `remove()`, and `remove_if()` to Copy a List into a Vector and Remove Zeros and Even Numbers

```
#include<algorithm>
#include<vector>
#include<list>
#include<iostream>
using namespace std;

template <typename T>
void DisplayContents(const T& container)
{
   for_each(container.begin(), container.end(),
      [](const auto& element) {cout << element << ' '; });

   cout << "| Number of elements: " << container.size() << endl;
}

int main()
{
   list<int> numsInList{ 2017, 0, -1, 42, 10101, 25 };

   cout << "Source(list) contains:" << endl;
   DisplayContents(numsInList);

   // Initialize vector to hold 2x elements as the list
   vector<int> numsInVec(numsInList.size() * 2);

   auto lastElement = copy(numsInList.cbegin(),    // start source range
                           numsInList.cend(),      // end source range
                           numsInVec.begin());     // start dest range
```

```
28:
29:     // copy odd numbers from list into vector
30:     copy_if(numsInList.cbegin(), numsInList.cend(),
31:             lastElement,
32:             [](int element){return((element % 2) != 0);});
33:
34:     cout << "Destination(vector) after copy and copy_if:\n";
35:     DisplayContents(numsInVec);
36:
37:     // Remove all instances of '0', resize vector using erase()
38:     auto newEnd = remove(numsInVec.begin(), numsInVec.end(), 0);
39:     numsInVec.erase(newEnd, numsInVec.end());
40:
41:     // Remove all odd numbers from the vector using remove_if
42:     newEnd = remove_if(numsInVec.begin(), numsInVec.end(),
43:                [](int element) {return((element % 2) != 0);});
44:     numsInVec.erase(newEnd , numsInVec.end());  // resizing
45:
46:     cout << "Destination(vector) after remove, remove_if, erase:\n";
47:     DisplayContents(numsInVec);
48:
49:     return 0;
50: }
```


Output ▼

```
Source(list) contains:
2017 0 -1 42 10101 25 | Number of elements: 6
Destination(vector) after copy and copy_if:
2017 0 -1 42 10101 25 2017 -1 10101 25 0 0 | Number of elements: 12
Destination (vector) after remove, remove_if, erase:
42 | Number of elements: 1
```

Analysis ▼

The use of `copy()` is demonstrated in Line 25, where it copies the contents of the list into the vector. `copy_if()` is used in Line 30 and copies all odd numbers from the source range `numsInList` into the destination range `numsInVec`, starting at the iterator position `lastElement` returned by `copy()`. `remove()` in Line 38 rids `numsInVec` of all instances of `0`. `remove_if()` in Line 42 removes all odd numbers.

NOTE

> Listing 23.8 features a version of the `DisplayContainer<>` function that differs from the one in Listing 23.3, given its use of `for_each()` and a lambda expression.

CAUTION

> Listing 23.8 demonstrates that both `remove()` and `remove_if()` return an iterator that points to the new end of the container. However, the container `numsInVec` has not been resized yet. Elements have been deleted by the remove algorithms, and other elements have been shifted forward, but the size has remained unaltered, meaning there are values at the end of the vector. To resize the container (and this is important; otherwise, it has unwanted values at the end), you need to use the iterator returned by `remove()` or `remove_if()` in a subsequent call to `erase()`, as shown in Lines 39 and 44.

Replacing Values and Replacing Elements Given a Condition

`replace()` and `replace_if()` are the STL algorithms that can replace elements in a collection that are equivalent to a supplied value or that satisfy a given condition, respectively. `replace()` replaces elements based on the return value of the comparison operator (==):

```
cout << "Using 'std::replace' to replace value 5 by 8" << endl;
replace(numsInVec.begin(), numsInVec.end(), 5, 8);
```

`replace_if()` expects a user-specified unary predicate that returns `true` for every value that needs to be replaced:

```
cout << "Using 'std::replace_if' to replace even values by -1" << endl;
replace_if(numsInVec.begin(), numsInVec.end(),
   [](int element) {return ((element % 2) == 0); }, -1);
```

The use of these functions is demonstrated by Listing 23.9.

Input ▼

LISTING 23.9 Using `replace()` and `replace_if()` to Replace Values in a Specified Range

```
#include<iostream>
#include<algorithm>
#include<vector>
using namespace std;

template <typename T>
void DisplayContents(const T& container)
{
    for_each(container.begin(), container.end(),
        [](const auto& element) {cout << element << ' '; });

    cout << endl;
```

```
12: }
13:
14: int main()
15: {
16:     vector<int> numsInVec{232, 5, -98, -3, 5, 0, 987};
17:
18:     cout << "The initial contents of vector:\n";
19:     DisplayContents(numsInVec);
20:
21:     replace(numsInVec.begin(), numsInVec.end(), 5, 8);
22:     cout << "After replacing value 5 by 8\n";
23:     DisplayContents(numsInVec);
24:
25:     replace_if(numsInVec.begin(), numsInVec.end(),
26:         [](int element) {return((element % 2) == 0); }, -1);
27:     cout << "After replacing even values by -1:\n";
28:     DisplayContents(numsInVec);
29:
30:     return 0;
31: }
```

Output ▼

```
The initial contents of vector:
232 5 -98 -3 5 0 987
After replacing value 5 by 8
232 8 -98 -3 8 0 987
After replacing even values by -1:
-1 -1 -1 -3 -1 -1 987
```

Analysis ▼

This example creates a `vector<int>` container with initial values. Line 21 demonstrates the use of `replace()` to replace all `5`s with `8`s. Line 25 demonstrates the use of `replace_if()` with a predicate that identifies even numbers. Each of these even numbers is replaced with `-1`, as shown in the output.

Sorting and Searching in a Sorted Collection and Erasing Duplicates

Sorting and searching a sorted range are requirements that come up in practical applications. Very often you have an array of information that needs to be sorted, such as for presentation's sake. You can use STL's `sort()` algorithm to sort a container:

```
sort(numsInVec.begin(), numsInVec.end()); // ascending order
```

This version of `sort()` uses `std::less<>` as a default binary predicate that uses the operator `<` implemented by the type in the vector. You can supply your own predicate to change the sort order using an overloaded version:

```
sort(numsInVec.begin(), numsInVec.end(),
    [](int lhs, int rhs) {return (lhs > rhs);} ); // descending order
```

Similarly, duplicates need to be deleted before the collection is displayed. To remove adjacently placed repeating values, you use the algorithm `unique()`:

```
auto newEnd = unique(numsInVec.begin(), numsInVec.end());
numsInVec.erase(newEnd, numsInVec.end());  // to resize
```

To search in a sorted container, you use `binary_search()`:

```
bool elementFound = binary_search(numsInVec.begin(), numsInVec.end(), 2021);

if(elementFound)
   cout << "Element found in the vector!" << endl;
```

Listing 23.10 demonstrates the STL algorithms `std::sort()`, which can sort a range; `std::binary_search()`, which can search a sorted range; and `std::unique()`, which eliminates duplicate neighboring elements (that become neighbors after a `sort()` operation).

Input ▼

LISTING 23.10 Using `sort()`, `binary_search()`, and `unique()`

```
#include<algorithm>
#include<vector>
#include<string>
#include<iostream>
using namespace std;

template <typename T>
void DisplayContents(const T& container)
{
   for_each(container.begin(), container.end(),
      [](const auto& element) {cout << element << ' '; });
}

int main()
{
   vector<string> names{"John", "jack", "sean", "Anna"};

   // insert a duplicate
   names.push_back("jack");

   cout << "The initial contents of the vector are:\n";
   DisplayContents(names);

   cout << "\nThe sorted vector contains names in the order:\n";
```

```
24:     sort(names.begin(), names.end());
25:     DisplayContents(names);
26:
27:     cout << "\nSearching for \"John\" using 'binary_search':\n";
28:     bool found = binary_search(names.begin(), names.end(), "John");
29:
30:     if(found)
31:        cout << "Result: \"John\" was found in the vector!\n";
32:     else
33:        cout << "Element not found " << endl;
34:
35:     // Erase adjacent duplicates
36:     auto newEnd = unique(names.begin(), names.end());
37:     names.erase(newEnd, names.end());
38:
39:     cout << "The contents of the vector after using 'unique':\n";
40:     DisplayContents(names);
41:
42:     return 0;
43: }
```

Output ▼

```
The initial contents of the vector are:
John jack sean Anna jack
The sorted vector contains names in the order:
Anna John jack jack sean
Searching for "John" using 'binary_search':
Result: "John" was found in the vector!
The contents of the vector after using 'unique':
Anna John jack sean
```

Analysis ▼

The listing first sorts the sample vector `names` in Line 24, before using `binary_search()` in Line 28 to find `"John"` in it. Similarly, `std::unique()` is used in Line 36 to delete the second occurrence of an adjacent duplicate. Note that `unique()`, like `remove()`, does not resize the container. It results in values being shifted but not a reduction in the total number of elements. To ensure that you don't have unwanted or unknown values at the tail end of the container, always follow a call to `unique()` with `vector::erase()`, using the iterator returned by `unique()`, as demonstrated in Line 37.

CAUTION

Algorithms such as `binary_search()` are effective only in sorted containers. Use of this algorithm on an unsorted vector can have undesirable consequences.

NOTE

> The usage of `stable_sort()` is the same as the usage of `sort()`, which you saw earlier. `stable_sort()` ensures that the relative order of the sorted elements is maintained. Maintaining relative order comes at the cost of performance—a factor that needs to be kept in mind, especially if the relative ordering of elements is not essential.

Partitioning a Range

`std::partition()` helps partition an input range into two sections—one that satisfies a unary predicate and another that doesn't:

```
bool IsEven(const int& num)  // unary predicate
{
   return ((num % 2) == 0);
}
...
partition(numsInVec.begin(), numsInVec.end(), IsEven);
```

`std::partition()`, however, does not guarantee the relative order of elements within each partition. To maintain relative order, when that is important, you should use `std::stable_partition()`:

```
stable_partition(numsInVec.begin(), numsInVec.end(), IsEven);
```

Listing 23.11 demonstrates the use of these algorithms.

Input ▼

LISTING 23.11 Using `partition()` and `stable_partition()` to Partition a Range of Integers into Even and Odd Values

```
#include<algorithm>
#include<vector>
#include<iostream>
using namespace std;

auto IsEven = [](const int& num) { return((num % 2) == 0); };

template <typename T>
void DisplayContents(const T& container)
{
   for_each(container.begin(), container.end(),
      [](const auto& element) {cout << element << ' '; });

   cout << "| Number of elements: " << container.size() << endl;
}
```

```
15:
16: int main()
17: {
18:    vector<int> numsInVec{ 2017, 0, -1, 42, 10101, 25 };
19:
20:    cout << "The initial contents: " << endl;
21:    DisplayContents(numsInVec);
22:
23:    vector<int> vecCopy(numsInVec);
24:
25:    cout << "The effect of using partition():" << endl;
26:    partition(numsInVec.begin(), numsInVec.end(), IsEven);
27:    DisplayContents(numsInVec);
28:
29:    cout << "The effect of using stable_partition():" << endl;
30:    stable_partition(vecCopy.begin(), vecCopy.end(), IsEven);
31:    DisplayContents(vecCopy);
32:
33:    return 0;
34: }
```

Output ▼

```
The initial contents:
2017 0 -1 42 10101 25 | Number of elements: 6
The effect of using partition():
42 0 -1 2017 10101 25 | Number of elements: 6
The effect of using stable_partition():
0 42 2017 -1 10101 25 | Number of elements: 6
```

Analysis ▼

The code partitions a range of integers, as contained inside the vector `numsInVec`, into even and odd values. This partitioning is first done using `std::partition()`, as shown in Line 26, and is repeated on a copy, using `stable_partition()` in Line 30. For the sake of being able to compare, you copy the sample range `numsInVec` into `vecCopy`; the former is partitioned using `partition()`, and the latter is partitioned using `stable_partition()`. The effect of using `stable_partition()` rather than `partition()` is apparent in the output. `stable_partition()` maintains the relative order of elements in each partition. Note that maintaining this order comes with a performance penalty, which might be small, as in this case, or significant, depending on the type of object contained in the range.

NOTE

> `stable_partition()` is slower than `partition()`, and therefore you should use it only when the relative order of elements in a container is important.

Inserting Elements in a Sorted Collection

It is important that new elements be inserted in a sorted collection at the correct relative positions. STL supplies functions, such as `lower_bound()` and `upper_bound()`, to assist in meeting this need:

```
auto minInsertPos = lower_bound(names.begin(), names.end(),
                                "Brad Pitt");
// alternatively:
auto maxInsertPos = upper_bound(names.begin(), names.end(),
                                "Brad Pitt");
```

Hence, `lower_bound()` and `upper_bound()` return iterators pointing to the minimal and maximal positions in a sorted range where an element can be inserted without breaking the order of the sort.

Listing 23.12 demonstrates the use of `lower_bound()` in inserting an element at the minimal position in a sorted list of names.

Input ▼

LISTING 23.12 Using `lower_bound()` and `upper_bound()` to Insert in a Sorted Collection

```
#include<algorithm>
#include<list>
#include<string>
#include<iostream>
using namespace std;

template <typename T>
void DisplayContents(const T& container)
{
   for_each(container.begin(), container.end(),
      [](const auto& element) {cout << element << ' '; });
}

int main()
{
   list<string> names{ "John", "Brad", "jack", "sean", "Anna" };

   cout << "Sorted contents of the list are: " << endl;
```

```
18:     names.sort();
19:     DisplayContents(names);
20:
21:     cout << "\nLowest index where \"Brad\" can be inserted is: ";
22:     auto minPos = lower_bound(names.begin(), names.end(), "Brad");
23:     cout << distance(names.begin(), minPos) << endl;
24:
25:     cout << "The highest index where \"Brad\" can be inserted is: ";
26:     auto maxPos = upper_bound(names.begin(), names.end(), "Brad");
27:     cout << distance(names.begin(), maxPos) << endl;
28:
29:     cout << "List after inserting Brad in sorted order: " << endl;
30:     names.insert(minPos, "Brad");
31:     DisplayContents(names);
32:
33:     return 0;
34: }
```


Output ▼

```
Sorted contents of the list are:
Anna Brad John jack sean
Lowest index where "Brad" can be inserted is: 1
The highest index where "Brad" can be inserted is: 2
List after inserting Brad in sorted order:
Anna Brad Brad John jack sean
```

Analysis ▼

An element can be inserted into a sorted collection at two potential positions: One is returned by `lower_bound()` and is the lowest (the closest to the beginning of the collection), and the other is the iterator returned by `upper_bound()` that is the highest (the furthest away from the beginning of the collection). In the case of Listing 23.12, where the string `"Brad"` that is inserted into the sorted collection already exists in it, the lower and upper bounds are different (otherwise, they would've been identical). The use of these functions is shown in Lines 22 and 26, respectively. As the output demonstrates, the iterator returned by `lower_bound()`, when used in inserting the string into the list, as shown in Line 30, results in the list keeping its sorted state. Thus, these algorithms help you make an insertion at a point in the collection without breaking the sorted nature of the contents. Using the iterator returned by `upper_bound()` would work fine as well.

Performing Fold Operations Using `std::accumulate()` in C++20

`std::accumulate`, introduced in 2020, helps you perform an accumulatory action on elements in a container. The simplest form of `accumulate` can add or multiply elements, as in this example:

```
accumulate(container.cbegin(), // start source range
           container.cend(), // end source range
          0, // initial value of the sum
          binaryfunc); // optional, binary function to apply
```

TIP

> To use the algorithm `std::accumulate`, include this header:
>
> `#include<numeric>`

Listing 23.13 demonstrates the versatility of this algorithm in delivering the sum and product of all numbers in a container.

Input ▼

LISTING 23.13 Using `std::accumulate` to Determine the Sum and Product of All Elements in a Container

```
#include<numeric>
#include<vector>
#include<iostream>
using namespace std;

int main()
{
   vector<int> integers{ 1, 2, 3, 4 };
   int sum = std::accumulate(integers.cbegin(), integers.cend(), 0);
   cout << "Sum of elements: " << sum << endl;

   int product = std::accumulate(integers.cbegin(), integers.cend(), 1,
      [](auto mul1, auto mul2) {return mul1 * mul2; });

   cout << "The product is: " << product << endl;

   return 0;
}
```

Output ▼

```
Sum of elements: 10
The product is: 24
```

Analysis ▼

Line 8 demonstrates the simplest variant, where `std::accumulate` performs the default function of adding elements in the container. The initializing value has been supplied as `0`, and if you were to give it another value, that would influence the result of the addition as well. In Lines 11 and 12, you see a variant where a binary function has been supplied in the form of a lambda expression that returns the multiple of the supplied two arguments. `std::accumulate` is a generic implementation and can be used on all STL containers as well as a variety of types.

C++20 Constrained Algorithms

You might have noticed that algorithms introduced so far are required to explicitly specify the range. For instance, when using `std::find()` in Listing 23.1:

```
auto element = find(numsInVec.cbegin(),     // Start of range
                    numsInVec.cend(),       // End of range
                    numToFind);             // Element to find

if(element != numsInVec.cend())
   cout << "Value " << *element << " found!" << endl;
```

This example specifies the range to be operated upon as starting at `numsInVec.cbegin()` and ending before `numsInVec.end()`.

Beginning with C++20, you can use constrained versions of the algorithms in the namespace `std::ranges`. You simply supply the container object, without needing to specify the beginning and end of the range when you need the algorithm to work on every element contained, as shown here:

```
auto element = std::ranges::find(numsInVec, numToFind);
if (element != numsInVec.end())
    cout << "Value " << *element << " found!" << endl;
```

The good news is that many—perhaps even most—algorithms are available in constrained versions, as demonstrated in Listing 23.14.

Input ▼

LISTING 23.14 Using C++20 Constrained Algorithms to Find, Sort, Fill, and Modify Elements in a Range

```
#include<algorithm>
#include<vector>
#include<string>
#include<iostream>
using namespace std;

```

```
template <typename T>
void DisplayContents(const T& container)
{
    for (const auto& element : container)
        cout << element << ' ';

    cout << endl;
}

int main()
{
    vector<int> numsInVec{ 2021, -1, 42, 404949, -981 };
    cout << "Initial contents of vector: ";
    DisplayContents(numsInVec);

    cout << "Enter integer to search for: ";
    int numToFind = 0;
    cin >> numToFind;

    auto element = std::ranges::find(numsInVec, numToFind);
    if (element != numsInVec.end())
        cout << "Value " << *element << " found!" << endl;
    else
        cout << "The number isn't in the range\n";

    std::ranges::sort(numsInVec);
    cout << "Sorting the range now\n";
    DisplayContents(numsInVec);

    std::ranges::fill(numsInVec, 0);
    cout << "Reset vector contains: ";
    DisplayContents(numsInVec);

    string strHello("Hello C++20 constrained algorithms");
    cout << "Original string: " << strHello << endl;
    std::ranges::for_each(strHello, [](auto& c) {c = ::tolower(c); });
    cout << "In lower case: " << strHello << endl;

    return 0;
}
```

Output ▼

```
Initial contents of vector: 2021 -1 42 404949 -981
Enter integer to search for: 42
Value 42 found!
Sorting the range now
-981 -1 42 2021 404949
Reset vector contains: 0 0 0 0 0
```

```
Original string: Hello to C++20 constrained algorithms
In lower case: hello to c++20 constrained algorithms
```

Analysis ▼

The example uses `ranges::find()` in Line 25 to find an integer supplied by you in the range. `ranges::sort()` in Line 31 organizes the contents of the vector in ascending order. `ranges::fill()` is used to reset all elements, and `ranges::for_each()` is used to convert every character in the string to lowercase. What's special about these constrained algorithms is that they didn't necessarily require you to specify the starting and ending limits of the range (but you may do so if you need the algorithm to work on a part of the input collection).

DO	DON'T
DO remember to use a container's `erase()` member method after using the algorithms `remove()`, `remove_if()`, or `unique()` to resize the container. **DO** always check the iterator returned by the `find()`, `find_if()`, `search()`, or `search_n()` functions for validity before using it by comparing against the end of the container. **DO** choose `stable_partition()` over `partition()` and `stable_sort()` over `sort()` when the relative ordering of sorted elements is important.	**DON'T** forget to sort a container using `sort()` before calling `unique()` to remove repeating adjacent values. `sort()` ensures that all elements of a value are aligned adjacent to each other, making `unique()` effective. **DON'T** insert elements into a sorted container at randomly chosen positions. Rather, insert them using positions returned by `lower_bound()` or `upper_bound()` to ensure that the sorted order of elements remains undisturbed. **DON'T** forget that `binary_search()` is used only on a sorted container.

Summary

In this lesson, you learned about one of the most important and powerful aspects of STL, algorithms. You gained insights about the different types of algorithms, and thanks to the listings, you should now have a clearer understanding of the application of algorithms.

Q&A

Q Would I use a mutating algorithm, such as `std::transform()`, on an associative container, such as `std::set`?

A Even if it were possible, this should not be done. Associative containers sort elements on insertion, and the relative positions of the elements play an important role in functions such as `find()` and also in the efficiency of the container. For this reason, mutating algorithms, such as `std::transform()`, should not be used on STL sets.

Q I need to set the content of every element of a sequential container to a particular value. Would I use `std::transform()` to do this?

A Although `std::transform()` could be used to do this, `fill()` and `fill_n()` are better suited to the task.

Q Does `copy_backward()` reverse the contents of the elements in the destination container?

A No, it doesn't. The STL algorithm `copy_backward()` reverses the order in which elements are copied but not the order in which elements are stored; that is, it starts with the end of the range and reaches the top. To reverse the contents of a collection, you should use `std::reverse()`.

Q Should I use `std::sort()` on a list?

A `std::sort()` can be used on a list in the same way it can be used on any other sequential container. However, the list needs to maintain a special property such that an operation on the list does not invalidate existing iterators—a property that `std::sort()` cannot guarantee to uphold. For this reason, STL `list` supplies the `sort()` algorithm in the form of the member function `list::sort()`, which should be used because it guarantees that iterators to elements in the list are not invalidated even if their relative positions in the list have changed.

Q Why is it important to use functions such as `lower_bound()` or `upper_bound()` while inserting into a sorted range?

A These functions supply the first and the last positions, respectively, where an element can be inserted into a sorted collection without disturbing the sort order.

Workshop

The Workshop provides quiz questions to help you solidify your understanding of the material covered and exercises to provide you with experience using what you've learned. Try to answer the quiz and exercise questions before checking the answers in Appendix E and be certain you understand the answers before continuing to the next lesson.

Quiz

1. You need to remove from a list items that meet a specific condition. Would you use `std::remove_if()` or `list::remove_if()`?
2. You have a list of a class type `ContactItem`. How does the `list::sort()` function sort items of this type in the absence of an explicitly specified binary predicate?
3. How often does the `generate()` STL algorithm invoke the generator function?
4. What differentiates `std::transform()` from `std::for_each()`?

Exercises

1. Write a binary predicate that accepts strings as input arguments and returns a value based on a case-insensitive comparison.
2. Demonstrate how STL algorithms such as `copy()` use iterators to do their functions without needing to know the nature of the destination collections by copying between two sequences held in two dissimilar containers.
3. You are writing an application that records the characteristics of stars that come up on the horizon, in the order in which they rise. In astronomy, the sizes of stars as well as information on their relative rise and set sequences are important. If you're sorting this collection of stars on the basis of their sizes, would you use `std::sort` or `std::stable_sort`?

LESSON 24
Adaptive Containers: Stack and Queue

The Standard Template Library (STL) features containers that adapt other containers to simulate stack and queue behavior. Containers that internally use other containers and present a distinct behavior are called *adaptive containers*.

In this lesson, you learn

- The behavioral characteristics of stacks and queues
- Using the STL `stack`
- Using the STL `queue`
- Using the STL `priority_queue`

The Behavioral Characteristics of Stacks and Queues

Stacks and queues are like arrays or lists but present restrictions on how elements are inserted, accessed, and removed. Their behavioral characteristics are decided exactly by the placement of elements on insertion or the position of the element that can be erased from the container.

Stacks

Stacks are LIFO (last-in, first-out) systems in which elements can be inserted or removed at the top of the container. A stack can be visualized as a stack of plates. The last plate added to the stack is going to be the first one taken off. Plates in the middle and at the bottom cannot be inspected. This method of organizing elements, involving addition and removal at the top, is illustrated in Figure 24.1.

FIGURE 24.1
Operations on a stack.

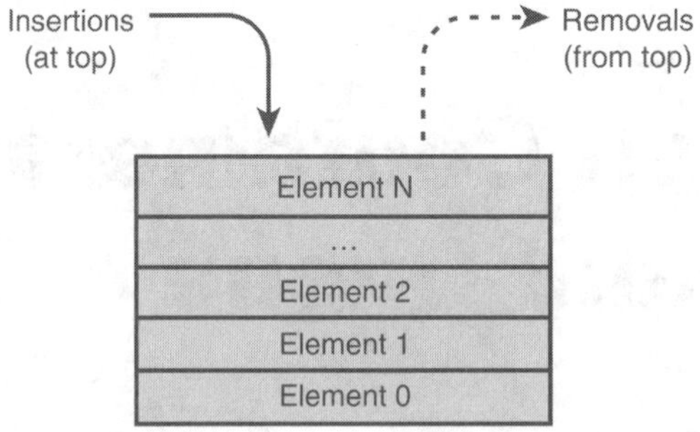

This behavior of a stack of plates is simulated in the generic STL container `std::stack`.

TIP

To use `std::stack`, include the header

```
#include<stack>
```

Queues

Queues are FIFO (first-in, first-out) systems in which an element can be inserted behind the previous one, and the one inserted first gets removed first. A queue can be visualized as a queue of people waiting for stamps at the post office, where those who join the queue earlier leave earlier. This method of organizing elements, involving addition at the back but removal at the front, is illustrated in Figure 24.2.

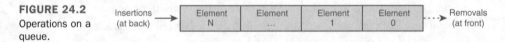

FIGURE 24.2
Operations on a queue.

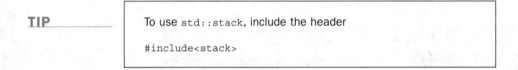

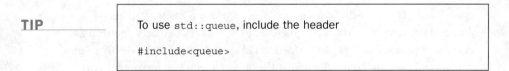

This behavior of a queue is simulated in the generic STL container `std::queue`.

TIP

To use `std::queue`, include the header

```
#include<queue>
```

Using the STL `stack` Class

`stack` is an STL class that needs to include the header `<stack>`. It is a generic class that allows insertions and removal of elements at the top and does not permit any access or inspection of elements in the middle. In that sense, `std::stack` is quite similar in behavior to a stack of plates.

Instantiating a Stack

`std::stack` is defined by some implementations of the STL as follows:

```
template <
   class elementType,
   class Container=deque<Type>
> class stack;
```

The parameter *elementType* is the type of object that is collected by the stack. The second template parameter, *Container*, is the stack's default underlying container implementation class. `std::deque` is the default for the stack's internal data storage and can be replaced by `std::vector` or `std::list`. Thus, the instantiation of a stack of integers looks like this:

```
std::stack<int> numsInStack;
```


If you want to create a stack of objects of any type, such as in the `Tuna`, you would use the following:

```
std::stack <Tuna> tunasInStack;
```

To create a stack that uses a different underlying container, use

```
std::stack<double, vector <double> > doublesStackedInVec;
```

Listing 24.1 demonstrates different instantiation techniques.

Input ▼

LISTING 24.1 Instantiating an STL Stack

```
#include<stack>
#include<vector>

int main()
{
   using namespace std;

   // A stack of integers
   stack<int> numsInStack;

   // A stack of doubles
   stack <double> dblsInStack;

   // A stack of doubles contained in a vector
   stack<double, vector<double>> doublesStackedInVec;
```

```
15:
16:     // initializing one stack to be a copy of another
17:     stack<int> numsInStackCopy(numsInStack);
18:
19:     return 0;
20: }
```

Output ▼

This code snippet produces no output

Analysis ▼

This example produces no output but demonstrates the template instantiation of the STL `stack` container. Lines 8 and 11 instantiate two `stack` objects to hold elements of type `int` and `double`, respectively. Line 14 also instantiates a stack of `doubles` but specifies a second template parameter—the type of collection class that the stack should use internally, a vector. If this second template parameter is not supplied, the stack automatically defaults to using `std::deque` instead. Finally, Line 17 demonstrates that one `stack` object can be constructed as a copy of another.

Stack Member Functions

The stack, which adapts another container, such as a deque, list, or vector, implements its functionality by restricting the manner in which elements can be inserted or removed to supply a behavior that is expected strictly from a stack-like mechanism. Table 24.1 describes the public member functions of the `stack` class and demonstrates their use for a stack of integers.

TABLE 24.1 Popular Member Functions of `std::stack`

Function	Description	Example
`push()`	Inserts an element at the top of the stack	`numsInStack.push(25);`
`pop()`	Removes the element at the top of the stack	`numsInStack.pop();`
`empty()`	Tests whether the stack is empty; returns `bool`	`if (numsInStack.empty())` `   DoSomething();`
`size()`	Returns the number of elements in the stack	`size_t numElements = numsInStack.size();`
`top()`	Gets a reference to the topmost element in the stack	`cout << "Element at the top = " << numsInStack.top();`

As the table indicates, the public member functions of the stack expose only methods that allow insertion and removal at positions that are compliant with a stack's behavior. That is, even though the underlying container might be a deque, a vector, or a list, the functionality of that container has not been revealed to enforce the behavioral characteristics of a stack.

Insertion and Removal at the Top, Using `push()` and `pop()`

Insertion of elements is done by using the member method `stack<T>::push()`:

```
numsInStack.push(25); // 25 is atop the stack
```

The stack, by definition, allows access to elements at the top. You use the member method `top()`:

```
cout << numsInStack.top() << endl;
```


If you want to remove an element at the top, you can use the function `pop()` to do so:

```
numsInStack.pop(); // pop: removes topmost element
```

Listing 24.2 demonstrates inserting elements in a stack using `push()` and removing elements using `pop()`.

Input ▼

LISTING 24.2 Working with a Stack of Integers

```
#include<stack>
#include<iostream>

int main()
{
    using namespace std;
    stack<int> numsInStack;

    // push: insert values at top of the stack
    cout << "Pushing {25, 10, -1, 5} on stack in that order:\n";
    numsInStack.push(25);
    numsInStack.push(10);
    numsInStack.push(-1);
    numsInStack.push(5);

    cout << "Stack contains " << numsInStack.size() << " elements\n";
    while(numsInStack.size() != 0)
    {
```

```
18:         cout << "Popping topmost element: " << numsInStack.top() << endl;
19:         numsInStack.pop(); // pop: removes topmost element
20:      }
21:
22:      if(numsInStack.empty())   // true: due to previous pop()s
23:         cout << "Popping all elements empties stack!\n";
24:
25:      return 0;
26: }
```

Output ▼

```
Pushing {25, 10, -1, 5} on stack in that order:
Stack contains 4 elements
Popping topmost element: 5
Popping topmost element: -1
Popping topmost element: 10
Popping topmost element: 25
Popping all elements empties stack!
```

Analysis ▼

This example first inserts numbers into a stack of integers, `numsInStack`, by using the `stack::push()` function in Lines 9 through 13. It then proceeds to delete elements by using `stack::pop()`. As `stack` permits access to only the topmost element, an element at the top can be accessed using the member method `stack::top()`, as shown in Line 18. Elements can be deleted from the stack one at a time by using `stack::pop()`, as shown in Line 19. The `while` loop around it ensures that the `pop()` operation is repeated until the stack is empty. As you can see from the order of the elements that were popped, the element inserted last was popped first, demonstrating the typical LIFO behavior of a stack.

Listing 24.2 demonstrates five member functions of the `stack` class. Note that `push_back()` and `insert()`, which are available with all STL sequential containers used as underlying containers by the `stack` class, are not available as public member functions of a stack. The same is true of iterators that help you peek at elements that are not at the top of the container. The stack exposes only the element at the top and nothing else.

Using the STL `queue` Class

In the STL, `queue` is a template class that requires the inclusion of the header `<queue>`. It is a generic class that allows insertion only at the end and removal of elements only at the front. A queue does not permit any access or inspection of elements in the middle;

however, elements at the beginning and the end can be accessed. In a sense, `std::queue` is quite similar in behavior to a queue of people at the cashier in a supermarket.

Instantiating a Queue

`std::queue` is defined as

```
template <
   class elementType,
   class Container = deque<Type>
> class queue;
```

Here, *`elementType`* is the type of elements collected by the queue object. *`Container`* is the type of collection that the `std::queue` class uses to maintain its data. The `std::list`, `vector`, and `deque` are possible candidates for this template parameter, and `deque` is the default.

The simplest instantiation of a queue of integers would be the following:

```
std::queue<int> numsInQ;
```

If you want to create a queue containing elements of type `double` inside a `std::list` (instead of a `deque`, which is the default), use the following:

```
std::queue<double, list <double>> dblsInQInList;
```

Just like a stack, a queue can also be instantiated as a copy of another queue:

```
std::queue<int> copyQ(numsInQ);
```

Listing 24.3 demonstrates the various instantiation techniques for `std::queue`.

Input ▼

LISTING 24.3 Instantiating an STL Queue

```
#include<queue>
#include<list>

int main()
{
   using namespace std;

   // A queue of integers
   queue<int> numsInQ;

   // A queue of doubles
   queue <double> dblsInQ;

   // A queue of doubles stored internally in a list
```

```
14:     queue <double, list<double>> dblsInQInList;
15:
16:     // one queue created as a copy of another
17:     queue<int> copyQ(numsInQ);
18:
19:     return 0;
20: }
```

Output ▼

This code snippet produces no output

Analysis ▼

This example demonstrates how the generic STL class `queue` can be instantiated to create a queue of integers, as shown in Line 8, or a queue for objects of type `double`, as shown in Line 11. `dblsInQInList`, as instantiated in Line 14, is a queue that has explicitly specified in the second template parameter that the underlying container to be adapted should be a `std::list`. In the absence of the second template parameter, as in the first two queues, `std::deque` is used as the default underlying container for the contents of the queue.

Member Functions of the `queue` Class

`std::queue`, like `std::stack`, bases its implementation on an STL container such as a vector, list, or deque. The `queue` class exposes only those member functions that implement the behavioral characteristics of a queue. Table 24.2 describes the popular member functions using `numsInQ`, which Listing 24.3 demonstrates is a queue of integers.

TABLE 24.2 Popular Member Functions in `std::queue`

Function	Description	Example
`push()`	Inserts an element at the back of the queue (that is, at the last position)	`numsInQ.push(10);`
`pop()`	Removes the element at the front of the queue (that is, at the first position)	`numsInQ.pop();`
`front()`	Returns a reference to the element at the front of the queue	`cout << "Element at front: " << numsInQ.front();`
`back()`	Returns a reference to the element at the back of the queue (that is, the last inserted element)	`cout << "Element at back: " << numsInQ.back();`

Function	Description	Example
`empty()`	Tests whether the queue is empty; returns a Boolean value	`if(numsInQ.empty())` `cout << "Queue is empty!";`
`size()`	Returns the number of elements in the queue	`size_t numElements = numsInQ.size();`

The STL `queue` class does not feature functions such as `begin()` and `end()`, which are supplied by most STL containers, including the underlying `deque`, `vector`, or `list` containers, as used by the `queue` class. This is by intention so that the only permissible operations on a queue are those that comply with the queue's behavioral characteristics.

Insertion at the End and Removal at the Beginning of a Queue via `push()` and `pop()`

Insertion of elements in a queue happens at the end and is done using the member method `push()`:

```
numsInQ.push(5);  // elements pushed are inserted at the end
```

Removal, on the other hand, happens at the beginning and via `pop()`:

```
numsInQ.pop();  // removes element at front
```

Unlike `stack`, `queue` allows elements at both ends—that is, the front and back of the container—to be inspected:

```
cout << "Element at front: " << numsInQ.front() << endl;
cout << "Element at back: " << numsInQ.back() << endl;
```

Insertion, removal, and inspection are demonstrated in Listing 24.4.

Input ▼

LISTING 24.4 Inserting, Removing, and Inspecting Elements in a Queue of Integers

```
#include<queue>
#include<iostream>

int main()
{
   using namespace std;
   queue<int> numsInQ;

   cout << "Inserting {10, 5, -1, 20} into queue\n";
   numsInQ.push(10);
```

```
10:     numsInQ.push(5);  // elements are inserted at the end
11:     numsInQ.push(-1);
12:     numsInQ.push(20);
13:
14:     cout << "Queue contains " << numsInQ.size() << " elements\n";
15:     cout << "Element at front: " << numsInQ.front() << endl;
16:     cout << "Element at back: " << numsInQ.back() << endl;
17:
18:     while(numsInQ.size() != 0)
19:     {
20:        cout << "Deleting element: " << numsInQ.front() << endl;
21:        numsInQ.pop();  // removes element at front
22:     }
23:
24:     if(numsInQ.empty())
25:        cout << "The queue is now empty!" << endl;
26:
27:     return 0;
28: }
```

Output ▼

```
Inserting {10, 5, -1, 20} into queue
Queue contains 4 elements
Element at front: 10
Element at back: 20
Deleting element: 10
Deleting element: 5
Deleting element: -1
Deleting element: 20
The queue is now empty!
```

Analysis ▼

In this example, elements are added to `numsInQ` using `push()`, which inserts the elements at the end (or back) of the queue in Lines 9 through 12. The methods `front()` and `back()` are used to reference elements at the beginning and end positions of the queue, as shown in Lines 15 and 16. The `while` loop in Lines 18 through 22 displays the element at the beginning of the queue, before removing it using a `pop()` operation at Line 21. It continues doing this until the queue is empty. The output demonstrates that elements are erased from the queue in the same order in which they were inserted: Elements are inserted at the rear of the queue and deleted from the front.

Using the STL Priority Queue

In the STL, `priority_queue` is a template class that also requires the inclusion of the header `<queue>`. `priority_queue` is different from `queue` in that the element with the highest value (or the value deemed to be highest by a binary predicate) is available at the front of the queue, and queue operations are restricted to the front.

Instantiating the `priority_queue` Class

The `std::priority_queue` class is defined as

```
template <
   class elementType,
   class Container=vector<Type>,
      class Compare=less<typename Container::value_type>
>
class priority_queue
```


Here, *`elementType`* is the template parameter that conveys the type of elements to be collected in the priority queue. The second template parameter tells the collection class to be internally used by `priority_queue` for holding data, and the third parameter allows the programmer to specify a binary predicate that helps the queue determine the element that is at the top. In the absence of a specified binary predicate, the `priority_queue` class uses the default in `std::less<>`, which compares two objects using the operator `<`.

The simplest instantiation of a priority queue of integers would be

```
std::priority_queue<int> numsInPrioQ;
```

Here is how you can create a priority queue containing elements of type `double` inside `std::deque`:

```
priority_queue<int, deque<int>, greater<int>> numsInDescendingQ;
```

Just like a stack, a priority queue can be instantiated as a copy of another:

```
std::priority_queue<int> copyQ(numsInPrioQ);
```

The instantiation of a `priority_queue` object is demonstrated in Listing 24.5.

Input ▼

LISTING 24.5 Instantiating an STL `priority_queue` Object

```
#include<queue>
#include<functional>

int main()
```

```
 4: {
 5:     using namespace std;
 6:
 7:     // Priority queue of int sorted using std::less <>(default)
 8:     priority_queue<int> numsInPrioQ;
 9:
10:     // A priority queue of doubles
11:     priority_queue<double> dblsInPrioQ;
12:
13:     // A priority queue of integers sorted using std::greater <>
14:     priority_queue<int, deque<int>, greater<int>> numsInDescendingQ;
15:
16:     // a priority queue created as a copy of another
17:     priority_queue<int> copyQ(numsInPrioQ);
18:
19:     return 0;
20: }
```

Output ▼

This code snippet produces no output.

Analysis ▼

Lines 8 and 11 demonstrate the instantiation of priority queues for objects of type int and double, respectively. The absence of any other template parameter results in the use of std::vector as the internal container of data, and the default comparison criterion is provided by std::less<>. These queues are therefore so prioritized that the integer of the highest value is available at the front of the priority queue. numsInDescendingQ, however, supplies a deque for the second parameter as the internal container and std::greater as the predicate. This predicate results in a queue where the smallest number is available at the front.

The effect of using the predicate std::greater<T> is illustrated in Listing 24.7, later in this lesson.

NOTE

> Listing 24.5 includes the standard header <functional> to use std::greater<>.

Member Functions of `priority_queue`

The member functions `front()` and `back()`, available in the `queue` class, are not available in the `priority_queue` class. Table 24.3 introduces the member functions of the `priority_queue` class.

TABLE 24.3 Popular Member Functions in `std::priority_queue`

Function	Description	Example
`push()`	Inserts an element into the priority queue	`numsInPrioQ.push(10);`
`pop()`	Removes the element at the top of the queue (that is, the largest element in the queue)	`numsInPrioQ.pop();`
`top()`	Returns a reference to the largest element in the queue (which also holds the topmost position)	`cout << "The largest element in the priority queue is: " << numsInPrioQ.top();`
`empty()`	Tests whether the priority queue is empty; returns a `boolean` value	`if(numsInPrioQ.empty()) cout << "The queue is empty!";`
`size()`	Returns the number of elements in the priority queue	`size_t numElements = numsInPrioQ.size();`

As the table indicates, queue members can only be accessed by using `top()`, which returns the element with the highest value, and they can be evaluated using the user-defined predicate or by `std::less` in the absence of a user-defined predicate.

Insertion at the End and Removal at the Beginning of a Priority Queue via `push()` and `pop()`

Insertion of elements in a priority queue is done using the member method `push()`:

```
numsInPrioQ.push(5);   // elements are organized in sorted order
```

Removal, on the other hand, happens at the beginning via `pop()`:

```
numsInPrioQ.pop();   // removes element at front
```

The use of priority queue members is demonstrated in Listing 24.6.

Input ▼

LISTING 24.6 Working with a Priority Queue Using `push()`, `top()`, and `pop()`

```
 0: #include<queue>
 1: #include<iostream>
 2:
 3: int main()
 4: {
 5:     using namespace std;
 6:
 7:     priority_queue<int> numsInPrioQ;
 8:     cout << "Inserting {10, 5, -1, 20} into the priority_queue" << endl;
 9:     numsInPrioQ.push(10);
10:     numsInPrioQ.push(5);
11:     numsInPrioQ.push(-1);
12:     numsInPrioQ.push(20);
13:
14:     cout << "Deleting the " << numsInPrioQ.size() << " elements" << endl;
15:     while(!numsInPrioQ.empty())
16:     {
17:         cout << "Deleting topmost element: " << numsInPrioQ.top() << endl;
18:         numsInPrioQ.pop();
19:     }
20:
21:     return 0;
22: }
```

Output ▼

```
Inserting {10, 5, -1, 20} into the priority_queue
Deleting the 4 elements
Deleting topmost element: 20
Deleting topmost element: 10
Deleting topmost element: 5
Deleting topmost element: -1
```

Analysis ▼

Listing 24.6 inserts sample integers into a priority queue, as shown in Lines 9 through 12, and then erases the element on the top/front by using `pop()`, as shown in Line 18. The output indicates that the element of greatest value is available at the top of the queue. Usage of `priority_queue::pop()` therefore effectively deletes the element that evaluates to having the greatest value among all elements in the container, which is also exposed as the value at the top, via the method `top()` in Line 17. Given that you have not supplied a prioritization predicate, the queue has automatically resorted to sorting elements in descending order (with the highest value at the top).

Listing 24.7 demonstrates the instantiation of a priority queue with `std::greater<int>` as the predicate. This predicate results in the queue evaluating the smallest number as the element with the greatest value, which is then available at the front of the priority queue.

Input ▼

LISTING 24.7 Instantiating a Priority Queue That Holds the Smallest Value at the Top

```
0: #include<queue>
1: #include<iostream>
2: #include<functional>
3: int main()
4: {
5:     using namespace std;
6:
7:     // Define a priority_queue object with greater<int> as predicate
8:     priority_queue <int, vector<int>, greater<int>> numsInPrioQ;
9:
10:    cout << "Inserting {10, 5, -1, 20} into the priority queue" << endl;
11:    numsInPrioQ.push(10);
12:    numsInPrioQ.push(5);
13:    numsInPrioQ.push(-1);
14:    numsInPrioQ.push(20);
15:
16:    cout << "Deleting " << numsInPrioQ.size() << " elements" << endl;
17:    while(!numsInPrioQ.empty())
18:    {
19:        cout << "Deleting topmost element " << numsInPrioQ.top() << endl;
20:        numsInPrioQ.pop();
21:    }
22:
23:    return 0;
24: }
```

24

Output ▼

```
Inserting {10, 5, -1, 20} into the priority queue
Deleting 4 elements
Deleting topmost element -1
Deleting topmost element 5
Deleting topmost element 10
Deleting topmost element 20
```

Analysis ▼

Most of the code and all the values supplied to the priority queue in this example are intentionally the same as those in Listing 24.6. However, the output shows how the two queues behave differently. The elements in the priority queue are compared using the predicate `greater<int>` in Line 8. As a result of this predicate, the integer with the lowest magnitude is evaluated as greater than others and is therefore placed at the top position. So, the function `top()` used in Line 19 displays the smallest integer number in the priority queue, and it is deleted soon after using by a `pop()` operation in Line 20.

Thus, when elements are popped, this priority queue pops the integers in order of increasing magnitude.

Summary

This lesson explained the use of the three key adaptive containers—the STL `stack`, `queue`, and `priority_queue` containers. These classes adapt sequential containers for their internal storage requirements, but via their member functions they present the behavioral characteristics that make stacks and queues so unique.

Q&A

Q Can an element in the middle of a stack be modified?

A No, it cannot be modified because modification would contradict the purpose of a stack, which is supposed to be a last-in, first-out container.

Q Can I iterate through all the elements of a queue?

A A queue does not feature iterators, and elements in a queue can be accessed only at the ends by using the member methods `front()` and `back()`.

Q Can STL algorithms work with adaptive containers?

A STL algorithms work using iterators. Because neither the `stack` class nor the `queue` class supplies iterators that mark the ends of the ranges, the use of STL algorithms with these containers is not possible.

Workshop

The Workshop provides quiz questions to help you solidify your understanding of the material covered and exercises to provide you with experience using what you've learned. Try to answer the quiz and exercise questions before checking the answers in Appendix E and be certain you understand the answers before continuing to the next lesson.

Quiz

1. Can you change the behavior of the priority_queue class for a certain element, such that the element with the greatest value is popped last?
2. You have a priority queue of class Coin. What member operator do you need to define for the priority_queue class to present the coin with the greater value at the top position?
3. You have a stack of class Coin and have pushed six objects into it. Can you access or delete the first coin inserted?

Exercises

1. A queue of people (in class Person) are lining up at the post office. Person contains member attributes that hold age and gender and are defined as

```
class Person
{
    public:
        int age;
        bool isFemale;
};
```

   Amend this class such that a priority queue containing objects of it would offer elderly people and women (in that order) priority service.

2. Write a program that reverses the user's string input using the stack class.

LESSON 25

Working with Bit Flags Using the STL

Using bits is an efficient way of storing settings and flags. The Standard Template Library (STL) supplies classes that help organize and manipulate bitwise information. This lesson introduces you to

- The `bitset` class
- The `vector<bool>` class

The `bitset` Class

`std::bitset` is the STL class designed for handling information in bits and bit flags. `std::bitset` is not an STL container class because it cannot resize itself. It is a utility class that is optimized for working with a sequence of bits whose length is known at compile time.

TIP

To use the class `std::bitset`, include the header `<bitset>`:

```
#include<bitset>
```

Instantiating `std::bitset`

The `bitset` template class requires you to supply one template parameter that contains the number of bits the instance of the class has to manage:

```
bitset<4> fourBits;  // 4 bits initialized to 0000
```

You can also initialize the bitset to a bit sequence represented in a `char*` string literal:

```
bitset<5> fiveBits("10101"); // 5 bits 10101
```

Copying from one bitset while instantiating another is quite simple:

```
bitset<5> fiveBitsCopy(fiveBits);
```

Some instantiation techniques of the `bitset` class are demonstrated in Listing 25.1.

Input ▼

LISTING 25.1 Instantiating `std::bitset`

```
 0: #include<bitset>
 1: #include<iostream>
 2: #include<string>
 3:
 4: int main()
 5: {
 6:     using namespace std;
 7:
 8:     bitset<4> fourBits;  // 4 bits initialized to 0000
 9:     cout << "Initial contents of fourBits: " << fourBits << endl;
10:
11:     bitset<5> fiveBits("10101"); // 5 bits 10101
12:     cout << "Initial contents of fiveBits: " << fiveBits << endl;
13:
14:     bitset<6> sixBits(0b100001); // binary literal introduced in C++14
15:     cout << "Initial contents of sixBits: " << sixBits << endl;
16:
17:     bitset<8> eightBits(255); // 8 bits initialized to long int 255
18:     cout << "Initial contents of eightBits: " << eightBits << endl;
19:
20:     // instantiate one bitset as a copy of another
21:     bitset<8> eightBitsCopy(eightBits);
21:
23:     return 0;
24: }
```

Output ▼

```
Initial contents of fourBits: 0000
Initial contents of fiveBits: 10101
Initial contents of sixBits: 100001
Initial contents of eightBits: 11111111
```

Analysis ▼

This example demonstrates four different ways of constructing a `bitset` object. The default constructor initializes the bit sequence to `0` in Line 8. A string literal that contains the representation of the desired bit sequence is used in Line 11. Lines 14 and 17 demonstrate the use of a binary literal and an integer to initialize the `bitset`, while Line 21 demonstrates the use of the copy constructor in initializing from another `bitset` object. Note that in each of these instances, you have to supply the number of bits that the bitset is supposed to contain as a template parameter. This number is fixed at compile time; it isn't dynamic. You can't insert more bits into a bitset than you specified in your code; this is different from a vector, where you can insert more elements than the size planned at compile time.

TIP

> Note the use of the binary literal `0b100001` in Line 14. The prefix `0b` or `0B` tells the compiler that the following digits are a binary representation of an integer.

Using `std::bitset` and Its Members

The `bitset` class supplies member functions that help perform insertions into the bitset, set or reset contents, read the bits, or write the bits into a stream. It also supplies operators that help display the contents of a bitset and perform bitwise logical operations, among other things.

Useful Operators in `std::bitset`

You learned about operators in Lesson 12, "Operator Types and Operator Overloading," and you also learned that the most important role played by operators is increasing the usability of a class. `std::bitset` provides operators that make using this class really easy. These operators, listed in Table 25.1, are explained using the sample bitset from Listing 25.1, `fourBits`.

TABLE 25.1 Operators Supported by `std::bitset`

<table>
<tr><th>Operator</th><th>Description</th><th>Example</th></tr>
<tr><td><<</td><td>Inserts a text representation of the bit sequence into the output stream</td><td>cout << fourBits;</td></tr>
<tr><td>>></td><td>Inserts a string into the bitset object</td><td>"0101" >> fourBits;</td></tr>
<tr><td>&</td><td>Performs a bitwise AND operation</td><td>bitset<4> result(fourBits1 & fourBits2);</td></tr>
<tr><td>|</td><td>Performs a bitwise OR operation</td><td>bitset<4> result(fourBits1 | fourBits2);</td></tr>
</table>

Operator	Description	Example
^	Performs a bitwise XOR operation	`bitset<4> result(fourBits1 ^ fourBits2);`
~	Performs a bitwise NOT operation	`bitset<4> result(~fourBits1);`
>>=	Performs a bitwise right shift	`fourBits >>= (2);` `// Shift two bits to the right`
<<=	Performs a bitwise left shift	`fourBits <<= (2);` `// Shift bits two positions left`

[N]	Returns a reference to the Nth bit in the sequence	`fourBits[2] = 0;`
		`// sets the third bit to 0`
		`bool flag = fourBits[2];`
		`// reads the third bit`

In addition, `std::bitset` also features operators such as `|=`, `&=`, `^=`, and `~=`, which help perform bitwise operations on a `bitset` object.

`std::bitset` Member Methods

Bits can hold two states: set (`1`) or reset (`0`). To help manipulate the contents of a bitset, you can use the member functions listed in Table 25.2, which can help you work with a bit or with all the bits in a bitset.

TABLE 25.2 Popular Member Methods in `std::bitset`

Function	Description	Example
`set()`	Sets all bits in the sequence to `1`	`fourBits.set();` `// sequence now contains: '1111'`
`set(N, val=1)`	Sets the `N`th bit with the value specified in `val` (the default is `1`)	`fourBits.set(2, 0);` `// sets third bit to 0`
`reset()`	Resets all bits in the sequence to `0`	`fourBits.reset();` `// sequence contains: '0000'`
`reset(N)`	Clears the `N`th bit	`fourBits.reset(2);` `// the third bit is now 0`
`flip()`	Toggles all bits in the sequence	`fourBits.flip();` `// 0101 changes to 1010`
`size()`	Returns the number of bits in the sequence	`size_t numBits = fourBits.size();` `// returns 4`

Function	Description	Example
`count()`	Returns the number of bits that hold `true`	`size_t numBitsSet = fourBits.count();` `size_t numBitsReset = fourBits.size() - fourBits.count();`
`to_ulong()`	Returns the `unsigned long` value corresponding to the contents of the `bitset`	`unsigned long value = fourBits.to_ulong()`
`to_ullong()`	Returns the `unsigned long long` value corresponding to the contents of the `bitset`	`unsigned long long value = fourBits.to_ullong();`
`all()`	Returns `true` if all bits are set to `true`; otherwise, returns `false`	`if(fourBits.all())` `{/* do something*/}`
`any()`	Returns `true` if any one bit is set to `true`; otherwise, returns `false`	`if(fourBits.any())` `{/* do something*/}`
`none()`	Returns `true` if no bits are set to `true`; otherwise, returns `false`	`if(fourBits.none())` `{/* do something*/}`

The use of these member methods and operators is demonstrated in Listing 25.2.

25

Input ▼
LISTING 25.2 Performing Logical Operations Using a Bitset

```
0: #include<bitset>
1: #include<string>
2: #include<iostream>
3:
4: int main()
5: {
6:    using namespace std;
7:    bitset<8> inputBits;
8:    cout << "Enter a 8-bit sequence: ";
9:
10:    cin >> inputBits;  // store user input in bitset
11:
12:    cout << "Num 1s you supplied: " << inputBits.count() << endl;
13:    cout << "Num 0s you supplied: ";
14:    cout << inputBits.size() - inputBits.count() << endl;
15:
16:    bitset<8> inputFlipped(inputBits);  // copy
17:    inputFlipped.flip(); // toggle the bits
```

```
19:     cout << "Flipped version is: " << inputFlipped << endl;
20:
21:     cout << "Result of AND, OR and XOR between the two:" << endl;
22:     cout << inputBits << " & " << inputFlipped << " = ";
23:     cout << (inputBits & inputFlipped) << endl;  // bitwise AND
24:
25:     cout << inputBits << " | " << inputFlipped << " = ";
26:     cout << (inputBits | inputFlipped) << endl;  // bitwise OR
27:
28:     cout << inputBits << " ^ " << inputFlipped << " = ";
29:     cout << (inputBits ^ inputFlipped) << endl; // bitwise XOR
30:
31:     return 0;
32: }
```

Output ▼

```
Enter a 8-bit sequence: 10110101
Num 1s you supplied: 5
Num 0s you supplied: 3
Flipped version is: 01001010
Result of AND, OR and XOR between the two:
10110101 & 01001010 = 00000000
10110101 | 01001010 = 11111111
10110101 ^ 01001010 = 11111111
```

Analysis ▼

This interactive program demonstrates how easy it is to perform bitwise operations between two-bit sequences using `std::bitset`, and it also shows the utility of its `stream` operators. Shift operators (>> and <<) implemented by `std::bitset` make writing a bit sequence to the screen and reading a bit sequence from the user in string format a simple task. `inputBits` contains a user-supplied sequence that is fed into it in Line 10. `count()`, used in Line 12, tells the number of 1s in the sequence, and the number of 0s is evaluated as the difference between `size()`, which returns the number of bits in the bitset, and `count()`, as shown in Line 14. `inputFlipped` begins as a copy of `inputBits` and then is flipped using `flip()`, as shown in Line 17. It then contains the sequence with individual bits flipped—that is, toggled (so that 0s become 1s and vice versa). The rest of the program demonstrates the result of bitwise AND, OR, and XOR operations between the two bitsets.

NOTE

> bitset<> cannot resize itself dynamically. You can use a bitset only where the number of bits to be stored in the sequence is known at compile time.
>
> The STL supplies a programmer with the class vector<bool> (also called bit_vector in some implementations of STL) that overcomes this shortcoming.

The vector<bool> Class

The vector<bool> class is a partial specialization of std::vector and is intended for storing Boolean data. This class is able to dynamically size itself. Therefore, a programmer does not need to know the number of Boolean flags to be stored at compile time.

TIP

> To use the class std::vector<bool>, include the header <vector>:
>
> ```
> #include<vector>
> ```


Instantiating vector<bool>

Instantiating vector<bool> is similar to instantiating vector, with some convenient overloads:

```
vector<bool> boolFlags1;
```

For instance, you can create a vector with 10 Boolean values to start with, each initialized to 1 (that is, true):

```
vector<bool> boolFlags2(10, true);
```

You can also create an object as a copy of another:

```
vector<bool> boolFlags2Copy(boolFlags2);
```

Some of the instantiation techniques for vector<bool> are demonstrated in Listing 25.3.

Input ▼

LISTING 25.3 Instantiating vector<bool>

```
 0: #include<vector>
 1:
 2: int main()
 3: {
 4:     using namespace std;
 5:
 6:     // Instantiate an object using the default constructor
 7:     vector <bool> boolFlags1;
 8:
 9:     // Initialize a vector with 10 elements with value true
10:     vector <bool> boolFlags2(10, true);
11:
12:     // Instantiate one object as a copy of another
13:     vector <bool> boolFlags2Copy(boolFlags2);
14:
15:     return 0;
16: }
```

Output ▼

This code snippet produces no output.

Analysis ▼

This example presents some of the ways in which a vector<bool> object can be constructed. Line 7 uses the default constructor. Line 10 demonstrates the creation of an object that is initialized to contain 10 Boolean flags, each holding the value true. Line 13 demonstrates how one vector<bool> can be constructed as a copy of another.

vector<bool> Functions and Operators

The vector<bool> class features the function flip(), which toggles the state of the Boolean values in the sequence; its function is similar to that of bitset<>::flip().

Otherwise, the vector<bool> class is quite similar to std::vector in the sense that you can, for example, even push back flags into the sequence. Listing 25.4 demonstrates the use of the vector<bool> class in further detail.

Input ▼

LISTING 25.4 Using the vector<bool> Class

```
 0: #include<vector>
 1: #include<iostream>
 2: #include<algorithm>
 3: using namespace std;
 4:
 5: int main()
 6: {
 7:    vector<bool> boolFlags{ true, true, false }; // 3 bool flags
 8:    boolFlags [0] = true;
 9:    boolFlags [1] = true;
10:    boolFlags [2] = false;
11:
12:    boolFlags.push_back(true); // insert a fourth bool at the end
13:
14:    cout << "The contents of the vector are: " << endl;
15:    for (size_t index = 0; index < boolFlags.size(); ++ index)
16:       cout << boolFlags [index] << ' ';
17:
18:    cout << endl;
19:    boolFlags.flip();
20:
21:    cout << "The contents of the vector are: " << endl;
22:    for_each(boolFlags.cbegin(), boolFlags.cend(),
23:       [](const auto& b) {cout << b << ' '; });
24:
25:    cout << endl;
26:
27:    return 0;
28: }
```


Output ▼

```
The contents of the vector are:
1 1 0 1
The contents of the vector are:
0 0 1 0
```

Analysis ▼

In this example, the Boolean flags in the vector have been accessed using the operator `[]`, as shown in Lines 7 through 9, just the way a regular vector would be accessed. The function `flip()` in Line 18 toggles individual bit flags, essentially converting all `0`s to `1`s and vice versa. Note the use of `push_back()` in Line 11. Even though you initialize `boolFlags` to contain three flags in Line 6, you can add more to it dynamically in

Line 11. Adding more flags than the number specified at compile time is something you cannot do with `std::bitset`. Line 22 uses the `for_each()` algorithm instead of the `for` loop in Line 15 to display individual bits on the screen, thereby taking advantage of the iterator support provided by `vector<bool>`.

> **TIP**
>
> You can instantiate `boolFlags` in Listing 25.4 with initial values by using list initialization:
>
> ```
> vector <bool> boolFlags{ true, true, false };
> ```

Summary

In this lesson, you learned about the most effective tool for handling bit sequences and bit flags: the `std::bitset` class. You also gained knowledge about the `vector<bool>` class, which allows you to store Boolean flags—the number of which does not need to be known at compile time.

Q&A

Q Given a situation in which the number of bits to be stored is known, which of the two classes, `bitset` or `vector<bool>`, should I use to hold my binary flags?

A You should use `std::bitset` because it is best suited for this requirement.

Q I have a `std::bitset` object called `myBitSet` that contains a certain number of stored bits. How would I determine the number of bits that are at value `0` (or `false`)?

A `bitset::count()` supplies the number of bits at value `1`. This number, when subtracted from `bitset::size()` (which indicates the total number of bits stored), would give you the number of `0`s in the sequence.

Q Can I use iterators to access the individual elements in a `vector<bool>`?

A Yes. Because `vector<bool>` is a partial specialization of `std::vector`, iterators are supported, as demonstrated in Listing 25.4.

Q Can I specify the number of elements to be held in a `vector<bool>` at compile time?

A. Yes, you can specify the number of elements to be held in a `vector<bool>` at compile time by either specifying the number in the overloaded constructor or by using the `vector<bool>::resize()` function in a later instance.

Workshop

The Workshop provides quiz questions to help you solidify your understanding of the material covered and exercises to provide you with experience using what you've learned. Try to answer the quiz and exercise questions before checking the answers in Appendix E and be certain you understand the answers before continuing to the next lesson.

Quiz

1. Can a `bitset` expand its internal buffer to hold a variable number of elements?
2. Why is `bitset` not classified as an STL container class?
3. Would you use `std::vector` to hold a number of bits that is fixed and known at compile time?

Exercises

1. Write a `bitset` class that contains 4 bits. Initialize it to a number, display the result, and add it to another bitset object. (The catch: Bitsets don't allow bitsetA = bitsetX + bitsetY.)
2. Demonstrate how you would toggle (that is, switch) the bits in a bitset.

LESSON 26

Understanding Smart Pointers

C++ programmers do not necessarily need to use plain pointer types when managing memory on the heap (or the free store); they can make use of smart pointers.

In this lesson, you learn

- What smart pointers are and why you need them
- How smart pointers are implemented
- Different smart pointer types
- Why you should not use the deprecated `std::auto_ptr`
- The C++ Standard Library smart pointer `std::unique_ptr`
- Popular smart pointer libraries

What Are Smart Pointers?

Put simply, a *smart pointer* is a class that uses overloaded operators to help you use it like a conventional pointer. However, it adds value by ensuring proper and timely destruction of dynamically allocated data and facilitates a well-defined object life cycle.

The Problem with Using Conventional (Raw) Pointers

Unlike other programming languages, C++ supplies full flexibility in terms of memory allocation, deallocation, and management. Unfortunately, this flexibility is a double-edged sword. On one side, it makes C++ a powerful language, but on the other, it requires a programmer to meticulously manage memory and resources. Without rigorous management, problems such as memory leaks crop up. These can be difficult to diagnose and fix, and are best avoided at the outset.

Consider this example:

```
SomeClass* ptrData = anObject.GetData();
/*
   Questions: Is object pointed by ptrData dynamically allocated using new?
   If so, who calls delete? Caller or the called?
   Answer: No idea!
*/
ptrData->DoSomething();
```

In this code, there is no obvious way to tell whether the memory pointed to by `ptrData`

- Was allocated on the heap and, therefore, eventually needs to be deallocated
- Should be deallocated by the caller
- Will automatically be destroyed by the object's destructor

Although such ambiguities can be partially solved by inserting comments and enforcing good coding practices, these mechanisms are much too loose to efficiently prevent all errors related to abuse of dynamically allocated data and pointers.

How Do Smart Pointers Help?

As you have already seen in this lesson, there are problems with using conventional pointers and memory management techniques. However, as a C++ programmer, you are not forced to use those pointers and techniques when you need to manage data on the heap/free store. You can choose a smarter way to allocate and manage dynamic data—by adopting the use of smart pointers in your programs:

```
smart_pointer<SomeClass> spData = anObject.GetData();

// Use a smart pointer like a conventional pointer!
spData->Display();
(*spData).Display();

// Don't have to worry about de-allocation
// (the smart pointer's destructor does it for you)
```

Smart pointers behave like conventional pointers (which we can call *raw pointers*), but smart pointers supply useful features via their *overloaded operators* and *destructors* to ensure that dynamically allocated data is destroyed in a timely manner.

How Are Smart Pointers Implemented?

This question can for the moment be simplified to ask specifically about the example in the preceding section: "How did the smart pointer `spData` function like a conventional pointer?" The answer is this: Smart pointer classes overload the dereferencing operator (*) and the member selection operator (->) so that you can use them as conventional pointers. (Operator overloading was discussed previously in Lesson 12, "Operator Types and Operator Overloading.")

In addition, a smart pointer class is typically a template class that contains a generic implementation of its functionality. As template classes, these classes are versatile and can be specialized to manage objects of any type.

Listing 26.1 shows a sample implementation of a simple smart pointer class.

Input ▼

LISTING 26.1 The Minimal Essential Components of a Smart Pointer Class

```
template <typename T>
class smart_pointer
{
private:
    T* rawPtr;
public:
    smart_pointer(T* pData) : rawPtr(pData) {}  // constructor
    ~smart_pointer() {delete rawPtr;};            // destructor

    // copy constructor
    smart_pointer(const smart_pointer & anotherSP);
    // copy assignment operator
    smart_pointer& operator=(const smart_pointer& anotherSP);

    T& operator*() const    // dereferencing operator
    {
        return *(rawPtr);
    }

    T* operator->() const    // member selection operator
    {
        return rawPtr;
    }
};
```


Output ▼

This code snippet produces no output.

Analysis ▼

This example illustrates the implementation of the two operators * and ->, as declared in Lines 14 through 17 and 19 through 22, which help this class function as a pointer in the conventional sense. For instance, to use the smart pointer on an object of the class Tuna, you would instantiate it like this:

```
smart_pointer<Tuna> smartTuna(new Tuna);
smartTuna->Swim();
// Alternatively:
(*smartTuna).Swim();
```

This class smart_pointer doesn't display or implement any functionality that would make this pointer class very smart or make using it more beneficial than using a conventional pointer. The constructor, as shown in Line 6, accepts a pointer that is saved as the internal pointer object in the smart_pointer class. The destructor frees this pointer, allowing for automatic memory release.

NOTE

The implementations that make a smart pointer really "smart" are the implementations of the copy constructor, the assignment operator, and the destructor. They determine the behavior of the smart pointer object when it is passed across functions, when it is assigned, or when it goes out of scope (that is, gets destroyed). So, before looking at a complete smart pointer implementation, you should understand some smart pointer types.

Types of Smart Pointers

The management of a memory resource (that is, the ownership model implemented) is what sets smart pointer classes apart. Smart pointers decide what they do with a resource when they are copied and assigned to it. The simplest implementations often result in performance issues, but the fastest ones might not suit all applications. It is therefore important that you understand how smart pointers function before you use them.

Smart pointers are classified on the basis of their memory resource management strategies:

- Deep copy
- Copy on write (COW)
- Reference counted

- Reference linked
- Destructive copy

Let's take a brief look at each of these strategies before studying the smart pointer supplied by the C++ Standard Library: `std::unique_ptr`.

Deep Copy

In a smart pointer that implements deep copy, every smart pointer instance holds a complete copy of the object that is being managed. Whenever the smart pointer is copied, the object pointed to is also copied (hence the term *deep copy*). When the smart pointer goes out of scope, it releases the memory it points to (via the destructor).

Although a deep-copy smart pointer does not seem to be useful when passing objects by value, its advantage becomes apparent in the treatment of polymorphic objects, where it can avoid slicing, as shown here:

```
// Example of Slicing When Passing Polymorphic Objects by Value
// Fish is a base class for Tuna and Carp, Fish::Swim() is virtual
void MakeFishSwim(Fish aFish)    // attention: parameter type
{
    aFish.Swim(); // virtual function
}

// ... Some function
Carp freshWaterFish;
MakeFishSwim(freshWaterFish);  // Carp will be 'sliced' to Fish
// Slicing: only the Fish part of Carp is copied and passed

Tuna marineFish;
MakeFishSwim(marineFish); // Slicing again
```


You can resolve slicing issues by choosing a deep-copy smart pointer, as shown in Listing 26.2.

Input ▼

LISTING 26.2 Using a Deep-Copy Smart Pointer to Pass Polymorphic Objects by Their Base Types

```
template <typename T>
class deepcopy_smart_ptr
{
private:
    T* object;
public:
```

```
 6:     //... other functions
 7:
 8:     // copy constructor of the deepcopy pointer
 9:     deepcopy_smart_ptr(const deepcopy_smart_ptr& source)
10:     {
11:         // Clone() is virtual: ensures deep copy of Derived class object
12:         object = source->Clone();
13:     }
14:
15:    // copy assignment operator
16:     deepcopy_smart_ptr& operator=(const deepcopy_smart_ptr& source)
17:     {
18:       if(object)
19:          delete object;
20:
21:       object = source->Clone();
22:     }
23: };
```

Output ▼

This code snippet produces no output.

Analysis ▼

As you can see, `deepcopy_smart_ptr` implements a copy constructor in Lines 9 through 13 that enables a deep copy of the polymorphic object via the `Clone()` function, which the class needs to implement. Similarly, it implements a copy assignment operator in Lines 16 through 22. For the sake of simplicity, we assume in this example that the virtual function implemented by the base class `Fish` is called `Clone()`. Typically, smart pointers that implement deep-copy models have this function supplied as either a template parameter or a function object.

Thus, the smart pointer is passed as a pointer to base class type `Fish`:

```
deepcopy_smart_ptr<Carp> freshWaterFish(new Carp);
MakeFishSwim(freshWaterFish);  // Carp will not be 'sliced'
```

The deep copy implemented in the smart pointer's constructor kicks in to ensure that the object being passed is not sliced, even though syntactically only the base part of it is required by the destination function `MakeFishSwim()`.

The disadvantage of the deep-copy mechanism is performance. This might not be a factor for some applications, but for many others, it might inhibit the programmer from using a smart pointer for the application. Instead, the programmer might simply pass a base type pointer (conventional pointer, `Fish*`) to functions such as `MakeFishSwim()`. Other pointer types try to address this performance issue in various ways.

Copy on Write

Copy on write (*COW*, as it is popularly called) is a mechanism that attempts to optimize the performance of deep-copy smart pointers by sharing pointers until the first attempt at writing to the object is made. On the first attempt at invoking a non-`const` function, a COW pointer typically creates a copy of the object on which the non-`const` function is invoked, whereas other instances of the pointer continue sharing the source object.

COW has its fair share of fans. For those who swear by COW, implementing the operators `*` and `->` in their `const` and non-`const` versions is key to the functionality of the COW pointer. The latter creates a copy.

TIP

> When you choose a pointer implementation that follows the COW philosophy, be sure that you understand the implementation details before you proceed to use the implementation. Otherwise, you might land in a situation where you have a copy too few or a copy too many.

Reference-Counted Smart Pointers

Reference counting is a mechanism that keeps a count of the number of users of an object. When the count reduces to zero, the object is released. Reference counting is a very good mechanism for sharing objects without having to copy them.

Such smart pointers, when copied, need to have the reference count of the object in question incremented. There are at least two popular ways to keep this count:

- Reference count maintained in the object being pointed to
- Reference count maintained by the pointer class in a shared object

The first variant, where the reference count is maintained in the object, is called *intrusive reference counting* because the object needs to be modified. The object in this case maintains, increments, and supplies the reference count to any smart pointer class that manages it. The second variant, where the reference count is maintained in a shared object, is a mechanism where the smart pointer class can keep the reference count on the free store (a dynamically allocated integer, for example) and, when copied, the copy constructor increments this value.

The reference-counting mechanism requires you to work with smart pointers only and does not rely on any raw pointer copies. A raw pointer pointing to an object that is being managed by a reference-counted smart pointer can cause problems when the smart pointer releases the object. The raw pointer continues pointing to the part of the memory that is no longer valid. Similarly, reference counting can cause issues peculiar to their situation: Two objects that hold a pointer to each other are never released because their cyclic dependency holds their reference counts at a minimum of 1.

TIP

`std::shared_ptr` is a popular reference-counted smart pointer that retains shared ownership of the object being pointed to (that is, managed). `std::weak_ptr` is often used in tandem with `shared_ptr`. `weak_ptr` holds a weak reference to the object—that is, it can be used to view the object but not to execute operations that require ownership. Consequently, an object being observed through a `weak_ptr` may be deleted by anyone else. To gain temporary ownership of the object, the `weak_ptr` must be converted into a `shared_ptr` first.

Reference-Linked Smart Pointers

Reference-linked smart pointers are smart pointers that don't proactively count the number of references using the object; rather, they just need to know when the number comes down to zero so that the object can be released.

These smart pointers are called *reference linked* because their implementation is based on a double-linked list. When you create a new smart pointer by copying an existing one, the copy is appended to the list. When a smart pointer goes out of scope or is destroyed, the destructor de-indexes the smart pointer from this list. Reference linking also suffers from the problem caused by cyclic dependency that also affects reference-counted pointers.

Destructive Copy

Destructive copy is a mechanism whereby a smart pointer, when copied, transfers complete ownership of the object being handled to the destination and resets itself:

```
destructive_copy_smartptr<SampleClass> smartPtr(new SampleClass());

SomeFunc(smartPtr);     // Ownership transferred to SomeFunc
// Don't use smartPtr in the caller any more!
```

This mechanism is obviously not intuitive to use. Howev... e adva... tive copy smart pointers is that they ensure that at any point in time, only one active p... points to an object. So, destructive copy is a good mechanism for returning pointers from functions, and you can use the "destructive" properties of smart pointers to your advantage.

The implementation of destructive copy pointers deviates from the implementation of other pointers, as shown in Listing 26.3.

CAUTION

> `std::auto_ptr` is by far the most popular (or notorious, depending on how you look at it) pointer that follows the principles of destructive copy. Such a smart pointer is useless after it has been passed to a function or copied into another pointer.
>
> `std::auto_ptr` was deprecated in C++11. Use `std::unique_ptr` instead.

Input ▼

LISTING 26.3 A Sample Destructive Copy Smart Pointer

```
template <typename T>
class destructivecopy_ptr
{
private:
   T* object;
public:
   destructivecopy_ptr(T* input):object(input) {}
   ~destructivecopy_ptr() { delete object; }

   // copy constructor
   destructivecopy_ptr(destructivecopy_ptr& source)
   {
      // Take ownership on copy
      object = source.object;

      // destroy source
      source.object = 0;
   }

   // copy assignment operator
   destructivecopy_ptr& operator=(destructivecopy_ptr& source)
   {
      if(object != source.object)
      {
         delete object;
         object = source.object;
         source.object = 0;
      }
   }
```

```
29: };
30:
31: int main()
32: {
33:     destructivecopy_ptr<int> num(new int);
34:     destructivecopy_ptr<int> copy = num;
35:
36:     // num is now invalid
37:     return 0;
38: }
```

Output ▼

This code snippet produces no output.

Analysis ▼

Listing 26.3 demonstrates the implementation of a destructive-copy smart pointer. Lines 10 through 17 and 20 through 28 contain the copy constructor and the copy assignment operator, respectively. These functions invalidate the source when making a copy; that is, the copy constructor sets the pointer contained by the source to `NULL` after copying it—hence the name *destructive copy*. The assignment operator does the same thing. Thus, `num` is actually invalidated in Line 34 when it is assigned to another pointer. This behavior is counterintuitive to the act of assignment.

CAUTION

The copy constructor and copy assignment operators that are critical to the implementation of destructive-copy smart pointers as shown in Listing 26.3 also attract a lot of criticism. Unlike most C++ classes, this smart pointer class cannot have the copy constructor and assignment operator accept `const` references, as it needs to invalidate the source after copying it. This is a deviation from traditional copy-constructor and assignment-operator semantics, and it also makes using the smart pointer class counterintuitive. Few programmers expect the copy source or the assignment source to be damaged after a copy or assignment step. The fact that such smart pointers destroy the source also makes them unsuitable for use in STL containers such as `std::vector`, or any other dynamic collection class that you might use. These containers need to copy your content internally and end up invalidating the pointers.

So, for more than one reason, you are advised to avoid using destructive-copy smart pointers in your programs.

TIP

> Use `std::unique_ptr` instead of the deprecated `std::auto_ptr`. However, note that `std::unique_ptr` cannot be passed by value due to its private copy constructor and copy assignment operator. It can only be passed as a reference argument.

Using `std::unique_ptr`

`std::unique_ptr` was introduced in C++11, and is different from `auto_ptr` in the sense that it does not allow copy or assignment.

TIP

> To use the class `std::unique_ptr`, include this header:
>
> `#include<memory>`

`unique_ptr` is a simple smart pointer similar to what's shown in Listing 26.1, but with an explicitly deleted (that is, disabled) copy constructor and assignment operator. Therefore, it's not possible to create a copy when passing as an argument to a function by value or via assignment. Listing 26.4 demonstrates the use of `unique_ptr`.

Input ▼

LISTING 26.4 Using `std::unique_ptr`

```
#include<iostream>
#include<memory>  // include this to use std::unique_ptr
using namespace std;

class Fish
{
public:
    Fish() {cout << "Fish: Constructed!" << endl;}
    ~Fish() {cout << "Fish: Destructed!" << endl;}

    void Swim() const {cout << "Fish swims in water" << endl;}
};

void MakeFishSwim(const unique_ptr<Fish>& inFish)
{
   inFish->Swim();
}

```

```
18: int main()
19: {
20:     unique_ptr<Fish> smartFish(new Fish);
21:
22:     smartFish->Swim();
23:     MakeFishSwim(smartFish); // OK, as MakeFishSwim accepts reference
24:
25:     unique_ptr<Fish> copySmartFish;
26:     // copySmartFish = smartFish; // error: operator= is disabled
27:
28:     return 0;
29: }
```

Output ▼

```
Fish: Constructed!
Fish swims in watersw
Fish swims in water
Fish: Destructed!
```

Analysis ▼

Follow the construction and destruction sequence, which is visible in the output. Note that even though the object pointed to by `smartFish` was constructed in `main()`, as expected, it was destroyed (and automatically so) even without your having invoked the operator `delete`. This is the behavior of `unique_ptr`: The pointer that goes out of scope releases the object on its own via the destructor. Note in Line 23 how you can pass `smartFish` as an argument to `MakeFishSwim()`. This is not a copy step because `MakeFishSwim()` accepts the parameter by reference, as shown in Line 13. If you were to remove the reference symbol `&` from Line 13, you would immediately encounter a compile error caused by the private copy constructor. Similarly, assignment of one `unique_ptr` object to another, as shown in Line 26, is not permitted due to a private copy assignment operator.

In a nutshell, `unique_ptr` is safer to use than `auto_ptr` as it does not invalidate the source smart pointer object during a copy or an assignment. However, it allows simple memory management by releasing the object at the time of destruction.

TIP

Listing 26.4 demonstrates that `unique_ptr` doesn't support copy:

```
copySmartFish = smartFish; // error: operator= is
private
```

It does, however, support move semantics. Therefore, an option that would work is

```
unique_ptr<Fish> sameFish(std::move(smartFish));
// smartFish is empty henceforth
```

If you were to write a lambda expression that needed to capture `unique_ptr`, you would use the `std::move()` function (introduced in C++14) in your lambda capture:

```
std::unique_ptr<char> alphabet(new char);
*alphabet = 's';
auto lambda = [capture = std::move(alphabet)]() {
std::cout << *capture << endl; };

// alphabet is empty as contents have been 'moved'

lambda();
```

Don't be frustrated if the preceding code seems too exotic; it is complicated and covers a use case that most professional programmers would possibly never come across.

TIP

When programming multithreaded applications, use `std::shared_ptr` together with `std::atomic<T>` for thread-safe operations on shared data. C++20 introduces partial template specialization via `std::atomic<std::shared_ptr<T> >` for thread-safe object sharing using a smart pointer.

Popular Smart Pointer Libraries

It's pretty apparent that the version of the smart pointer shipped with the C++ Standard Library is not going to meet every programmer's requirements. This is precisely why there are many smart pointer libraries out there.

Boost (www.boost.org) supplies some well-tested and well-documented smart pointer classes, among many other useful utility classes. You can find information on Boost smart pointers and downloads at http://www.boost.org/libs/smart_ptr/smart_ptr.htm.

DO	DON'T
DO use smart pointer classes to manage memory and resources.	**DON'T** use deprecated smart pointers such as the `std::auto_ptr`. Use `std::unique_ptr` instead.

Summary

In this lesson, you learned the basics of smart pointers. You saw how using the right smart pointers can help reduce allocation and object ownership–related problems. You also explored the different smart pointer types and learned that it is important to know the behavior of a smart pointer class before adopting it in an application. You now know that you should not use `std::auto_ptr` as it invalidates the source during a copy or an assignment. You also learned about smart pointer classes such as `std::unique_ptr`.

Q&A

Q I need a vector of pointers. Should I choose `auto_ptr` as the object type to be held in the vector?

A As a rule, you should never use `std::auto_ptr`. It has been deprecated. A single copy or assignment operation can render the source object unusable.

Q What two operators does a class always need to load in order to be called a smart pointer class?

A A class always need to load the operators `*` and `->`. They help use objects of the class with regular pointer semantics.

Q I have an application in which `Class1` and `Class2` each hold member attributes that point to objects of the other's type. Should I use a reference-counted pointer in this scenario?

A You probably shouldn't do this because of the cyclic dependency that will keep the reference count from going down to zero and that will consequently keep objects of the two classes permanently in the heap.

Q A string class dynamically manages character arrays on the free store. Is a string class therefore a smart pointer, too?

A No, it isn't. A string class typically doesn't implement the operators `*` and `->` and therefore cannot be classified as a smart pointer.

Workshop

The Workshop provides quiz questions to help you solidify your understanding of the material covered and exercises to provide you with experience using what you've learned. Try to answer the quiz and exercise questions before checking the answers in Appendix E and be certain you understand the answers before continuing to the next lesson.

Quiz

1. Where would you look before writing your own smart pointer for an application?
2. Would a smart pointer slow down an application significantly?
3. Where can reference-counted smart pointers hold the reference count data?
4. Should the linked list mechanism used by reference-linked pointers be singly or doubly linked?

Exercises

1. **BUG BUSTERS:** What is the error in the following code?

```
std::auto_ptr<SampleClass> object(new SampleClass());
std::auto_ptr<SampleClass> anotherObject(object);
object->DoSomething();
anotherObject->DoSomething();
```

2. Use the `unique_ptr` class to instantiate a `Carp` that inherits from `Fish`. Pass the object as a `Fish` pointer and comment on slicing, if any.
3. **BUG BUSTERS:** What is the error in the following code?

```
std::unique_ptr<Tuna> myTuna(new Tuna);
unique_ptr<Tuna> copyTuna;
copyTuna = myTuna;
```

LESSON 27
Using Streams for Input and Output

You have actually been using streams all through this book, starting with Lesson 1, "Getting Started," in which you displayed "Hello World" on the screen by using `std::cout`. It's time to give this part of C++ its due attention and examine streams from a practical point of view.

In this lesson, you find out

- What streams are and how they are used
- How to write to and read from files by using streams
- Useful C++ stream operations

The Concept of Streams

Say that you are developing a program that reads from the disk, writes data to the display, reads user input from the keyboard, and saves data on the disk. Wouldn't it be useful if you could treat all read activities and write activities using similar patterns, regardless of what device or location the data is coming from or going to? This is exactly what C++ streams offer you!

Streams offer a consistent way of programming read and write logic (in other words, input and output). You use the same stream syntax in reading data from the disk as you would in accepting user input from the keyboard. Similarly, you use the same stream syntax in writing data to the display as you would in writing data to the disk. You need to use the right stream class, and the implementation within the class takes care of device- and OS-specific details.

To see how streams work, we can refer to a relevant line from your first C++ program, Listing 1.1 in Lesson 1:

```
std::cout << "Hello World!" << std::endl;
```

That's right: `std::cout` is a stream object of the class `ostream` for console output. To use `std::cout` in Listing 1.1, you included the header `<iostream>`, which supplies this and other functionality, such as `std::cin`, which enables you to read from a stream.

So, what do I mean when I say that streams allow consistent and device-specific access? If you were to write `"Hello World!"` to a text file, you would use this syntax on the file stream object `fsHello`:

```
fsHello << "Hello World!" << endl;  // "Hello World!" into a file stream
```

As you can see, after you've chosen the right stream class in C++, writing `"Hello World!"` to a file isn't too different from writing it to the display.

TIP

> The operator `<<`, which you use when writing into a stream, is called the *stream insertion operator*. You use it when writing to the display, to a file, and so on.
>
> The operator `>>`, which you use when writing a stream into a variable, is called the *stream extraction operator*. You use it when reading input from the keyboard, from a file, and so on.

In this lesson, you study streams from a practical point of view.

Important C++ Stream Classes and Objects

C++ provides a set of standard classes and headers that help you perform some important and commonly used I/O operations. Table 27.1 lists commonly used C++ stream classes.

TABLE 27.1 Commonly Used C++ Stream Classes in the `std` Namespace

Class/Object	Description
`Cout`	Standard output stream, typically redirected to the console
`Cin`	Standard input stream, typically used to read data into variables
`Cerr`	Standard output stream for errors
`Fstream`	Input and output stream class for file operations; inherits from `ofstream` and `ifstream`

Class/Object	Description
`Ofstream`	Output stream class for file operations—that is, used to create files
`Ifstream`	Input stream class for file operations—that is, used to read files
`Stringsstream`	Input and output stream class for string operations; inherits from `istringstream` and `ostringstream`; typically used to perform conversions from (or to) string and other types

NOTE

`cout`, `cin`, and `cerr` are global objects of the stream classes `ostream`, `istream`, and `ostream`, respectively. As global objects, they're initialized before `main()` starts.

When using a stream class, you have the option of specifying manipulators that perform specific actions for you. `std::endl` is one such manipulator that you have been using throughout this book to insert a newline character:

```
std::cout  << "This lines ends here" << std::endl;
```

Table 27.2 describes a few other manipulators.

TABLE 27.2 Frequently Used Manipulators in the `std` Namespace for Working with Streams

Manipulator	Description
Output Manipulators	
`Endl`	Inserts a newline character and flushes the stream buffer
`Ends`	Inserts a null character
Radix Manipulators	
`Dec`	Instructs a stream to interpret input or display output in decimal
`Hex`	Instructs a stream to interpret input or display output in hexadecimal
`Oct`	Instructs a stream to interpret input or display output in octal
Representation Manipulators	
`Fixed`	Instructs a stream to display in fixed-point notation

27

Manipulator	Description
`Scientific`	Instructs a stream to display in scientific notation
Manipulators Supplied by Header `<iomanip>`	
`Setprecision`	Sets decimal point precision as a parameter
`Setw`	Sets field width as a parameter
`Setfill`	Sets fill character as a parameter
`Setbase`	Sets the radix/base, akin to using `dec`, `hex`, or `oct` as a parameter
`Setiosflag`	Sets flags via a mask input parameter of type `std::ios_base::fmtflags`
`Resetiosflag`	Restores defaults for a particular type specified by the type contained in `std::ios_base::fmtflags`

Using `std::cout` for Writing Formatted Data to the Console

`std::cout`, which you use for writing to the standard output stream, is possibly the most used stream in this book thus far. It's time to revisit `cout` and use some manipulators to change the way you align and display data.

Changing the Display Number Format by Using `std::cout`

It is possible to ask `cout` to display an integer in hexadecimal notation or in octal notation. Listing 27.1 demonstrates the use of `cout` to display an input number in various formats.

Input ▼

LISTING 27.1 Displaying an Integer in Decimal, Octal, and Hexadecimal Formats by Using `cout` and the `<iomanip>` Flag

```
#include<iostream>
#include<iomanip>
using namespace std;

int main()
```

```
 5: {
 6:     cout << "Enter an integer: ";
 7:     int input = 0;
 8:     cin >> input;
 9:
10:     cout << "Integer in octal: " << oct << input << endl;
11:     cout << "Integer in hexadecimal: " << hex << input << endl;
12:
13:     cout << "Integer in hex using base notation: ";
14:     cout <<setiosflags(ios_base::hex|ios_base::showbase|ios_base::uppercase);
15:     cout << input << endl;
16:
17:     cout << "Integer after resetting I/O flags: ";
18:     cout <<resetiosflags(ios_base::hex|ios_base::showbase|
        ios_base::uppercase);
19:     cout << input << endl;
20:
21:     return 0;
22: }
```

Output ▼

```
Enter an integer: 253
Integer in octal: 375
Integer in hexadecimal: fd
Integer in hex using base notation: 0XFD
Integer after resetting I/O flags: 253
```

Analysis ▼

This example uses the manipulators presented in Table 27.2 to change the way `cout` displays the same integer object `input` that is supplied by the user. Note how the manipulators `oct` and `hex` are used in Lines 10 and 11. In Line 14, you tell `setiosflags()` to display the numbers in hex, using uppercase letters, resulting in `cout` displaying the integer input `253` as `0XFD`. The effect of `resetioflags()` used in Line 18 is demonstrated by the integer being displayed by `cout` using decimal notation again.

Another way to change the radix used in displaying integer to decimal would be the following:

```
cout << dec << input << endl;  // displays in decimal
```

It is also possible to format the manner in which `cout` displays numbers such as pi: You can specify the precision by using fixed-point notation to indicate the number of places after the decimal to show, or you can display a number using scientific notation. This and more is demonstrated by Listing 27.2.

Input ▼

LISTING 27.2 Using `cout` to Display Pi and a Circle's Area Using Fixed-Point and Scientific Notations

```
#include<iostream>
#include<iomanip>
using namespace std;

int main()
{
    const double Pi = (double)22.0 / 7;
    cout << "Pi = " << Pi << endl;

    cout << endl << "Setting precision to 7: " << endl;
    cout << setprecision(7);
    cout << "Pi = " << Pi << endl;
    cout << fixed << "Fixed Pi = " << Pi << endl;
    cout << scientific << "Scientific Pi = " << Pi << endl;

    cout << endl << "Setting precision to 10: " << endl;
    cout << setprecision(10);
    cout << "Pi = " << Pi << endl;
    cout << fixed << "Fixed Pi = " << Pi << endl;
    cout << scientific << "Scientific Pi = " << Pi << endl;

    cout << endl << "Enter a radius: ";
    double radius = 0.0;
    cin >> radius;
    cout << "Area of circle: " << 2*Pi*radius*radius << endl;

    return 0;
}
```

Output ▼

```
Pi = 3.14286

Setting precision to 7:
Pi = 3.142857
Fixed Pi = 3.1428571
Scientific Pi = 3.1428571e+000

Setting precision to 10:
Pi = 3.1428571429e+000
Fixed Pi = 3.1428571429
```

```
Scientific Pi = 3.1428571429e+000

Enter a radius: 9.99
Area of circle: 6.2731491429e+002
```

Analysis ▼

The output demonstrates how increasing the precision to 7 in Line 10 and to 10 in Line 16 changes the display of the value of pi. Also note how the manipulator `scientific` results in the calculated area of the circle being displayed as `6.2731491429e+002`.

Aligning Text and Setting Field Width by Using `std::cout`

You can use manipulators such as `setw()` to set the width of a field, in characters. Then, any insertion made to the stream is right-aligned in the specified width. Similarly, you can use `setfill()` to determine what character fills the empty area in such a situation, as demonstrated in Listing 27.3.

Input ▼

LISTING 27.3 Setting the Width of a Field via `setw()` and the Fill Characters by Using `setfill()` Manipulators

```
#include<iostream>
#include<iomanip>
using namespace std;

int main()
{
    cout << "Hey - default!" << endl;

    cout << setw(35);  // set field width to 25 columns
    cout << "Hey - right aligned!" << endl;

    cout << setw(35) << setfill('*');
    cout << "Hey - right aligned!" << endl;

    cout << "Hey - back to default!" << endl;

    return 0;
}
```

Output ▼

```
Hey - default!
               Hey - right aligned!
***************Hey - right aligned!
Hey - back to default!
```

Analysis ▼

The output demonstrates the effect of `setw(35)` supplied to `cout` in Line 8 and `setfill('*')` supplied together with `setw(35)` in Line 11. You see that the latter results in the free space preceding the text being displayed with asterisks, as specified in `setfill()`.

Using `std::cin` for Input

`std::cin` is versatile and enables you to read input into the plain old data types, such as `int`, `double`, and `char*`, and you can also read lines or characters from the screen by using methods such as `getline()`.

Using `std::cin` for Input into a Plain Old Data Type

You can feed integers, doubles, and chars directly from the standard input via `cin`. Listing 27.4 demonstrates the use of `cin` in reading simple data types from the user.

Input ▼

LISTING 27.4 Using `cin` to Read Input into an `int`, a Floating-Point Number Using Scientific Notation into a `double`, and Three Letters into a `char`

```
#include<iostream>
using namespace std;

int main()
{
   cout << "Enter an integer: ";
   int inputNum = 0;
   cin >> inputNum;

   cout << "Enter the value of Pi: ";
   double Pi = 0.0;
   cin >> Pi;

   cout << "Enter three characters separated by space: " << endl;
   char char1 = '\0', char2 = '\0', char3 = '\0';
```

```
15:     cin >> char1 >> char2 >> char3;
16:
17:     cout << "The recorded variable values are: " << endl;
18:     cout << "inputNum: " << inputNum << endl;
19:     cout << "Pi: " << Pi << endl;
20:     cout << "The three characters: " << char1 << char2 << char3 << endl;
21:
22:     return 0;
23: }
```

Output ▼

```
Enter an integer: 32
Enter the value of Pi: 0.314159265e1
Enter three characters separated by space:
c + +
The recorded variable values are:
inputNum: 32
Pi: 3.14159
The three characters: c++
```

Analysis ▼

The most interesting part about Listing 27.4 is that you entered the value of pi using exponential notation, which is reflected in the output, and `cin` fills that data into `double Pi`. Note that you can fill three-character variables within a single line, as shown in Line 15.

Using `std::cin::get` for Input into the `char*` Buffer

Just as `cin` allows you to write directly into an `int`, you can do the same with a C-style `char` array:

```
cout << "Enter a line: " << endl;
char charBuf[10]; // can contain max 10 chars
cin >> charBuf;    // Danger: user may enter more than 10 chars
```


When writing into a C-style string buffer, it is very important not to exceed the bounds of the buffer to avoid a crash or a security vulnerability. So, a better way of reading into a C-style `char` buffer is this:

```
cout << "Enter a line: " << endl;
char charBuf[10] = {0};
cin.get(charBuf, 9);  // stop inserting at the 9th character
```

Listing 27.5 demonstrates this safer way of inserting text into a C-style buffer.

Input ▼

LISTING 27.5 Inserting Text into a `char` Buffer Without Exceeding Its Bounds

```
 0: #include<iostream>
 1: #include<string>
 2: using namespace std;
 3:
 4: int main()
 5: {
 6:     cout << "Enter a line: " << endl;
 7:     char charBuf[10];
 8:     cin.get(charBuf, 10);
 9:     cout << "charBuf: " << charBuf << endl;
10:
11:     return 0;
12: }
```

Output ▼

```
Enter a line:
Testing if I can cross the bounds of the buffer
charBuf: Testing i
```

Analysis ▼

As the output indicates, in this case you only take the first nine characters input by the user into the `char` buffer due to the use of `cin::get` in Line 8. This is the safest way to deal with buffers of a given length.

> **TIP**
>
> If possible, don't use `char` arrays at all! Use `std::string` instead of `char*` or `char[]`.

Using `std::cin` for Input into `std::string`

`cin` is a versatile tool, and you can even use it to scan a string from a user directly into a `std::string`:

```
std::string input;
cin >> input;  // stops insertion at the first space
```

Listing 27.6 demonstrates using `cin` for input into `std::string`.

Input ▼

LISTING 27.6 Inserting Text into `std::string` by Using `cin`

```
#include<iostream>
#include<string>
using namespace std;

int main()
{
   cout << "Enter your name: ";
   string name;
   cin >> name;
   cout << "Hi " << name << endl;

   return 0;
}
```

Output ▼

```
Enter your name: Siddhartha Rao
Hi Siddhartha
```

Analysis ▼

The output perhaps surprises you as it displays only my first name and not the entire input string. So what happened? Apparently, `cin` stops insertion when it encounters the first whitespace.

To allow a user to enter a complete line, including spaces, you need to use `getline()`:

```
string name;
getline(cin, name);
```

This use of `getline()` with `cin` is demonstrated in Listing 27.7.

Input ▼

LISTING 27.7 Reading a Complete Line Input by a User by Using `getline()` and `cin`

```
#include<iostream>
#include<string>
using namespace std;

int main()
{
   cout << "Enter your name: ";
   string name;
```

```
 8:     getline(cin, name);
 9:     cout << "Hi " << name << endl;
10:
11:     return 0;
12: }
```

Output ▼

```
Enter your name: Siddhartha Rao
Hi Siddhartha Rao
```

Analysis ▼

`getline()`, as shown in Line 8, does the job of ensuring that whitespace characters are not skipped. The output now contains the complete line fed by the user.

Using `std::fstream` for File Handling

`std:fstream` is a class that C++ provides for (relatively) platform-independent file access. `std::fstream` inherits from `std::ofstream` for writing a file and `std::ifstream` for reading one.

In other words, `std::fstream` provides you with both read and write functionality.

TIP

To use the class `std::fstream` or its base classes, include this header:

```
#include<fstream>
```

Opening and Closing a File Using `open()` and `close()`

To use an `fstream`, `ofstream`, or `ifstream` class, you need to open a file by using the method `open()`:

```
fstream myFile;
myFile.open("HelloFile.txt",ios_base::in|ios_base::out|ios_base::trunc);

if(myFile.is_open()) // check if open() succeeded
{
   // do reading or writing here

   myFile.close();
}
```

`open()` takes two arguments. The first is the path and name of the file being opened. (If you don't supply a path, it assumes the current directory settings for the application.) The second argument is the mode in which the file is being opened. The modes chosen enable the file to be created even if one exists (`ios_base::trunc`) and allow you to read and write into the file (`in | out`).

Note the use of `is_open()` to test whether `open()` succeeded.

CAUTION

Closing a stream by using `close()` is essential to saving a file. There is an alternative way of opening a file stream, which is via the constructor:

```
fstream myFile("HelloFile.txt",
ios_base::in|ios_base::out|ios_base::trunc);
```

Alternatively, if you want to open a file for writing only, use the following:

```
ofstream myFile("HelloFile.txt", ios_base::out);
```

If you want to open a file for reading, use this:

```
ifstream myFile("HelloFile.txt", ios_base::in);
```

TIP

Regardless of whether you use the constructor or the member method `open()`, it is recommended that you check for the successful opening of the file by using `is_open()` before continuing to use the corresponding file stream object.

A file stream can be opened in various modes:

- **`ios_base::app`:** Appends to the end of existing files rather than truncating them
- **`ios_base::ate`:** Places you at the end of the file, but you can write data anywhere in the file
- **`ios_base::trunc`:** Causes existing files to be truncated; this is the default
- **`ios_base::binary`:** Creates a binary file; the default is text

- **`ios_base::in`:** Opens a file for read operations only
- **`ios_base::out`:** Opens a file for write operations only

Creating and Writing a Text File by Using `open()` and the Operator `<<`

After you have opened a file stream, you can write to it using insertion operator `<<`, as Listing 27.8 demonstrates.

Input ▼

LISTING 27.8 Creating a New Text File and Writing Text into It by Using `ofstream`

```
#include<fstream>
#include<iostream>
using namespace std;

int main()
{
   ofstream myFile;
   myFile.open("HelloFile.txt", ios_base::out);

   if(myFile.is_open())
   {
      cout << "File open successful" << endl;

      myFile << "My first text file!" << endl;
      myFile << "Hello file!";

      cout << "Finished writing to file, will close now\n";
      myFile.close();
   }

   return 0;
}
```

Output ▼

```
File open successful
Finished writing to file, will close now
```

Content of file HelloFile.txt:

```
My first text file!
Hello file!
```

Analysis ▼

Line 7 opens the file in mode `ios_base::out`—that is, exclusively for writing. In Line 9 you test if `open()` succeeded and then proceed to write to the file stream using the insertion operator `<<` as shown in Lines 13 and 14. Finally, you close at Line 17 and return.

> **NOTE**
>
> Listing 27.8 demonstrates how you are able to write into a file stream the same way as you would write to the standard output (console) using `cout`.
>
> This indicates how streams in C++ allow for a similar way of handling different devices, writing text to the display via `cout` in the same way one would write to a file via `ofstream`.

Reading a Text File by Using `open()` and the Operator `>>`

You can read a file by using `fstream` and open it by using the flag `ios_base::in` or by using `ifstream`. Listing 27.9 shows how to read text from the file `HelloFile.txt`, created in Listing 27.8.

Input ▼

LISTING 27.9 Reading Text from the File `HelloFile.txt` (Created in Listing 27.8)

```
#include<fstream>
#include<iostream>
#include<string>
using namespace std;

int main()
{
   ifstream myFile;
   myFile.open("HelloFile.txt", ios_base::in);

   if(myFile.is_open())
   {
```

```
12:       cout << "File open successful. It contains: \n";
13:       string fileContents;
14:
15:       while(myFile.good())
16:       {
17:          getline(myFile, fileContents);
18:          cout << fileContents << endl;
19:       }
20:
21:       cout << "Finished reading file, will close now\n";
22:       myFile.close();
23:    }
24:    else
25:       cout << "open() failed: check if file is in right folder\n";
26:
27:    return 0;
28: }
```

Output ▼

```
File open successful. It contains:
My first text file!
Hello file!
Finished reading file, will close now
```

> **NOTE** Because Listing 27.9 reads the text file `"HelloFile.txt"` created using Listing 27.8, you need to move that file into this project's working directory.

Analysis ▼

As always, you use `is_open()` to verify whether the call to `open()` in Line 8 succeeded. You read the file, one line at a time, for as long as the method `good()` in Line 15 returns `true`. Note the use of the extraction operator (`>>`) in reading the contents of the file directly into a string that is then displayed using `cout` in Line 18. You use `getline()` in this example to read input from a file stream in exactly the same way as in Listing 27.7, where you used it to read input from the user, one complete line at a time.

Writing to and Reading from a Binary File

The process of writing to a binary file is not too different from what you have learned thus far. It is important to use `ios_base::binary flag` as a mask when opening the file. You typically use `ofstream::write` or `ifstream::read` to write to or read from a binary file, as Listing 27.10 demonstrates.

Input ▼

LISTING 27.10 Writing a `struct` to a Binary File and Reconstructing It

```
#include<fstream>
#include<iomanip>
#include<string>
#include<iostream>
using namespace std;

struct Human
{
   char name[20] = "John";
   int age = 40;
   char DOB[20] = "1981 Sep 1";
};

int main()
{
   Human aPerson;

   ofstream fsOut ("MyBinary.bin", ios_base::out | ios_base::binary);
   if (fsOut.is_open())
   {
      cout << "Writing one Human to a binary file" << endl;
      fsOut.write(reinterpret_cast<char*>(&aPerson), sizeof(aPerson));
      fsOut.close();
   }

   ifstream fsIn ("MyBinary.bin", ios_base::in | ios_base::binary);
   if(fsIn.is_open())
   {
      Human readHuman;
      fsIn.read((char*)&readHuman, sizeof(readHuman));

      cout << "Reading information from binary file: " << endl;
      cout << "Name = " << readHuman.name << endl;
      cout << "Age = " << readHuman.age << endl;
      cout << "Date of Birth = " << readHuman.DOB << endl;
   }

   return 0;
}
```

Output ▼

```
Writing one Human to a binary file
Reading information from binary file:
Name = John
Age = 40
Date of Birth = 1981 Sep 1
```

Analysis ▼

In Lines 15 through 23, you create an instance of `struct Human` and persist it to the disk in the binary file `MyBinary.bin` using `ofstream`. This information is then read using another stream object of type `ifstream` in Lines 25 through 35. The output of attributes such as `name` is via the information that has been read from the binary file. This example also demonstrates the use of `ifstream` and `ofstream` for reading and writing a file using `ifstream::read` and `ofstream::write`, respectively. Note the use of `reinterpret_cast` in Line 21, which instructs the compiler to interpret the `struct*` as `char*`. In Line 29, you use the C-style cast version instead of `reinterpret_cast`.

> **NOTE**
>
> Typically, I would persist `struct Human` with all its attributes using an extensible format like XML or a more readable format like JSON. I didn't do that here because this listing is for demonstration purposes only.
>
> If `struct Human` were to be delivered in the version shown in Listing 27.10 and after delivery if you were to add new attributes to it (like `numChildren`, for instance), you would need to worry about `ifstream::read` functionality being able to correctly read binary data created using the older versions.

Using `std::stringstream` for String Conversions

Say that you have a string, and it contains a string value `45`. How do you convert this string value into an integer with the value `45`? And how do you do the opposite: convert an integer into a string? One of the most useful utilities provided by C++ is `class stringstream`, which enables you to perform a host of conversion activities.

TIP

> To use class `std::stringstream`, include this header:
> `#include<sstream>`

Listing 27.11 demonstrates some simple `stringstream` operations.

Input ▼

LISTING 27.11 Converting an Integer Value into a String Representation and Vice Versa by Using `std::stringstream`

```
#include<fstream>
#include<sstream>
#include<iostream>
using namespace std;

int main()
{
    cout << "Enter an integer: ";
    int input = 0;
    cin >> input;

    stringstream converterStream;
    converterStream << input;
    string inputAsStr;
    converterStream >> inputAsStr;

    cout << "Integer Input = " << input << endl;
    cout << "String gained from integer = " << inputAsStr << endl;

    stringstream anotherStream;
    anotherStream << inputAsStr;
    int copy = 0;
    anotherStream >> copy;

    cout << "Integer gained from string, copy = " << copy << endl;

    return 0;
}
```


Output ▼

```
Enter an integer: 45
Integer Input = 45
String gained from integer = 45
Integer gained from string, copy = 45
```

Analysis ▼

In this example, you ask the user to enter an integer value. You insert this integer into the `stringstream` object, as shown in Line 12, using the operator `<<`. Then, you use the extraction operator (`>>`) in Line 14 to convert the integer into a string. After that, you use the string as a starting point and get an integer representation copy of the numeric value held in the string `inputAsStr`.

DO	DON'T
DO use `ifstream` when you only intend to read from a file. **DO** use `ofstream` when you only intend to write to a file. **DO** remember to check whether a file stream has been opened successfully via `is_open()` before inserting into or extracting from the stream.	**DON'T** forget to close a file stream by using method `close()` after you are done using it. **DON'T** forget that extracting from `cin` to a `string` via `cin >> strData;` typically results in `strData` containing text until the first whitespace and not containing the entire line. **DON'T** forget that the function `getline(cin, strData);` fetches an entire line from the input stream, including whitespace.

Summary

This lesson taught you about C++ streams from a practical perspective. You learned that you have been using streams such as the I/O streams `cout` and `cin` since the very beginning of this book. You now know how to create simple text files and how to read or write from them. You learned how `stringstream` can help you convert simple types such as integers into strings and vice versa.

Q&A

Q I see that I can use `fstream` for both writing to and reading from a file, so when should I use `ofstream` and `ifstream`?

A If your code or module needs to only be reading from a file, you should use `ifstream`. Similarly, if it needs to only write to a file, you should use `ofstream`. `fstream` would work in both cases, but for the sake of ensuring data and code integrity, it is better to have a restrictive policy similar to using `const` (which is also not required).

Q When should I use `cin.get()`, and when should I use `cin.getline()`?

A `cin.getline()` ensures that you capture an entire line entered by a user, including whitespace. `cin.get()` helps you capture user input one character at a time.

Q When should I use `stringstream`?

A Use `stringstream` to convert integers and other simple types into strings and vice versa, as demonstrated in Listing 27.11.

Workshop

The Workshop provides quiz questions to help you solidify your understanding of the material covered and exercises to provide you with experience using what you've learned. Try to answer the quiz and exercise questions before checking the answers in Appendix E and be certain you understand the answers before continuing to the next lesson.

Quiz

1. You need to only write to a file. What stream should you use?
2. How do you use `cin` to get a complete line from the input stream?
3. You need to write `std::string` objects to a file. Should you choose `ios_base::binary` mode?
4. You opened a stream using `open()`. Why bother using `is_open()`?

Exercises

1. **BUG BUSTERS:** What is the error in the following code?

```
fstream myFile;
myFile.open("HelloFile.txt", ios_base::out);
myFile << "Hello file!";
myFile.close();
```

2. **BUG BUSTERS:** What is the error in the following code?

```
ifstream myFile("SomeFile.txt");
if(myFile.is_open())
{
   myFile << "This is some text" << endl;
   myFile.close();
}
```

LESSON 28
Exception Handling

This lesson teaches you how to deal with extraordinary situations that disrupt the flow of a program. The lessons thus far have mostly taken an exceedingly positive approach, assuming that memory allocations will succeed, files will be found, and so on. Reality doesn't always work that way.

In this lesson, you learn

- What an exception is
- How to handle exceptions
- How exception handling helps you deliver stable C++ applications

What Is an Exception?

Say that a program allocates memory, reads and writes data, saves to a file—the works. It executes flawlessly on your awesome development environment, and you are proud of the fact that your application doesn't leak a byte, though it manages a gigabyte! You ship your application, and the customer deploys it on a landscape of 1000 workstations. Some of the computers are 10 years old. It doesn't take much time for the first complaint to reach you. Some users complain about an "access violation," and others say they are getting an "unhandled exception."

Your application was doing well inside your environment, so why all the problems now?

The fact is that the world out there is very heterogeneous. No two computers, even if they have the same hardware configuration, are alike. The software running on each computer and the state of the machine determine the amount of resources that are available at a particular time. Memory allocation that works perfectly in your environment could fail in another environment. Such failures result in exceptions.

Exceptions disrupt the normal flow of an application. After all, if there is no memory available, there may be no way your application can achieve what it set out to do. However, your application can handle an exception and display a friendly error message to the user, perform any minimal rescue operation needed, and exit gracefully.

Handling exceptions help avoid those "unhandled exception" screens and error messages. Let's see what tools C++ provides for dealing with exceptions.

What Causes Exceptions?

Exceptions can be caused by external factors, such as a system with insufficient resources, or by factors internal to an application, such as a pointer that is used despite containing an invalid value or a divide-by-zero error. Some modules are designed to communicate errors by throwing exceptions to the caller.

NOTE To protect your code against exceptions, you "handle" exceptions, thereby making your code "exception safe."

Implementing Exception Safety via `try` and `catch`

`try` and `catch` are the most important keywords in C++ when it comes to implementing exception safety. To make statements exception safe, you enclose them within a `try` block and use a `catch` block to handle the exceptions that emerge out of the `try` block:

```
void SomeFunc()
{
   try
   {
      int* numPtr = new int;
      *numPtr = 999;
      delete numPtr;
   }
   catch(...)  // ... catches all exceptions
   {
      cout << "Exception in SomeFunc()" << endl;
   }
}
```

Using catch(...) to Handle All Exceptions

In Lesson 8, “Pointers and References Explained,” I mentioned that the default form of new returns a valid pointer to a location in memory when it succeeds but throws an exception when it fails. Listing 28.1 demonstrates how you can make memory allocations exception safe by using new and handle situations where the computer is not able to allocate the memory you requested.

Input ▼

LISTING 28.1 Using try and catch to Ensure Exception Safety in Memory Allocation

```
#include<iostream>
using namespace std;

int main()
{
   cout << "Enter number of integers you wish to reserve: ";
   try
   {
      int input = 0;
      cin >> input;

      // Request memory space and then return it
      int* numArray = new int[input];
      delete[] numArray;
   }
   catch (...)
   {
      cout << "Exception occurred. Got to end, sorry!" << endl;
   }
   return 0;
}
```

Output ▼

```
Enter number of integers you wish to reserve: -1
Exception occurred. Got to end, sorry!
```

Analysis ▼

In this example, I used -1 as the number of integers to reserve. This input is ridiculous, but users do ridiculous things all the time. In the absence of the exception handler, the program would encounter a very ugly end. But thanks to the exception handler, you see that the output displays a decent message: Got to end, sorry!

Listing 28.1 demonstrates the use of `try` and `catch` blocks. `catch()` takes parameters, just like a function does, and ... means that this `catch` block accepts all kinds of exceptions. In this case, however, you might want to specifically isolate exceptions of type `std::bad_alloc` as these exceptions are thrown when `new` fails. Catching a specific type will help you handle that type of problem in particular; you can, for instance, show the user a message telling what exactly went wrong.

Catching Exceptions of a Type

The exception in Listing 28.1 was thrown from the C++ Standard Library. Such exceptions are of a known type, and catching exceptions of a particular type is good for you because it means you can pinpoint the reason for the exception, do better cleanup, or at least show a precise message to the user, as Listing 28.2 does.

Input ▼

LISTING 28.2 Catching Exceptions of Type `std::bad_alloc`

```
#include<iostream>
#include<exception>  // to catch exception bad_alloc
using namespace std;

int main()
{
   cout << "Enter number of integers you wish to reserve: ";
   try
   {
      int input = 0;
      cin >> input;

      // Request memory space and then return it
      int* numArray = new int [input];
      delete[] numArray;
   }
   catch (std::bad_alloc& exp)
   {
      cout << "Exception encountered: " << exp.what() << endl;
      cout << "Got to end, sorry!" << endl;
   }
   catch(...)
   {
      cout << "Exception encountered. Got to end, sorry!" << endl;
   }
   return 0;
}
```

Output ▼

```
Enter number of integers you wish to reserve: -1
Exception encountered: bad array new length
Got to end, sorry!
```

Analysis ▼

Compare the output of Listing 28.2 to the output of Listing 28.1. The code in Listing 28.2 can supply a more precise reason for the abrupt ending of the application: `bad array new length`. This listing has an additional `catch` block (yes, two `catch` blocks). One of them traps exceptions of the type `catch(bad_alloc&)`, shown in Lines 16 through 20, which is thrown by `new`.

TIP

> In general, you can insert as many `catch()` blocks as you like, one after another, depending on the exceptions you expect and the blocks that would help.
>
> In Listing 28.2, `catch(...)` catches all the exception types that have not been explicitly caught by other `catch` statements.

Throwing Exceptions of a Type by Using `throw`

When you caught `std::bad_alloc` in Listing 28.2, you actually caught an object of class `std::bad_alloc` thrown by `new`. It is possible to throw an exception of your own choosing. All you need is the keyword `throw`:

```
void DoSomething()
{
   if(something_unwanted)
      throw object;
}
```

Let's study the use of `throw` in a custom-defined exception in Listing 28.3, which divides two numbers.

Input ▼

LISTING 28.3 Throwing a Custom Exception at an Attempt to Divide by Zero

```
 0: #include<iostream>
 1: using namespace std;
 2:
 3: double Divide(double dividend, double divisor)
 4: {
 5:    if(divisor == 0)
 6:       throw "Dividing by 0 is a crime";
 7:
 8:    return (dividend / divisor);
 9: }
10:
11: int main()
12: {
13:    cout << "Enter dividend: ";
14:    double dividend = 0;
15:    cin >> dividend;
16:    cout << "Enter divisor: ";
17:    double divisor = 0;
18:    cin >> divisor;
19:
20:    try
21:    {
22:       cout << "Result is: " << Divide(dividend, divisor);
23:    }
24:    catch(const char* exp)
25:    {
26:       cout << "Exception: " << exp << endl;
27:       cout << "Sorry, can't continue!" << endl;
28:    }
29:
30:    return 0;
31: }
```

Output ▼

```
Enter dividend: 2021
Enter divisor: 0
Exception: Dividing by 0 is a crime
Sorry, can't continue!
```

Analysis ▼

This example not only demonstrates that you can catch exceptions of type `const char*`, as shown in Line 24, but also that you caught an exception thrown in a called function `Divide()` in Line 6. Note that you did not include all of `main()` within `try {}`; you only included the part of it that you expected to throw. This is generally a good practice, as exception handling can reduce the execution performance of your code.

How Exception Handling Works

In Listing 28.3, you threw an exception of type `char*` in the function `Divide()` that was caught in the `catch(char*)` handler in the calling function `main()`.

Where an exception is thrown using `throw`, the compiler inserts a dynamic lookup for a compatible `catch(Type)` that can handle the exception. The exception handling logic first checks whether the line throwing the exception is within a `try` block. If so, it seeks the `catch(Type)` that can handle the exception of this type. If the `throw` statement is not within a `try` block or if there is no compatible `catch()` for the exception type, the exception handling logic looks in the calling function. So, the exception handling logic climbs the stack, calling one function after another, seeking a suitable `catch(Type)` that can handle the exception. At each step in the stack unwinding procedure, the variables local to that function are destroyed, in reverse sequence of their construction. This is demonstrated in Listing 28.4.

Input ▼

LISTING 28.4 The Destruction Order of Local Objects in the Event of an Exception

```
#include<iostream>
using namespace std;

struct StructA
{
   StructA() {cout << "StructA constructor" << endl; }
   ~StructA() {cout << "StructA destructor" << endl;  }
};

struct StructB
{
   StructB() {cout << "StructB constructor" << endl; }
   ~StructB() {cout << "StructB destructor" << endl; }
};

void FuncB()   // throws
{
   cout << "In Func B" << endl;
   StructA objA;
   StructB objB;
   cout << "About to throw up!" << endl;
   throw "Throwing for the heck of it";
}

```

```
void FuncA()
{
   try
   {
      cout << "In Func A" << endl;
      StructA objA;
      StructB objB;
      FuncB();
     cout << "FuncA: returning to caller" << endl;
   }
   catch(const char* exp)
   {
      cout << "FuncA: Caught exception: " << exp << endl;
      cout << "Handled it, will not throw to caller" << endl;
      // throw;  // uncomment this line to throw to main()
   }
}

int main()
{
   cout << "main(): Started execution" << endl;
   try
   {
      FuncA();
   }
   catch(const char* exp)
   {
      cout << "Exception: " << exp << endl;
   }
   cout << "main(): exiting gracefully" << endl;
   return 0;
}
```

Output ▼

```
main(): Started execution
In Func A
StructA constructor
StructB constructor
In Func B
StructA constructor
StructB constructor
About to throw up!
StructB destructor
StructA destructor
StructB destructor
StructA destructor
FuncA: Caught exception: Throwing for the heck of it
Handled it, will not throw to caller
main(): exiting gracefully
```

Analysis ▼

In Listing 28.4, `main()` invokes `FuncA()`, which invokes `FuncB()`, which throws an exception in Line 21. Both calling functions `FuncA()` and `main()` are exception safe as they both have a `catch(const char*)` block implemented. `FuncB()`, which throws the exception, has no `catch()` blocks, and hence the catch block within `FuncA()` at Lines 34 through 39 is the first handler for the thrown exception from `FuncB()`, as `FuncA()` is the caller of `FuncB()`. Note that `FuncA()` decided that this exception is not of a serious nature and did not propagate it to `main()`. Hence, `main()` continues as if no problem happened. If you uncomment Line 38, the exception is thrown to the caller of `FuncB()`—that is, `main()` receives it, too.

The output also indicates the order in which objects are created (the same order in which their instantiations were coded) and the order in which they're destroyed as soon as an exception is thrown (in the reverse order of instantiations). This happens not only in `FuncB()`, which threw the exception, but also in `FuncA()`, which invoked `FuncB()` and handled the thrown exception.

CAUTION

> Listing 28.4 demonstrates how destructors of local objects are invoked when an exception is thrown.
>
> If the destructor of an object invoked due to an exception also throws an exception, it results in an abnormal termination of your application. This is why you are advised to not throw exceptions from destructors.

Class `std::exception`

In catching `std::bad_alloc` in Listing 28.2, you actually caught an object of class `std::bad_alloc` thrown by `new`. `std::bad_alloc` is a class that inherits from the C++ standard class `std::exception`, declared in the header `<exception>`.

`std::exception` is the base class for the following important exceptions:

- **`bad_alloc`**: Thrown when a request for memory using new fails
- **`bad_cast`**: Thrown by dynamic_cast when you try to cast a wrong type (that is, a type that has no inheritance relationship)
- **`ios_base::failure`**: Thrown by the functions and methods in the iostream library

Class `std::exception`, which is the base class, supports the very useful and important virtual method `what()`, which gives a more descriptive explanation about the nature of the problem causing the exception. In Listing 28.2, `exp.what()` in Line 18 gives the information `bad array new length` to tell you what went wrong. You can make use of `std::exception` being a base class for many exceptions types and create one `catch(const exception&)` that can catch all exceptions that have `std::exception` as the base:

```
void SomeFunc()
{
   try
   {
      // code made exception safe
   }
   catch (const std::exception& exp) // catch bad_alloc, bad_cast, etc
   {
      cout << "Exception encountered: " << exp.what() << endl;
   }
}
```

A Custom Exception Class Derived from `std::exception`

You can throw an exception of whatever type you want. However, there is a benefit in inheriting from `std::exception`: All existing exception handlers with `catch(const std::exception&)` that work for `bad_alloc`, `bad_cast`, and the like will automatically scale up to catch your new exception class as well because it has the base class in common with them. This is demonstrated in Listing 28.5.

Input ▼

LISTING 28.5 The Class `CustomException`, Which Inherits from `std::exception`

```
#include<exception>
#include<iostream>
#include<string>
using namespace std;

class CustomException: public std::exception
{
   string reason;
public:
```

```
    // constructor, needs reason
    CustomException(const char* why):reason(why) {}

    // redefining virtual function to return 'reason'
    virtual const char* what() const throw()
    {
       return reason.c_str();
    }
};

double Divide(double dividend, double divisor)
{
    if(divisor == 0)
       throw CustomException("CustomException: Division by 0");

    return (dividend / divisor);
}

int main()
{
    cout << "Enter dividend: ";
    double dividend = 0;
    cin >> dividend;
    cout << "Enter divisor: ";
    double divisor = 0;
    cin >> divisor;
    try
    {
       cout << "Result is: " << Divide(dividend, divisor);
    }
    catch(exception& exp)// catch CustomException, bad_alloc, etc
    {
       cout << exp.what() << endl;
       cout << "Sorry, can't continue!" << endl;
    }

    return 0;
}
```

Output ▼

```
Enter dividend: 2021
Enter divisor: 0
CustomException: Division by 0
Sorry, can't continue!
```

Analysis ▼

This example is an improvement to Listing 28.3, which throws a simple `char*` exception on divide by zero. In here, we instantiate an object of class `CustomException`, defined in Lines 5 through 17, that inherits from `std::exception`, and throw it in Line 22 when an attempt to divide by zero is encountered. Note how the custom exception class implements the virtual function `what()` in Lines 13 through 16, essentially returning the reason the exception was thrown. The `catch(exception&)` logic in `main()` in Lines 39 through 43 handles not only the class `CustomException` but also other exceptions of type `bad_alloc` that have the same base class `exception`.

NOTE

Note the declaration of the virtual method `CustomException::what()` in Line 13 in Listing 28.5:

```
virtual const char* what() const throw()
```

It ends with `throw()`, which means that this function itself is not expected to throw an exception—which is a very important and relevant restriction on a class used as an exception object. If you still insert a throw within this function, you can expect a compiler warning.

If a function ends with `throw(int)`, it means that the function is expected to throw an exception of type `int`.

DO	DON'T
DO remember to catch exceptions of type `std::exception`.	**DON'T** throw exceptions from destructors.
DO remember to inherit a custom exception class (if any) from `std::exception`.	**DON'T** take memory allocations for granted; code that uses `new` should always be exception safe and within a `try` block with `catch(std::exception&)`.
DO throw exceptions—but with discretion. They're not a substitute for return values.	**DON'T** insert any heavy logic or resource allocations inside a `catch()` block. You don't want to cause new exceptions when you're handling one.

Summary

In this lesson, you learned an important part of practical C++ programming. Making your applications stable beyond your own development environment is important for customer satisfaction and intuitive user experiences, and exception handling is a necessary part of ensuring this stability. You found out that code that allocates resources or memory can fail and hence needs to be made exception safe. You learned about the C++ exception class `std::exception` and that if you need to program a custom exception class, you ideally want to inherit from `std::exception`.

Q&A

Q Why should I raise exceptions instead of returning an error?

A You may not always have the luxury of being able to return an error. If a call to `new` fails, you need to handle exceptions thrown by `new` to prevent your application from crashing. In addition, if an error is very severe and makes the future functioning of your application impossible, you should consider throwing an exception.

Q Why should my exception class inherit from `std::exception`?

A Inheriting from `std::exception` is not compulsory, but it helps you reuse all those `catch()` blocks that already catch exceptions of type `std::exception`. You can write your own exception class that doesn't inherit from anything else, but then you have to insert new `catch(MyNewExceptionType&)` statements at all the relevant points.

Q I have a function that throws an exception. Does it need to be caught at the very same function that throws the exception?

A Not at all. Just ensure that the exception type thrown is caught at one of the calling functions in the call stack.

Q Can a constructor throw an exception?

A Constructors actually have no choice! They don't have return values, and throwing an exception is the best way to demonstrate disagreement.

Q Can a destructor throw an exception?

A Technically, yes. However, this is a bad practice as destructors are also called when the stack is unwound due to an exception. So, a destructor invoked due to an exception throwing an exception itself can clearly result in quite an ugly situation for an already unstable application trying to make a clean exit.

Workshop

The Workshop provides quiz questions to help you solidify your understanding of the material covered and exercises to provide you with experience using what you've learned. Try to answer the quiz and exercise questions before checking the answers in Appendix E and be certain you understand the answers before continuing to the next lesson.

Quiz

1. What is `std::exception`?
2. What type of exception is thrown when an allocation using `new` fails?
3. Is it acceptable to allocate a million integers in an exception handler (that is, a `catch` block) to back up existing data, for instance?
4. How would you catch an exception object of class `MyException` that inherits from `std::exception`?

Exercises

1. **BUG BUSTERS:** What is wrong with the following code?

```
class SomeIntelligentStuff
{
   bool isStuffGoneBad;
public:
   ~SomeIntelligentStuff()
   {
      if(isStuffGoneBad)
         throw "Big problem in this class, just FYI";
   }
};
```

2. **BUG BUSTERS:** What is wrong with the following code?

```
int main()
{
   int* millionNums = new int[1000000];
   // do something with the million integers

   delete[] millionNums;
}
```

3. **BUG BUSTERS:** What is wrong with the following code?

```
int main()
{
   try
   {
      int* millionNums = new int[1000000];
      // do something with the million integers

      delete[] millionNums;
   }
   catch(exception& exp)
   {
      int* anotherMillion = new int[1000000];
      // take back up of millionNums and save it to disk
   }
}
```

LESSON 29
C++20 Concepts, Ranges, Views, and Adaptors

You have already learned the basics of C++ programming. In fact, you have gone beyond theoretical boundaries in understanding how using the Standard Template Library (STL), templates, and the Standard Library can help you write efficient and compact code. It is time to look at the new additions in C++20.

In this lesson, you learn

- The basics of concepts
- Defining your own concepts
- The basics of ranges, views, and adaptors
- Using adaptors to create views on ranges

TIP

> As of this writing, popular compilers do not fully support C++20. GNU g++ and MSVC currently provide the most support for the features presented in this lesson. Compiler support is constantly improving, and it is important to use the latest version of your favorite compiler, especially when using new C++ features, such as those described in this lesson.
>
> You also need to explicitly activate supported C++20 features. When using g++ or clang++, add -std=c++20 to the command line. MSVC users can enable /std:c++20 via the option C++ Language Standard under Project Properties.

Concepts

In Lesson 14, "An Introduction to Macros and Templates," you learned the basics of generic programming using templates. You learned that template classes can support attributes of different types and that template functions can be used with parameters of different types, depending on the instantiation, as seen below:

```
template <typename T>
double DivideNums(T dividend, T divisor)
{
   return (dividend / divisor);
}
```

Template instantiation works like this:

```
double pi = DivideNums(22.0, 7.0); // for float, float
```

It's clear that DivideNums() returns the result of the division of two numbers. Say that you try to instantiate this template function for two elements of type string:

```
std::string str1, str2;
double crazyCompileErrror = DivideNums(str1, str2);
```

You end up getting a compiler error, indicating that the type string does not support the operator /. However, what you ideally need is for the compiler to deny compilation at the outset and indicate that the function DivideNums() can be used only with numeric types. That is, you want to limit the template instantiation of DivideNums() to numeric types, preferably floating point, and you want the compiler to validate that for you. C++20 introduces *concepts*, which help you do exactly that.

You use concepts to define constraints governing the types that a template class or function can be instantiated with. The compiler validates concepts for you and enforces them. Furthermore, the Standard Library supplies basic concepts such as `std::floating_point`, which helps you constrain the template instantiation in this particular case:

```
template <std::floating_point T> // concept constraining T
double DivideNums(T dividend, T divisor)
{
   return (dividend / divisor);
}
```

If you were to now use the function `DivideNums()` for a non-numeric type such as `std::string`, the compiler wouldn't even start by seeking the operator / in the class `std::string`. It would supply a simpler error message, telling you at the outset that the constraints defined for `DivideNums()` haven't been met. Trivial as this feature may seem at first, concepts represent a massive improvement because they enable easy and safe use of template classes.

TIP

> To use C++20 concepts, include this header:
>
> `#include<concepts>`

Using Concepts Provided by the Standard Library

Listing 29.1 presents a full-fledged program using the concept `std:: floating_point` to constrain the parameters used in `DivideNums` to floating-point types (namely `float` and `double`).

Input ▼

LISTING 29.1 Using a Simple Concept to Constrain the Parameter Type of a Template Function to Floating Point

```
#include<concepts>
#include<iostream>
using namespace std;

template <std::floating_point T> // enforce floating point
double DivideNums(T dividend, T divisor)
{
   return (dividend / divisor);
}

int main()
{
   cout << "Pi = " << DivideNums(22.0, 7.0); // OK
   // cout << "Pi = " << DivideNums(22, 7); // err: not floating pt
```

```
14:
15:     return 0;
16: }
```

Output ▼

```
Pi = 3.14286
```

Analysis ▼

Listing 29.1 shows the concept `std::floating_point` used in Line 4. It constrains `T` to a floating-point type. The template instantiation of `DivideNums()` will be validated by the compiler for floating-point types. If you were to uncomment Line 13, you would face a compilation failure, as intended, because this line invokes `DivideNums()` using arguments that are not floating-point numbers.

Table 29.1 describes some popular concepts provided by the Standard Library.

TABLE 29.1 Key Concepts Provided by the Standard Library

Concept	Description
`integral`	Validates an integral type. Examples include `int`, `long`, and unsigned and signed variants of `int` and `long`.
`signed_integral`	Validates a signed integral type. Examples include `int`, `long`, and `long long`.
`unsigned_integral`	Validates an unsigned integral type. Examples include `unsigned int` and `unsigned long`.
`floating_point`	Validates a floating-point type. Examples include `float` and `double`.
`same_as`	Validates that one type is the same as another.
`derived_from`	Validates that one type is derived from another.
`convertible_to`	Validates that one type can be converted to another.

Defining Custom Concepts by Using the Keyword `requires`

One of the drawbacks of the template function `DivideNums()` in Listing 29.1 is that it expects both `dividend` and `divisor` to be of the same floating-point type `T`. That is, you cannot use it to divide `22.0` by `7` or `22` by `7.0`, although both operations should definitely be possible. You could solve this problem by defining a concept that combines `floating_point` and `integral` types:

```
template <typename T>
concept AnyNumericType = floating_point<T> || integral<T>;
```

Furthermore, to ensure that the dividend and divisor are allowed to be of different types, you could use the keyword `requires` in defining the template function:

```
template <typename T1, typename T2>
requires AnyNumericType<T1> && AnyNumericType<T2>
double DivideAnyNumericType(T1 dividend, T2 divisor)
{
   return (dividend / divisor);
}
```

Listing 29.2 integrates these ideas into an example that shows how you can use concepts in constraining one or the other or both parameters of a function. It also uses a variadic template function to display on the screen.

Input ▼

LISTING 29.2 Combining Multiple Concepts, Using Different Constraints for Different Parameters

```
#include<concepts>
#include<iostream>
using namespace std;

template <typename T>
concept AnyNumericType = floating_point<T> || integral<T>;

template <integral T>
double DivideOnlyInts(T dividend, T divisor)
{
   return (dividend / divisor);
}

template <typename T1, typename T2>
requires AnyNumericType<T1> && AnyNumericType<T2>
double DivideAnyNumType(T1 dividend, T2 divisor)
{
   return (dividend / divisor);
```

```
}

template <typename T1, typename T2>
requires same_as<T1, T2>
double DivideIdenticalTypes(T1 dividend,T2 divisor)
{
   return (dividend / divisor);
}

void DisplayNums() { cout << endl; }

template <typename T, typename... Types>
void DisplayNums(T num1, Types... numN)
{
   cout << num1 << ' ';
   DisplayNums(numN ...);
}

int main()
{
   double q1 = DivideOnlyInts(22, 7); // OK
   // double q2 = DivideOnlyInts(22.0, 7); // error: 22.0 isn't integral

   double q3 = DivideAnyNumType(22.0, 7); // OK
   double q4 = DivideAnyNumType(22.0, 7.0); // OK
   double q5 = DivideAnyNumType(22.0, '7'); // OK: type char is numeric
   // double q6 = DivideAnyNumType("22.0", 7); // error: char* isn't numeric

   double q7 = DivideIdenticalTypes(22.0, 7.0); // OK
   double q8 = DivideIdenticalTypes(22.0, 7.0); // OK
   // double q9 = DivideIdenticalTypes(22.0, 7); // error: unidentical types

   DisplayNums("q1 =", q1, "q3 =", q3, "q4 =", q4);
   DisplayNums("q5 =", q5, "q7 =", q7, "q8 =", q8);

   return 0;
}
```

Output ▼

```
q1 = 3 q3 = 3.14286 q4 = 3.14286
q5 = 0.4 q7 = 3.14286 q8 =  3.14286
```

Analysis ▼

This example gets rid of the constraint from Listing 29.1 that both parameters of the function that divides two numbers need to be of the same type. It defines a new concept,

`AnyNumericType`, in Lines 4 and 5 that permits the parameter type that fulfills the concept to be either an integral type or a floating-point type. This concept is then used in the template function `DivideAnyNumType()`, defined in Lines 13 through 18, which accepts a dividend and a divisor of different types, as long as they're numeric types that fulfill the concept `AnyNumType`.

In addition, this example demonstrates the concept `std::same_as` in the function `DivideIdenticalTypes()`, which is defined in Lines 20 through 25. Commented Line 48 demonstrates how `std::same_as` is used to enforce the use of identical types in the two parameters and produce a compilation error if is a floating-point type and the other an integral type.

TIP

> Note the use of variadic templates in the function `DisplayNums()`, which is defined in Lines 27 through 34 and used in Lines 50 and 51. This function is used to display types that are string literals and a double.
>
> The compiler identifies the ellipsis (`...`) as an instruction to expand `DisplayNums()` and generate a compile-time recursive version that prints all arguments on the screen.

Using Concepts with Classes and Objects

Thus far in the lesson, you have used concepts with template functions to learn the basics of concepts. Using concepts with classes is not too different. You use templates with classes to generically program the nature of member attributes contained by the classes and the behavior of methods contained in the classes. You can use concepts to validate and constrain the types that these template classes can be instantiated with, as shown in Listing 29.3.

Input ▼

LISTING 29.3 Using Concepts to Constrain and Validate Template Parameters Used with Classes

```
#include<concepts>
using namespace std;

template <typename T>
concept AnyNumericType = floating_point<T> || integral<T>;

template<AnyNumericType T1, AnyNumericType T2>
class Person
```

```
 8: {
 9: public:
10:    T1 age;
11:    T2 yearsEmployed;
12:
13:    Person(T1 num1, T2 num2) : age(num1), yearsEmployed(num2) {}
14: };
15:
16: int main()
17: {
18:    Person<int, double> p1(21, 3.4); // OK
19:    Person<double, float> p2(32.6, 3.4f); // OK
20:
21:    // Person<string, double> p3("lara", 3.4); // error: "lara" isn't numeric
22:
23:    return 0;
24: }
```

Output ▼

This code snippet produces no output.

Analysis ▼

Line 6 demonstrates the use of the now-familiar concept `AnyNumericType<>` (which was initially used in Listing 29.2) to constrain the types with which the class `Person<>` can be instantiated. Basically, you are ensuring that the compiler verifies that `Person<>` is instantiated for only numeric types because you do not want the attributes `age` or `yearsEmployed` to contain anything else. In the absence of constraints imposed by the concept `AnyNumericType<>`, you can compile even Line 21, which instantiates an instance with age as `"lara"`. This is not what you would ideally want.

Thus, concepts give the designer of a template class a powerful tool for ensuring that the class is instantiated in accordance with its intended use and function.

Listing 29.4 demonstrates how to ensure that the object being passed to a function is of a type that is related to `Base`. Remember from Lesson 10, "Implementing Inheritance," that public derivation gives you an is-a relationship between the derived class and the base class. `derived_from<>` validates exactly this relationship, evaluating to `false` for private inheritance as well as for unrelated types.

Input ▼

LISTING 29.4 Using the Concept `derived_from`

```
 0: #include<concepts>
 1: #include<iostream>
 2: using namespace std;
 3:
 4: class Base {};
 5: class PublicDerived : public Base {};
 6: class PrivateDerived : private Base {};
 7: class Unrelated {};
 8:
 9: template<derived_from<Base> T>
10: void ProcessBaseTypesOnly(T& input)
11: {
12:    cout << "Processing an instance of Base" << endl;
13: }
14:
15: int main()
16: {
17:    static_assert(derived_from<PublicDerived, Base> /* == true */);
18:    static_assert(derived_from<PrivateDerived, Base> == false);
19:    static_assert(derived_from<Unrelated, Base> == false);
20:
21:    PublicDerived d1;
22:    PrivateDerived d2;
23:    Unrelated u;
24:    ProcessBaseTypesOnly(d1); // OK, d1 is also type Base
25:    // ProcessBaseTypesOnly(d2); // Error: d2 isn't a Base
26:    // ProcessBaseTypesOnly(u); // Error: u is unrelated to Base
27:
28:    return 0;
29: }
```

Output ▼

```
Processing an instance of Base
```

Analysis ▼

This example uses `static_assert` to demonstrate what the compiler agrees with and what it doesn't (see Lines 17 through 19). Furthermore, you can see the concept `derived_from<T>` in Line 9, where it is used to constrain the parameter type of the function `ProcessBaseTypesOnly()`. Because of this concept and the constraints it imposes, Line 24 will compile, but Lines 25 and 26 won't.

The Ranges Library, Views, and Adaptors

When learning about containers in Lesson 15, "An Introduction to the Standard Template Library," you saw that STL containers consistently support the following methods:

- **`begin()`:** This method returns the beginning of the container (that is, it points to the first element).
- **`end()`:** This method returns the end of the container, *after* the last element.

A *range* is an abstraction of a collection. Any collection that fulfills the properties mentioned above is also a range. C++20 introduces a new library, the ranges library, which uses this abstraction and further develops on it to provide alternatives to STL algorithms in the form of *views* and *adaptors*.

TIP

> To use the ranges library, include this header:
>
> ```
> #include<ranges>
> ```

The ranges library features concepts such as `ranges::range`, which you can use to validate a collection as a range. Ranges are classified on the basis of known properties of the collections and provide concepts that can validate range type. The prominent ones among them are `input_range`, `output_range`, `forward_range`, `bidirectional_range`, and `random_access_range`, as demonstrated by Listing 29.5.

Input ▼

LISTING 29.5 Using `std::ranges` to Validate Popular Containers as Ranges and Types of Ranges

```
#include<ranges>
#include<vector>
#include<list>
#include<set>
#include<map>
#include<stack>
#include<forward_list>
using namespace std;

int main()
{
    static_assert(ranges::range<int[5]>);
    static_assert(ranges::range<vector<int>>);
    static_assert(ranges::range<list<int>>);
```

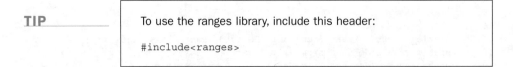

```
14:     static_assert(ranges::range<set<int>>);
15:     static_assert(ranges::range<map<int, int>>);
16:
17:     static_assert(ranges::forward_range<vector<int>>);
18:     static_assert(ranges::random_access_range<vector<int>>);
19:     static_assert(ranges::bidirectional_range<vector<int>>);
20:
21:     //static_assert(ranges::range<stack<int>>);//err: stack isn't a range
22:     //static_assert(ranges::bidirectional_range<forward_list<int>>);//error
23:     //static_assert(ranges::random_access_range<set<int>>); // error
24:
25:     return 0;
26: }
```

Output ▼

This code snippet produces no output.

Analysis ▼

This example uses `static_assert` to get the compiler to validate the concepts `std::ranges::range`, `std::ranges::forward_range`, `std::ranges::random_access_range`, and `std::ranges::bidirectional_range`. Lines 11 through 19 demonstrate that typical STL containers such as `vector`, `list`, `set`, and `map` fulfill the criteria of a range. In Line 21, you see that `stack` doesn't. This is because the `stack` container has modified the behavior of an underlying container (such as `vector`) to restrict certain freedoms in implementing last-in, first-out (LIFO) functionality. It doesn't support iterations and doesn't feature the methods `begin()` and `end()`, and hence it cannot be a range. Similarly, Line 22 demonstrates that `forward_list` isn't accepted as a bidirectional range, and Line 23 demonstrates that `std::set` doesn't permit random access to elements within it.

Having seen what ranges are, let us now visit views and adaptors and use them in combination with ranges.

Views and Adaptors

Views are ranges that also assure constant-time copies, moves, and assignments. Therefore, a view is a special kind of range. Every view is a range, but not every range qualifies as a view.

In Lesson 16, "The STL String Class," you learned how `std::string_view` helps give a peek into a string, substring, or character without the expensive task of creating copies. C++20 views fulfill a similar objective over ranges (or collections). You can use a view to operate an algorithm on a range. Such algorithms are called *adaptors*. An adaptor returns a view comprising data resulting from the execution of the adaptor.

Say that you want to construct a view that comprises the elements in an input collection, in reverse order. Listing 29.6 demonstrates the use of the adaptor `std::views::reverse` to view a collection in reverse—that is, with the last element first.

Input ▼

LISTING 29.6 Viewing a Collection in the Reverse Order

```
#include<ranges>
#include<vector>
#include<iostream>
using namespace std;

int main()
{
    vector<int> nums{ 1, 5, 202, -99, 42, 50 };

    // create a view using adaptor reverse
    auto viewReverse = nums | std::views::reverse;

    cout << "View of collection in reverse: ";
    // range-based for: because, a view is also a range
    for (int num : viewReverse)
       cout << num << ' ';

    cout << endl << "Original collection (unchanged): ";
    for (int num : nums)
       cout << num << ' ';

    return 0;
}
```

Output ▼

```
View of collection in reverse: 50 42 -99 202 5 1
Original collection (unchanged): 1 5 202 -99 42 50
```

Analysis ▼

This example demonstrates the creation of a view called `viewReverse`, using the adaptor `std::views::reverse`. You first print the view on the screen and then print the contents of the original `vector` container, demonstrating that the creation of the view does not alter the original collection in any way. If you were to use the algorithm `std::reverse()` instead, you would alter the collection. Furthermore, Line 14 uses the range-based `for` loop on `viewReverse` because, as explained earlier, a view is a special case of a range. Remember that all views are ranges, but some ranges are not views.

Adaptors Provided by the Ranges Library

In Listing 29.6, you saw how to use the adaptor `std::views::reverse` to generate a view of a collection in the reverse order of element insertion. Table 29.2 lists some common adaptors provided by the STL.

TABLE 29.2 Common Adaptors

Adaptor	Description
`std::views::reverse`	View elements in a collection in the reverse order (that is, last element first)
`std::views::all`	View all elements in a collection
`std::views::filter(p)`	View only elements that satisfy a supplied predicate `p`
`std::views::drop(n)`	View elements in the collection, ignoring the first `n` elements
`std::views::take(n)`	View the first `n` elements in a collection
`std::views::transform(f)`	View the result of a transforming function `f` applied individually to elements in the supplied range

Listing 29.7 shows how to use these adaptors to generate different views on a collection.

Input ▼

LISTING 29.7 Using Range Adaptors to Generate Views on a Given Collection

```
#include<ranges>
#include<vector>
#include<iostream>

using namespace std;

template<ranges::view T>
void DisplayView(T& view)
{
    for (auto element : view)
```

```
      cout << element << ' ';

   cout << endl;
}

int main()
{
   vector<int> nums{ 1, 5, 202, -99, 42, 50 };

   // Adaptor all creates a view comprising all elements
   auto viewAllElements = nums | std::views::all;
   cout << "View of all elements in the collection: ";
   DisplayView(viewAllElements);

   // Adaptor filter creates a view comprising even numbers
   auto viewOnlyEven = nums | \
      std::views::filter([](auto num) {return ((num % 2) == 0); });
   cout << "View of even numbers in collection: ";
   DisplayView(viewOnlyEven);

   // Adaptor reverse creates a view of elements in reverse order
   auto viewReverse = nums | std::views::reverse;
   cout << "View of collection in reverse: ";
   DisplayView(viewReverse);

   // Adaptor drop creates a view of elements without first 3
   auto viewSkip3 = nums | std::views::drop(3);
   cout << "View of collection ignoring first 3 elements: ";
   DisplayView(viewSkip3);

   // Adaptor take creates a view comprising first 3 elements
   auto viewFirst3 = nums | std::views::take(3);
   cout << "View of first 3 elements: ";
   DisplayView(viewFirst3);

   // Adaptor transform creates a view comprising -1, 0 or 1
   auto viewTransform = nums | \
      std::views::transform([](auto num) {return (num % 2); });
   cout << "Transformed view ";
   DisplayView(viewTransform);

   return 0;
}
```

Output ▼

```
View of all elements in the collection: 1 5 202 -99 42 50
View of even numbers in collection: 202 42 50
View of collection in reverse: 50 42 -99 202 5 1
View of collection ignoring first 3 elements: -99 42 50
View of first 3 elements: 1 5 202
Transformed view 1 1 0 -1 0 0
```

Analysis ▼

The code in this example is quite self-explanatory. It starts with a simple collection called `nums`, in the form `vector<int>`, that is initialized to contain some sample numbers. You then create different views of this collection by using the adaptors `all`, `filter`, `reverse`, `drop`, `take`, and `transform`.

In this example, note how the function `DisplayView()` is programmed. By using the concept `ranges::view`, you tell the compiler that this function can only be used with arguments that are a view. If you were to pass a range (such as the vector `nums`) to this function, the compiler would protest.

TIP

> C++20 views feature lazy initialization. The performance cost of defining a view is negligible, and not influenced by the size of the range it is intended to be operated upon. *Lazy initialization* means that the expense of execution is incurred when a view is used for the first time. Furthermore, a composite view can be created by combining (or *chaining*) multiple adaptors to each other by using the pipe symbol (|). These features make views and adaptors superior to STL algorithms.

Combining Multiple Adaptors

Say that you need to reverse elements and identify the even numbers among them. Generating such a view is a one-step process when you combine the adaptors `reverse` and `filter` as follows:

```
auto lambdaIsEven = [](auto num) {return ((num % 2) == 0); };
auto viewEvenInRev = nums | views::reverse | views::filter(lambdaIsEven);
```

If you now intend to further restrict the view to only two elements, you need to add the adaptor `take` to your chain:

```
auto viewEvenInReverseTopTwo = nums | views::reverse
              | views::filter(lambdaIsEven) | views::take(2);
```

Listing 29.8 demonstrates the use of these adaptors.

Input ▼

LISTING 29.8 Combining Adaptors by Using the Pipe Symbol (|)

```
#include<ranges>
#include<vector>
#include<iostream>
using namespace std;

// concept ranges::view limits parameter type to view
template<ranges::view T>
void DisplayView(T& view)
{
    for (auto element : view)
        cout << element << ' ';

    cout << endl;
}

int main()
{
    vector<int> nums{ 1, 5, 202, -99, 42, 50 };
    auto viewAllElements = nums | std::views::all;
    cout << "View of all elements in the collection: ";
    DisplayView(viewAllElements);

    auto lambdaIsEven = [](auto num) {return ((num % 2) == 0); };
    auto viewEvenInRev = nums | views::reverse | views::filter(lambdaIsEven);
    cout << "View even numbers in reverse: ";
    DisplayView(viewEvenInRev);

    auto viewEvenInReverseTopTwo = nums | views::reverse
                | views::filter(lambdaIsEven) | views::take(2);
    cout << "View first two even numbers in reverse: ";
    DisplayView(viewEvenInReverseTopTwo);

    return 0;
}
```

Output ▼

```
View of all elements in the collection: 1 5 202 -99 42 50
View even numbers in reverse: 50 42 202
View first two even numbers in reverse: 50 42
```

Analysis ▼

Lines 18, 23, and 27 demonstrate how adaptors are combined to give you the view you seek. Using adaptors is a new way of programming in C++, and it might seem foreign at first. However, you'll come to appreciate the fact that you can quickly use adaptors to implement the same logic that would require multiple steps using algorithms. Using algorithms would require more lines of code and might be slow as well. Views and adaptors have made C++ code more intuitive and can save you a good number of lines of code and processing steps as well!

Summary

This lesson familiarized you with the dramatic changes introduced with C++20, including concepts, ranges, views, and adaptors. These new features are not required to write good C++ programs, but they represent a major modernization to the language. In the next few years, you will see more and more C++ code adopting these changes, and you're now set up to understand such code and develop your skills further. Don't stop at the examples in this book; explore the ranges library online to develop your skills further.

Q&A

Q I am not able to compile the examples in this lesson. What am I doing wrong?

A As of this writing, not every compiler consistently and completely supports C++20 features. This code has been successfully tested using `g++` Version 12.0 and MSVC Version 16.10. You have to specifically enable C++20 language features in your compiler, as mentioned earlier in this lesson.

Q Why use concepts when you can use `DisplayView()` (as shown in Listing 27.8) without concepts?

A You can program `DisplayView()` to accept an `auto` parameter without using a concept to restrict the parameter type, like this:

```
void DisplayView(auto& view)
```

If you used this parameter, the code in Listing 29.8 would compile. You would even save a line of code. The use of concepts is optional. When things go wrong, though, and `DisplayView()` is used for types that are not necessarily views, the compiler may deliver complicated error messages. Concepts help the designer of a template class or function enforce the use of that class or function within specified constraints. Any failure to meet these defined constraints (that is, concepts) will result in simpler compiler error messages that accelerate the correction process.

Workshop

The Workshop provides quiz questions to help you solidify your understanding of the material covered and exercises to provide you with experience using what you've learned. Try to answer the quiz and exercise questions before checking the answers in Appendix E and be certain you understand the answers before continuing to the next lesson.

Quiz

1. What header would you include to use concepts to help validate a type as integral?
2. Are all views ranges, and are all ranges also views?
3. What do you call the logic (algorithm) that acts on a collection to create a view?

Exercises

1. **BUG BUSTERS:** If you replace Line 20 in Listing 29.8 with the following code, it won't compile:

   ```
   DisplayView(nums);
   ```

   Why is this the case?
2. What changes would you need to make to the declaration of `DisplayView()` so that the code in Listing 29.8, with the change shown in Exercise 1, will compile?
3. Compose a view that consists of the square of three elements taken from the end of a collection.

LESSON 30
C++20 Threads

The ability to write high-performance applications is one reason why C++ is often chosen over other programming languages. The time has come to learn how recent developments in C++ help you program multithreaded applications for high-performance computing.

In this lesson, you learn

- The basics of threads and multithreading
- C++20 multithreading support improvements

Multithreading

Multithreaded applications take advantage of processor capabilities to perform certain tasks concurrently. The threads run in parallel, enabling the OS to utilize multiple cores. Although it is beyond the scope of this book to discuss threads and multithreading in detail, I introduce this topic and give you a head start toward high-performance computing.

What Is a Thread?

Application code always runs in a thread. A *thread* is a synchronous execution entity in which instructions are executed one after another. The code inside `main()` is considered to execute the main thread of the application. In this main thread, you can create new threads that can run in parallel. Applications that are composed of one or more threads running in parallel, in addition to the main thread, are called *multithreaded* applications.

The OS dictates how threads are to be created. You create threads by calling application programming interfaces (APIs) supplied by the OS. Different OSs support different APIs for multithreading, and there have been many attempts at wrapper libraries that support portable thread creation and synchronization. C++20 has standardized the creation and simple synchronization of threads. You can therefore use platform-independent C++ code in creating multithreaded applications.

Why Program Multithreaded Applications?

Multithreading is useful in scenarios where certain activities need to be executed in parallel. Imagine that you are one among 100,000 users using a popular shopping portal at a given moment. The web server, of course, cannot keep thousands of users waiting. The web server creates multiple threads to service multiple users at the same time. If the web server is running on a multiple-core processor or a multiple-processor cloud, the multithreaded architecture gets to extract the best out of the available infrastructure and provide optimal user experience.

Another common example of multithreading is an application that does some work in addition to interacting with the user, such as via a progress bar. Such applications are often divided into a user interface thread, which displays and updates the user interface and accepts user input, and a worker thread, which does the work in the background. A tool that defragments your disk is one such application. After you press the start button, a worker thread is created that starts with the scan and defragmenting activity. At the same time, the user interface thread displays progress and also gives you the option to cancel the defragmentation. Note that for the user interface thread to show progress, the worker thread that does the defragmentation needs to regularly communicate what is happening. Similarly, for the worker thread to stop working when you cancel, the user interface thread needs to communicate a stop message.

NOTE

> A multithreaded application typically needs threads to "talk" to each other so that the application can function as a unit. Sequence is important, too. In the preceding example, you want the user interface thread to end after the defragmenting worker thread has ended—and not before. In such situations, one thread needs to wait on another.
>
> The act of making threads wait on one another is called *thread synchronization*.

Using the C++20 Thread Library

C++2020 has simplified programming of multithreaded applications through the helper class `std::jthread`.

TIP

> To use multithreading functionalities, include this header:
>
> ```
> #include<thread>
> ```

Listing 30.1 shows a simple application comprising a main thread and a worker thread. It displays a line on the screen at one-second intervals.

NOTE

As of this writing, popular compilers do not consistently support the C++20 features explained in this lesson. Be sure to use the latest versions of your favorite compiler when trying the code examples provided in this lesson. Do not let compiler errors dishearten you. Use this lesson to understand the features so that you're ready to consume them as soon as they're better supported by your compiler.

TIP

Remember to explicitly activate supported C++20 features. When using `g++` or `clang++`, add `-std=c++20` to the command line. MSVC users can enable `/std:c++20` via the option C++ Language Standard under Project Properties.

Input ▼

LISTING 30.1 A Simple Multithreading Application Using `std::jthread`

```
#include<thread>
#include<stop_token>
#include<iostream>
using namespace std;

void ThreadFunction(std::stop_token stopSoon)
{
    while (true)
    {
        cout << "Worker thread: Hello!\n";
        std::this_thread::sleep_for(1s);

        if (stopSoon.stop_requested())
        {
            cout << "Worker thread: asked to end, bye\n";
            break;
        }
    }
}

int main()
{
    cout << "Main thread: Starting a worker thread\n";
```

```
23:
24:     // Construct a thread object (it starts execution too)
25:     jthread thSayHello(ThreadFunction);
26:
27:     // pause the main thread for 5 seconds
28:     this_thread::sleep_for(5s);
29:
30:     cout << "Main thread: Sending a stop request to worker\n";
31:     // send a stop "request" to child thread (not a kill)
32:     thSayHello.request_stop();
33:
34:     if (thSayHello.joinable())
35:     {
36:        cout << "Main thread: Waiting on worker to end\n";
37:        thSayHello.join(); // waiting on thread to end
38:        cout << "Main thread: wait has ended. Exiting now\n";
39:     }
40:
41:     return 0;
42: }
```

Output ▼

```
Main thread: Starting a worker thread
Worker thread: Hello!
Worker thread: Hello!
Worker thread: Hello!
Worker thread: Hello!
Worker thread: Hello!
Main thread: Sending a stop request to worker
Main thread: Waiting on worker to end
Worker thread: asked to end, bye
Main thread: wait has ended. Exiting now
```

Analysis ▼

The program in this example comprises two parts: `main()` and `ThreadFunction()`. `main()` executes the main thread of the application. It instantiates a worker thread that executes `ThreadFunction()` in parallel. `ThreadFunction()`, defined in Lines 5 through 18, does nothing but output `Worker thread: Hello!` on the screen every second. It's programmed to keep doing this forever until a stop signal is received, in the form `std::stop_token.stop_requested()`. The main thread triggers the execution of the worker thread in Line 25, where `ThreadFunction` is passed as a parameter to the constructor of `jthread`.

In Line 32, the main thread sends a signal requesting the worker to end. If `ThreadFunction()` chose not to handle the stop token in Line 12, this request is ignored. The method `joinable()` returns `false` if it was invoked from the same thread object. It helps ensure that a thread doesn't use `join()` on itself. For demonstration purposes, method `joinable()` is queried in Line 34 from the main thread on the worker thread object even though `joinable()` is certain to return `true` in this simple program. The actual act of getting `main()` to wait on the worker thread is executed in Line 37, using `join()`.

Obviously, this is a very simple application that demonstrates the basics of instantiating a thread and waiting on it. Practical applications include sharing data between threads and therefore come with the added challenge of ensuring data integrity.

How Can Threads Transact Data?

Threads can share variables. Threads have access to globally placed data. A thread can be created with a pointer to a shared object (`struct` or `class`) with data in it, as shown in Figure 30.1.

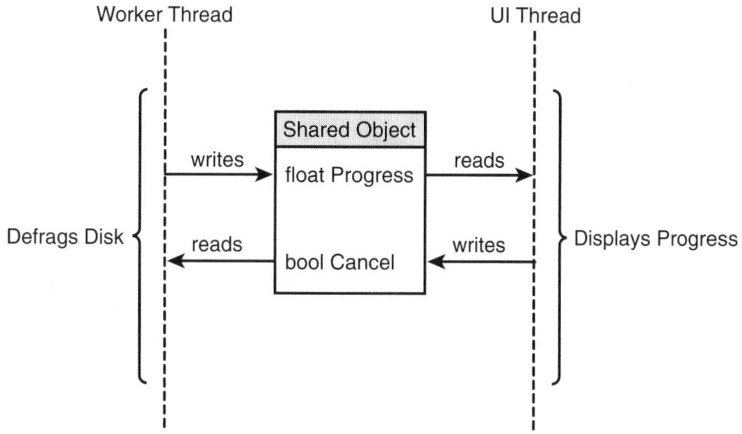

FIGURE 30.1
Worker and user interface threads sharing data.

Different threads can communicate by accessing or writing data that is stored in a location in memory that can be accessed by all the threads and is therefore shared. In the previously mentioned example of the defragmenter where the worker thread knows the progress and the user interface thread needs to be informed of it, the worker thread can constantly store the progress, in percentage, as an integer that the user interface thread uses to display the progress.

This is a simple case, though: One thread creates information and the other consumes it. What would happen if multiple threads wrote to and read from the same location? Some threads might start reading data when some other threads have not finished writing it. The integrity of the data in question would be compromised. This is why we need thread synchronization.

Using Mutexes and Semaphores to Synchronize Threads

Threads are OS-level entities, and the objects that you use to synchronize them are supplied by the OS, too. Most operating systems provide you with *semaphores* and *mutexes* for performing thread synchronization activity.

You use a *mutex*—that is, a *mutual exclusion synchronization* object—to ensure that one thread has access to a piece of code at a time. In other words, a mutex is used to bracket a section of code where a thread has to wait until another thread that is currently executing it is done and releases the mutex. The next thread acquires the mutex, does its job, and releases it. C++ supplies you with an implementation of a mutex in the class `std::mutex`, which is available via the header `<mutex>`.

By using *semaphores*, you can control the number of threads that execute a section of code. A semaphore that allows access to only one thread at a time is also called a *binary semaphore*.

C++20 Coroutines

C++20 introduces coroutines as an alternative that helps with efficient thread synchronization. Coroutines are functions that can be paused; that is, their execution can be suspended and restarted when suitable. The other thing that sets them apart from regular functions is that they do not use a stack. When suspended, a coroutine stores the state necessary to resume reliably outside the stack (for example, heap or free store).

Summary

Multithreading isn't a necessity in every scenario, and the decision to use it must be taken carefully, keeping the objectives of the application in perspective. Programming multithreaded applications requires patience and thoroughness. This lesson familiarized you with key terms related to multithreading so that you can continue your learning through hands-on practice assisted by online resources.

Q&A

Q I am quite happy with the performance of my application. Should I still implement multithreaded capabilities?

A No, not at all. Multithreading isn't required in every application. Only applications that need to perform tasks concurrently or that serve many users in parallel need multithreading.

Workshop

The Workshop contains exercises to help solidify your understanding of the material covered. Try to complete the exercises before checking the answers in Appendix E.

Exercise

1. What would happen to the worker thread in Listing 30.1 if the main thread didn't use `join()`?

LESSON 31
C++20 Modules and C++23

You are now familiar with C++ programming. You have learned recent additions that modernize the language: lambda expressions, automatic type deductions, ranges, views, and adaptors to mention a few. We'll now visit modules that have been introduced by the standard in C++20 but are yet to be consistently supported by popular compilers as of this writing. Before we close this lesson, we also briefly visit the amendments that C++23 is expected to bring.

In this lesson, you learn

- C++20 modules that are poised to replace header files
- New features expected in C++23
- Improving your C++ skills beyond this book

Modules

Modules are an advancement of one of the most primitive yet well-established C++ features: header files. By now, you're undoubtedly familiar with syntax such as

```
#include<header>
```

For instance:

```
#include<iostream>
```

The Problem with #include<*header*>

`#include<header>` is a relic inherited from C. This directive is executed by the preprocessor and inserts the entire contents of `<header>` at the point in code where the inclusion is declared. When multiple headers are included, the preprocessor goes about inserting the text content inline, in the order of insertion. Headers often include other headers, and the preprocessor just adds to the burden on the compiler. This rather simple inclusion logic as a precursor to compilation brings a bunch of problems:

- It is unintelligent, and artifacts common to multiple headers are included repeatedly.
- It causes code explosion because code that is not relevant to the program being compiled also gets included and evaluated by the compiler.
- It slows down compilation time significantly and increases the probability of errors caused by duplicate artifact definition.
- The order of inclusion is important because other preprocessor directives such as `#define` *`MACRO`* with `#ifdef` and `#ifndef` influence the code that is to be compiled.

C++20 Modules

Modules are compartmentalized sections of code, where each module has a unique name. Modules can *export* functions, variables, and classes. They need to be *imported* in order for the artifacts that are exported to be consumed. A variant of the `"Hello World!"` program created using modules is demonstrated in Listing 31.1.

CAUTION

> As of this writing, C++20 module support in popular compilers is incomplete and often buggy.
>
> The modularization of standard headers such as `<iostream>` has not yet been standardized. This standardization is earmarked for completion in C++23.
>
> So, don't be surprised if Listing 31.1 doesn't and cannot compile in your favorite environment. For now, you just need to understand the subject matter and should not worry about implementation details.

Input ▼

LISTING 31.1 A Simple `"Hello World!"` Program Using Modules (Compiler Compatibility Limited to MSVC)

```
import std.core; // module containing core utilities like cout

int main()
{
     std::cout << "Hello World!" << std::endl;
     return 0;
}
```

Output ▼

```
Hello World!
```

Analysis ▼

The special thing about this program is that it uses modules, which are some of the newest introductions to C++. Note that this example doesn't include the header <iostream>. The keyword import instructs the compiler to include the module std.core. In the current implementation of MSVC, the module std.core supplies all the core functions, including those supplied by <iostream>.

Programming a Module

A module has two key parts:

- **The module interface unit:** This is the file where the module declares artifacts that are visible outside the module (that is, artifacts that are exported from the module). It is characterized by the declaration

  ```
  export module ModuleName;
  ```

  For instance, a module called MyFirstModule in the file MyFirstModule.ixx would be declared like this:

  ```
  // file MyFirstModule.ixx (extension ixx for MSVC)
  export module MyFirstModule;
  ```

  Functions and variables that the module chooses to expose to its consumers are declared in the module interface unit using the keyword export:

  ```
  export int AddIntegers(int a, int b);
  void FuncNotVisibleOutsideModule(); // not exported
  ```

  Functions, classes, and variables that are not exported from the module continue to be visible and usable within the module but are not available outside it.

TIP

Header files cannot be included in a module unit. You can import like this them instead (don't forget the semicolon!):

```
import <header>;
```

- **The module implementation unit:** This defines (that is, implements) the functions and artifacts that are declared in the module interface unit:

```
// file MyFirstModule.cpp
module MyFirstModule;

int AddIntegers(int a, int b)
{
   return (a + b);
}
```

TIP

Headers can be included in the global module fragment. When a module interface unit starts with

```
export module; // no module name supplied
```

the code that follows is said to be part of the global module fragment:

```
// file MyFirstModule.ixx
export module;
#include<header> // in global module fragment
export module MyFirstModule;
export int AddIntegers(int a, int b); // in module
MyFirstModule
```

You use the global module fragment to include header files that may be required.

Consuming a Module

After you create the module `MyFirstModule`, you want to consume the functions it exposes. You need to import a module in the location where you need to be using it:

```
// main.cpp
import MyFirstModule;
int main()
{
   int sum = AddIntegers(500, 50); // exported by MyFirstModule

   // FuncNotVisibleOutsideModule(); // error: not exported, hence unavailable

   return 0;
}
```

TIP

> An example showing modules with multiple files and demonstrating `module` definition, `export`, and `import` is available in Listing 31.1 and among the code files that you can download.

Why `import` *`Module;`* Is Superior to the Preprocessor `#include<`*`header`*`>`

Importing modules is more efficient than using the preprocessor to include header files for several reasons:

- Modules are compiled individually, unlike header files, which are inserted by the preprocessor as text within the contents of the `.CPP` file at the point of header inclusion.
- There are no dependencies between modules; therefore, the order of module import is irrelevant. (In contrast, in many cases, the order of header inclusion is relevant.)
- Only artifacts that are exported by a module are relevant outside it, and other artifacts are not. This helps speed up compilation.

C++23 Expected Features

One of the great things about C++ is that the Standards Committee is active and constantly improves the language. Building on the radical amendments introduced in C++20, the next wave of improvements to the standard is expected to complete support for these features in C++23.

NOTE

> The features discussed in this section are likely to make it to the C++ standard but aren't currently part of it. C++23 may not necessarily support every feature introduced here.

Key features that are expected to make it to the 2023 revision to C++ include

- **A modular standard library:** When learning modules, you probably noticed the disclaimers related to importing `std.core`. Although modularized versions of the Standard Library have been introduced, compilers don't yet have clear guidance on the names of the modules and what they're required to support or export.

The expectation is that C++23 will provide clarity on modularizing the Standard Library, and the changes then will be consistent across compilers and platforms.

- **Library support for coroutines:** Coroutines, introduced in C++20, help with thread synchronization. However, missing library support is going to hamper adoption. This barrier is expected to be lifted in C++23.

C++23 is expected to complete features introduced by C++20, such as full ranges support with relevant algorithms, including those from `<numeric>`. C++23 is also expected to add support for networking applications. There might be support added for *executors*, which are expected to govern the execution of code (functions, methods, and so on), including scheduling and processor details.

Learning C++ Doesn't Stop Here!

Throughout these lessons, you have made great progress in learning C++. The best way to continue is to code and code some more! C++ is a sophisticated language. The more you program, the greater the understanding you will have of how it all works behind the scenes. Visit Appendix C, "Writing Great C++ Code," to learn best practices that will help you program good, maintainable C++ code. Visit online resources and be an active participant in development communities!

Online Documentation

You are encouraged to learn more about the signatures of STL containers, their methods, algorithms, ranges, views, and adaptors by using online resources and documents. One popular site with structured resources is www.cppreference.com.

Communities for Guidance and Help

To take advantage of the rich and vibrant online communities around C++, consider these suggestions:

- Enroll at sites such as Stack Overflow (www.stackoverflow.com) and CodeGuru (www.codeguru.com), and when you have technical queries, you can get answers from those communities.
- Participate in open source C++ projects and contribute to GitHub.
- Program together with other experienced programmers.
- Be curious, learn, and share.

Summary

This concluding lesson is an invitation to keep learning more C++ on your own. You are now familiar with basic and advanced concepts of the language. You know that good code requires more than the adoption of the newest language features. You've learned that you typically don't need to reinvent the wheel but can use Standard Library algorithms and features. You are ready for the world of professional programming in C++, and we wish you all the best!

Q&A

Q I am not able to compile modules. What do I need to change?

A As of this writing, the implementation of C++20 modules is inconsistent across compilers. You need to consult your compiler documentation. For example, when using Visual Studio, you need to ensure that the optional component on C++ modules is installed, ensure that your project is configured for C++20 (`/std:c++20`), and ensure that the experimental mode is switched on (`/experimental:module`).

Q Why have modules been introduced in the book if the compiler support is not yet complete?

A Modules introduced in C++20 are here to stay. It takes a while for compilers to adopt the newest standard and support new features. In exercising ample caution to ensure that stable builds are not broken, new features are introduced using switches like `-std=c++20` in `g++` and `clang++`, or `/std:c++20` in MSVC that have to be explicitly enabled.

Workshop

The Workshop contains exercises to help solidify your understanding of the material covered. Try to complete the exercises before checking the answers in Appendix E.

Exercise

1. **BUG BUSTERS:** What is the error in the following code?

```
// module interface file Calculations.ixx
export module Calculations;
int AddNums(int a, int b)
{
   return (a + b);
}
// main.cpp
import Calculations;
int main()
{
   int sum = AddNums(3, 4);
   return 0;
}
```

APPENDIX A

Working with Numbers: Binary and Hexadecimal

Understanding how the binary and hexadecimal number systems work is not critical to programming better applications in C++, but it helps you to better understand what happens under the hood.

Decimal Numeral System

Numbers that we use on a daily basis are in the range of 0 through 9. This set of numbers is called the *decimal numeral system*. Because this system is composed of 10 unique digits, it's a system with a base of 10.

Hence, as the base is 10, the zero-based position of each digit denotes the power of 10 that the digit is multiplied with. For example, in the number 957, the zero-based position of 7 is 0, that of 5 is 1, and that of 9 is 2. These position indexes become powers of the base 10, as shown in the following example:

```
957 = 9 x 102 + 5 x 101 + 7 x 100 = 9 x 100 + 5 x 10 + 7
```

Remember that any number to the power 0 is 1 (so, 10^0 is the same as 1000^0 as both evaluate to 1).

NOTE

> In the decimal system, powers of 10 are important. Digits in a number are multiplied by 10, 100, 1000, and so on to determine the magnitude of the number.

Binary Numeral System

A system with a base of 2 is called a *binary system*. The binary numeral system allows only two states and is represented by the numbers 0 and 1. These numbers in C++ typically evaluate to `false` and `true` (`true` being nonzero).

Just as numbers in the decimal system are evaluated to powers of base 10, those in binary are evaluated to powers of their base 2:

$$101 \text{ (binary)} = 1 \times 2^2 + 0 \times 2^1 + 1 \times 2^0 = 4 + 0 + 1 = 5 \text{ (decimal)}$$

So, the decimal equivalent of binary 101 is 5.

NOTE

> Digits in a binary number are multiplied by powers of 2—such as 4, 8, 16, 32, and so on—to determine the magnitude of the number. The power is decided by the zero-based place of the digit in question.

To understand the binary numeral system better, examine Table A.1, which lists the various powers of 2.

TABLE A.1 Powers of 2

Power	Value	Binary Representation
0	$2^0 = 1$	1
1	$2^1 = 2$	10
2	$2^2 = 4$	100
3	$2^3 = 8$	1000
4	$2^4 = 16$	10,000
5	$2^5 = 32$	100,000
6	$2^6 = 64$	1,000,000
7	$2^7 = 128$	10,000,000

Why Do Computers Use Binary?

The binary system has been in widespread use for a comparatively short period of time. Its use has been accelerated by the development of electronics and computers. The evolution of electronics and electronic components resulted in a system that detected states of a component as being ON (that is, under a significant potential difference or voltage) or OFF (that is, no or low potential difference).

These ON and OFF states were conveniently interpreted as 1 and 0, completely representing the binary number set and making it the method of choice for performing arithmetic calculations. Logical operations, such as NOT, AND, OR, and XOR, as covered in Lesson 5, "Working with Expressions, Statements, and Operators" (in Tables 5.2 through 5.5), were easily supported by the development of electronic gates, resulting in the binary system being wholeheartedly adopted as conditional processing became easy.

What Are Bits and Bytes?

A *bit* is a basic unit in a computational system that contains a binary state. Thus, a bit is said to be "set" if it contains state 1 or "reset" if it contains state 0. A collection of bits is a *byte*. The number of bits in a byte is theoretically not fixed and is a hardware-dependent number. However, most computational systems assume 8 bits in a byte—for the simple, convenient reason that 8 is a power of 2. Assuming 8 bits in a byte also allows the transmission of up to 2^8 different values, allowing for 255 distinct values. These 255 distinct values are enough for the display or transaction of all characters in the ASCII character set—and more.

How Many Bytes Make a Kilobyte?

1024 bytes (210 bytes) make a kilobyte. Similarly, 1024 kilobytes make a megabyte. 1024 megabytes make a gigabyte. 1024 gigabytes make a terabyte.

Hexadecimal Numeral System

The *hexadecimal numeral system* has a base of 16. A digit in the hexadecimal system can be in the range 0 through 9 and A through F. For example, 10 in decimal is equivalent to A in hexadecimal, and 15 in decimal is equivalent to F in hexadecimal. Table A.2 shows how the hexadecimal digits translate to decimal.

TABLE A.2 Decimal and Hexadecimal Equivalents

Decimal	Hexadecimal	Decimal (continued)	Hexadecimal (continued)
0	0	8	8
1	1	9	9
2	2	10	A
3	3	11	B
4	4	12	C
5	5	13	D
6	6	14	E
7	7	15	F

Just as numbers in a decimal system are evaluated to powers of base 10 and numbers in binary are evaluated to powers of their base 2, those in hexadecimal are evaluated to powers of base 16. Consider this example:

$$0x31F = 3 \times 16^2 + 1 \times 16^1 + F \times 16^0 = 3 \times 256 + 16 + 15 \text{ (in decimal)} = 799$$

NOTE By convention, hexadecimal numbers are represented with the prefix 0x.

Why Do We Need Hexadecimal?

Computers use the binary numeral system, and the state of each unit of memory in a computer is a 0 or a 1. However, if we humans were to interact with computer- or programming-specific information using 0s and 1s, we would need a lot of space to record even small pieces of information. A hexadecimal representation can very efficiently represent the state of 4 bits in a digit by using a maximum of two hexadecimal digits to represent the state of a byte. For example, instead of writing 1111 in binary, you are a lot more efficient writing F in hexadecimal.

NOTE

> A less-used number system is the *octal numeral system*. This is a system with base 8, comprising the numbers 0 through 7.

Converting to a Different Base

When dealing with numbers, you might sometimes need to view a number in a different base. For instance, you might need to know the value of a binary number in decimal or the value of a decimal number in hexadecimal.

Earlier in this appendix, you saw how numbers can be converted from binary or hexadecimal into decimal. The following section gives you a look at converting binary and hexadecimal numbers into decimal.

The Generic Conversion Process

When converting a number in one system to another system, you successively divide with the base, starting with the number being converted. Each remainder fills places in the destination numeral system, starting with the lowest place. The next division uses the quotient of the previous division operation with the base as the divisor.

This continues until the remainder is within the destination numeral system and the quotient is 0.

This process is also called the *breakdown method*.

Converting Decimal to Binary

To convert decimal 33 into binary, you follow the steps shown below:

Place 1: 33 / 2 = quotient 16, remainder 1

Place 2: 16 / 2 = quotient 8, remainder 0

Place 3: 8 / 2 = quotient 4, remainder 0

Place 4: 4 / 2 = quotient 2, remainder 0

Place 5: 2 / 2 = quotient 1, remainder 0

Place 6: 1 / 2 = quotient 0, remainder 1

Therefore, the binary equivalent of 33 (reading places) is 100001.

Similarly, the binary equivalent of 156 is

Place 1: 156 / 2 = quotient 78, remainder 0

Place 2: 78 / 2 = quotient 39, remainder 0

Place 3: 39 / 2 = quotient 19, remainder 1

Place 4: 19 / 2 = quotient 9, remainder 1

Place 5: 9 / 2 = quotient 4, remainder 1

Place 6: 4 / 2 = quotient 2, remainder 0

Place 7: 2 / 2 = quotient 1, remainder 0

Place 9: 1 / 0 = quotient 0, remainder 1

Therefore, the binary equivalent of 156 is 10011100.

Converting Decimal to Hexadecimal

The process of converting decimal to hexadecimal is the same as for converting decimal to binary—but you divide by base 16 instead of 2.

So, to convert decimal 5211 to hex:

Place 1: 5211 / 16 = quotient 325, remainder B_{16} (11_{10} is B_{16})

Place 2: 325 / 16 = quotient 20, remainder 5

Place 3: 20 / 16 = quotient 1, remainder 4

Place 4: 1 / 16 = quotient 0, remainder 1

Therefore, $5211_{10} = 145B_{16}$.

TIP

> To better understand how different number systems work, you can write a simple C++ program similar to Listing 27.1 in Lesson 27, "Using Streams for Input and Output." It uses `std::cout` with manipulators for displaying an integer in hex, decimal, and octal notations.
>
> To display an integer in binary, you can use `std::bitset`, as explained in Lesson 25, "Working with Bit Flags Using the STL," deriving inspiration from Listing 25.1.

APPENDIX B
C++ Keywords

Keywords are reserved in a compiler for use by the C++ language. You cannot define classes, variables, or functions that have the following keywords as their names.

```
alignas         dynamic_cast       requires
alignof         else               return
and             enum               short
and_eq          explicit           signed
asm             export             sizeof
auto            extern             static
bitand          false              static_assert
bitor           float              static_cast
bool            for                struct
break           friend             switch
case            goto               template
catch           if                 this
char            inline             thread_local
char8_t         int                throw
char16_t        long               true
char32_t        mutable            try
class           namespace          typedef
compl           new                typeid
concept         noexcept           typename
const           not                union
consteval       not_eq             unsigned
constexpr       nullptr            using
constinit       operator           virtual
const_cast      or                 void
continue        or_eq              volatile
decltype        private            wchar_t
default         protected          while
delete          public             xor
do              register           xor_eq
double          reinterpret_cast
```

NOTE

Lesson 10, "Implementing Inheritance," and Lesson 11, "Polymorphism," introduce two identifiers: `final` and `override`. These are not reserved C++ keywords, and you can name your objects and functions after them. However, they carry special meanings when accompanying certain constructs, as explained in Lessons 10 and 11. Similarly, `import` and `module`, introduced in Lesson 31, "C++20 Modules and C++23," are also identifiers.

APPENDIX C

Writing Great C++ Code

C++ has evolved significantly since it was first conceived. In addition, standardization efforts made by major compiler manufacturers and the availability of utilities and functions help you write compact and clean C++ code. It is indeed easy to program readable and reliable C++ applications.

Here is a short list of best practices that help you create good C++ applications:

- Give your variables names that make sense (to others as well as to you). Thoughtfully named variables increase the maintainability of code.
- Always initialize a pointer value to a valid address, such as the address returned by the operator `new`.
- Never take the success of the operator `new` for granted. Code that performs resource allocation should always be made exception safe (that is, bracketed within `try` with corresponding `catch()` blocks).
- When using arrays, never cross the bounds of the array buffer. Doing so is called a *buffer overflow* and can be exploited as a security vulnerability.
- Don't use `char*` string buffers or functions such as `strlen()` and `strcpy()`. `std::string` is safer and provides many useful utility methods, including methods that help you find the length, copy, and append.
- Use a static array only when you are certain of the number of elements it will contain. If you are not certain of the number, use a dynamic array such as `std::vector`.
- When declaring and defining functions that take non-POD (plain old data) types as input, consider declaring parameters as reference parameters to avoid the unnecessary copy step when the function is called.
- If a class contains a raw pointer member (or members), give thought to how memory resource ownership needs to be managed in the event of a copy or an assignment. That is, consider programming the copy constructor and copy assignment operator.
- When writing a utility class that manages dynamically allocated resources, remember to program the move constructor and the move assignment operator for better performance.
- Remember to make your code `const` correct. A `get()` function should ideally not be able to modify the class's members and hence should be a `const`. Similarly, function parameters should be `const` references unless you want to change the values they contain.
- Avoid using raw pointers. Instead, use the appropriate smart pointers where possible.
- When programming a utility class, make the effort to support operators that will make consuming and using the class easy.

- Given an option, choose a template version over a macro. Templates offer type safety and are generic.
- When programming a class that will be collected in a container, such as a vector or a list, or a class that will be used as a key element in a map, remember to support the operator `<`, which helps define the default sort criteria.
- If a lambda function gets too large, consider making a function object of it. A class with `operator()` as the functor is reusable and provides a single point of maintenance.
- Never throw from the destructor of a class.
- Comment your code adequately.
- Use constants such as `std::numbers::pi` that are supplied by C++20 in the header `<numbers>` instead of defining your own.

This is not an exhaustive list, but it covers some of the most important points that will help you write good and maintainable C++ code.

APPENDIX D
ASCII Codes

Computers work using bits and bytes, which are essentially numbers. To represent character data in this numeric system, the standard American Standard Code for Information Interchange (ASCII) is prevalently used. ASCII assigns 7-bit numeric codes to Latin characters A–Z, a–z, numbers 0–9, some special keystrokes (for example, Delete), and special characters (such as backspace).

7 bits allow for 128 combinations, with the first 32 (0–31) reserved as control characters used to interface with peripherals such as printers.

ASCII Table of Printable Characters

ASCII codes 32–127 are used for printable characters such as 0–9, A–Z, and a–z, as well as a few others, such as space. Table D.1 shows the decimal and hexadecimal values reserved for these symbols.

TABLE D.1 Printable Characters

Symbol	Decimal	Hexadecimal	Description
	32	20	Space
!	33	21	Exclamation point
"	34	22	Double quotes (or speech marks)
#	35	23	Number
$	36	24	Dollar
%	37	25	Percent sign
&	38	26	Ampersand
'	39	27	Single quote
(	40	28	Open parenthesis
)	41	29	Close parenthesis
*	42	2A	Asterisk
+	43	2B	Plus
,	44	2C	Comma
-	45	2D	Hyphen
.	46	2E	Period, dot, or full stop
/	47	2F	Slash (or divide)
0	48	30	Zero
1	49	31	One
2	50	32	Two
3	51	33	Three
4	52	34	Four
5	53	35	Five

Symbol	Decimal	Hexadecimal	Description
6	54	36	Six
7	55	37	Seven
8	56	38	Eight
9	57	39	Nine
:	58	3A	Colon
;	59	3B	Semicolon
<	60	3C	Less than (or open angled bracket)
=	61	3D	Equals
>	62	3E	Greater than (or close angled bracket)
?	63	3F	Question mark
@	64	40	At symbol
A	65	41	Uppercase A
B	66	42	Uppercase B
C	67	43	Uppercase C
D	68	44	Uppercase D
E	69	45	Uppercase E
F	70	46	Uppercase F
G	71	47	Uppercase G
H	72	48	Uppercase H
I	73	49	Uppercase I
J	74	4A	Uppercase J
K	75	4B	Uppercase K
L	76	4C	Uppercase L
M	77	4D	Uppercase M
N	78	4E	Uppercase N
O	79	4F	Uppercase O
P	80	50	Uppercase P
Q	81	51	Uppercase Q
R	82	52	Uppercase R

Symbol	Decimal	Hexadecimal	Description
S	83	53	Uppercase S
T	84	54	Uppercase T
U	85	55	Uppercase U
V	86	56	Uppercase V
W	87	57	Uppercase W
X	88	58	Uppercase X
Y	89	59	Uppercase Y
Z	90	5A	Uppercase Z
[	91	5B	Opening bracket
\	92	5C	Backslash
]	93	5D	Closing bracket
^	94	5E	Caret (or circumflex)
_	95	5F	Underscore
`	96	60	Grave accent
a	97	61	Lowercase a
b	98	62	Lowercase b
c	99	63	Lowercase c
d	100	64	Lowercase d
e	101	65	Lowercase e
f	102	66	Lowercase f
g	103	67	Lowercase g
h	104	68	Lowercase h
i	105	69	Lowercase i
j	106	6A	Lowercase j
k	107	6B	Lowercase k
l	108	6C	Lowercase l
m	109	6D	Lowercase m
n	110	6E	Lowercase n
o	111	6F	Lowercase o
p	112	70	Lowercase p

Symbol	Decimal	Hexadecimal	Description
q	113	71	Lowercase q
r	114	72	Lowercase r
s	115	73	Lowercase s
t	116	74	Lowercase t
u	117	75	Lowercase u
v	118	76	Lowercase v
w	119	77	Lowercase w
x	120	78	Lowercase x
y	121	79	Lowercase y
z	122	7A	Lowercase z
{	123	7B	Opening brace
		124	7C	Vertical bar (or pipe)
}	125	7D	Closing brace
~	126	7E	Equivalency sign (or tilde)
	127	7F	Delete

APPENDIX E
Answers

Answers for Lesson 1

Quiz

1. A compiled language like C++ helps create executables—that is, instructions that run natively on a processor. An interpreted language like JavaScript needs an interpreter at runtime. An interpreter is a tool that reads the content of the script file and performs the desired actions.
2. A compiler takes C++ code files as input and generates the corresponding object files in machine language. In doing so, dependencies on functions and libraries used by other code files remain unresolved. The linker then takes over and generates an executable that is the final output of the build process, wherein all dependencies are resolved and linked.
3. Code. Compile to create object file. Link to create an executable. Execute to test. Debug. Fix errors in code. Deploy, especially in a cloud environment. Repeat. In many cases, compilation and linking are completed as one step.

Exercises

1. Display the result of subtracting y from x, multiplying the two, and adding the two.
2. Output should be

```
2 48 14
```

3. A preprocessor command to include `iostream`, as seen in Line 1, should start with `#`, as in this example:

```
#include<iostream>
```

4. It displays the following:

```
Hello Buggy World
```

Answers for Lesson 2

Quiz

1. Code in C++ is case-sensitive. Int is not acceptable to the compiler as an integer type `int`.
2. Yes.

```
/*  if you comment using this C-style syntax
then you can span your comment over multiple lines */
```

Exercises

1. It fails because case-sensitive C++ compilers don't know what `std::Cout` is or why the string following it doesn't start with an opening quote (`"`). In addition, the declaration of `main` should always return an `int`.
2. Here is the corrected version:

```
#include<iostream>
int main()
{
      std::cout << "Is there a bug here?"; // no bug anymore
      return 0;
}
```

3. This program, derived from Listing 2.4, demonstrates subtraction and multiplication:

```
#include<iostream>
using namespace std;

// Function declaration
int DemoConsoleOutput();

int main()
{
    // Call i.e. invoke the function
    DemoConsoleOutput();

    return 0;
}

// Function definition
int DemoConsoleOutput()
```

```
{
    cout << "10 - 5 = "
    cout << "10 * 5 = "

    return 0;
}
```

Output ▼

```
10 - 5 = 5
10 * 5 = 50
```

Answers for Lesson 3

Quiz

1. In a signed integer, the most-significant-bit (MSB) functions as the sign bit and indicates whether the value of the integer is positive or negative. An unsigned integer, in comparison, is used to contain only positive integer values.
2. `#define` is a preprocessor directive that directs the compiler to do a text replacement wherever the defined value is seen. However, it is not type safe, and using `#define` is a primitive way of defining constants. Therefore, it is to be avoided.
3. To ensure that it contains a definite, non-random value.
4. 2.
5. There is nothing wrong syntactically, but the name is nondescriptive and not reader friendly. Although this statement would compile, code like this becomes difficult to maintain and should be avoided. An integer is better declared using a name that reveals its purpose. For example:

   ```
   int age = 0;
   ```


Exercises

1. There are many ways of achieving this, including the following:

   ```
   enum YourCards {Ace = 43, Jack, Queen, King};
   // Ace is 43, Jack is 44, Queen is 45, King is 46
   // Alternatively..
   enum YourCards {Ace, Jack, Queen = 45, King};
   // Ace is 0, Jack is 1, Queen is 45 and King is 46
   ```

2. See Listing 3.4 and adapt it (reduce it) to get the answer to this question.

3. Here is a program that asks you to enter the radius of a circle and then calculates the area and circumference for you:

```
#include<iostream>
using namespace std;

int main()
{
   const double Pi = 3.1416;

   cout << "Enter circle's radius: ";
   double radius = 0;
   cin >> radius;

   cout << "Area = " << Pi * radius * radius << endl;
   cout << "Circumference = " << 2 * Pi * radius << endl;

   return 0;
}
```

Output ▼

```
Enter circle's radius: 4
Area = 50.2656
Circumference = 25.1328
```

4. You get a compilation warning (not an error) if you store the result of calculating area and circumference in an integer. The output looks like this:

```
Enter circle's radius: 4
Area = 50
Circumference = 25
```

5. `auto` is a construct with which the compiler automatically deduces the type of variable by using the value it is being initialized to. The code in question does not contain an initialization and hence fails compilation. Here is an improvement:

```
auto age = 21; // initialized to 21
```

Answers for Lesson 4

Quiz

1. 0 and 4 are the zero-based indexes of the first and last elements of an array with five elements.

2. No. They are unsafe, especially in handling user input, giving the user an opportunity to enter a string longer than the length of the array.

3. One null-terminating character.
4. It depends on how you use it. If you use it in a `cout` statement, for instance, the display logic reads successive characters, seeking a terminating null, and crosses the bounds of the array, possibly causing your application to crash.
5. That would simply replace the `int` in the vector's declaration by `char`:

```
vector<char> dynArrChars(3);
```

Exercises

1. This example initializes for rooks, but it's enough for you to get an idea:

```
int main()
{
   enum Square
   {
      Empty = 0,
      Pawn,
      Rook,
      Knight,
      Bishop,
      King,
      Queen
   };

   Square chessBoard[8][8];   // 8 rows x 8 columns

   // Initialize the squares containing rooks
   chessBoard[0][0] = chessBoard[0][7] = Rook;
   chessBoard[7][0] = chessBoard[7][7] = Rook;

   return 0;
}
```

2. To set the fifth element of an array, you need to access the element at index 4 (that is, `myNums[4]`) because arrays use a zero-based index.

Answers for Lesson 5

Quiz

1. Integer types cannot contain decimal values that are possibly relevant for the user who wants to divide two numbers. So, you would use `float`.
2. As the compiler interprets them to be an integer, it is 4.

3. As the numerator is 32.0 and not 32, the compiler interprets this to be a floating-point operation and creates a result in a `float` that is akin to 4.571.
4. No. `sizeof` is an operator.
5. It does not work as intended because the addition operator has priority over shift, resulting in a shift of 1 + 5 = 6 bits instead of just 1 bit.
6. The result of XOR is `false`, as also indicated in Table 5.5.

Exercises

1. Here is a correct solution:

```
int result = ((number << 1) + 5) << 1;
```

2. The result contains the number shifted 7 bits left, as the operator + takes priority over the operator <<.
3. Here is a program that stores two Boolean values entered by the user and demonstrates the result of using bitwise operators on them:

```
#include<iostream>
using namespace std;

int main()
{
    cout << "Enter a boolean value true(1) or false(0): ";
    bool value1 = false;
    cin >> value1;

    cout << "Enter another boolean value true(1) or false(0): ";
    bool value2 = false;
    cin >> value2;

    cout << "Result of bitwise operators on these operands: " << endl;
    cout << "Bitwise AND: " << (value1 & value2) << endl;
    cout << "Bitwise OR: " << (value1 | value2) << endl;
    cout << "Bitwise XOR: " << (value1 ^ value2) << endl;

    return 0;
}
```

Output ▼

```
Enter a boolean value true(1) or false(0): 1
Enter another boolean value true(1) or false(0): 0
Result of bitwise operators on these operands:
Bitwise AND: 0
Bitwise OR: 1
Bitwise XOR: 1
```

Answers for Lesson 6

Quiz

1. You indent not for sake of the compiler but for the sake of other programmers (humans) who might need to read or understand your code.
2. You avoid it to keep your code from getting unintuitive and expensive to maintain.
3. See the code in the solution to Exercise 1 that uses the decrement operator.
4. Because the condition in the for statement is not satisfied, the loop won't execute even once, and the cout statement it contains is never executed.

Exercises

1. You need to be aware that array indexes are zero based, and the last element is at index Length – 1:

```
#include<iostream>
using namespace std;

int main()
{
    const int ARRAY_LEN = 5;
    int myNums[ARRAY_LEN]= {-55, 45, 9889, 0, 45};

    for(int index = ARRAY_LEN - 1; index >= 0; --index)
        cout << "myNums[" << index << "] = " << myNums[index] << endl;

    return 0;
}
```

Output ▼

```
myNums[4] = 45
myNums[3] = 0
myNums[2] = 9889
myNums [1] = 45
myNums [0] = -55
```


2. One nested loop equivalent of Listing 6.13 that adds elements in two arrays in the reverse order is provided here:

```
#include<iostream>
using namespace std;

int main()
{
```

```
    const int ARRAY1_LEN = 3;
    const int ARRAY2_LEN = 2;

    int myNums1[ARRAY1_LEN] = {35, -3, 0};
    int MyInts2[ARRAY2_LEN] = {20, -1};

    cout << "Adding each int in myNums1 by each in MyInts2:" << endl;

    for(int index1 = ARRAY1_LEN - 1; index1 >= 0; --index1)
       for(int index2 = ARRAY2_LEN - 1; index2 >= 0; --index2)
          cout << myNums1[index1] << " + " << MyInts2[index2] \
          << " = " << myNums1[index1] + MyInts2[index2] << endl;

    return 0;
}
```

Output ▼

```
Adding each int in myNums1 by each in myNums2:
0 + -1 = -1
0 + 20 = 20
-3 + -1 = -4
-3 + 20 = 17
35 + -1 = 34
35 + 20 = 55
```

3. You need to replace the constant integer `numsToCalculate` with a value fixed at 5 with code that asks the user the following:

```
cout << "How many Fibonacci numbers you wish to calculate: ";
int numsToCalculate = 0; // no const
cin >> numsToCalculate;
```

4. The following is a `switch-case` construct using enumerated constants that tells if a color is in the rainbow:

```
#include<iostream>
using namespace std;


int main()
{
   enum Colors
   {
      Violet = 0,
      Indigo,
      Blue,
      Green,
      Yellow,
```

```
        Orange,
        Red,
        Crimson,
        Beige,
        Brown,
        Peach,
        Pink,
        White,
    };

    cout << "Here are the available colors: " << endl;
    cout << "Violet: " << Violet << endl;
    cout << "Indigo: " << Indigo << endl;
    cout << "Blue: " << Blue << endl;
    cout << "Green: " << Green << endl;
    cout << "Yellow: " << Yellow << endl;
    cout << "Orange: " << Orange << endl;
    cout << "Red: " << Red << endl;
    cout << "Crimson: " << Crimson << endl;
    cout << "Beige: " << Beige << endl;
    cout << "Brown: " << Brown << endl;
    cout << "Peach: " << Peach << endl;
    cout << "Pink: " << Pink << endl;
    cout << "White: " << White << endl;

    cout << "Choose one by entering code: ";
    int YourChoice = Blue; // initial
    cin >> YourChoice;

    switch(YourChoice)
    {
    case Violet:
    case Indigo:
    case Blue:
    case Green:
    case Yellow:
    case Orange:
    case Red:
        cout << "Bingo, your choice is a Rainbow color!" << endl;
        break;

    default:
        cout << "The color you chose is not in the rainbow" << endl;
        break;
    }

    return 0;
}
```

E

Output ▼

```
Here are the available colors:
Violet: 0
Indigo: 1
Blue: 2
Green: 3
Yellow: 4
Orange: 5
RED: 6
Crimson: 7
Beige: 8
Brown: 9
Peach: 10
Pink: 11
White: 12
Choose one by entering code: 4
Bingo, your choice is a Rainbow color!
```

5. The programmer unintentionally made an assignment to `10` in the `for` loop condition statement.
6. The `while` statement is followed by the null statement `;` on the same line. Thus, the intended loop following the `while` is never reached, and because `loopCounter`, which governs the `while` is never incremented, the `while` does not end, and the statements following it are never executed.
7. There is a missing `break` statement under `case 4` (which means the `default` case always executes).

Answers for Lesson 7

Quiz

1. The scope of these variables is the life of the function.
2. `someNumber` is a reference to the variable in the calling function. It does not hold a copy.
3. A recursive function.
4. Overloaded functions.
5. Top! Visualize a stack of plates; the one at the top is available for withdrawal, and that is what the stack pointer points to.

Exercises

1. The function prototypes would look like this:

```
double Volume(double radius); // sphere
double Volume (double radius, double height); // cylinder
```

   The function implementations (definitions) use the respective formulas supplied in the question and return the area to the caller as a return value.

2. Let Listing 7.8 inspire you. The function prototype is as follows:

```
void ProcessArray(double numbers[], int length);
```

3. The parameter `result` ought to be a reference for the function `Area()` to be effective:

```
void Area(double radius, double &result)
```

4. The default parameter should be listed at the end; otherwise, you will have a compile error. Alternatively, all parameters should have default values specified.
5. The function needs to return its output data by reference to the caller:

```
void Calculate(double radius, double &Area, double &Circumference)
{
    Area = 3.14 * radius * radius;
    Circumference = 2 * 3.14 * radius;
}
```

Answers for Lesson 8

Quiz

1. If the compiler let you do that, it would be an easy way to break exactly what `const` references were meant to protect: the data being referred to that cannot be changed.
2. They're operators.
3. A memory address.
4. The operator `*`.

Exercises

1. 40.
2. In the first overloaded variant, the arguments are copied to the called function. In the second variant, they're not copied as they're references to the variables in the caller,

and the function can change them. The third variant uses pointers, which (unlike references) can be `NULL` or invalid, and validity needs to be ensured in such a system.

3. Use the `const` keyword:

```
1: const int* pNum1 = &number;
```

4. It is assigning an integer to a pointer directly (that is, overwriting the contained memory address by an integer value). This is the correct version:

```
*pointToAnInt = 9; // previously: pointToAnInt = 9;
```

5. There is a double `delete` on the same memory address returned by `new` to `pNumber` and duplicated in `pNumberCopy`. Remove one `delete`.

6. 30.

Answers for Lesson 9

Quiz

1. On the free store. This is the same as it would be if you allocated for an `int` using `new`.
2. `sizeof()` calculates the size of a class on the basis of the declared data members. As `sizeof(pointer)` is constant and independent of the mass of data being pointed to, the `sizeof(Class)` containing one such pointer member isn't affected by the number of integers being pointed to.
3. None except member methods of the same class.
4. Yes, it can.
5. A constructor is typically used to initialize data members and resources.
6. Destructors are typically used for releasing resources and deallocating memory.

Exercises

1. C++ is case-sensitive. A class declaration should start with `class`, not `Class`, and it should end with a semicolon (`;`), as shown here:

```
class Human
{
    int Age;
    string Name;

public:
    Human() {}
};
```

2. Remember that members of a class, unlike those in a struct, are `private` by default. As `Human::Age` is a private member and as there is no public accessor function, there is no way that the user of this class can access `Age`.

3. Here is a version of the class `Human` with an initialization list in the constructor:

```
class Human
{
   int Age;
   string Name;

public:
   Human(string inputName, int inputAge)
         : Name(inputName), Age(inputAge) {}
};
```

4. Note that pi has not been exposed outside the class, as required:

```
#include<iostream>
using namespace std;

class Circle
{
   const double Pi;
   double radius;

public:
   Circle(double InputRadius) : radius(InputRadius), Pi(3.1416) {}

   double GetCircumference()
   {
      return 2*Pi*radius;
   }

   double GetArea()
   {
      return Pi*radius*radius;
   }
};

int main()
{
   cout << "Enter a radius: ";
   double radius = 0;
   cin >> radius;

   Circle myCircle(radius);
```

```
    cout << "Circumference = " << myCircle.GetCircumference() << endl;
    cout << "Area = " << myCircle.GetArea() << endl;

    return 0;
}
```

Answers for Lesson 10

Quiz

1. Use the access specifier `protected` to ensure that members of the base class are visible to the derived class.
2. The base part of the derived class object gets copied and passed as an argument. The resulting behavior due to "slicing" can be unpredictable. Avoid slicing by ensuring that functions accept parameters by reference instead of by value. This avoids the copy step and the slicing that is a result of copying.
3. Composition for design flexibility.
4. Use it to unhide base class methods.
5. No. The first class that specializes `Base`—that is, the class `Derived`—has a private inheritance relationship with `Base`. Thus, public members of the class `Base` are private to the class `SubDerived` and hence are not accessible.

Exercises

1. Construction occurs in the order mentioned in the class declaration: `Mammal`, `Bird`, `Reptile`, and `Platypus`. Destruction occurs in the reverse order.
2. Like this:

```
class Shape
{
    // ... Shape members
};

class Polygon: public Shape
{
    // ... Polygon members
};

class Triangle: public Polygon
{
    // ... Triangle members
};
```

3. The inheritance relationship between the classes `D1` and `Base` should be private to restrict the class `D2` from accessing the public members of `Base`.

4. Classes inherit `private` by default. If `Derived` were a `struct`, the inheritance would be `public`.

5. `SomeFunc()` accepts a parameter of type `Base` by value. Calling `SomeFunc()` using an instance of `Derived` will result in slicing, which leads to instability and unpredictable output:

```
Derived objectDerived;
SomeFunc(objectDerived); // slicing problems
```

You would solve this problem by ensuring that `SomeFunc()` accepts the parameter by reference:

```
void SomeFunc(Base& value) // avoids copy and slicing
{
   // ...
}
```

Answers for Lesson 11

Quiz

1. Declare an abstract base class `Shape` with `Area()` and `Print()` as pure virtual functions, thereby forcing `Circle` and `Triangle` to implement pure virtual functions. `Circle` and `Triangle` are then forced to comply with your criteria requiring support for `Area()` and `Print()`.

2. No. It creates virtual function tables only for classes that contain virtual functions.

3. Yes. It still cannot be instantiated. As long as a class has at least one pure virtual function, it remains an abstract base class (ABC), regardless of the presence or absence of other fully defined functions or parameters.

E

Exercises

1. The inheritance hierarchy using an abstract base class `Shape` for the classes `Circle` and `Triangle` is shown here:

```
#include<iostream>
using namespace std;

class Shape
{
public:
   virtual double Area() = 0;
   virtual void Print() = 0;
```

```
   virtual ~Shape() {};
};

class Circle
{
   double radius;
public:
   Circle(double inputRadius) : radius(inputRadius) {}

   double Area()
   {
      return 3.1415 * radius * radius;
   }

   void Print()
   {
      cout << "Circle says hello!"
   }
};

class Triangle
{
   double base, height;
public:
   Triangle(double inputBase, double inputHeight) : base(inputBase),
height(inputHeight) {}

   double Area()
   {
      return 0.5 * base * height;
   }

   void Print()
   {
      cout << "Triangle says hello!"
   }
};

int main()
{
   Circle myRing(5);
   Triangle myWarningTriangle(6.6, 2);

   cout << "Area of circle : " << myRing.Area() << endl;
   cout << "Area of triangle : " << myWarningTriangle.Area() << endl;

   myRing.Print();
   myWarningTriangle.Print();

   return 0;
}
```

There is a missing virtual destructor! Correct the code to
`virtual ~Vehicle(){}`

3. Without a virtual destructor, the constructor sequence would be `Vehicle()` followed by `Car()`, whereas the nonvirtual destructor would result only in `~Vehicle()` being invoked. The destructor `~Car()` isn't invoked.

Answers for Lesson 12

Quiz

1. You can program two implementations of the operator `[]`: one defined as a `const` function and the other not. In this case, the C++ compiler picks the `const` version for `const` instances of the class:

```
const Type& operator[](int index) const;
Type& operator[](int Index);
```

2. Yes, but only if you don't want your class to allow copying or assignment. Such a restriction would be necessary when programming a singleton—that is, a class that permits the existence of only one instance. Listing 9.10 in Lesson 9, "Classes and Objects," demonstrates a singleton class.
3. Because there are no dynamically allocated resources contained within the class `Date` that cause redundant memory allocation and deallocation cycles within the copy constructor or copy assignment operator, this class is not a good candidate for a move constructor or move assignment operator.

Exercises

1. The conversion operator `int()` can be as shown here:

```
class Date
{
   int day, month, year;
public:
   explicit operator int()
   {
      return ((year * 10000) + (month * 100) + day);
   }

   // constructor etc
};
```

2. Use the move constructor and move assignment operators from Listing 12.12 as inspiration. Modify code defining the class `MyBuffer` to manage a pointer to `float` instead of `int`.

Answers for Lesson 13

Quiz

1. `dynamic_cast`.
2. Correct the function, of course. Using `const_cast` and casting operators in general should be a last resort.
3. True.
4. Yes, true.

Exercises

1. The result of a `dynamic_cast` operation should always be checked for validity:

```
void DoSomething(base* pBase)
{
   Derived* objDerived = dynamic_cast <Derived*>(pBase);

   if(objDerived) // check for validity
      objDerived->DerivedClassMethod();
}
```

2. Use `static_cast` as you know that the object being pointed to is of type `Tuna`. Using Listing 13.1 as a base, here is what `main()` would look like:

```
int main()
{
   Fish* objFish = new Tuna;
   Tuna* objTuna = static_cast<Tuna*>(objFish);

   // Tuna::BecomeDinner will work only using valid Tuna*
   objTuna->BecomeDinner();

   // virtual destructor in Fish ensures invocation of ~Tuna()
   delete objFish;

   return 0;
}
```

Answers for Lesson 14

Quiz

1. A preprocessor construct that keeps you from recursively including header files.

2. 4.

3. 10 + 10 / 5 = 10 + 2 = 12.

4. Use parentheses:

```
#define SPLIT(x) ((x) / 5)
```

Exercises

1. Here it is:

```
#define MULTIPLY(a,b) ((a)*(b))
```

2. This is the template version of the macro in the answer to Quiz Question 4:

```
template<typename T> double Split(const T& input)
{
   return (input / 5);
}
```

3. The template version of `swap` would be:

```
template <typename T>
void Swap(T& x, T& y)
{
     T temp = x;
     x = y;
     y = temp;
}
```

4. `#define QUARTER(x) ((x)/ 4)`

5. The `template` class definition would look like this:

```
template <typename Array1Type, typename Array2Type>
class TwoArrays
{
private:
        Array1Type Array1 [10];
        Array2Type Array2 [10];
public:
        Array1Type& GetArray1Element(unsigned int index){return
Array1[index];}
        Array2Type& GetArray2Element(unsigned int index){return
Array2[index];}
};
```

6. Here is a full sample containing a `Display()` function that features variable templates:

```
#include<iostream>
using namespace std;

void Display()
{
}

template <typename First, typename ...Last> void Display(First a,
Last... U)
{
   cout << a << endl;
   Display(U...);
}

int main()
{
   Display('a');
   Display(3.14);
   Display('a', 3.14);
   Display('z', 3.14567, "The power of variadic templates!");

   return 0;
}
```

Output ▼

```
a
3.14
a
3.14
z
3.14567
The power of variadic templates!
```

Answers for Lesson 15

Quiz

1. `std::deque`. Only a deque simulates a dynamic array and also allows constant-time insertions at the beginning and at the end of the container. `std::vector` does not allow insertions at the beginning and is therefore not suitable.

2. You would use `std::set`. Alternatively, you could use `std::map` if you have key/value pairs. If the keys are required to be non-unique, too, then you can choose `std::multiset` or `std::multimap`.
3. Yes. When you instantiate a `std::set` template, you can optionally supply a second template parameter that is a binary predicate that the `set` class uses as the sort criterion. Program this binary predicate to criteria that are relevant to your requirements. It needs to be strict-weak ordering compliant.
4. These are called *iterators*. Iterators form the bridge between algorithms and containers so that algorithms (which are generic) can work on containers without having to know (that is, be customized for) every container type possible.
5. `hash_set` is not a C++ Standard-compliant container. So, you should not use it in any application that has portability listed as one of its requirements. Use `std::unordered_set` instead.

Answers for Lesson 16

Quiz

1. `std::basic_string<T>`.
2. Copy the two strings into two string objects. Convert each copied string into either lowercase or uppercase. Return the result of comparison of the converted copied strings.

Exercises

1. The program needs to use `std::reverse()`:

```
#include<string>
#include<iostream>
#include<algorithm>

int main()
{
   using namespace std;

   cout << "Please enter a word for palindrome-check:"
   string strInput;
   cin >> strInput;

   string strCopy(strInput);
   reverse(strCopy.begin(), strCopy.end());
```

E

```
    if(strCopy == strInput)
       cout << strInput << " is a palindrome!" << endl;
    else
       cout << strInput << " is not a palindrome." << endl;

    return 0;
}
```

2. Use `std::find()`:

```
#include<string>
#include<iostream>
using namespace std;

// Find the number of character 'chToFind' in string "strInput"
int GetNumCharacters(string& strInput, char chToFind)
{
    int nNumCharactersFound = 0;

    size_t nCharOffset = strInput.find(chToFind);
    while(nCharOffset != string::npos)
    {
       ++nNumCharactersFound;

       nCharOffset = strInput.find(chToFind, nCharOffset + 1);
    }

    return nNumCharactersFound;
}

int main()
{

    cout << "Please enter a string:""> ";
    string strInput;
    getline(cin, strInput);

    int nNumVowels = GetNumCharacters(strInput, 'a');
    nNumVowels += GetNumCharacters(strInput, 'e');
    nNumVowels += GetNumCharacters(strInput, 'i');
    nNumVowels += GetNumCharacters(strInput, 'o');
    nNumVowels += GetNumCharacters(strInput, 'u');

    // DIY: handle capitals too..

    cout << "The number of vowels in that sentence is:" << nNumVowels;

    return 0;
}
```

3. Use the function `toupper()`:

```
#include<string>
#include<iostream>
#include<algorithm>

int main()
{
   using namespace std;

   cout << "Please enter a string for case-conversion:" << endl;
   cout << "> ";

   string strInput;
   getline(cin, strInput);
   cout << endl;

   for(size_t nCharIndex = 0
      ; nCharIndex < strInput.length()
      ; nCharIndex += 2)
      strInput[nCharIndex] = toupper(strInput[nCharIndex]);

   cout << "The string converted to upper case is: "
   cout << strInput << endl << endl;

   return 0;
}
```

4. This can be simply programmed as

```
#include<string>
#include<iostream>

int main()
{
   using namespace std;

   const string str1 = "I";
   const string str2 = "Love";
   const string str3 = "STL";
   const string str4 = "String.";

   string strResult = str1 + " " + str2 + " " + str3 + " " + str4;

   cout << "The sentence reads:"
   cout << strResult;

   return 0;
}
```

5. Use `std::string::find()`:

```
#include<iostream>
#include<string>

int main()
{
   using namespace std;

   string sampleStr("Good day String! Today is beautiful!");
   cout << "Sample string is: " << sampleStr << endl;
   cout << "Locating all instances of character 'a'" << endl;

   auto charPos = sampleStr.find('a', 0);

   while(charPos != string::npos)
   {
      cout << "'" << 'a' << "' found";
      cout << " at position: " << charPos << endl;

      // resume find starting with next character
      size_t charSearchPos = charPos + 1;

      charPos = sampleStr.find('a', charSearchPos);
   }

   return 0;
}
```

Output ▼

```
Sample string is: Good day String! Today is beautiful!
Locating all instances of character 'a'
'a' found at position: 6
'a' found at position: 20
'a' found at position: 28
```

Answers for Lesson 17

Quiz

1. No, they can't. Elements can only be added at the back (that is, the end) of a vector sequence in constant time. Insertion at the beginning or the middle of a vector is a linear-time activity.

2. 10 more. At the 11th insertion, you trigger a reallocation.

3. Deletes the last element; that is, removes the element at the back.
4. Type `Mammal`.
5. Via the subscript operator (`[]`) or the method `at()`.
6. Random-access iterator.

Exercises

1. One solution is

```
#include<vector>
#include<iostream>

using namespace std;

char DisplayOptions()
{
    cout << "What would you like to do?" << endl;
    cout << "Select 1: To enter an integer" << endl;
    cout << "Select 2: Query a value given an index" << endl;
    cout << "Select 3: To display the vector" << endl;
    cout << "Select 4: To quit!" << endl << "> ";

    char ch;
    cin >> ch;

    return ch;
}

int main()
{
    vector<int> vecData;

    char chUserChoice = '\0';
    while((chUserChoice = DisplayOptions()) != '4')
    {
        if(chUserChoice == '1')
        {
            cout << "Please enter an integer to be inserted: ";
            int dataInput = 0;
            cin >> dataInput;

            vecData.push_back(dataInput);
        }
        else if(chUserChoice == '2')
        {
            cout << "Please enter an index between 0 and ";
            cout << (vecData.size() - 1) << ": ";
```

```
                size_t index = 0;
                cin >> index;

                if(index < (vecData.size()))
                {
                    cout<<"Element ["<<index<<"] = "<<vecData[index];
                    cout << endl;
                }
            }
            else if(chUserChoice == '3')
            {
                cout << "The contents of the vector are: ";
                for(size_t index = 0; index < vecData.size(); ++ index)
                    cout << vecData [index] << ' ';
                cout << endl;
            }
        }
        return 0;
    }
```

2. There are many possible solutions. The simplest one is to use the `std::find()` algorithm:

```
auto elementFound = std::find(vecData.begin(),
                              vecData.end(), value);
if(elementFound != vecData.end())
   cout << "Element found!" << endl;
```

3. Here is a possible solution:

```
#include<vector>
#include<iostream>
#include<string>
#include<sstream>

using namespace std;

char DisplayOptions()
{
   cout << "What would you like to do?" << endl;
   cout << "Select 1: To enter length & breadth " << endl;
   cout << "Select 2: Query a value given an index" << endl;
   cout << "Select 3: To display dimensions of all packages" << endl;
   cout << "Select 4: To quit!" << endl << "> ";

   char ch;
   cin >> ch;

   return ch;
}
```

```
class Dimensions
{
   int length, breadth;
   string strOut;
public:
   Dimensions(int inL, int inB) : length(inL), breadth(inB) {}

   operator const char*()
   {
      stringstream os;
      os << "Length "s << length<<", Breadth: "s << breadth << endl;
      strOut = os.str();
      return strOut.c_str();
   }
};

int main()
{
   vector <Dimensions> vecData;

   char chUserChoice = '\0';
   while((chUserChoice = DisplayOptions()) != '4')
   {
      if(chUserChoice == '1')
      {
         cout << "Please enter length and breadth: " << endl;
         int length = 0, breadth = 0;
         cin >> length;
         cin >> breadth;

         vecData.push_back(Dimensions(length, breadth));
      }
      else if(chUserChoice == '2')
      {
         cout << "Please enter an index between 0 and ";
         cout <<(vecData.size() - 1) << ": ";
         size_t index = 0;
         cin >> index;

         if(index <(vecData.size()))
         {
            cout << "Element [" << index << "] = " <<
            vecData[index];
            cout << endl;
         }
      }
      else if(chUserChoice == '3')
      {
         cout << "The contents of the vector are: ";
         for(size_t index = 0; index < vecData.size(); ++index)
            cout << vecData[index] << ' ';
```

E

```
            cout << endl;
        }
    }
    return 0;
}
```

Note the use of `vector` to store instances of the class `Dimensions`. Also note how `Dimensions` implements the operator `const char*` so that `std::cout` can directly work on instances of it.

4. List initializations, introduced in 2011, make the code compact:

```
#include<deque>
#include<string>
#include<iostream>
using namespace std;

template<typename T>
void DisplayDeque(deque<T> inDQ)
{
    for(auto element = inDQ.cbegin();
    element != inDQ.cend();
        ++element)
        cout << *element << endl;
}

int main()
{
    deque<string> strDq{ "Hello"s, "Containers are cool"s,
                         "C++ is evolving!"s };
    DisplayDeque(strDq);

    return 0;
}
```

Answers for Lesson 18

Quiz

1. Elements can be inserted in the middle of the list as they can be at either end. There is no gain or loss in performance due to position.

2. The specialty of the list is that operations such as these don't invalidate existing iterators.

3. `theList.clear();`

or

`theList.erase(theList.begin(), theList.end());`

4. Yes, an overloaded version of the `insert()` function enables you to insert a range from a source collection.

Exercises

1. This is like the solution for Exercise 1 for `vector` in Lesson 17, "STL Dynamic Array Classes." The only change is that you use the `list::insert()` function as
`List.insert(List.begin(), dataInput);`

2. Store iterators to two elements in a list. Insert an element in the middle, using the list's `insert()` function. Use the iterators to demonstrate that they are still able to fetch the values they pointed to before the insertion.

3. A possible solution is

```
#include<vector>
#include<list>
#include<iostream>

using namespace std;

int main()
{
   vector<int> vecData{ 0, 10, 20, 30 };

   list<int> linkInts;

   // Insert contents of vector into beginning of list
   linkInts.insert(linkInts.begin(),
      vecData.begin(), vecData.end());

   cout << "The contents of the list are: ";

   list<int>::const_iterator element;
   for(element = linkInts.begin();
      element != linkInts.end();
      ++element)
      cout << *element << " ";

   return 0;
}
```

4. A possible solution is

```
#include<list>
#include<string>
#include<iostream>

using namespace std;

int main()
```

E

```
{
    list <string> names;
    names.push_back("Jack");
    names.push_back("John");
    names.push_back("Anna");
    names.push_back("Skate");

    cout << "The contents of the list are: ";

    list <string>::const_iterator element;
    for(element = names.begin(); element != names.end(); ++element)
       cout << *element << " ";
    cout << endl;

    cout << "The contents after reversing are: ";
    names.reverse();
    for(element = names.begin(); element != names.end(); ++element)
       cout << *element << " ";
    cout << endl;

    cout << "The contents after sorting are: ";
    names.sort();
    for(element = names.begin(); element != names.end(); ++element)
       cout << *element << " ";
    cout << endl;

    return 0;
}
```

Answers for Lesson 19

Quiz

1. The default sort criterion is specified by `std::less<>`, which effectively uses the operator < to compare two integers and returns true if the first is less than the second.
2. Given that a multiset sorts elements on insertion, you would find the two elements of equal value together, one after another.
3. `size()`, as is the case with all other STL containers.

Exercises

1. One solution is

```
#include<set>
#include<iostream>
```

```
#include<string>
using namespace std;

template <typename T>
void DisplayContents(const T& container)
{
   for(auto iElement = container.cbegin();
   iElement != container.cend();
      ++iElement)
      cout << *iElement << endl;

   cout << endl;
}

struct ContactItem
{
   string name;
   string phoneNum;
   string displayAs;

   ContactItem(const string& nameInit, const string & phone)
   {
      name = nameInit;
      phoneNum = phone;
      displayAs =(name + ": " + phoneNum);
   }

   // used by set::find() given contact list item
   bool operator ==(const ContactItem& itemToCompare) const
   {
      return(itemToCompare.phoneNum == this->phoneNum);
   }

   // used to sort
   bool operator <(const ContactItem& itemToCompare) const
   {
      return(this->phoneNum < itemToCompare.phoneNum);
   }

   // Used in DisplayContents via cout
   operator const char*() const
   {
      return displayAs.c_str();
   }
};

int main()
{
   set<ContactItem> setContacts;
   setContacts.insert(ContactItem("Oprah Winfrey", "+1 7889 879
879"));
```

E

```
    setContacts.insert(ContactItem("Bill Gates", "+1 97 7897 8799 8"));
    setContacts.insert(ContactItem("Angi Merkel", "+49 23456 5466"));
    setContacts.insert(ContactItem("Vlad Putin", "+7 6645 4564 797"));
    setContacts.insert(ContactItem("John Travolta", "91 234 4564 789"));
    setContacts.insert(ContactItem("Angelina Jolie", "+1 745 641 314"));
    DisplayContents(setContacts);

    cout << "Enter a number you wish to search: ";
    string input;
    getline(cin, input);

    auto contactFound = setContacts.find(ContactItem("", input));
    if(contactFound != setContacts.end())
       cout << "The number belongs to " <<(*contactFound).name << endl;
    else
       cout << "Contact not found"

    return 0;
}
```

2. The structure and the multiset definition would be

```
#include<set>
#include<iostream>
#include<string>

using namespace std;

struct PAIR_WORD_MEANING
{
   string word;
   string meaning;

   PAIR_WORD_MEANING(const string& sWord, const string& sMeaning)
      : word(sWord), meaning(sMeaning) {}

   bool operator<(const PAIR_WORD_MEANING& pairAnotherWord) const
   {
      return(word < pairAnotherWord.word);
   }

   bool operator==(const string& key)
   {
      return(key == this->word);
   }
};

int main()
{
```

```
    multiset <PAIR_WORD_MEANING> msetDictionary;
    PAIR_WORD_MEANING word1("C++", "A programming language");
    PAIR_WORD_MEANING word2("Programmer", "A geek!");

    msetDictionary.insert(word1);
    msetDictionary.insert(word2);

    cout << "Enter a word you wish to find the meaning of" << endl;
    string input;
    getline(cin, input);
    auto element = msetDictionary.find(PAIR_WORD_MEANING(input, ""));
    if(element != msetDictionary.end())
        cout << "Meaning is: " <<(*element).meaning << endl;

    return 0;
}
```

3. One solution is

```
#include<set>
#include<iostream>

using namespace std;

template <typename T>
void DisplayContent(const T& cont)
{
    for(auto element = cont.cbegin(); element != cont.cend();
++element)
        cout << *element << " ";
}

int main()
{
multiset<int> msetIntegers;

msetIntegers.insert(5);
msetIntegers.insert(5);
msetIntegers.insert(5);

set<int> setIntegers;
setIntegers.insert(5);
setIntegers.insert(5);
setIntegers.insert(5);

cout << "Displaying the contents of the multiset: ";
DisplayContent(msetIntegers);
cout << endl;

cout << "Displaying the contents of the set: ";
DisplayContent(setIntegers);
```

E

```
cout << endl;

return 0;
}
```

Answers for Lesson 20

Quiz

1. The default sort criterion is specified by `std::less<>`.
2. Next to each other.
3. `size()`. In fact, this member function would tell you the number of elements in every container supplied by the STL.
4. You would not find duplicate elements in a map.

Exercises

1. An associative container that allows duplicate entries. For example, `std::multimap`:

   ```
   std::multimap<string, string> mapNamesToNumbers;
   ```

2. An associative container that allows duplicate entries. For example:

   ```
   struct fPredicate
   {
      bool operator< (const WordProperty& lsh, const WordProperty& rsh)
   const
      {
          return (lsh.word < rsh.word);
      }
   };
   ```

3. Take a hint from the similarly solved Exercise 3 in Lesson 19, "STL `set` and `multiset`."

Answers for Lesson 21

Quiz

1. A unary predicate.

2. It can display data, count elements, or return a value computed using supplied input. See the use of `std::transform()` in Listing 21.7 with the function `tolower()`, which returns the lowercase equivalent of a supplied character.
3. All entities that exist during the runtime of an application are objects. In this case, even structures and classes can be made to work as functions—hence the term *function objects*. Note that functions can also be available via function pointers, which are function objects, too.

Exercises

1. A solution is

```
#include<vector>
#include<iostream>
#include<algorithm>
using namespace std;

template <typename elementType = int>
struct Double
{
   void operator()(const elementType element) const
   {
      cout << element * 2 << ' ';
   }
};

int main()
{
   vector<int> numsInVec;

   for(int count = 0; count < 10; ++count)
      numsInVec.push_back(count);

   cout << "Displaying the vector of integers: "

   // Display the array of integers
   for_each(numsInVec.begin(),   // Start of range
            numsInVec.end(), // End of range
            Double<>()); // Unary function object

   return 0;
}
```

2. Add a member integer that is incremented every time `operator()` is used. Note that such a functor cannot be a `const` function.

```
#include<vector>
#include<iostream>
```

E

```
#include<algorithm>
using namespace std;

template <typename elementType = int>
struct Double
{
   int count = 0;
   void operator()(const elementType element)
   {
      ++count;
      cout << element * 2 << ' ';
   }
};

int main()
{
   vector<int> numsInVec;

   for(int count = 0; count < 10; ++count)
      numsInVec.push_back(count);

   cout << "Displaying the vector of integers: " << endl;

   Double<int> doubleElement;
   // Display the array of integers
   doubleElement = for_each(numsInVec.begin(),  // Start of range
            numsInVec.end(), // End of range
            Double<>()); // Unary function object

   cout << "\nFunctor called: "" times\n"; << doubleElement.count
   << " times\n";

   return 0;
}
```

3. The binary predicate is as follows:

```
template <typename elementType>
template <typename elementType>
class SortAscending
{
public:
   bool operator() (const elementType& num1,
      const elementType& num2) const
   {
      return (num1 < num2);
   }
};
```

This predicate can be used as

```
#include<iostream>
```

```
#include<vector>
#include<algorithm>
int main()
{
   std::vector<int> numsInVec;

   // Insert sample numbers: 100, 90... 20, 10
   for(int sample = 10; sample > 0; --sample)
      numsInVec.push_back(sample * 10);

   std::sort(numsInVec.begin(), numsInVec.end(),
      SortAscending<int>());

   for(size_t index = 0; index < numsInVec.size(); ++index)
      std::cout << numsInVec[index] << ' ';

   return 0;
}
```

Answers for Lesson 22

Quiz

1. A lambda starts with square brackets: `[...]`.
2. Via a capture list: `[var1, var2, ...](Type& param) { ...; }`
3. Like this:

```
[var1, var2, ...](Type& param) -> ReturnType { ...; }
```

Exercises

1. One solution for the lambda is

```
sort(container.begin(),container.end(),
     [](auto& lhs, auto& rhs) {return(lhs > rhs);} );
```

The working sample that contains it:

```
#include<iostream>
#include<algorithm>
#include<vector>
using namespace std;

int main()
{
   vector<int> vecNumbers{25, -5, 122, 2021, -10001};
```

```
    // template lambda that displays element on screen
    auto displayElement = [] <typename T>(const T& element)
                         { cout << element << ' ';};

    cout << "Elements in vector in initial order:\n";
    for_each(vecNumbers.cbegin(), vecNumbers.cend(), displayElement);

    sort(vecNumbers.begin(), vecNumbers.end());

    cout << "\nAfter sort using default predicate:\n";
    for_each(vecNumbers.cbegin(), vecNumbers.cend(), displayElement);

    sort(vecNumbers.begin(), vecNumbers.end(),
        [](auto& lhs, auto& rhs) {return(lhs > rhs); });

    cout << "\nAfter sort in descending order:\n";
    for_each(vecNumbers.cbegin(), vecNumbers.cend(), displayElement);

    return 0;
}
```

2. This is what the lambda would look like:

```
[=](int& element) {element += num; }
```

The working sample that contains it:

```
#include<iostream>
#include<algorithm>
#include<vector>
using namespace std;

int main()
{
    vector<int> vecNumbers{25, -5, 122, 2021, -10001};

    // template lambda that displays element on screen
    auto displayElement = [] <typename T>(const T& element)
                         { cout << element << ' ';};

    cout << "Elements in vector in initial order:\n";
    for_each(vecNumbers.cbegin(), vecNumbers.cend(), displayElement);

    cout << "\nEnter number to add to all elements: ";
    int num = 0;
    cin >> num;

    for_each(vecNumbers.begin(), vecNumbers.end(),
```

```
            [=](int& element) {element += num; });

    cout << "\nElements after adding the supplied number:\n";
    for_each(vecNumbers.cbegin(), vecNumbers.cend(), displayElement);

    return 0;
}
```

Answers for Lesson 23

Quiz

1. Use the `std::list::remove_if()` function because it ensures that existing iterators to elements in the list (that were not removed) remain valid.
2. `list::sort()` (or even `std::sort()`) in the absence of an explicitly supplied predicate resorts to a sort using `std::less<>`, which in turn uses the operator `<` to sort objects in a collection.
3. Once per element in the range supplied.
4. `for_each()` accepts a unary predicate and returns the function object that can be used to contain state information. `std::transform()` can work with unary or binary predicates and features an overloaded version that can therefore work on two input ranges.

Exercises

1. Here is one solution:

```
struct CaseInsensitiveCompare
{
    bool operator() (const string& str1, const string& str2) const
    {
        string str1Copy(str1), str2Copy(str2);

        transform(str1Copy.begin(),
                  str1Copy.end(), str1Copy.begin(), tolower);
        transform(str2Copy.begin(),
                  str2Copy.end(), str2Copy.begin(), tolower);

        return (str1Copy < str2Copy);
    }
};
```

2. Here is the demonstration:

```
#include<vector>
#include<algorithm>
#include<list>
#include<string>
#include<iostream>

using namespace std;

int main()
{
    list <string> listNames;
    listNames.push_back("Jack");
    listNames.push_back("John");
    listNames.push_back("Anna");
    listNames.push_back("Skate");

    vector <string> vecNames(4);
    copy(listNames.begin(), listNames.end(), vecNames.begin());

    vector <string> ::const_iterator iNames;
    for_each(vecNames.begin(), vecNames.end(),
             [](const auto& name) {cout << name << ' '; });

    return 0;
}
```

Note how `std::copy()` works in copying contents from `std::list` to `std::vector`, without requiring you to really know the types of the collections involved. It simply works using iterators.

3. The difference between `std::sort()` and `std::stable_sort()` is that the latter maintains the relative positions of the elements. In this case, the application needs to store data in the sequence of occurrence, and therefore you would choose `stable_sort()` to maintain the relative ordering between the celestial events.

Answers for Lesson 24

Quiz

1. Yes, by supplying a binary predicate as a template instantiation parameter.
2. The class `Coin` needs to implement the operator `<`.
3. No, you can only use elements at the top of the stack. You can't access the first coin because it is at the bottom of the stack.

Exercises

1. The binary predicate could be `operator<`:

```
class Person
{
public:
    int age = 0;
    bool isFemale = false;

    Person(int ageIn, bool isFemaleIn) : age(ageIn),
isFemale(isFemaleIn) {};
    bool operator<(const Person& anotherPerson) const
    {
        if (age > anotherPerson.age)
            return false;
        else if (isFemale && (!anotherPerson.isFemale))
            return false;

        return true;
    }
};
```

2. Push individual characters into a stack. As you pop data, you effectively reverse the contents because a stack is a LIFO type of container.

Answers for Lesson 25

Quiz

1. No. The number of bits `bitset` can hold is fixed at compile time.

2. Because `bitset` can't resize itself dynamically the way STL containers can; and also because it doesn't support iterators in the way STL containers do.

3. No. `std::bitset` is best suited for this purpose and performs better.

E

Exercises

1. `std::bitset` featuring instantiation, initialization, display, and addition (by converting to `unsigned long`) is demonstrated here:

```
#include<bitset>
#include<iostream>
using namespace std;

int main()
{
```

```
    // Initialize the bitset to 1001
    bitset<4> fourBits("1001");

    cout << "fourBits: "

    // Initialize another bitset to 0010
    bitset<4> fourMoreBits("0010");

    cout << "fourMoreBits: "

    bitset<8> addResult(fourBits.to_ulong() + fourMoreBits.to_ulong());
    cout << "The result of the addition is: "

    return 0;
}
```

2. Call the `flip()` function on any of the bitset objects in the preceding example:

```
addResult.flip();
cout << "The result of the flip is: " << addResult << endl;
```

Answers for Lesson 26

Quiz

1. I would look at www.boost.org. I hope you would, too!
2. No, typically well-programmed (and correctly chosen) smart pointers would not.
3. When intrusive, objects that they own need to hold it; otherwise, they can hold this information in a shared object on the free store.
4. The list needs to be traversed in both directions, so it needs to be doubly linked.

Exercises

1. `object->DoSomething();` will cause problems because the pointer lost ownership of the object during the previous copy step. This is why `auto_ptr` was deprecated and should never be used.
2. The code would look like this:

```
#include<memory>
#include<iostream>
using namespace std;

class Fish
{
public:
```

```
    Fish() {cout << "Fish: Constructed!" << endl;}
    ~Fish() {cout << "Fish: Destructed!" << endl;}

    void Swim() const {cout << "Fish swims in water" << endl;}
};

class Carp: public Fish
{
};

void MakeFishSwim(const unique_ptr<Fish>& inFish)
{
    inFish->Swim();
}

int main()
{
    unique_ptr<Fish> myCarp(new Carp); // note this
    MakeFishSwim(myCarp);

    return 0;
}
```

As there is no copy step involved, given that `MakeFishSwim()` accepts the argument as a reference, there is no question of slicing. Also, note the instantiation syntax of the variable `myCarp`. If `MakeFishSwim()` were to accept the parameter by value instead of by reference, the compilation would fail because `unique_ptr` doesn't support a copy constructor and protects you from slicing errors.

3. `unique_ptr` does not allow copy or assignment. The copy constructor and copy assignment operator are explicitly marked as deleted.

Answers for Lesson 27

Quiz

1. Use `ofstream` to only write to a file.
2. You would use `cin.getline()`. See Listing 27.7.
3. You wouldn't because `std::string` contains text information, and you can stay with the default mode, which is text; there is no need for binary.
4. To check whether `open()` succeeded. If it fails, you may want to show an error and suspend file processing.

E

Exercises

1. You opened the file but didn't check for the success of `open()` using `is_open()` before using the stream or closing it.
2. You cannot insert into `ifstream`, which is designed for input and not output and hence does not support the stream insertion operator (`<<`).

Answers for Lesson 28

Quiz

1. A class just like any other but created expressly as a base class for some other exception classes, such as `bad_alloc`.
2. `std::bad_alloc`.
3. That's a bad idea because it's possible that the exception was thrown in the first place due to a lack of memory.
4. Use the same `catch(std::exception& exp)` that you can also use for type `bad_alloc`.

Exercises

1. Never throw in a destructor.
2. You forgot to make the code exception safe; it is missing a `try` and `catch` block.
3. Don't allocate in a `catch` block! Assume that the data allocated within `try` is lost and continue with damage control.

Answers for Lesson 29

Quiz

1. To use concepts, use `#include<concepts>` and enable the compiler settings specific to C++20.
2. Views are a special case of ranges that feature constant time copy, move, and assignment. All views are ranges, but not all ranges fulfill the criteria for being views.
3. Adaptors.

Exercises

1. It won't compile because `DisplayView()` has been constrained by the concept `ranges::view` to accept parameters that are views, as shown below:

```
template<ranges::view T>
void DisplayView(T& view)
{
   for (auto element : view)
      cout << element << ' ';

   cout << endl;
}
```

The variable `nums` is type `vector<int>`. It is a range, but it is not a view.

2. If you want `DisplayView()` to work with collections/ranges like `vector<int>`, you need to modify the governing concept accordingly (and change the name, too, perhaps):

```
template<ranges::range T>
void DisplayRange(T& view)
{
   for (auto element : view)
      cout << element << ' ';

   cout << endl;
}
```

3. The view would combine `reverse`, `transform`, and `take`:

```
auto viewSquare3Rev = nums | views::reverse | views::take(3)
      | views::transform([](auto num) {return num * num; });
```

A working example:

```
#include<ranges>
#include<vector>
#include<iostream>
using namespace std;

// concept ranges::view limits parameter type to view
template<ranges::view T>
void DisplayView(T& view)
{
   for (auto element : view)
      cout << element << ' ';

   cout << endl;
}
```

```
int main()
{
   vector<int> nums{ 1, 5, 202, -99, 42, 50 };
   auto viewAllElements = nums | std::views::all;
   cout << "View of all elements in the collection: ";
   DisplayView(viewAllElements);

   auto viewSquare3Rev = nums | views::reverse | views::take(3)
      | views::transform([](auto num) {return num * num; });
   cout << "View square of numbers, ignoring first three: ";
   DisplayView(viewSquare3Rev);

   return 0;
}
```

Answers for Lesson 30

Exercise

1. If `main()` doesn't call `join()` in Listing 30.1, the main thread is likely to terminate before the worker thread.

Answers for Lesson 31

Exercise

1. The bug is that `AddNums()` isn't exported from the module and hence cannot be accessed in `main()`. Fix the issue by using the keyword `export`:

```
// module interface file Calculations.ixx
export module Calculations;
export int AddNums(int a, int b)
{
   return (a + b);
}
```

Index

A

D

E

J-K

L

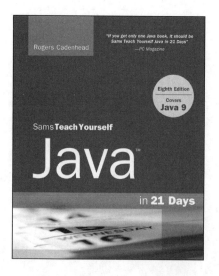

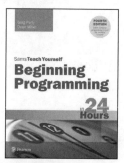

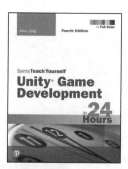

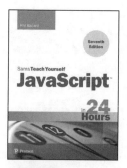

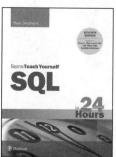